KARL MARX
FREDERICK ENGELS
COLLECTED WORKS
VOLUME
26

KARL MARX
FREDERICK ENGELS

COLLECTED WORKS

INTERNATIONAL PUBLISHERS
NEW YORK

KARL MARX
FREDERICK ENGELS

Volume
26

FREDERICK ENGELS: 1882-89

INTERNATIONAL PUBLISHERS

NEW YORK

This volume has been prepared jointly by Lawrence & Wishart Ltd., London, International Publishers Co. Inc., New York, and Progress Publishers, Moscow, in collaboration with the Institute of Marxism-Leninism, Moscow.

Editorial commissions:
GREAT BRITAIN: Eric Hobsbawm, John Hoffman, Nicholas Jacobs, Monty Johnstone, Martin Milligan, Jeff Skelley, Ernst Wangermann.
USA: Louis Diskin, Philip S. Foner, James E. Jackson, Leonard B. Levenson, Victor Perlo, Betty Smith, Dirk J. Struik.
USSR: for Progress Publishers—A. K. Avelichev, N. P. Karmanova, Yu. V. Semyonov, M. K. Shcheglova; for the Institute of Marxism-Leninism— P. N. Fedoseyev, L. I. Golman, N. Yu. Kolpinsky, A. I. Malysh, M. P. Mchedlov, V. N. Pospelova, G. L. Smirnov.

Library of Congress Cataloging in Publication Data

Marx, Karl, 1818-1883.
Karl Marx, Frederick Engels: collected works.

1. Socialism—Collected works. 2. Economics—Collected works. I. Engels, Friedrich, 1820-1895. Works. English. 1975. II. Title.
HX 39. 5 A 16 1975   335.4   73-84671
ISBN 0-7178-0526-3 (v. 26)

Printed in the Union of Soviet Socialist Republics

CONTENTS

FREDERICK ENGELS

WORKS

August 1882-December 1889

1882
August

Manuscripts on Early German History

1883

May

June

1884

March

April-May

June

October

1885
January

February

NOTES AND INDEXES

ILLUSTRATIONS

TRANSLATORS:

K. M. COOK: Works 14; Appendix 2
NICHOLAS JACOBS: Works 23
R. S. LIVINGSTONE: Works 13, 31
BARBARA RUHEMANN: Works 1
SALO RYAZANSKAYA: Works 2
BARRIE SELMAN: Works 2 (Note), 16, 17, 19, 22, 25, 29,
      30, 33; From the Preparatory Materials 1-5, 8, 9;
      Appendices 3, 4, 5, 8
STEPHEN SMITH: From the Preparatory Materials 6
JOAN and TREVOR WALMSLY: Works 3, 10

Preface

Volume 26 of the *Collected Works* of Karl Marx and Frederick Engels contains works by Frederick Engels, most of which were written between August 1882 and December 1889.

After Marx's death Engels took upon himself the complex tasks of the development of the theory and the ideological leadership of the international socialist movement, which for many decades had been performed by himself and Marx in close collaboration. "For after all, we wish to maintain intact, in so far as it is in my power, the many threads from all over the world which spontaneously converged upon Marx's study," he wrote to August Bebel on April 30, 1883 (see present edition, Vol. 47).

Throughout the 1880s Engels' links with members of the socialist working-class movement of various countries grew stronger and broader. The working-class struggle for emancipation acquired greater dimensions, and was joined by new strata of the proletariat. The process of forming independent working-class political parties begun in the preceding years continued, and by the end of the decade they had been set up or were in the stage of being set up in almost all the countries of Europe. Most of them based their programmes on the principles of scientific socialism. These principles were also reflected in the decisions of the Paris International Socialist Congress of 1889, which .marked the beginning of the Second International. The creation of parties was an important new step in the process of combining socialism with the working-class movement.

Engels constantly helped the young socialist parties and working-class organisations to draw up their programmes, tactics and political line. He contributed actively to the socialist press and did his utmost to promote the dissemination of Marxism. He carried on an extensive correspondence with members of the working-class and socialist movement of different countries. Alongside the preparation for the press of volumes II and III of *Capital,* a major part of Engels' activity consisted of publishing new editions of Marx's and his own works and organising translations of them into other languages. The prefaces to these editions published in this volume constitute an important part of his literary heritage.

During this period Engels wrote two major theoretical works which occupy a central place in the volume: *The Origin of the Family, Private Property and the State* and *Ludwig Feuerbach and the End of Classical German Philosophy.*

The Origin of the Family, Private Property and the State was an important contribution to the development of the materialist conception of history. The scientifically argued theses advanced in this work about the role of production in the development of society, the origin and evolution of the family, the origin of private property and classes, and the emergence and class essence of the state, fully retain their significance today. This work remains, to quote Lenin, "one of the fundamental works" of scientific communism (*Collected Works,* Vol. 29, Progress Publishers, Moscow, 1977, p. 473). It contains a profound theoretical generalisation of scientific achievements in the sphere of the history of primitive society and ethnography, first and foremost, of the studies of the progressive American scientist Lewis H. Morgan, whose results were set out in his book *Ancient Society.* This book was based to a large extent on many years of studying the life and customs of North American Indians. Morgan, Engels wrote in his preface to the first edition of *The Origin of the Family,* "rediscovered ..., in his own way, the materialist conception of history that had been discovered by Marx forty years ago" (this volume, p. 131). The extensive material contained in Morgan's book provided Engels with "a factual basis we have hitherto lacked" (Engels to Karl Kautsky, April 26, 1884, present edition, Vol. 47), which enabled him to analyse the early stages of human development from the viewpoint of the materialist conception of history.

Engels regarded his work as, "in a sense, the fulfilment of a behest" of Marx (p. 131), who himself had planned to write a book on the early period of human history drawing on the results of Morgan's studies. Engels made full use of Marx's notes in the latter's conspectus of Morgan's book, drawn up shortly before his death, and made the structure of this conspectus, which differed from that of Morgan, the basis for his work. He also drew on a great deal of additional material, including his own studies on the early history of Ireland and of the Germans, carried out in preceding years (all this is referred to in the Notes to this volume). In preparing a fourth edition of the book (1891) Engels made certain changes and important additions based on a study of the most recent scientific literature of his day.

Engels based his work on the idea of two types of production, remarking in the preface: "According to the materialist conception, the determining factor in history is, in the last resort, the production and reproduction of immediate life. But this itself is again of a twofold character. On the one hand, the production of the means of subsistence, of food, clothing and shelter and the implements required for this; on the other, the production of human beings themselves, the propagation of the species. The social institutions under which men of a definite historical epoch and of a definite country live are determined by both kinds of production: by the stage of development of labour, on the one hand, and of the family, on the other" (pp. 131-32).

Tracing the evolution of the family, Engels examined how its forms had changed under the influence of the development of productive forces and changes in the mode of production. He showed that at the early stages of human history, when private property and the division of society into classes had not yet arisen, family relations, ties of kinship played a very important part. With the growth of productive forces, however, this role was gradually reduced, and with the emergence of private property and classes the family became totally subjected to property relations.

Substantiating in detail the thesis already advanced by him in *Socialism: Utopian and Scientific,* to the effect that human society at the early stages of its development was a classless society based on a gentile structure and common ownership of the means of production, Engels summed up, as it were, his and Marx's many years of research in this sphere. He supplemented Marx's view of socio-economic formations expounded in the preface to *A Contribution to the Critique of Political Economy,* Part One (present edition, Vol. 29).

In a note to the 1888 English edition of the *Manifesto of the Communist Party* he made a major correction, quoting *The Origin of the Family,* to the *Manifesto*'s thesis, that "the history of all hitherto existing society is the history of class struggles" (present edition, Vol. 6, p. 482). The emergence of classes, he pointed out, was preceded by a lengthy period when communal, tribal ownership of the means of production reigned supreme.

The periodisation of the early periods in the history of humanity, which Engels adopted from Morgan, i.e. the division into epochs of savagery and barbarism each sub-divided into three stages, is now regarded as obsolete in the light of new scientific data and recent research and is no longer used by scholars. However, in present-day research account is taken of Engels' outline of the main stages of development of the primitive-communal system. Ideas of the individual stages in the development of the family and the origin of the gens have also changed considerably. This applies, for example, to such stages in the evolution of the family, advanced by Morgan and accepted by Engels (although with certain reservations in the fourth edition of the book), as the consanguine family and the punaluan family, and also to certain other concrete theses which have not been confirmed by subsequent archaeological and ethnographic investigations.

At the same time the methodological principles on which Engels based his work remain fully valid. Here for the first time he applied the dialectical-materialist method to the study of the history of the family, which enabled him to draw the highly important conclusion as to the dependence of forms of the family on the development of productive forces and changes in the mode of production. This was a major step forward in the development of the materialist conception of history.

Equally important and relevant today is Engels' explanation of the causes of the inequality of women in a class society. Engels showed that this inequality is determined not by biological factors, but in the final analysis by economic causes, and that its very emergence is connected with the appearance of private ownership of the means of production. Thus the way was pointed to the establishment of the full equality of the sexes.

Drawing on factual material from Morgan's book and other sources, Engels examined the process of the formation of antagonistic classes and showed that it was based on the development of productive forces, the growth of labour productivity.

It was in *The Origin of the Family* that Engels, for the first time in Marxist literature, gave such a detailed picture of the emergence of the state. He showed that the state had not always existed, but arose at a certain stage of economic development. Its appearance was the result of the division of society into antagonistic classes. It is proof that "society has become entangled in an insoluble contradiction with itself, that it has split into irreconcilable opposites which it is powerless to dispel" (p. 269) and therefore needs some force that could restrain them. The state is such a force.

Developing the theory of the state set out by Marx most fully in *The Eighteenth Brumaire of Louis Bonaparte* and *The Civil War in France*, and also in his own works *The Housing Question* and *Anti-Dühring* (see present edition, vols 11, 22, 23 and 25), Engels analysed the essence of the state, revealed the scientific invalidity of the view of the state as a kind of "supra-class" force, and characterised it as an organ "of the most powerful, economically dominant class, which, through the medium of the state, becomes also the politically dominant class" (p. 271). The state retains this character in a bourgeois democratic republic as well.

Engels did not limit himself to analysing the causes of the emergence of the state, and characterising its essence and explaining its structure, which already in itself meant developing further the theory of the state. He showed, in addition, that with the growth of productive forces the existence of antagonistic classes becomes an obstacle to the development of social production and that this, in the final analysis, leads to their destruction on the basis of the nationalisation of the means of production and, consequently, the withering away of the state.

The society of the future "which will reorganise production on the basis of a free and equal association of the producers, will put the whole machinery of state where it will then belong: into the museum of antiquities, by the side of the spinning-wheel and the bronze axe" (p. 272).

This volume also contains one of the most famous Marxist philosophical works, *Ludwig Feuerbach and the End of Classical German Philosophy*. Although the direct aim of this work was a critique of the book on Feuerbach by the Danish philosopher and sociologist Carl Starcke, its polemical aspect took second place. Here Engels expounded in positive form some vital philosophical problems: the subject of philosophy, the laws of its development and the struggle of materialism and idealism, the attitude of Marxism to its philosophical predecessors, above all, to Hegel and Feuerbach. Finally, he revealed the essence of Marxist philosophy, namely, dialectical and historical materialism, and showed how it differed fundamentally from preceding philosophical systems.

Engels' work was particularly important for the socialist movement, because some Social-Democratic intellectuals were influenced by idealist philosophical trends popular at that time, above
all, by Neo-Kantianism.

In his book Engels broached some of the main questions of
philosophy, namely, the relationship of thinking to being, of mind
to matter, a question which divides philosophers into two major
camps: the idealists, who believe that the mind is primary, and the
materialists, who believe in the primacy of matter. The answer to
this question predetermines to a large extent the solution of other
philosophical problems. The struggle between idealism and
materialism is the main characteristic feature of the history of
philosophy. Engels stresses that the question of the relationship of
thinking to being has yet another aspect: is the reflection of being
by the human consciousness identical to the real world? And is this
world cognisable? Arguing that being is cognisable and criticising
philosophers who deny the possibility of cognising it, Engels points
out that the main criterion for the cognisability of the world is
practical human activity. "The most telling refutation of this as of all
other philosophical quirks is practice, namely, experimentation and
industry" (p. 367).

Here for the first time Engels advanced the thesis on the three
great discoveries in natural science: the discovery of the cell, the
theory of the transformation of energy and Darwin's theory of
evolution, "which have advanced our knowledge of the interconnection of natural processes by leaps and bounds" (p. 385) and
thanks to which the dialectical nature of this connection was
established.

Engels regards Hegelian dialectics and Feuerbach's materialist
views as the most important philosophical sources of Marxism. He
characterises Hegelian philosophy as "the termination of the
whole movement since Kant" (p. 359), and sees Hegel's dialectical
method as "the way ... to real positive cognition of the world"
(p. 362). In doing this Engels reveals the contradiction between
this method and Hegelian idealism.

Characterising the philosophical views of Feuerbach, Engels
stresses his importance in reviving materialism in philosophy. At
the same time he shows the limitations of Feuerbach's materialism,
which did not extend to the materialist interpretation of social life.
In criticising Hegel's idealism Feuerbach also rejected the main
positive feature of Hegel's philosophy, his dialectical method.
Feuerbach, wrote Engels, "as a philosopher, ... stopped halfway,
was a materialist below and an idealist above" (p. 382).

The final chapter of Engels' work examines the essence of dialectical and historical materialism. The combining of the dialectical method with a consistently materialist world outlook meant in fact a revolutionary change in philosophy. "Thus dialectics reduced itself to the science of the general laws of motion, both of the external world and of human thinking" (p. 383). And the extension of the dialectical-materialist method to the study of the history of human society, the materialist conception of history, made it possible for the first time to reveal the objective laws of social development. It was established that the historical process is based on the development of productive forces and economic relations, changes in which bring about alterations in the political system and, eventually, in the forms and types of social consciousness—in other words, in the whole ideological superstructure. Here Engels notes the relative independence of the political superstructure and different forms of social consciousness and their ability to exert a reciprocal influence on the economic basis.

The volume also includes a number of works defending Marx's economic teaching against the attacks of his ideological adversaries.

During the period to which the works published in this volume belong Engels prepared for the press Volume II of *Capital,* which came out in 1885, and the third (1884) and fourth (1890) German editions of Volume I, and also edited its English translation which appeared in 1887. All these editions were provided with prefaces written by him. In the preface to Volume II (see present edition, Vol. 36) and in the article "Marx and Rodbertus" published in this volume and written as a preface to the first German edition of Marx's work *The Poverty of Philosophy,* Engels criticised the views of the German economist Karl Rodbertus, whose works had served as the theoretical basis for the "state-socialist" measures of Bismarck and become the banner of the so-called armchair socialists who advocated bourgeois reforms in solving the social question, disguised in pseudo-socialist phraseology. Rodbertus also had apologists within the ranks of the Social-Democrats. Engels convincingly disproved the fabrications of certain bourgeois economists who accused Marx of plagiarising Rodbertus' ideas on the origin of value, by showing the fundamental difference between Marx's theory of value and Rodbertus' views. He exposed the reactionary-utopian nature of his views on the formation of

2*

value, his theory of "labour money" (pp. 288-89), and his statements on the ability of the modern state by means of legislative reforms to radically improve the position of the workers and to solve the social question, without touching the basis of the capitalist mode of production.

With the aim of making Marx's great work accessible to the socialists of all countries, Engels did his utmost to promote translations of *Capital* into other languages, in particular, Russian, Polish and English. He showed constant concern as to their accuracy. The present volume contains his article "How Not to Translate Marx", written in connection with the publication in the London journal *To-Day* of an English translation of a few paragraphs from chapter one of Volume I of *Capital*. The translator was the leader of the English Social-Democratic Federation H. M. Hyndman, who used the pseudonym Broadhouse. Engels demanded that the translator should possess not only a perfect knowledge of both languages, but also a profound understanding of the content of the work to be translated.

Engels was a careful observer of the development of the capitalist economy, particularly the new phenomena which emerged in it. Evidence of this can be found, among others, in the article "Protection and Free Trade" written as a preface to the American edition of Marx's "Speech on the Question of Free Trade" published on the initiative of American socialists. For the United States, where the struggle between the supporters and opponents of protectionism was continuing at this time, this publication was of great topical importance. Basing himself on an analysis of historical facts, Engels showed that whereas the protectionist system had for a certain time stimulated the development of capitalist production, with the growth of productive forces and technological progress it was becoming an obstacle to this development. "Free trade has become a necessity for the industrial capitalists," he noted (p. 536). One of the signs that protectionism had become obsolete in the United States, Engels considered, was the formation of large monopolies which, on the one hand, led to increased competition on the world market, but on the other, threatened the interests of the home consumer by setting up monopolistic prices. Engels stresses that the rapid development of capitalism, whether under protectionism or free trade, is inevitably accompanied by the growth of a revolutionary working class, "that is to say, the class which is fated one day to destroy the system itself" (p. 536).

Many of the articles published in the present volume reflect the great attention paid by Engels to the proletarian struggle for emancipation in various countries, and to the development of the international working-class and socialist movement. As well as corresponding regularly with the leaders and active members of the movement in almost all European countries and the United States, he maintained personal contact with them. Engels readily contributed to the German, French and English socialist press. He not only had his articles printed in the German Social-Democratic newspaper *Der Sozialdemokrat,* but gave daily assistance to its editors. His articles were published in the French newspaper *Le Socialiste,* the English organs *The Commonweal, The Labour Elector* and *The Labour Leader,* the German theoretical journal *Die Neue Zeit,* and others. The contents of the present volume provide a full picture of this collaboration.

Engels devoted a great deal of energy to disseminating the major theoretical works by Marx and himself. With his participation and, as a rule, under his editorship the following works were published: a German translation of *The Poverty of Philosophy* and a French translation of *The Eighteenth Brumaire of Louis Bonaparte* by Marx, the Italian and Danish editions of *The Origin of the Family, Private Property and the State* and many others. The present volume contains the prefaces to a new German edition (1883) prepared with Engels' participation and the English edition (1888) edited by him of the *Manifesto of the Communist Party.* In the latter he noted with satisfaction that "at present" the *Manifesto* "is undoubtedly the most widespread, the most international production of all Socialist Literature, the common platform acknowledged by millions of working men from Siberia to California" (p. 516).

Engels paid special attention to German Social-Democracy, at that time the strongest, best organised and most militant detachment of the international socialist movement, which rightly held pride of place in the latter. Engels gave it the utmost assistance to overcome reformist influences, to struggle against opportunist elements, to work out correct revolutionary tactics and to propagate scientific socialism. This assistance was all the more important because in the 1880s the party was operating in the intensely difficult conditions of the Anti-Socialist Law when its legal methods of activity were reduced to a minimum. In spite of the outstanding successes of the socialist working-class movement in Germany, it had not freed itself entirely from ideological influences alien to the interests of the working class. In the preface to the second edition of his work *The Housing Question,* published in this volume, Engels noted that "bourgeois and petty-bourgeois socialism is strongly represented in Germany down to this very hour". And in the Social-Democratic Party itself there was "a certain petty-bourgeois socialism" (p. 427), which was explained by the special features of the country's historical development.

Considering it most important in these conditions that progressive German workers be educated in the spirit of revolutionary and internationalist traditions, Engels undertook in the 1880s the reprinting of a number of Marx's works relating to the period of the revolution of 1848-49, and also some of his own works, providing them with prefaces which are of specific scientific interest. Appearing, as a rule, in periodicals before the publication of the books for which they were intended, these prefaces, which substantiated revolutionary tactics, were extremely relevant in the conditions of the Anti-Socialist Law and were aimed directly against the opportunist elements within Social-Democracy.

In his article "Marx and the *Neue Rheinische Zeitung*" about the history of this newspaper, Engels reveals the special features of the Communist League's tactics in the bourgeois-democratic revolution of 1848-49. On the experience of the revolution he urged German Social-Democrats to struggle for the leading role of the working class in the solution of general democratic tasks, provided that it retained its independence, and spoke of the need not only to struggle against direct enemies, but also to denounce the false friends of the revolution.

The work *On the History of the Communist League* was written as an introduction to a new edition of Marx's pamphlet *Revelations Concerning the Communist Trial in Cologne*. It drew attention to one of the most vivid pages in the history of the German workers' struggle, stressing the historical continuity between the first international and German proletarian organisation, the ideological banner of which was the programme of scientific socialism, and German Social-Democracy. In so doing Engels demonstrated the invalidity of the statement that the foundations of the working-class movement in Germany were laid by Lassalle's General Association of German Workers in 1863. He noted in particular the significance of the Communist League as an organisation which had educated many active members of the international working-class movement who subsequently played a major role in the First International and the socialist parties. He emphasised the vital importance of the international solidarity of the struggling proletariat, noting with satisfaction the enormous progress made by the working-class movement and pointing out that the theoretical principles of the League "constitute today the strongest international bond of the entire proletarian movement in both Europe and America" (p. 312).

In his preface to the pamphlet *Karl Marx Before the Cologne Jury,* containing Marx's speech at the trial of the Rhenish District Committee of Democrats in February 1849, Engels described this speech as a model defence of revolutionary principles before a bourgeois court. In denouncing the hypocrisy of the ruling circles in the German Empire, who persecuted the socialist working-class movement under the guise of "legality" while actually trampling upon it, Engels defended the right of the working class to struggle against reactionary orders with revolutionary means. Engels ridiculed attempts by reactionary circles, which to some extent found support in the moods of reformist elements within the party itself, to force German Social-Democracy to renounce its ultimate aims and thereby turn it into a party of the German philistines.

These three articles of Engels, particularly *On the History of the Communist League,* are fine examples of Marxist historical research, combining a profound analysis of events of the comparatively recent past with the current problems of the struggle for emancipation of the working class.

Also included in the present volume, the article "The Ruhr Miners' Strike of 1889" shows how much importance Engels attached to the entry of new detachments of the German working class into the organised labour movement.

Engels paid increasing attention to socialist tactics in relation to the peasantry. On his initiative Wilhelm Wolff's series of articles, *The Silesian Milliard,* about the tragic state of the peasants in Silesia, printed in the *Neue Rheinische Zeitung* in 1849, was published as a separate pamphlet. The article "On the History of the Prussian Peasants", also contained in this volume, was written as part of the introduction to this pamphlet.

After describing the history of the enserfment of the peasantry in Prussia, Engels showed that the abolition of feudal obligations after the revolution of 1848 was accompanied by large-scale robbery of the mass of the peasants. Consequently, the objective conditions made the peasants the natural ally of the proletariat in the struggle against the bourgeois-Junker order. The same idea also pervades the above-mentioned preface to the second edition of *The Housing Question.* Here Engels showed that the broad development of domestic industry in Germany led to the ruin of many peasant farms. And the inevitable destruction of these industries as a result of the development of large-scale machine production would lead to the complete expropriation of a considerable section of the peasantry and put it on the path of revolutionary struggle.

An important place in the ideological education of progressive German workers and socialist intellectuals was allotted by Engels to the materialist explanation of German history in opposition to the reactionary, nationalist historiography that prevailed in the discipline at that time. An explanation of the historical roots of the reactionary practices which had grown up in Germany was also essential for a correct assessment of the policy of the ruling circles at that time. And this was extremely important for elaborating the strategy and tactics of Social-Democracy and determining its long-term activity.

In the 1880s Engels continued his studies of German history. The present volume contains two large manuscripts dealing with the history of the emergence and development of a class society among the Germans. They are based on a large amount of factual material: various historical sources, archaeological data, accounts by ancient writers, etc.

Chronologically these manuscripts belong to 1881-82, but the reason for including them in the present volume is that Engels made extensive use of them in his work *The Origin of the Family, Private Property and the State.*

The first of them, *On the Early History of the Germans,* covers the history of the Germans from the point when they appeared on the territory of present-day Europe up to the beginning of the migration of peoples. The clash of the Germanic tribes with the slave-owning Roman Empire which was declining is seen here as a major factor of social revolution, which led to the decay of the primitive-communal system of the conquerors themselves and to the emergence of a class of big land-owning feudal lords, to the development of feudalism and the formation of the Frankish state.

In the manuscript *The Frankish Period* attention is focused on the agrarian relations in the age of early feudalism in Western Europe during the reigns of the Merovingians and Carolingians. Taking the history of the Franks as an example, Engels sought to trace the formation of the foundations of feudalism, the emergence of the main classes of feudal society. Pointing out the significant role of political factors in this process, he stressed however that they "only advance and accelerate an inevitable economic process" (p. 60).

In the mid-1880s Engels began preparing a new edition of his work *The Peasant War in Germany,* in which he presented the Reformation and the Peasant War as the first, albeit unsuccessful, bourgeois revolution, as an event which largely determined the whole subsequent history of Germany. He intended to revise his book thoroughly, in particular to provide it with a detailed introduction, the draft for which is published in this volume under the editors' title *On the Decline of Feudalism and the Emergence of National States* in the section "From the Preparatory Materials". Engels showed here the process of the emergence of capitalist relations and the formation of nations and national states in Western Europe during the decline of feudalism. He also revealed the progressive centralising role of the monarchy, a counterforce to feudal anarchy.

Judging from these drafts, Engels intended to analyse the reasons why feudal fragmentation had lasted much longer in Germany than in most other European countries, which had a negative influence on her further development.

Other commitments prevented Engels from completing the work which he had begun.

The present volume also contains the unfinished work *The Role of Force in History* which deals with the history of the unification of Germany under Prussia. It was to form the fourth chapter of a pamphlet of the same name as a supplement to the chapters of *Anti-Dühring* which contain a critique of the theory of force. Engels revealed the economic and political causes which led to the unification of Germany not in a revolutionary democratic way, but "from above", by means of wars and territorial aggrandizement, "blood and iron". He gave a profound and vivid description of the German Empire, its constitution, class structure, political parties, the domestic contradictions inherent in it and also the reforms carried out by Bismarck in the 1870s. A considerable section of the work was devoted to criticising Bismarck's aggressive foreign policy, and his policy of militarising the country, which threatened to cause an all-European war.

The surviving preparatory materials for this work, its general plan and a plan of the final part, which are included in the present volume in the section "From the Preparatory Materials", indicate that Engels intended to continue his account up to the second half of the 1880s, to show the inevitability of the failure of Bismarck's domestic policies and the growing influence of revolutionary Social-Democracy.

In a number of articles in this volume, "England in 1845 and in

1885", "Appendix to the American Edition of *The Condition of the Working Class in England*", "The Abdication of the Bourgeoisie", and others, Engels examines the condition and prospects of the English working-class movement. Analysing the changes in the position of the English working class over the last forty years, Engels notes a certain improvement in the conditions of its life and labour, particularly of factory-workers, and also a growth in the influence of the large trade unions uniting qualified workers. With regard to the majority of the working people, however, the state of misery and insecurity of their existence was "as low as ever, if not lower" (p. 299). An analysis of the tendencies in the development of the English economy in the 1870s and 1880s led Engels to conclude that signs had appeared which heralded England's loss of her industrial monopoly in the relatively near future. He assumed that this fact would lead to the loss by the English working class of its relatively privileged position compared with that of the proletariat of other countries and would stimulate the socialist movement in England. Engels placed great hopes on the process which began in the late 1880s of drawing the broad mass of unqualified workers into an organised struggle for their rights. "It is a glorious movement," he wrote in connection with a strike by the London dockers (p. 545).

Engels' great interest in the revolutionary traditions of the struggle for emancipation of the English proletariat can be seen from his manuscript "Chartist Agitation" published here in English for the first time. In this manuscript, which is essentially a brief conspectus of the history of Chartism, the activity of its revolutionary wing headed by Ernest Jones was brought out clearly for the first time.

The material published in this volume testifies to Engels' keen interest in various aspects of the social life of the United States, in this country's remarkably rapid economic development and the special features of its history. In the summer of 1888, accompanied by Mr. and Mrs. Aveling and Carl Schorlemmer, he made a journey to the United States. He intended to record his impressions in travel notes, but this intention was not realised. The outlines for these notes are published in the section "From the Preparatory Materials".

Engels paid constant attention to the struggle of the working class in the United States, which assumed a particularly turbulent nature in the 1880s.

Engels maintained regular contacts with members of the American working-class movement and was well informed about its state.

Engels attached great importance to the dissemination of the ideas of scientific socialism among the American workers, and he willingly agreed to the suggestion to publish his work *The Condition of the Working-Class in England* in the United States, editing the translation of it himself. The present volume includes the article "The Labor Movement in America" written as a preface to this edition. It was translated into many languages at that time and was published in the socialist press of a number of European countries. Noting the exceptionally rapid development and wide scope of the struggle of the American proletariat and the growth of its class consciousness, and describing the working-class organisations which existed at that time in the United States, Engels stressed that most of the participants in the struggle of the working class for its rights did not have a clear, scientifically based programme and were therefore easily influenced by all manner of utopian theories which did not express their true interests. A specific feature of the working-class movement in the United States was its lack of unity, the result primarily of the diverse national composition of the proletariat. At the same time the existence of free land in the West gave the American worker illusory hopes of becoming a small proprietor. Engels made a critical analysis of the programme of the American economist Henry George, who was the leader of the United Labor Party in New York in the mid-1880s, and showed that his theory, according to which the main cause of the poverty of the broad mass of the people was private ownership of land, did not explain the essence of capitalist exploitation and could therefore not serve as a theoretical basis for the programme of a party of the working class.

Engels regarded the unification of the separate workers' organisations into "one national Labor Army, with no matter how inadequate a provisional platform, provided it be a truly working class platform" (p. 441), as the main condition for the development of the working-class movement in the United States. He therefore showed a special interest in the activity of the Knights of Labor, and believed that this organisation, then highly influential among the working masses, could become the basis of such a unification.

Engels regarded this unification as the first step towards the creation of a mass working-class party, the programme of which "must and will be essentially the same as that now adopted by the whole militant working class of Europe" (p. 440), i.e. be based on the principles of scientific socialism.

Engels criticised the Socialist Labor Party of North America which, although it proclaimed Marxist programme principles, remained—being in terms of composition to a large extent the party of German émigrés—far removed from the main mass of workers, the indigenous inhabitants of the country. He urged the party to overcome sectarian tendencies and carry on work in all the mass working-class organisations.

The volume includes several articles, "The Situation", "To the Editorial Committee of *Le Socialiste*", "On the Anniversary of the Paris Commune" and others, which characterise Engels' relations with the working-class movement in France. His regular correspondence with Paul and Laura Lafargue, and other members of the French Workers' Party, enabled him to keep constantly in touch with the events taking place in the country. Some of his letters were printed as articles in the French socialist press. Through his advice and reports in the press he helped the leaders of the party to solve theoretical problems and tactical tasks, to overcome errors of a sectarian nature and to struggle against opportunists.

He welcomed the actions of workers' deputies in parliament and the formation of a socialist faction, noting that this "was sufficient to throw the ranks of all the bourgeois parties into disarray" (p. 407).

Some of the material published here characterises Engels' attitude to the prospects for the revolutionary movement in Russia. He was deeply convinced that a democratic revolution would take place in this country in the not too distant future and would have a great influence on the whole international situation. "...Revolution ... in Russia," he said on September 19, 1888 in an interview for the socialist newspaper *New Yorker Volkszeitung*, "would revolutionise the whole European political situation" (p. 627). And in a talk with the Russian revolutionary Narodnik Hermann Lopatin five years earlier he is said by the latter to have remarked as follows: "Russia is the France of the present century. The revolutionary initiative of a *new* social reorganisation legally and rightly belongs to it" (p. 592).

A number of articles analyse the international situation and the tasks of socialist parties in the struggle against the threat of war and the arms race. In his article "The Political Situation in Europe" Engels examined the reasons for the aggravation of relations between the major European powers, stressing that their rulers saw war as a means of preventing the coming revolution. "*They see the spectre of social revolution looming up ahead of them, and*

they know but one means of salvation: war" (p. 416). He urged the
socialists of these countries to fight for peace.

In his "Introduction to Sigismund Borkheim's pamphlet *In
Memory of the German Blood-and-Thunder Patriots. 1806-1807*",
Engels made a prophetic prediction of the nature, scale and
consequences of the future war on the basis of an analysis of
inter-state contradictions and the alignment of forces in Europe. It
would be "a world war, moreover, of an extent and violence
hitherto unimagined," he wrote. "Eight to ten million soldiers will
be at each other's throats and in the process they will strip Europe
barer than a swarm of locusts. The depredations of the Thirty
Years' War compressed into three to four years and extended over
the entire continent; famine, disease, the universal lapse into
barbarism, both of the armies and the people, in the wake of acute
misery; irretrievable dislocation of our artificial system of trade,
industry and credit, ending in universal bankruptcy; collapse of
the old states and their conventional political wisdom to the point
where crowns will roll into the gutters by the dozen, and no one
will be around to pick them up; the absolute impossibility of
foreseeing how it will all end and who will emerge as victor
from the battle" (p. 451).

In drawing this terrible picture of the consequences of the
future war, Engels never for a moment lost his historical
optimism. He foresaw that the universal exhaustion caused by the
war would aggravate the contradictions inherent in capitalism and
could create the conditions for the victory of the working class.
Thirty years later this prediction of his found confirmation in the
Great October Revolution in Russia.

Engels devoted much energy to strengthening the international
relations of socialists of different countries. He took a most active
part in the preparation of the International Socialist Labour
Congress held in Paris in 1889. Largely thanks to his efforts the
attempts of opportunist elements—the French Possibilists and the
leaders of the English Social-Democratic Federation—to take over
leadership of the international working-class movement were
thwarted. Materials published in this volume (the article "Possibilist Credentials" and a letter to the editors of *The Labour Elector*)
reflect this activity of his.

* * *

The present volume contains 41 works by Engels, six of which
are published in English for the first time, including the articles

"The Situation", "The Political Situation in Europe", "Real Imperial Russian Privy Dynamiters" and others. All eight documents in the section entitled "From the Preparatory Materials" are published in English for the first time, as are six of the eight documents in the Appendices.

The material in the volume is arranged in chronological order.

In cases where an edition other than the first is taken as the basis for publication, points of divergence with the first edition are given in the footnotes.

In cases where there are different language versions of this or that work by Engels the English text is taken as the basis for publication and points of divergence are set out in the footnotes.

The explanatory words in square brackets belong to the editors.

Misprints in proper names, geographical names, statistical data, dates, etc., have, as a rule, been corrected without comment on the basis of checking the sources used by Engels. The relevant literary and documentary sources are mentioned in the footnotes and in the index of quoted and mentioned literature.

The compilation of the volume, preparation of the text and writing of the notes was by Tatiana Andrushchenko. The preface was written by Boris Tartakovsky and Tatiana Andrushchenko. Engels' manuscripts *On the Early History of the Germans, The Frankish Period* and the notes for them were prepared by Valentina Ostrikova and edited by Valentina Smirnova.

The name index, the index of periodicals and the glossary of geographical names were compiled by Georgy Volovik.

The index of quoted and mentioned literature was compiled by Tatiana Andrushchenko.

The indexes for the manuscripts *On the Early History of the Germans* and *The Frankish Period* were prepared by Yelena Kofanova.

The volume was edited by Boris Tartakovsky (Institute of Marxism-Leninism of the CC CPSU).

The translations were made by Nicholas Jacobs, R. S. Livingstone, Barbara Ruhemann, Barrie Selman, Joan and Trevor Walmsly (Lawrence & Wishart), K. M. Cook, Salo Ryazanskaya and Stephen Smith (Progress Publishers) and edited by Yelena Chistyakova, Yelena Kalinina, Margarita Lopukhina, Victor Schnittke, Stephen Smith, Yelena Vorotnikova (Progress Publishers) and Norire Ter-Akopyan, scientific editor (USSR Academy of Sciences).

The volume was prepared for the press by Yelena Vorotnikova (Progress Publishers).

FREDERICK ENGELS

WORKS

August 1882-December 1889

MANUSCRIPTS
ON EARLY GERMAN HISTORY [1]

[Draft plan]

1. Caesar and Tacitus.
2. The district and army structure.
3. The first battles against Rome.
4. Progress until the migration period.

Notes

1. in the text
2. the German peoples
3. the Franconian dialect

Written in mid-1878-early August 1882

First published in *MEGA*, Abt. I. Bd. 25, S. 307

Printed according to the manuscript

Published in English for the first time

[ON THE EARLY HISTORY OF THE GERMANS]

CAESAR AND TACITUS

The Germans are by no means the first inhabitants of the country they now occupy.* At least three races preceded them.

The oldest traces of man in Europe are found in certain strata of southern England, which it has not yet been possible to date with accuracy, but which probably fall between the two glacial periods of the so-called Ice Age.

After the second glacial period, as the climate gradually grew warmer, man appears all over Europe, North Africa and Anterior Asia up to India, together with the extinct great pachyderms (mammoth, straight-tusked elephant, woolly rhinoceros) and carnivores (cave lion, cave bear), and with still surviving animals (reindeer, horse, hyena, lion, bison, aurochs). The tools belonging to this period indicate a very primitive level of culture—crude stone knives, lozenge-shaped stone hatchets or axes, used without handles, scrapers for the preparation of animal skins, and borers, all made of flint—approximately corresponding to the stage of development of the present aborigines of Australia. The skeletal remains found so far do not enable us to form an idea of the physique of these men, from whose wide distribution and overall uniform culture it may be inferred that this period was of very long duration.

We do not know what became of these early palaeolithic people. In none of the countries where they appeared, including India, have races survived that could be considered their representatives in present-day mankind.

---

* I here follow in the main Boyd Dawkins, *Early Man in Britain*, London, 1880.

In the caves of England, France, Switzerland, Belgium and Southern Germany the tools of these extinct people are found for the most part in the lowest layers of stratified deposits. Above this lowest cultural stratum, and frequently separated from it by a more or less substantial layer of stalagmite, a second tool-bearing layer is found. These tools belong to a later period and are already much more skilfully made, and also of more varied material. Although the stone implements are not yet polished, they are designed and fashioned in a manner more suited to their purpose; with them are found arrow- and spear-points of stone, reindeer antler and bone; daggers and sewing needles of bone or antler, necklaces of pierced animal teeth, etc. Individual pieces are in part ornamented with very vivid drawings of animals, reindeer, mammoth, aurochs, seal, whale, and also hunting scenes with naked people; we find even beginnings of sculpture in horn.

If early palaeolithic people appeared in the company of animals of predominantly southern origin, animals of northern origin appear with the later palaeolithic people: two still surviving kinds of northern bear, the polar fox, the wolverine, the snowy owl. These people probably came in with these animals from the north-east, and the Eskimos would appear to be their last remaining descendants in the modern world. The tools of both correspond completely, not only in detail but in the ensemble. So do the drawings; the food of both is supplied by almost exactly the same animals. Their way of life, as far as we can reconstruct it for the extinct race, corresponds exactly.

These Eskimos, who so far have only been traced north of the Pyrenees and the Alps, have also disappeared from European soil. As the American Redskins even in the last century, by an inexorable war of extermination, pressed the Eskimos back to the extreme north, so in Europe the now appearing new race seems gradually to have driven them back and eventually exterminated them without mixing with them.

This new race came from the south, at least in Western Europe; it probably penetrated from Africa into Europe at a time when the two continents were still linked by land, both at Gibraltar and at Sicily. It stood on a considerably higher stage of culture than its predecessors. It knew agriculture; it had domestic animals (dogs, horses, sheep, goats, pigs and cattle). It knew hand pottery, spinning and weaving. Although its tools were still made of stone, they were already worked with great care and for the most part polished smooth (they are distinguished as neolithic from those of the earlier periods). The axes have handles and are thus for the

first time usable for felling trees; it thus became possible to hollow
out tree trunks for boats in which one could cross over to the
British Isles, now separated from the continent by the gradual
sinking of the ground.

In contrast to their predecessors they buried their dead with
care; we therefore have sufficient skeletons and skulls to judge of
their physique. The long skulls, small stature (average for women
1.46 metres, for men 1.65 metres), the low forehead, the aquiline
nose, strong brows and weak cheekbones and moderately developed jaw bones indicate a race whose last modern representatives would seem to be the *Basques.* The neolithic inhabitants not
only of Spain but of France, Britain and the whole region at least
as far as the Rhine were in all probability of Iberian race. Before
the arrival of the Aryans[2] Italy also was inhabited by a similar
small, dark-haired race, the closeness of whose relationship to the
Basques is today difficult to judge.

Virchow traces these long Basque skulls deep into northern
Germany and Denmark,[a] and the oldest neolithic pile dwellings of
the northern slopes of the Alps also belong to them.
Schaaffhausen, on the other hand, declares a series of skulls found
near the Rhine to be decidedly Finnish, in particular Lappish,[b]
and the oldest history knows only Finns as the northern
neighbours of the Germans in Scandinavia, of the Lithuanians and
Slavs in Russia. These two small, dark-haired races, one from
beyond the Mediterranean, the other directly from Asia north of
the Caspian Sea, appear to have run into one another in Germany.
It remains totally obscure in what circumstances this took place.

These various immigrations were eventually followed, also still
in prehistoric times, by that of the last great stock, the *Aryans,* the
peoples whose languages are grouped around the most ancient of
them, Sanscrit. The earliest immigrants were the Greeks and
Latins, who took possession of the two south-eastern peninsulas of
Europe; in addition probably also the now lost Scythians,
inhabitants of the steppes north of the Black Sea, very likely most
closely related to the tribes of the Medes and Persians. Then the
Celts followed. We know of their migrations only that they took

---

a *Verhandlungen der Berliner Gesellschaft für Anthropologie, Ethnologie und Urgeschichte.* Jahrg. 1878.— *Zeitschrift für Ethnologie.* Vol. X, Berlin, 1878, pp. 418-24.
Quoted in W. B. Dawkins, op. cit., p. 314.— *Ed.*

b H. Schaaffhausen [Paper presented to the Sixth General Congress of the
German Society of Anthropology, Ethnology and Early History on August 11,
1875], *Correspondenz-Blatt der deutschen Gesellschaft für Anthropologie, Ethnologie und
Urgeschichte,* Brunswick, Munich, 1875 [Supplement], pp. 67, 81.— *Ed.*

place north of the Black Sea and by way of Germany. Their vanguard pressed through to France, conquered the country to the Garonne and subjugated even a part of western and central Spain. They were brought to a halt, here by the sea, there by the resistance of the Iberians, while behind them other Celtic tribes from both sides of the Danube pressed after them. They are known to Herodotus here at the ocean coast and at the sources of the Danube.[3] But they must have arrived much earlier. The graves and other finds from France and Belgium prove that the Celts did not know any metal tools when they took possession of the country; in Britain, however, they appear from the beginning with bronze tools. Between the conquest of Gaul and the move to Britain a certain time must have gone by, during which the Celts acquired the knowledge of bronze, through their trading connections with Italy and Marseilles, and introduced it at home.

In the meantime the Celtic peoples behind them, themselves pressed by the Germans, were pressing more and more strongly; before them the ways were barred, and thus a move in a south-easterly direction took place, as we find later also with the Germanic and Slav migrations. Celtic tribes crossed the Alps, moved through Italy, the Thracian Peninsula and Greece, and either met with destruction or found permanent settlement in the Po plain and in Asia Minor. The mass of the tribe is found about that time (−400 to −300*) in Gaul, as far as the Garonne, in Britain and Ireland, and north of the Alps on both sides of the Danube, as far as the Main and the Riesengebirge, if not beyond. For, even if Celtic mountain and river names are less frequent and more disputed in North Germany than in the south, it is not to be assumed that the Celts only chose the more difficult way through mountainous South Germany without at the same time using the more convenient way through the open North German plain.

The Celtic immigration only partially displaced the existing inhabitants; especially in the south and west of Gaul these still formed the majority of the population, even if as an oppressed race, and the present population has inherited their physique. It is clear from the custom of bleaching the hair with soap existing among both Celts and Germans in their new places of settlement that both dominated over a pre-existing dark-haired population. Fair hair was a feature of the ruling race, and where this was lost through mixing of the races, soap had to' come to the aid.

---

* I distinguish the years *before* our era mathematically, by a minus sign (−), for brevity's sake.

The Celts were followed by the Germans, and here we can determine the time of their immigration with some probability, at least approximately. It will hardly have begun long before −400 and was not yet quite completed in Caesar's time.

About the year −325 Pytheas' account of his voyage gives us the first authentic information on the Germans.[4] He went from Marseilles to the Amber coast and there mentions Guttons and Teutons, without doubt German peoples. But where was the Amber coast? It is true that we usually think only of the East Prussian one, and when Guttons are named as neighbours of that coast that certainly fits. However, the distances given by Pytheas do not fit this region but fit rather well the great bay of the North Sea between the North German coast and the Cimbric Peninsula.[a] The Teutons, also named as neighbours, fit in there, too. There—on the western side of Schleswig and Jutland—is another Amber coast; Ringkjöbing to this day has a considerable trade in the amber found there. It also seems most improbable that Pytheas should so early have already penetrated so far into quite unknown waters, and still more so that the complicated voyage from the Kattegat to East Prussia should not only remain entirely without mention in his very careful statements, but not fit into them at all. One should therefore decidedly declare for the view, first pronounced by Lelewel, that Pytheas' Amber coast must be sought on the North Sea,[b] were it not for the name of Guttons, who can only belong to the Baltic. A step towards removing this last obstacle has been taken by Müllenhoff, who reads Guttons as a distortion of Teutons.[c]

About 180 before our era the Bastarnae, undoubtedly Germans, appear on the lower Danube and a few years later are noted as soldiers in the army of the Macedonian King Perseus against the Romans—the first mercenaries. They are savage warriors:

> "Men who do not know how to plough or sail the seas, who did not follow the life of herdsmen, but who were ever practising one business and one art, that of fighting and conquering their antagonists."

It is Plutarch who gives us this first information of the way of life of a German people.[d] Centuries later we find these same Bastarnae north of the Danube, although in a more westerly

---

    a Jutland.—*Ed.*

    b J. Lelewel, *Pythéas de Marseille et la géographie de son temps*, Brussels, 1836, pp. 59-60.—*Ed.*

    c K. Müllenhoff, *Deutsche Altertumskunde*, Vol. 1, Berlin, 1870, p. 479.—*Ed.*

    d Plutarchus, *Vitae parallelae: Aemilius Paullus*, 12, 2.—*Ed.*

region. Fifty years later Cimbri and Teutons broke into the Celtic Danube region, were repelled by the Celtic Boii, living in Bohemia, moved in several bands to Gaul and into Spain, and defeated one Roman army after another until at last Marius put an end to their almost twenty years of migration by destroying their no doubt already greatly weakened troops, the Teutons at Aix-en-Provence (−102) and the Cimbri at Vercelli in Northern Italy (−101).

Half a century later Caesar met two new German armies in Gaul: first, on the Upper Rhine, that of Ariovistus in which seven different peoples were represented, including the Marcomanni and Suebi; soon afterwards, on the lower Rhine, that of the Usipetes and Tencteri, who, pressed by the Suebi, had left their former seats and reached the Rhine after wandering for three years. Both armies succumbed to orderly Roman warfare, the Usipetes and the Tencteri also to Roman breach of treaty. In the first years of Augustus, Dio Cassius reports an invasion of Thrace by the Bastarnae; Marcus Crassus defeated them on the Hebrus (the present-day Maritza). The same historian also mentions a move of the Hermunduri, who at the beginning of our era left their homeland for unknown reasons and were settled by the Roman general Domitius Ahenobarbus "in a part of the country of the Marcomanni".[a] These are the last migrations of that epoch. The consolidation of Roman rule on the Rhine and the Danube put a stop to them for quite a long time; but there are many signs which indicate that the peoples of the north-east, beyond the Elbe and the Riesengebirge, did not achieve permanent settlement for a long time.

These expeditions of Germans formed the first act of that migration of peoples[5] which, halted for three centuries by Roman resistance, towards the end of the third century swept irresistibly across the two border rivers, flooded Southern Europe and Northern Africa and only came to an end with the conquest of Italy by the Langobardi in 568—an end in so far as the Germans took part in them, but not for the Slavs, who long remained in movement in their rear. These were literally migrations of peoples. Entire peoples, or at least large parts of them, went on the move with wife and child, with goods and chattels. Wagons covered in skins served as dwellings and for the transport of women and children as well as of the paltry household effects; the

---

[a] Dio Cassius, *Historia Romana*, LI, 24; LV, 10a. Quoted in *Die Geschichtschreiber der deutschen Vorzeit...*, pp. 265-66, 307.— *Ed.*

cattle were driven along with them. The men were armed and ready to overcome any resistance, to repel any attack; a military host by day, a military camp fortified by the wagons at night. The human losses during these moves, through constant fighting, through misery, hunger and sickness, must have been colossal. It was a life-and-death adventure. If the move succeeded, the survivors settled on foreign soil; if it failed, the migrating tribe disappeared from the earth. Those who were not killed in the slaughter of battle perished in slavery. The Helvetii and their allies, whose migration was halted by Caesar, started out with 368,000 head, including 92,000 fit to bear arms. After their defeat by the Romans only 110,000 were left, whom Caesar, exceptionally, sent back home, for political reasons. The Usipetes and Tencteri crossed the Rhine with 180,000 head; almost all of them perished in battle or fleeing from pursuit. No wonder that during this long period of migration entire tribes often disappeared without trace.

This migratory way of life of the Germans is fully matched by the conditions Caesar found on the Rhine. The Rhine was by no means a sharply defined border between Gauls and Germans. Belgic-Gallic Menapii had villages and fields on the right bank of the Rhine in the area of Wesel; on the other hand, the part of the Maas delta, on the left bank of the Rhine, was occupied by the German Batavi, and round Worms as far as Strassburg there lived German Vangiones, Tribocci and Nemetes, whether since Ariovistus or even earlier is uncertain. The Belgae made constant wars upon the Germans, everywhere territory was still disputed. As yet no Germans were living south of the Main and the Erzgebirge; only shortly before, the Helvetii had been driven by the Suebi from the region between Main, Rhine, Danube and the Bohemian Forest, as had the Boii from Bohemia (Boihemum), which bears their name to this day. The Suebi did not occupy the land, however; they transformed it into that wooded wilderness, 600 Roman [a] (150 German) miles long, which was to protect them from the south. Further east Caesar indicated more Celts (Volcae Tectosages) north of the Danube, where Tacitus later places the German Quadi.[b] Not until Augustus' time did Maroboduus lead his Suebian Marcomanni to Bohemia, while the Romans cut off the angle between Rhine and Danube with entrenchments and

---

[a] The Roman mile equals approximately 1.5 km.— *Ed.*

[b] Caesar, *Commentarii de bello Gallico*, VI, 24, 2; Tacitus, *Germania*, 42. Quoted in *Die Geschichtschreiber...*, pp. 215, 669-70.— *Ed.*

peopled it with Gauls. The area beyond this fortified frontier seems to have been settled by Hermunduri. This shows conclusively that the Germans moved to Germany via the plains north of the Carpathians and the Bohemian border mountains; only after they had occupied the northern plains did they drive the Celts, who lived in the mountains more to the south, across the Danube.

The way of life of the Germans as described by Caesar also proves that they were by no means yet settled in their country. They lived in the main by raising cattle, on cheese, milk and meat, less on corn; the chief occupation of the men was hunting and military training. They tilled the soil a little, but only as a sideline and in the most primitive forest fashion. Caesar reports that they worked the fields for just one year, the next year always taking new land under the plough.[a] It seems to have been slash-and-burn cultivation, as is still practised today in northern Scandinavia and Finland; the forest—and outside the forest there were only swamps and peet-bogs, in those days useless for agriculture—was burnt down, the roots superficially removed and also burnt, together with the turf; the corn was sown into the soil fertilised by the ash. But even in that case Caesar's statement on the annual renewal of arable land is not to be taken literally and as a rule is to be understood as applying to a habitual passing on to new land after at least two or three harvests. The entire passage, the un-German distribution of land by princes and officials, and particularly the motivation attributed to the Germans for this rapid change, smacks of Roman concepts. This change of land was inexplicable to the Romans. To the Rhenish Germans, already in the process of transition to permanent settlement, it may already have appeared as an inherited custom, more and more losing purpose and meaning. To the Germans of the interior, the Suebi who were just arriving on the Rhine, and for whom it was mainly valid, it was still, however, an essential condition of a way of life by which the whole people moved slowly forward in whatever direction and at whatever pace the resistance they met permitted. Their constitution, too, was tailored to this way of life: the Suebi were divided into a hundred districts, every one of which supplied a thousand men annually to the army, while the rest of the men stayed at home, looking after cattle and fields and taking their turn in the army the second year. The mass of the people, with the women and children, only followed the army when it had

---

[a] Caesar, op. cit., IV, 1, VI, 22. Quoted in *Die Geschichtschreiber...*, pp. 163, 214.— *Ed.*

conquered new territory. This is already an advance towards settlement compared with the migrating hosts of the time of the Cimbri.

Caesar speaks repeatedly of the custom of the Germans to make themselves secure on the side facing an enemy, that is any alien people, by deep forest wildernesses.[a] This is the same custom which lasted into the late Middle Ages. The Saxons north of the Elbe were protected by the border forest between Eider and Schlei (Old Danish *Jarnwidhr*) against the Danes, by the Saxon forest between the Bay of Kiel and the Elbe against the Slavs, and the Slav name of Brandenburg, *Branibor,* is again only a designation of such a protective forest (Czech *braniti*—to defend, *bor*—pine and pinewood).

After all that there can be no doubt about the stage of civilisation of the Germans encountered by Caesar. They were far from being nomads in the sense of the contemporary Asiatic horse-riding peoples. Nomads need the steppe, and the Germans were living in the virgin forest. But they were equally far removed from the stage of settled peasant peoples. Strabo, sixty years later, still says of them:

"It is a common characteristic of all these" (Germanic) "peoples that they *migrate* with ease, because of their simple way of life, for they do not till the soil or accumulate wealth; they live in huts which they can build in one day; and they live for the most part off their livestock, as the nomads do, and like the nomads they load their belongings on their wagons and with their herds move whithersoever they think best."[b]

Comparative language studies prove that they had already brought with them from Asia a knowledge of agriculture; Caesar shows that they had not forgotten it. But it was the kind of agriculture that serves semi-nomadic warrior tribes, slowly proceeding through the wooded plains of central Europe, as a makeshift and subordinate source of livelihood.

It follows from the above that in Caesar's time the immigration of the Germans into their new homeland between Danube, Rhine and North Sea was not yet completed or was at most in process of completion. That is by no means to say that at the time of Pytheas, Teutons, and perhaps also Cimbri, could not have reached the Jutland Peninsula, or the furthest advanced Germans the Rhine, as may be concluded from the absence of any signs of their arrival. A way of life compatible only with constant movement,

---

[a] Quoted in *Die Geschichtschreiber...,* p. 164.— *Ed.*

[b] Strabo, *Geographica,* VII, 1. Quoted in *Die Geschichtschreiber...,* pp. 373-74.—*Ed.*

repeated moves to the west and south and lastly the fact that Caesar encountered the largest mass known to him, the Suebi, still in full movement, admit only one conclusion: obviously, we have here glimpses of the last moments of the great Germanic immigration into their main European settlement area. It was the Roman resistance on the Rhine and later on the Danube which put an end to this movement, confined the Germans to the region they were then occupying, and thus forced them to adopt permanent habitation.

For the rest, our ancestors, as Caesar saw them, were proper barbarians. They only allowed merchants into the country to secure purchasers for their booty rather than to buy anything from them; for what need had they for foreign things, anyway? They even preferred their ill-favoured ponies to the fine, strong horses of the Gauls. The Suebi suffered no importation of wine whatever, believing the men were thereby rendered effeminate.[a] In this respect their Bastarnae cousins were more civilised; on the occasion of their invasion of Thrace[b] they sent envoys to Crassus, who made them drunk and elicited from them all he needed to know concerning the positions and intentions of the Bastarnae, whom he then lured into an ambush and destroyed. Even before the battle on the Idistavisus (16 of our era) Germanicus described the Germans to his soldiers as without armour or helmets, protected only by shields made of wicker or light boards, only the first rank having real lances, posterior ranks nothing but sharpened poles hardened by fire.[c] Metal working was then therefore still scarcely known to the inhabitants of the Weser region, and the Romans will have taken good care not to let merchants carry arms into Germany.

Fully a century and a half after Caesar, Tacitus gives us his famous description of the Germans.[d] Here much already looks quite different. As far as the Elbe and beyond, the migrating tribes had come to a halt and settled down permanently. To be sure, for a long time there was still no question of towns; settlement was made in villages consisting of individual farmsteads, either widely spaced or close together, but even in the latter case every house was free standing in its own space. Houses were built without quarry-stones or roof-tiles, roughly put together of

---

a See *Die Geschichtschreiber...*, p. 164.— *Ed.*

b See this volume, p. 11.—*Ed.*

c Tacitus, *Annales*, II, 14. Quoted in *Die Geschichtschreiber...*, pp. 457-58.—*Ed.*

d Tacitus, *Germania*, 16. See *Die Geschichtschreiber...*, pp. 655-56.— *Ed.*

untrimmed timber (*materia informi* must here mean this in
contrast to *caementa* and *tegulae*); blockhouses, as still in northern
Scandinavia, but no longer huts which can be built in one day, as
with Strabo.[a] We shall deal later with the agrarian constitution.
The Germans also already had subterranean storage chambers, a
kind of cellar where they dwelt in the winter for warmth and
where the women practised weaving, according to Pliny.[b] Agriculture is therefore already more important, but cattle is still the
chief wealth; it is numerous, but of poor breed, the horses ugly
and no runners, sheep and cattle small, the latter without horns.
Under "nourishment" meat, milk and crab apples are listed, but
no bread. Hunting was no longer much practised, hence the stock
of game was already much reduced since Caesar. Clothing was also
still very primitive, a rough blanket for the mass, otherwise naked
(almost as among the Zulu Kaffirs), but the wealthiest already had
closely fitting clothes; animal skins were also used; the women
dressed much like the men, but already more often wore linen
garments without sleeves. The children all ran about naked.
Reading and writing were unknown, but one passage indicates that
priests were already using runes, characters derived from the
Latin, which they cut into wooden staves.[c] Gold and silver were
not treasured by the Germans of the interior, silver vessels
presented by Romans to princes and envoys served the same
common uses as earthenware. The insignificant trade was by
simple barter.

The men still had the custom common to all primitive peoples
of leaving the work in the home and field to the women, old
people and children, as something unmanly. They had, however,
adopted two civilised customs: drinking and gambling, and they
practised both with all the abandon of untouched barbarians,
gambling to the extreme of throwing dice for their own persons.
In the interior their drink was barley or wheat beer; if schnapps
had already been invented, world history might well have taken a
different course.

At the borders of Roman territory further progress had been
made: imported wine was drunk; to some extent people had
become used to money, preference naturally being given to silver,
as more handy for limited exchange, and, according to barbarian

---

[a] Strabo, *Geographica,* VII, 1. Quoted in *Die Geschichtschreiber...,* pp. 373-74.— *Ed.*
[b] Plinius, *Naturalis historia,* XIX, 1. Quoted in *Die Geschichtschreiber...,*
p. 716.— *Ed.*
[c] Tacitus, *Germania,* 10. See *Die Geschichtschreiber...,* p. 651.— *Ed.*

custom, to coin with a stamp well-known of old. We shall see that they had good cause for such precaution. Trade with the Germans was only conducted on the banks of the Rhine itself; only the Hermunduri, straddling the Limes Germanicus, went at this time in and out of Gaul and Rhaetia for trading purposes.

Hence the first great phase of German history, the final transition from a migratory life to permanent habitations, occurred in the period between Caesar and Tacitus, at least for the greater part of the people, from the Rhine to far beyond the Elbe. The names of the individual tribes begin more or less to coalesce with certain tracts of land. Information from ancient writers being contradictory, and names fluctuating and changing, it is, however, often impossible to assign a definite settlement area to every tribe. It would also lead us too far from our subject. A general statement found in Pliny must suffice here:

> "There are five principal Germanic stocks: the *Vindili,* who include the Burgundiones, Varini, Carini and Guttons; the second stock consists of the *Ingaevones,* including the Cimbri, Teutons and the tribes of the Chauci. The *Iscaevones,* including the Sugambri, live close to the Rhine. The *Hermiones,* comprising the Suebi, Hermunduri, Chatti and Cherusci, occupy the middle of the country. The fifth stock comprises the Peucini, and the Bastarnae, whose neighbours are the Dacians." [a]

A sixth branch may be added to these: the Hilleviones, living in Scandinavia.[b]

Of all the information we gather from the ancient writers this fits best with the later facts and with the preserved linguistic remains.

The Vindili comprise peoples of the *Gothic* tongue who occupied the Baltic coast between Elbe and Vistula and deep inland; the Guttons (Goths) were settled beyond the Vistula around the Frische Haff. The scarce linguistic remains which have been preserved leave not the slightest doubt that the Vandals (who must have formed part of Pliny's Vindili, since he transfers their name to the whole main stock) and the Burgundians spoke Gothic dialects. Only the Warni (or Varini), who are usually, on the basis of information from the 5 and 6 centuries, reckoned among the Thuringians, can cause doubts; we know nothing of their language.

---

[a] Plinius, *Naturalis historia,* IV, 14. Quoted in J. Grimm's *Geschichte der deutschen Sprache,* Vol. 2, Leipzig, 1848, p. 830.— *Ed.*

[b] Engels marks the passage from "Peucini..." to "Scandinavia" with a vertical line in the margin of his manuscript.— *Ed.*

The second stock, the Ingaevones, first of all includes peoples speaking the *Frisian* tongues, inhabitants of the North Sea coast and the Cimbric Peninsula, and most probably also speakers of the Saxon tongue between Elbe and Weser, in which case the Cherusci must also be reckoned among them.

The Iscaevones are at once singled out by the Sugambri, who joined them, as the later Franks, the inhabitants of the right bank of the Rhine from the Taunus down to the sources of the Lahn, Sieg, Ruhr, Lippe and Ems, bordered on the north by Frisians and Chauci.

The Hermiones, or Herminones, as Tacitus calls them more correctly,[a] are the later High Germans: the Hermunduri (Thuringians), Suebi (Swabians and Marcomanni-Bavarians), Chatti (Hessians), etc. The Cherusci are without doubt placed here in error. It is the only indubitable error in the whole of Pliny's list.

The fifth stock, Peucini and Bastarnae, is lost. No doubt Jacob Grimm is right in reckoning it to the Gothic.[b]

Finally, the sixth stock, the Hilleviones, comprises the inhabitants of the Danish islands and the great Scandinavian peninsula.

Hence the division of Pliny corresponds with surprising accuracy to the grouping of the German dialects which later actually appear. We know no dialects which do not belong to either Gothic, Frisian-Low Saxon, Franconian, High German or Scandinavian, and even today we can still acknowledge Pliny's division as exemplary. I shall examine anything that might possibly be said against it in my note on the German peoples.[c]

We must therefore conceive of the original immigration of the Germans into their new homeland approximately as follows: In the first instance the Iscaevones advanced into the middle of the North German plain, between the southern mountains and the Baltic and North seas; close after them, but nearer to the coast, the Ingaevones. These appear to have been followed by the Hilleviones, who turned off to the islands, however. They are followed by the Goths (Pliny's Vindili), who left the Peucini and Bastarnae behind in the south-east; the Gothic name in Sweden testifies that individual sections joined the migrating Hilleviones. Finally, south of the Goths, the Herminones, who, at least for the greater part, moved only in Caesar's and even Augustus' time

---

[a] See *Die Geschichtschreiber...*, p. 647.— *Ed.*

[b] J. Grimm, op. cit., Vol. 1, p. 462.—*Ed.*

[c] See this volume, pp. 44-57.—*Ed.*

into their settlements, which they retained until the migration of peoples.[a]

THE FIRST BATTLES AGAINST ROME

Since Caesar, Romans and Germans faced each other across the Rhine, and since the subjection of Rhaetia, Noricum and Pannonia by Augustus across the Danube. In the meantime Roman rule had been consolidated in Gaul; Agrippa had covered the whole country with a network of military roads, fortresses had been built, a new generation, born under the Roman yoke, had grown up. Brought into the most direct communication with Italy by the Alpine roads over the Little and Great St. Bernard, built by Augustus, Gaul could serve as the base for the conquest of Germania from the Rhine. Augustus entrusted his stepson (or real son?) Drusus with the accomplishment of this conquest with the eight legions stationed on the Rhine.

Pretexts were provided by constant friction among the border-dwellers, by German intrusions into Gaul and by an alleged or actual conspiracy of the disaffected Belgae with the Sugambri, according to which the latter were to cross the Rhine and effect a general rising. Drusus made sure of the Belgic leaders (−12), crossed the river close by the island of Batavia above the Rhine delta, devastated the country of the Usipetes and partly that of the Sugambri, sailed down the Rhine, forced the Frisians to supply him with auxiliary foot soldiers and sailed with the fleet along the coast and into the mouth of the Ems to make war on the Chauci. But here his Roman seamen, unaccustomed to the tides, grounded the fleet during the ebb; he got it free only with the help of the allied Frisian troops, who were better acquainted with the matter, and returned home.

This first campaign was only an extensive reconnaissance. In the following year (−11) he began the actual conquest. He crossed the Rhine again below the mouth of the Lippe, subjugated the Usipetes living there, threw a bridge across the Lippe and invaded the country of the Sugambri, who had just taken the field against the Chatti because these did not want to join the alliance against the Romans under the leadership of the Sugambri. On the confluence of the Lippe and the Eliso he then made a fortified camp (Aliso) and retreated again across the Rhine when winter

---

[a] In the manuscript Engels inserted in pencil: "Here follows the chapter on the agrarian and military constitutions."[6] — Ed.

approached. During this retreat he was ambushed in a narrow defile by the Germans, and it was only with the greatest difficulty that his army escaped annihilation. This year he also made another fortified camp "in the land of the Chatti, close to the Rhine".[a]

This second campaign of Drusus already contains the complete plan of conquest as it was afterwards consistently followed. The region immediately to be conquered was fairly sharply delimited: the Iscaevonian interior to the border with the Cherusci and Chatti and the coastal strip belonging to it as far as the Ems, if possible to the Weser. The main job of subjecting the coastlands was allotted to the fleet. In the south, the base of operations was Mainz, founded by Agrippa and extended by Drusus, in the neighbourhood of which we must look for the fort built "in the land of the Chatti" (nowadays it is being sought in the Saalburg at Homburg). From here the course of the lower Main leads into the open country of the Wetterau and the upper Lahn, the occupation of which would separate Iscaevones and Chatti. In the centre of the front of attack the flat country through which the Lippe flows and particularly the broad ridge of hills between the Lippe and the Ruhr offered the most convenient line of operations to the main Roman force; by its occupation it could divide the region to be conquered into two approximately equal areas and at the same time separate the Bructeri from the Sugambri. From this position it could coordinate its action with the fleet, on the left; together with the column debouching from the Wetterau isolate the Iscaevonian slate mountains on the right, and in front keep the Cherusci in check. The fort of Aliso formed the most advanced stronghold of this line of operations; it was situated near the sources of the Lippe, either at Elsen near Paderborn at the confluence of the Alme and the Lippe, or at Lippstadt, where a big Roman fort has recently been discovered.[b]

In the following year (−10) the Chatti, realising the common danger, at last allied themselves to the Sugambri. But Drusus attacked and forced them into subjection, at least in part. This cannot have outlasted the winter, however, for in the next spring (−9) he attacked once more, advanced as far as the Suebi (i.e., probably Thuringians, according to Florus and Orosius also

---

[a] Dio Cassius, *Historia Romana*, LIV, 33. See *Die Geschichtschreiber...*, p. 276.—*Ed.*

[b] See H. von Abendroth, *Terrainstudien zu dem Rückzuge des Varus und den Feldzügen des Germanicus*, Leipzig, 1862, p. 8.—*Ed.*

Marcomanni,[a] who at that time still lived north of the Erzgebirge), then attacked the Cherusci, crossed the Weser and only turned back at the Elbe. He devastated the whole land he moved through, but met everywhere with heavy resistance. On the way back he died, thirty years old, even before he reached the Rhine.

To the above account, taken from Dio Cassius, we add from Suetonius that Drusus had the canal dug from the Rhine to the Ijssel by which he led his fleet to the North Sea through Frisia and the Flevo (Vliestrom—the present fairway between Vlieland and Terschelling, out of the Zuider Zee)[b]; from Florus, that he erected over 50 forts along the Rhine and a bridge at Bonn and also fortified the line of the Maas, thus securing the position of the Rhenish legions both against risings of the Gauls and against incursions of the Germans. Florus' fables of forts and earthworks on the Weser and Elbe are empty boasting[c]; he [Drusus] may have thrown up entrenchments there during his marches, but he was too good a general to leave even a single man as garrison there. But there is surely no doubt that he had the line of operations along the Lippe provided with fortified bases. He also fortified the passes over the Taunus.

Tiberius, Drusus' successor on the Rhine, crossed the river in the following year (−8); the Germans, except the Sugambri, sent peace negotiators; Augustus, who was in Gaul, refused all negotiations as long as the Sugambri were not represented. When at last they also sent envoys, "numerous and respected men", says Dio, Augustus had them taken prisoner and interned them in various towns in the interior of the empire; "distressed at this, they took their own lives".[d] In the following year (−7), Tiberius went again with an army to Germania, where already nothing had any longer to be combated, except a few insignificant instances of unrest. Velleius says of this time:

"Tiberius so subdued the country (Germania) that it differed but little from a tributary province."[e]

This success will probably have to be attributed not only to Roman arms and to the much vaunted diplomatic "wisdom" of

---

[a] Florus, *Epitomae de Tito Livio*, IV, 12, 21-40 and Orosius, *Historiae adversus paganos*, VI, 21. See *Die Geschichtschreiber...*, pp. 279-80.— *Ed.*

[b] Dio Cassius, op. cit., LV, 1, 2; Suetonius, *De vita Caesarum: Claudius*, 1. See *Die Geschichtschreiber...*, pp. 276-77, 280-81.— *Ed.*

[c] See *Die Geschichtschreiber...*, pp. 279-80.— *Ed.*

[d] Dio Cassius, op. cit., LV, 6. Quoted in *Die Geschichtschreiber...*, pp. 304-05.—*Ed.*

[e] Velleius Paterculus, *Historia Romana*, II, 97. Quoted in *Die Geschichtschreiber...*, p. 305.—*Ed.*

Tiberius, but in particular to the transplanting of Germans to the Roman bank of the Rhine. Already Agrippa had shifted the Ubii, who were always much attached to the Romans, to the left bank of the Rhine at Cologne, with their consent. Tiberius forced 40,000 Sugambri to go over and settle, and with that he broke this powerful people's strength to resist for a considerable time.

Tiberius now retired for some time from all affairs of state and we learn nothing of what went on in Germany during several years. A fragment from Dio tells of a move of Domitius Ahenobarbus from the Danube to beyond the Elbe.[a] Soon after that, however, about the first year of our era, the Germans rose. According to Velleius' statements, Marcus Vinicius, the Roman supreme commander, fought on the whole with success and in recognition received rewards.[b] Nevertheless, in the year 4, soon after his adoption by Augustus, Tiberius had to cross the Rhine once more to restore the shaken Roman power. He subjected first the Canninefates and Chattuari, living next to the river, then the Bructeri, and "won over" the Cherusci. Further details are not given by Velleius, who participated in this and the following campaigns. The mild winter allowed the legions to remain in movement until December; then they went into winter quarters in Germany itself, probably at the sources of the Lippe.

The campaign of the following year (5) was to complete the subjugation of western Germany. While Tiberius advanced from Aliso and defeated the Langobardi on the lower Elbe, the fleet sailed along the coast and "won over" the Chauci. On the lower Elbe the army met the fleet sailing up the river. With the success of this campaign the work of the Romans in the north appeared to be done, according to Velleius[c]; in the following year Tiberius turned to the Danube, where the Marcomanni, who had recently moved to Bohemia under Maroboduus, were threatening the frontier. Educated in Rome and familiar with Roman tactics, Maroboduus had an army of 70,000 foot and 4,000 cavalry, organised on the Roman pattern. Tiberius attacked this army on the Danube in the front, while Sentius Saturninus was to lead the legions from the Rhine through the country of the Chatti into the rear and the flank of the enemy. Then the Pannonians rose in Tiberius' own rear, and the army had to turn and reconquer its

---

[a] See *Die Geschichtschreiber..*, p. 307.— *Ed.*

[b] Velleius Paterculus, op. cit., II, 104. See *Die Geschichtschreiber...*, pp. 309-10.— *Ed.*

[c] Ibid., II, 109. See *Die Geschichtschreiber...*, pp. 313-14.—*Ed.*

base of operations. The fighting lasted three years; but the Pannonians had only just been defeated when in northern Germany things also took such a turn that there could no longer be any question of conquests in the land of the Marcomanni.

Drusus' plan of conquest had been fully retained; but to carry it out in security, campaigns by land and by sea had become necessary as far as the Elbe. In the plan of campaign against Maroboduus the idea transpired of shifting the border to the Little Carpathians, the Riesengebirge and the Elbe as far as its mouth; but for the time being that was still in the remote future and soon became quite impracticable. We do not know how far up the Wetterau Roman forts may have reached; to all appearances this line of operations was at the time neglected in favour of the more important line along the Lippe. There, however, the Romans appeared to have made themselves fairly well at home. The Rhine plain on the right bank from Bonn downwards belonged to them; the Westphalian lowland from the Ruhr northwards to beyond the Ems, to the borders of the Frisians and the Chauci, remained in military occupation. In the rear, Batavi and Frisians were at that time still reliable friends; further west the Chauci, Cherusci and Chatti could be held to be mastered sufficiently, after their repeated defeats and after the blow which had also struck the Langobardi. And in any case, in those three peoples a fairly powerful party existed at the time which saw salvation only in joining Rome. In the south, the power of the Sugambri was broken for the time being; part of their territory, between Lippe and Ruhr, and also in the Rhine plain, was occupied, the rest was surrounded on three sides by the Roman positions on the Rhine, the Ruhr and in the Wetterau, and certainly often enough traversed by Roman columns. In the direction of the Lippe sources, from Neuwied to the Sieg, from Deutz and Neuss to the Wupper, Roman roads leading over dominating mountain ridges have recently been traced at least as far as the border of Berg and Mark.[a] Still further off the Hermunduri, in agreement with Domitius Ahenobarbus, occupied part of the area abandoned by the Marcomanni and were in peaceful intercourse with the Romans. And, finally, the well-known disunity of the German peoples justified the expectation that the Romans would only have to conduct such minor wars as

---

[a] See J. Schneider, *Die römischen Militärstraßen an der Lippe und das Castell Aliso. Nach eigenen Lokalforschungen dargestellt*, Düsseldorf, 1878.— *Ed.*

they themselves must have thought desirable for the purpose of gradually transforming their allies into subjects.

The core of the Roman position was the country on both sides of the Lippe as far as the Osning. Here Roman rule and Roman customs were made acceptable by the constant presence of the legions in fortified camps and "virtually transformed" the barbarians, according to Dio.[a] Here, near the permanent army quarters, there arose those towns and markets of which the same historian writes and whose peaceful intercourse contributed most to the consolidation of the alien rule. Everything seemed to go splendidly. But it was to be otherwise.

Quintilius Varus was appointed supreme commander of the troops in Germany. A Roman of the beginning decline, phlegmatic and indolent, inclined to rest on the laurels of his predecessors, and still more to take advantage of these laurels for himself.

"That he was no despiser of money is demonstrated by his governorship of Syria: he entered the rich province a poor man, but left it a rich man and the province poor" (Velleius).[b]

Otherwise he was "a man of mild character"; but this mild character must have been greatly upset by the transfer to a country where extortion was made so difficult for him because there was almost nothing to extort. Varus nevertheless tried, and that by the method which had long become customary with Roman proconsuls and propraetors.[7] First of all it was necessary as quickly as possible to arrange the occupied part of Germany on the footing of a Roman province, to replace the indigenous public authority, which had hitherto continued to function under the military rule, by Roman authority and thus to turn the country into a source of revenue—both for the fisc and for the proconsul. Varus accordingly tried to "transform" the Germans "more rapidly and effectively". He "issued orders to them as if they were slaves and exacted money as he would from subject nations" (Dio).[c] And the main instrument of subjugation and extortion he used there was the well-tried one of the power of supreme judge exercised by Roman provincial governors, which he here arrogated to himself and on the strength of which he sought to force Roman law on the Germans.

Unfortunately Varus and his civilising mission were nearly one and a half thousand years in advance of history; for that was

---

[a] Dio Cassius, op. cit., LVI, 18. Quoted in *Die Geschichtschreiber...*, p. 326.— *Ed.*
[b] Quoted in *Die Geschichtschreiber...*, p. 321.— *Ed.*
[c] Dio Cassius, op. cit., LVI, 18. Quoted in *Die Geschichtschreiber...*, p. 326.—*Ed.*

roughly how long it was before Germany was ready to "receive Roman law".[8] In fact, Roman law with its classical dissection of private property relations must have appeared as pure nonsense to the Germans, whose title to the little private property that had developed amongst them derived solely from their common property in land. Similarly the solemn forms and procedural challenges, the constant adjournments that are a feature of Roman legal proceedings, must have seemed to them, who were used to finding judgment and sentence themselves in open public court within a few hours according to inherited custom, as just so much denial of justice; just as the swarm of officials and legal sharks surrounding the proconsul must have seemed to them what they in fact were—nothing but cut-throats. And now the Germans were supposed to surrender their free Thing, where fellow tribesmen judged fellow tribesman, and submit to the peremptory sentence of a single man who conducted the proceedings in a foreign language, and who at best based himself on a law unknown and quite inapplicable to them—and who himself was an interested party. The free German, whom according to Tacitus only a priest could physically chastise in seldom cases,[a] who could forfeit life and limb only through treason against his people, but could otherwise atone for every offence, even murder, by a fine (*wergeld*), and who was moreover used to exercising blood revenge for himself and his relations on his own—this free German was now supposed to submit to the scourge and the axe of the Roman lictor.[9] And all for no other reason than to throw the doors wide open to the exchequer bleeding the land white through taxation, and to the extortion and corruption of the proconsul and his accomplices.

But Varus had miscalculated. The Germans were no Syrians. He impressed them with his enforced Roman civilisation only in one respect. He merely showed the neighbouring peoples pressed into alliance what an intolerable yoke awaited them also, and thus forced on them a unity which they had never before been able to achieve.

Varus stood in Germany with three legions, Asprenas with another two on Lower Rhine, only five or six marches from Aliso, the centre of the position. In the face of such a force only a long and carefully prepared, but then suddenly struck, decisive blow offered a prospect of success. Conspiracy was therefore imperative. Arminius undertook to organise it.

---

[a] Tacitus, *Germania*, 12. Quoted in *Die Geschichtschreiber...*, p. 653.— *Ed.*

Arminius, of the Cheruscan nobility, son of Segimerus, who seems to have been a military leader of his people, had spent his early youth in Roman military service, mastered the Roman language and custom, and was a frequent and well received guest at the Roman headquarters, whose loyalty seemed beyond all doubt. Even on the eve of the surprise attack Varus relied on him as a rock. Velleius called him

"a young man of noble birth, brave in action and alert in mind, more so than barbarians usually are; a young man whose countenance and eyes shone with the fire of the mind. He had been our constant companion on previous campaigns," (that is, against Germans) "and in addition to Roman citizenship, enjoyed the Roman dignity of equestrian rank".[a]

But Arminius was more than all that, he was a great statesman and a considerable general. Once resolved to put an end to Roman rule on the right bank of the Rhine, he took the necessary steps without hesitation. The Cheruscan military nobility, already much dominated by Roman influence, had to be won over at least in great part, and the Chatti and Chauci, and even more so the Bructeri and Sugambri, who were directly under Roman yoke, had to be drawn into the conspiracy. All that took time, even though Varus' extortions had prepared the ground; and during this time it was necessary to lull Varus into security. This was done by taking him in with his hobby of dispensing justice and making a complete fool of him with it. Velleius tells us that the Germans,

"who with their extreme savagery combine great cunning, to an extent scarcely credible to one who has had no experience with them, and are a race of born liars, by trumping up a series of fictitious lawsuits, now suing one another without cause, and now thanking him for settling their disputes with Roman justice, so that their own barbarous nature was being softened down by this new and hitherto unknown discipline and order, and that quarrels which had usually been settled by arms were now being settled by law—the Germans brought him to such a complete degree of negligence, that he came to look upon himself as a city praetor, administering justice in the forum, and not a general in command of an army in the heart of Germany"[b]

So passed the summer of the year 9. To make still more certain of success, Varus was induced to split up his troops by detaching them in various ways, which cannot have been difficult given the character of the man and the circumstances.

"Varus," Dio says, "did not keep his troops properly together, as was necessary in a hostile country, but lent teams of soldiers to people who needed help and

---

[a] Quoted in *Die Geschichtschreiber...*, p. 322.— *Ed.*
[b] Here and above Engels quotes from Velleius Paterculus, *Historia Romana*, II, 118. See *Die Geschichtschreiber...*, pp. 321-22.— *Ed.*

asked for it, either to guard a fortified place, to catch robbers, or to escort grain transports."[a]

In the meantime the chief conspirators, in particular Arminius and Segimerus, were constantly round him and frequently at his table. According to Dio, Varus was now already warned, but his confidence knew no bounds. At length, in the autumn, when all was ready for striking the blow, and Varus with the bulk of his troops had been lured deep into the land of the Cherusci, as far as the Weser, a feigned rising at some distance gave the signal. Even as Varus received the news and gave orders for departure, he was warned by another leader of the Cherusci, Segestes, who seems to have maintained a sort of clan feud with the family of Arminius. Varus would not believe him. Segestes thereupon proposed that he himself, Arminius and the other leaders of the Cherusci should be put in chains before Varus marched off; success would show who was right. But Varus' confidence was unshakeable, even when on his departure the conspirators stayed behind, under the pretext that they were gathering allies to join him with them.

This happened, indeed, though not as Varus expected. The troops of the Cherusci were already assembled. The first thing they did was to massacre the Roman detachments stationed with them at their own earlier request, and then to attack Varus on the flank while he was on the march. The latter was moving along bad forest paths, for here, in the land of the Cherusci, there were not yet any paved Roman military roads. Taken by surprise, he at last realised his situation, braced himself and from now on showed that he was a Roman general—but too late. He let his troops close up, had his large train of women, children, waggons, pack animals, etc., lined up in order and protected as well as was possible considering the narrow paths and dense woods, and turned towards his base of operations—which we must take to have been Aliso. Pouring rain softened the ground, hindered the march, constantly breaking up again the order of the ponderous train. With heavy losses Varus succeeded in reaching a densely wooded mountain, which, however, offered open space for a temporary camp. This was occupied and fortified still in fairly good order and according to regulations; the army of Germanicus, visiting the place six years later, still recognised there distinctly "the work of three legions".[b] With a resolve appropriate to the

---

[a] Dio Cassius, op. cit., LVI, 19. Quoted in *Die Geschichtschreiber...*, pp. 326-27.—*Ed.*

[b] Tacitus, *Annales*, I, 61. Quoted in *Die Geschichtschreiber...*, p. 443.—*Ed.*

situation Varus here had all the not absolutely necessary waggons and baggage burnt. The next day he moved through open country, but again suffered so heavily that the troops were separated still more widely, and in the evening the camp could no longer be fortified according to regulations; Germanicus found only one half-ruined mound and a shallow ditch. On the third day the march led again through wooded mountains, and here Varus and most of the leaders lost heart. Varus killed himself, the legions were destroyed almost to the last man. Only the cavalry escaped under Vala Numonius; individual refugees from the infantry also appear to have managed to get to Aliso. Aliso itself held out at least for some time, since the Germans did not know the regular siege attack; later the garrison somehow fought its way through, wholly or in part. Asprenas, intimidated, appears to have confined himself to a short advance to receive them. Bructeri, Sugambri and all the lesser peoples rose, and Roman power was again thrown back across the Rhine.

The localities of this expedition have been much disputed. Most likely, before the battle Varus was stationed in the hollow of the Rinteln valley, somewhere between Hausberge and Hameln; the retreat decided upon after the first attack was in the direction of the Dören gap near Detmold, which forms a plain and broad pass through the Osning. This is the general view which has become traditional and fits in with the sources as well as the military exigencies of the war situation. Whether Varus reached the Dören gap remains uncertain; the breakthrough of the cavalry and perhaps the first ranks of the infantry would appear to show that he did.[a]

The news of the annihilation of the three legions and the rising of the whole of western Germany struck Rome like a thunder clap. Some already saw Arminius marching across the Rhine and spreading insurrection in Gaul, Maroboduus on the other side crossing the Danube and carrying with him the barely subdued Pannonians on a march across the Alps. And Italy was already so exhausted that it could hardly supply men any longer. Dio reports that there were only few young men capable of bearing arms left among the citizenry, that the older men refused to join the army so that Augustus punished them with confiscation of their wealth, and some even with death; that the emperor eventually managed to raise a few troops for the protection of Rome from among

---

[a] H. von Abendroth, op. cit., p. 14.— Ed.

freedmen and veterans, disarmed his German bodyguard and banned all Germans from the city.[a]

Arminius did not cross the Rhine, however; Maroboduus was not thinking of any attack, and so Rome could indulge undisturbed in outbursts of fury at the "perfidious Germans". We have already seen Velleius' description of them as people who "with their extreme savagery combine great cunning ... and are a race of born liars". Similarly Strabo. He knows nothing of "German loyalty" and "Celtic perfidy"; quite to the contrary. While he calls the Celts "simple and straightforward", so simple-minded that they "gather for battle in full view of everybody and without any circumspection, thus making it easy for the enemy to carry the day",[b] he says of the Germans:

> "In dealing with them it was always advisable not to trust them, those who have been trusted have done great harm as, for instance, the Cherusci, in whose country three legions, with their general Varus, were destroyed by an ambush in violation of the treaties." [c]

Not to speak of the indignant and vindictive verses of Ovid.[d] One could imagine to be reading French authors of the most chauvinistic period, boiling with rage at Yorck's breach of faith or the treachery of the Saxons at Leipzig.[10] The Germans had become well acquainted with Roman loyalty to agreements and probity when Caesar attacked the Usipetes and Tencteri during the negotiations and the truce; they had become acquainted with it when Augustus had the envoys of the Sugambri taken prisoner, while before their arrival he had rejected any negotiations with the German peoples. All conquering nations have this in common that they will try to outwit their opponents by any means; and they find this quite in order; no sooner do their adversaries do the same thing, however, than they call this breach of faith and treachery. But the instruments of subjection must also be allowed to serve to throw off the yoke. So long as there are exploiting and ruling nations and classes on the one hand, and exploited and ruled ones on the other, so long the use of cunning side by side with force will for both sides be a necessity against which all moral preaching will be powerless.

However childish the fantastic statue of Arminius erected at Detmold may be—it had only one good side, that it induced Louis

---

[a] Dio Cassius, op. cit., LVI, 23. Quoted in *Die Geschichtschreiber...*, pp. 330-31.—*Ed.*

[b] Strabo, *Geographica*, IV, 4. Quoted in *Die Geschichtschreiber...*, pp. 370-71.— *Ed.*

[c] Quoted in *Die Geschichtschreiber...*, pp. 374-75.— *Ed.*

[d] Ovidius, *Ex Ponto* and *Tristia.* See *Die Geschichtschreiber...*, p. 365.—*Ed.*

Napoleon to erect a similarly ridiculous, fantastic colossus of
Vercingetorix on a mountain at Aliso [-Sainte-Reine]—it remains
true that the Varus battle was one of the most decisive turning
points in history. It decided Germany's independence of Rome
once and for all. One can argue at length to no purpose about
whether or not this independence was such a great gain for the
Germans themselves; it is certain that without it the whole of
history would have taken a different course. And even if in fact all
the subsequent history of the Germans has been almost nothing
but a long series of national disasters, mostly through their own
fault, so much so that even the most brilliant successes almost
always turned out to the detriment of the people, one must
nevertheless say that here, at the beginning of their history, the
Germans were decidedly fortunate.

Caesar used the last vital forces of the dying Republic to
subjugate Gaul. The legions, since Marius consisting of recruited
mercenaries but still exclusively Italic men, since Caesar literally
died out in the measure in which the Italic people themselves died
out under the rapidly spreading latifundia and their slave
economy. The 150,000 men who made up the compact infantry of
the 25 legions could only be kept together by extreme measures.
The 20-year service was not observed; veterans who had completed their service were forced to remain with the colours for an
indefinite period. That was the chief reason for the mutiny of the
Rhenish legions on the death of Augustus which Tacitus describes
so imaginatively,[a] and which with its extraordinary mixture of
refractoriness and discipline recalls so vividly the mutinies of the
Spanish soldiers of Philip II in the Netherlands,[11] in both cases
testifying to the solidity of the army at a time when the Prince had
broken the word he had given it. We saw how vain Augustus'
attempt remained after the Varus battle to reinstate the old levy
laws which had long gone out of use; how he had to fall back on
veterans and even freedmen—he had used these once before,
during the Pannonian insurrection.[12] The reserve of free Italic
peasants' sons had disappeared with the free Italic peasants
themselves. Every new reserve contingent introduced into the
legions worsened the army's quality. And since these legions, this
core of the entire might of the army, which was difficult to
maintain, had nevertheless to be spared as much as possible, the
auxiliary troops came more and more to the fore and fought
battles in which the legions only formed the reserve, so that

---

[a] Tacitus, *Annales,* I, 31-52. See *Die Geschichtschreiber...,* pp. 421-37.— *Ed.*

already in Claudius' time the Batavi could say: the provinces were being conquered with the blood of the provinces.

With such an army, more and more alienating itself from the ancient Roman discipline and solidity and therewith from the ancient Roman manner of fighting, increasingly composed of provincials and eventually of barbarians alien to the empire, almost no great aggressive wars could any longer be conducted— soon no great offensive battles could be fought. The deterioration of the army placed the state on the defensive, which was first fought aggressively, then more and more passively, until at length the weight of the attack, now shifted completely to the side of the Germans, broke through irresistibly across the Rhine and Danube along the whole line from the North Sea to the Black Sea.

In the meantime it was necessary, even to safeguard the line of the Rhine, to let the Germans feel once more, on their own territory, the superior strength of Roman arms. For this purpose Tiberius hastened to the Rhine, restored weakened discipline by his own example and strict punishment, limited the train of the mobile army to the absolutely necessary and marched through western Germany in two expeditions (years 10 and 11). The Germans did not present themselves for decisive battles, the Romans did not dare to occupy their winter camps on the right bank of the Rhine. There is no evidence that Aliso and the fort set up at the mouth of the Ems in the country of the Chauci retained their permanent garrison also in the winter, but it is probable.

In the year 14, in August, Augustus died. The Rhenish legions, who after completing their service were neither dismissed nor given their pay, refused to recognise Tiberius and proclaimed Germanicus, son of Drusus, emperor. He calmed the rising himself, returned the troops to obedience, and led them into Germany in three expeditions which have been described by Tacitus.[a] Here Arminius confronted him and proved a general fully worthy of his opponent. He sought to avoid any decisive battles in open country, to hinder the Romans' march as much as possible, and to attack them only in swamps and defiles where they could not deploy their forces. But the Germans did not always follow him. Pugnacity often carried them away into fighting in unfavourable circumstances; greed for booty more than once saved Romans who were already sitting firmly in a trap. So Germanicus gained the two fruitless victories on the Idistavisus and on the Angrivarian limes,[13] barely escaped on the retreats

---

[a] Tacitus, *Annales*, I, 31-52. See *Die Geschichtschreiber...*, pp. 421-37.—*Ed.*

through narrow swamp passes, lost ships and crews through storms and floods on the Frisian coast, and was eventually recalled by Tiberius after the expedition of the year 16. With that the Roman expeditions into the interior of Germany came to an end.

But the Romans knew only too well that a river line is only held if one also holds the crossings to the other bank. Far from retreating passively beyond the Rhine, the Romans transferred their defence to the right bank. The Roman fortifications which cover the regions of the lower Lippe, Ruhr and Wupper in big groups, at least in some cases corresponding to later districts, [and] the military roads built from the Rhine to the border of the Duchy of Mark, lead us to surmise here a system of defence works along a line from the Ijssel to the Sieg, corresponding to the present frontier line between Franks and Saxons, with occasional deviations of the border of the Rhine province in the direction of Westphalia. This system, which was probably still to some extent defensible in the 7th century, must then also have kept the Saxons, who were advancing at that time, from reaching the Rhine, and thereby fixed their present ethnic border against the Franks. The most interesting discoveries have been made here in recent years (by J. Schneider)[a]; we may well expect further discoveries.

Farther up the Rhine the great Roman Limes was gradually built up, especially under Domitian and Hadrian; it runs from below Neuwied over the heights of Montabaur to Ems, there crosses the Lahn, turns west at Adolfseck, following the northern slopes of the Taunus, envelopes Grüningen in the Wetterau as its northernmost point, and thence, running in a south-south-easterly direction, reaches the Main south of Hanau. From here the Limes runs on the left bank of the Main to Miltenberg; thence in an only once broken straight line to the Württemberg Rems, near the castle of Hohenstaufen. Here the line, built further at a later time, probably under Hadrian, turns eastward via Dinkelsbühl, Gunzenhausen, Ellingen and Kipfenberg, and reaches the Danube at Irnsing above Kehlheim. Smaller entrenchments lay behind the Limes, and larger forts as support points at a greater distance. Thus enclosed, the country to the right of the Rhine, which at least south of the Main had lain deserted since the Helvetii were driven out by the Suebi, was peopled by Gallic vagrants, stragglers of the troops, according to Tacitus.[b]

---

[a] See J. Schneider, *Die römischen Militärstraßen an der Lippe und das Castell Aliso. Nach eigenen Lokalforschungen dargestellt*, Düsseldorf, 1878.— *Ed.*

[b] Tacitus, *Germania*, 28. See *Die Geschichtschreiber...*, pp. 662-63.—*Ed.*

Thus conditions gradually became calmer and safer on the Rhine, the Limes and the Danube. Fighting and expeditions continued, but the mutual borders remained unchanged for some centuries.

PROGRESS UNTIL THE MIGRATION PERIOD

Written sources on the situation and the events in the interior of Germany fail after Tacitus and Ptolemy. Instead a series of other, much more vivid sources is opening up for us: finds of antiquities in so far as they can be attributed to the period under discussion.

We have seen that at the time of Pliny and Tacitus Roman trade with the interior of Germany was virtually non-existent. But we find in Pliny an indication of an old trade route, which in his time was still used occasionally, from Carnuntum (opposite the confluence of the March with the Danube), along the March and the Oder to the Amber coast.[a] This route, and also another, through Bohemia along the Elbe, was probably used at a very early period by the Etruscans, whose presence in the northern valleys of the Alps is documented by numerous finds, particularly the Hallstatt find.[14] The invasion of the Gauls into northern Italy will have put an end to this trade (ca.—400) (Boyd Dawkins).[b] If this view is confirmed, this Etruscan trade, especially the importation of bronze goods, must have been conducted with the peoples who occupied the land on the Vistula and the Elbe before the Germans, probably with Celts, and the immigration of the Germans would have had as much to do with its interruption as the backflow of the Celts into Italy. The more easterly trade route, from the Greek cities on the Black Sea along Dniester and Dnieper to the area of the Vistula mouth, would then appear to have come into use only after this interruption. The ancient Greek coins found near Bromberg, in the island of Oesel and elsewhere suggest this interpretation; among them are pieces of the fourth, possibly the fifth century before our era, coined in Greece, Italy, Sicily, Cyrene, etc.

The interrupted trade routes along the Oder and Elbe were bound to be restored again as soon as the migrating people came to a halt. At the time of Ptolemy not only these, but other roads of

---

a Plinius, *Naturalis historia*, XXXVII, 45.— *Ed.*

b W. Boyd Dawkins, *Early Man in Britain and His Place in the Tertiary Period*, London, 1880, p. 472.—*Ed.*

traffic through Germany seem to have come into use again, and where Ptolemy's evidence fails, finds continue to bear witness.

C. F. Wiberg* has clarified much here by careful compilation of the finds, and has provided the evidence that in the second century of our era the trade routes both through Silesia down the Oder and through Bohemia down the Elbe were used again. In Bohemia Tacitus already mentions

"traders in booty and merchants" (*lixae ac negotiatores*) "out of our provinces whom avarice and oblivion of their homes have led into enemy territory and to Maroboduus' army camp".[a]

So also the Hermunduri, who, long since friends of the Romans, had, according to Tacitus,[b] unhindered access to the *Agri Decumates*[15] and Rhaetia as far as Augsburg, will surely have traded Roman goods and coins from the upper Main further to the Saale and Werra. Traces of a trade route into the interior have also been revealed further down the Roman Limes, on the Lahn.

The route through Moravia and Silesia appears to have remained the most important one. The only watershed that has to be crossed, that between the March, or Bečva, and Oder, passes through open hill country and lies less than 325 metres above sea level; even now the railway passes along here. Beginning with Lower Silesia the north German lowlands open up, so that roads can branch out in all directions to the Vistula and the Elbe. Roman merchants must have resided in Silesia and Brandenburg in the second and third centuries. There we find not only urns of glass, tear bottles and burial urns with Latin inscriptions (Massel near Trebnitz in Silesia and elsewhere), but even complete Roman sepulchral vaults with recesses for urns (*columbaria*), (Nacheln near Glogau). Undoubted Roman graves have also been found at Warin in Mecklenburg. Similarly, finds of coins, Roman metal ware, clay lamps, etc., are evidence of trade along this route. Generally speaking, the whole of eastern Germany, although never entered by Roman armies, is studded with Roman coins and manufactures, the latter frequently documented by the same trade marks as occur on finds in the provinces of the Roman Empire. Clay lamps found in Silesia bear the same trade mark as others found in Dalmatia, Vienna, etc. The mark: *Ti. Robilius Sitalces,* for instance,

---

* *Bidrag till kännedomen om Grekers och Romares förbindelse med Norden.* German by Mestorf: *Der Einfluß der klassischen Völker* etc., Hamburg, 1867.

---

a Tacitus, *Annales*, II, 62.— *Ed.*
b Op. cit.— *Ed.*

is stamped on bronze vases of which one was found in Mecklenburg, another in Bohemia; this indicates a trade route along the Elbe.

Moreover, in the first centuries after Augustus Roman merchant vessels sailed on the North Sea. This is proved by the find in Neuhaus on the Oste (Elbe mouth) of 344 Roman silver coins from Nero to Marcus Aurelius with remains of a ship which probably foundered there. Shipping also went along the southern coast of the Baltic, reaching the Danish islands, Sweden and Gotland, and we shall have to study this more closely. The distances given by Ptolemy and Marcianus (about the year 400) between the various points on the coast can only have been derived from the reports of merchants who sailed along that coast. They are given from the coast of Mecklenburg to Danzig and thence to Scandia. Finally, this trade is proved by innumerable other finds of Roman origin in Holstein, Schleswig, Mecklenburg, Western Pomerania, the Danish islands and southern Sweden, on sites lying closest to each other near the coast.

How far this Roman traffic included the import of weapons into Germany is difficult to determine. The numerous Roman weapons found in Germany could equally well be booty, and the Roman border authorities naturally did everything to cut off supplies of arms to the Germans. Some could have come by sea, however, particularly to the more distant peoples such as those of the Cimbric peninsula.

The rest of the Roman products which came to Germany by these various routes consisted of household goods, jewellery, toilet articles, etc. Household goods include bowls, measures, tumblers, vessels, cooking pots, sieves, spoons, scissors, ladles, etc., of bronze; a few vessels of gold or silver; clay lamps, which are very widespread; jewellery made of bronze, silver or gold: necklaces, diadems, bracelets and rings, clips rather like our brooches; among the toilet articles we find combs, pincers, ear spoons, etc.—not to mention articles the use of which is disputable. Most of these manufactures, according to Worsaae, were made under the influence of the tastes dominant in Rome in the first century.[a]

The difference between the Germans of Caesar, and even of Tacitus, and the people who used these wares is great, even if we admit that they were used only by the nobler and wealthier families. The "simple dishes without much preparation" (*sine*

---

[a] J. J. A. Worsaae, *Die Vorgeschichte des Nordens nach gleichzeitigen Denkmälern*, Hamburg, 1878, p. 109.— *Ed.*

apparatu) "or condiments" with which the Germans, according to Tacitus, "banished their hunger"[a] had given way to a cuisine which already used a fairly sophisticated apparatus and in addition probably also obtained the corresponding condiments from the Romans. Contempt for gold- and silver-ware had given way to the desire to adorn oneself with them; indifference to Roman money to its spread all over German territory. And especially the toilet articles—what a transformation of customs is revealed by their mere presence among a people which, as far as we know, invented soap, indeed, but used it only to bleach the hair!

Concerning the goods which the Germans provided to the Roman traders in exchange for all this cash and these wares we are in the first instance dependent on the information of the ancient writers, who, as we have said, leave us almost completely in the dark. Pliny mentions vegetables, goose quills, woollen stuffs and soap as articles which the empire imported from Germany.[b] But this insipient trade at the border cannot be a standard for the later period. The chief article of trade of which we know was amber; it does not suffice, however, to explain a traffic which was spreading all over the country. Cattle, the chief wealth of the Germans, will also have been the most important export; the legions stationed at the border alone guaranteed a big demand for meat. Hides and furs, which in the time of Jornandes were sent from Scandinavia to the Vistula mouth, and thence into Roman territory, no doubt found their way there from the East German forests even in earlier periods. Wild beasts for the circus were brought in from the north by Roman seafarers, Wiberg thinks. But nothing could be got there save bears, wolves and possibly aurochs, and lions, leopards and even bears were easier to procure nearer home in Africa and Asia.—Slaves? asks Wiberg eventually, almost bashfully, and there he has probably got the right idea.[c] Indeed, apart from cattle, slaves were the only article Germany could export in sufficient quantities to balance its trade with Rome. The cities and latifundia of Italy alone used up an enormous slave population, which propagated itself only to a very small extent. The entire Roman large landed property economy had as its precondition that colossal importation of traded prisoners of war which flooded into Italy in the ceaseless wars of conquest of the decaying Republic, and even of Augustus. That

[a] Tacitus, *Germania*, 23. Quoted in *Die Geschichtschreiber...*, p. 659.—*Ed.*

[b] Plinius, *Naturalis historia*, XVIII, 17.—*Ed.*

[c] C. F. Wiberg, *Der Einfluß der klassischen Völker...*, p. 44.—*Ed.*

had now come to an end. The empire was on the defensive within fixed borders. Defeated enemies, from whom the bulk of the slaves were recruited, were being supplied in decreasing numbers by the Roman army. One had to buy them from the barbarians. And should not the Germans also have appeared on the market as sellers? The Germans who were already selling slaves according to Tacitus (*Germania,* 24),[a] who were constantly at war with each other, who, like the Frisians, when money was scarce paid their tax to the Romans by giving their wives and children into slavery and who already in the third century, if not before, sailed on the Baltic Sea and whose maritime expeditions in the North Sea, from the Saxon voyages of the third century to the Norman voyages of the tenth, had as their main object, alongside other forms of piracy, the hunt for slaves—almost exclusively for the trade?—the same Germans who, a few centuries later, both during the migration of the peoples and in their wars against the Slavs acted as the prime slave hunters and slave traders of their time? Either we must assume that the Germans of the second and third centuries were quite different people from all the other neighbours of the Romans, and quite different from their own descendants of the third, fourth and fifth centuries and later, or we must admit that they also largely participated in the slave trade to Italy, which at the time was held to be quite decent and even honourable. And then the mysterious veil falls, which otherwise conceals the German export trade of that time.

Here we must return to the Baltic traffic of those times. While the coast of the Kattegat has almost no Roman finds to show, the southern coast of the Baltic as far as Livland, Schleswig-Holstein, the southern fringes and the interior of the Danish islands, the southern and south-eastern coasts of Sweden, Oeland and Gotland are very rich in them. By far the greater part of these finds belongs to the so-called denarius period, of which we shall have more to say later, and which lasted until the first years of the reign of Septimius Severus, i.e. to about 200. Tacitus already calls the Suiones strong by virtue of their rowing fleets and says that they honour wealth[b]; hence they surely already practised maritime trade. Shipping, which first developed in the Belts and in the Oeresund and Oelandsund and in coastal navigation, had to dare on to the high seas to draw Bornholm and Gotland into its circle; it had to have acquired considerable assurance in the handling of

---

[a] See *Die Geschichtschreiber...,* p. 660.— *Ed.*
[b] Tacitus, *Germania,* 44. See *Die Geschichtschreiber...,* p. 671.—*Ed.*

vessels to develop the lively traffic the centre of which was the island of Gotland, farthest away from the continent. Here, indeed, more than 3,200 Roman silver denarii have been found up to 1873,* against about 100 on Oeland, barely 50 on the Swedish mainland, 200 on Bornholm and 600 in Denmark and Schleswig (of these 428 in a single find, Slagelse on Zealand).[16] An analysis of these finds shows that down to the year 161, when Marcus Aurelius became emperor, only a few, but from then on to the end of the century, masses of Roman denarii came to Gotland. In the last half of the second century shipping in the Baltic must already have achieved a considerable development; that it existed already earlier is shown by Ptolemy's statement[a] that the distance from the Vistula mouth to Scandia was 1,200 to 1,600 stadia (30 to 40 geographical miles[b]). Both distances are about right for the eastern point of Blekinge as for the southern tip of Oeland or Gotland, depending on whether one measures from Rixhöft or Neufahrwasser and Pillau respectively. They can only rest on seamen's reports, just like the other distance measurements along the German coast to the mouths of the Vistula.

That this sea traffic on the Baltic was not practised by the Romans is indicated, firstly, by their altogether nebulous concepts about Scandinavia and, secondly, by the absence of any finds of Roman coins on the Kattegat and in Norway. The Cimbric Cape (Skagen), which the Romans reached under Augustus, and from which they saw the endless sea spreading out, seems to have remained the limit of their direct sea traffic. Hence the Germans themselves sailed on the Baltic and maintained the intercourse which brought Roman money and Roman manufactures to Scandinavia. Nor could it have been otherwise. Beginning with the second half of the third century the Saxon maritime expeditions appear quite suddenly on the coasts of Gaul and Britain, and that with a daring and assurance which they could not have acquired overnight, which rather presupposes long familiarity with navigation on the open sea. And the Saxons, by whom we must here also understand all the peoples of the Cimbric peninsula, hence also Frisians, Angles and Jutes, could only have acquired this familiarity on the Baltic. This big inland sea, without tides, where

---

* Hans Hildebrand, *Das heidnische Zeitalter in Schweden.* Translated into German by J. Mestorf. Hamburg, 1873.

---

[a] Ptolemaeus, *Geographia,* II, 11, 2.— *Ed.*
[b] A German geographical mile equals 4.66 English geographical miles.— *Ed.*

the Atlantic sou'westers only arrive having exhausted their fury in great part on the North Sea, this extensive, long basin with its many islands, its shallow, closed-in bays and straits, where on crossing from shore to shore one cannot see land only for short distances, was as if made to serve a newly developing navigation as training waters. Here the Swedish rock drawings, attributed to the bronze age, with their many representations of rowing boats, indicate a maritime traffic of great antiquity. Here the Nydam bog-find in Schleswig presents us with a boat made of oak timbers, 70 feet long and eight to nine feet wide, dated to the beginning of the third century, and quite suitable for voyaging on the high seas.[a] Here that boat-building technique and sea-faring experience quietly grew which made possible the later conquering expeditions of Saxons and Normans on the high seas and laid the foundations which enabled the Germanic people to stand at the head of all sea-faring peoples of the world to this day.

Roman coins which reached Germany before the end of the second century were predominantly silver denarii (1 denarius = 1.06 mark). And moreover, as Tacitus informs us, the Germans preferred the old, well-known coins with serrated rim, the design including a team of two horses.[b] Indeed, among the older coins many of these *serrati bigatique* have been found. These old coins only had some 5 to 10 per cent copper added to the silver; Trajan already ordered that 20 per cent copper be added to the silver and the Germans do not seem to have noticed this. But when Septimius Severus from 198 onwards raised the addition to 50-60 per cent, the Germans thought it too bad; these devalued later denarii occur in the finds only quite exceptionally, the importation of Roman money ceased. It only began again after Constantine, in the year 312, established the gold solidus as the monetary unit (72 solidi to the Roman pound of 327 g of fine gold, hence 1 solidus = 4.55 g fine = 12.70 marks) and then it was predominantly gold coins, solidi, which came to Germany, but even more so to Oeland and particularly Gotland. This second period of Roman money importation, the solidus period, lasted to the end of the Western Empire for West Roman coins, and for Byzantine coins up to Anastasius (died 518). Most of the finds have been made in Sweden, on the Danish islands, and a few on the German Baltic coast; in the German interior they are sporadic.

The counterfeiting of coins by Septimius Severus and his

---

[a] See C. F. Wiberg, op. cit., p. 119.— *Ed.*

[b] Tacitus, *Germania*, 5. See *Die Geschichtschreiber...*, pp. 648-49.—*Ed.*

successors does not, however, suffice to explain the sudden cessation of trade relations between Germans and Romans. Other causes must have come into play. One is evidently to be sought in the political situation. In the beginning of the third century the aggressive war of the Germans against Rome started, and by 250 it had flared up all along the line from the Danube mouths to the Rhine delta. Of course, no regular trade could be conducted by the warring parties in these circumstances. But these sudden, general, persistent aggressive wars themselves require an explanation. Internal Roman conditions do not explain them; on the contrary, as yet the empire resisted everywhere successfully and between individual periods of wild anarchy strong emperors were still produced, particularly around this time. The attacks must therefore have been conditioned by changes among the Germans themselves. And here again the finds provide the explanation.

At the beginning of the sixties of our century finds of outstanding importance were made in two Schleswig peatbogs, which, carefully studied by Engelhardt in Copenhagen, have now, after various wanderings, been deposited in the Museum in Kiel. They are distinguished from other, similar finds by the coins belonging to them, which establish their age with fair certainty. One of these finds, from the Taschberg (Danish Thorsbjerg) moor near Süderbrarup, contains 37 coins from Nero to Septimius Severus; the other, from the Nydam moor, a peat-covered, silted-up sea bay, 34 coins from Tiberius to Macrinus (218).[a] Hence the finds are without doubt from the period between 220 and 250. They contain not only objects of Roman origin but also numerous others, made in the country itself and which, being almost perfectly preserved thanks to the ferrous peat water, reveal with amazing clarity the state of the north German metal industry, weaving and shipbuilding, and through the runic letters even the writing in use in the first half of the third century.

Here we are even more struck by the level of the industry itself. The fine fabrics, the delicate sandals, and the neatly worked leather straps bear witness to a much higher stage of culture than that of the Germans of Tacitus; but what arouses particular amazement is the local metal work.

Linguistic comparisons show that the Germans brought the knowledge of metals and their uses with them from their Asiatic homeland. The art of smelting and working metal was perhaps

---

[a] C. Engelhardt, *Thorsbjerg Mosefund,* Copenhagen, 1863. Quoted in C. F. Wiberg, *Der Einfluß der klassischen Völker...,* pp. 104, 118-19.— *Ed.*

also known to them, but they had barely retained it at the time when they came into collision with the Romans. At least the writers of the first century give no indication that iron or bronze were produced and worked between Rhine and Elbe; they rather suggest the opposite. Tacitus, it is true, says of the Gothines (in Upper Silesia?) that they were digging for iron,[a] and Ptolemy attributes ironworks to the neighbouring Quadi[b]; both may again have acquired a knowledge of smelting from the Danube area. Nor do the finds of the first century documented by coins contain any local metal products anywhere, but only Roman ones; and how could the masses of Roman metal ware have got to Germany if a home metalworking industry had existed there? Ancient casting moulds, incomplete castings and waste of bronze are indeed found there, but never with coins to document their age; in all probability these are traces of pre-Germanic times, the residue of the work of itinerant Etruscan bronze casters. In any case, the question whether the German immigrants had lost the art of metalworking *completely* is pointless; all the evidence goes to show that no, or hardly any, metalworking was practised in the first century.

Here now the Taschberg moor finds suddenly turn up, and reveal to us an unexpectedly high level of the indigenous metal industry. Buckles, metal plates for mountings, decorated with animal and human heads; a silver helmet which completely frames the face, leaving only eyes, nose and mouth free; chain armour of wire netting, which presupposes very laborious operations, since the wire had first to be hammered (wire drawing was not invented until 1306), and a head ring of gold, not to mention other objects the indigenous origin of which might be disputed. These finds agree with others—those from the Nydam moor and bog finds from Fyn, and lastly a find from Bohemia (Hořovice), likewise discovered at the beginning of the sixties, which contains magnificent bronze disks with human heads, buckle clips, etc., quite in the manner of the Taschberg finds, hence probably also of the same period.

Beginning with the third century the metal industry will have spread over the whole German area, being increasingly perfected; by the time of the migration of the peoples, say by the end of the fifth century, it reached a relatively very high level. Not only iron

---

[a] Tacitus, *Germania*, 43. See *Die Geschichtschreiber...*, p. 670.— *Ed.*
[b] Ptolemaeus, *Geographia*, II, 11.—*Ed.*

and bronze, gold and silver also were worked regularly, Roman coins imitated in gold bracteates,[a] the base metals gilded; inlaid work, enamel and filigree work occur; highly artistic ornaments in good taste, only in part imitating Roman work, are found on otherwise often crudely made pieces, especially on clips and buckles or fibulae, which have certain characteristic forms in common. Buckles from Kerch on the Sea of Azov are lying in the British Museum next to quite similar ones found in England; they could be from the same manufactory. The style of these pieces is basically the same, from Sweden to the Lower Danube and from the Black Sea to France and England, though often with quite clearly distinguishable local peculiarities. This first period of the German metal industry came to an end on the continent with the end of the migration of the peoples and the general acceptance of Christianity; in England and Scandinavia it lasted a little longer.

That this industry was widespread among the Germans in the 6th and 7th centuries and that it had already become a separate branch of industry is proved by local laws [Volksrechte].[17] Smiths, swordmakers, gold- and silversmiths are frequently mentioned, in the Alamannic law[18] even smiths who have passed a public examination (*publice probati*). Bavarian law punishes theft from a church, a ducal court, a smithy or a mill with harsher penalties "because these four are public buildings and are always open".[19] In Frisian law[20] the goldsmith has a higher *wergeld* by one fourth than other people of his estate; Salic law[21] estimates the simple bondsman at 12 solidi, but one who is a smith (*faber*) at 35.

We have already mentioned *shipbuilding*. The Nydam boats are rowing boats, the bigger one, made of oak, for fourteen pairs of rowers; the smaller one is of pine. Oars, rudder and scoops were still lying inside. It was not until the Germans began to navigate the North Sea, too, that they seem to have adopted sails from the Romans and Celts.

They knew *pottery* already at the time of Tacitus, but probably only hand pottery. The Romans had large potteries on the borders, particularly inside the Limes in Swabia and Bavaria, which also employed Germans, as is proved by the workers' names burnt into the pots. With these workers the knowledge of glazing

---

[a] A very thin coin usually of silver having a design stamped on one side only.— *Ed.*

and the potter's wheel and also higher technical skill will have come to Germany. Glassmaking, too, was known to the Germans who broke in across the Danube; glass vessels, coloured glass beads and glass insets in metal ware, all of German origin, have often been found in Bavaria and Swabia.

Finally, we now find runic writing widely spread and generally used. The Taschberg find has a sword sheath and a shieldboss which are ornamented with runes. The same runes are found on a gold ring found in Walachia, on buckles from Bavaria and Burgundy, and lastly, on the oldest runic stones in Scandinavia. It is the more complete runic alphabet, the one from which the Anglo-Saxon runes were later derived; it contains seven more characters than the Norse runic writing which predominated later in Scandinavia and indicates also an older linguistic form than the one in which the oldest Norse has been preserved. It was, incidentally, an extremely clumsy system of writing, consisting of Roman and Greek letters so changed that they were easily scratched [*eingeritzt* = writan] on stone, metal and especially on wooden staves. The rounded forms had to give way to angular shapes; only vertical or inclined strokes were possible, not horizontal ones on account of the wood grain; this way, however, it became a very clumsy writing for parchment or paper. And indeed, as far as we can see, it has only served for religious and magic purposes and for inscriptions, perhaps also for other brief communications; as soon as the need for real literary writing was felt, as among the Goths and later the Anglo-Saxons, it was discarded and a new adaptation of the Greek or Roman alphabet made which preserved only individual runic characters.

Finally, the Germans will also have made considerable progress in tillage and cattle raising in the period here discussed. The restriction to permanent settlement forced them to it; the enormous population growth, which overflowed in the migration of the peoples, would have been impossible without it. Many a stretch of virgin forest must have been cleared, and most of the "Hochäcker"—stretches of wood which show traces of ancient cultivation—among them, in as far as they are situated on territory that was then German. Special proofs are here, of course, lacking. But if Probus already, towards the end of the third century, preferred German horses for his cavalry, and if the large white cattle, which replaced the small, black Celtic cattle in the Saxon areas of Britain, got here through the Anglo-Saxons, as is now assumed, this indicates a complete revolution also in the cattle raising, and consequently in the agriculture, of the Germans.

* * *

The result of our study is that the Germans made considerable progress in civilisation in the period from Caesar to Tacitus, but that they progressed even more rapidly from Tacitus to the migration of the peoples—about 400. Trade came to them, brought to them Roman industrial products and with these at least some Roman needs; it awakened an industry of their own, which leaned on Roman patterns, to be sure, but at the same time developed quite independently. The bog finds in Schleswig represent the first phase of this industry which can be dated; the finds of the time of the migration of the peoples represent the second phase, showing a higher development. Here it is remarkable that the more westerly peoples were decidedly more backward than those of the interior, and especially of the Baltic coasts. The Franks and Alamanni, and later still the Saxons, produced metal work of a quality inferior to that of the Anglo-Saxons, Scandinavians, and the peoples who had moved out from the interior—the Goths on the Black Sea and the Lower Danube, the Burgundians in France. The influence of the old trade routes from the Middle Danube along the Elbe and Oder is here not to be gainsaid. At the same time the inhabitants of the coast turned themselves into skilled shipbuilders and bold seafarers; everywhere population was rapidly growing; the territory restricted by the Romans no longer sufficed. New movements of landseeking peoples arose, at first far in the east, until finally the billowing masses irresistibly overflowed at every point, over land and sea, to new territories.

NOTE: THE GERMAN PEOPLES

Roman armies only reached the interior of Germany proper by a few routes of march and during a short period of time, and then only as far as the Elbe; nor did merchants and other travellers get there often, or far into it up to Tacitus' time. Hence it is not surprising that intelligence on this country and its inhabitants is so meagre and contradictory; it is rather surprising that we learn as much for certain as we do.

Even the two Greek geographers among our sources can only be used without reservations where they find independent confirmation. Both had only book learning. They were collectors and in their own way and according to their resources also critical sifters of material now largely lost to us. They lacked personal knowledge of the country. Strabo makes the Lippe, so well known to the Romans, flow into the North Sea parallel with the Ems and Weser, instead of into the Rhine, and is honest enough to admit that the country beyond the Elbe is completely unknown.[a] While he disposes of the contradictions in his sources and his own doubts by means of a naive rationalism which often recalls the beginning of our century, the scientific geographer Ptolemy attempts to allot to the individual German peoples mentioned in his sources mathematically determined locations in the inexorable grid of his map. Ptolemy's geography of Germany is as misleading as his work as a whole is grandiose for his time.[b] In the first place the material available to him is for the greater part vague and contradictory, often directly wrong. Secondly, however, his map is wrongly drawn, many rivers and mountain ranges are quite wrongly entered. It is as if an untravelled Berlin geographer, say about 1820, felt obliged to fill the empty spaces on the map of Africa by bringing into harmony the information of all sources since Leo Africanus and allotting to every river and every mountain range a definite location, to every people a precise seat. Such attempts to do the impossible can only worsen the errors of the sources used. Thus, Ptolemy entered many peoples twice, Laccobardi on the lower Elbe, Langobardi from the middle Rhine to the middle Elbe; he has two Bohemias, one inhabited by Marcomanni, the other by Bainochaimi, etc.[c] While Tacitus says specifically that there are no cities in Germany,[d] Ptolemy, barely 50 years later, already is able to name 96 places.[e] Many of those names may well be true place names; Ptolemy seems to have gathered much intelligence from merchants, who at this time already visited the east of Germany in greater numbers and began to learn the names of the places they visited, which were gradually becoming fixed. The origin of certain others is shown by the example of the alleged town of Siatutanda, which our geographer thinks he reads in Tacitus, probably from a bad manuscript, who wrote: *ad sua tutanda.*[f] Side by side we find information of surprising accuracy and of the greatest historical value. Thus Ptolemy is the only ancient writer who places the Langobardi, under the distorted name Laccobardi, it is true, exactly where to this day we find

---

[a] Strabo, *Geographica*, VII, 1. Quoted in *Die Geschichtschreiber...*, p. 374.— *Ed.*
[b] Ptolemy describes Germany in his *Geographia*, II and III.— *Ed.*
[c] Ptolemaeus, *Geographia*, II, 11, 12.—*Ed.*
[d] Tacitus, *Germania*, 16. Quoted in *Die Geschichtschreiber...*, p. 655.—*Ed.*
[e] Ptolemaeus, op. cit., II, 12-15.—*Ed.*
[f] "For his protection." See ibid., II, 11, 12. Tacitus, *Annales*, IV, 73.—*Ed.*

Bardengau and Bardenwik bear witness to them; similarly, Ingrioni in Engersgau where today we still find Engers on the Rhine at Neuwied.[a] He, also alone, gives the names of the Lithuanian Galindi and Suditi which to this day continue in the East Prussian districts Galinden and Sudauen. But such cases only show his great scholarship, not the correctness of his other statements. Moreover, the text is terribly distorted, especially where the main thing, the names, are concerned.

The Romans remain the most direct sources, particularly those who visited the country themselves. Velleius was in Germany as a soldier and writes as a soldier, approximately in the manner of an officer of the *grande armée*[22] writing of the expeditions of 1812 and 1813. His account does not enable us to establish the localities even for military events; not surprising in a country without towns. Pliny also served in Germany as a cavalry officer and visited the Chaucian coast among other places. He described all the wars conducted against the Germans in twenty books[23]; this was Tacitus' source. Moreover Pliny was the first Roman to take a more than military and political interest in the affairs of the barbarian land; his interest was theoretical.[b] His information on the German peoples must therefore be of special importance as resting on the Roman scientific encyclopaedist's own enquiries. It is traditionally maintained that Tacitus had been in Germany, but I cannot find the evidence. At all events, at that time he could have gathered direct information only from near the Rhine and Danube.

Two classical works have tried in vain to square the charts of peoples in the *Germania* [of Tacitus] and of Ptolemy with one another and with the chaos of other ancient information: Kaspar Zeuss' *Deutsche* and Jacob Grimm's *Geschichte der deutschen Sprache*. Where these two brilliant scholars did not succeed, nor anybody since, we will have to regard the task as insoluble with our present resources. The inadequacy of the resources is clear from the fact alone that both had to resort to the construction of false auxiliary theories; Zeuss thought that Ptolemy should have the last word in all disputed questions, although nobody has criticised Ptolemy's fundamental errors more sharply than he did; Grimm believed that the might which overthrew the Roman world empire must have grown on more extensive ground than the area between

---

[a] Ptolemaeus, op. cit., II, 11, 9.— *Ed.*

[b] Here the sentence "Moreover, he was a naturalist" is crossed out in the manuscript.— *Ed.*

Rhine, Danube and Vistula, and that therefore, with the Goths and Dacians, the greater part of the country in the north and north-east of the lower Danube should be taken as German, too. The assumptions of both Zeuss and Grimm are today obsolete.

Let us try to bring at least some clarity into the matter by limiting the subject. If we succeed in establishing a more general grouping of the peoples into a few principal branches, later investigations into detail will have gained firm ground. And here we are offered a point of departure by Pliny[a] in a passage which has proved more and more reliable in the course of the enquiry and certainly leads to fewer difficulties and involves us in fewer contradictions than any other.

When we begin with Pliny we must indeed drop the unconditional validity of Tacitus' triad and the old legend of Mannus and his three sons Ing, Isk and Ermin.[b] But firstly, Tacitus himself is unable to do anything with his Ingaevones, Iscaevones, and Herminones. He makes not the least attempt to group the peoples he lists individually under these three principal branches, and secondly, no one else has succeeded in doing this. Zeuss makes a terrific effort to force the Gothic peoples, whom he conceives as "Istaevones", into the triad, and thereby only aggravates the confusion. As for the Scandinavians, he does not even attempt to bring them into it and construes them as a fourth principal branch. But with that the triad is destroyed quite as much as with the five principal branches of Pliny.

Now let us look at these five branches individually.

I. *Vindili, quorum pars Burgundiones, Varini, Carini, Guttones.*[c]

Here we have three peoples, the Vandals, Burgundians and the Goths themselves, of whom it is established, firstly, that they spoke Gothic dialects, and secondly that at that time they lived deep in the east of Germany: Goths at and beyond the Vistula mouth; Burgundians, placed by Ptolemy in the area of the Warta and as far as the Vistula,[d] and Vandals, placed in Silesia by Dio Cassius, who calls the Riesengebirge after them.[e] We should surely also reckon to this *Gothic* main branch, to name it by the language, all those peoples whose dialects Grimm derives from the Gothic, that is, in the first place the areas to which Procopius directly ascribes

a Plinius, *Naturalis historia*, IV, 14. See *Die Geschichtschreiber...*, p. 681.— *Ed.*

b Tacitus, *Germania*, 2. See *Die Geschichtschreiber...*, pp. 646-47.— *Ed.*

c The Vindili, to whom the Burgundians, Varini, Carini and Guttons belong.— *Ed.*

d Ptolemaeus, *Geographia*, II, 11, 8.—*Ed.*

e Dio Cassius, *Historia Romana*, XV, 1, 3.—*Ed.*

the Gothic language, including the Vandals.[a] We know nothing of their earlier domicile, nor of that of the Heruli, whom Grimm places among the Goths, side by side with Skiri and Rugii.[b] Pliny names the Skiri on the Vistula,[c] Tacitus the Rugii immediately next to the Goths on the coast.[d] Hence the Gothic dialect occupied a fairly compact region between the Vandal mountains (Riesengebirge), the Oder and the Baltic up to and beyond the Vistula.

We do not know who the Carini were. Some difficulty is caused by the Varini. Tacitus lists them next to the Angles among the seven peoples who sacrifice to Nerthus,[e] of whom Zeuss already remarked, rightly, that they look uncommonly like Ingaevones[f] But the Angles are counted by Ptolemy among the Suebi,[g] which is obviously wrong. Zeuss sees in one or two names distorted by the same geographer the Varini and accordingly he places them in the Havelland and counts them as Suebi.[h] The heading of the ancient common law identifies Varini and Thuringians[i] without qualification; but the law itself is common to Varini and Angles. After all this we must leave it in doubt whether the Varini are to be reckoned to the Gothic or the Ingaevonian branch; since they have completely disappeared the question is not of great importance.

II. *Altera pars Ingaevones, quorum pars Cimbri, Teutoni ac Chaucorum gentes.*[j]

Pliny here allocates the Cimbric Peninsula and the coastal districts between Elbe and Ems to the Ingaevones as their domicile. Of the three peoples here named, the Chauci were surely very close relatives of the Frisians. To this day the Frisian language predominates along the North Sea, in Dutch West Friesland, in Oldenburg Saterland and in Schleswig North Friesland. During the Carolingian period[24] Frisian was spoken almost exclusively along the whole coast, from the Sinkfal (the bay which today still

---

[a] Procopius, *De bello Vandalico*, 1, 2. See J. Grimm, *Geschichte...*, Vol. 1, pp. 476-77.—*Ed.*

[b] J. Grimm, op. cit., Vol. 1, p. 471.—*Ed.*

[c] Plinius, *Naturalis historia*, IV, 13, 27. See J. Grimm, op. cit., p. 465.—*Ed.*

[d] Tacitus, *Germania*, 44. See *Die Geschichtschreiber...*, p. 669.—*Ed.*

[e] Ibid., p. 668.—*Ed.*

[f] K. Zeuss, *Die Deutschen und die Nachbarstämme*, p. 79.—*Ed.*

[g] Ptolemaeus, *Geographia*, II, 11, 8.—*Ed.*

[h] K. Zeuss, op. cit., pp. 132-33.—*Ed.*

[i] *Lex Angliorum et Werinorum, hoc est Thuringorum.* Quoted in K. Zeuss, op. cit., p. 363.—*Ed.*

[j] Another group—the Ingaevones, which include the Cimbri, Teutons and Chauci.—*Ed.*

forms the boundary between Belgian Flanders and Dutch Zeeland) to Sylt and Schleswig Widau, and probably still a good deal further north; the Saxon language only on both sides of the Elbe mouth, to the sea.

Pliny evidently understands by the Cimbri and Teutons the then inhabitants of the Cimbric Chersonesus,[a] who therefore belonged to the Chauci-Frisian language branch. With Zeuss and Grimm we must therefore see in the North Frisians direct descendants of these oldest peninsular Germans.

It is true that Dahlmann (*Geschichte von Dänemark*)[b] maintains that the north Frisians immigrated into the peninsula only in the fifth century, from the south-west. But he does not cite the smallest evidence for this statement which has rightly been left quite out of consideration in all later studies.

Ingaevonian would accordingly here be in the first place synonymous with Frisian, in the sense that we name the entire linguistic branch after the dialect of which alone older memorials and surviving dialects remain. But is the extent of the Ingaevonian branch thereby exhausted? Or is Grimm right when he comprises in it the totality of what he, not quite accurately, terms Low German, that is alongside the Frisians also the Saxons?[c]

To begin with, we may admit that Pliny allots to the Saxons quite the wrong place when he reckons the Cherusci among the Herminones. We shall find later that indeed no option is left but to reckon the Saxons also among the Ingaevones and thus to understand this main branch as the Frisian-Saxon one.

Here it is in place to mention the Angles, whom Tacitus possibly, Ptolemy definitely reckons among the Suebi. The latter places them on the right bank of the Elbe,[d] opposite the Langobardi, by whom he can only mean the *true* Langobardi on the lower Elbe if the statement is at all to be taken to imply anything reliable; hence the Angles must have come from Lauenburg approximately as far as the Prignitz. Later we find them in the peninsula itself, where their name has been preserved and whence they went to Britain together with the Saxons. Their language now appears as an element of Anglo-Saxon, in particular the decidedly *Frisian* element of this newly formed dialect.

---

[a] Plinius, *Naturalis historia*, IV, 99.— *Ed.*

[b] F. C. Dahlmann, *Geschichte von Dännemark*, Vol. I, Hamburg, 1840, p. 16.— *Ed.*

[c] J. Grimm, op. cit., Vol. 2, p. 608.—*Ed.*

[d] Tacitus, *Germania*, 40. Quoted in *Die Geschichtschreiber...*, p. 668; Ptolemaeus, *Geographia*, II, 11, 8.—*Ed.*

Whatever may have become of those Angles who either remained behind in the interior of Germany or strayed there, this fact alone compels us to reckon the Angles among the Ingaevones, in particular to their Frisian branch. To them is due the far more Frisian than Saxon vocalisation of Anglo-Saxon and the fact that the further development of this language in many cases proceeds strikingly in parallel with that of the Frisian dialects. Of all the continental dialects the Frisian are today closest to the English. Similarly, the change of guttural sounds into sibilants in English is not of French but of Frisian origin. English *ch* = *č* instead of *k*, English *dž* for *g* before soft vowels could certainly originate from Frisian *tz*, *tj* for *k*, *dz* for *g*, but never from French *ch* and *g*.

With the Angles we must also count the Jutes to the Frisian-Ingaevonian branch, whether they were already occupying the peninsula in the time of Pliny or Tacitus or did not immigrate there until later. Grimm finds their name in that of the *Eudoses,* one of Tacitus' peoples who worshipped Nerthus[a]; if the Angles are Ingaevonian, it becomes difficult to allot the remaining peoples of this group to another branch. In that case the Ingaevones would extend to the area of the Oder mouth, and the gap between them and the Gothic peoples is filled.

III. *Proximi autem Rheno Iscaevones* (*alias Istaevones*), *quorum pars Sicambri.*[b]

Already Grimm, and others after him, Waitz for example,[c] more or less identify the Iscaevones and Franks. But their language confuses Grimm. From the middle of the 9th century all German documents of the realm of the Franks were composed in a dialect which cannot be distinguished from Old High German; hence Grimm assumes that Old Franconian perished in the alien country and at home was replaced by High German, and so he eventually reckoned the Franks to the High Germans.

Grimm himself asserts as a result of his investigation of preserved linguistic remains that Old Franconian has the value of an independent dialect holding an intermediary position between Saxon and High German.[d] This suffices here for the time being; a closer investigation of the Frankish linguistic situation, where much is still unclear, must be reserved for a special note.[e]

---

[a] J. Grimm, op. cit., Vol. 2, p. 738.—*Ed.*

[b] Closer to the Rhine, however, the Iscaevones (or Istaevones), including the Sugambri.—*Ed.*

[c] G. Waitz, *Deutsche Verfassungsgeschichte,* Vol. 1, Kiel, 1844, p. XVII.—*Ed.*

[d] J. Grimm, op. cit., Vol. 1, p. 547.—*Ed.*

[e] See this volume, pp. 81-107.— *Ed.*

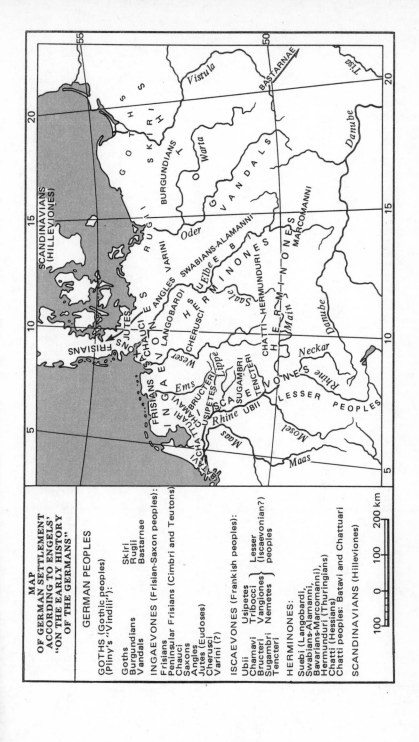

MAP
OF GERMAN SETTLEMENT
ACCORDING TO ENGELS'
"ON THE EARLY HISTORY
OF THE GERMANS"

GERMAN PEOPLES

GOTHS (Gothic peoples)
(Pliny's "Vindili"):

Goths   Skiri
Burgundians   Rugii
Vandals   Bastarnae

INGAEVONES (Frisian-Saxon peoples):

Frisians
Peninsular Frisians (Cimbri and Teutons)
Chauci
Saxons
Angles
Jutes (Eudoses)
Cherusci
Varini (?)

ISCAEVONES (Frankish peoples):

Ubii   Usipetes
Chamavi   Tribocci   } Lesser
Bructeri   Vangiones   } (Iscaevonian?)
Sugambri   Nemetes   } peoples
Tencteri

HERMINONES:

Suebi (Langobardi,
Swabians-Alamanni,
Bavarians-Marcomanni),
Hermunduri (Thuringians),
Chatti (Hessians)
Chatti peoples: Batavi and Chattuari

SCANDINAVIANS (Hilleviones)

100   0   100   200 km

True enough, the area allotted to the Iscaevonian branch is comparatively small for an entire main German branch, and moreover one which has played such a mighty role in history. From the Rheingau onwards it accompanies the Rhine, extending inland to the sources of the Dill, Sieg, Ruhr, Lippe and Ems, northwards cut off from the sea by the Frisians and Chauci, and at the mouth of the Rhine penetrated by splinters of other peoples, mostly of Chattish origin: Batavi, Chattuari, etc. The Germans settled on the left bank of the lower Rhine will then also belong to the Franks; but also the Tribocci, Vangiones and Nemetes? The small extent of this area is explained, however, by the resistance offered to the expansion of the Iscaevones on the Rhine by the Celts and since Caesar the Romans; while in their rear the Cherusci had already settled, and on their flank Suebi, particularly the Chatti, hemmed them in more and more, as Caesar attests.[a] Here a dense population, for German conditions, was compressed into a small space, as is proved by the constant pressing across the Rhine: at first by conquering hordes, later by voluntary transfer to Roman territory, as with the Ubii. For the same reason the Romans easily succeeded here, and only here, in transferring considerable sections of Iscaevonian peoples to Roman territory already at an early period.

The investigation to be made in the note on the Franconian dialect will prove that the Franks form a separate group of Germans, composed of various branches, speaking a particular dialect divided into many subdialects, in short possessing all the marks of a main German branch, as is required if they are to be declared identical with the Iscaevones. On the individual peoples of this main branch J. Grimm has already said what is necessary.[b] In addition to the Sugambri he reckons among them Ubii, Chamavi, Bructeri, Tencteri and Usipetes, that is the peoples who inhabited the area on the right bank of the Rhine which we have earlier designated as Iscaevonic.

IV. *Mediterranei Hermiones, quorum Suevi, Hermunduri, Chatti, Cherusci.*[c]

J. Grimm already identified the Herminones, to use the more correct spelling of Tacitus, with the High Germans.[d] The name

---

[a] Caesar, *Commentarii de bello Gallico*, IV, 4. Cf. *Die Geschichtschreiber...*, p. 165.— *Ed.*

[b] J. Grimm, op. cit., Vol. 2, p. 831.— *Ed.*

[c] In the middle of the country, the Hermiones, comprising the Suebi, Hermunduri, Chatti and Cherusci.— *Ed.*

[d] J. Grimm, op. cit., Vol. 1, p. 547.— *Ed.*

Suebi, which according to Caesar covered all High Germans as far
as he knew them,[a] is beginning to become differentiated.
Thuringians (Hermunduri) and Hessians (Chatti) appear as
separate peoples. The rest of the Suebi still remain undifferen-
tiated. Leaving aside as inscrutable the many mysterious names
which get lost already in the next centuries, we must, however,
distinguish among these Suebi three great branches of High
German tongue which later played their part in history: the
Alamanni-Swabians, the Bavarians and the Langobardi. We know
for certain that the Langobardi lived on the left bank of the lower
Elbe, about the Bardengau, separated from their other branch
comrades, advanced into the midst of Ingaevonian peoples.
Tacitus describes this isolated position, which had to be maintained by prolonged fighting, excellently, without knowing its
cause.[b] We also know since Zeuss and Grimm[c] that the Bavarians
lived in Bohemia under the name of Marcomanni, the Hessians
and Thuringians in their present abodes and in the neighbouring
areas to the south. Since Roman territory began south of the
Franks, Hessians and Thuringians, no other space remained for
the Swabians-Alamanni than that between Elbe and Oder, in the
modern Mark Brandenburg and the Kingdom of Saxony; and
here we find a Suebian people, the Semnones. Thus they were
probably identical with these, bordering on Ingaevones in the
north-west and on Gothic branches in the north-east and east.

So far everything seems to go fairly smoothly. But now Pliny
reckons also the Cherusci among the Herminones,[d] and here he
decidedly makes a slip. Caesar already distinguishes them definitely
from the Suebi, among whom he still reckons the Chatti.[e] Nor does
Tacitus know anything of Cherusci belonging to any High German branch. Neither does Ptolemy, who extends the name
Suebi to the Angles.[f] The mere fact that the Cherusci filled the
space between Chatti and Hermunduri in the south and Langobardi in the north-east is not enough by a long way to conclude
from that on any close branch kinship; although it may have been
precisely that which misled Pliny here.[g]

---

[a] Caesar, op. cit., VI, 10. Cf. *Die Geschichtschreiber...*, p. 207.— *Ed.*
[b] Tacitus, *Germania,* 40. Cf. *Die Geschichtschreiber...*, pp. 668-69.— *Ed.*
[c] K. Zeuss, op. cit., pp. 364-80; J. Grimm, op. cit., Vol. 1, p. 502.— *Ed.*
[d] Plinius, *Naturalis historia,* IV, 14.— *Ed.*
[e] Caesar, *Commentarii de bello Gallico,* VI, 10. Cf. *Die Geschichtschreiber...*,
p. 207.— *Ed.*
[f] Ptolemaeus, *Geographia,* II, 11, 8.— *Ed.*
[g] Plinius, *Naturalis historia,* IV, 14.— *Ed.*

As far as I know, no scholar whose opinion matters counts the Cherusci among the High Germans. This only leaves the question whether they are to be reckoned among the Ingaevones or the Iscaevones. The few names which have come down to us show a Frankish stamp; *ch* instead of the later *h* in *Cherusci, Chariomerus*; *e* instead of *i* in *Segestes, Segimerus, Segimundus*. But almost all German names which came to the Romans from the banks of the Rhine seem to have been handed down to them by Franks in Frankish form. Moreover, we do not know whether the guttural aspirate of the first shift of the consonants, in the seventh century still *ch* with the Franks, did not sound *ch* with all West Germans in the first century and was only later weakened to the *h* common to them all. Nor do we otherwise find any branch kinship of the Cherusci with the Iscaevones, such as showed itself when the Sugambri took in the remaining Usipetes and Tencteri after they had escaped from Caesar. Moreover, the country on the right bank of the Rhine occupied at the time of Varus by the Romans and treated by them as a province coincides with Iscaevonian-Frankish territory. Here Aliso and the other Roman forts were situated; of the Cheruscan country at most only the strip between the Osning and the Weser seems to have been actually occupied. Beyond it, the Chatti, Cherusci, Chauci and Frisians were more or less uncertain allies, held in check by fear, but autonomous in their internal affairs and free of permanent Roman garrisons. In this area the Romans, when met with resistance of any strength, always made the branch boundary the limit of conquest for the time being. Thus Caesar had done in Gaul; at the border of the Belgae he halted and only crossed it when he thought that he had made sure of Gaul proper, so-called Celtic Gaul.[a]

Nothing remains but to reckon the Cherusci and their nearest relatives among the smaller neighbouring peoples to the Saxon branch, and hence among the Ingaevones, after J. Grimm[b] and the usual view. The fact that the old Saxon *a* is purest preserved just in the old Cheruscan area, against the *o* in the genitive plural and weak masculine which predominates in Westphalia, suggests the same thing. In this way all the difficulties disappear; the Ingaevonian branch, like the others, is given a fairly rounded territory into which only the Herminonian Langobardi penetrate a little. Of the two great divisions of the branch, the Frisian-Anglian-Jutish occupies the coast and at least the northern and western

a Caesar, op. cit., II, 3, 7, 1.— *Ed.*
b J. Grimm, op. cit., Vol. 2, p. 612.— *Ed.*

parts of the peninsula, the Saxon division the inner country and perhaps also now already a part of North Albingia, where soon afterwards Ptolemy first mentions the *Saxones* by name.[a]

V. *Quinta pars Peucini, Bastarnae contermini Dacis.*[b]

The little we know of these two peoples stamps them as branch relatives of the Goths, as does even the form of the name, *Bastarnae.* If Pliny lists them as a separate branch, this is probably due to the fact that he heard of them from the lower Danube, through Greek intermediaries,[25] while his knowledge of the Gothic peoples on the Oder and Vistula had been gained on the Rhine and the North Sea, so that the connection between Goths and Bastarnae escaped him. Both Bastarnae and Peucini are German peoples who stayed behind at the Carpathians and the Danube mouths and continued migrating for some time, preparing the later great realm of the Goths, in which they became immersed.

VI. I mention the Hilleviones, the collective name under which Pliny lists the German Scandinavians,[c] only for the sake of completeness and in order once more to establish that all the ancient authors allot to this main branch only the islands (which include Sweden and Norway), excluding them from the Cimbric peninsula.

Thus we have five main German branches with five principal dialects.

The Gothic, in the east and north-east, has -*ê* in the genitive plural of the masculine and neuter, -*ô* and -*ê* in the feminine; the weak masculine has -*a.* The inflected forms of the present tense (the indicative) are still close to those of the originally related languages, in particular Greek and Latin, if the shifting of the consonants is borne in mind.

The Ingaevonic, in the north-west, has -*a* in the genitive plural, and also for the weak masculine; in the present indicative all three persons in the plural end in -*d* or -*dh,* all nasal sounds being expunged. It is divided into the two main branches of the Saxon and Frisian, which merge again into one in the Anglo-Saxon. Close to the Frisian branch is

the Scandinavian; genitive plural ending in -*a,* weak masculine in -*i,* weakened from -*a,* as shown by the whole declension. In the present indicative the original -*s* of the second person singular

---

[a] Ptolemaeus, *Geographia,* II, 11, 7.— *Ed.*

[b] The fifth group: Peucini and Bastarnae, whose neighbours are the Dacians.— *Ed.*

[c] Plinius, *Naturalis historia,* IV, 13.— *Ed.*

passes into -r, the first person plural retains -m, the second -dh, the remaining persons are more or less mutilated.

These three face the two southern branches: the Iscaevonic and Herminonic, in the later mode of expression the Franconian and the High German. The two have in common the weak masculine ending -o; most probably also the genitive plural ending -ô, although it is not substantiated in the Franconian, and in the oldest western (Salic) documents the accusative plural ends in -as. In the present tense the two dialects, as far as we can document this for the Franconian, are close and, in this respect like Gothic, closely correspond with the originally related languages. But the whole course of linguistic history, from the very significant, archaic peculiarities of the oldest Franconian to the great differences between the modern dialects of both, precludes us from throwing the two dialects together into one; just as the whole course of the history of the peoples themselves makes it impossible for us to put them both into one main branch.

If throughout this investigation I have considered only the forms of inflection and not the phonetic relations, this is to be explained from the considerable changes which have occurred in the latter—at least in many dialects—between the first century and the time when our oldest linguistic sources were drawn up. In Germany I need only recall the second shift of the consonants; in Scandinavia the alliterations of the oldest songs show how much the language altered between the time when they were composed and when they were written down. Whatever it may still be possible to do in this respect will most likely be done by competent German linguists; here it would only have made the investigation unnecessarily complicated.

Written in mid-1878-early August 1882

First published in: Marx and Engels, *Works*, First Russian Edition, Vol.XVI, Part I, Moscow, 1937

Printed according to the manuscript

THE FRANKISH PERIOD [26]

THE RADICAL TRANSFORMATION OF THE RELATIONS OF LANDOWNERSHIP UNDER THE MEROVINGIANS [27] AND CAROLINGIANS

The mark system [28] remained the basis of almost the entire life of the German nation till the end of the Middle Ages. Eventually, after an existence of one and a half millennia, it gradually disintegrated for purely economic reasons. It succumbed to economic advances with which it was unable to keep pace. We shall later examine its decline and ultimate destruction and we shall see that remnants of the mark system continue to exist even today.

It was only at the expense of its political importance that it was able to survive for so long. For centuries it had been the form embodying the freedom of the Germanic tribes. Then it became the basis of the people's bondage for a thousand years. How was this possible?

The earliest community, as we have seen, comprised the whole people. Originally the people owned all the appropriated land. Later the whole body of inhabitants of a district [Gau], who were closely interrelated, became the owners of the territory settled by them, and the people as such retained only the right to dispose of the tracts which had not yet been claimed. The populace of the district in their turn handed over their field and forest marks to individual village communities, which likewise consisted of closely kindred people, and in this case too the land that was left over was retained by the district. The same procedure was followed when the original villages set up new village colonies—they were provided with land from the old mark by the parent village.

With the growth of the population and the further development of the people the blood-ties, on which here as everywhere the entire national structure was based, increasingly fell into oblivion.

This was first the case with regard to the people as a whole. The common descent was less and less seen as real consanguinity, the memory of it became fainter and fainter and what remained was merely the common history and the dialect. On the other hand, the inhabitants of a district naturally retained an awareness of their consanguinity for a longer time. The people thus came to mean merely a more or less stable confederation of districts. This seems to have been the state of affairs among the Germans at the time of the great migrations. Ammianus Marcellinus reports this definitely about the Alamanni,[a] and in the local law[29] it is still everywhere apparent. The Saxons were still at this stage of development during Charlemagne's time and the Frisians until they lost their independence.

But the migration on to Roman soil broke the blood-ties, as it was bound to. Although the intention was to settle by tribes and kindreds, it was impossible to carry this through. The long marches had mixed together not only tribes and kindreds but also entire peoples. Only with difficulty could the blood-ties of the individual village communities still be held together, and these became thus the real political units of which the people consisted. The new districts on Roman territory were from the start, or soon became, judicial divisions set up more or less arbitrarily—or occasioned by conditions found already in existence.

The people thus disintegrated into an association of small village communities, between which there existed no or virtually no economic connection, for every mark was self-sufficient, producing enough to satisfy its own needs, and moreover the products of the various neighbouring marks being almost exactly the same. Hardly any exchange could therefore take place between them. And since the people consisted entirely of small communities, which had identical economic interests, but for that very reason no common ones, the continued existence of the nation depended on a state power which did not derive from these communities but confronted them as something alien and exploited them to an ever increasing extent.

The form of this state power depends in its turn on the form of the communities at the time in question. Where, as among the Aryan peoples of Asia and the Russians, it arises at a time when the fields are still cultivated by the community for the common account, or when at any rate the fields are only temporarily

---

[a] Ammianus Marcellinus, *Rerum gestarum*, XVIII, 2, 1; XX, 4, 1; XXX, 3, 1.—*Ed.*

allotted by it to individual families, i.e. when there is as yet no private property in land, the state power appears as despotism. On the other hand, in the Roman lands conquered by the Germans, the individual shares in arable land and meadows already take, as we have seen, the form of the allodium, the owners' free property subject only to the ordinary mark obligations. We must now examine how on the basis of this allodium a social and political structure arose, which—with the usual irony of history—in the end dissolved the state and completely abolished the allodium in its classical form.

The allodium made the transformation of the original equality of landed property into its opposite not only possible but inevitable. From the moment it was established on formerly Roman soil, the German allodium became what the Roman landed property adjacent to it had long been—a commodity. It is an inexorable law of all societies based on commodity production and commodity exchange that the distribution of property within them becomes increasingly unequal, the opposition of wealth and poverty constantly grows and property is more and more concentrated in a few hands. It is true that this law reaches its full development in modern capitalist production, but it is by no means only in it that this law operates. From the moment therefore that allodium, freely disposable landed property, landed property as commodity, arose, from that moment the emergence of large-scale landed property was merely a matter of time.

But in the period we are concerned with, farming and stock-breeding were the principal branches of production. Landed property and its products constituted the by far largest part of wealth at that time. Other types of movable wealth that existed then followed landed property as a matter of course, and gradually accumulated in the same hands as landed property. Industry and trade had already deteriorated during the decline of the Roman empire; the German invasion ruined them almost completely. The little that was left was for the most part carried on by unfree men and aliens and remained a despised occupation. The ruling class which, with the emerging inequality in property, gradually arose could only be a class of big landowners, its form of political rule that of an aristocracy. Though, as we shall see, political levers, violence and deceit contribute frequently, and as it seems even predominantly, to the formation and development of this class, we must not forget that these political levers only advance and accelerate an inevitable economic process. We shall indeed see just as often that these political levers impede economic development; this happens quite frequently, and invariably when the different parties concerned apply them in opposite or intersecting directions.

How did this class of big landowners come into being?

First of all we know that even after the Frankish conquest a large number of big Roman landowners remained in Gaul, whose estates were for the most part cultivated by free or bound copyholders against payment of rent (*canon*).

Furthermore we have seen that as a result of the wars of conquest the monarchy had become a permanent institution and real power among all Germans who had moved out, and that it had turned the land which had formerly belonged to the people into royal domains and had likewise appropriated the Roman state lands. These crown lands were constantly augmented by the wholesale seizure of the estates of so-called rebels during the many civil wars resulting from the partitions of the empire. But rapidly as these lands increased, they were just as rapidly squandered in donations to the Church and to private individuals, Franks and Romans, retainers (antrustions[30]) and other favourites of the king. Once the rudiments of a ruling class comprising the big and the powerful, landlords, officials and generals had formed, during and because of the civil wars, local rulers tried to purchase their support by grants of land. Roth has conclusively proved that in most cases these were real grants, transfers of land which became free, inheritable and alienable property, until this was changed by Charles Martel.*

When Charles took over the helm of state, the power of the kings was completely broken but, as yet, by no means replaced by that of the major-domos.[31] The class of grandees, created under the Merovingians at the expense of the Crown, furthered the ruin of royal power in every way, but certainly not in order to submit to the major-domos, their compeers. On the contrary, the whole of Gaul was, as Einhard says, in the hands of these

"tyrants, who were arrogating power to themselves everywhere" (*tyrannos per totam Galliam dominatum sibi vindicantes*).[a]

This was done not only by secular grandees but also by bishops, who appropriated adjacent counties and duchies in many areas,

---

* P. Roth, *Geschichte des Beneficialwesens*, Erlangen, 1850. One of the best books of the pre-Maurer period. I have borrowed a good deal from it in this chapter.

---

[a] Einhardus, *Vita Caroli Magni*, 2. Quoted in P. Roth, *Geschichte des Beneficialwesens...*, Erlangen, 1850, p. 352.— *Ed.*

and were protected by their immunity and the strong organisation
of the Church. The internal disintegration of the empire was
followed by incursions of external enemies. The Saxons invaded
Rhenish Franconia, the Avars Bavaria, and the Arabs moved
across the Pyrenees into Aquitania.[32] In such a situation, mere
subjection of the internal enemies and expulsion of the external
ones could provide no long-term solution. A method had to be
found of binding the humbled grandees, or their successors
appointed by Charles, more firmly to the Crown. And since their
power was up to then based on large-scale landed property, the
first prerequisite for this was a total transformation of the
relations of landownership. This transformation was the principal
achievement of the Carolingian dynasty.[33] The distinctive feature
of this transformation is that the means chosen to unite the
empire, to tie the grandees permanently to the Crown and thus to
make the latter more powerful, in the end led to the complete
impotence of the Crown, the independence of the grandees and
the dissolution of the empire.

To understand how Charles came to choose this means, we must
first examine the property relations of the Church at the time,
which anyway cannot be passed over here, being an essential
element of contemporary agrarian relations.

Even during the Roman era, the Church in Gaul owned
considerable landed property, the revenue from which was further
increased by its great privileges with regard to taxes and other
obligations. But it was only after the conversion of the Franks to
Christianity[34] that the golden age began for the Gallic Church.
The kings vied with one another in making donations of land,
money, jewels, church utensils, etc., to the Church. Already
Chilperic used to say (according to Gregory of Tours):

"See how poor our treasury has become, see, all our wealth has been
transferred to the Church." [a]

Under Guntram, the darling and lackey of the priests, the
donations exceeded all bounds. Thus the confiscated lands of free
Franks accused of rebellion mostly became the property of the
Church.

The people followed the lead of the kings. Small man and big
could not give enough to the Church.

"A miraculous cure of a real or imagined ailment, the fulfilment of an ardent
wish, e.g. the birth of a son or deliverance from danger, brought the Church whose

---

[a] Gregorius Turonensis, *Historia Francorum,* VI, 46. Quoted in P. Roth, op. cit.,
pp. 248-49, Note 6.— *Ed.*

saint had proved helpful a gift. It was deemed the more necessary to be always open-handed as both among high and low the view was widespread that gifts to the Church led to the remission of sins" (Roth, p. 250).

Added to this was the immunity protecting the property of the Church from violation at a time of incessant civil wars, looting and confiscation. Many a small man thought it wise to cede his property to the Church provided he retained its usufruct at a moderate rent.

Yet all this was not sufficient for the pious priests. With threats of eternal punishment in hell they virtually extorted more and more donations, so that as late as 811 Charlemagne reproaches them with this in the Aachen Capitulary,[35] adding that they induce people

"to commit perjury and bear false witness, so as to increase your" (the bishops' and abbots') "wealth".[a]

Unlawful donations were obtained by hook or by crook in the hope that, apart from its privileged judicial status, the Church had sufficient means to cock a snook at the judiciary. There was hardly any Gallic Church Council in the sixth and seventh centuries that did not threaten to excommunicate anyone trying to contest donations to the Church. In this way even formally invalid donations were to be made valid, and the private debts of individual clerics protected against collection.

"We see that truly contemptible means were employed to arouse, again and again, the desire for making donations. When descriptions of heavenly bliss and infernal torment were no longer effective, relics were brought from distant parts, translations were arranged and new churches built; this was a veritable business in the ninth century" (Roth, p. 254). "When the emissaries of the St. Medard monastery in Soissons by much assiduous begging obtained the body of Saint Sebastian in Rome and in addition stole that of Gregory, and both bodies were deposited in the monastery, so many people flocked to see the new saints that the whole area seemed to be swarming with locusts, and those seeking relief were cured not individually but in whole herds. The result was that the monks measured the money by the bushel, counting as many as 85, and their stock of gold amounted to 900 pounds" (p. 255).

Deceit, legerdemain, the appearance of the dead, especially of saints, and finally also, and even predominantly, the forging of documents, were used to obtain riches for the Church. The forging of documents was—to let Roth speak again—

"practised by many clerics on a vast scale ... this business began very early.... The extent of this practice can be seen from the large number of forged documents contained in our collections. Of Bréquigny's 360 Merovingian certifi-

---

[a] Quoted in P. Roth, *Geschichte des Beneficialwesens...*, p. 253.— *Ed.*

cates[a] nearly 130 are definitely forgeries.... The forged testament of Remigius was used by Hincmar of Reims[b] to procure his church a number of properties, which were not mentioned in the genuine testament, although the latter had never been lost and Hincmar knew very well that the former was spurious."[c]

Even Pope John VIII tried to obtain the possessions of the St. Denis monastery near Paris by means of a document which he knew to be a forgery. (Roth, pp. 256 ff.)

No wonder then that the landed property the Church amassed through donations, extortion, guile, fraud, forgery and other criminal activities assumed enormous proportions within a few centuries. The monastery of Saint-Germain-des-Prés, now within the perimeter of Paris, at the beginning of the ninth century owned landed property of 8,000 mansi or hides,[d] an area which Guérard estimates at 429,987 hectares with an annual yield of one million francs=800,000 marks.[36] If we use the same average, i.e. an area of 54 hectares with a yield of 125 francs=100 marks per hide of land, then the monasteries St. Denis, Luxeuil, St. Martin de Tours, each owning 15,000 mansi at that time, held landed property of 810,000 hectares with an income of 1¹/₂ million marks. And this was the position *after* the confiscation of Church property by Pepin the Short![e] Roth estimates (p. 249) that the entire property of the Church in Gaul at the end of the seventh century was probably above, rather than below, one-third of the total area.

These enormous estates were cultivated partly by unfree and in part also by free copyholders of the Church. Of the unfree, the slaves (*servi*) were originally subject to unmeasured service to their lords, since they were not persons in law. But it seems that for the resident slaves too a customary amount of duties and services was soon established. On the other hand, the services of the other two unfree classes, the colons and lites[37] (we have no information about the difference in their legal position at that time) were fixed and consisted in certain personal services and corvée as well as a definite part of the produce of their plot. These were long established relations of dependence. But for the Germans it was something quite new that free men were cultivating not their own or common land. It is true that the

---

[a] L. G. O. F. de Bréquigny, F. J. G. La Porte du Theil, *Diplomata, chartae, epistolae, et alia documenta...* In P. Roth, *Geschichte des Beneficialwesens...*, p. XVII.— *Ed.*

[b] Hincmar Remensis, *Vita Remigii.* Quoted in P. Roth, op. cit., pp. XIX, 258.— *Ed.*

[c] Quoted in P. Roth, op. cit., pp. 256-58.— *Ed.*

[d] Hide—a variable unit of area of land, enough for a household.— *Ed.*

[e] See this volume, p. 66.— *Ed.*

Germans met quite frequently free Roman tenants in Gaul and in general in territories where Roman law prevailed; however during the settlement of the country care was taken to ensure that they themselves did not have to become tenants but could settle on their own land. Hence before free Franks could become somebody's copyholders they must have in some way or other lost the allodium they received when the country was being occupied, a distinct class of landless free Franks must have come into existence.

This class arose as a result of the beginning concentration of landed property, owing to the same causes as led to this concentration, i.e., on the one hand civil wars and confiscations and on the other the transfer of land to the Church mainly due to the pressure of circumstances and the desire for security. The Church soon discovered a specific means to encourage such transfers, it allowed the donor not only to enjoy the usufruct of his land for a rent, but also to rent a piece of Church land as well. For such donations were made in two forms. Either the donor retained the usufruct of his farm during his lifetime, so that it became the property of the Church only after his death (*donatio post obitum*). In this case it was usual, and was later expressly laid down in the kings' Capitularies, that the donor should be able to rent twice as much land from the Church as he had donated. Or the donation took effect immediately (*cessio a die praesente*) and in this case the donor could rent three times as much Church land as well as his own farm, by means of a document known as precaria, issued by the Church—which transferred the land to him, usually for the duration of his life, but sometimes for a longer or shorter period. Once a class of landless free men had come into being, some of them likewise entered into such a relationship. The precaria they were granted seem at first to have been mostly issued for five years, but in their case too they were soon made out for life.

There is scarcely any doubt that even under the Merovingians relations very similar to those obtaining on Church estates developed also on the estates of the secular magnates, and that here too free and unfree rent-paying tenants were living side by side. They must have been very numerous as early as Charles Martel's rule for otherwise at least *one* aspect of the transformation of landownership relations initiated by him and completed by his són and grandson[a] would be inexplicable.

---

[a] Pepin III (the Short) and Charlemagne.— *Ed.*

This transformation depended basically on two new institutions. First, in order to keep the barons of the empire tied to the Crown, the Crown lands they received were now as a rule no longer a gift, but only a "beneficium", granted for life, and moreover on certain conditions nonfulfilment of which entailed the forfeiture of the land. Thus they became themselves tenants of the Crown. And secondly, in order to ensure that the free tenants of the barons turned up for military service, the latter were granted some of the district count's official powers over the free men living on their estates and appointed their "seniores". For the present we need only consider the first of these two changes.

When subduing the rebellious small "tyrants" Charles proba-bly—we have no information regarding this—confiscated their landed property according to old custom, but in so far as he reinstated them in their offices and dignities he will have granted it to them entirely or in part as a benefice. He did not yet dare to treat the Church land of recalcitrant bishops in the same way. He deposed them and gave their positions to people devoted to him, though the only clerical trait of many of them was their tonsure (*sola tonsura clericus*). These new bishops and abbots then began at his bidding to transfer large tracts of Church land to laymen as precaria. Such instances had occurred earlier too, but it was now done on a mass scale. His son Pepin went considerably further. The Church was in decay, the clergy despised, the Pope,[a] hard pressed by the Langobardi, depended exclusively on Pepin's support. He helped the Pope, favoured the extension of his ecclesiastical rule and held the Pope's stirrup.[38] But as a remuneration he incorporated the by far largest part of the Church land into the Crown estates and left the bishops and monasteries an amount just sufficient for their maintenance. The Church acquiesced passively in this first large-scale secularisation, the synod of Lestines[39] confirmed it, albeit with a restrictive clause, which was, however, never observed. This huge mass of land placed the exhausted Crown estate once more on a secure footing and was to a large extent used for further grants, which in fact soon assumed the form of ordinary benefices.

Let us add here that the Church was soon able to recover from this blow. Directly after the conflict with Pepin the worthy men of God resumed their old practices. Donations came once more thick and fast from all directions, the small free peasants were still in the same sorry plight between hammer and anvil as they had been

---

[a] Stephen II.— *Ed.*

for the past 200 years. Under Charlemagne and his successors they fared far worse still and many entrusted themselves and all their possessions to the protection of the crosier. The kings returned some of their booty to favoured monasteries, and donated vast stretches of Crown land to others, especially in Germany. The blessed times of Guntram seemed to have returned for the Church during the reign of Louis the Pious. The monastery archives contain especially numerous records of donations made in the ninth century.

The benefice, this new institution, which we must now examine closer, was not yet the future fief, but certainly its embryo. It was from the outset granted for the common span of life of both the conferrer and the recipient. If one or the other died, it reverted to the owner or his heirs. To renew the former relationship, a new transfer of property to the recipient or his heirs had to be made. Hence the benefice was subject to both "throne-fall" and "home-fall", to use a later terminology. Throne-fall soon fell into desuetude; the great beneficiaries became more powerful than the king. Home-fall, even at an early stage, not infrequently entailed the re-transfer of the estate to the heir of the former beneficiary. Patriciacum (Percy), an estate near Autun, which Charles Martel granted as a benefice to Hildebrannus, remained in the family passing from father to son for four generations, until in 839 the king presented it to the brother of the fourth beneficiary as full property. Similar cases occur quite frequently since the mid-eighth century.

The benefice could be withdrawn by the conferrer in all cases in which confiscation of property was applicable. And there was no shortage of such cases under the Carolingians. The risings in Alamannia under Pepin the Short, the conspiracy of the Thuringians and the repeated risings of the Saxons[40] invariably led to new confiscations, either of free peasant land or of magnates' estates and benefices. This occurred also, despite all treaty stipulations to the contrary, during the internal wars under Louis the Pious and his sons.[41] Certain non-political crimes were also punished by confiscation.

The Crown could moreover withdraw benefices if the beneficiary neglected his general obligations as a subject, e.g., did not hand over a robber who had sought asylum, did not turn up armed for a campaign, did not pay heed to royal letters, etc.

Furthermore benefices were conferred on special terms, the infringement of which entailed their withdrawal, which of course did not extend to the rest of the property of the beneficiary. This was the case, for example, when former Church estates were granted and the beneficiary failed to pay the Church the dues that went with them (*nonae et decimae*[a]). Or if he let the estate deteriorate, in which case a year's notice was usually first given as a warning so that the beneficiary could improve matters to avert confiscation which would otherwise follow, etc. The transfer of an estate could also be tied to definite services and this was indeed done more and more frequently as the benefice gradually developed into the fief proper. But initially this was by no means necessary, especially with regard to military service, for many benefices were conferred on lower clerics, monks, and women both spiritual and lay.

Finally it is by no means impossible that in the beginning the Crown also conferred land subject to recall or for a definite period, i.e. as precaria. Some of the information and the procedure of the Church make this probable. But at any rate this ceased soon for the granting of land as a benefice became prevalent in the ninth century.

For the Church—and we must assume that this applied to the big landowners and beneficiaries as well—the Church, which previously granted estates to its free tenants mostly only as precaria for a definite period of time, had to follow the stimulus given by the Crown. The Church not only began to grant benefices as well, but this kind of grant became so predominant that already existing precaria were turned into lifelong ones and imperceptibly became benefices, until the former merged almost completely into the latter in the ninth century. Beneficiaries of the Church and also of secular magnates must have played an important part in the state as early as the second half of the ninth century, some of them must have been men of substantial property, the founders of the future lower nobility. Otherwise Charles the Bald would not have so vigorously helped those who had been without reason deprived of their benefices by Hincmar of Laon.

The benefice, as we see, has many aspects which recur in the developed fief. Throne-fall and home-fall are common to both. The benefice, like the fief, can only be revoked under certain conditions. The social hierarchy created by the benefices, which descends from the Crown through the big beneficiaries—the predecessors of the imperial princes—to the medium be-

---

[a] Ninth and tenth part of the harvest or other revenues. See P. Roth, op. cit., pp. 363-64.— *Ed.*

Page 17 of Engels' manuscript *The Frankish Period*

neficiaries—the future nobility—and from them to the free and unfree peasants, the bulk of whom lived in mark communities, formed the foundation for the future compact feudal hierarchy. Whereas the subsequent fief is, in all circumstances, held in return for services and entails military service for the feudal lord, the benefice does not yet require military service and other services are by no means inevitable. But the tendency of the benefice to become an estate held in return for services is already obvious, and spreads steadily during the ninth century; and in the same measure as it unfolds, the benefice develops into the fief.

Another factor contributed to this development, i.e., the changes which took place in the district and army structure first under the influence of big landed property and later under that of the big benefices, into which big landed property was increasingly transformed as a result of the incessant internal wars and the confiscations and retransfers associated with them.

It is evident that only the pure, classical form of the benefice has been examined in this chapter, which was certainly only a transitory form and did not even appear everywhere simultaneously. But such historical manifestations of economic relations can only be understood if they are considered in their pure state, and it is one of the chief merits of Roth that he has laid bare this classical form of the benefice, stripping it of all its confusing appendages.

THE DISTRICT AND ARMY STRUCTURE

The transformation in the position of landed property just described was bound to influence the old structure. It caused just as significant changes in the latter, and these in their turn had repercussions on the relations of landed property. For the present we shall leave aside the remodelling of the political structure as a whole and confine ourselves to an examination of the influence the new economic position exerted on the still existing remnants of the old popular structure in the districts and the army.

As early as the Merovingian period we frequently encounter counts and dukes as administrators of Crown estates. But it was not until the ninth century that certain Crown estates were definitely linked to the countship in such a way that the count of the day received their revenue. The formerly honorary office had been transformed into a paid one. In addition to this we find the counts holding royal benefices granted to them personally, which is something self-evident under the conditions of that time. The count thus became a powerful landowner within his county.

First of all it is obvious that the authority of the count was bound to suffer when big landed proprietors arose under him and side by side with him. People who had often enough scorned the commands of the kings under the Merovingians and early Carolingians could be expected to show even less respect for the orders of the count. Their free tenants, confident 'of the protection of powerful landlords, just as frequently disregarded the count's summons to appear in court or turn up for his levy to the army. This was one of the reasons that led to grants being made in the form of benefices instead of allodial grants and later to the gradual transformation of most of the formerly free big estates into benefices.

This alone was not enough to ensure that the free men living on the estates of the magnates did in fact perform their services to the State. A further change had to be introduced. The king saw himself compelled to make the big landlords responsible for the appearance of their free tenants at court and for their performance of military and other traditional services to the State in the same way as hitherto the count was held accountable for all free inhabitants of his county. And this could only be accomplished if the king gave the magnates some of the count's official powers over their tenants. It was the landlord or beneficiary who had to make sure that his people appeared before the court, they therefore had to be summoned through him. He had to bring them to the army, therefore the levy had to be effected by him, and so that he might always be held accountable for them he had to lead them and have the right to impose military discipline on them. But it was and continued to be the king's service that the tenants performed, and the recalcitrant was punished not by the landlord but by the royal count, and the fine went to the royal fisc.

This innovation too goes back to Charles Martel. At any rate only since his time do we find the custom of high ecclesiastical dignitaries taking the field themselves, a custom which, according to Roth, was due to the fact that Charles made his bishops join the army at the head of their tenants in order to ensure that the latter turned up.[a] Undoubtedly this also applied to the secular magnates and their tenants. Under Charlemagne the new arrangement is already firmly established and universally enforced.

---

[a] See P. Roth, op. cit., p. 356.— *Ed.*

But this caused a substantial change also in the political position of the free tenants. They who had formerly been on an equal footing with their landlord before the law, however much they depended on him economically, now became his subordinates also in the legal sphere. Their economic subjection was politically sanctioned. The landlord becomes Senior, Seigneur, the tenants become his *homines*, the "lord" becomes the master of his "man". The legal equality of the free men has disappeared; the man on the lowest rung of the ladder, his full freedom already greatly impaired by the loss of his ancestral land, moves down another step nearer the unfree. The new "lord" rises that much higher above the level of the old communal freedom. The basis of the new aristocracy, already established economically, is recognised by the State and becomes one of the fully operative driving wheels of the State machinery.

But alongside these *homines* made up of free tenants there existed yet another kind. These were impoverished free men who had voluntarily entered into the service or become retainers of a magnate. The retinue of the Merovingians were the antrustions, the magnates of that time will likewise have had their retainers. The retainers of the king were, under the Carolingians, called *vassi, vasalli* or *gasindi*, terms which had been used for unfree men in the oldest codes of common law, but had now come to mean usually free retainers. The same expressions were applied to the grandee's retainers, who now occur quite commonly and become an increasingly numerous and important element of society and State.

Old treaty formulas show how the grandees came to have such retainers. One of them (Formulae Sirmondicae 44) for instance says:

"Since it is known to one and all that I have not the wherewithal to feed and clothe myself, I ask of your" (the lord's) "piety that I may betake and commend myself into your protection" (*mundoburdum*—guardianship, as it were) "so that ... you will be obliged to aid me with food and clothing, according as I shall serve you and merit the same; in return, may I be obliged to render you service and obedience in the manner of a freeman (*ingenuili ordine*); nor shall it be in my power to withdraw from your authority and patronage during my lifetime but I shall spend my days under your authority and protection." [42]

This formula provides full information about the origin and nature of the ordinary relations of allegiance stripped of all alien admixtures, and it is especially revealing because it presents the extreme case of a poor devil who has been reduced to absolute penury. The entry into the seignior's retinue was effected by the

two parties reaching a free agreement—free in the sense of
Roman and modern law—often rather similar to the entry of a
present-day worker into the service of a manufacturer. The
"man" commended himself to the lord, and the latter accepted his
commendation. It was confirmed by a handshake and an oath of
allegiance. The agreement was lifelong and was only dissolved by
the death of one of the two contractors. The liege man was
obliged to carry out all services consistent with the position of a
free man which his lord might impose on him. In return the lord
provided for his keep and rewarded him as he thought fit. A
grant of land was by no means necessarily involved and in fact it
certainly did not take place in all cases.

Under the Carolingians, especially since Charlemagne, this
relationship was not only tolerated but directly encouraged and
eventually, it seems, made compulsory for all ordinary free
men—by a Capitulary of 847—and regulated by the State. For
example, the liege man could unilaterally annul the relationship
with his lord only if the latter attempted to kill him, hit him with a
stick, dishonour his wife or daughter or deprive him of his
hereditary property (Capitulary of 813). The liege man moreover
was bound to his lord as soon as he had received a value
equivalent to one solidus from him. This again clearly shows how
little at that time the vassal relationship was linked with the
granting of land. The same stipulations are repeated in a
Capitulary of 816, with the addition that the liege man was
released from his obligations if his lord wrongfully attempted to
reduce him to the status of an unfree man or failed to afford him
the promised protection although he was able to do so.[43]

With regard to his retainers the liege lord now had the same
rights and duties towards the State as the landlord or beneficiary
had with regard to his tenants. As before they were liable to serve
the king, but here too the liege lord was interposed between the
king and his counts. The liege lord brought the vassals to court,
he called them up, led them in war and maintained discipline
among them, he was responsible for them and their regulation
equipment. This gave him a certain degree of penal authority over
his subordinates, and was the starting point of the feudal lord's
jurisdiction over his vassals, which developed later.

In these two additional institutions, the formation of the
retainer system and the transfer of the official powers of the
counts, that is the State, to the landlord, the holder of a Crown
benefice, and the liege lord over his subordinates—both tenants
and landless retainers, who were soon all to be called *vassi, vasalli*

or *homines*—in this political confirmation and strengthening of the actual power of the lord over his vassals we see an important further development of the germ of the fief system contained in the benefices. The hierarchy of social estates, from the king downwards through the big beneficiaries to their free tenants and finally to the unfree men, has in its official capacity become a recognised element of the political organisation. The State recognises that it cannot exist without its help. We shall see later how in actual fact this help was given.

The differentiation between retainers and tenants is only important in the beginning, in order to show that the dependence of free men came about in two ways. The two types of vassals very soon merged inseparably, in name as well as in fact. It became more and more customary for the big beneficiaries to commend themselves to the king, so that they were not only his beneficiaries but also his vassals. It was in the interest of the kings to make the magnates, bishops, abbots, counts and vassals swear the oath of allegiance to them personally (*Annales Bertiniani* 837 [44] and other documents of the ninth century); consequently the distinction between the general oath of the subject and the specific oath of the vassal was bound to disappear soon. Thus all the great men gradually became vassals of the king. The slow transformation of the big landowners into a special estate, an aristocracy, was herewith recognised by the State, incorporated into the State structure and became one of its officially functioning elements.

Similarly the retainers of the individual big landowners gradually became tenants. Apart from providing board at the manor-house, which after all could only be done for a small number of people, there was but one way of assuring oneself of retainers, that is by settling them on the ground, by granting them land as a benefice. A numerous militant retinue, the main prerequisite for the existence of the magnates in those times of perpetual fighting, could therefore only be obtained by granting land to the vassals. Consequently landless retainers gradually disappear from the manor while the mass of those settled on the lord's land grows.

But the more this new element penetrated the old structure, the more it was bound to weaken the latter. The old direct exercise of State power by the king and the counts was more and more replaced by an indirect method; the seignior, to whom the common free men were increasingly tied by personal allegiance, now stood between them and the State. The count, the mainspring of the mechanism of State, was bound to recede into the background more and more, and so he did. In this situation

Charlemagne acted as he generally used to do. First he encouraged the spread of the vassal relationship, as we have seen, until the independent small free men had almost disappeared, and when the weakening of his power to which this led became obvious, he tried to help it on its feet again by State intervention. Under such an energetic and formidable ruler this could be successful in some cases, but the force of circumstances created with his help asserted itself inexorably under his weak successors.

Charlemagne's favourite method was to send out royal emissaries (*missi dominici*) with plenipotentiary powers. Where the ordinary royal official, the count, was unable to stem the spread of disorder, a special envoy was expected to do so. (This has to be historically substantiated and amplified.)

There was, however, another method, and this was to put the count in such a position that he had at his disposal material means to enforce his authority which were at least equal to those of the magnates in his county. This was only possible if the count too became a big landowner, which again could be brought about in two ways. Certain estates could be attached to the office of the count in the various districts as a sort of endowment, so that the count of the day administered them ex officio and received the revenue they yielded. Many examples of this kind can be found, especially in documents, from as early as the end of the eighth century, and this arrangement is quite usual from the ninth century onwards. It is self-evident that such endowments come for the most part from the king's fiscal estates, and as early as the time of the Merovingians we often find counts and dukes administering the king's fiscal estates situated in their territory.

Strangely enough there are also a good many examples (and even a formula for this purpose) of bishops using Church property to endow the office of the count, of course in the form of some sort of benefice since Church property was inalienable. The munificence of the Church is too well known to allow of any other reason for this but dire need. Under the growing pressure of neighbouring secular magnates no other resort was left to the Church but to ally itself with the remnants of the state authority.

These appurtenances associated with the count's post (*res comitatus, pertinentiae comitatus*) were originally quite distinct from the benefices which were granted personally to the count of the day. These too were usually distributed generously, so that, endowment and benefices taken together, countships, originally honorary positions, had by then become very lucrative posts, and since Louis the Pious they were, like other royal favours, bestowed on people whom the king wanted to win over to his side or of whom he wanted to be sure. Thus it is said of Louis the Stammerer that he "*quos potuit conciliavit [sibi], dans eis comitatus et abbatias ac villas*" (*Annales Bertiniani* 877).[a] The term honor, formely used to designate the office with reference to the honorary rights connected with it, acquired the same meaning as benefice in the course of the ninth century. And this necessarily caused a substantial change in the character of the count's office, as Roth rightly emphasises (p. 408). Originally the seigniory, in so far as it was of a public character, was modelled upon the office of the count and invested with some of the count's powers. Then, in the second half of the ninth century, the seigniory had become so widespread that it threatened to outweigh the count's office and the latter could only maintain its authority by more and more assuming the characteristics of seigniory. The counts increasingly sought, and not without success, to usurp the position of a seignior vis-à-vis the inhabitants of their districts (*pagenses*) with regard to both their private and their public relations. Just as the other "lords" sought to subordinate the small people in their neighbour-hood, so the counts tried, in an amicable way or by force, to induce the less well-off free inhabitants of their district to become their vassals. They succeeded the more easily as the mere fact that the counts could thus abuse their official power was the best proof that the remaining common free men could expect very little protection from the royal authority and its organs. Exposed to oppression from all quarters, the smaller free men had to be glad to find a patron, even at the cost of relinquishing their allodium and receiving it back as a mere benefice. Already in the Capitulary of 811 Charlemagne complained that bishops, abbots, counts, judges and *centenarii*[b] by continuous legal chicanery and repeated summonses to the army reduced the small people to such a state that they agreed to transfer or sell their allodium to them, and that the poor bitterly lamented that they were being robbed of their property, etc. The greater part of free property in Gaul had in this way already passed into the hands of the Church, the counts and other magnates by the end of the ninth century (Hincmar, *Annales Remenses* 869). And somewhat later no free landed property belonging to small free men existed any longer in

---

a "Tried to win the support of all he could by giving them countships, abbacies and estates." See P. Roth, *Geschichte des Beneficialwesens...*, p. 420, Note 10.— *Ed.*

b Subordinate judges, responsible to the court.— *Ed.*

some provinces (Maurer, *Einleitung,* p. 212).[a] When the increasing
power of the beneficiaries and the declining power of the Crown
had gradually caused benefices to become hereditary, the count's
office as a rule became hereditary too. If we saw the beginnings of
the subsequent nobility in the large number of royal beneficiaries,
here we see the seed of the territorial sovereignty of the future
princes that evolved from the district counts.

While thus the social and political system changed completely,
the old constitution of the army, based on the military service of
all free men—a service which was both their right and their
duty—remained outwardly unchanged, except that where the new
relations of dependence existed, the seignior interposed himself
between his vassals and the count. However, year by year the
common free men were less able to carry the burden of military
service. This consisted not only of personal service; the conscript
had also to equip himself and to live at his own expense during
the first six months. This continued until Charlemagne's incessant
wars knocked the bottom out of the barrel. The burden became so
unbearable that in order to rid themselves of it the small free men
began en masse to transfer not only their remaining property but
also their own person and their descendants to the magnates, and
especially to the Church. Charlemagne had reduced the free
warlike Franks to such a state that they preferred to become
bondsmen or serfs to avoid going to war. That was the
consequence of Charlemagne's insistence on maintaining, and even
carrying to the extreme, a military system based on universal and
equal landownership by all free men, at a time when the bulk of
the free men had lost all or most of their landed property.

The facts, however, were stronger than Charlemagne's obstinacy
and ambition. The old army system was no longer tenable. To
equip and provision the army at the expense of the State was even
less feasible in that age of a subsistence economy run practically
without money or commerce. Charlemagne was therefore obliged
to restrict the liability to service in such a way that equipment and
food could still remain the responsibility of the men themselves.
This was done in the Aachen Capitulary of 807, at a time when

---

[a] Hincmar Remensis, *Annales Remenses: Annales ad annum 869* in G. L. Maurer,
*Einleitung zur Geschichte der Mark-, Hof-, Dorf- und Stadt-Verfassung und der öffentlichen
Gewalt,* Munich, 1854, pp. 210-12 and notes 61 and 71.— *Ed.*

the wars were reduced to mere border fights, and the continued existence of the empire seemed, on the whole, ensured. Firstly all the king's beneficiaries without exception had to turn up, then those owning twelve hides (*mansi*) of land were to appear clad in armour, and therefore presumably also on horseback (the word *caballarius*—knight is used in the same Capitulary). Owners of three to five hides of land were also obliged to serve. Two owners having two hides of land each, three owners having one hide of land each, or six owners each possessing half a hide of land, had to send one man equipped by the others. As to free men who had no land at all but personal property worth five solidi, every sixth of them was to take the field and receive one solidus as pecuniary aid from each of the other five men. Moreover the obligation of the various parts of the country to take part in the fighting, an obligation which applied fully when the war was waged in the neighbourhood, was in the case of more distant wars reduced to between one-half and one-sixth of the total manpower, depending on the distance from the theatre of war.[a]

Charlemagne evidently attempted to adapt the old system to the changed economic position of the men liable to military service, to rescue what he could still rescue. But even these concessions were of no avail, and he was soon compelled to grant further exemptions in the *Capitulare de exercitu promovendo*.[b] The whole contents of this Capitulary, which is usually regarded as antecedent to that of Aachen, shows that it was undoubtedly drawn up several years later. According to it, one man has to do military service from every four hides of land, instead of three as previously. The owners of half a hide of land and those without land appear to be exempt from military service, and as regards beneficiaries their obligation is also restricted to the provision of one man for every four hides of land. Under Charlemagne's successors the minimum number of hides of land obliged to provide one man seems even to have been raised to *five*.[c]

It is strange that the mobilisation of the armoured owners of twelve hides of land seems to have encountered the greatest difficulties. At any rate, the order that they must turn up clad in armour is repeated innumerable times in the Capitularies.

Thus the common free men disappeared to an increasing extent. Just as the gradual separation from the land had driven

---

[a] P. Roth, *Geschichte des Beneficialwesens...*, pp. 398-401.— *Ed.*

[b] Capitulary on the levy for military service.— *Ed.*

[c] See P. Roth, op. cit., pp. 399-400.— *Ed.*

part of them to become vassals of the new big landlords, so the
fear of being completely ruined by military service actually drove
the other part into serfdom. How rapidly this submission to
servitude proceeded can be seen from the polyptychon (land
register) of the Saint-Germain-des-Prés monastery, which then still
lay outside Paris. It was compiled by abbot Irminon early in the
ninth century, and among the tenants of the monastery it lists
2,080 families of colons, 35 of lites, 220 of slaves (*servi*), but only
eight free families.[a] In the Gaul of those days, however, the word
colonus definitely denoted a serf. The marriage of a free woman
to a colonus *or* slave subjected her to the lord as defiled
(*deturpatam*) (Capitulary of 817). Louis the Pious commanded that
"*colonus vel servus*" (of a monastery at Poitiers) "*ad naturale
servitium velit nolit redeat*".[b] They received blows (Capitularies of
853, 861, 864 and 873) and were sometimes set free (see Guérard,
Irmino).[c] And these enthralled peasants were by no means of
Romance stock, but according to the testimony of Jacob Grimm
(*Geschichte der deutschen Sprache*, I, p. [537]), who examined their
names, "almost exclusively Frankish, far outweighing the small
number of Romance ones".

This huge rise in the unfree population in its turn changed the
class relations of the Frankish society. Alongside the big landlords,
who at that time rapidly emerged as a social estate in its own right,
and alongside their free vassals there appeared now a class of
unfree men which gradually absorbed the remnants of the
common free men. But these unfree men had either themselves
been free or were children of free men; those who had lived for
three or more generations in hereditary bondage formed a small
minority. Moreover, for the most part they were not Saxon,
Wendish, or other prisoners of war brought in from outside, but
natives of Frankish or Romance origin. Such people, especially
when they began to constitute the bulk of the population, were not
as easy to deal with as inherited or foreign serfs. They were not
yet used to servitude, the blows which even the colonus received
(Capitularies of 853, 861, 873) were still seen as a humiliation and
not as something natural. Hence the many plots and risings of
unfree men and even peasant vassals. Charlemagne himself

---

a B. E. Ch. Guérard, *Polyptyque de l'abbé Irminon* in P. Roth, op. cit.,
p. 378.— *Ed.*

b "A colon or slave has to return to his natural servitude whether he is willing
or not."— *Ed.*

c Quoted according to P. Roth, op. cit., pp. 376-77.— *Ed.*

brutally crushed an uprising of the tenants of the bishopric of Reims. In a Capitulary of 821 Louis the Pious mentions slaves (*servorum*) plotting in Flanders and Menapiscus (on the upper Lys). Risings of the liege men (*homines*) of the Mainz bishopric had to be put down in 848 and 866.[a] Orders to stamp out such plots are reiterated in capitularies from 779 onwards. The rising of the Stellinga in Saxony[45] must likewise be included here. The fact that from the end of the eighth century and the beginning of the ninth gradually a definite limit was fixed for the obligations of the unfree men, and even of the settled slaves, and that this limit, which was not to be exceeded, was laid down by Charlemagne in his Capitularies, was obviously a consequence of the threatening attitude of the enthralled masses.

The price therefore which Charlemagne had to pay for his new Roman Empire[46] was the annihilation of the social estate of common free men, who had constituted the entire Frankish people at the time of the conquest of Gaul, and the division of the people into big landlords, vassals and serfs. But with the common free men the old military system collapsed, and with these two the monarchy went down. Charlemagne had destroyed the foundation of his own power. It could still sustain him, but under his successors it became evident what the work of his hands had been in reality.

NOTE: THE FRANCONIAN DIALECT[47]

This dialect has received curious treatment from philologists. Whereas Grimm let it disappear into French and High German,[b] more recent ones grant it a spread extending from Dunkirk and Amsterdam to the Unstrut, Saale and Rezat, and in some cases even as far as the Danube and, through colonisation, to the Riesengebirge. While even a philologist like Moritz Heyne constructs an Old Low Franconian language[c] from a manuscript of the Heliand prepared in Werden,[48] a language that is almost pure Old Saxon with a very faint tinge of Franconian, Braune lumps together all the truly Low Franconian dialects without further comment as Saxon here and Dutch there.[d] And finally

[a] See P. Roth, op. cit., p. 378, Note 47.— *Ed.*

[b] J. Grimm, *Geschichte der deutschen Sprache*, Vol. 1, Leipzig, 1848, p. 535.— *Ed.*

[c] M. Heyne, *Kleine altsächsische und altniederfränkische Grammatik*, Paderborn, 1873, p. 2.— *Ed.*

[d] W. Braune, *Zur Kenntnis des Fränkischen und zur hochdeutschen Lautverschiebung.* In: *Beiträge zur Geschichte der deutschen Sprache und Literatur*, Vol. I, Halle, 1874, pp. 1-56.— *Ed.*

Arnold limits the territory conquered by the Ripuarians to the
area north of the watershed of the Ahr and the Mosel, letting
everything situated to the south and south-west be occupied, first
by Alamanni, later exclusively by the Chatti (whom he also lumps
together with the Franks), thus letting them speak Alamannic-
Chattish.[a]

First let us reduce the Franconian language area to its real
limits. Thuringia, Hesse and Main Franconia have no other claim
whatever to be included in it except that in the Carolingian period
they were part of what was called Francia. The language spoken
east of the Spessart and Vogelsberg and the Kahler Asten is
anything but Franconian. Hesse and Thuringia have their own
independent dialects, being inhabited by independent peoples; in
Main Franconia a mixed Slav, Thuringian and Hessian population
was permeated with Bavarian and Frankish elements and evolved
its own peculiar dialect. Only if one employs as the main criterion
the extent to which the High German sound shift penetrated into
these dialects can these three linguistic branches be assigned to
Franconian. Yet as we shall see, it is precisely this procedure which
creates all the confusion when the Franconian language is assessed
by non-Franks.

Let us commence with the oldest records and first view Moritz
Heyne's[*] so-called Old Low Franconian in the correct light. The
so-called Cotton Manuscript of the Heliand, prepared in Werden
and now preserved in Oxford, is supposed to be Old Low
Franconian because it was produced in the monastery of Werden,
still on Frankish soil though close to the Saxon frontier. Here the
old tribal boundary is, to this day, the boundary between Berg and
Mark; of the abbeys situated in between, Werden belongs to
Franconia, Essen to Saxony. Werden is bounded in the immediate
vicinity, to the east and north, by indisputably Saxon communities;
in the plain between the Ruhr and the Lippe the Saxon language
pushes forward in places almost to the Rhine. The fact that a
Saxon work is copied in Werden, obviously by a Frank, and that
here and there this Frank has let slip from his pen Franconian
word forms, is far from being sufficient reason to declare the
language of the copy to be Franconian. Apart from the Cotton
Heliand Heyne considers as Low Franconian a number of

---

[*] *Kleine altsächsische und altniederfränkische Grammatik* by Moritz Heyne,
Paderborn, 1873.

---

[a] W. Arnold, *Deutsche Urzeit*, Gotha, 1879, pp. 150-53.— *Ed.*

fragments from Werden that show the same character, and the remains of a psalm translation,[a] which according to him originated in the area of Aachen, whereas Kern (*Glossen in der Lex Salica*)[b] states quite simply that it is Dutch. In fact it does contain purely Dutch forms on the one hand, but also genuine Rhenish Franconian forms and even traces of the High German sound shift. It obviously originated on the frontier between Dutch and Rhenish Franconian, say between Aachen and Maastricht. Its language is much later than that of the two Heliand manuscripts.

The Cotton Heliand alone is enough, however, for us to establish beyond doubt from the few Franconian forms that occur in it some of the main differences between Franconian and Saxon.

I. In all Ingaevonian dialects the three persons of the present indicative plural all have the same ending, namely a dental preceded by a vowel: Old Saxon -*d*, Anglo-Saxon -*dh*, Old Frisian -*th* (which probably also stands for -*dh*). Thus Old Saxon *hebbiad* means "we have, you have, they have"; similarly, all three persons of *fallan, gewinnan* are the same: *fallad, winnad*. It is the third person that has taken over all three, but, mark well, with the specifically Ingaevonian loss of *n* before -*d* or -*dh*, the loss affecting all the three dialects mentioned. Of all living dialects, only Westphalian has preserved this peculiarity; to this very day Westphalian has *wi, ji, se hebbed*, etc. The other Saxon dialects no longer retain this feature, nor does West Frisian; they differentiate the three persons.[c]

The West Rhenish psalms[d] have, like Middle High German, -*n* in the first person plural, -*t* in the second, -*nt* in the third. However, at times the Cotton Heliand has, besides the Saxon forms, quite different forms: *tholônd*—they suffer, *gornônd*—you complain, and as the imperative, *mârient*—announce, *seggient*—say, where Saxon requires *tholôd, gornôd, mâriad, seggiad*. These forms are not merely Franconian, they are in fact genuine local Werden, Berg dialect to this day. In Bergish we also find that all three persons of the present plural are the same, but end not as in

---

a *Altniederdeutsche Interlinearversion der Psalmen.* In: *Kleinere altniederdeutsche Denkmäler* published by Moritz Heyne, 2nd ed., Paderborn, 1867, pp. 1-40. For a description of the psalms see M. Heyne, *Kleine altsächsische und altniederfränkische Grammatik*, p. 2.— *Ed.*

b H. Kern, *Die Glossen in der Lex Salica und die Sprache der salischen Franken. Beitrag zur Geschichte der deutschen Sprachen*, The Hague, 1869, p. 2, Note 1.— *Ed.*

c Engels added in pencil here "and the 3rd person from the 2nd".— *Ed.*

d See *Altniederdeutsche Interlinearversion der Psalmen.*— *Ed.*

Saxon in -d, but as in Franconian in -nt. As opposed to Märkish *wi hebbed*, there right on the border they say *wi hant*, and as in the above imperative *seggient* they say *seient ens*—[German] *sagt einmal* (tell me). On the basis of this simple observation, that here in Bergish the three persons have been levelled, Braune and others [a] have quite simply declared the entire Bergish highlands to be Saxon. The rule certainly advanced into the area from Saxony; unfortunately, however, it is put into effect in the Franconian manner, thus proving the reverse of what it is intended to prove.

The loss of *n* before dentals in the Ingaevonian dialects is not restricted to this case; it is less common in Old Frisian, but fairly widespread in Old Saxon and Anglo-Saxon: *mudh*—*Mund* [mouth], *kudh*—*kund* [known], *us*—*uns* [us], *odhar*—*ein anderer* [other]. The Frankish copyist of the Heliand in Werden twice has the Franconian form *andar* for *odhar*.[b] The Werden tax registers [49] alternate between the Franconian form of the names *Reinswind, Meginswind* and the Saxon *Reinswid* and *Meginswid*. The psalms of the left bank of the Rhine,[c] on the other hand, regularly have *munt, kunt, uns*; only once have the so-called Lipsius Glosses [50] (excerpted from the lost manuscript of these psalms) *farkutha abominabiles* instead of *farkuntha*. Similarly, the Old Salic records have consistently preserved the *n* in the names *Gund, Segenand, Chlodosindis, Ansbertus,* etc., which is irrelevant. The modern Franconian dialects regularly have the *n* (sole exception in Bergish is the form *os*—*uns* [us]).

II. The linguistic records from which the so-called Old Saxon grammar is usually constructed all belong to south-western Westphalia, Münster, Freckenhorst, Essen. The language of these records shows a few essential deviations not only from the general Ingaevonian forms, but also from such forms as have been preserved for us in proper names from Engern and Eastphalia as genuine Old Saxon; however, they are in curious agreement with Franconian and Old High German. The latest grammarian of the dialect, Cosijn, therefore even terms it Old West Saxon.[d]

Since in this investigation we must almost totally rely on proper names in Latin documents, the demonstrable differences in form between West and East Saxon can only be few in number; they are restricted to two cases, but these are very important.

---

[a] See W. Braune, *Zur Kenntnis des Fränkischen...*, pp. 12, 16 and M. Heyne, *Kleine altsächsische und altniederfränkische Grammatik*, p. 50.— *Ed.*

[b] M. Heyne, *Kleine altsächsische und altniederfränkische Grammatik*, p. 2.— *Ed.*

[c] *Altniederdeutsche Interlinearversion der Psalmen.— Ed.*

[d] P. J. Cosijn, *Kurzgefaßte altwestsächsische Grammatik*, Leiden, 1881.— *Ed.*

1. Anglo-Saxon and Old Frisian have -*a* in the genitive plural of all declensions. Old West Saxon, Old Franconian and Old High German, on the other hand, have -*ô*. So what is the correct Old Saxon form? Should this dialect in fact deviate from the Ingaevonian rule on this point?

The documents from Engern and Eastphalia provide the answer. In *Stedieraburg, Horsadal, Winethahûsen, Edingahûsun, Magathaburg* and many other names, the first part of the compound is in the genitive plural and has -*a*. Even in Westphalia the -*a* has still not entirely disappeared: the Freckenhorst Roll once has *Aningera lô* and *Wernera-Holthûson*,[a] and the -*a* in Osnabrück is likewise an old genitive plural.

2. Similarly, the weak masculine in Franconian, as in Old High German, ends in -*o*, as opposed to Gothic-Ingaevonian -*a*. In Old West Saxon -*o* is likewise established as the rule; thus another deviation from Ingaevonian usage. But this by no means applies to Old Saxon as a whole. Not even in Westphalia did -*o* apply without exception; alongside -*o* the Freckenhorst Roll already has a whole succession of names in -*a* (*Sîboda, Uffa, Asica, Hassa, Wenda,* etc.,); the Paderborn records in Wigand[51] nearly always show -*a*, only exceptionally -*o*; in documents from Eastphalia -*a* dominates almost exclusively; so that Jakob Grimm (*Geschichte der deutschen Sprache*)[b] already comes to the conclusion that there can be no mistaking the fact that -*a* and -*an* (in oblique cases) was the original Saxon form common to all parts of the nation. The advance of -*o* instead of -*a* was not restricted to Westphalia either. At the beginning of the 15th century the East Frisian men's names of the chronicles, etc., almost regularly have -*o*; *Fokko, Occo, Enno, Smelo,* etc., as opposed to the earlier -*a* still preserved in odd cases in West Frisian.

It may therefore be taken for established that both deviations of West Saxon from the Ingaevonian rule are not originally Saxon but caused by foreign influence. This influence is easily explained by the fact that West Saxony *was formerly Frankish territory*. Only after the departure of the main mass of the Franks did the Saxons move across the Osning and Egge gradually up to the line that even today divides Mark and Sauerland from Berg and Siegerland. The influence of the Franks who remained behind and have now merged with the Saxons shows in those two cases of -*o*

---

[a] Freckenhorster Heberolle. In: *Kleinere altniederdeutsche Denkmäler*, pp. 70, 72.— *Ed.*

[b] J. Grimm, op. cit., Vol. 2. Leipzig, 1848, p. 649.— *Ed.*

instead of -a; it is still unmistakable in the present-day dialects.

III. A peculiarity of the Rhenish Franconian language which extends from the Ruhr to the Mosel is the ending of the 1st [person] present indicative in -n, which is best preserved in cases[a] where it is followed by a vowel: dat don ek—das tue ich [I do that], ek han—ich habe [I have] (Bergish). This verb form applies to the whole lower Rhine and the Mosel, at least as far as the Lotharingian border: don, han. The same peculiarity is already found in the left-bank Rhenish psalms: biddon—ich bitte [I ask], wirthon—ich werde [I become], though not consistently.[b] This-n is lacking in the Salic dialect; there even the oldest record[53] has ec forsacho, gelôbo. It is also missing in Dutch. Old West Saxon is here distinct from Franconian in so far as it knows this -n in one conjugation only (the so-called second weak): skawôn—ich schaue [I look], thionôn—ich diene [I serve], etc. It is quite alien to Anglo-Saxon and Old Frisian. We may therefore assume that this -n is also a Franconian remnant in Old West Saxon.

Apart from the numerous proper names preserved in documents, etc., and the glosses of the Lex Salica, which are often distorted past recognition, we have almost no remains of the Salic dialect at all. Nevertheless, Kern (Die Glossen in der Lex Salica) has removed a considerable number of these distortions and established the text, in many cases with certainty, in others with great likelihood, demonstrating that it is written in a language that is the immediate precursor of Middle and Modern Dutch. But the material reconstructed in this way is naturally not directly applicable for the grammar. Apart from this, all we possess is the brief abjuration charm[c] added to the Capitulary of Carloman of 743 and probably drawn up at the synod of Lestines, thus in Belgium. And here we come across two characteristic Franconian words right at the outset: ec forsacho—ich entsage [I renounce]. Ec for ich [I] is widespread among the Franks even today. In Trier and Luxemburg eich, in Cologne and Aachen êch, in Bergish ek. Though written Dutch has ik, ek is often heard in the vernacular, particularly in Flanders. The Old Salic names Segenandus, Segemundus, Segefredus are unanimous in showing e for i.

In forsacho, ch stands for g between vowels: this occurs elsewhere in the records (rachineburgius) and is even today a sign

---

    [a] Engels' note in pencil in the margin: "Otfried".[52]— Ed.

    [b] See M. Heyne, Kleine altsächsische und altniederfränkische Grammatik, p. 50.— Ed.

    [c] Taufgelöbnis. In: Kleinere altniederdeutsche Denkmäler, p. 85.— Ed.

of all the Franconian dialects from the Palatinate to the North Sea. We shall return to these two chief characteristics of Franconian— *e* often for *i,* and *ch* between vowels for *g*—in the individual dialects.

As the result of the above investigation, which may be compared with Grimm's statements about Old Franconian in the *Geschichte der deutschen Sprache* at the end of the first volume [p. 547], we may posit this thesis, which anyway is hardly disputed now: that in the 6th and 7th centuries Franconian was already a dialect of its own, forming the transition between High German, in particular Alamannic, and Ingaevonian, in particular Saxon and Frisian, and at that time still completely at the Gothic-Low German stage of shifting. But once this has been conceded it has also been acknowledged that the Franks were not a mish-mash of different peoples allied by external circumstances, but a main German people in their own right, the Iscaevonians, who probably absorbed foreign constituents at different times but also had the strength to assimilate them. Similarly we may regard it as proven that each of the main branches of the Franconian people already spoke a peculiar dialect at an early stage, that the language divided into Salic and Ripuarian and that many distinguishing peculiarities of the old dialects still live on in the present-day vernacular.

Let us now move on to these still living dialects.

1. There is no longer any doubt that Salic lives on in the two Netherlands dialects, Flemish and Dutch, and at its purest in the areas that have been Frankish ever since the 6th century. For after the great tidal waves of the 12th, 13th and 14th centuries had wiped out almost all Zeeland and formed the Zuider Zee, the Dollart and the Jade, thus breaking the geographical, and also the political, cohesion of the Frisians, the remains of old Frisian liberty succumbed to the pressure of the surrounding landed gentry,[54] and with it, almost everywhere, the Frisian language, too. To the west it was hemmed in or wholly suppressed by Dutch, to the east and north by Saxon and Danish, in all cases leaving behind strong traces in the invading language. In the 16th and 17th centuries the old Frisian area of Zeeland and Holland became the centre and mainstay of the struggle for independence in the Netherlands,[55] just as they were already the seat of the main trading towns of the country. Thus it was chiefly here that the modern

written language of the Netherlands came into being, absorbing Frisian elements, words and word forms, which can be clearly distinguished from the Franconian foundation. On the other hand, the Saxon language advanced from the east on to formerly Frisian and Frankish territory. It must be left to detailed research to draw up the exact boundaries; purely Salic are only the Flemish-speaking parts of Belgium, North Brabant, Utrecht, along with Gelderland and Overijssel with the exception of the easterly, Saxon areas.

Between the French linguistic boundary on the Maas and the Saxon boundary north of the Rhine, the Salians and the Ripuarians clashed. We shall discuss later the matter of the demarcation line, which here too has yet to be ascertained by detailed study. But first let us consider the grammatical peculiarities of Dutch.

As for the vowels, we see at once that *i* is replaced by *e* in the true Franconian manner: *brengen—bringen* [bring], *kreb—Krippe* [crib], *hemel—Himmel* [sky], *geweten—Gewissen* [conscience], *ben—bin* [am], *stem—Stimme* [voice]. This is even more frequently the case in Middle Dutch: *gewes—gewiss* [certain], *es—ist* [is], *selver—Silber* [silver], *blent—blind* [blind], where Modern Dutch has *gewis, is, zilver, blind*. Similarly in the vicinity of Ghent I find two places, *Destelbergen* and *Desteldonck*, according to which *Distel* [thistle] is to this day *Destel*. Middle Dutch, raised on pure Franconian soil, is here in exact agreement with Ripuarian, while the Modern Dutch written language, having been exposed to Frisian influence, is less so.

Further, again in agreement with Ripuarian, *o* replaces *u* before *m* or *n* plus following consonant, though not so consistently as in Middle Dutch and Ripuarian. Beside *konst, gonst, kond,* Modern Dutch has *kunst, gunst, kund* [art, favour, known]; yet both agree in having *mond—Mund* [mouth], *hond—Hund* [dog], *jong—jung* [young], *ons—uns* [us].

In contrast to Ripuarian, the long *i* (*ij*) has become *ei* as far as pronunciation is concerned, which does not yet seem to have been the case in Middle Dutch. However, this *ei* is not pronounced as High German *ei* = *ai*, but really as *e* + *i*, though not quite as thin as, e.g., the *ej* of the Danes and Slavs. Scarcely divergent from this sound is the diphthong written not *ij* but *ei*. Corresponding to High German *au* we find *ou, ouw*.

The umlaut has disappeared from the inflexion. In the declension singular and plural have the same stem vowel, as do indicative and subjunctive in the conjugation. On the other hand, umlaut does occur in word formation in two forms: 1. in the [mutation] of *a* to *e* by *i* common to all post-Gothic dialects; 2. in a form peculiar to Dutch that did not develop until later. Middle Dutch and Ripuarian still both have *hus—Haus* [house], *brun—braun* [brown], *rum—geräumig* [roomy], *tun—Zaun* [fence], plural *huse, brune.* Modern Dutch has only the forms *huis, bruin, ruim, tuin* (*ui*=High German *eu*), which are alien to Middle Dutch and Ripuarian. On the other hand, *eu* is already displacing short *o* (High German *u*) in Middle Dutch: *jeughet,* beside *joghet,* Modern Dutch *jeugd—Jugend* [youth]; *doghet—Tugend* [virtue], *dor—Tür* [door], *kor—Wahl* [choice], alongside the forms with *eu*; Modern Dutch permits the forms *deugd, keur, deur* only. This is in perfect agreement with the *eu* that developed from the 12th century in Northern French for Latin stressed *o.* Kern draws attention to a third case [a]: the mutated form *ei* from *ê* (*ee*) in Modern Dutch. All these three forms of umlaut are unknown in Ripuarian, as in the other dialects, and are a special characteristic of Dutch.

Ald, alt, old, olt, uld, ult turn into *oud, out.* This transition is already present in Middle Dutch, in which, however, *guldin, hulde, sculde* still occur alongside *goudin, houde, scoude* (*sollte*) [should], so that it is possible to establish roughly the time when it was introduced. It is also peculiar to Dutch, at least as opposed to all the other continental Germanic dialects; it does, however, exist in the Lancashire dialect of English: *gowd, howd, owd* for *gold, hold, old.*

As far as the consonants are concerned, Dutch has no pure *g* (the guttural Italian, French or English *g*). This consonant is pronounced as a strongly aspirated *gh,* which in certain sound combinations does not differ from the deeply guttural (Swiss, Modern Greek or Russian) *ch.* We have seen that this transition of *g* into *ch* was already known in Old Salic. It is also found in a part of Ripuarian and the Saxon dialects that developed on formerly Frankish soil, e.g. in Münsterland, where, as in Bergish, even initial *j,* especially in foreign words, on occasion sounds like *ch,* and it is possible to hear *Choseph* and even *Chahr* (*Jahr*) [year]. If M. Heyne had taken this into account,[b] he might have spared himself his difficulty with the frequent confusion and mutual alliteration of *j, g* and *ch* in the Heliand.

In some cases Dutch retains the initial *wr*: *wringen—ringen* [ring], *wreed*—cruel, harsh, *wreken—rächen* [avenge]. There is also a remnant of this in Ripuarian.

---

[a] H. Kern, *Die Glossen in der Lex Salica...,* p. 111, Note 1.—*Ed.*
[b] M. Heyne, *Kleine altsächsische und altniederfränkische Grammatik,* p. 21.—*Ed.*

The softening of the diminutive -*ken* to -*tje*, -*je* is derived from Frisian: *mannetje*—*Männchen* [little man], *bietje*—*Bienchen* [little bee], *halsje*—*Hälschen* [little throat], etc. But *k* is also retained: *vrouken*—*Frauchen* [little woman], *hoedeken*—*Hütchen* [little hat]. Flemish better preserves the *k*, at least in the vernacular; the famous little man in Brussels is called *Manneken-Pis*.[56] The French have thus borrowed their *mannequin,* and the English their *manikin,* from Flemish. The plural of both endings is -*s*: *vroukens, mannetjes.* We shall come across this -*s* again in Ripuarian.

In common with Saxon and even Scandinavian dialects, Dutch shows the loss of *d* between vowels, especially betwen two *e*'s: *leder* and *leer, weder* and *weer, neder* and *neer, vader* and *vaer, moeder* and *moer*—*Mutter* [mother].

The Dutch declension shows a complete mixture of strong and weak forms, so that, as the plural umlaut is also lacking, the Dutch plural forms only in the rarest cases agree with even the Ripuarian or Saxon ones, and this, too, is a very tangible characteristic of the language.

Common to Salic and Ripuarian and all the Ingaevonian dialects is the loss of the nominative indicator in *er, der, wer* [he, the, who]: Dutch *hij, de* (article) and *die* (demonstrative pronoun), *wie.*

To go into the conjugation would take us too far. What has been said here will suffice to distinguish the present-day Salic language everywhere from the neighbouring dialects. Closer examination of the Dutch dialects is bound to bring to light much of importance.

II. *Rhenish Franconian.* With this term I denote all the remaining Franconian dialects. I do not place Salic in opposition to Ripuarian in the old manner, and there is a very good reason for this.

Even Arnold[a] has drawn attention to the fact that the Ripuarians in the proper sense occupied a relatively limited area, the southern boundary of which is more or less marked by the two places Reifferscheid near Adenau and near Schleiden. This is correct in so far as in this way the *purely Ripuarian* territory is demarcated linguistically too from the territories occupied by genuine Ripuarians after, or at the same time as, other German tribes. Since the name Low Franconian has already acquired another meaning which also includes Salic, I am left only with the

---

[a] W. Arnold, *Deutsche Urzeit,* Gotha, 1879, p. 150.—*Ed.*

term Ripuarian—in the narrower sense—to denote the group of closely related dialects which extend from the Salic linguistic boundary up to this line.

1. *Ripuarian*. The dividing line between this group of dialects and the Salic by no means coincides with the Dutch-German border. On the contrary, the major part of the district Rees, where in the area of Wesel Salic, Ripuarian and Saxon meet, still belongs to Salic on the right bank of the Rhine. On the left bank the areas of Kleve and Geldern are Salic, roughly as far as a line drawn from the Rhine between Xanten and Wesel, south of the village of Vluyn (west of Mörs) and from there south-west towards Venlo. A more exact definition of the boundary is only possible on the spot since many Ripuarian names have been preserved on the maps in Salic-Dutch form as the result of many years of Dutch administration not only in Geldern but also in the county of Mörs.

From the area of Venlo upwards the greater part of the right bank of the Maas seems to be Ripuarian, so that here the political border nowhere crosses Salic territory but only Ripuarian and this extends almost as far as Maastricht. Names in *-heim* (not *-hem*) and the specifically Ripuarian ending *-ich* occur here in great numbers on Dutch territory, further south already names in *-broich* (Dutch *-broek*), e.g. *Dallenbroich* near Roermond; likewise in *-rade* (*Bingelrade* near Sittard, plus *Amstenrade*, *Hobbelrade* and 6 or 7 others); the little piece of German territory that has fallen to Belgium to the right of the Maas, is entirely Ripuarian (cf. *Krützenberg*, 9 kilometres from the Maas, with *Kruisberg*, north of Venlo). Indeed, left of the Maas, in the Belgian so-called Limburg I find *Kessenich* near Maaseyk, *Stockheim* and *Reekheim* on the Maas, *Gellik* near Maastricht as proof that no purely Salic population lives here.

The Ripuarian border with Saxony starts from the area of Wesel, running south-east at an increasing distance from the Rhine, between Mülheim on the Ruhr and Werden on the Franconian side and Essen on the Saxon side, to the border between Berg and Mark, here even now the border between the Rhine Province and Westphalia. It does not leave this border until south of Olpe, where it proceeds eastwards, dividing the Siegerland as Franconian from the Saxon Sauerland. Further east, the Hessian dialect soon takes over.

The above-mentioned southern border with the dialect which I term Middle Franconian is in rough agreement with the southern borders of the old districts of Avalgau, Bonngau and Eiflia, and from there runs westwards to Wallonia, keeping rather to the south. This area thus circumscribed includes the big old district of Ripuaria as well as parts of the districts adjoining it to the north and west.

As already stated, Ripuarian agrees in many respects with Dutch, but in such a way that Middle Dutch is closer to it than Modern Dutch. Ripuarian agrees with Modern Dutch in its pronunciation of *ei* = *e* + *i* and *ou* for *au*, the transition of *i* to *e*, which goes much further in Ripuarian and Middle Dutch than in Modern Dutch: the Middle Dutch *gewes, es, blend, selver* (silver) are still good Ripuarian to this day. Similarly, and consistently so, *u* changes into *o* before *m* or *n* with a following consonant: *jong, lomp, domm, konst*. If this following consonant is a *d* or a *t*, this changes to *g* or *k* in some dialects; e.g. *honk—Hund* [dog], plural *höng*, where the softening to *g* is an aftereffect of the loss of the final vowel, *e*.

However, the situation as regards umlaut in Ripuarian is very different from that of Dutch; it is in general agreement with High German, and in odd exceptions with Saxon (e.g. *hanen* for *Hähne* [cocks]).

Initial *wr* has become hardened to *fr*, retained in *fringen*—to wring water out of a cloth, etc., and *frêd* (Dutch *wreed*) with the meaning hardy, weather-beaten.

For *er, der, wer* it has *hê, dê, wê*.

The declension is midway between High German and Saxon. Plural forms in *-s* are common, but are hardly ever in agreement with the Dutch; this *-s* becomes *-r* in local High German in correct memory of the linguistic development.

The diminutive *-ken, -chen* is changed to *-schen* after *n*: *männschen*; the plural has *-s* as in Dutch (*männsches*). Both forms extend all the way into Lorraine.

r is lost before *s, st, d, t, z*, the preceding vowel remaining short in some dialects, being lengthened in others. Thus *hart* [hard] becomes *hatt* (Bergish), *haad* (Cologne). In the process *st* becomes *scht* through Upper German influence: *Durst* [thirst]—*doascht* (Bergish), *dôscht* (Cologne).

Similarly, initial *sl, sw, st, sp* have become *schl*, etc., through High German influence.

As in Dutch, pure *g* is unknown in Ripuarian. Some of the dialects on the Salic border, as well as Bergish, have aspirated *gh* for initial and medial *g*, though softer than in Dutch. The rest have *j*. Final *g* is everywhere pronounced as *ch*, though not like the hard Dutch sound, but like the soft Rhenish Franconian *ch*, which sounds like a hardened *j*. The essentially Low German character of Ripuarian is attested by terms such as *boven* for *oben* [above].

The majority of the voiceless consonants are everywhere at the first stage of the sound shift. Only *t* and medial and final *k*, occasionally *p*, show the High German sound shift in the southern dialects: they have *lôsze* for *lôten—lassen* [let], *holz* for *holt* [wood], *rîch* for *rîk—reich* [rich], *êch* for *ek—ich* [I], *pief* for *pîpe—Pfeife* [pipe]. But *et, dat, wat* and a few others are retained.

It is this not even consistently carried out intrusion of the High German sound shift in three cases on which the usual demarcation of Middle and Low Franconian is based. But in this way a group of dialects that belong together on account of definite features in the sound system, as demonstrated, which are still recognised in the popular mind as belonging together, are torn apart arbitrarily and on the basis of a characteristic that is here quite fortuitous.

Quite fortuitous, I say. Each of the other Central German dialects, Hessian, Thuringian, Upper Saxon, etc., is generally speaking at a specific stage of the High German sound shift. They may show rather less shifting on the Low Saxon border and rather more on the Upper German border, but that is at most only enough to justify local differences. Franconian, on the other hand, shows no shifting at all on the North Sea, Maas and Lower Rhine, on the Alamannic border almost entirely Alamannic shifting; in between there are at least three intermediate stages. The shift thus penetrated into Rhenish Franconian when it had already developed independently, splitting it up into several pieces. The last trace of this shift need not by any means vanish on the border of a particular group of dialects that was already in existence; it may die out in the midst of such a group, as it in fact does. On the other hand, the truly dialect-forming influence of the shift, as we shall see, does indeed cease on the border of two dialect groups that were already different beforehand. And did not the *schl, schw,* etc., and the final *scht* come to us from High German in a similar way and at an even later date? These however—at least the first—even go deep into Westphalia.

The Ripuarian dialects formed a fixed group long before some of them learnt to shift *t* and medial and final *k* and *p*. How far this change was able to advance within the group was and remains for the group a matter of chance. The dialect of Neuss is identical with that of Krefeld and München-Gladbach—apart from minor differences that a stranger cannot hear at all. Nevertheless, one is supposed to be Middle Franconian, the other Low Franconian. The dialect of the Berg industrial country merges into that of the

south-west Rhine plain in imperceptible stages. And yet they are
supposed to belong to two totally different groups. For anyone
who is at home in the region it is obvious that book-learning is
here forcing the living dialects, with which it is scarcely acquainted
if at all, into the Procrustean bed of characteristics constructed *a
priori.*

As a result of this purely superficial distinction the southern
Ripuarian dialects are lumped together into a so-called Middle
Franconian with other dialects from which they diverge, as we
shall see, far more than they do from the so-called Low
Franconian. Owing to the same superficial distinction, a narrow
strip is held back because you are at a loss what to do with it and
are finally obliged to declare one part Saxon and another Dutch,
which is in glaring contradiction to the state of affairs in these
dialects.

Let us take, for instance, the Bergish dialect, which Braune
without much ado calls Saxon.[a] It forms, as we have seen, all three
persons plural of the present indicative in the same way, but as in
Franconian, with the ancient form *-nt.* It regularly has *o* instead of
u before *m* and *n* followed by a consonant, which according to
the same Braune is definitely un-Saxon and specifically Low
Franconian. It agrees with the other Ripuarian dialects in all the
characteristics set out above. While it imperceptibly merges into the
dialect of the Rhine plain from village to village, from farm
to farm, it is most sharply separated from the Saxon dialect on the
Westphalian border. Perhaps nowhere else in all Germany is there
such an abruptly drawn linguistic border as here. And what a
distance between the languages! The whole vowel system seems to
be turned upside down; the sharp Low Franconian *ei* contrasts
abruptly with the broadest *ai,* just as *ou* contrasts with *au*; not one
of the many diphthongs and vocalic glides is in agreement; here
sch as in the rest of Germany, there *s-ch* as in Holland; here *wi
hant,* there *wi hebbed*; here the dual forms *get* and *enk* used as the
plural (German *ihr* and *euch*), there only *i, ji,* and *ü, jü*; here the
sparrow is called common Ripuarian *Mösche,* there common
Westphalian *Lüning.* Not to mention other peculiarities specific to
the Bergish dialect which also suddenly vanish here on the border.

The individuality of a dialect is most apparent to the stranger if
the person in question is not speaking dialect but High German,
which is more intelligible to the stranger, and which in the case of
most Germans is, of course, strongly coloured by their respective

---

[a] W. Braune, *Zur Kenntnis des Fränkischen...,* p. 11.— *Ed.*

dialect. But then the allegedly Saxon inhabitant of the Berg industrial district is for the non-native quite indistinguishable from the inhabitant of the Rhine plain, who is supposed to be Middle Franconian, except for the somewhat more harshly aspirated *gh*, where the other says *j*. A man from Heckinghaus in Berg (from Oberbarmen, left of the Wupper), however, and a man from Langerfeld in Mark, who lives scarcely a kilometre further east, are further apart in the local High German of everyday life than the man from Heckinghaus and one from Coblenz, let alone anyone from Aachen or Bonn.

The advance of the shift of *t* and final *k* makes such a small impression on the Rhenish Frank himself as a linguistic boundary that even in an area well known to him he will first have to reflect where the border runs between *t* and *z*, *k* and *ch*, and that, when crossing this border, he finds that one comes almost as naturally to him as the other. This is made even easier by the many High German words with shifted *sz*, *z*, *ch* and *f* that have entered the dialects. A striking example is afforded by the old Bergish penal code from the 14th century (Lacomblet, *Archiv*, I, p. 79 ff.[a]). There we find *zo, uiss* (*aus*), *zween, bezahlen*; alongside them in the same sentence: *setten, dat nutteste* (*nützeste*); likewise *Dache, redelich* beside *reicket* (*reicht*); *Upladen, upheven, hulper* (*Helfer*) beside *verkouffen*. In another paragraph p. 85 it has alternately *zo* and *tho—zu*. In short, the dialects of the mountain and the plain are continually getting mixed up without this disturbing the scribe in the slightest. As usual, this final wave with which the High German sound shift washed over Frankish territory was also the weakest and shallowest. It is surely of interest to mark out the line showing how far this wave extends. But this line cannot be a dialect boundary; it is not able to tear apart an independent group of anciently and closely related dialects and provide the pretext for allocating the fragments thus violently divided to more distant groups in contradiction with all linguistic facts.

2. *Middle Franconian*. From the above it is quite obvious that I place the northern border of Middle Franconian much further to the south than is customary.

From the fact that the Middle Franconian region on the left bank of the Rhine *seems* to have been in the possession of the Alamanni at the time of Clovis, Arnold[b] finds reason to investigate

---

[a] *Archiv für die Geschichte des Niederrheins.* Hrsg. von T. J. Lacomblet, Abt. 1: Sprach- und Rechtsalterthümer, Bd. 1, Heft 1, Düsseldorf, 1831, pp. 79-110.— *Ed.*
[b] W. Arnold, *Deutsche Urzeit*, pp. 140-41.— *Ed.*

the place-names there for traces of Alamannic settlement, and comes to the result that it is possible to prove the existence of a pre-Frankish, Alamannic population as far as the line Cologne-Aachen; the traces, most numerous in the south, naturally becoming rarer and rarer to the north. The place-names, so he says, point to

"a temporary advance by the Alamanni as far as and beyond the area around Coblenz and Aachen, and also a longer occupation of the Wetterau and the southern areas of Nassau. For the names with the genuine Alamannic endings -ach, -brunn, -felden, -hofen, -ingen, -schwand, -stetten, -wangen, and -weiler, which nowhere occur in purely Frankish territory, are found scattered from Alsace onwards over the entire Palatinate, Rhenish Hesse and Rhenish Prussia, only they become rarer to the north, giving way more and more to the Franconian names par excellence in -bach, -berg, -dorf, -born, -feld, -hausen, -heim, and -scheid" (Deutsche Urzeit, p. [140]).

Let us first examine the allegedly Alamannic names of the Middle Franconian country. I have not found the endings -brunn, -stetten, -felden, -wangen anywhere on the Reymann map [57] (which I am using here, let it be said once and for all). The ending -schwand occurs once: Metzelschwander Hof near Winnweiler, and then again Schwanden north of Landstuhl. Thus both in the Upper Franconian Palatinate, with which we are not concerned here. In -ach we have along the Rhine Kreuznach, Bacharach, Hirzenach near St. Goar, Rübenach near Coblenz (Ribiniacus of the Spruner-Menke District Map [58]), Andernach (Antunnacum of the Romans), as well as Wassenach. Now, as the Romanised Celtic ending -acum occurs generally the whole length of the left bank of the Rhine in Roman times — Tolbiacum (Zülpich), Juliacum (Jülich), Tiberiacum (Ziewerich) near Bergheim, Mederiacum — in the majority of these cases the choice of the form -ach for -ich, at most, might betray Alamannic influence. Only one, Hirzenach (=Hirschenbach), is definitely German, and this was formerly called Hirzenowe, Hirschenau, not Hirschenbach, according to the district map. But how then do we explain Wallach, between Büderich and Rheinberg, close by the Salic border? At any rate it is certainly not Alamannic.

In the Mosel region there are also a few -ach: Irmenach east of Bernkastel, Waltrach, Crettenach near Trier, Mettlach on the Saar. In Luxemburg Echternach, Medernach, Kanach; in Lorraine on the right of the Mosel only: Montenach, Rodelach, Brettnach. Even if we wished to concede that these names indicate an Alamannic settlement, then it is only a thinly scattered one, which, moreover, does not extend beyond the southernmost part of the Middle Franconian territory.

There remain -weiler, -hofen, and -ingen which require closer examination.

Firstly, the ending -weiler is not properly speaking Alamannic but the provincial Latin villarium, villare, and is found only very exceptionally outside the old frontiers of the Roman Empire. The Germanisation of villare to weiler was not the privilege of the Alamanni, but they had a predilection for using this ending also for new settlements in large numbers. In so far as Roman villaria occurred, the Franks too were obliged to take over the ending, Germanising it as wilare, later weiler, or drop it altogether. Probably they did now one, now the other, just as they certainly gave new settlements names in -weiler here and there, but far more rarely than the Alamanni. Arnold[a] cannot find any important places in -weiler north of Eschweiler near Aachen and Ahrweiler. But the present importance of the place has nothing to do with it; the fact of the matter is that on the left bank of the Rhine the names in -weiler extend almost as far as the Salic border to the north (Garzweiler and Holzweiler are less than five miles from the nearest Dutch-speaking place of the Geldern area) and north of the line Eschweiler-Ahrweiler there are at least twenty of them. They are, understandably, commonest in the vicinity of the old Roman road from Maastricht via Jülich to Cologne, two of them, Walwiller and Nyswiller, even being on Dutch territory; are these Alamannic settlements too?

Further south they hardly occur in the Eifel at all; the Malmedy section (Reymann, No. 159) has not one single case. In Luxemburg, too, they are rare, as on the lower Mosel and as far as the crest of the Hunsrück. Yet they frequently occur on the upper Mosel on both sides of the river, becoming increasingly common towards the east, becoming more and more the dominating ending to the east of Saarlouis. But this is where the Upper Franconian language begins, and here it is not disputed by anyone that the Alamanni had occupied the country before the Franks.

Thus for the Middle Franconian and Ripuarian area the -weiler do not indicate Alamannic settlement any more than do the many -villers in France.

Let us move on to -hofen. This ending is still less exclusively Alamannic. It occurs throughout the Franconian area, including present-day Westphalia, which was later occupied by the Saxons. On the right bank of the Rhine just a few examples: Wehofen near Ruhrort, Mellinghofen and Eppinghofen near Duisburg, Benningho-

---

fen near Mettmann, another *Eppinghofen* near Dinslaken, in Westphalia *Kellinghofen* near Dorsten, *Westhofen* near Castrop, *Wellinghofen, Wichlinghofen, Niederhofen,* two *Benninghofens, Berghofen, Westhofen, Wandhofen,* all on the Hellweg, etc. *Ereshofen* on the Agger, *Martis villa,* reaches back into pagan times, and the very designation of the god of war as *Eru* proves that no Alamanni are conceivable here: they called themselves *Tiuwâri,* thus calling the god not *Eru* but *Tiu,* later shifted to *Ziu.*[a]

On the left bank of the Rhine it is even more difficult to demonstrate the Alamannic derivation of *-hofen.* There is another *Eppinghofen* south-east of Xanten, hence possibly Salic already, and from there on to the south the whole Ripuarian area is teeming with *-hofen,* alongside *-hof* for single farms. But if we proceed to Salic country, it gets even worse. The Maas is accompanied by *-hofen* on either side, from the French linguistic boundary onwards. For the sake of brevity let us pass to the west bank straight away. In Holland and Belgium we find at least seven *Ophovens,* in Holland *Kinckhoven,* etc; for Belgium let us first turn to the section for Löwen (Reymann, No. 139). Here we find *Ruykhoven, Schalkhoven, Bommershoven, Wintershoven, Mettecoven, Helshoven, Engelmannshoven* near Tongern; *Zonhoven, Reekhoven, Konings-Hoven* near Hasselt, further west *Bogenhoven, Schuerhoven, Nieuwenhoven, Gippershoven, Baulershoven* near St. Truyen; most westerlv *Gussenhoven* and *Droenhoven* east and north-east Tirlemont (Thien'en). The section for Turnhout (No. 120) has at least 33 *-hoven,* most of them on Belgian territory. Further to the south-west the *-hove* (the dative *-n* is regularly dropped here) skirt the entire French linguistic border: from *Heerlinkhove* and *Nieuwenhove* near *Ninove,* which is itself a Romanised *-hove,*— omitting the intermediate ones, about ten in number—to *Ghyverinckhove* and *Pollinchove* near Dixmuyden and *Volckerinckhove* near St. Omer in French Flanders. *Nieuwenhove* occurs three times, which proves that the ending is still living among the people. In addition a great number of single farms in *-hof.* On this basis the supposedly exclusively Alamannic character of *-hofen* may be judged.

Finally to *-ingen.* The designation of common descent with *-ing, -ung,* is common to all the Germanic peoples. Since settlement took place by kin, the ending plays an important part in place-names everywhere. Sometimes it is linked, in the genitive plural, with a local ending: *Wolvarad-inga-husun* near Minden, *Snotingaham*

---

[a] J. Grimm, op. cit., Vol. I, p. 508.— *Ed.*

(Nottingham) in England. Sometimes the plural alone stands for the designation of place: *Flissingha* (Vlissingen), *Phladirtinga* (Vlaardingen), *Crastlingi* in Dutch Frisia; *Grupilinga, Britlinga, Otlinga* in Old Saxony. These names have mostly been reduced to the dative nowadays, ending in *-ingen,* rarely in *-ing.* Most peoples know and employ both forms; the Alamanni, so it seems, chiefly the latter, at any rate now.* Since, however, this also occurs among the Franks, Saxons and Frisians, it is very audacious to immediately deduce Alamannic settlement from the occurrence of place-names in *-ingen.*

The above mentioned names prove that names in *-ingas* (nominative plural) and *-ingum, -ingon* (dative plural) were nothing unusual either among the Frisians or among the Saxons, from the Schelde to the Elbe. Even today the *-ingen* are no rarity throughout Lower Saxony. In Westphalia on either side of the Ruhr, south of the line Unna-Soest, there are at least twelve *-ingen,* alongside *-ingsen* and *-inghausen.* And as far as Franconian territory extends, we find names in *-ingen.*

On the right bank of the Rhine we first find in Holland *Wageningen* on the Rhine and *Genderingen* on the Ijssel (and we exclude all possibly Frisian names), in the Berg country *Huckingen, Ratingen, Ehingen* (close behind them on Saxon territory *Hattingen, Sodingen, Ummingen*), *Heisingen* near Werden (which Grimm derives from the *Silva Caesia* of Tacitus[c] and which would thus be very ancient), *Solingen, Husingen, Leichlingen* (on the district map[d] *Leigelingon,* thus almost a thousand years old), *Quettingen* and on the Sieg *Bödingen* and *Röcklingen,* not counting two names in *-ing. Hönningen* near Rheinbrohl and *Ellingen* in the Wied area provide the link with the area between Rhine, Lahn and Dill, which at a low estimate counts 12 *-ingen.* It is pointless to go any further south, since here begins the country that indisputably passed through a period of Alamannic settlement.

---

* *Rümmingen* near Lörrach was formerly (764) called *Romaninchova,* so that sometimes the Swabian *-ingen* are also only of recent origin (Mone, *Urzeit des badischen Landes,* I, p. 213).[a] The Swiss *-kon* and *-kofen* have nearly all been contracted from *-inghofen*: *Zollinchovun—Zollikhofen, Smarinchova—Schmerikon,* etc. Cf. F. Beust, *Historischer Atlas des Kantons Zürich,*[b] where there are dozens of them on map 3, representing the Alamannic period.

---

[a] F. J. Mone, *Urgeschichte des badischen Landes bis zu Ende des siebenten Jahrhunderts,* Vol. 1, "Die Römer im oberrheinischen Gränzland", Karlsruhe, 1845, p. 213.— *Ed.*

[b] F. Beust, *Kleiner historischer Atlas des Kantons Zürich,* Zurich, 1873.— *Ed.*

[c] J. Grimm, op. cit., Vol. 1, p. 483.— *Ed.*

[d] Spruner-Menke, *Hand-Atlas...— Ed.*

Left of the Rhine we have *Millingen* in Holland above
Nimwegen, *Lüttingen* below Xanten, another *Millingen* below
Rheinberg, then *Kippingen, Rödingen, Höningen, Worringen,*
Fühlingen, all further north than Cologne, *Wesselingen* and
Köttingen near Brühl. From here the names in *-ingen* follow two
directions. In the High Eifel they are rare; we find near Malmedy
on the French linguistic border: *Büllingen, Hünningen, Mürringen,*
Iveldingen, Eibertingen as a transition to the very numerous *-ingen*
in Luxemburg and on the Prussian and Lotharingian upper
Mosel. Another connecting line follows the Rhine and the side
valleys (in the Ahr area 7 or 8) and finally the Mosel valley,
likewise after the area above Trier, where the *-ingen* predominate,
but cut off from the great mass of Alamannic-Swabian *-ingen* first
by the *-weiler* and then by the *-heim*. So if we, according to
Arnold's demand, "consider all the facts in their context",[a] we
shall come to the conclusion that the *-ingen* of the upper German
Mosel area are Franconian and not Alamannic.

How little we need Alamannic help here becomes even clearer
as soon as we trace the *-ingen* from the French-Ripuarian
linguistic border near Aachen on to Salic territory. Near Maaseyk
west of the Maas lies *Geystingen,* further west near Brée *Gerdingen.*
Then we find, turning back to section No. 139, Löwen: *Moperting-*
en, Vlytingen, Rixingen, Aerdelingen, Grimmersingen, Gravelingen,
Ordange (for *Ordingen*), *Bevingen, Hatingen, Buvingen, Hundeling-*
en, Bovelingen, Curange, Raepertingen, Boswinningen, Wimmertingen,
and others, in the area of Tongern, St. Truyen and Hasselt. The
most westerly, not far from Löwen, are *Willebringen, Redingen,*
Grinningen. Here the connection seems to break off. But if we
move on to territory that is now French-speaking but from the 6th
to the 9th century was in dispute between the two languages, we
find from the Maas onwards an entire belt of French *-ange,* a form
which corresponds to *-ingen* in Lorraine and Luxemburg too,
stretching from east to west: *Ballenge, Roclenge, Ortrange, Lan-*
tremange, Roclange, Libertange, Noderange, Herdange, Oderinge,
Odange, Gobertang, Wahenges; slightly further west *Louvrenge* near
Wavre and *Revelinge* near Waterloo form the link with *Huysinghen*
and *Buisinghen,* the outpost of a group of over 20 *-inghen,*
stretching south-west of Brussels from Hal to Grammont along the
linguistic boundary. And finally in French Flanders: *Gravelingen,*
Wulverdinghe (thus exactly the Old Saxon *Wolvaradinges-hûsun*),
Leubringhen, Leulinghen, Bonninghen, Peuplingue, Hardinghen, Her-

---

[a] W. Arnold, op. cit., p. 141.— *Ed.*

melinghen, near St. Omer and as far as behind Boulogne *Herbinghen, Hocquinghen, Velinghen, Lottinghen, Ardinghen,* all sharply distinguished from the even more numerous names in *-inghem* (= *-ingheim*) in the same area.

Thus the three endings which Arnold regards as typically Alamannic turn out to be every bit as much Franconian, and the attempt to prove an Alamannic settlement on Middle Franconian territory *before* the Franconian one on the basis of these names must be considered to have failed. While the possibility of a not very strong Alamannic element in the south-eastern part of this territory can still be conceded.

From the Alamanni, Arnold leads us to the Chatti. With the exception of the Ripuarians proper, they are supposed to have occupied the area south of the Ripuaria district, the same one, in other words, as we call Middle and Upper Franconia, after and alongside the Alamanni. This too is substantiated by references to the Hessian place-names found in the area beside the Alamannic ones.

"The agreement in the place-names on this and the other side of the Rhine as far as the Alamannic border is so peculiar and so striking that it would be a miracle indeed if it were coincidental; on the other hand, it seems quite natural as soon as we assume that the immigrants gave their native place-names to their new domiciles, as still occurs in America all the time." [a]

There is little to object to in this sentence. But all the more to object to in the conclusion that the Ripuarians proper had nothing to do with the settlement of the whole Middle and Upper Franconian country, that we only find Alamanni and Chatti here. Most of the Chatti who left their home for the west seem to have joined the Iscaevones from time immemorial (as did the Batavi, Canninefates and Chattuari); and where else should they turn? In the first two centuries A. D. the Chatti were only linked with the other Herminones in the rear through the Thuringians; on the one side they had the Ingaevonian Cherusci, on the other the Iscaevones, and before them the Romans. The Herminonian tribes, which later appear united as Alamanni, came from the heart of Germania, having been separated from the Chatti for centuries by Thuringians and other peoples and having become more alien to them than the Iscaevonian Franks, with whom they were allied by a centuries-old brotherhood in arms. The Chatti's participation in the occupation of the area in question is thus not doubted. But the exclusion of the Ripuarians is. This can only be

---

[a] W. Arnold, op. cit., p. 156.— *Ed.*

proved if no specifically Ripuarian names occur there. The situation is quite the reverse.

Of the endings stated by Arnold[a] to be specifically Franconian, *-hausen* is common to Franks, Saxons, Hessians and Thuringians; *-heim* is Salic *-ham*; *-bach* Salic and Lower Ripuarian *-beek*; of the others, only *-scheid* is really characteristic. It is specifically Ripuarian, just like *-ich, -rath* or *-rade* and *-siepen.* Further, common to both Franconian dialects are *-loo* (*-loh*), *-donk* and *-bruch* or *-broich* (Salic *broek*).

-scheid occurs only in the mountains and, as a rule, in places on the watershed. The Franks left this ending behind throughout Westphalian Sauerland as far as the Hessian border, where it occurs, only as mountain names, as far as eastern Korbach. On the Ruhr Old Franconian *-scheid* encounters the ending in its Saxon form, *-schede: Melschede, Selschede, Meschede*; in the near vicinity, *Langscheid, Ramscheid, Bremscheid.* Frequent in the Berg area, it is found as far as the Westerwald and into it, but not further south, on the right side of the Rhine. Left of the Rhine, however, the *-scheid* understandably do not commence until the Eifel*; in Luxemburg there are at least 21 of them, in the Hochwald and Hunsrück they are common. But as south of the Lahn, here too, on the eastern and southern sides of the Hunsrück and Soonwald, they are joined by the form *-schied,* which seems to be a Hessian adaption. Both forms together move southwards across the Nahe as far as the Vosges, where we find: *Bisterscheid* west of Donnersberg, *Langenscheid* near Kaiserslautern, a plateau called *Breitscheid* south of Hochspeyer, *Haspelscheid* near Bitsch, the *Scheidwald* north of Lützelstein, and finally as the southernmost outpost *Walscheid* on the north slope of the Donon, even further south than the village of Hessen near Saarburg, the most advanced Chattic outpost in Arnold.[b]

Also specifically Ripuarian is *-ich,* from the same root, Gothic *-ahva* (water), as *-ach*; both are also German forms of the Belgian-Roman *-acum,* as proved by *Tiberiacum,* on the district map[c] *Civiraha,* today *Ziewerich.* It is not very frequent on the right side of the Rhine; *Meiderich* and *Lirich* near Ruhrort are the most

---

* In the plain I can only find *Waterscheid,* east of Hasselt in Belgian Limburg, where we have already observed a strong Ripuarian mixture above [see this volume, p. 90].

a Ibid., p. 141.— *Ed.*
b Ibid., p. 144.— *Ed.*
c Spruner-Menke, *Hand-Atlas...*— *Ed.*

northerly, from where they skirt the Rhine as far as *Biebrich*. The plain on the left of the Rhine, from *Büderich* opposite Wesel onwards, is full of them; they cross the Eifel as far as the Hochwald and Hunsrück, but vanish in the Soonwald and the region of the Nahe, even before *-scheid* and *-roth* stop. In the western part of our territory, however, they continue to the French linguistic border and beyond. The Trier area, which has a lot of them, we shall pass over; in Dutch Luxemburg I count twelve, on the other side, in the Belgian part, *Törnich* and *Merzig* (Messancy—the spelling *-ig* makes no difference, etymology and pronunciation are the same), in Lorraine, *Soetrich, Sentzich, Marspich, Daspich* west of the Mosel; east of it *Kuntzich, Penserich, Cemplich, Destrich,* twice *Kerprich, Hibrich, Hilsprich*.

The ending *-rade, -rad,* on the left bank of the Rhine *-rath,* also considerably exceeds the bounds of its old Ripuarian homeland. It fills the whole Eifel and the middle and lower Mosel valley, as well as its side valleys. In the same area where *-scheid* mixes with *-schied, -rod, -roth* occurs alongside *-rad* and *-rath* on both banks of the Rhine, also of Hessian origin, except that on the right bank, in the Westerwald, the *-rod* extend further north. In the Hochwald the northern slope has *-rath,* the southern slope *-roth,* as a rule.

The least advanced is *-siepen,* shifted *-seifen.* The word means a small stream-valley with a steep fall and is still in general use with this meaning. Left of the Rhine it does not extend far beyond the old Ripuarian border; on the right it is found in the Westerwald on the Nister and even near Langenschwalbach (*Langenseifen*).

To examine the other endings would take us too far. But at any rate we may assert that the countless *-heim,* which accompany the Rhine upstream from Bingen deep into Alamannic territory and are found everywhere where the Franks settled, are not Chattic but Ripuarian. Their home is not in Hesse, where they rarely occur and seem to have entered later, but in the Salic country and the Rhine plain around Cologne, where they occur alongside the other specifically Ripuarian names in almost equal numbers.

Thus the result of this investigation is that the Ripuarians, far from being held back by the stream of Hessian immigration at the Westerwald and Eifel, on the contrary overran the entire Middle Franconian area themselves. And more strongly in a south-westerly direction, towards the upper Mosel area, than to the south-east towards the Taunus and the area of the Nahe. This is also corroborated by the language. The south-western dialects, right into Luxemburg and western Lorraine, are much closer to Ripuarian than the eastern ones, particularly those on the right bank of the Rhine. The former might be regarded as a more High German shifted extension of Ripuarian.

The characteristic thing about the Middle Franconian dialects is firstly the penetration of the High German sound shift. Not the mere shift of a few tenues to aspirates, applying to relatively few words and not affecting the character of the dialect, but the beginning shift of the *voiced-stopped consonants,* which brings about the peculiarly Middle and Upper German confusion of *b* and *p, g* and *k, d* and *t.* Only where the impossibility of making a sharp distinction between initial *b* and *p, d* and *t, g* and *k* appears, in other words what the French particularly mean by *accent allemand*—only then does the Low German feel the great cleft which the second sound shift has torn through the German language. And this cleft runs in between the Sieg and the Lahn, the Ahr and the Mosel. Accordingly, Middle Franconian has an initial *g* which is lacking in more northern dialects, whereas medially and finally it still pronounces a soft *ch* for *g.* Furthermore, the *ei* and *ou* of the northern dialects turn into *ai* and *au.*

A few genuinely Franconian peculiarities: in all the Salic and Ripuarian dialects *Bach,* unshifted *Beek,* is feminine. This is also true at least of the largest, western part of Middle Franconian. Like the numerous other *-bachs* with the same name in the Netherlands and on the lower Rhine, the Luxemburg *Glabach* (*Gladbach,* Dutch *Glabeek*) is also feminine. On the other hand, girls' names are treated as neuter: it is not only *das* Mädchen, *das* Mariechen, *das* Lisbethchen, but also *das* Marie, *das* Lisbeth, from Barmen to Trier and beyond. Near Forbach in Lorraine the map, originally made by the French, shows a "*Karninschesberg*" (Kaninchenberg). Thus the same diminutive *-schen,* plural *-sches,* which we found above to be Ripuarian.

With the watershed between Mosel and Nahe and on the right bank of the Rhine with the hill-country south of the Lahn, a new group of dialects begins:

3. *Upper Franconian.* Here we are in a region which was indisputably first Alamannic territory by conquest (disregarding the earlier occupation by Vangiones, etc., of whose tribal affinities and language we know nothing) and where a fairly strong Chattic admixture can be readily conceded. But here too the place-names, as we need not repeat, indicate the presence of not insignificant Ripuarian elements, especially in the Rhine plain. And the language even more so. Let us take the southernmost definable dialect which at the same time has a literature, that of the Palatinate. Here we again encounter the general Franconian

inability to pronounce medial and final *g* in any other way but as a soft *ch*.* They say there: *Vöchel, Flechel, geleche* (gelegen) [lain], *gsacht*—gesagt, *licht*—liegt, etc. Similarly the general Franconian *w* instead of *b* in the medial position: *Bûwe*—Buben, *glâwe*—glauben (but *i glâb*), *bleiwe, selwer*—selbst, *halwe*—halbe. The shift is far from being as complete as it looks; there is even reverse shifting, particularly in foreign words, i.e. the initial voiceless consonant is shifted not one stage forwards, but backwards: *t* becomes *d, p* becomes *b,* as will be seen; initial *d* and *p* remain at the Low German stage: *dûn*—tun, *dag, danze, dür, dodt*; but before *r*: *trinke, trage*; *paff*—Pfaff, *peife, palz*—Pfalz, *parre*—Pfarrer. Now as *d* and *p* stand for High German *t* and *pf*, initial *t* is shifted back to *d*, and initial *p* to *b*, even in foreign words: *derke*—Türke, *dafel*—Tafel, *babeer*—Papier, *borzlan*—Porzellan, *bulwer*—Pulver. Then the Palatinate dialect, agreeing only with Danish on this score, cannot tolerate any tenues between vowels: *ebbes*—etwas, *labbe*—Lappen, *schlubbe*—schlüpfen, *schobbe*—Schoppen, *Peder*—Peter, *dridde*—dritte, *rodhe*—raten. The only exception is *k*: *brocke, backe.* But in foreign words *g*: *musigande*—Musikanten. This is also a relic of the Low German stage of the sound system which has spread out further by means of reverse shifting [a]; only because *dridde, hadde* remained unshifted could Peter become *Peder* and the corresponding High German *t* receive the same impartial treatment. Similarly, the *d* in *halde*—halten, *alde*—alte, etc., remains at the Low German stage.

Despite the decidedly High German impression it makes on Low Germans, the dialect of the Palatinate is far from having adopted the High German sound shift even to the extent that our written language has preserved it. On the contrary, by means of its reverse shift the Palatinate dialect is protesting against the High German stage, which, having entered from without, proves to be a foreign element in the dialect to this day.

This is the place to look at a feature that is usually misunderstood: the confusion between *d* and *t, b* and *p* and even *g* and *k* among those Germans in whose dialects the voiced-stopped consonants have undergone the High German sound shift. This confusion does not arise as long as everyone speaks *his own*

---

* All quotations are from *Fröhlich Palz, Gott erhalts! Gedichte in Pfälzer Mundart,* by K. G. Nadler, Frankfurt am Main, 1851.

[a] Engels' note in pencil in the margin: "Agrees with Otfrid." (See Otfrid, *Liber Evangeliorum domini gratia theotisce conscriptus.* In: W. Braune, *Zur Kenntnis des Fränkischen...*, pp. 3, 52).—*Ed.*

dialect. On the contrary. We have just seen that the native of the Palatinate, for example, makes a very nice distinction here, so much so that he even shifts back foreign words in order to adapt them to the requirements of his dialect. The foreign initial *t* only becomes *d* for him because written German *t* corresponds to his *d*, foreign *p* only becomes *b* because his *p* corresponds to written German *pf*. Nor do the voiceless consonants get mixed up in the other Upper German dialects as long as people speak dialect. Each of these dialects has its own, precisely applied sound-shift law. But the position is different as soon as the written language or a foreign language is spoken. The attempt to apply to it the shifting law of the dialect concerned—and this attempt is made involuntarily—collides with the attempt to speak the new language correctly. In the process the written *b* and *p*, *d* and *t* lose all fixed meaning, and thus it is that Börne, for instance, in his letters from Paris complains that the French were unable to distinguish between *b* and *p*, because they obstinately insisted that his name, which he pronounced *Perne*, commenced with a *p*.[a]

But back to the Palatinate dialect. The evidence that the High German sound shift was foisted on it from without, so to speak, and has remained a foreign element to this day, not even reaching the sound-system stage of the written language either (far exceeding which the Alamanni and the Bavarians on the whole preserve one Old High German stage or another)—this proof alone suffices to establish the predominantly Franconian character of the Palatinate dialect. For even in Hesse, which is much further north, the shift has, on the whole, been carried further, thus reducing the allegedly chiefly Hessian character of the Palatinate dialect to modest proportions. In order to offer such resistance to the High German sound shift hard by the Alamannic border among the Alamanni that remained behind, there must have been at least as many Ripuarians alongside the Hessians, who were themselves essentially High Germans. And their presence is further proved—apart from the place-names—by two generally Franconian peculiarities: the preservation of the Franconian *w* instead of *b* medially, and the pronunciation of *g* as *ch* in medial and final positions. To this may be added a lot of individual cases of agreement. With the Palatinate *Gundach*—"guten Tag"—you will get by as far as to Dunkirk and Amsterdam. Just as "a certain man" is ein *sichrer Mann* in the Palatinate, in the entire

---

[a] L. Börne, *Schilderungen aus Paris* (*1822 und 1823*). In: L. Börne, *Gesammelte Schriften*, Vol. 3, Hamburg, Frankfurt am Main, 1862, pp. 19-21.—*Ed.*

Netherlands it is een *zekeren man*. *Handsching* for *Handschuh* [glove] corresponds to the Ripuarian *Händschen*. Even *g* for *j* in *Ghannisnacht* (*Johannisnacht* [midsummer night]) is Ripuarian and extends, as we have seen, into the Münster area. And *baten* (to improve, be of use, from *bat*—better), common to all the Franks, and the Netherlanders too, is in current use in the Palatinate: *'s badd alles nix*—it's all no use—where the *t* is not even shifted to High German *tz* but is softened to *d* between vowels in the Palatinate manner.

Written in mid-1878-early August 1882

First published in full in: Marx and Engels, *Works*, First Russian Edition, Vol. XVI, Part 1, Moscow, 1937

"The Franconian Dialect" was first published, as a book in Russian, in 1935

Printed according to the manuscript

Published in English in full for the first time

Der Sozialdemokrat

Zentral-Organ der deutschen Sozialdemokratie.

№: 24. Donnerstag, 7. Juni. **1883.**

[GEORG WEERTH]

"SONG OF THE APPRENTICES" by Georg Weerth (1846)[59]

At the time when the cherries blossomed,
In Frankfurt we did stay.
At the time when the cherries blossomed,
In that city we did stay.

Up spake mine host, the landlord:
"Your coats are frayed and worn."
"Look here, you lousy landlord,
That's none of your concern.

"Now give us of your wine,
And give us of your beer,
And with the beer and wine,
Bring us a roast in here."

The cock crows in the bunghole,
Out comes a goodly flow,
And in our mouths it tastes
Like urinatio.

And then he brought a hare
In parsley leaves bedight,
And at this poor dead hare
We all of us took fright.

And when we were in bed,
Our nightly prayers reciting,
Early and late in bed
The bed-bugs kept on biting.

It happened once in Frankfurt,
That town so fine and fair,
That knows who did once dwell
And who did suffer there.[a]

---

[a] Translated into English by Alex Miller.— *Ed.*

I came across this poem by our friend Weerth once again when looking through Marx's estate. Weerth, the German proletariat's first and most important poet, was born in Detmold of Rhenish parents, where his father was a superintendent of churches. When I was staying in Manchester in 1843, Weerth came to Bradford as a clerk for his German firm, and we spent many an enjoyable Sunday together. In 1845, when Marx and I were living in Brussels, Weerth took over the continental agency of his trading house, and organised things in such a way that he could set up his headquarters in Brussels as well.[60] After[a] the March Revolution of 1848 we all met up in Cologne for the founding of the *Neue Rheinische Zeitung*. Weerth took charge of the feuilleton, and I doubt whether any other newspaper ever had such a witty and spirited feuilleton. One of his main contributions was *Leben und Thaten des berühmten Ritters Schnapphahnski,* describing the adventures of Prince Lichnowski, who was given that name by Heine in *Atta Troll.*[b] The facts are all true; how we found out about them we shall perhaps leave to another time. Those Schnapphahnski feuilletons were published together as a book by Hoffmann and Campe in 1849, and are still today most entertaining. However, since Schnapphahnski-Lichnowski, together with the Prussian General von Auerswald (also a member of parliament), went riding out on September 18, 1848 to spy on the columns of peasants who were joining up with the Frankfurt fighters at the barricades, on which occasion he and Auerswald received their just deserts and were beaten to death by the peasants for spying, the German Imperial Vice-Regent brought charges against Weerth for libelling the deceased Lichnowski, and Weerth, who had now been in England for some time, was given a three months' prison sentence long after the forces of reaction had put paid to the *Neue Rheinische Zeitung*. He then duly served his three months' sentence, because his business interests obliged him to visit Germany from time to time.

In 1850-51 he travelled to Spain on behalf of another Bradford firm, and then to the West Indies and across almost all of South America. After a short visit to Europe he returned to his beloved West Indies. He did not wish to forego the pleasure there of seeing, just once, the real original of Louis Napoleon III, the

---

[a] The text to the end of the article is checked with the available manuscript.— *Ed.*

[b] H. Heine, *Atta Troll,* I.— *Ed.*

black King Soulouque of Haiti. But, as W. Wolff wrote to Marx on
August 28, 1856, he had

"problems with the quarantine authorities, had to give up his project, and on
the trip contracted (yellow) fever, with which he arrived in Havana. He took to his
bed, his condition was complicated by inflammation of the brain, and—on
July 30—our Weerth died in Havana".

I called him the first and *most important* poet of the German
proletariat. His socialist and political poems are indeed far
superior to Freiligrath's in terms of their originality and wit, and
particularly in their fervent passion. He often employed forms of
Heine's, but only in order to fill them with an entirely original and
independent content. At the same time, he differed from most
other poets inasmuch as he was totally unconcerned about his
poems once he had written them down. Once he had sent a copy
to Marx or me, he would forget about the poems and it was often
difficult to persuade him to have them printed. Only during the
time of the *Neue Rheinische Zeitung* was it otherwise. The reason
why is shown by the following extract from a letter Weerth wrote
to Marx from Hamburg, April 28, 1851:

"By the way, I hope to see you again in London at the beginning of July, for I
cannot bear these GRASSHOPPERS in Hamburg any longer. I stand under threat here
of a splendid existence, but it frightens me. Anyone else would seize it with both
hands. But I am too old to become a philistine, and across the sea there is the far
West...

"Recently I have written all kinds of things, but have completed nothing for I
see no point at all, no aim in writing. When *you* write something on economics
there is a point and meaning to it. But *me?* Cracking feeble jokes, making up
cheap jibes in order to squeeze a stupid smile from the faces of the rascals at
home—in all seriousness, I know nothing more pitiable! My days as a writer ended
well and truly with the *Neue Rheinische Zeitung.*

"I must admit: much as it grieves me to have wasted the last three years on
absolutely nothing, it thrills me when I think of the time we spent at Cologne. We
did *not* compromise ourselves. That is the main thing! Since Frederick the Great
nobody has treated the German people so completely *en canaille*[a] as the *Neue
Rheinische Zeitung.*

"I don't mean to say that the entire credit was due to me; but I was there...

"O Portugal! O Spain!" (Weerth had just come from there.) "If only we had
your beautiful skies, your wine, your oranges and myrtles! But not even that!
Nothing but rain and long noses and smoked meat!

"Yours in the rain and with a long nose,

G. Weerth."

Where Weerth was a master, where he outstripped Heine
(because he was more wholesome and unadulterated) and where

---

[a] Ungraciously.— *Ed.*

he is only surpassed by Goethe in the German language, is in his expression of natural, robust sensuality and carnal lust. Many a reader of the *Sozialdemokrat* would be horrified were I to have reprinted here some of the articles from the *Neue Rheinische Zeitung*. I have no intention of doing that, however. Nevertheless I cannot help remarking that the moment must come for the German socialists too when they openly reject this last German philistine prejudice, that deceitful, petty-bourgeois moral prudery, which in any case is no more than a cover for furtively cracking dirty jokes. If one reads Freiligrath's poetry, for example, one might well believe that human beings were completely devoid of sex organs. And yet nobody took more pleasure in slipping in a piece of filth than the very same Freiligrath who was so extremely chaste in his poetry. It is high time that the German workers at least got used to speaking just as freely about things they themselves do every day or every night, about natural, essential and extremely pleasurable things, as the Romance peoples do, like Homer and Plato did, like Horace and Juvenal, like the Old Testament and the *Neue Rheinische Zeitung*.

Moreover Weerth also wrote less offensive things, and I shall allow myself the liberty, from time to time, to send some of them to the feuilleton of the *Sozialdemokrat*.

Written in late May 1883

First published in *Der Sozialdemokrat*, No. 24, June 7, 1883

Printed according to the newspaper

THE BOOK OF REVELATION [61]

A science almost unknown in this country, except to a few liberalising theologians, who contrive to keep it as secret as they can, is the historical and linguistic criticism of the Bible, the inquiry into the age, origin, and historical value of the various writings comprising the Old and New Testament.

This science is almost exclusively German. And, moreover, what little of it has penetrated beyond the limits of Germany is not exactly the best part of it: it is that latitudinarian criticism which prides itself upon being unprejudiced and thoroughgoing, and, at the same time, Christian. The books are not exactly revealed by the holy ghost, but they are revelations of divinity through the sacred spirit of humanity, etc. Thus, the Tübingen school (Baur, Gfrörer, etc.) [62] are the great favorites in Holland and Switzerland, as well as in England, and, if people will go a little further, they follow Strauss. The same mild, but utterly unhistorical, spirit dominates the renowned Ernest Renan, who is but a poor plagiarist of the German critics. Of all his works nothing belongs to him but the aesthetic sentimentalism of the pervading thought, and the milk-and-water language which wraps it up.

One good thing, however, Ernest Renan has said:

"When you want to get a distinct idea of what the first Christian communities were, do not compare them to the parish congregations of our day; they were rather like local sections of the International Working Men's Association."

And this is correct. Christianity got hold of the masses, exactly as modern socialism does, under the shape of a variety of sects, and still more of conflicting individual views—some clearer, some more confused, these latter the great majority—but all opposed to the ruling system, to "the powers that be".

Take, for instance, our Book of Revelation, of which we shall see that, instead of being the darkest and most mysterious, it is the simplest and clearest book of the whole New Testament. For the present we must ask the reader to believe what we are going to prove by-and-bye. That it was written in the year of our era 68 or January, 69, and that it is therefore not only the only book of the New Testament, the date of which is really fixed, but also the oldest book. How Christianity looked in 68 we can here see as in a mirror.

First of all, sects over and over again. In the messages to the seven churches of Asia[a] there are at least three sects mentioned, of which, otherwise, we know nothing at all: the Nicolaitanes, the Balaamites, and the followers of a woman typified here by the name of Jezebel. Of all the three it is said that they permitted their adherents to eat of things sacrificed to idols, and that they were fond of fornication. It is a curious fact that with every great revolutionary movement the question of "free love" comes in to the foreground. With one set of people as a revolutionary progress, as a shaking off of old traditional fetters, no longer necessary; with others as a welcome doctrine, comfortably covering all sorts of free and easy practices between man and woman. The latter, the philistine sort, appear here soon to have got the upper hand; for the "fornication" is always associated with the eating of "things sacrificed to idols", which Jews and Christians were strictly forbidden to do, but which it might be dangerous, or at least unpleasant, at times to refuse. This shows evidently that the free lovers mentioned here were generally inclined to be everybody's friend, and anything but stuff for martyrs.

Christianity, like every great revolutionary movement, was made by the masses. It arose in Palestine, in a manner utterly unknown to us, at a time when new sects, new religions, new prophets arose by the hundred. It is, in fact, a mere average, formed spontaneously out of the mutual friction, of the more progressive of such sects, and afterwards formed into a doctrine by the addition of theorems of the Alexandrian Jew, Philo, and later on of strong stoic infiltrations.[63] In fact, if we may call Philo the doctrinal father of Christianity, Seneca was her uncle. Whole passages in the New Testament seem almost literally copied from his works[b]; and you

---

a Revelation 2:6, 14, 20.— Ed.

b See the chapter "Seneca im Neuen Testament" in B. Bauer's *Christus und die Caesaren*, pp. 47-61.— Ed.

will find, on the other hand, passages in Persius' satires which seem copied from the then unwritten New Testament.[a] Of all these doctrinal elements there is not a trace to be found in our Book of Revelation. Here we have Christianity in the crudest form in which it has been preserved to us. There is only one dominant dogmatic point: that the faithful have been saved by the sacrifice of Christ. But how, and why is completely indefinable. There is nothing but the old Jewish and heathen notion, that God, or the gods, must be propitiated by sacrifices, transformed into the specific Christian notion (which, indeed, made Christianity the universal religion) that the death of Christ is the great sacrifice which suffices once for all.

Of original sin, not a trace. Nothing of the trinity. Jesus is "the lamb", but subordinate to God. In fact, in one passage (15:3) he is placed upon an equal footing with Moses. Instead of one holy ghost there are "the seven spirits of god" (3:1 and 4:5). The murdered saints (the martyrs) cry to God for revenge:

"How long, O Lord, dost thou not judge and avenge our blood on them that dwell on the earth?" (6:10)—

a sentiment which has, later on, been carefully struck out from the theoretical code of morals of Christianity, but carried out practically with a vengeance as soon as the Christians got the upper hand over the heathens.

As a matter of course, Christianity presents itself as a mere sect of Judaism. Thus, in the messages to the seven churches:

"I know the blasphemy of them which say that they are Jews" (not Christians), "and are not, but are the synagogue of Satan" (2:9);

and again, 3:9:

"Them of the synagogue of Satan, which say they are Jews, but are not."

Thus, our author, in the 69th year of our era, had not the remotest idea that he represented a new phase of religious development, destined to become one of the greatest elements of revolution. Thus also, when the saints appear before the throne of God, there are at first 144,000 Jews, 12,000 of each of the twelve tribes, and only after them are admitted the heathens who have joined this new phase of Judaism.

Such was Christianity in the year 68, as depicted in the oldest, and the only, book of the New Testament, the authenticity of which cannot be disputed. Who the author was we do not know.

---

[a] [A. Persius Flacus,] A. Persii Flacci satirarum liber.— Ed.

He calls himself John. He does not even pretend to be the "apostle" John, for in the foundations of the "new Jerusalem" are "the names of the twelve apostles of the lamb" (21:14). They therefore must have been dead when he wrote. That he was a Jew is clear from the Hebraisms abounding in his Greek, which exceeds in bad grammar, by far, even the other books of the New Testament. That the so-called Gospel of John, the epistles of John, and this book have at least three different authors, their language clearly proves, if the doctrines they contain, completely clashing one with another, did not prove it.

The apocalyptic visions which make up almost the whole of the Revelation, are taken in most cases literally, from the classic prophets of the Old Testament and their later imitators, beginning with the Book of Daniel (about 160 before our era, and prophesying things which had occurred centuries before) and ending with the "Book of Henoch", an apocryphal concoction in Greek written not long before the beginning of our era. The original invention, even the grouping of the purloined visions, is extremely poor. Professor Ferdinand Benary, to whose course of lectures in Berlin University, in 1841, I am indebted for what follows,[64] has proved, chapter and verse, whence our author borrowed every one of his pretended visions. It is therefore no use to follow our "John" through all his vagaries. We had better come at once to the point which discovers the mystery of this at all events curious book.

In complete opposition with all his orthodox commentators, who all expect his prophecies are still to come off, after more than 1,800 years, "John" never ceases to say,

"The time is at hand", all this will happen shortly.[a]

And this is especially the case with the crisis which he predicts, and which he evidently expects to see.

This crisis is the great final fight between God and the "Antichrist", as others have named him. The decisive chapters are 13 and 17. To leave out all unnecessary ornamentations, "John" sees a beast arising from the sea which has seven heads and ten horns (the horns do not concern us at all)

"and I saw one of his heads, as it were, wounded as to death; and his deadly wound was healed".

This beast was to have power over the earth, against God and the lamb for forty-two months (one half of the sacred seven years),

---

[a] Revelation 1:3.— *Ed.*

and all men were compelled during that time to have the mark of
the beast or the number of his name in their right hand, or in
their forehead.

"Here is wisdom. Let him that hath understanding *count the number of the beast:
for it is the number of a man, and his number is six hundred threescore and six.*"

Irenaeus, in the second century, knew still that by the head
which was wounded and healed, the Emperor Nero was meant.
He had been the first great persecutor of the Christians. At his
death a rumour spread, especially through Achaia and Asia, that
he was not dead, but only wounded, and that he would one day
reappear and spread terror throughout the world (Tacitus, Ann.
VI, 22).[a] At the same time Irenaeus knew another very old
reading, which made the number of the name 616, instead of
666.[b]

In Chapter 17, the beast with the seven heads appears again,
this time mounted by the well-known scarlet lady, the elegant
description of whom the reader may look out in the book itself.
Here an angel explains to John:

"The beast that thou sawest was, and is not.... The seven heads are seven
mountains, on which the woman sitteth; and there are seven kings: *five are fallen,
and one is, and the other is not yet come*; and when he cometh, he must continue a
short space. And the beast that was, and is not, *even he is the eighth, and is of the
seven*.... And the woman which thou sawest is the great city, which reigneth over
the kings of the earth."

Here, then, we have two clear statements: (1) The scarlet lady is
Rome, the great city which reigneth over the kings of the earth;
(2) at the time the book is written the sixth Roman emperor
reigns; after him another will come to reign for a short time; and
then comes the return of one who "is of the seven," who was
wounded but healed, and whose name is contained in that
mysterious number, and whom Irenaeus still knew to be Nero.

Counting from Augustus, we have Augustus, Tiberius, Caligula,
Claudius, Nero the fifth. The sixth, who is, is Galba, whose
ascension to the throne was the signal for an insurrection of the
legions, especially in Gaul, led by Otho, Galba's successor.[65] Thus
our book must have been written under Galba, who reigned from
June 9th, 68, to January 15th, 69. And it predicts the return of
Nero as imminent.

---

[a] The reference is inaccurate. See Tacitus, *Historiarum*, II, 8.— *Ed.*

[b] Irenaeus, *Refutation and Overthrow of Gnosis falsely so called.* (*Against the
Heresies*), V, 28-30.— *Ed.*

But now for the final proof—the number. This also has been discovered by Ferdinand Benary, and since then it has never been disputed in the scientific world.

About 300 years before our era the Jews began to use their letters as symbols for numbers. The speculative Rabbis saw in this a new method for mystic interpretation or Kabbala. Secret words were expressed by the figure, produced by the addition of the numerical values of the letters contained in them. This new science they called *gematriah,* geometry. Now this science is applied here by our "John". We have to prove (1) that the number contains the name of a man, and that man is Nero; and (2) that the solution given holds good for the reading 666 as well as for the equally old reading 616. We take Hebrew letters and their values—

נ (nun)	n = 50		ק (kof)	k = 100
ר (resh)	r = 200		ס (samech)	s = 60
ו (vav) for	o = 6		ר (resh)	r = 200
ן (nun)	n = 50			

Neron Kesar, the Emperor Neron, Greek Nêron Kaisar. Now, if instead of the Greek spelling, we transfer the Latin Nero Caesar into Hebrew characters, the *nun* at the end of *Neron* disappears, and with it the value of fifty. That brings us to the other old reading of 616, and thus the proof is as perfect as can be desired.*

The mysterious book, then, is now perfectly clear. "John" predicts the return of Nero for about the year 70, and a reign of terror under him which is to last forty-two months, or 1,260 days. After that term God arises, vanquishes Nero, the Antichrist, destroys the great city by fire, and binds the devil for a thousand years. The millennium begins, and so forth. All this now has lost all interest, except for ignorant persons who may still try to calculate the day of the last judgment. But as an authentic picture of almost primitive Christianity, drawn by one of themselves, the book is worth more than all the rest of the New Testament put together.

Frederick Engels

Written in June-July 1883

First published in *Progress*, Vol. II, No. 2, August, 1883

Reproduced from the magazine

---

* The above spelling of the name, both with and without the second *nun*, is the one which occurs in the Talmud, and is therefore authentic.

[PREFACE TO THE 1883 GERMAN EDITION OF THE *MANIFESTO OF THE COMMUNIST PARTY*][66]

The preface to the present edition I must, alas, sign alone. Marx, the man to whom the whole working class of Europe and America owes more than to anyone else, rests at Highgate Cemetery and over his grave the first grass is already growing. Since his death, there can even be less thought of revising or supplementing the *Manifesto.* All the more do I consider it necessary again to state here the following expressly:

The basic thought running through the *Manifesto*—that economic production and the structure of society of every historical epoch necessarily arising therefrom constitute the foundation for the political and intellectual history of that epoch; that consequently (ever since the dissolution of the primeval communal ownership of land) all history has been a history of class struggles, struggles between exploited and exploiting, between dominated and dominating classes at various stages of social development; that this struggle, however, has now reached a stage where the exploited and oppressed class (the proletariat) can no longer emancipate itself from the class which exploits and oppresses it (the bourgeoisie), without at the same time forever freeing the whole of society from exploitation, oppression and class struggles—the basic thought belongs solely and exclusively to Marx.*

* "This proposition," I wrote in the preface to the English translation,[a] "which, in my opinion, is destined to do for history what Darwin's theory has done for biology, we, both of us, had been gradually approaching for some years before 1845. How far I had independently progressed towards it, is best shown by my

---

a See this volume, p. 517.— *Ed.*

I have already stated this many times; but precisely now it is necessary that it also stand in front of the *Manifesto* itself.

London, June 28, 1883

F. Engels

First published in *Das Kommunistische Manifest*, Hottingen-Zurich, 1883

Printed according to the 1890 German edition, checked with the 1883 edition

---

Condition of the Working Class in England. But when I again met Marx at Brussels, in spring, 1845, he had it ready worked out, and put it before me, in terms almost as clear as those in which I have stated it here." [*Note by Engels to the 1890 German edition.*]

MARX AND THE *NEUE RHEINISCHE ZEITUNG* (1848-49) [67]

On the outbreak of the February Revolution, the German "Communist Party", as we called it, consisted only of a small core, the Communist League, which was organised as a secret propaganda society. The League was secret only because at that time no freedom of association or assembly existed in Germany. Besides the workers' associations abroad, from which it obtained recruits, it had about thirty communities, or sections, in the country itself and, in addition, individual members in many places. This inconsiderable fighting force, however, possessed a leader, *Marx*, to whom all willingly subordinated themselves, a leader of the first rank, and, thanks to him, a programme of principles and tactics that still has full validity today: the *Communist Manifesto*.

It is the tactical part of the programme that concerns us here in the first instance. This part stated in general:

"The Communists do not form a separate party opposed to other working-class parties.

"They have no interests separate and apart from those of the proletariat as a whole.

"They do not set up any sectarian principles of their own, by which to shape and mould the proletarian movement.

"The Communists are distinguished from the other working-class parties by this only: 1. In the national struggles of the proletarians of the different countries, they point out and bring to the front the *common interests* of the entire proletariat, *independently of all nationality*. 2. In the various stages of development which the struggle of the working class against the bourgeoisie has to pass through, they always and everywhere represent *the interests of the movement as a whole*.

"The Communists, therefore, are on the one hand, *practically*, the most resolute section of the working-class parties of every country, that section which pushes forward all others; on the other hand, *theoretically*, they have over the great mass of the proletariat the advantage of clearly understanding the line of march, the conditions, and the ultimate general results of the proletarian movement." [a]

And for the German party it stated in particular:

"In Germany the Communist Party fights with the bourgeoisie whenever it acts in a revolutionary way, against the absolute monarchy, the feudal landowners and philistinism.

"But they never cease, for a single instant, to instil into the working class the clearest possible recognition of the hostile antagonism between bourgeoisie and proletariat, in order that the German workers may straightway use, as so many weapons against the bourgeoisie, the social and political conditions that the bourgeoisie must necessarily introduce along with its supremacy, and in order that, after the fall of the reactionary classes in Germany, the fight against the bourgeoisie itself may immediately begin.

"The Communists turn their attention chiefly to Germany, because that country is on the eve of a bourgeois revolution," etc. (*Manifesto*, Section IV.) [b]

Never has a tactical programme proved its worth as well as this one. Devised on the eve of a revolution, it stood the test of this revolution; whenever, since this period, a workers' party has deviated from it, the deviation has met its punishment; and today, after almost forty years, it serves as the guiding line of all resolute and self-confident workers' parties in Europe, from Madrid to St. Petersburg.

The February events in Paris precipitated the imminent German revolution and thereby modified its character. The German bourgeoisie, instead of conquering by virtue of its own power, conquered in the tow of a French workers' revolution. Before it had yet conclusively overthrown its old adversaries—the absolute monarchy, feudal landownership, the bureaucracy and the cowardly petty bourgeosie—it had to confront a new enemy, the proletariat. However, the effects of the economic conditions, which lagged far behind those of France and England, and thus of the

---

[a] See present edition, Vol. 6, p. 497. Engels' italics.— *Ed.*
[b] Ibid., p. 519.— *Ed.*

backward class situation in Germany resulting therefrom, immediately showed themselves here.

The German bourgeoisie, which had only just begun to establish
its large-scale industry, had neither the strength nor the courage
to win for itself unconditional domination in the state, nor was
there any compelling necessity for it to do so. The proletariat,
undeveloped to an equal degree, having grown up in complete
intellectual enslavement, being unorganised and still not even
capable of independent organisation, possessed only a vague
feeling of the profound conflict of interests between it and the
bourgeoisie. Hence, although in point of fact the mortal enemy of
the latter, it remained, on the other hand, its political appendage.
Terrified not by what the German proletariat was, but by what it
threatened to become and what the French proletariat already
was, the bourgeoisie saw its sole salvation in some compromise,
even the most cowardly, with the monarchy and nobility; as the
proletariat was still unaware of its own historical role, the bulk of
it had, at the start, to take on the role of the forward-pressing,
extreme left wing of the bourgeoisie. The German workers had
above all to win those rights which were indispensable to their
independent organisation as a class party: freedom of the press,
association and assembly—rights which the bourgeoisie, in the
interest of its own rule, ought to have fought for, but which it
itself in its fear now began to dispute when it came to the workers.
The few hundred separate League members vanished in the
enormous mass that had been suddenly hurled into the movement. Thus, the German proletariat at first appeared on the
political stage as the extreme democratic party.

In this way, when we founded a major newspaper in Germany,
our banner was determined as a matter of course. It could only be
that of democracy, but that of a democracy which everywhere
emphasised in every point the specific proletarian character which
it could not yet inscribe once for all on its banner. If we did not
want to do that, if we did not want to take up the movement,
adhere to its already existing, most advanced, actually proletarian
side and to advance it further, then there was nothing left for us
to do but to preach communism in a little provincial sheet and to
found a tiny sect instead of a great party of action. But we had
already been spoilt for the role of preachers in the wilderness; we
had studied the utopians too well for that, nor was it for that we
had drafted our programme.

When we came to Cologne, preparations by the democrats, and
partly by the Communists, had been made there for a major

newspaper; they wanted to make this a purely local Cologne paper and to banish us to Berlin. But in twenty-four hours, especially thanks to Marx, we had conquered the field, and the newspaper became ours, in return for the concession of taking *Heinrich Bürgers** into the editorial board. The latter wrote *one* article (in No. 2) and never another.

Cologne was where we had to go, and not Berlin. First, Cologne was the centre of the Rhine Province, which had gone through the French Revolution, which had provided itself with *modern* legal conceptions in the *Code Napoléon*,[68] which had developed by far the most important large-scale industry and which was in every respect the most advanced part of Germany at that time. The Berlin of that time we knew only too well from our own observation, with its hardly hatched bourgeoisie, its cringing petty bourgeoisie, audacious in words but craven in deeds, its still wholly undeveloped workers, its mass of bureaucrats, aristocratic and court riff-raff, its entire character of a mere "*Residenz*".[a] Decisive, however, was the following: in Berlin the wretched Prussian *Landrecht*[69] prevailed and political cases were tried by professional magistrates; on the Rhine the *Code Napoléon* was in force, which knows no press trials, because it presupposes censorship, and if one did not commit political misdemeanours but only *crimes,* one came before a jury; in Berlin *after* the revolution young Schlöffel was sentenced to a year's imprisonment for a trifle,[70] while on the Rhine we had unconditional freedom of the press—and we used it to the last drop.

Thus we began, on June 1, 1848, with very limited share capital, of which only a little had been paid up and the shareholders themselves were more than unreliable. Half of them deserted us immediately after the first number came out and by the end of the month we no longer had any at all.

The editorial constitution was simply the dictatorship of Marx. A major daily paper, which has to be ready at a definite hour, cannot observe a consistent policy with any other constitution. Moreover, Marx's dictatorship was a matter of course here, undisputed and willingly recognised by all of us. It was above all his clear vision and firm attitude that made this publication the most famous German newspaper of the years of revolution.

The political programme of the *Neue Rheinische Zeitung* consisted of two main points:

---

* Later became a liberal. [Note by the *Sozialdemokrat* editors.]

---

[a] *Residenz*: Seat of the reigning prince.— *Ed.*

A single, indivisible, democratic German republic, and war with Russia, including the restoration of Poland.

The petty-bourgeois democracy were divided at that time into two factions: the North German, which would not mind putting up with a democratic Prussian emperor, and the South German, then almost all specifically Baden, which wanted to transform Germany into a federative republic after the Swiss model. We had to fight both of them. The interests of the proletariat forbade the Prussianisation of Germany just as much as the perpetuation of its division into petty states. These interests called for the unification of Germany at long last into a *nation,* which alone could provide the battlefield, cleared of all traditional petty obstacles, on which proletariat and bourgeoisie were to measure their strength. But they equally forbade the establishment of Prussia as the head. The Prussian state with its set-up, its tradition and its dynasty[a] was precisely the sole serious internal adversary which the revolution in Germany had to overthrow; and, moreover, Prussia could unify Germany only by tearing Germany apart, by excluding German Austria. Dissolution of the Prussian and disintegration of the Austrian state, real unification of Germany as a republic—we could not have any other immediate revolutionary programme. And this could be accomplished through war with Russia and only through such a war. I will come back to this last point later.

Incidentally, the tone of the newspaper was by no means solemn, serious or enthusiastic. We had altogether contemptible opponents and treated them, without exception, with the utmost scorn. The conspiring monarchy, the *camarilla,* the nobility, the *Kreuz-Zeitung,* the entire "reaction", about which the philistines were morally indignant—we treated them only with mockery and derision. No less so the new idols that had appeared on the scene through the revolution: the March ministers,[71] the Frankfurt and Berlin Assemblies, both the Rights and the Lefts in them. The very first number began with an article which mocked at the inanity of the Frankfurt parliament, the pointlessness of its long-winded speeches, the superfluity of its cowardly resolutions.[b] It cost us half the shareholders. The Frankfurt parliament was not even a debating club; hardly any debates took place there, but for the most part only academic dissertations prepared beforehand

---

[a] The Hohenzollerns.— *Ed.*
[b] F. Engels, "The Assembly at Frankfurt".— *Ed.*

were ground out and resolutions adopted which were intended to inspire the German philistines but of which no one else took any notice.

The Berlin Assembly was of more importance: it confronted a real power, it did not debate and pass resolutions in the air, in a Frankfurt cloud-cuckoo land. Consequently, it was dealt with in more detail. But there too, the idols of the Lefts, Schulze-Delitzsch, Berends, Elsner, Stein, etc., were just as sharply attacked as those in Frankfurt; their indecisiveness, hesitancy and pettiness were mercilessly exposed, and it was proved how step by step they compromised themselves into betraying the revolution. This, of course, evoked a shudder in the democratic petty bourgeois, who had only just manufactured these idols for his own use. To us, this shudder was a sign that we had hit the bull's eye.

We came out likewise against the illusion, zealously spread by the petty bourgeoisie, that the revolution had come to an end with the March days and that now one had only to pocket the fruits. To us, February and March could have the significance of a real revolution only if they were not the conclusion but, on the contrary, the starting-points of a long revolutionary movement in which, as in the Great French Revolution, the people developed further through its own struggles and the parties became more and more sharply differentiated until they coincided entirely with the great classes, bourgeoisie, petty bourgeoisie and proletariat, and in which the separate positions were won one after another by the proletariat in a series of battles. Hence, we everywhere opposed the democratic petty bourgeoisie as well when it tried to gloss over its class antagonism to the proletariat with the favourite phrase: after all, we all want the same thing; all the differences rest on mere misunderstandings. But the less we allowed the petty bourgeoisie to misunderstand our proletarian democracy, the tamer and more amenable it became towards us. The more sharply and resolutely one opposes it, the more readily it ducks and the more concessions it makes to the workers' party. We have seen this for ourselves.

Finally, we exposed the parliamentary cretinism (as Marx called it) of the various so-called National Assemblies.[72] These gentlemen had allowed all means of power to slip out of their hands, in part had voluntarily surrendered them again to the governments. In Berlin, as in Frankfurt, alongside newly strengthened, reactionary governments there stood powerless assemblies, which nevertheless imagined that their impotent resolutions would shake the world in its foundations. This cretinous self-deception prevailed right to the extreme Lefts. We told them plainly that their parliamentary victory would coincide with their real defeat.

And it so happened both in Berlin and in Frankfurt. When the "Lefts" obtained the majority, the government dispersed the entire Assembly; it could do so because the Assembly had forfeited all credit with the people.

When later I read *Bougeart's* book on *Marat*,[a] I found that in more than one respect we had only unconsciously imitated the great model of the genuine "*Ami du Peuple*" (not the one forged by the royalists) and that the whole outburst of rage and the whole falsification of history, by virtue of which for almost a century only an entirely distorted Marat had been known, were solely due to the fact that Marat mercilessly removed the veil from the idols of the moment, Lafayette, Bailly and others, and exposed them as ready-made traitors to the revolution; and that he, like us, did not want the revolution declared complete, but lasting.

We openly proclaimed that the trend we represented could enter the struggle for the attainment of our real party aims only when the most extreme of the official parties existing in Germany came to the helm: then we would form the opposition to it.

Events, however, saw to it that besides mockery at our German opponents there also appeared fiery passion. The insurrection of the Paris workers in June 1848 found us at our post. From the first shot we were unconditionally on the side of the insurgents. After their defeat, Marx paid tribute to the vanquished in one of his most powerful articles.[b]

Then the last remaining shareholders deserted us. But we had the satisfaction of being the only paper in Germany, and almost in Europe, that had held aloft the banner of the crushed proletariat at the moment when the bourgeois and petty bourgeois of all countries were trampling the vanquished in the ground with a torrent of slander.

Our foreign policy was simple: to support every revolutionary people, and to call for a general war of revolutionary Europe against the mighty bulwark of European reaction—Russia. From February 24[73] onwards it was clear to us that the revolution had only *one* really formidable enemy, Russia, and that the more the movement took on European dimensions the more this enemy was compelled to enter the struggle. The Vienna, Milan and Berlin events were bound to delay the Russian attack, but its final coming

---

[a] A. Bougeart, *Marat, L'ami du peuple*, vols I-II.— *Ed.*

[b] K. Marx, "The June Revolution".— *Ed.*

became all the more certain the closer the revolution came to Russia. But if Germany could be successfully brought to make war against Russia, it would be the end for the Habsburgs and Hohenzollerns and the revolution would triumph along the whole line.

This policy pervaded every issue of the newspaper until the moment of the actual invasion of Hungary by the Russians, which fully confirmed our forecast and decided the defeat of the revolution.

When, in the spring of 1849, the decisive battle drew near, the language of the paper became more vehement and passionate with every issue. *Wilhelm Wolff* reminded the Silesian peasants in the "Silesian Milliard" (eight articles),[74] how on being emancipated from feudal services they had been cheated out of money and land by the landlords with the help of the government, and he demanded a thousand million talers in compensation.

It was at the same time, in April, that *Marx's* essay on wage labour and capital appeared in the form of a series of editorial articles[a] as a clear indication of the social goal of our policy. Every issue, every special number, pointed to the great battle that was in the making, to the sharpening of antagonisms in France, Italy, Germany and Hungary. In particular, the special numbers in April and May were as much proclamations to the people to hold themselves in readiness for direct action.

"Out there, in the Reich", wonder was expressed that we carried on our activities so unconcernedly within a Prussian fortress of the first rank, in the face of a garrison of 8,000 troops and confronting the guardhouse; but, on account of the eight rifles with bayonets and 250 live cartridges in the editorial room, and the red Jacobin caps of the compositors, our house was reckoned by the officers likewise as a fortress which was not to be taken by a mere *coup de main*.

At last, on May 18, 1849, the blow came.

The insurrection in Dresden and Elberfeld was suppressed, that in Iserlohn was encircled; the Rhine Province and Westphalia bristled with bayonets which, after completing the rape of the Prussian Rhineland, were intended to march against the Palatinate and Baden. Then at last the government ventured to come to close quarters with us. Half of the editorial staff were prosecuted, the other half were liable to deportation as non-Prussians. Nothing could be done about it, as long as a whole army corps stood

---

[a] K. Marx, "Wage Labour and Capital".— *Ed.*

behind the government. We had to surrender our fortress, but we withdrew with our arms and baggage, with band playing and flag flying, the flag of the last, red issue, in which we warned the Cologne workers against hopeless putsches, and called to them:

"In bidding you farewell, the editors of the *Neue Rheinische Zeitung* thank you for the sympathy you have shown them. Their last word everywhere and always will be: *emancipation of the working class!*" [a]

Thus the *Neue Rheinische Zeitung* came to an end, shortly before it had completed its first year. Begun almost without financial resources—the little that had been promised it very soon, as we said, was lost—it had achieved a circulation of almost 5,000 by September. The state of siege in Cologne suspended it; in the middle of October it had to begin again from the start. But in May 1849, when it was suppressed, it again had 6,000 subscribers, while the *Kölnische,* at that time, according to its own admission, had not more than 9,000. No German newspaper, before or since, has ever had the same power and influence or been able to electrify the proletarian masses as effectively as the *Neue Rheinische Zeitung.*

And that it owed above all to *Marx.*

When the blow fell, the editorial staff dispersed. *Marx* went to Paris where the *dénouement,* then in preparation there, took place on June 13, 1849 [75]; *Wilhelm Wolff* took his seat in the Frankfurt parliament—now that the Assembly had to choose between being dispersed from above or joining the revolution; and I went to the Palatinate and became an adjutant in Willich's volunteer corps. [76]

Fr. Engels

Written in mid-February and early March, 1884

First published in *Der Sozialdemokrat,* No. 11, March 13, 1884

Printed according to the newspaper

---

[a] K. Marx, F. Engels, "To the Workers of Cologne" (see present edition, Vol. 9, p. 467).— *Ed.*

THE ORIGIN OF THE FAMILY,
PRIVATE PROPERTY AND THE STATE

IN THE LIGHT OF THE RESEARCHES
BY LEWIS H. MORGAN [77]

Written in early April-May 26, 1884

First published as a book in Zurich in 1884

Signed: *Frederick Engels*

Printed according to the 1891 edition collated with the 1884 edition

Der Ursprung der Familie,

des

Privateigenthums

und des Staats.

Im Anschluss

an

Lewis H. Morgan's Forschungen

von

Friedrich-Engels.

Hottingen-Zürich.
Verlag der Schweizerischen Volksbuchhandlung.
1884.

Cover of the first edition
of *The Origin of the Family,
Private Property and the State*

PREFACE [TO THE FIRST EDITION]

The following chapters constitute, in a sense, the fulfilment of a behest. It was no less a person than Karl Marx who had planned to present the results of Morgan's researches in connection with the conclusions arrived at by his own—within certain limits I might say our own—materialist investigation of history and only thus to make clear their whole significance. For Morgan rediscovered in America, in his own way, the materialist conception of history that had been discovered by Marx forty years ago, and in his comparison of barbarism and civilisation was led by this conception to the same conclusions, in the main points, as Marx. And just as *Capital* was for years both zealously plagiarised and persistently hushed up by the official economists in Germany, so was Morgan's *Ancient Society** treated by the spokesmen of "prehistoric" science in England. My work can offer but a meagre substitute for that which my departed friend was not destined to accomplish. However, I have before me, in his extensive extracts from Morgan,[78] critical notes which I reproduce here as far as they refer to the subject in any way.

According to the materialist conception, the determining factor in history is, in the last resort, the production and reproduction of immediate life. But this itself is again of a twofold character. On

---

* *Ancient Society, or Researches in the Lines of Human Progress from Savagery through Barbarism to Civilization.* By Lewis H. Morgan, London, MacMillan & Co., 1877. This book was printed in America, and is remarkably difficult to obtain in London. The author died a few years ago.

the one hand, the production of the means of subsistence, of food, clothing and shelter and the implements required for this; on the other, the production of human beings themselves, the propagation of the species. The social institutions under which men of a definite historical epoch and of a definite country live are determined by both kinds of production: by the stage of development of labour, on the one hand, and of the family, on the other. The less labour is developed and the more limited the volume of its products and, therefore, the wealth of society, the more predominantly the social order appears to be dominated by ties of kinship. However, within this structure of society based on ties of kinship, the productivity of labour develops more and more; with it, private property and exchange, differences in wealth, the possibility of utilising the labour power of others, and thereby the basis of class antagonisms: new social elements, which strive in the course of generations to adapt the old structure of society to the new conditions, until, finally, incompatibility of the two leads to a complete transformation. The old society, based on ties of kinship, bursts asunder with the collision of the newly developed social classes; in its place a new society appears, constituted in a state, the lower units of which are no longer groups based on ties of kinship but territorial groups, a society in which the family system is entirely dominated by the property system, and in which the class antagonisms and class struggle, which make up the content of all hitherto *written* history now freely unfold.

Morgan's great merit lies in having discovered and reconstructed this prehistoric foundation of our written history in its main features, and in having found in the ties of kinship of the North American Indians the key to the most important, hitherto insoluble, riddles of the earliest Greek, Roman and German history. His book, however, was not the work of one day. He grappled with his material for nearly forty years until he completely mastered it. But for this reason his book is one of the few epoch-making works of our time.

In the following exposition the reader will, on the whole, easily be able to distinguish between what has been taken from Morgan and what I have added myself. In the historical sections dealing with Greece and Rome I have not limited myself to Morgan's evidence, but have added what I had at my disposal. The sections dealing with the Celts and the Germans are substantially my own; here Morgan had at his disposal almost exclusively second-hand sources, and, as far as German conditions were concerned—with the exception of Tacitus—only the wretched liberal falsification of

Mr. Freeman.[a] The economic arguments, sufficient for Morgan's purpose but wholly inadequate for my own, have all been elaborated afresh by myself. And, finally, I, of course, am responsible for all conclusions wherever Morgan is not expressly quoted.

Written in late May 1884

First published in F. Engels, *Der Ursprung der Familie, des Privateigenthums und des Staats*, Hottingen-Zurich, 1884   Printed according to the book

---

[a] E. A. Freeman, *Comparative Politics.—Ed.*

I

PREHISTORIC STAGES OF CULTURE

Morgan was the first specialist to attempt to introduce a definite order into the prehistory of man; unless important additional material necessitates alterations, his classification may be expected to remain in force.

Of the three main epochs, savagery, barbarism and civilisation, he is naturally concerned only with the first two, and with the transition to the third. He subdivides each of these two epochs into a lower, middle and upper stage, according to the progress made in the production of the means of subsistence; for, as he says:

"Upon their skill in this direction, the whole question of human supremacy on the earth depended. Mankind are the only beings who may be said to have gained an absolute control over the production of food. [...] The great epochs of human progress have been identified, more or less directly, with the enlargement of the sources of subsistence." [a]

The evolution of the family proceeds concurrently, but does not offer such conclusive criteria for the delimitation of the periods.

1. SAVAGERY

1. *Lower Stage.* Infancy of the human race. Man still lived in his original habitat, tropical or subtropical forests, dwelling, at least partially, in trees; this alone explains his survival in face of the large beasts of prey. Fruits, nuts and roots served him as food; the

---

[a] L. H. Morgan, *Ancient Society,* p. 19. This proposition is also set forth in "Marx's Excerpts from Lewis Henry Morgan, *Ancient Society*" in *The Ethnological Notebooks of Karl Marx,* p. 99.— *Ed.*

formation of articulate speech was the main achievement of this period. None of the peoples that became known during the historical period were any longer in this primeval state. Although this period may have lasted for many thousands of years, we have no direct evidence to prove its existence; but once we admit the descent of man from the animal kingdom, the acceptance of this transitional stage is inevitable.

2. *Middle Stage*. Begins with the utilisation of fish (under which heading, we also include crabs, shellfish and other aquatic animals) for food and with the employment of fire. These two are complementary, since fish food becomes fully available only by the use of fire. This new food, however, made men independent of climate and locality. By following the rivers and coasts they were able, even in their savage state, to spread over the greater part of the earth's surface. The crudely fashioned, unpolished stone implements of the earlier Stone Age—the so-called palaeolithic— which belong wholly, or predominantly, to this period, being scattered over all the continents, are evidence of these migrations. The newly occupied territories as well as the unceasingly active urge for discovery, linked with the command of the art of producing fire by friction, made available new foodstuffs, such as farinaceous roots and tubers, baked in hot ashes or in baking pits (ground ovens), and game, which was occasionally added to the diet after the invention of the first weapons—the club and the spear. Exclusively hunting peoples, such as figure in books, that is, peoples subsisting *solely* by hunting, have never existed, since the fruits of the chase are much too precarious for that. As a consequence of the continued uncertainty with regard to sources of food, cannibalism appears to have arisen at this stage, and continued for a long time. The Australians and many Polynesians are to this day in this middle stage of savagery.

3. *Upper Stage*. Begins with the invention of the bow and arrow, making game a regular item of food and hunting one of the normal occupations. To be sure, bow, string and arrow constitute a very composite instrument, the invention of which presupposes long accumulated experience and sharpened mental powers, and, consequently, a simultaneous acquaintance with a host of other inventions. If we compare the peoples which, although familiar with the bow and arrow, are not yet acquainted with the art of pottery (from which point Morgan dates the transition to barbarism), we actually already find a few beginnings of settlement in villages, a certain mastery of the production of means of subsistence: wooden vessels and utensils, finger weaving (without

looms) with filaments of bast, baskets woven from bast or rushes, and polished (neolithic) stone implements. Also for the most part, fire and the stone axe have already provided the dug-out canoe and, in places, timber and planks for house-building. All these advances are to be found, for example, among the Indians of the American North-West, who, although familiar with the bow and arrow, know nothing of pottery. The bow and arrow was for savagery what the iron sword was for barbarism and the firearm for civilisation, namely, the decisive weapon.

2. BARBARISM

1. *Lower Stage.* Dates from the introduction of pottery. The latter had its origin, demonstrably in many cases and probably everywhere, in the coating of woven or wooden vessels with clay in order to render them fire-proof; though it was soon discovered that moulded clay also served the purpose without the inner vessel.

Up to this point we have been able to regard the course of evolution as being generally valid for a definite period among all peoples, irrespective of locality. With the advent of barbarism, however, we reach a stage where the difference in natural endowment of the two great continents begins to assert itself. The characteristic feature of the period of barbarism is the domestication and breeding of animals and the cultivation of plants. Now the Eastern Continent, the so-called Old World, possessed almost all the animals suitable for domestication and all the cultivable cereals with one exception; while the Western one, America, possessed only one domesticable mammal, the llama, and even this only in a part of the South; and of all cultivable cereals only one, but the best: maize. The effect of these different natural conditions was that from now on the population of each hemisphere went its own separate way, and the landmarks on the borderlines between the various stages are different in each of the two cases.

2. *Middle Stage.* Begins, in the East, with the domestication of animals; in the West, with the cultivation of edible plants by means of irrigation, and with the use of adobes (bricks dried in the sun) and stone for buildings.

We shall commence with the West, because there this stage was nowhere surpassed until the European Conquest.

At the time of their discovery, the Indians in the lower stage of barbarism (to which all those found east of the Mississippi belonged) already engaged to a certain extent in the garden cultivation of maize and perhaps also of pumpkins, melons and other garden plants, which supplied a very substantial part of their food. They lived in wooden houses, in villages surrounded by stockades. The tribes of the North-West, particularly those living in the region of the Columbia River, still remained in the upper stage of savagery and were familiar neither with pottery nor with any kind of plant cultivation. On the other hand, the so-called Pueblo Indians of New Mexico,[79] the Mexicans, Central Americans and Peruvians were in the middle stage of barbarism at the time of the Conquest. They lived in fort-like houses built of adobe or stone; they cultivated, in artificially irrigated gardens, maize and other edible plants, varying according to location and climate, which constituted their chief source of food, and they had even domesticated a few animals—the Mexicans the turkey and other birds, and the Peruvians the llama. They were furthermore acquainted with the working of metals—except iron, which was the reason why they could not yet dispense with stone weapons and stone implements. The Spanish Conquest cut short all further independent development.

In the East, the middle stage of barbarism commenced with the domestication of milk and meat-yielding cattle, while plant cultivation appears to have remained unknown until well into this period. The domestication and breeding of cattle and the formation of large herds seem to have been the cause of the differentiation of the Aryans and the Semites from the remaining mass of barbarians. Names of cattle are still common to the European and the Asiatic Aryans, the names of cultivable plants hardly at all.

The formation of herds led in suitable places to pastoral life; among the Semites, on the grassy plains of the Euphrates and the Tigris; among the Aryans, on those of India, of the Oxus and the Jaxartes, of the Don and the Dnieper. The domestication of animals must have been first accomplished on the borders of such pasture lands. It thus appears to later generations that the pastoral peoples originated in areas which, far from being the cradle of mankind, were, on the contrary, almost uninhabitable for their savage forebears and even for people in the lower stage of barbarism. Conversely, once these barbarians of the middle stage had taken to pastoral life, it would never have occurred to them to leave the grassy watered plains of their own accord and return to the forest regions which had been the home of their ancestors.

Even when the Semites and Aryans were driven farther north and west, they found it impossible to settle in the forest regions of Western Asia and Europe until they were enabled, by the cultivation of cereals, to feed their cattle on this less favourable soil, and particularly to pass the winter there. It is more than probable that the cultivation of cereals was introduced here primarily because of the need to provide fodder for cattle and only later became important for human nourishment.

The abundant diet of meat and milk among the Aryans and the Semites, and particularly the beneficial effects of these foods on the development of children, may, perhaps, explain the superior development of these two races. In fact, the Pueblo Indians of New Mexico, who are reduced to an almost exclusively vegetarian diet, have a smaller brain than the Indians at the lower stage of barbarism who ate more meat and fish. At any rate, cannibalism gradually disappears at this stage, and survives only as a religious rite or, what is almost identical in this instance, sorcery.

3. *Upper Stage.* Begins with the smelting of iron ore and passes into civilisation through the invention of alphabetic script and its utilisation for literary records. At this stage, which, as we have already noted, was traversed independently only in the eastern hemisphere, more progress was made in production than in all the previous stages put together. To it belong the Greeks of the Heroic Age, the Italic tribes shortly before the foundation of Rome, the Germans of Tacitus and the Normans of the days of the Vikings.[a]

Above all, we encounter here for the first time the iron ploughshare drawn by cattle, making possible land cultivation on a wide scale — *tillage* — and, in the conditions of that time, a practically unlimited increase in the means of subsistence; in connection with this we find also the clearing of forests and their transformation into arable and pasture land — which, again, would have been impossible on a wide scale without the iron axe and spade. But with this there also came a rapid increase in the population and dense population of small areas. Prior to tillage only very exceptional circumstances could have brought together half a million people under a single central leadership; in all probability this had never happened.

In the poems of Homer, particularly the *Iliad*, we find the

---

[a] The 1884 edition had "and the Germans of Caesar (or, as we would rather say, of Tacitus)" instead of "the Germans of Tacitus and the Normans of the days of the Vikings".— *Ed.*

upper stage of barbarism at its zenith. Improved iron tools, the bellows, the handmill, the potter's wheel, the making of oil and wine, the advanced working of metals developing into a craft, waggons and war chariots, shipbuilding with beams and planks, the beginnings of architecture as an art, walled towns with towers and battlements, the Homeric epic and the whole of mythology— these are the chief heritages carried over by the Greeks from barbarism to civilisation. If we compare with this Caesar's and even Tacitus' descriptions of the Germans,[a] who were at the beginning of that stage of culture from which the Homeric Greeks were preparing to advance to a higher one, we will see what wealth was embodied in the development of production at the upper stage of barbarism.

The picture of the evolution of mankind through savagery and barbarism to the beginnings of civilisation that I have here sketched after Morgan is already rich enough in new and, what is more, incontestable features, incontestable because they are taken straight from production; nevertheless it will appear faint and meagre compared with the picture which will unfold at the end of our journey. Only then will it be possible to give a full view of the transition from barbarism to civilisation and the striking contrast between the two. For the time being we can generalise Morgan's periodisation as follows: Savagery—the period in which the appropriation of natural products, ready for use, predominated; the things produced by man are, in the main, instruments that facilitate this appropriation. Barbarism—the period in which knowledge of cattle breeding and land cultivation is acquired, in which methods of increasing the yield of nature's products through human activity are learnt. Civilisation—the period in which knowledge of the further processing of nature's products, of industry proper, and of art are acquired.

II

THE FAMILY

Morgan, who spent the greater part of his life among the Iroquois—who still inhabit the State of New York—and was adopted by one of their tribes (the Senecas), found a system of consanguinity prevailing among them that stood in contradiction to their actual family relations. Marriage between single pairs, with

---

[a] See Caesar, *Commentarii de bello Gallico* and Tacitus, *Germania.—Ed.*

easy dissolution by either side, which Morgan termed the "pairing family", was the rule among them. The offspring of such a married couple was known and recognised by all, and no doubt could arise as to the person to whom the designation father, mother, son, daughter, brother, sister should be applied. But the actual use of these terms contradicted this. The Iroquois calls not only his own children sons and daughters, but those of his brothers also; and they call him father. On the other hand, he calls his sisters' children his nephews and nieces; and they call him uncle. Conversely, the Iroquois woman calls her sisters' children her sons and daughters along with her own; and they call her mother. On the other hand, she calls her brothers' children her nephews and nieces; and she is called their aunt. In the same way, the children of brothers call one another brothers and sisters, and so do the children of sisters. The children of a woman and those of her brother, in contrast, call each other cousins. And these are no mere empty terms, but expressions of ideas actually in force concerning proximity and remoteness, equality and inequality of blood relationship; and these ideas serve as the foundation of a fully elaborated system of consanguinity, capable of expressing several hundred different relationships of a single individual. Furthermore, this system not only exists in full force among all American Indians (no exceptions have as yet been discovered), but also prevails almost unchanged among the aborigines of India, among the Dravidian tribes in the Deccan and the Gaura tribes in Hindustan. The terms of kinship current among the Tamils of South India and the Seneca Iroquois in the State of New York are identical even at the present day for more than two hundred different relationships. And among these tribes in India, too, as among all the American Indians, the relationships arising out of the prevailing form of the family stand in contradiction to the system of consanguinity.

How is this to be explained? In view of the decisive role which kinship plays in the social order of all peoples in the stage of savagery and barbarism, the significance of so widespread a system cannot be explained away by mere phrases. A system which is generally prevalent throughout America, which likewise exists in Asia among peoples of an entirely different race, and more or less modified forms of which abound everywhere throughout Africa and Australia, needs to be historically explained, not talked away, as McLennan, for example, attempted to do.[a] The terms father,

---

[a] See J. F. McLennan, *Primitive Marriage* and *Studies in Ancient History.—Ed.*

child, brother and sister are no mere honorary titles, but carry with them absolutely definite and very serious mutual obligations, the totality of which forms an essential part of the social constitution of these peoples. And the explanation was found. In the Sandwich Islands (Hawaii) there existed as late as the first half of the present century a form of the family which yielded just such fathers and mothers, brothers and sisters, sons and daughters, uncles and aunts, nephews and nieces, as are demanded by the American and ancient Indian system of consanguinity. But strangely enough, the system of consanguinity prevalent in Hawaii again did not coincide with the actual form of the family existing there. There, all first cousins, without exception, are regarded as brothers and sisters, and as the common children, not only of their mother and her sisters, or of their father and his brothers, but of all the brothers and sisters of their parents without distinction. Thus, if the American system of consanguinity presupposes a more primitive form of the family, no longer existing in America itself, but actually still found in Hawaii, the Hawaiian system of consanguinity, on the other hand, points to an even more primitive form of the family, which, though we cannot prove it still exists anywhere, *must* nevertheless have existed, for otherwise the system of consanguinity corresponding to it could not have arisen.

"The family," says Morgan, "represents an active principle. It is never stationary, but advances from a lower to a higher form as society advances from a lower to a higher condition. [...] Systems of consanguinity, on the contrary, are passive; recording the progress made by the family at long intervals apart, and only changing radically when the family has radically changed." [a]

"And," adds Marx, "the same applies to political, juridical, religious and philosophical systems generally." [b] While the family continues to live, the system of consanguinity becomes ossified, and while this latter continues to exist in the customary form, the family outgrows it. However, just as Cuvier could with certainty conclude, from the pouch bones of an animal skeleton found near Paris, that this belonged to a marsupial and that now extinct marsupials had once lived there, so we, with the same certainty, can conclude, from a historically transmitted system of consanguinity, that an extinct form of the family corresponding to it did once exist.

---

[a] L. H. Morgan, *Ancient Society,* p. 435.— *Ed.*
[b] "Marx's Excerpts...", op. cit., p. 112.— *Ed.*

The systems of consanguinity and forms of the family just referred to differ from those which prevail today in that each child has several fathers and mothers. According to the American system of consanguinity, to which the Hawaiian family corresponds, brother and sister cannot be the father and the mother of one and the same child; but the Hawaiian system of consanguinity presupposes a family in which this, on the contrary, was the rule. We are confronted with a series of forms of the family which directly contradict the forms hitherto generally accepted as being the only ones prevailing. The traditional conception knows monogamy only, along with polygamy on the part of individual men, and even, perhaps, polyandry on the part of individual women, and hushes up the fact—as is the way with moralising philistines—that in practice these bounds imposed by official society are silently but unblushingly transgressed. The study of primeval history, on the contrary, reveals to us conditions in which men live in polygamy and their wives simultaneously in polyandry, and the common children are, therefore, regarded as being common to them all; in their turn, these conditions undergo a whole series of modifications until they are ultimately dissolved in monogamy. These modifications are of such a character that the circle of people embraced by the common tie of marriage—very wide originally—becomes narrower and narrower, until, finally, only the single couple is left, which predominates today.

By thus constructing the history of the family in reverse, Morgan, in agreement with the majority of his professional colleagues, arrived at a primitive stage at which promiscuous intercourse prevailed within a tribe, so that every woman belonged equally to every man and every man to every woman.[a] There had been talk about such a primitive condition ever since the last century, but only in general clichés; Bachofen was the first—and this was one of his great services—to take this condition seriously and to search for traces of it in historical and religious traditions.[b] We know today that the traces he discovered do not at all lead back to a social stage of sexual promiscuity, but to a much later form, group marriage. That primitive social stage, if it really existed, belongs to so remote an epoch that we can scarcely expect

---

[a] The 1884 edition had after this: "The discovery of this primitive stage is Bachofen's first great merit.* It is probable that at a very early stage there developed from this primitive condition:". In the 1891 edition this sentence was replaced by the text that follows below, up to the paragraph "1. The *Consanguine Family*" (see p. 147).— *Ed.*

[b] J. J. Bachofen, *Das Mutterrecht.*— *Ed.*

to find *direct* evidence of its one-time existence in social fossils, among backward savages. What Bachofen deserves credit for is that he placed this question in the forefront of investigation.*

It has become the fashion of late to deny the existence of this initial stage in the sexual life of mankind. The aim is to spare humanity this "shame". Apart from pointing to the absence of any direct evidence, reference is particularly made to the example of the rest of the animal world; wherefrom Letourneau (*L'évolution du mariage et de la famille,* 1888) collected numerous facts purporting to show that here, too, complete sexual promiscuity belongs to a lower stage. The only conclusion I can draw from all these facts, however, is that they prove absolutely nothing as far as man and his primeval conditions of life are concerned. The fact that vertebrates mate for lengthy periods of time can be sufficiently explained on physiological grounds; for example, among birds, the female's need for assistance during brooding time; the examples of faithful monogamy among birds prove nothing whatsoever for human beings, since these are not actually descended from birds. And if strict monogamy is to be regarded as the acme of all virtue, then the palm must be given to the tapeworm, which possesses complete male and female genitals in every one of its 50 to 200 proglottides or body segments, and passes the whole of its life cohabiting with itself in every one of these segments. If, however, we limit ourselves to mammals, we find all forms of sexual life among them: promiscuity, suggestions of group marriage, polygamy and monogamy. Only polyandry is absent. This was only achieved by humans. Even our nearest relatives, the tetrapods, exhibit all possible variations in the grouping of male and female; and, if we draw the line closer and consider only the four anthropoid apes, Letourneau can tell us only that they are sometimes monogamous and sometimes polygamous, while Saussure, quoted by Giraud-Teulon, asserts

---

* How little Bachofen understood what he had discovered, or rather guessed, is proved by his description of this primitive condition as *hetaerism.* This word was used by the Greeks, when they introduced it, to describe intercourse between unmarried men, or those living in monogamy, and unmarried women; it always presupposes the existence of a definite form of marriage outside of which this intercourse takes place, and includes prostitution, at least as a possibility. The word has never been used in any other sense and I use it in this sense like Morgan. Bachofen's highly important discoveries are everywhere incredibly mystified by his fantastic belief that the historically arisen relations between man and woman sprang from human beings' religious ideas in each given period and not from their actual conditions of life.

that they are monogamous.[a] The recent assertions by Westermarck
(*The History of Human Marriage,* London, 1891) regarding
monogamy among anthropoid apes are no proof by any means. In
short, the reports are of such a character that the honest
Letourneau admits:

> "For the rest, there exists among the mammals absolutely no strict relations
> between the degree of intellectual development and the form of sexual union."[b]

And Espinas (*Des sociétés animales,* 1877) says point-blank:

> "The horde is the highest social group observable among animals. It *seems* to be
> composed of families, but right from the outset *the family and the horde stand in
> antagonism to each other,* they develop in inverse ratio."[c]

As is evident from the above, we know next to nothing
conclusive about the family and other gregarious groupings of the
anthropoid apes. The reports directly contradict one another. Nor
is this surprising. How contradictory, how much in need of critical
examination and sifting are the reports in our possession
concerning even savage human tribes! But ape communities are still
more difficult to observe than human ones. We must, therefore, for
the present reject every conclusion drawn from such absolutely
unreliable reports.

The passage from Espinas, quoted above, however, provides us
with a better clue. Among the higher animals the horde and the
family are not complementary, but antagonistic to each other.
Espinas describes very neatly how jealousy amongst the males in
the rutting season loosens, or temporarily dissolves, every gregarious horde.

> "Where the family is closely bound together hordes are rare exceptions. On the
> other hand, the horde arises almost naturally where free sexual intercourse or
> polygamy is the rule.... For a horde to arise the family ties must have been loosened
> and the individual freed again. That is why we so rarely find organised flocks
> among birds.... Among mammals, on the other hand, more or less organised
> communities are to be found, precisely because the individual in this case is not
> merged in the family.... Thus, at its inception, the collective feeling of the horde can
> have no greater enemy than the collective feeling of the family. Let us not hesitate to
> say: if a higher social form than the family has evolved, it can have been due solely to
> the fact that it incorporated within itself families which had undergone a fundamental
> transformation; which does not exclude the possibility that, precisely for this reason,
> these families were later able to reconstitute themselves under infinitely more
> favourable circumstances" (Espinas, op. cit. [Ch. I]; quoted by Giraud-Teulon in his
> *Origines du mariage et de la famille,* 1884, pp. 518-20).

---

[a] A. Giraud-Teulon, *Les origines du mariage et de la famille,* p. XV.— *Ed.*
[b] Ch. Letourneau, *L'évolution du mariage et de la famille,* p. 41.— *Ed.*
[c] Quoted from Giraud-Teulon's book, p. 518, Note "a".— *Ed.*

From this it becomes apparent that animal communities have, to be sure, a certain value in drawing conclusions regarding human ones—but only in a negative sense. As far as we have ascertained, the higher vertebrates know only two forms of the family: polygamy or the single pair. In both cases only *one* adult male, only *one* husband is permissible. The jealousy of the male, representing both the ties and limits of the family, brings the animal family into conflict with the horde. The horde, the higher form of gregariousness, is rendered impossible here, loosened there, or dissolved altogether during the rutting season; at best, its continued development is hindered by the jealousy of the male. This alone suffices to prove that the animal family and primitive human society are incompatible things; that primitive man, working his way up out of the animal stage, either knew no family whatsoever, or at the most knew a family that is non-existent among animals. Such an unarmed animal as man in the making could survive in small numbers even in isolation, which knows monogamy as its highest form of gregariousness, as ascribed by Westermarck to the gorilla and chimpanzee on the basis of hunters' reports. For evolution out of the animal stage, for the accomplishment of the greatest advance known to nature, an additional element was needed: the replacement of the individual's inadequate power of defence by the united strength and joint effort of the horde. The transition to the human stage out of conditions such as those under which the anthropoid apes live today would be absolutely inexplicable. These apes rather give the impression of being stray sidelines gradually approaching extinction, and, at any rate, in process of decline. This alone is sufficient reason for rejecting all conclusions based on parallels drawn between their family forms and those of primitive man. Mutual toleration among the adult males, freedom from jealousy, was, however, the first condition for the formation of those large and enduring groups in the sole midst of which the transition from animal to man could take place. And indeed, what do we find as the oldest, most primitive form of the family, of which undeniable evidence can be found in history, and which even today can be studied here and there? Group marriage, the form in which whole groups of men and whole groups of women belong to one another, and which leaves but little scope for jealousy. And further, we find at a later stage of development the exceptional form of polyandry, which still more militates against all feeling of jealousy, and is, therefore, unknown to animals. Since, however, the forms of group marriage known to us are accompanied by such peculiarly complicated conditions that they necessarily point to earlier, simpler forms of sexual behaviour and thus, in the last analysis, to a period of promiscuous intercourse coinciding with the period of transition from animality to humanity, references to the forms of marriage among animals bring us back again to the very point from which they were supposed to have led us away once and for all.

What, then, does promiscuous sexual intercourse mean? That the prohibitive restrictions in force at present or in earlier times did not exist. We have already witnessed the collapse of the barrier of jealousy. If anything is certain, it is that jealousy is an emotion of comparatively late development. The same applies to the conception of incest. Not only did brother and sister live as man and wife originally, but sexual intercourse between parents and children is permitted among many peoples to this day. Bancroft (*The Native Races of the Pacific States of North America*, 1875, Vol. I) testifies to the existence of this among the Kadiaks of the Bering Strait, the Kadiaks near Alaska and the Tinnehs in the interior of British North America. Letourneau has collected reports of the same fact among the Chippewa Indians, the Cucus in Chile, the Caribbeans and the Karens of Indo-China, not to mention the accounts of the ancient Greeks and Romans concerning the Parthians, Persians, Scythians, Huns, etc. Prior to the discovery of incest (and it *is* a discovery, and one of the utmost value), sexual intercourse between parents and children could be no more disgusting than between other persons belonging to different generations—such as indeed occurs today even in the most Philistine countries without exciting great horror; in fact, even old "maids" of over sixty, if they are rich enough, sometimes marry young men of about thirty. However, if we eliminate from the most primitive forms of the family known to us the conceptions of incest that are associated with them— conceptions totally different from our own and often in direct contradiction to them—we arrive at a form of sexual intercourse which can only be described as promiscuous—promiscuous insofar as the restrictions later established by custom did not yet exist. But it by no means necessarily follows from this that a higgledy-piggledy promiscuity was daily practice. Temporary monogamous pairings are by no means excluded; in fact, even in group marriage they now constitute the majority of cases. And if Westermarck, the latest to deny this original state, defines as marriage every case where the two sexes remain mated until the birth of offspring, then it may be said that this kind of marriage could very well occur under the conditions of promiscuous intercourse, without in any way contradicting promiscuity, that is, the absence of barriers to sexual intercourse set up by custom. Westermarck, to be sure, starts out from the viewpoint that

"promiscuity involves a suppression of individual inclinations," so that "prostitution is its most genuine form".[a]

To me it rather seems that all understanding of primitive conditions remains impossible so long as we regard them through brothel spectacles. We shall return to this point again when dealing with group marriage.

According to Morgan, there developed out of this original condition of promiscuous intercourse, probably at a very early stage:

1. The *Consanguine Family,* the first stage of the family. Here the marriage groups are ranged according to generations: all the grandfathers and grandmothers within the limits of the family are all mutual husbands and wives, the same being the case with their children, the fathers and mothers, whose children will again form a third circle of common marriage partners, their children—the great-grandchildren of the first—in turn, forming a fourth circle. Thus, in this form of the family, only ancestors and descendants, parents and children, are excluded from the rights and obligations (as we would say) of marriage with one another. Brothers and sisters, male and female cousins of the first, second and more remote degrees are all mutually brothers and sisters, and *precisely because of this* are all mutually husbands and wives. At this stage the relation of brother and sister includes the exercise of sexual intercourse with one another as a matter of course.* In its typical

* Marx, in a letter written in the spring of 1882,[80] expresses himself in the strongest possible terms about the utter falsification of primeval times appearing in Wagner's *Nibelung* text.[81] "Whoever heard of a brother embracing his sister as his bride?" [b] To these "lewd gods" of Wagner's, who in quite modern style spiced their love affairs with a little incest, Marx gave the answer: "In primeval times the sister *was* the wife, *and that was moral."* [*Note by Engels to the 1884 edition.*]

A French friend and admirer of Wagner does not agree with this note, and points out that already in the *Ögisdrekka,* the *Elder Edda,*[82] which Wagner took as his model, Loki reproaches Freya thus: "Thine own brother has thou embraced before the gods." [c] Marriage between brother and sister, he claimed, was

---

[a] E. Westermarck, *The History of Human Marriage,* pp. 70, 71.— *Ed.*

[b] R. Wagner, *Die Walküre. Erster Tag aus der Trilogie: der Ring des Nibelungen.* Zweiter Aufzug, S. 29.— *Ed.*

[c] Here and below see *Die Edda die ältere und jüngere... Die ältere Edda,* pp. 68-69.— *Ed.*

form, such a family would consist of the descendants of a couple, among whom, again, the descendants of each degree are all brothers and sisters, and, precisely for that reason, all mutual husbands and wives.

The consanguine family has become extinct. Even the crudest peoples known to history furnish no verifiable example of this form of the family. The conclusion that it *must* have existed, however, is forced upon us by the Hawaiian system of consanguinity, still prevalent throughout Polynesia, which expresses degrees of consanguinity such as can arise only under such a form of the family; and we are forced to the same conclusion by the entire further development of the family, which postulates this form as a necessary preliminary stage.

2. The *Punaluan Family.* If the first advance in organisation was the exclusion of parents and children from mutual sexual intercourse, the second was the exclusion of brothers and sisters. In view of the greater similarity in the ages of the participants, this step forward was infinitely more important, but also more difficult, than the first. It was accomplished gradually, commencing most probably[c] with the exclusion of natural brothers and sisters (that is, on the maternal side) from sexual intercourse, at first in isolated cases, then gradually becoming the rule (in Hawaii exceptions to this rule still existed in the present century), and ending with the prohibition of marriage even between collateral brothers and sisters, or, as we would call them, between first, second and third cousins. According to Morgan it

proscribed already at that time. The *Ögisdrekka* is the expression of a time when belief in the ancient myths was completely shattered; it is a truly Lucianian satire on the gods. If Loki, as Mephistopheles, thus reproaches Freya, it argues rather against Wagner. A few verses later, Loki also says to Njordr: "You begat [such] a son by your sister" (*vidh systur thinni gaztu slikan mög*). Now, Njordr is not an Asa but a Vana, and says, in the Ynglinga saga,[83] that marriages between brothers and sisters are customary in Vanaland, which is not the case amongst the Asas.[a] This would seem to indicate that the Vanas were older gods than the Asas. At any rate, Njordr lived among the Asas as their equal, and the *Ögisdrekka* is thus rather proof that intermarriage between brothers and sisters, at least among the gods, did not yet arouse any revulsion at the time the Norwegian Sagas of the gods originated. If one wants to excuse Wagner, one would do better to cite Goethe instead of the *Edda,* for Goethe, in his ballad of God and the Bayadere,[b] makes a similar mistake regarding the religious surrender of women, which he likens far too closely to modern prostitution. [*Addition by Engels in the 1891 edition.*]

---

[a] Snorri Sturluson, *Ynglinga Saga,* 4.— *Ed.*
[b] J. W. Goethe, "Der Gott und die Bajadere".— *Ed.*
[c] The words "most probably" were added in the 1891 edition.— *Ed.*

"affords a good illustration of the operation of the principle of natural selection".[a]

It is beyond question that tribes among whom inbreeding was restricted by this advance were bound to develop more rapidly and fully than those among whom intermarriage between brothers and sisters remained both rule and duty. And how powerfully the effect of this advance was felt is proved by the institution of the *gens,* which arose directly from it and shot far beyond the mark. The gens was the foundation of the social order of most, if not all, the barbarian peoples of the world, and in Greece and Rome we pass directly from it into civilisation.

Every primeval family had to split up after a couple of generations, at the latest. The original communistic common household, which prevailed without exception until the late middle stage of barbarism, determined a certain maximum size of the family community, varying according to circumstances but fairly definite in each locality. As soon as the conception of the impropriety of sexual intercourse between the children of a common mother arose, it was bound to have an effect upon such divisions of old and the foundation of new household communities (which, however, did not necessarily coincide with the family group). One or more groups of sisters became the nucleus of one household, their natural brothers the nucleus of the other. In this or some similar way the form of the family which Morgan calls the punaluan family developed out of the consanguine family. According to the Hawaiian custom, a number of sisters, either natural or collateral (that is, first, second or more distant cousins), were the common wives of their common husbands, from which relation, however, their brothers were excluded. These husbands no longer addressed one another as brothers—which indeed they no longer had to be—but as punalua, that is, intimate companion, *associé,* as it were. In the same way, a group of natural or collateral brothers held in common marriage a number of women, who were *not* their sisters, and these women addressed one another as punalua. This is the classical form of family structure which later admitted of a series of variations, and the essential characteristic feature of which was: mutual community of husbands and wives within a definite family circle, from which, however, the brothers of the wives—first the natural brothers, and later the collateral brothers also—were excluded, the same applying conversely to the sisters of the husbands.

---

[a] L. H. Morgan, *Ancient Society,* p. 425.— *Ed.*

This form of the family now furnishes us with the most complete accuracy the degrees of kinship as expressed in the American system. The children of my mother's sisters still remain her children, the children of my father's brothers being likewise his children, and all of them are my brothers and sisters; but the children of my mother's brothers are now her nephews and nieces, the children of my father's sisters are his nephews and nieces, and they all are my cousins. For while my mother's sisters' husbands still remain her husbands, and my father's brothers' wives likewise still remain his wives—by right, if not always in actual fact—the social proscription of sexual intercourse between brothers and sisters now divided the first cousins, hitherto indiscriminately regarded as brothers and sisters, into two classes: some remain (collateral) brothers and sisters as before; the others, the children of brothers on the one hand and of sisters on the other, *can* no longer be brothers and sisters, can no longer have common parents, whether father, mother, or both, and therefore the class of nephews and nieces, male and female cousins—which would have been senseless in the previous family system—becomes necessary for the first time. The American system of consanguinity, which appears to be utterly absurd in every family form based on some kind of individual marriage, is rationally explained, and naturally justified, down to its minutest details, by the punaluan family. To the extent that this system of consanguinity was prevalent, to exactly the same extent, at least, must the punaluan family, or a form similar to it,[a] have existed.

This form of the family, proved actually to have existed in Hawaii, would probably have been demonstrable throughout Polynesia, had the pious missionaries—like the quondam Spanish monks in America—been able to perceive in these unchristian relations something more than mere "abomination".* When Caesar tells us of the Britons, who at that time were in the middle stage of barbarism, that "by tens and by twelves they possessed their wives in common; and it was mostly brothers with brothers

---

* There can no longer be any doubt that the traces of indiscriminate sexual intercourse, his so-called "*Sumpfzeugung*" which Bachofen believes he has discovered, lead back to group marriage. "If Bachofen regards these punaluan marriages as 'lawless', a man of that period would likewise regard most present-day marriages between near and distant cousins on the father's or the mother's side as incestuous, that is, as marriages between consanguineous brothers and sisters" (Marx).[b]

---

a The words "or a form similar to it" were added in the 1891 edition.— *Ed.*
b "Marx's Excerpts...", op. cit. p. 237. Engels quotes with slight changes.— *Ed.*

and parents with their children",[a] this is best explained as group marriage.[b] Barbarian mothers have not ten or twelve sons old enough to be able to keep wives in common, but the American system of consanguinity, which corresponds to the punaluan family, provides many brothers, since all a man's near and distant cousins are his brothers. The expression "parents with their children" may be a misunderstanding on Caesar's part; this system, however, does not absolutely exclude the presence of father and son, or mother and daughter, in the same marriage group, though it does exclude the presence of father and daughter, or mother and son. In the same way, this or a similar form of group marriage[c] provides the simplest explanation of the reports by Herodotus[d] and other ancient writers concerning community of wives among savage and barbarian peoples. This also applies to the description of the Tikurs of Oudh (north of the Ganges) given by Watson and Kaye in *The People of India* [Vol. II, p. 85]:

"They live together" (that is, sexually) "almost indiscriminately in large communities, and when two people are regarded as married, the tie is but nominal."

In by far the majority of cases the institution of the *gens* seems to have originated directly from the punaluan family. To be sure, the Australian class system[84] also offers a starting-point for it: the Australians have gentes; but they have not yet the punaluan family; they have a cruder form of group marriage.[e]

In all forms of the group family it is uncertain who the father of a child is, but it is certain who the mother is. Although she calls *all* the children of the aggregate family her children and is charged with the duties of a mother towards them, she, nevertheless, knows her natural children from the others. It is thus clear that, wherever group marriage exists, descent is traceable only on the *maternal* side, and thus the *female line* alone is recognised. This, in fact, is the case among all savage peoples and among those belonging to the lower stage of barbarism; and it is Bachofen's second great service to have been the first to discover this. He terms this exclusive recognition of lineage through the mother,

---

[a] Caesar, *Commentarii de bello Gallico*, V, 14.— *Ed.*

[b] The 1884 edition has "punaluan family" instead of "group marriage".— *Ed.*

[c] The 1884 edition has "form of the family" instead of "or a similar form of group marriage".— *Ed.*

[d] Herodotus, *Historiae*, I, 216; IV, 104.— *Ed.*

[e] The 1884 edition has "their organisation, however, is too isolated for us to consider it" instead of "they have a cruder form of group marriage".— *Ed.*

and the inheritance relations that arose out of it in the course of
time, mother right. I retain this term for the sake of brevity. It is,
however, an unhappy choice, for at this stage of society, there is as
yet no such thing as right in the legal sense.

Now if we take from the punaluan family one of the two typical
groups—namely, that consisting of a number of natural and
collateral sisters (i.e., those descendant from natural sisters of the
first, second or more remote degree), together with their children
and their natural or collateral brothers on the mother's side (who
according to our premiss are *not* their husbands), we obtain
exactly that circle of persons who later appear as members of a
gens in the original form of this institution. They all have a
common ancestress, whose female descendants, generation by
generation, are sisters by virtue of descent from her. These sisters'
husbands, however, can no longer be their brothers, i.e., cannot be
descended from this ancestress, and, therefore, do not belong to
the consanguineous group, later the gens; but their children do
belong to this group, since descent on the mother's side alone is
decisive, because it alone is certain. Once the proscription of
sexual intercourse between all brothers and sisters, including even
the most remote collateral relations on the mother's side, becomes
established, the above group is transformed into a gens—i.e.,
constitutes itself as a defined circle of blood relatives in the female
line, who are not allowed to marry one another; from now on it
increasingly consolidates itself through other common institutions
of a social and religious character, and differentiates itself from
the other gentes of the same tribe. We shall deal with this in detail
later. If, however, we find that the gens not only necessarily, but
even obviously, evolved out of the punaluan family, then there is
ground for assuming almost for certain that this form of the
family used to exist among all peoples for whom gentile
institutions can be established—i.e., virtually all barbarian and
civilised peoples.[a]

At the time Morgan wrote his book our knowledge of group
marriage was still very limited. A little was known about the group
marriages current among the Australians, who were organised in
classes, and, in addition, Morgan, as early as 1871, had published
the information that reached him concerning the Hawaiian
punaluan family.[b] On the one hand, the punaluan family provided

---

[a] The text below, up to the paragraph: "3. The *Pairing Family*" (see p. 156), was
added by Engels in the 1891 edition.— *Ed.*

[b] See L. H. Morgan, *Systems of Consanguinity and Affinity of the Human
Family.— Ed.*

a complete explanation of the system of consanguinity prevalent among the American Indians—the system which was the starting-point of all Morgan's investigations; on the other hand, it constituted a ready-made point of departure for the derivation of the mother-right gens; and, finally, it represented a far higher stage of development than the Australian classes. It was, therefore, comprehensible that Morgan should conceive the punaluan family as a stage of development necessarily preceding the pairing family, and assume that it was generally prevalent in earlier times. Since then we have learned of a number of other forms of group marriage and now know that Morgan went too far in this respect. Nevertheless, in his punaluan family, he had the good fortune to come across the highest, the classical form of group marriage, the form from which the transition to a higher stage is most easily explained.

We are indebted to the English missionary Lorimer Fison for the most substantial enrichment of our knowledge of group marriage, for he studied this form of the family for years in its classical home, Australia.[a] He found the lowest stage of develop-ment among the Australian Negroes of Mount Gambier in South Australia. The whole tribe is here divided into two large classes—Kroki and Kumite. Sexual intercourse within each of these classes is strictly proscribed; on the other hand, every man of one class is the born husband of every woman of the other class, and she is his born wife. Not individuals, but entire groups are married to one another, class to class. And let it be noted, no reservations at all are made here concerning difference of age, or special blood relationship, other than those determined by the division into two exogamous classes. A Kroki has every Kumite woman as his legitimate wife; since, however, his own daughter, being the daughter of a Kumite woman, is, according to mother right, also a Kumite, she is thereby the born wife of every Kroki, and thus also her father. At all events, the class organisation, as we know it, imposes no restriction here. Hence, this organisation either arose at a time when, despite all dim impulses to limit inbreeding, sexual intercourse between parents and children was not yet regarded with any particular horror, in which case the class system would have arisen directly out of a condition of promiscuous sexual behaviour. Or intercourse between parents and children *had already been* proscribed by custom when the classes arose, in which case the present position points back to the

---

[a] L. Fison and A. Howitt, *Kamilaroi and Kurnai.*—*Ed.*

consanguine family, and is the first advance beyond it. The latter
is the more probable. Cases of marital contacts between parents
and children have not, as far as I am aware, been reported from
Australia; and the later form of exogamy, the mother-right gens,
also, as a rule, tacitly presupposes the prohibition of such contacts
as something already existing upon its establishment.

Apart from Mount Gambier, in South Australia, the *two*-class
system is likewise to be found along the Darling River, farther
east, and in Queensland, in the North-East, thus being very
widespread. This system excludes only marriage between brothers
and sisters, between the children of brothers and between the
children of sisters on the mother's side, because these belong to
the same class; on the other hand, the children of brother and
sister are permitted to marry. A further step towards the
prevention of inbreeding is to be found among the Kamilaroi,
along the Darling River, in New South Wales, where the two
original classes are split into four, and each of these four classes is
likewise married lock, stock and barrel to a certain other class. The
first two classes are the born spouses of each other; the children
become members of the third or the fourth class, depending on
whether the mother belongs to the first or the second class; and
the children of the third and fourth classes, which are likewise
married to each other, belong again to the first and second classes.
So that one generation always belongs to the first and second
classes, the next belongs to the third and fourth, and the next
again to the first and second. According to this system, the
children of brothers and sisters (on the mother's side) may not
become man and wife—their grandchildren, however, may. This
strangely complicated system is made even more intricate by
the—at any rate, subsequent—superimposition of mother-right
gentes; but we cannot go into this here. We see, then, how the
impulse towards the prevention of inbreeding asserts itself time
and again, but in a groping, spontaneous way, without a clear
consciousness of the purpose.

Group marriage, which in the case of Australia is still class
marriage, the state of marriage of a whole class of men, often
scattered over the whole breadth of the continent, with an equally
widely distributed class of women—this group marriage, when
observed more closely, does not appear quite so horrible as is
fancied by the Philistine in his brothel-tainted imagination. On the
contrary, long years passed before its existence was even suspected, and indeed, it has again been disputed only quite recently.
To the superficial observer it appears to be a kind of loose

monogamy and, in places, polygamy, accompanied by occasional infidelity. One must spend years, as Fison and Howitt did, in order to discover the law that regulates these states of marriage—which in practice rather remind the average European of his own marital customs—the law according to which an Australian Negro, even when a stranger thousands of miles away from his home, among people whose language he does not understand, nevertheless, quite often, in roaming from camp to camp, from tribe to tribe, finds women who guilelessly, without resistance, give themselves to him; and according to which he who has several wives cedes one of them to his guest for the night. Where the European can see only immorality and lawlessness, strict law actually reigns. The women belong to the stranger's marriage class, and are therefore his born wives; the same moral law which assigns one to the other, prohibits, on pain of banishment, all intercourse outside the marriage classes that belong to each other. Even where women are abducted, which is frequently the case, and in some areas the rule, the class law is scrupulously observed.

Incidentally, the abduction of women reveals even here a trace of the transition to monogamy—at least in the form of the pairing marriage: After the young man has abducted, or eloped with, the girl with the assistance of his friends, all of them have sexual intercourse with her one after the other, whereupon, however, she is regarded the wife of the young man who initiated the abduction. And, conversely, should the abducted woman run away from the man and be captured by another, she becomes the latter's wife, and the first man loses his privilege. Thus, exclusive relations, pairing for longer or shorter periods, and also polygamy, establish themselves alongside and within the system of group marriage, which, in general, continues to exist; so that here too group marriage is gradually dying out, the only question being which will disappear first from the scene as a result of European influence—group marriage or the Australian Negroes who indulge in it.

In any case, marriage based on whole classes, such as prevails in Australia, is a very low and primitive form of group marriage; whereas the punaluan family is, as far as we know, its highest stage of development. The former would seem to be the form corresponding to the social status of roving savages, while the latter already presupposes relatively stable settlements of communistic communities and leads directly to the next higher stage of development. Some intermediate stages will assuredly be found between these two; here an only just opened and barely trodden field of investigation lies before us.

3. The *Pairing Family*. A certain pairing for longer or shorter periods took place already under group marriage, or even earlier. Among his numerous wives, the man had a principal wife (one can scarcely yet call her his favourite wife) and he was the principal one of all her husbands. This situation contributed in no small degree to the confusion among missionaries, who saw in group marriage,[a] now promiscuous community of wives, now wanton adultery. Such habitual pairing, however, necessarily became more and more established as the gens developed and as the numbers of classes of "brothers" and "sisters" between which marriage was now impossible increased. The impetus given by the gens to the prevention of marriage between blood relatives drove things still further. Thus we find that among the Iroquois and most other Indian tribes in the lower stage of barbarism marriage is prohibited between *all* relatives recognised by their system, and these are of several hundred kinds. This growing complexity of marriage prohibitions rendered group marriages more and more impossible; they were supplanted by the *pairing family*. At this stage one man lives with one woman, yet in such a manner that polygamy and occasional infidelity remain men's prerogative, even though the former is seldom practised for economic reasons; at the same time, the strictest fidelity is usually demanded of the woman during the period of cohabitation, adultery on her part being cruelly punished. The marriage bond can, however, be easily dissolved by either side, and the children still belong solely to the mother.

Even in this ever widening exclusion of blood relatives from marriage bonds, natural selection continues to have its effect. In Morgan's words,

"marriage between non-consanguineous gentes tended to create a more vigorous stock physically and mentally. ... When two advancing tribes ... are blended into one people the new skull and brain would ... widen and lengthen to the sum of the capabilities of both".[b]

Tribes constituted according to gentes were bound, therefore, to gain the upper hand over the more backward ones, or carry them along by force of their example.

---

[a] The 1884 edition has "the punaluan family" instead of "group marriage".— *Ed.*

[b] This is a rendering of the passage from L. H. Morgan's *Ancient Society,* p. 459. See also "Marx's Excerpts...", op. cit., p. 118.— *Ed.*

Thus, the evolution of the family in prehistoric times consisted in the continual narrowing of the circle—originally embracing the whole tribe—within which marital community between the two sexes prevailed. By the successive exclusion, first of closer, then of ever more remote relatives, and finally even of those merely related by marriage, every kind of group marriage was ultimately rendered practically impossible; and in the end there remained only the couple, for the moment still loosely united, the molecule, with the dissolution of which marriage itself ceases completely. This fact alone shows how little individual sex love, in the modern sense of the word, had to do with the origin of monogamy. The practice of all peoples in this stage affords still further proof of this. Whereas under previous forms of the family men were never in want of women but, on the contrary, had a surfeit of them, women now became scarce and were sought after. Consequently, with pairing marriage there begins the abduction and purchase of women—widespread *symptoms,* but nothing more, of a much more deeply rooted change that had set in. These symptoms, mere methods of obtaining women, McLennan, the pedantic Scot, nevertheless metamorphosed into special classes of families which he called "marriage by abduction" and "marriage by purchase".[a] Moreover, among the American Indians, and elsewhere (at the same stage), the arrangement of a marriage is not the affair of the two parties to the same, who are often not even consulted at all, but of their respective mothers. Two complete strangers are thus often betrothed and only learn of the conclusion of the deal when the marriage day approaches. Prior to the marriage, presents are given by the bridegroom to the gentile relatives of the bride (that is, to her relatives on her mother's side, not to the father and his relatives), these presents serving as purchase gifts for the ceded girl. The marriage may, as before, be dissolved at the discretion of either of the two spouses. Nevertheless, among many tribes, for example, the Iroquois, public sentiment gradually developed against such separations. When conflicts arise, the gentile relatives of both parties intervene and attempt a reconciliation, and separation takes place only if this proves fruitless, the children remaining with the mother and each party being free to marry again.

The pairing family, itself too weak and unstable to make an independent household necessary, or even desirable, did not by any means dissolve the communistic household inherited from

---

[a] J. F. McLennan, *Primitive Marriage,* particularly Ch. I and II.— *Ed.*

earlier times. But the communistic household implies the supremacy of women in the house, just as the exclusive recognition of a natural mother, because of the impossibility of determining the natural father with certainty, signifies high esteem for the women, i.e. for the mothers. That woman was the slave of man at the commencement of society is one of the most absurd notions that have come down to us from the Enlightenment of the eighteenth century. Woman occupied not only a free but also a highly respected position among all savages and all barbarians of the lower and middle stages and partly even of the upper stage. Let Arthur [a] Wright,[85] missionary for many years among the Seneca Iroquois, testify what her place still was in the pairing marriage:

"As to their family system, when occupying the old long houses"

(communistic households embracing several families)

"it is probable that some one clan" (gens) "predominated, the women taking in husbands ... from other clans" (gentes). "...Usually, the female portion ruled the house...; the stores were in common; but woe to the luckless husband or lover who was too shiftless to do his share of the providing. No matter how many children, or whatever goods he might have in the house, he might at any time be ordered to pick up his blanket and budge; and after such orders it would not be healthful for him to attempt to disobey. The house would be too hot for him; and ... he had to retreat to his own clan" (gens); "or, as was often done, go and start a new matrimonial alliance in some other. The women were the great power among the clans" (gentes), "as everywhere else. They did not hesitate, when occasion required, ... to knock off the horns, as it was technically called, from the head of the chief and send him back to the ranks of the warriors." [b]

The communistic household, in which most or even all of the women belong to one and the same gens, while the men come from various other gentes, is the material foundation of that predominancy of women which universally obtained in primitive times; and Bachofen's discovery of this constitutes his third great service.—I may add, furthermore, that the reports of travellers and missionaries about women among savages and barbarians being burdened with excessive toil in no way conflict with what has been said above. The division of labour between the two sexes is determined by causes entirely different from those that determine the status of women in society. Peoples whose women have to work much harder than we would consider proper often have far more real respect for women than our Europeans have for theirs. The social status of the lady of civilisation, surrounded by sham homage and estranged from all real work, is infinitely lower than

---

[a] Should be: Asher.— *Ed.*

[b] Quoted from L. H. Morgan's *Ancient Society,* p. 455. See also "Marx's Excerpts...", op. cit., p. 116.— *Ed.*

that of the hard-working woman of barbarism, who was regarded among her people as a real lady (LADY, *frowa, Frau*=mistress) and was such by the nature of her position.

Whether or not the pairing marriage has totally supplanted group marriage[a] in America today must be determined by closer investigation among the North-Western, and particularly among the South American, peoples, who are still in the higher stage of savagery. So very many instances of sexual freedom are reported with regard to the latter that the complete suppression of the old group marriage can scarcely be assumed.[b] At any rate, not all traces of it have as yet disappeared. Among at least forty North American tribes, the man who marries an eldest sister is entitled to all her sisters as wives as soon as they reach the requisite age—a survival of the community of husbands for the whole group of sisters. And Bancroft relates that the inhabitants of the Californian peninsula (in the upper stage of savagery) have certain festivities during which several "tribes" congregate for the purpose of indiscriminate sexual intercourse.[c] These are manifestly gentes for whom these festivities represent dim memories of the times when the women of one gens had all the men of another as their common husbands, and vice versa.[d] The same custom still prevails in Australia. Among a few peoples it happens that the older men, the chiefs and sorcerer-priests, exploit the community of wives for their own ends and monopolise most of the women for themselves; but they, in their turn, have to allow the old common possession to be restored during certain feasts and great public gatherings and permit their wives to enjoy themselves with the young men. Westermarck (pp. 28 and 29) adduces a whole series of examples of such periodical Saturnalian feasts[86] during which the old free sexual intercourse comes into force again for a short period, as, for example, among the Hos, the Santals, the Panjas

---

[a] The 1884 edition has "punaluan family" instead of "group marriage".— *Ed.*

[b] This sentence was added by Engels in the 1891 edition.— *Ed.*

[c] H. Bancroft, *The Native Races of the Pacific States of North America,* pp. 352-53.— *Ed.*

[d] The text below, up to the words "The pairing family arose on the borderline between savagery and barbarism" (see p. 162), was added by Engels in the 1891 edition. In the 1884 edition this paragraph ended with the following text, partly used in the 1891 edition and partly omitted: "Similar remnants from the world of antiquity are familiar enough, such as the surrender of Phoenician girls in the temple at the festivals of the Astarte: even the medieval right of the first night, which was very well established despite neoromantic German whitewashing, was presumably a piece of the punaluan family passed on by the Celtic gens (clan)."— *Ed.*

and Kotars of India, among some African peoples, etc. Curiously enough, Westermarck concludes from this that they are relics, not of group marriage, which he rejects, but—of the rutting season common alike to primitive man and the other animals.

We now come to Bachofen's fourth great discovery, that of the widespread transitionary form between group marriage and pairing. What Bachofen construes as a penance for infringing the ancient commandments of the gods, the penance with which the woman buys her right to chastity, is in fact nothing more than a mystical expression for the penance by means of which the woman purchases her redemption from the ancient community of husbands and acquires the right to give herself to one man only. This penance takes the form of limited surrender: the Babylonian women had to surrender themselves once a year in the Temple of Mylitta. Other Middle Eastern peoples sent their girls for years to the Temple of Anaitis, where they had to practise free love with favourites of their own choice before they were allowed to marry. Similar customs bearing a religious guise are common to nearly all Asiatic peoples between the Mediterranean and the Ganges. The expiatory sacrifice for the purpose of redemption becomes ever lighter in the course of time, as Bachofen notes:

"The annually repeated offering yields place to the single performance; the hetaerism of the matrons is succeeded by that of the maidens, its practice during marriage by practice before marriage, the indiscriminate surrender to all by surrender to certain persons" (*Mutterrecht*, p. XIX).

Among other peoples, the religious guise is absent; among some—the Thracians, Celts, etc., of antiquity, and many aboriginal inhabitants of India, the Malay peoples, South Sea Islanders and many American Indians even to this day—the girls enjoy the greatest sexual freedom until their marriage. Particularly is this the case throughout almost the whole of South America, as anybody who has penetrated a little into the interior can testify. Thus, Agassiz (*A Journey in Brazil,* Boston and New York, 1868, p. 266) relates the following about a rich family of Indian descent. When he was introduced to the daughter and enquired after her father, who, he supposed, as the mother's husband, an officer on active service in the war against Paraguay, the mother answered smilingly: "*naõ tem pai, é filha da fortuna*"—she has no father, she is the daughter of chance.

"It is the way the Indian or half-breed women here always speak of their illegitimate children, unconscious of any wrong or shame. So far is this from being an unusual case that the opposite seems the exception. Children [often] know [only] about their mother, for all the care and responsibility falls upon her; but they have no knowledge of their father, nor does it seem to occur to the woman that she or her children have any claim upon him."[a]

What appears so strange to the civilised man here is simply the rule according to mother right and in group marriage.

Among still other peoples, the bridegroom's friends and relatives, or the wedding guests, exercise their old traditional right to the bride at the wedding itself, and the bridegroom has his turn last of all; for instance, on the Balearic Islands and among the African Augilas of antiquity, and among the Bareas of Abyssinia even now. In the case of still other peoples, again, an official person—the chief of the tribe or of the gens, the cacique, shaman, priest, prince or whatever his title—represents the community and exercises the right of the first night with the bride. Despite all neoromantic whitewashing, this *jus primae noctis*[b] persists to this day as a relic of group marriage among most of the natives of the Alaska territory (Bancroft, *Native Races,* I, p. 81), among the Tahus in North Mexico (ibid., p. 584) and among other peoples; and it existed throughout the Middle Ages at least in the originally Celtic countries, where it was directly transmitted from group marriage; for instance, in Aragon. While the peasant in Castile was never a serf, in Aragon the most ignominious serfdom prevailed until abolished by the decree issued by Ferdinand the Catholic in 1486.[87] This public act states:

"We pass judgment and declare that the aforementioned lords" (*señores,* barons) "... also shall not sleep the first night with the woman taken in wedlock by a peasant, nor on the wedding night, after she has gone to bed, stride over it and over the woman as a sign of their authority; not shall the aforementioned lords avail themselves of the services of the sons or daughters of the peasant, with or without payment, against their will." (Quoted in the Catalonian original by Sugenheim, *Leibeigenschaft,* Petersburg, 1861, p. 35.[c])

Bachofen is again absolutely right when he contends throughout that the transition from what he terms "hetaerism" or "*Sumpfzeugung*" to monogamy was brought about essentially by the women. The more the old traditional sexual relations lost their naïve, primeval character, as a result of the development of the economic conditions of life, that is, with the undermining of the old communism and the growing density of the population, the more degrading and oppressive they must have appeared to the

---

[a] Op. cit., pp. 266-67.— *Ed.*
[b] Right of the first night.— *Ed.*
[c] S. Sugenheim, *Geschichte der Aufhebung der Leibeigenschaft und Hörigkeit in Europa bis um die Mitte des Neunzehnten Jahrhunderts.— Ed.*

women; the more fervently they must have longed for the right to chastity, to temporary or permanent marriage with one man only, as a deliverance. This advance could not have originated from the men, if only for the reason that they have never—not even to the present day—dreamed of renouncing the pleasures of actual group marriage. Only after the transition to pairing marriage had been effected by the women could the men introduce strict monogamy—for the women only, of course.

The pairing family arose on the borderline between savagery and barbarism, mostly at the upper stage of savagery already, and here and there only at the lower stage of barbarism. It is the form of the family characteristic of barbarism, in the same way as group marriage is characteristic of savagery and monogamy of civilisation. For its further development to stable monogamy, causes different from those we have hitherto found operating were required. In the pairing family, the group was already reduced to its last unit, its diatomic molecule—to one man and one woman. Natural selection had completed its work by constantly extending the circle excluded from the community of marriage; there was nothing more left for it to do in this direction. If no new, *social* driving forces had come into operation, there would have been no reason why a new form of the family should arise out of the pairing family. But these driving forces did begin to operate.

We now leave America, the classical soil of the pairing family. There is no evidence enabling us to conclude that a higher form of the family developed there, or that strict monogamy existed in any part of it at any time before its discovery and conquest. It was otherwise in the Old World.

Here the domestication of animals and the breeding of herds had developed a hitherto unsuspected source of wealth and created entirely new social relations. Until the lower stage of barbarism, fixed wealth consisted almost entirely of the house, clothing, crude ornaments and the implements for procuring and preparing food: boats, weapons and household utensils of the simplest kind. Food had to be won anew day by day. Now, with herds of horses, camels, donkeys, oxen, sheep, goats and pigs, the advancing pastoral peoples—the Aryans in the Indian land of the five rivers and the Ganges area, as well as in the then much more richly watered steppes of the Oxus and the Jaxartes, and the Semites on the Euphrates and the Tigris—acquired possessions demanding merely supervision and most elementary care in order to propagate in ever-increasing numbers and to yield the richest nutriment in milk and meat. All previous means of procuring food now sank into the background. Hunting, once a necessity, now became a luxury.

But to whom did this new wealth belong? Originally, doubtless, to the gens. But private ownership of herds must have developed at a very early stage. It is hard to say whether Father Abraham appeared to the author of what is known as the First Book of Moses as the owner of his herds and flocks in his own right as head of a family community or by virtue of his status as actual hereditary chief of a gens.[a] One thing, however, is certain, and that is that we must not regard him as a property owner in the modern sense of the term. Equally certain is that on the threshold of authenticated history we find everywhere the herds as already the separate property[b] of the family chiefs, in exactly the same way as were the artistic products of barbarism, metal utensils, articles of luxury and, finally, human cattle—the slaves.

For now slavery too had been invented. The slave was of no value to the barbarian of the lower stage. It was for this reason that the American Indians treated their vanquished foes quite differently from the way they were treated in the upper stage. The men were either killed or adopted as brothers by the tribe of the victors. The women were either taken in marriage or likewise just adopted along with their surviving children. Human labour power at this stage yielded no noticeable surplus as yet over the cost of its maintenance. With the introduction of cattle breeding, of metalworking, of weaving and, finally, of field cultivation, this changed. Just as the once so easily obtainable wives had now acquired an exchange value[c] and were bought, so it happened with labour power, especially after the herds had finally been converted into family[d] possessions. The family did not multiply as rapidly as the cattle. More people were required to mind them; the captives taken in war were useful for just this purpose, and, furthermore, they could be bred like the cattle themselves.

Such riches, once they had passed into the private possession of families[e] and there rapidly multiplied, struck a powerful blow at a society founded on pairing marriage and mother-right gens. Pairing marriage had introduced a new element into the family. By the side of the natural mother it had placed the attested

---

[a] Genesis 12:16, 13:2.— *Ed.*
[b] The 1884 edition has "private property" instead of "separate property".— *Ed.*
[c] The 1884 edition has "numerous wives had now acquired value" instead of "easily obtainable wives had now acquired an exchange value".— *Ed.*
[d] The 1884 edition has "private" instead of "family" here.— *Ed.*
[e] The words "of families" are added in the 1891 edition.— *Ed.*

natural father—who was probably better attested than many a
"father" of the present day. According to the division of labour
then prevailing in the family, the procurement of food and the
means of labour necessary thereto, and therefore, also, the
ownership of the latter, fell to the man; he took them with him in
case of separation, just as the woman retained the household
goods. Thus, according to the custom of society at that time, the
man was also the owner of the new sources of food—the
cattle—and later, of the new means of labour—the slaves.
According to the custom of the same society, however, his children
could not inherit from him, for the position in this respect was as
follows.

According to mother right, that is, as long as descent was
counted solely through the female line, and according to the
original custom of inheritance in the gens, it was the gentile
relatives that at first inherited from a deceased member of the
gens. The property had to remain within the gens. In view of the
insignificance of the objects in question, it may, from time
immemorial, have passed in practice to the nearest gentile
relatives—that is, to the blood relatives on the mother's side. The
children of the deceased man, however, belonged not to his gens,
but to that of their mother. In the beginning, they inherited from
their mother, along with the rest of their mother's blood relatives,
and later, perhaps, had first claim upon her property; but they
could not inherit from their father, because they did not belong
to his gens, and his property had to remain in the latter. On the
death of the herd owner, therefore, his herds passed, first of all,
to his brothers and sisters and to his sisters' children or to the
descendants of his mother's sisters. His own children, however,
were disinherited.

Thus, as wealth increased, it, on the one hand, gave the man a
more important status in the family than the woman, and, on the
other hand, created a stimulus to utilise this strengthened position
in order to overthrow the traditional order of inheritance in
favour of the children. But this was impossible as long as descent
according to mother right prevailed. This had, therefore, to be
overthrown, and it was overthrown. It was not so difficult to do
this as appears to us now. For this revolution—one of the most
far-reaching ever experienced by mankind—did not have to affect
one single living member of a gens. All the members could remain
what they had been previously. The simple decision sufficed that
in future the descendants of the male members should remain in
the gens, but that those of the females were to be excluded from

the gens by being transferred to that of their father. The reckoning of descent through the female line and the right of inheritance through the mother were thus overthrown and male lineage and right of inheritance from the father instituted. We know nothing as to how and when this revolution was effected among the civilised peoples. It falls entirely within prehistoric times. That it was actually *effected* is more than sufficiently proved by the abundant traces of mother right which have been collected, especially by Bachofen. How easily it is accomplished can be seen from a whole number of Indian tribes, among whom it has only recently taken place and is still proceeding, partly under the influence of increasing wealth and changed mode of life (relocation from the forests to the prairies), and partly under the moral influence of civilisation and the missionaries. Of eight Missouri tribes, six have male, and two still retain the female, lineage and inheritance line. Among the Shawnees, Miamis and Delawares it has become the custom to transfer the children to the father's gens by giving them one of the gentile names obtaining therein, in order that they may inherit from him. "Innate casuistry of man to change things by changing names! And to find loopholes for breaking through tradition within tradition itself, wherever actual interest provided a powerful motive!" (Marx.)[a] As a consequence, hopeless confusion arose; and matters could only be straightened out, and partly were straightened out, by the transition to father right. "This appears altogether to be the most natural transition." (Marx.)—As for what the experts on comparative method have to tell us regarding the ways and means by which this transition was effected among the civilised peoples of the Old World—almost only hypotheses, of course—see M. Kovalevsky, *Tableau des origines et de l'évolution de la famille et de la propriété*, Stockholm, 1890.[b]

The overthrow of mother right was the *world-historic defeat of the female sex*. The man seized the reins in the house too, the woman was degraded, enthralled, became the slave of the man's lust, a mere instrument for breeding children. This humiliated position of women, especially manifest among the Greeks of the Heroic and still more of the Classical Age, has become gradually embellished and dissembled and, in part, clothed in a milder form, but by no means abolished.

The first effect of the sole rule of the men that was now

---

[a] "Marx's Excerpts...", op. cit., p. 181.— *Ed.*
[b] This sentence was added by Engels in the 1891 edition.— *Ed.*

established is shown in the intermediate form of the family which now emerges, the patriarchal family. Its chief attribute is not polygamy—of which more anon—but

"the organisation of a number of persons, bond and free, into a family, under paternal power of the head of the family. In the Semitic form, this family chief lives in polygamy, the bondsman has a wife and children, and the purpose of the whole organisation is the care of flocks and herds over a limited area".[a]

The essential features are the incorporation of bondsmen and paternal power; the Roman family, accordingly, constitutes the perfected type of this form of the family. The word *familia* did not originally signify the ideal of our modern philistine, which is a compound of sentimentality and domestic discord. Among the Romans, in the beginning, it did not even refer to the married couple and their children, but to the slaves alone. *Famulus* means a household slave and *familia* signifies the totality of slaves belonging to one individual. Even in the time of Gaius the *familia, id est patrimonium* (i.e., the inheritance) was bequeathed by will. The expression was invented by the Romans to describe a new social organism, the head of which had under him wife and children and a number of slaves, under Roman paternal power, with power of life and death over them all.

"The term, therefore, is no older than the ironclad family system of the Latin tribes, which came in after field agriculture and after legalised servitude, as well as after the separation of the Greeks and (Aryan) Latins."[b]

To which Marx adds: "The modern family contains in embryo not only slavery (*servitus*) but serfdom also, since from the very beginning it is connected with agricultural services. It contains within itself in *miniature* all the antagonisms which later develop on a wide scale within society and its state."[c]

Such a form of the family shows the transition of the pairing marriage to monogamy. In order to guarantee the fidelity of the wife, that is, the paternity of the children, the woman is placed in the man's absolute power; if he kills her, he is but exercising his right.[d]

With the patriarchal family we enter the field of written history and, therewith, a field in which the science of comparative law can

---

[a] In the 1884 edition the quotation marks are missing. This passage is a summary of the text on pp. 465-66 of L. H. Morgan's *Ancient Society*. See also "Marx's Excerpts...", op. cit., pp. 118-19.—*Ed.*

[b] L. H. Morgan, op. cit., p. 470. Quoted with slight changes.—*Ed.*

[c] "Marx's Excerpts...", op. cit., p. 120.—*Ed.*

[d] The text below, up to the words "A few words more about polygamy" (see p. 169), was added by Engels in the 1891 edition.—*Ed.*

render us major assistance. And in fact it has brought us considerable progress here. We are indebted to Maxim Kovalevsky (*Tableau etc. de la famille et de la propriété*, Stockholm, 1890, pp. 60-100) for the proof that the patriarchal household community, such as we still find today among the Serbs and the Bulgars under the designations of *Zádruga* (meaning something like fraternity) or *Bratstvo* (brotherhood), and among the Oriental peoples in a modified form, constituted the transition stage between the mother-right family which evolved out of group marriage and the individual family of the modern world. This appears to be proved at least as far as the civilised peoples of the Old World, the Aryans and Semites, are concerned.

The South Slavic *Zádruga* provides the best still surviving example of such a family community. It embraces several generations of the descendants of one father and their wives, who all live together on one farm, till their fields in common, feed and clothe themselves from the common stocks and communally own all surplus yield. The community is under the supreme management of the master of the house (*domačin*), who represents it in external affairs, may dispose of smaller objects, and manages the finances, being responsible for the latter as well as for the regular conduct of business. He is elected and does not by any means need to be the eldest. The women and their work are under the direction of the mistress of the house (*domačica*), who is usually the *domačin*'s wife. In the choice of husbands for the girls she has an important, often the decisive voice. Supreme power, however, is vested in the Family Council, the assembly of all adult members, women as well as men. The master of the house reports back to this assembly; it makes all the important decisions, administers justice among the members, decides on purchases and sales of any importance, especially of landed property, etc.

It was only about ten years ago that the existence of such large family communities also in Russia was proved[a]; they are now generally recognised as being just as firmly rooted in the popular customs of the Russians as the *obščina*, or village community. They figure in the most ancient Russian law code—the *Pravda* of Yaroslav[88]—under the same name (*verv*) as in the Dalmatian Laws,[89] and references to them may be found also in Polish and Czech historical sources.

According to Heusler (*Institutionen des deutschen Rechts*[b]), the

[a] See М. Ковалевскій, *Первобытное право*, Вып. I Родъ, стр. 32-38.—*Ed.*

[b] A. Heusler, *Institutionen des Deutschen Privatrechts*, Vol. II, p. 271.—*Ed.*

economic unit among the Germans as well was not originally the individual family in the modern sense, but the "household community", consisting of several generations, or individual families, and often enough including bondsmen besides. The Roman family, too, has been traced back to this type, and in consequence the absolute power of the head of the house, as also the lack of rights of the remaining members of the family in relation to him, has recently been strongly questioned. Similar family communities are likewise supposed to have existed among the Celts in Ireland; in France they continued to exist in Nivernais under the name of *parçonneries* right up to the French Revolution, while in Franche-Comté they are not quite extinct even today. In the district of Louhans (Saône et Loire) there may be seen large peasant houses with a lofty communal central hall reaching up to the roof, surrounded by sleeping rooms to which access is had by staircases of six to eight·steps, and in which dwell several generations of the same family.[90]

In India, the household community with common tillage of the soil was already mentioned by Nearchus,[a] at the time of Alexander the Great, and exists to this day in the same area, in the Punjab and the entire North-Western part of the country. Kovalevsky himself was able to testify to its existence in the Caucasus. It still exists in Algeria among the Kabyles. It is said to have occurred even in America; attempts are being made to find it in the *calpullis* in ancient Mexico,[91] described by Zurita[b]; Cunow, on the other hand, has proved fairly clearly (in *Ausland*, Nos 42-44, 1890),[c] that a kind of Mark constitution existed in Peru (where, peculiarly enough, the Mark was called *marca*) at the time of the Conquest, with periodical allotment of the cultivated land, that is, individual tillage.

At any rate, the patriarchal household community with common land ownership and common tillage now assumes quite another significance than hitherto. We can no longer doubt the important transitional role which it played among the civilised and many other peoples of the Old World between the mother-right family and the monogamian family. We shall return later on to the further conclusion drawn by Kovalevsky, namely, that it was likewise the transition stage out of which developed the village,

---

a [Strabo] *Strabonis rerum geographicarum libri XVII*, XV, 1.—*Ed.*
b A. de Zurita, *Rapport sur les différentes classes de chefs de la Nouvelle-Espagne...* in *Voyages, relations et mémoires*, pp. 50-64.—*Ed.*
c H. Cunow, "Die altperuanischen Dorf- und Markgenossenschaften", *Das Ausland*, Nos 42-44, October 20, 27 and November 3, 1890.—*Ed.*

or Mark, community with individual cultivation and at first periodical, then definitive, allotment of arable and pasture lands.

As regards family life within these household communities, it should be noted that in Russia, at least, the head of the house is reputed to be strongly abusing his position as far as the younger women of the community, particularly his daughters-in-law, are concerned, and to be very often making a harem of them for himself; this is rather eloquently reflected in the Russian folk songs.[a]

A few words more about polygamy and polyandry before we deal with monogamy, which developed rapidly following the overthrow of mother right. Both these marriage forms can only be exceptions, historical luxury products, so to speak, unless they appeared side by side in one country, which, it will be recalled, is not the case. As, therefore, the men, excluded from polygamy, could not console themselves with the women left over from polyandry, the numerical strength of men and women without regard to social institutions having been fairly equal hitherto, it is evident that neither the one nor the other form of marriage could rise to general prevalence. Actually, polygamy on the part of a man was clearly a product of slavery and limited to a few exceptional positions. In the Semitic patriarchal family, only the patriarch himself and, at most, a couple of his sons lived in polygamy; the others had to be content with one wife each. It remains the same today throughout the entire Orient. Polygamy is a privilege of the rich and of the nobility, the wives being re-cruited chiefly by the purchase of female slaves; the mass of the people live in monogamy. Just such an exception is provided by polyandry in India and Tibet, the certainly not uninteresting origin of which from group marriage[b] requires closer investigation. In its practice, at any rate, it appears to be much more generous than the jealous harem system of the Mohammedans. At least, among the Nairs in India, the men, in groups of three, four or more, have, to be sure, one wife in common; but each of them can simultaneously have a second wife in common with three or more other men, and, in the same way, a third wife, a fourth and so on. It is a wonder that McLennan did not discover a new class—that of *club marriage*—in these marriage clubs, of which one could belong to several at a time, and which he himself described. This marriage club system, however, is by no means real polyandry; on

---

[a] M. Kovalevsky, op. cit., pp. 56-59.— *Ed.*

[b] The 1884 edition has "punaluan family" instead of "group marriage".— *Ed.*

the contrary, as has been noted by Giraud-Teulon, it is a specialised form of group marriage, the men living in polygamy, the women in polyandry.[a]

4. The *Monogamian Family*. As already indicated, this arises out of the pairing family in the transition period from the middle to the upper stage of barbarism, its final victory being one of the signs of fledgling civilisation. It is based on the supremacy of the man; its express aim is the procreation of children of undisputed paternity, this paternity being required in order that these children may in due time inherit their father's wealth as his natural heirs. The monogamian family differs from pairing marriage in the far greater rigidity of the marriage bond, which can now no longer be dissolved at the pleasure of either party. Now, as a rule, only the man can dissolve it and disown his wife. The right of conjugal infidelity remains his even now, sanctioned, at least, by custom (the *Code Napoléon* expressly concedes this right to the husband as long as he does not bring his concubine into the conjugal home [b]), and is exercised more and more with the growing development of society. Should the wife recall the ancient sexual practice and desire to revive it, she is punished more severely than ever before.

We are confronted with this new form of the family in all its severity among the Greeks. While, as Marx observes,[c] the position of the goddesses in mythology represents an earlier period, when women still occupied a freer and more respected place, in the Heroic Age we already find women degraded owing to the predominance of the man and the competition of female slaves.[d] One may read in the *Odyssey* how Telemachus cuts his mother short and enjoins silence upon her.[e] In Homer the young female captives become enslaved to the sensual lust of the victors; the military chiefs, one after the other, according to rank, choose the most beautiful ones for themselves. The whole of the *Iliad,* as we know, revolves around the quarrel between Achilles and Agamemnon over such a female slave. In connection with each Homeric

---

[a] The last sentence was added by Engels in the 1891 edition.— *Ed.*

[b] *Code Napoléon,* Art. 230.— *Ed.*

[c] "Marx's Excerpts...", op. cit., p. 121.— *Ed.*

[d] In the 1884 edition the end of this sentence reads: "find women in an isolation bordering on imprisonment to ensure their children proper paternity". The text below, up to the words "the Greek women found opportunities often enough for deceiving their husbands" (see p. 173), was almost entirely added by Engels in the 1891 edition, only a few sentences being used from the 1884 edition.— *Ed.*

[e] Homer, *Odyssey,* Canto I.— *Ed.*

hero of importance mention is made of a captive maiden with whom he shares tent and bed. These maidens are taken back home and into the conjugal house, as was Cassandra by Agamemnon in Aeschylus.[a] Sons born of these slaves receive a small share of their father's estate and are regarded as freemen. Teucer was such an illegitimate son of Telamon and was permitted to adopt his father's name. The wedded wife is expected to tolerate all this, but to maintain strict chastity and conjugal fidelity herself. True, in the Heroic Age the Greek wife is more respected than in the period of civilisation; for the husband, however, she is, in reality, merely the mother of his legitimate heirs, his chief housekeeper, and the superintendent of the female slaves, whom he may make, and does make, his concubines at will. It is the existence of slavery side by side with monogamy, the existence of beautiful young female slaves who belong to the *man* with all they have, that from the very beginning stamped on monogamy its specific character as monogamy *only for the woman*, but not for the man. And it retains this character to this day.

As regards the Greeks of later times, we must differentiate between the Dorians and the Ionians. The former, of whom Sparta was the classical example, have in many respects more ancient marriage relationships than even Homer indicates. In Sparta we find a form of pairing marriage—modified by the state in accordance with the conceptions there prevailing—which still displays many vestiges of group marriage. Childless marriages are dissolved: King Anaxandridas (about 560 B.C.) took another wife in addition to his first, childless one, and maintained two households; King Aristones of the same period added a third wife to two who were barren, one of whom he, however, let go. On the other hand, several brothers could have a wife in common. A person having a preference for his friend's wife could share her with him; and it was regarded as proper to place one's wife at the disposal of a strapping "stallion", as Bismarck would say, even when this person was not a citizen. A passage in Plutarch, where a Spartan woman refers a lover who is pursuing her with his attentions to her husband, would indicate, according to Schoemann, still greater freedom of manners.[b] Real adultery, the infidelity of the wife behind the back of her husband, was thus unheard of. On the other hand, domestic slavery was unknown in

---

[a] Aeschylus, *Oresteia: Agamemnon.*— *Ed.*

[b] G. F. Schoemann, *Griechische Alterthümer,* Vol. 1, p. 268. See also Plutarch, *Short Sayings of Spartan Women,* V.— *Ed.*

Sparta, at least in its heyday; the serf Helots lived separately on the estates and thus there was less temptation for the Spartiates[92] to pursue their women. That in all these circumstances the women of Sparta enjoyed a very much more respected position than all other Greek women was quite natural. The Spartan women and the *élite* of the Athenian *hetaerae* are the only Greek women of whom thê ancients speak with respect, and whose remarks they consider as being worthy of record.

Among the Ionians—of whom Athens is characteristic—things were quite different. Girls learned only spinning, weaving and sewing, at best a little reading and writing. They were practically kept in seclusion and consorted only with other women. The women's quarter was a separate part of the house, on the upper floor, or in the rear of the building, not easily accessible to men, particularly strangers; to this the women retired when male visitors came. The women did not go out unless accompanied by a female slave; at home they were positively kept under guard; Aristophanes speaks of Molossian hounds kept to frighten off adulterers, while in Asiatic towns, at least, eunuchs were maintained to keep guard over the women; they were manufactured for the trade in Chios as early as Herodotus' day, and according to Wachsmuth, not merely for the barbarians. In Euripides, the wife is described as *oikurema*,[a] a thing for housekeeping (the word is a neuter), and apart from the business of bearing children, she was nothing more to the Athenian than the chief housemaid. The husband had his gymnastic exercises, his public affairs, from which the wife was excluded; in addition, he often had female slaves at his disposal and, in the heyday of Athens, extensive prostitution, which was viewed with favour by the state, to say the least. It was precisely on the basis of this prostitution that the sole outstanding characters of Greek women developed, who by their *esprit* and artistic taste towered as much above the general level of ancient womanhood as the Spartan women did by virtue of their character. That one had first to become a *hetaera* in order to become a woman is the strongest indictment of the Athenian family.

In the course of time, this Athenian family became the model upon which not only the rest of the Ionians, but also all the Greeks of the mainland and of the colonies increasingly moulded

---

[a] W. Wachsmuth, *Hellenische Alterthumskunde aus dem Gesichtspunkte des Staates,* Part II, Section II, p. 77. See also Aristophanes, *Thesmophoriazusae*; Herodotus, *Historiae*, VIII, 105; Euripides, *Orestes.— Ed.*

their domestic relations. But despite all the seclusion and surveillance the Greek women found opportunities often enough for deceiving their husbands. The latter, who would have been ashamed to evince any love for their own wives, amused themselves with *hetaerae* in all kinds of amours. But the degradation of the women recoiled on the men and degraded them too, until they sank into the perversion of boy-love, degrading both themselves and their gods by the myth of Ganymede.

This was the origin of monogamy, as far as we can trace it among the most civilised and highly developed people of antiquity. It was not in any way the fruit of individual sex love, with which it had absolutely nothing to do, for the marriages remained marriages of convenience, as before. It was the first form of the family based not on natural but on economic conditions,[a] namely, on the victory of private property over original, naturally developed, common ownership. The rule of the man in the family, the procreation of children who could only be his, destined to be the heirs of his wealth—these alone were frankly avowed by the Greeks as the exclusive aims of monogamy. For the rest, it was a burden, a duty to the gods, to the state and to their own ancestors, which just had to be fulfilled. In Athens the law made not only marriage compulsory, but also the fulfilment by the man of a minimum of so-called conjugal duties.[b]

Thus, monogamy does not by any means make its appearance in history as the reconciliation of man and woman, still less as the highest form of such a reconciliation. On the contrary, it appears as the subjection of one sex by the other, as the proclamation of a conflict between the sexes hitherto unknown throughout preceding history. In an old unpublished manuscript, the work of Marx and myself in 1846, I find the following: "The first division of labour is that between man and woman for child breeding."[c] And today I can add: The first class antithesis which appears in history coincides with the development of the antagonism between man and woman in monogamian marriage, and the first class oppression with that of the female sex by the male. Monogamy was a great historical advance, but at the same time it inaugurated, along with slavery and private wealth, that epoch, surviving to this day,

---

a The 1884 edition has "social conditions" and the sentence ends here.— *Ed.*
b This sentence was added by Engels in the 1891 edition.— *Ed.*
c Cf. K. Marx and F. Engels, *The German Ideology* (see present edition, Vol. 5, p. 44).— *Ed.*

in which every advance is likewise a relative regression, in which the well-being and development of some are attained through the misery and repression of others. It is the cellular form of civilised society, in which we can already study the nature of the antitheses and contradictions which develop fully in the latter.

The old relative freedom of sexual intercourse by no means disappeared with the victory of the pairing marriage, or even of monogamy.

"The old conjugal system, now reduced to narrower limits by the gradual disappearance of the punaluan groups, still environed the advancing family, which it was to follow to the verge of civilisation.... It finally disappeared in the new form of hetaerism, which still follows mankind in civilisation as a dark shadow upon the family." [a]

By hetaerism Morgan means that extramarital sexual intercourse between men and unmarried women which exists *alongside monogamy*, and, as is well known, has flourished in the most diverse forms during the whole period of civilisation and is steadily developing into open prostitution.[b] This hetaerism is directly traceable to group marriage, to the sacrificial surrender of the women, whereby they purchased their right to chastity. The surrender for money was at first a religious act, taking place in the temple of the Goddess of Love, and the money originally flowed into the coffers of the temple. The hierodules[93] of Anaitis in Armenia, of Aphrodite in Corinth, as well as the religious dancing girls attached to the temples in India—the so-called bayaderes (the word is a corruption of the Portuguese *bailadeira,* a female dancer)—were the first prostitutes. This sacrificial surrender, originally obligatory for all women, was later practised by these priestesses alone on behalf of all other women. Hetaerism among other peoples grows out of the sexual freedom permitted to girls before marriage—hence likewise a survival of group marriage, only transmitted to us by another route. With the rise of property differentiation—that is, as far back as the upper stage of barbarism—wage labour appears sporadically alongside slave labour; and simultaneously, as its necessary correlate, the professional prostitution of free women appears side by side with the forced surrender of the female slave. Thus, the heritage bequeathed to civilisation by group marriage is double-sided, just as everything engendered by civilisation is double-sided, two-faced, self-contradictory and antagonistic: on the one hand,

---

[a] L. H. Morgan, op. cit., p. 504.—*Ed.*

[b] The text below, up to the words "Hetaerism is as much a social institution..." (see p. 175), was added in the 1891 edition.—*Ed.*

monogamy, on the other, hetaerism, including its most extreme form, prostitution. Hetaerism is as much a social institution as any other; it is a continuation of the old sexual freedom—in favour of the men. Although, in reality, it is not only tolerated but even practised with gusto, particularly by the ruling classes, it is condemned in words. In reality, however, this condemnation by no means falls on the men who indulge in it, it falls only on the women: they are scorned and cast out in order to proclaim once again the absolute domination of the men over the female sex as the fundamental law of society.

A second contradiction, however, is hereby developed within monogamy itself. By the side of the husband, whose life is embellished by hetaerism, stands the neglected wife.[a] And it is just as impossible to have one side of a contradiction without the other as it is to retain the whole of an apple in one's hand after eating half of it. Nevertheless, the men appear to have thought differently, until their wives taught them to know better. Two permanent social figures, previously unknown, appear on the scene along with monogamy—the wife's steady lover and the cuckold. The men had gained the victory over the women, but the act of crowning the victor was magnanimously undertaken by the vanquished. Adultery—proscribed, severely penalised, but irrepressible—became an unavoidable social institution alongside monogamy and hetaerism. The assured paternity of children was now, as before, based, at best, on moral conviction; and in order to solve the insoluble contradiction, Article 312 of the *Code Napoléon* decreed:

"*L'enfant conçu pendant le mariage a pour père le mari,*" "a child conceived during marriage has for its father the husband."

This is the final outcome of three thousand years of monogamy.

Thus, in the monogamian family, in those cases that faithfully reflect its historical origin and that clearly bring out the sharp conflict between man and woman resulting from the exclusive domination of the male, we have a picture in miniature of the very antagonisms and contradictions in which society, split up into classes since the commencement of civilisation, moves, without being able to resolve and overcome them. Naturally, I refer here only to those cases of monogamy where matrimonial life really takes its course according to the rules governing the original character of the whole institution, but where the wife rebels against the domination of the husband. That this is not the case

---

[a] These two sentences were added by Engels in the 1891 edition.—*Ed.*

with all marriages no one knows better than the German philistine, who is no more capable of ruling in the home than in the state, and whose wife, therefore, with full justification, wears the breeches of which he is unworthy. But in consolation he imagines himself to be far superior to his French companion in misfortune, who, more often than he, fares far worse.

The monogamian family, however, did not by any means appear everywhere and always in the classically harsh form which it assumed among the Greeks. Among the Romans, who as future world conquerors took a broader, if less refined, view than the Greeks, woman was more free and respected. The Roman believed the conjugal fidelity of his wife to be adequately safeguarded by his power of life and death over her. Besides, here the wife, just as well as the husband, could dissolve the marriage voluntarily. But the greatest advance in the development of monogamy definitely occurred with the entry of the Germans into history, because, probably owing to their poverty, monogamy does not yet appear to have completely evolved among them out of the pairing marriage. We conclude this from three circumstances mentioned by Tacitus: Firstly, despite their firm belief in the sanctity of marriage—"each man is contented with a single wife, and the women lived fenced around with chastity" [a]—polygamy existed for high society and the tribal chiefs, a situation similar to that of the Americans among whom pairing marriage prevailed. Secondly, the transition from mother right to father right could only have been accomplished a short time previously, for the mother's brother— the closest male gentile relative according to mother right—was still regarded as being an almost closer relative than one's own father, which likewise corresponds to the standpoint of the American Indians, among whom Marx found the key to the understanding of our own prehistoric past, as he often used to say. And thirdly, women among the Germans were highly respected and were influential in public affairs too—which directly conflicts with the domination of the male characteristic of monogamy. Nearly all these are points on which the Germans are in accord with the Spartans, among whom, likewise, as we have already seen, pairing marriage had not completely disappeared. [b] Thus, in this connection also, an entirely new element acquired world supremacy with the emergence of the Germans. The new monogamy, which now developed out of the mingling of races on

---

[a] Tacitus, *Germania*, 18-19.—*Ed.*
[b] This sentence was added in the 1891 edition.—*Ed.*

the ruins of the Roman world, clothed the domination of the men in milder forms and permitted women to occupy, at least externally, a far more respected and freer position than classical antiquity had ever known. This, for the first time, created the possibility for the greatest moral advance which we derive from and owe to monogamy—a development taking place within it, parallel with it, or in opposition to it, as the case may be, namely, modern individual sex love, previously unknown to the whole world.

This advance, however, definitely arose out of the circumstance that the Germans still lived in the pairing family, and as far as possible, superimposed the position of woman corresponding thereto onto monogamy. It by no means arose as a result of the legendary, wonderful moral purity of natural disposition of the Germans, which was limited to the fact that, in practice, the pairing marriage did not reveal the same glaring moral antagonisms as monogamy. On the contrary, the Germans, in their migrations, particularly south-eastwards, to the nomads of the steppes on the Black Sea, suffered considerable moral degeneration and, apart from their horsemanship, acquired serious unnatural vices from them, as is attested to explicitly by Ammianus about the Taifali, and by Procopius about the Heruli.[a]

Although monogamy was the only known form of the family under which modern sex love could develop, it does not follow that this love developed exclusively, or even predominantly, within it as the mutual love of the spouses. The whole nature of strict monogamian marriage under male domination ruled this out. Among all historically active classes, i.e., among all ruling classes, matrimony remained what it had been since pairing marriage—a matter of convenience arranged by the parents. And the first form of sex love that historically emerges as a passion, and as a passion in which any person (at least of the ruling classes) has a right to indulge, as the highest form of the sex drive—which is precisely its specific feature—this, its first form, the chivalrous love of the Middle Ages, was by no means conjugal love. On the contrary, in its classical form, among the Provençals, it steers under full sail towards adultery, and their poets praise this. The *Albas,* in German *Tagelieder,* are the flower of Provençal love poetry.[94] They describe in glowing colours how the knight lies in bed with his love—the wife of another—while the watchman stands guard

---

[a] Ammianus Marcellinus, *Rerum gestarum libri qui supersunt,* XXXI, 9 and Procopius of Caesarea, *The Histories. The Gothic War,* II, 14.—*Ed.*

outside, calling him at the first faint streaks of dawn (*alba*) so that he may yet escape unnoticed. The parting scene then constitutes the climax. The Northern French, as well as the worthy Germans, likewise adopted this style of poetry, along with the manners of chivalrous love which corresponded to it; and on this same suggestive theme our own old Wolfram von Eschenbach has left us three exquisite *Tagelieder,* which I prefer to his three long heroic poems.[95]

Bourgeois marriage of our own times is of two kinds. In Catholic countries the parents, as heretofore, still provide a suitable wife for their young bourgeois son, and the consequence is naturally the fullest unfolding of the contradiction inherent in monogamy—flourishing hetaerism on the part of the husband, and flourishing adultery on the part of the wife. The Catholic Church doubtless abolished divorce only because it was convinced that for adultery, as for death, there is no cure whatsoever. In Protestant countries, on the other hand, it is the rule that the bourgeois son is allowed to seek a wife for himself from his own class, more or less freely. Consequently, marriage can be based on a certain degree of love which, for decency's sake, is always assumed, in accordance with Protestant hypocrisy. In this case, hetaerism on the part of the man is less actively pursued, and adultery on the woman's part is not so much the rule. Since, in every kind of marriage, however, people remain what they were before they married, and since the bourgeoisie of Protestant countries are mostly philistines, this Protestant monogamy leads merely, if we take the average of the best cases, to a wedded life of leaden boredom, which is described as domestic bliss. The best mirror of these two ways of marriage is the novel; the French novel for the Catholic style, and the German[a] novel for the Protestant. In both cases "he gets it": in the German novel the young man gets the girl; in the French, the husband gets the cuckold's horns. Which of the two is in the worse plight is not always made out. For the dullness of the German novel excites the same horror in the French bourgeois as the "immorality" of the French novel excites in the German philistine, although lately, now that "Berlin is becoming a metropolis", the German novel has begun to deal a little less timidly with hetaerism and adultery, long known to exist there.

In both cases, however, marriage is determined by the class position of the participants, and to that extent always remains

---

[a] The 1884 edition has "and Swedish".— *Ed.*

marriage of convenience.[a] In both cases, this marriage of convenience often enough turns into the crassest prostitution—sometimes on both sides, but much more usually on the part of the wife, who differs from the ordinary courtesan only in that she does not hire out her body, like a wage worker, on piecework, but sells it into slavery once and for all. And Fourier's maxim holds good for all marriages of convenience:

"Just as in grammar two negatives make a positive, so in the morals of marriage, two prostitutions make one virtue."[b]

Sex love in the relationship of husband and wife is and can become the genuine rule only among the oppressed classes, that is, at the present day, among the proletariat, no matter whether this relationship is officially sanctioned or not. But here all the foundations of classical monogamy are removed. Here, there is a complete absence of all property, for the safeguarding and bequeathing of which monogamy and male domination were established. Therefore, there is no stimulus whatever here to assert male domination. What is more, the means, too, are absent; bourgeois law, which protects this domination, exists only for the propertied classes and their dealings with the proletarians. It costs money, and therefore, owing to the worker's poverty, has no validity in his position vis-à-vis his wife. Personal and social factors of quite a different sort are decisive here. Moreover, since large-scale industry has moved the woman from the house to the labour market and the factory, and made her, often enough, the bread-winner of the family, the last remnants of male domination in the proletarian home have lost all foundation—except, perhaps, for a bit of that brutality towards women which became firmly rooted with the establishment of monogamy. Thus, the proletarian family is no longer monogamian in the strict sense, even with most passionate love and strictest faithfulness of the two parties, and despite all spiritual and worldly benedictions which may have been received. The two eternal adjuncts of monogamy—hetaerism and adultery—therefore, play an almost negligible role here; the woman has regained, in fact, the right of dissolution of marriage, and when the man and woman cannot get along they prefer to part. In short, proletarian marriage is

---

[a] The text below, up to the words "Sex love in the relationship of husband and wife...", was added in the 1891 edition.— *Ed.*

[b] Ch. Fourier, *Théorie de l'unité universelle*, Vol. 3, p. 120.— *Ed.*

monogamous in the etymological sense of the word, but by no means in the historical sense.[a]

Our lawyers, to be sure, hold that the progress of legislation to an increasing degree removes all cause for complaint on the part of the woman. Modern civilised systems of law are recognising more and more, first, that, in order to be effective, marriage must be an agreement voluntarily entered into by both parties; and secondly, that during marriage, too, both parties must have equal rights and responsibilities vis-à-vis each other. If, however, these two demands were consistently carried into effect, women would have all they could ask for.

This typical lawyer's reasoning is exactly the same as that with which the radical republican bourgeois dismisses and enjoins silence on the proletarian. The labour contract is supposed to be voluntarily entered into by both parties. But it is taken to be voluntarily entered into as soon as the law has put both parties on an equal footing *on paper*. The power given to one party by its specific class position, the pressure it exercises on the other—the real economic position of the two—all this is no concern of the law. And both parties, again, are supposed to have equal rights for the duration of the labour contract, unless one or the other of the parties has explicitly waived them. That the concrete economic situation compels the worker to forego even the slightest semblance of equal rights—this again is something the law cannot help.

As far as marriage is concerned, even the most progressive law is fully satisfied as soon as the parties formally register their voluntary desire to get married. What happens behind the scenes of the law where real life is enacted, how this voluntary agreement is arrived at—is no concern of the law and the lawyer. And yet the simplest comparison of laws should serve to show the lawyer what this voluntary agreement really amounts to. In countries where the children are legally guaranteed an obligatory share of their parents' property and thus cannot be disinherited—in Germany, in the countries under French law, etc.—the children are bound by their parents' consent in the question of marriage. In countries under English law, where parental consent to marriage is not legally requisite, the parents have full testatory freedom over their property and can disinherit their children at

---

[a] The rest of the section, except the last paragraph beginning with the words "In the meantime, let us return to Morgan" (see p. 189), was added in the 1891 edition.— *Ed.*

their discretion. It is clear, therefore, that despite this, or rather just because of this, among those classes where there is something to inherit, freedom to marry is not one whit greater in England and America than in France or Germany.

The position is no better with regard to the legal equality of man and woman in marriage. The inequality of the two before the law, which is a legacy of previous social conditions, is not the cause but the effect of the economic oppression of women. In the old communistic household, which embraced numerous couples and their children, the administration of the household, entrusted to the women, was just as much a public, a socially necessary industry as the procurement of food by the men. This situation changed with the patriarchal family, and even more with the monogamian individual family. The administration of the household lost its public character. It was no longer the concern of society. It became a *private service*. The wife became the first domestic servant, pushed out of participation in social production. Only the large-scale industry of our time has again thrown open to her—and only to the proletarian woman at that—the avenue to social production; but in such a way that, if she fulfils her duties in the private service of her family, she remains excluded from public production and cannot earn anything; and if she wishes to take part in public industry and earn her living independently, she is not in a position to fulfil her family duties. What applies to the woman in the factory applies to her in all branches of business, right up to medicine and law. The modern individual family is based on the overt or covert domestic slavery of the woman; and modern society is a mass composed solely of individual families as its molecules. Today, in the great majority of cases, the man has to be the earner, the bread-winner of the family, at least among the propertied classes, and this gives him a dominating position which requires no special legal privileges. In the family, he is the bourgeois; the wife represents the proletariat. In the industrial world, however, the specific character of the economic oppression weighing down on the proletariat emerges in its full vividness only after all the special legal privileges of the capitalist class have been eliminated and the complete juridical equality of both classes established. The democratic republic does not abolish the antagonism between the two classes; on the contrary, it provides the field on which it is fought out. And, similarly, the peculiar character of man's domination over woman in the modern family, and the necessity, as well as the manner, of establishing real social equality between the two, will be brought out in full relief only when both

are completely equal before the law. It will then become evident
that the first precondition for the emancipation of women is the
reintroduction of the entire female sex into public industry; and
that this again demands that the quality possessed by the
individual family of being the economic unit of society be
eliminated.

* * *

We have, then, three chief forms of marriage, which, by and
large, conform to the three main stages of human development.
For savagery—group marriage; for barbarism—pairing marriage;
for civilisation—monogamy, supplemented by adultery and prostitution. In the upper stage of barbarism, between pairing
marriage and monogamy, are wedged in the dominion exercised
by men over female slaves, and polygamy.

As our whole exposition has shown, the advance which
manifests itself in this sequence is linked with the peculiar fact
that, while women are more and more deprived of the sexual
freedom of group marriage, the men are not. Actually, for men,
group marriage exists to this day. What for a woman is a crime
entailing dire legal and social consequences, is regarded in the case
of a man as being honourable or, at most, as a slight moral stigma
that one bears with pleasure. But the more the old traditional
hetaerism is changed in our day by capitalist commodity production and adapted to it, and the more it is transformed into
unconcealed prostitution, the more demoralising are its effects.
And it demoralises the men far more than it does the women.
Among women, prostitution degrades only those unfortunates
who fall into its clutches; and even these are not degraded to the
degree that is generally believed. On the other hand, it degrades
the character of the entire male world. Thus, in nine cases out of
ten, a long engagement is positively a preparatory school for
conjugal infidelity.

We are now approaching a social revolution in which the
hitherto existing economic foundations of monogamy will disappear just as certainly as those of its complement—prostitution.
Monogamy arose out of the concentration of considerable wealth
in the hands of one person—in those of a man—and out of the
desire to bequeath this wealth to this man's children and to no one
else's. For this purpose monogamy was essential on the woman's
part, but not on the man's; so that this monogamy of the woman
in no way hindered the overt or covert polygamy of the man. The

impending social revolution, however, by transforming at least by far the greater part of durable inheritable wealth—the means of production—into social property, will reduce all this anxiety about inheritance to a minimum. Since, however, monogamy arose from economic causes, will it disappear when these causes disappear?

One would not be wrong to reply: far from disappearing, it will only begin to be completely realised. For with the conversion of the means of production into social property, wage labour, the proletariat, also disappears, and therewith, also the necessity for a certain—statistically calculable—number of women to surrender themselves for money. Prostitution disappears; monogamy, instead of meeting its demise, finally becomes a reality—for the men as well.

At all events, the position of the men is thus greatly altered. But that of the women, of *all* women, also undergoes considerable change. With the passage of the means of production into common property, the individual family ceases to be the economic unit of society. Private housekeeping is transformed into a social industry. The care and upbringing of the children becomes a public affair. Society takes care of all children equally, irrespective of whether they are born in wedlock or not. Thus, the anxiety about the "consequences", which is today the most important social factor—both moral and economic—that hinders a girl from giving herself freely to the man she loves, disappears. Will this not be cause enough for a gradual rise of more unrestrained sexual intercourse, and along with it, a laxer public opinion regarding virginal honour and female shame? And finally, have we not seen that monogamy and prostitution in the modern world, although opposites, are nevertheless inseparable opposites, poles of the same social conditions? Can prostitution disappear without dragging monogamy with it into the abyss?

Here a new factor comes into operation, a factor that, at most, existed in embryonic form at the time when monogamy emerged, namely, individual sex love.

No such thing as individual sex love existed before the Middle Ages. That personal beauty, intimate association, similarity in inclinations, etc., aroused desire for sexual intercourse among people of opposite sexes, that men as well as women were not totally indifferent to the question of with whom they entered into this most intimate relation is obvious. But this is still a far cry from the sex love of our day. Throughout antiquity marriages were arranged by the parents; the parties quietly acquiesced. The little conjugal love that was known to antiquity was not in any way a subjective inclination, but an objective duty; not a reason for, but a correlate of, marriage. In antiquity, love affairs in the modern sense occur only outside official society. The shepherds, whose joys and sorrows in love are sung by Theocritus and Moschus, or by Longus' *Daphnis and Chloe*,[96] are mere slaves, who have no share in the state, the sphere of life of the free citizen. Except among slaves, however, we find love affairs only as disintegration products of the declining ancient world; and with women who are also beyond the pale of official society, with *hetaerae*, that is, with alien or freed women: in Athens beginning with the eve of its decline, in Rome at the time of the emperors. If love affairs really occurred between free male and female citizens, it was only in the form of adultery. And sex love in our sense of the term was so immaterial to that classical love poet of antiquity, old Anacreon, that even the sex of the beloved one was a matter of complete indifference to him.

Our sex love differs essentially from the simple sexual desire, the *eros*, of the ancients. First, it presupposes reciprocal love on the part of the loved one; in this respect, the woman stands on a par with the man; whereas in the ancient *eros*, the woman was by no means always consulted. Secondly, sex love attains a degree of intensity and permanency where the two parties regard non-possession or separation as a great, if not the greatest, misfortune; in order to possess each other they confront great hazards, even risking life itself—which in antiquity happened, at best, only in cases of adultery. And finally, a new moral standard arises for judging sexual contact. The question asked is not only whether such contact was in or out of wedlock, but also whether it arose from mutual love or not. It goes without saying that in feudal or bourgeois practice this new standard fares no better than all the other moral standards—it is simply ignored. But it fares no worse either. It is recognised in theory, on paper, like all the rest. And more than this cannot be expected for the present.

Where antiquity broke off with its start towards sex love, the Middle Ages began, namely, with adultery. We have already described chivalrous love, which gave rise to the *Tagelieder*. It is still a long way from this kind of love, which aimed at breaking up matrimony, to the love which was meant to establish it, a way never completely covered by the age of chivalry. Even when we pass from the frivolous Romance peoples to the virtuous Germans, we find, in the *Nibelungenlied*, that Kriemhild—although secretly in love with Siegfried every bit as much as he is with her—nevertheless, in reply to Gunther's intimation that he has plighted her to a knight whom he does not name, answers simply:

"You have no need to ask; as you command, so will I be for ever. He whom you, my lord, choose for my husband, to him will I gladly plight my troth." [a]

It never even occurs to her that her love could possibly be considered in this matter. Gunther seeks the hand of Brunhild without ever having seen her, and Etzel does the same with Kriemhild. The same occurs in the *Gutrun*,[97] where Siegebant of Ireland seeks the hand of Ute the Norwegian, Hettel of Hegelingen that of Hilde of Ireland; and lastly, Siegfried of Morland, Hartmut of Ormany and Herwig of Seeland seek the hand of Gutrun; and here for the first time it happens that Gutrun, of her own free will, decides in favour of the last named. As a rule, the bride of a young prince is selected by his parents if they are still alive; otherwise he chooses her himself with the counsel of his highest vassal chiefs, whose word carries great weight in all cases. Nor can it be otherwise. For the knight, or baron, just as for the prince himself, marriage is a political act, an opportunity for the enhancement of power through new alliances; the interest of the *House* and not individual discretion is the decisive factor. How can love here hope to have the last word regarding marriage?

It was the same for the guildsman of the medieval towns. The very privileges which protected him—the guild charters with their special stipulations, the artificial lines of demarcation which legally separated him from other guilds, from his own fellow guildsmen and from his journeymen and apprentices—considerably restricted the circle in which he could hope to secure a suitable spouse. And the question as to who was the most suitable was definitely decided under this complicated system, not by his discretion, but by family interest.

Up to the end of the Middle Ages, therefore, marriage, in the overwhelming majority of cases, remained what it had been right from the beginning, an affair that was not decided by the parties concerned. In the beginning one came into the world married, married to a whole group of the opposite sex. A similar relation probably existed in the later forms of group marriage, only with an ever increasing narrowing of the group. In pairing marriage it is the rule that the mothers arrange their children's marriages; and here also, considerations of new ties of relationship that are to strengthen the young couple's position in the gens and

---

[a] See *Nibelungenlied*, Song X.—*Ed.*

tribe are the decisive factor. And when, with the predominance of private property over common property, and with the interest in bequeathing, father right and monogamy came to dominate, marriage became more than ever dependent on economic considerations. The *form* of marriage by purchase disappears, the transaction itself is to an ever increasing degree carried out in such a way that not only the woman but the man also is appraised, not by his personal qualities but by his possessions. The idea that the mutual affection of the parties concerned should be the overriding reason for matrimony had been unheard of in the practice of the ruling classes from the very beginning. Such things took place, at best, in romance, or—among the oppressed classes, which did not count.

This was the situation encountered by capitalist production when, following the era of geographical discoveries, it set out to conquer the world through international trade and manufacture. One would think that this mode of matrimony should have suited it down to the ground, and such was indeed the case. And yet—the irony of world history is unfathomable—it was capitalist production that was to make the decisive breach in it. By transforming all things into commodities, it abolished all ancient traditional relations, and for inherited customs and historical rights it substituted purchase and sale, "free" contract. And H. S. Maine, the English legal scholar, believed he had made a colossal discovery when he said that our entire progress in comparison with previous epochs consisted in our having evolved FROM STATUS TO CONTRACT, from an inherited state of affairs to one voluntary contracted [a]—a statement which, insofar as it is correct, was contained long ago in the *Communist Manifesto.*[b]

But the conclusion of contracts presupposes people who can freely dispose of their persons, actions and possessions, and who meet each other on equal terms. To create such "free" and "equal" people was precisely one of the main achievements of capitalist production. Although in the beginning this took place only in a semi-conscious manner, and in religious guise to boot, neverthe-less, from the time of the Lutheran and Calvinistic Reformation it became a firm principle that a person was completely responsible for his actions only if he possessed full freedom of the will when performing them, and that it was a moral duty to resist all

---

[a] H. S. Maine, *Ancient Law: its connection with the early history of society, and its relation to modern ideas,* p. 170.— *Ed.*

[b] See present edition, Vol. 6, pp. 485-89.— *Ed.*

compulsion to commit immoral acts. But how did this fit in with the previous practice of matrimony? According to bourgeois conceptions, matrimony was a contract, a legal transaction, indeed the most important of all, since it disposed of the body and mind of two persons for life. True enough, formally the bargain was struck voluntarily; it could not be concluded without the consent of the parties; but how this consent was obtained, and who really arranged the marriage was known only too well. But if real freedom to decide was demanded for all other contracts, why not for this one? Had not the two young people about to be paired the right freely to dispose of themselves, their bodies and organs? Had not sex love become the fashion as a consequence of chivalry, and was not the love of the spouses its correct bourgeois form, as against the adulterous love of the knights? But if it was the duty of married people to love each other, was it not just as much the duty of lovers to marry each other and nobody else? And did not the right of these lovers stand higher than that of parents, relatives and other traditional marriage brokers and matchmakers? If the right of free personal examination unceremoniously forced its way into church and religion, how could it halt at the intolerable claim of the older generation to dispose of body and soul, the property, the happiness and unhappiness of the younger generation?

These questions were bound to arise in a period which loosened all the old social ties and which shook the foundations of all inherited conceptions. At one stroke the size of the world had increased nearly tenfold. Instead of only a quadrant of a hemisphere the whole globe was now open to the gaze of the West Europeans, who hastened to take possession of the other seven quadrants. And the thousand-year-old barriers set up by the medieval prescribed mode of thought vanished in the same way as did the old, narrow barriers of the homeland. An infinitely wider horizon opened up both to man's outer and inner eye. Of what avail were the good intentions of respectability, the honoured guild privileges handed down through the generations, to the young man who was allured by India's riches, by the gold and silver mines of Mexico and Potosi? It was the knight-errant period of the bourgeoisie; it had its romance also, and its love dreams, but on a bourgeois basis and, in the last analysis, with bourgeois ends in mind.

Thus it happened that the rising bourgeoisie, particularly in the Protestant countries, where the existing order was shaken up most of all, increasingly recognised freedom of contract for marriage as well and carried it through in the manner described above. Marriage remained class marriage, but, within the confines of the class, the parties were accorded a certain degree of freedom to choose. And on paper, in moral theory as in poetic description, nothing was more unshakably established than that every marriage not based on mutual sex love and on the really free agreement of the spouses was immoral. In short, love marriage was proclaimed a human right; not only as *droit de l'homme*[a] but also, by way of exception, as *droit de la femme*.[b]

But in one respect this human right differed from all other so-called human rights. While, in practice, the latter remained limited to the ruling class, the bourgeoisie—the oppressed class, the proletariat, being directly or indirectly deprived of them—the irony of history asserts itself here once again. The ruling class continues to be dominated by well-known economic influences and, therefore, only in exceptional cases does it bear witness to really voluntary marriages; whereas, as we have seen, these are the rule among the dominated class.

Thus, full freedom of marriage can become generally operative only when the abolition of capitalist production, and of the property relations created by it, has removed all those secondary economic considerations which still exert so powerful an influence on the choice of a partner. Then, no other motive remains than mutual affection.

Since sex love is by its very nature exclusive—although this exclusiveness is fully realised today only in the woman—then marriage based on sex love is by its very nature monogamy. We have seen how right Bachofen was when he regarded the advance from group marriage to individual marriage chiefly as the work of women; only the advance from pairing marriage to monogamy can be placed to the men's account, and, historically, this consisted essentially in a worsening of the position of women and in the facilitation of infidelity on the part of the men. With the disappearance of the economic considerations which compelled women to tolerate the customary infidelity of the men—the anxiety about their own livelihood and even more about the future of their children—the equality of woman thus achieved will, judging from all previous experience, be infinitely more effective in making the men really monogamous than in making the women polyandrous.

---

a Man's right.— *Ed.*
b Woman's right.— *Ed.*

What will most definitely disappear from monogamy, however, are all the characteristics stamped on it in consequence of its having arisen out of property relationships. These are, first, the predominance of the man, and secondly, the indissolubility of marriage. The predominance of the man in marriage is simply a consequence of his economic predominance and will vanish automatically with it. The indissolubility of marriage is partly the result of the economic conditions under which monogamy arose, and partly a tradition from the time when the connection between these economic conditions and monogamy was not yet correctly understood and was exaggerated by religion. Already today it has been breached a thousandfold. If only marriages that are based on love are moral, then, also, only those are moral in which love continues. The duration of the urge of individual sex love differs very much according to the individual, particularly among men; and a definite cessation of affection, or its displacement by a new passionate love, makes separation a blessing for both parties as well as for society. People will only be spared the experience of wading through the useless mire of divorce proceedings.

Thus, what we can conjecture at present about the regulation of sex relationships after the impending effacement of capitalist production is, in the main, of a negative character, limited mostly to what will vanish. But what will be added? That will be settled after a new generation has grown up: a generation of men who never in their lives have had occasion to purchase a woman's surrender either with money or with any other social means of power, and of women who have never had occasion to surrender to any man out of any consideration other than that of real love, or to refrain from giving themselves to their beloved for fear of the economic consequences. Once such people appear, they will not care a damn about what we today think they should do. They will establish their own practice and their own public opinion, conforming therewith, on the practice of each individual—and that's the end of it.

In the meantime, let us return to Morgan, from whom we have strayed quite considerably. The historical investigation of the social institutions which developed during the period of civilisation lies outside the scope of his book. Consequently, he concerns himself only briefly with the fate of monogamy during this period. He, too, regards the development of the monogamian family as an advance, as an approximation to the complete equality of the sexes, without, however, considering that this goal has been reached. But, he says, "when the fact is accepted that the family has passed through four successive forms, and is now in a fifth, the question at once arises whether this form can be permanent in the future. The only answer that can be given is that it must advance as society advances, and change as society changes, even as it has done in the past. It is the creature of the social system, and will reflect its culture. As the monogamian family has improved greatly since the commencement of civilisation, and very sensibly in modern times, it is at least supposable that it is capable of still farther improvement until the equality of the sexes is attained. Should the monogamian family in the distant future fail to answer the requirements of society [...] it is impossible to predict the nature of its successor".[a]

III

THE IROQUOIS GENS

We now come to a further discovery of Morgan's, which is at least as important as the reconstruction of the primitive form of the family out of the systems of consanguinity. The demonstration of the fact that the bodies of *consanguinei* within the American Indian tribe, designated by the names of animals, are in essence identical with the *genea* of the Greeks and the *gentes* of the Romans; that the American form was the original and the Greek and Roman the later, derivative; that the entire social organisation of the Greeks and Romans of primitive times in gens, phratry and tribe finds its faithful parallel in that of the American Indians; that (as far as our present sources of information go) the gens is an institution common to all barbarians up to their entry into civilisation, and even afterwards—this demonstration cleared up at one stroke the most difficult parts of the earliest Greek and Roman history. At the same time it has thrown unexpected light on the fundamental features of the social constitution of primitive times—before the introduction of the *state*. Simple as this may seem when one knows it—nevertheless, Morgan discovered it only very recently. In his previous work, published in 1871,[b] he had not yet hit upon the secret, the discovery of which since reduced for a time[c] the otherwise so confident English prehistorians to a mouse-like silence.

The Latin word *gens*, which Morgan employs as a general designation for this body of *consanguinei*, is, like its Greek equivalent, *genos*, derived from the common Aryan root *gan* (in

---

[a] L. H. Morgan, *Ancient Society*, pp. 491-92. See also "Marx's Excerpts...", op. cit., p. 124.— *Ed.*

[b] L. H. Morgan, *Systems of Consanguinity and Affinity of the Human Family.— Ed.*

[c] The words "for a time" were added in the 1891 edition.— *Ed.*

German, where the Aryan *g* is, according to rule, replaced by *k*, it is *kan*), which means to beget. *Gens, genos,* the Sanscrit *ganas,* the Gothic *kuni* (in accordance with the above-mentioned rule), the Old Norse and Anglo-Saxon *kyn,* the English *kin,* the Middle High German *künne,* all equally signify kinship, descent. However, *gens* in the Latin and *genos* in the Greek are specially used for a body of *consanguinei* which boasts a common descent (in this case from a common male ancestor) and which, owing to certain social and religious institutions, forms a separate community, whose origin and nature have hitherto, nevertheless, remained obscure to all our historians.

We have already seen above, in connection with the punaluan family, how a gens in its original form is constituted. It consists of all persons who, by virtue of punaluan marriage and in accordance with the conceptions necessarily predominating therein, constitute the recognised descendants of a definite individual ancestress, the founder of the gens. Since paternity is uncertain in this form of the family, female lineage alone is valid. Since the brothers may not marry their sisters, but only women of different descent, the children born of such alien women fall, according to mother right, outside the gens. Thus, only the offspring of the *daughters* of each generation remain in the body of *consanguinei,* while the offspring of the sons go over into the gentes of their mothers. What, then, becomes of this consanguine group once it constitutes itself as a separate group as against similar groups within the tribe?

Morgan takes the gens of the Iroquois, in particular that of the Seneca tribe, as the classical form of the original gens. They have eight gentes, named after the following animals: 1) Wolf; 2) Bear; 3) Turtle; 4) Beaver; 5) Deer; 6) Snipe; 7) Heron; 8) Hawk. The following usages prevail in each gens:

1. It elects its sachem (headman in times of peace) and its chief (leader in war). The sachem had to be elected from within the gens itself and his office was hereditary in the gens, in the sense that it had to be immediately filled whenever a vacancy occurred. The war chief could also be elected outside the gens and could at times be completely non-existent. The son of the previous sachem was never elected as his successor, since mother right prevailed among the Iroquois, and the son, therefore, belonged to a different gens. The brother or the sister's son, however, was often elected. All voted at the election—men and women alike. The choice, however, had to be endorsed by the remaining seven gentes and only then was the elected person ceremonially installed,

this being carried out by the general council of the entire Iroquois Confederacy. The significance of this will be seen later. The sachem's authority within the gens was of a paternal and purely moral character. He had no means of coercion at his command. He was by virtue of his office a member also of the tribal council of the Senecas, as well as of the Council of the Confederacy of all the Iroquois. The war chief could give orders only in military expeditions.

2. The gens can depose the sachem and war chief at will. This again is carried out jointly by the men and women. Thereafter, the deposed rank as simple warriors and private persons like the rest. The council of the tribe can also depose the sachems, even against the wishes of the gens.

3. No member is permitted to marry within the gens. This is the fundamental rule of the gens, the bond which keeps it together; it is the negative expression of the very positive blood relationship by virtue of which the individuals included in it become a gens at all. By the discovery of this simple fact Morgan, for the first time, revealed the nature of the gens. How little the gens had been understood until then is proved by the earlier reports concerning savages and barbarians, in which the various bodies constituting the gentile organisation are ignorantly and indiscriminately referred to as tribe, clan, thum, etc.; and regarding these it is sometimes asserted that marriage within any such body is prohibited. This gave rise to the hopeless confusion in which Mr. McLennan was able to intervene as a Napoleon, creating order by his fiat: All tribes are divided into those within which marriage is forbidden (exogamous) and those within which it is permitted (endogamous). And having thus thoroughly muddled matters, he was able to indulge in most profound investigations as to which of his two fatuous classes was the older, exogamy or endogamy. This nonsense ceased automatically with the discovery of the gens based on blood relationship and the consequent impossibility of marriage between its members.—Obviously, at the stage at which we find the Iroquois, the prohibition of marriage within the gens is strictly observed.

4. The property of deceased persons was distributed among the remaining members of the gens—it had to remain in the gens. In view of the insignificance of the effects which an Iroquois could leave, the heritage was divided among the nearest relatives in the gens; when a man died, among his natural brothers and sisters and his maternal uncle; when a woman died, then among her children and natural sisters, but not her brothers. That is precisely

the reason why it was impossible for man and wife to inherit from each other, and why children could not inherit from their father.

5. The members of the gens were bound to give one another assistance, protection and particularly support in avenging injuries inflicted by outsiders. The individual depended, and could depend, for his security on the protection of the gens. Whoever injured him injured the whole gens. From this—the blood ties of the gens—arose the obligation of blood revenge, which was recognised unconditionally by the Iroquois. If a non-member of a gens slew a member of the gens the whole gens to which the slain person belonged was bound to take blood revenge. First mediation was tried. A council of the slayer's gens was held and propositions were made to the council of the victim's gens for a settlement of the matter—mostly in the form of expressions of regret and presents of considerable value. If these were accepted, the affair was closed. If not, the injured gens appointed one or more avengers, whose duty it was to pursue and slay the murderer. If this happened the gens of the latter had no right to complain; the matter was regarded as even.

6. The gens has definite names or series of names which it alone, in the whole tribe, is entitled to use, so that an individual's name also indicates the gens to which he belongs. A gentile name carries gentile rights with it as a matter of course.

7. The gens can adopt strangers and thereby admit them into the tribe as a whole. Prisoners of war that were not slain became members of the Seneca tribe by adoption into a gens and thereby obtained full tribal and gentile rights. The adoption took place at the request of individual members of the gens—men placed the stranger in the relation of a brother or sister, women in that of a child. For confirmation of this, ceremonial acceptance into the gens was necessary. Individual, exceptionally depleted gentes were often replenished by mass adoption from another gens, with the latter's consent. Among the Iroquois, the ceremony of adoption into the gens was performed at a public meeting of the council of the tribe, which turned it practically into a religious rite.

8. It would be difficult to prove special religious rites among the Indian gentes—and yet the religious ceremonies of the Indians are more or less connected with the gentes. Among the Iroquois, at their six annual religious festivals, the sachems and war chiefs of the individual gentes were included among the "Keepers of the Faith" *ex officio* and exercised priestly functions.

9. The gens has a common burial place. That of the Iroquois of New York State, who have been hemmed in by the whites, has

now disappeared, but it did use to exist. It still survives amongst other Indian tribes, as, for instance, amongst the Tuscaroras, a tribe closely related to the Iroquois, who, although Christian, still retain in their cemetery a special row for each gens, so that the mother is buried in the same row as her children, but not the father. And also among the Iroquois, all the members of the gens are mourners at the funeral, prepare the grave, deliver funeral orations, etc.

10. The gens has a council, the democratic assembly of all adult male and female members of the gens, all with equal voice. This council elected and deposed the sachems and war chiefs and, likewise, the remaining "Keepers of the Faith". It decided about penance gifts (*wergeld*) or blood revenge, for murdered gentiles. It adopted strangers into the gens. In short, it was the sovereign power in the gens.

These are the powers of a typical Indian gens.

"All its members were personally free, and they were bound to defend each other's freedom; they were equal [...] in personal rights, the sachems and chiefs claiming no superiority; and they were a brotherhood bound together by the ties of kin. Liberty, equality, and fraternity, though never formulated, were cardinal principles of the gens. [...] The gens was the unit for a social system, the foundation upon which Indian society was organised. [...] [This] serves to explain that sense of independence and personal dignity universally an attribute of Indian character." [a]

At the time of their discovery the Indians throughout North America were organised in gentes in accordance with mother right. Only in a few tribes, as amongst the Dakotas, had the gentes fallen into decay, while in some others, such as the Ojibwas and Omahas, they were organised in accordance with father right.

Among numerous Indian tribes having more than five or six gentes, we find three, four and more gentes united in a special group which Morgan—faithfully translating the Indian term by its Greek counterpart—calls the phratry (brotherhood). Thus, the Senecas have two phratries, the first embracing gentes 1 to 4, and the second gentes 5 to 8. Closer investigation shows that these phratries, in the main, represent those original gentes into which the tribe split at the outset; for with the prohibition of marriage within the gens, each tribe had necessarily to consist of at least two gentes in order to be capable of surviving on its own. As the tribe multiplied, each gens again subdivided into two or more gentes, each of which now appears as a separate gens, while the original

---

[a] L. H. Morgan, *Ancient Society,* pp. 85-86. The quotation is somewhat abridged and slightly changed according to "Marx's Excerpts...", op. cit., p. 150.—*Ed.*

gens, which embraces all the daughter gentes, lives on as the phratry. Among the Senecas and most other Indians, the gentes in one phratry are brother gentes, while those in another are their cousin gentes—designations which, as we have seen, have a very real and expressive significance in the American system of consanguinity. Originally, indeed, no Seneca could marry within his phratry; but this prohibition has long since lapsed and is limited only to the gens. The Senecas had a tradition that the Bear and the Deer were the two original gentes, of which the others were offshoots. Once this new institution had become firmly rooted, it was modified according to need. In order to maintain equilibrium, whole gentes out of other phratries were occasionally transferred to those in which gentes had died out. This explains why we find in different tribes gentes of the same name variously grouped among the phratries.

Among the Iroquois the functions of the phratry are partly social and partly religious. 1) The ball game is played by phratries, one against the other; each phratry puts forward its best players, the remaining members of the phratry being spectators arranged according to phratry, who bet against each other on the success of their respective sides. 2) At the council of the tribe the sachems and war chiefs of each phratry sit together, the two groups facing each other, and each speaker addresses the representatives of each phratry as a separate body. 3) If a murder had been committed in the tribe and the slayer and the victim did not belong to the same phratry, the aggrieved gens often appealed to its brother gentes; these held a phratry council and addressed themselves to the other phratry as a whole, asking it also to summon a council for the adjustment of the matter. Here again the phratry appears as the original gens and with greater prospects of success than the weaker individual gens, its offspring. 4) On the death of persons of consequence, the opposite phratry undertook the arrangement of the funeral and the burial rites, while the phratry of the deceased went along as mourners. When a sachem died, the opposite phratry notified the federal council of the Iroquois of the vacant office. 5) The council of the phratry again appeared on the scene at the election of a sachem. Confirmation by the brother gentes was regarded as rather a matter of course, but the gentes of the other phratry might oppose. In such a case the council of this phratry met and, if it upheld the opposition, the election was null and void. 6) Previously, the Iroquois has special religious mysteries, which white men called "MEDICINE LODGES". Among the Senecas they were celebrated by two religious fraternities, one for

each phratry, with a regular initiation ritual for new members.
7) If, as is almost certain, the four LINEAGES (kinship groups) that
occupied the four quarters of Tlascala at the time of the
Conquest[98] were four phratries, this proves that the phratries, as
among the Greeks, and similar bodies of *consanguinei* among the
Germans, also served as military units. These four LINEAGES went
into battle, each one as a separate division, with its own uniform
and standard, and a leader of its own.

Just as several gentes constitute a phratry, so, in the classical
form, several phratries constitute a tribe. In many cases the middle
link, the phratry, is missing among greatly depleted tribes.
What are the distinctive features of the Indian tribe in America?

1. Its own territory and its own name. In addition to the area of
actual settlement, each tribe possessed considerable territory for
hunting and fishing. Beyond this there was a wide stretch of
neutral land reaching to the territory of the next tribe; the extent
of this neutral territory was less where the two tribes were related
linguistically, and greater where not. Such neutral ground was the
border forest of the Germans, the wasteland which Caesar's Suebi
created around their territory, the *îsarnholt* (Danish *jarnved, limes
Danicus*) between the Danes and the Germans, the Saxon forest
and the *branibor* (protective forest in Slavic)—from which
Brandenburg derives its name—between Germans and Slavs. The
territory thus marked out by imperfectly defined boundaries was
the common land of the tribe, recognised as such by neighbouring
tribes, and defended by the tribe against any encroachment. In
most cases, the uncertainty of the boundaries became a practical
inconvenience only when the population had greatly increased.—
The tribal names appear to have been the result more of accident
than of deliberate choice. As time passed it frequently happened
that neighbouring tribes designated a tribe by a name different
from that which it itself used, like the case of the Germans, whose
first all-embracing historical name—Teutons—was bestowed on
them by the Celts.

2. A separate *dialect* peculiar to this tribe only. In fact, tribe and
dialect are substantially co-extensive. The establishment of new
tribes and dialects through subdivision was in progress in America
until quite recently, and can hardly have ceased altogether even
now. Where two depleted tribes have amalgamated into one, it
happens, by way of exception, that two closely related dialects are
spoken in the same tribe. The average strength of American tribes
is under 2,000. The Cherokees, however, are nearly 26,000

strong—being the largest number of Indians in the United States that speak the same dialect.

3. The right of investing the sachems and war chiefs elected by the gentes, and

4. The right to depose them again, even against the wishes of their gens. As these sachems and war chiefs are members of the tribal council, these rights of the tribe in relation to them are self-explanatory. Wherever a confederacy of tribes was established and all the tribes were represented in a federal council, the above rights were transferred to this latter body.

5. The possession of common religious ideas (mythology) and rites of worship.

"After the fashion of barbarians the [...] Indians were a religious people."[a]

Their mythology has not yet been critically investigated at all. They already personified their religious ideas—spirits of all kinds—but in the lower stage of barbarism in which they lived there was as yet no graphic depictions, no so-called idols. It was a nature and element worship evolving towards polytheism. The various tribes had their regular festivals with definite forms of worship, particularly, dancing and games. Dances especially were an essential part of all religious ceremonies, each tribe performing its own separately.

6. A tribal council for common affairs. It consisted of all the sachems and war chiefs of the separate gentes—the real representatives of the latter, because they could always be deposed. The council sat in public, surrounded by the other members of the tribe, who had the right to join in the discussion and to secure a hearing for their opinions, and the council took the decisions. As a rule it was open to everyone present who desired to address it; even the women could express their views through a spokesman of their own choice. Among the Iroquois the final decisions had to be adopted unanimously, as was also the case with many of the decisions of the German Mark communities.* In particular, the

---

* In Germany the "Mark" constitution is the name given to the old system of land ownership, handed down by custom and usufruct, in which vestiges of the old Germanic common ownership of land have been preserved to this day. The area of land belonging to a community, called the "Mark", was divided into three parts: (1) the actual village, where every member of the community received a plot of equal size for house, farmyard and garden; (2) the divided "Mark", that is the area designated for arable land and meadowland; (3) the communal or undivided

---

[a] L. H. Morgan, *Ancient Society*, p. 115. See also "Marx's Excerpts...", op. cit., p. 162.— *Ed.*

regulation of relations with other tribes devolved upon the tribal council. It received and sent embassies, it declared war and made peace. When war broke out it was carried on mainly by volunteers. In principle each tribe was in a state of war with every other tribe

---

"Mark", that is all the remaining land—woods, grassland, heath, bog, waters, paths, etc.

The divided Mark was first divided into a number of plots according to location and fertility, called "gewanne". Each "gewanne" was, in turn, divided into as many plots of equal size as there were members of the community, i.e. heads of families. These plots were then distributed by lot in such a way that each member of the community received his share of each "gewanne", in other words, as much land—and as good—as everyone else. House and yard became each member's personal property at an early stage; the communal lands, on the other hand, were redistributed, annually to begin with, and later on every four, six or twelve years. But they, too, soon became the owner's hereditary and disposable property. Only around the Rhine did the constant cycle of redistribution persist—into this century, in the Palatinate and the now Prussian districts south of the Mosel—and may still exist in a few villages under the name of "gehöferschaften". But even where arable land and grassland had become private property it had to be tilled according to a communal plan laid down by the community (arable land was generally divided into winter fields, summer fields and fallow fields), and after harvest and when lying fallow it was open to all the members of the community as communal grazing.

The undivided or common "Mark" was the communal property of all members and was used equally by all for grazing, pannage, timber felling, hay-making, hunting, fishing, etc.

How it should be used, the rights of each individual, the cultivation and common use of the divided "Mark" and all other land matters, were discussed at the members' public assembly and decided by voting, as were all disputes and breaches of the land law. Here all members were equal, no matter if one man was a serf and the other his liege lord, as was often the case in the later Middle Ages; at the Mark assembly no man was more worth than the next: it was democracy in its most perfect form.

The original Mark communities embraced large districts (entire *Gaus*, or hundreds), with each village owning its own common land, while alongside it there still existed a large amount of common land that belonged to them all. In the Rheingau this existed right up into the sixteenth and seventeenth centuries. This was also the case in Scandinavia. The old Swedish law knew village commons, district commons, provincial commons and finally the King's (that is, properly speaking, the people's) commons; in other words, apart from village common land, common land belonging to the hundred, the province and ultimately land belonging to the King as the whole nation's representative. In Germany as late as the fourteenth century there were six to twelve villages to a "Mark"; later as a rule each village had only its own "Mark", that is to say, the large common "Mark" of earlier times had been stolen by the feudal lords.

Out of the "Mark" system developed the village system, and, where the villages were reorganised as towns, the town system. In such towns the former "Mark" members naturally had sole right, initially, to participate in the management of the town's business, that is, matters relating to their own land, while outsiders who had migrated to the towns and had no entitlement to the "Mark" were, and remained, without legal rights. In this way the original democracy practised in the Mark

with which it had not expressly concluded a treaty of peace. Military expeditions against such enemies were for the most part organised by a few outstanding warriors. They gave a war dance; whoever joined in the dance thereby declared his intention to participate in the expedition. A detachment was immediately formed and set out forthwith. When the tribal territory was attacked, its defence was likewise conducted mainly by volunteers. The departure and return of such detachments always provided an occasion for public festivities. The sanction of the tribal council for such expeditions was not necessary. It was neither sought nor given. They were exactly like the private war expeditions of the German retainers, as Tacitus has described them,[a] except that among the Germans the body of retainers had assumed a more permanent character, and constituted a strong nucleus, already organised in times of peace, around which the remaining volunteers grouped in the event of war. Such military detachments were seldom numerically strong. The most important expeditions of the Indians, even those covering great distances, were carried out by insignificant fighting forces. When several such retinues gathered for an important engagement, each group obeyed its own leader only. The cohesion of the plan of campaign was ensured, more or less, by a council of these leaders. It was the method of war adopted by the Alamanni of the Upper Rhine in the fourth century, as described by Ammianus Marcellinus.

7. In some tribes we find a head chief, whose powers, however, are very slight. He is one of the sachems, who in cases demanding

community became a closed aristocracy of the town's "families", the patricians. Newly arrived outsiders, artisans, etc. comprised the town's plebs, whose struggle for equal rights with the privileged families fills the history of whole towns all through the Middle Ages.

Where the "Mark" came under the control of a feudal lord, it was, initially, only transformed into a manorial system in so far as the lord became the permanent head of the Mark assembly and received a larger share of the cultivation of the common "Mark"; legislative, executive and judicial powers remained with the members as a whole. But early on the feudal lords encroached on the members' rights, undermining them until in the end there was little or nothing left of them.

The Mark system was the original system of all the Germanic tribes; it was at its strongest in Germany, Scandinavia, England and northern France; in all these countries remains of it are still to be found. But only in Germany has its history been studied in detail, namely by G. L. Maurer. [*Engels' note to the 1888 Danish edition.*]

---

[a] Tacitus, *Germania*, Vol. II.— *Ed.*

speedy action has to take provisional measures until such time as the council can assemble and take the final decision. This is a feeble but, subsequently, generally fruitless attempt to create an official with executive authority; actually, as will be seen, it was the supreme military commander who, in most cases, if not in all, developed into such an official.

The great majority of American Indians never got beyond the stage of tribal integration. Constituting numerically small tribes, separated from one another by wide border-lands, and enfeebled by perpetual warfare, they occupied an enormous territory with but few people. Alliances arising out of temporary emergencies were concluded here and there between kindred tribes and dissolved when they passed. But in certain areas originally kindred but subsequently disunited tribes reunited in lasting confederacies, and so took the first step towards the formation of nations. In the United States we find the most advanced form of such a confederacy among the Iroquois. Emigrating from their original home west of the Mississippi, where they probably constituted a branch of the great Dakota family, they settled down after protracted wanderings in what is today the State of New York. They were divided into five tribes: Senecas, Cayugas, Onondagas, Oneidas and Mohawks. Subsisting on fish, game and the produce of crude horticulture, they lived in villages protected mostly by palisades. Never more than 20,000 strong, they had a number of gentes common to all five tribes; they spoke closely related dialects of the same language and occupied a continuous tract of territory that was divided among the five tribes. Since this area had been newly conquered, habitual cooperation among these tribes against those they displaced was only natural. No later than the beginning of the fifteenth century, this developed into a regular "permanent league", a confederacy, which, conscious of its new-found strength, immediately assumed an offensive character and at the height of its power—about 1675—had conquered large stretches of the surrounding country, expelling some of the inhabitants and forcing others to pay tributes. The Iroquois Confederacy was the most advanced social organisation attained by the Indians who had not gone beyond the lower stage of barbarism (that is, excepting the Mexicans, New Mexicans[99] and Peruvians). The main rules of the Confederacy were as follows:

1. Perpetual alliance of the five consanguine tribes on the basis of complete equality and independence in all internal tribal affairs. This blood relationship constituted the true basis of the Confederacy. Of the five tribes, three were called the father tribes and were

brothers one to another; the other two were called son tribes and were likewise brother tribes to each other. Three gentes—the oldest—still had living representatives in all the five tribes, while another three had in three tribes. The members of each of these gentes were all brothers throughout the five tribes. The common language, with mere dialectal differences, was the expression and the proof of common descent.

2. The organ of the Confederacy was a Federal Council comprised of fifty sachems, all of equal rank and dignity; this council passed final decisions on all matters pertaining to the Confederacy.

3. At the time the Confederacy was constituted these fifty sachems were distributed among the tribes and gentes as the bearers of new offices especially created to suit the aims of the Confederacy. They were elected anew by the gentes concerned whenever a vacancy arose, and could always be removed by them. The right to invest them with office belonged, however, to the Federal Council.

4. These federal sachems were also sachems in their own respective tribes, and each had a seat and a vote in the tribal council.

5. All decisions of the Federal Council had to be unanimous.

6. Voting was by tribes, so that each tribe and all the council members in each tribe had to agree before a binding decision could be made.

7. Each of the five tribal councils could convene the Federal Council, but the latter had no power to convene itself.

8. Its meetings took place before the assembled people. Every Iroquois had the right to speak; the council alone decided.

9. The Confederacy had no official head, no chief executive.

10. It did, however, have two supreme war chiefs, enjoying equal authority and equal power (the two "kings" of the Spartans, the two consuls in Rome).

This was the entire social constitution under which the Iroquois lived for over four hundred years, and still do live. I have described it in some detail after Morgan because it gives us the opportunity of studying the organisation of a society which as yet knows no *state*. The state presupposes a special public authority separated from the totality of those respectively concerned; and Maurer's instinct is correct in recognising the German Mark constitution as a purely social institution, differing essentially from the state, although it largely served as its foundation later on. In all his writings, therefore, Maurer investigates the gradual rise of public authority out of and side by side with the original constitutions of the Marks, villages, manors and towns.[100] The North American Indians show how an originally united tribe gradually spread over an immense continent; how tribes, by breaking up, became peoples, whole groups of tribes; how the languages changed not only until they became mutually unintelligible, but until nearly every trace of original unity disappeared; and how at the same time individual gentes within the tribes broke up to become several; how the old mother gentes persisted as phratries, and yet the names of these oldest gentes still remain the same among very remote and long-separated tribes—the Wolf and the Bear are still gentile names among a majority of Indian tribes. Generally speaking, the constitution described above can be applied to them all—except that many of them did not get as far as a confederation of kindred tribes.

But we also see that once the gens existed as a social unit, the entire system of gentes, phratries and tribe developed with almost compelling necessity—because naturally—out of this unit. All three are groups of various degrees of consanguinity, each complete in itself and managing its own affairs, but each also complementing the rest. And the sphere of affairs devolving on them comprised the totality of the public affairs of the barbarians in the lower stage. Wherever, therefore, we find among a people the gens as the social unit, we may look for an organisation of the tribe similar to that described here; and where sufficient sources are available, as, for example, amongst the Greeks and the Romans, we shall not only find it, but also convince ourselves that, where the sources fail us, a comparison with the American social constitution will help us out of the most difficult doubts and enigmas.

And this gentile constitution is wonderful in all its childlike simplicity! Everything runs smoothly without soldiers, gendarmes or police; without nobles, kings, governors, prefects or judges; without prisons; without trials. All quarrels and disputes are settled by the whole body of those concerned—the gens or the tribe or the individual gentes among themselves. Blood revenge is threatened only as an extreme, rarely applied measure, of which our capital punishment is only the civilised form, possessed of all the advantages and drawbacks of civilisation. Although there are many more affairs in common than at present—the household is run in common and communistically by a number of families, the land is tribal property, only the small gardens being temporarily assigned to the households—still, not a bit of our extensive and complicated machinery of administration is required. Those concerned decide, and in most cases centuries-old custom has already settled everything. There can be no poor and needy—the communistic household and gens know their obligations towards the aged, the sick and those disabled in war. All are free and equal—including the women. There is as yet no room for slaves, nor, as a rule, for the subjugation of alien tribes. When the Iroquois conquered the Eries and the "Neutral Nations" [101] about the year 1651, they invited them to join the Confederacy as equal members; only when the vanquished refused were they driven out of their territory. And the kind of the men and women that are produced by such a society is indicated by the admiration felt by all white men who came into contact with uncorrupted Indians, admiration of the personal dignity, rectitude, strength of character and bravery of these barbarians.

We have witnessed quite recently examples of this bravery in Africa. The Zulu Kaffirs a few years ago, like the Nubians a couple of months ago—both tribes in which gentile institutions have not yet died out—did what no European army can do. [102] Armed only with pikes and spears and without firearms, they advanced, under a hail of bullets from the breech loaders, right up to the bayonets of the English infantry—acknowledged as the best in the world for fighting at close formation—throwing them into disorder more than once and even beating them back; and this, despite the colossal disparity in arms and despite the fact that they have no such thing as military service, and do not know what military exercises are. Their capacity and endurance are proved by the complaint of the English that a Kaffir can move faster and cover a longer distance in twenty-four hours than a horse. As an English painter says, their smallest muscle stands out, hard and steely, like whipcord.

This is what mankind and human society were like before class divisions arose. And if we compare their condition with that of the overwhelming majority of civilised people today, we will find an enormous gulf between the present-day proletarian and small peasant and the ancient free member of a gens.

This is one side of the matter. Let us not forget, however, that this organisation was doomed to extinction. It never developed beyond the tribe; the confederacy of tribes already signified the commencement of its downfall, as we shall see later, and as the attempts of the Iroquois to subjugate others have shown. What was outside the tribe was outside the law. Where no express treaty of peace existed, war raged between tribe and tribe; and war was waged with the cruelty that distinguishes man from all other animals and which was abated only later in self-interest. The gentile constitution in full bloom, as we have seen it in America, presupposed extremely undeveloped production, thus an extremely sparse population spread over a wide territory, and therefore the almost complete domination of man confronted by an alien and incomprehensible external nature, a domination reflected in his childish religious ideas. The tribe remained the boundary for man, in relation to outsider as well as himself: the tribe, the gens and their institutions were sacred and inviolable, a superior power, instituted by nature, to which the individual remained absolutely subject in feeling, thought and deed. Impressive as the people of this epoch may appear to us, they differ in no way one from another, they are still bound, as Marx says, to the umbilical cord of naturally evolved community. The power of these naturally evolved communities had to be broken, and it was broken. But it was broken by influences which from the outset appear to us as a degradation, a fall from the simple moral grandeur of the old gentile society. The lowest interests—base greed, brutal sensuality, sordid avarice, selfish plunder of common possessions—usher in the new, civilised society, class society; the most outrageous means—theft, rape, deceit and treachery— undermine and topple the old, classless, gentile society. And the new society, during all the 2,500 years of its existence, has never been anything but the development of the small minority at the expense of the exploited and oppressed great majority; and it is so today more than ever before.

IV

THE GRECIAN GENS

Greeks, as well as Pelasgians and other peoples of the same tribal origin, were constituted since prehistoric times in the same organic series as the Americans: gens, phratry, tribe, confederacy of tribes. The phratry might be missing, as among the Dorians; the confederacy of tribes might not yet be developed everywhere, but in every case the gens was the unit. At the time the Greeks entered history, they were on the threshold of civilisation. Almost two entire great periods of development lie between the Greeks and the above-mentioned American tribes, the Greeks of the Heroic Age being by this much ahead of the Iroquois. For this reason the Grecian gens no longer bore the archaic character of the Iroquois gens; the stamp of group marriage[a] was becoming considerably blurred. Mother right had given way to father right; thereby rising private wealth made its first breach in the gentile constitution. A second breach naturally followed the first: after the introduction of father right, the fortune of a wealthy heiress would, by virtue of her marriage, fall to her husband, that is to say, to another gens; and so the foundation of all gentile law was broken, and in such cases the girl was not only permitted, but *obliged* to marry within the gens, in order that the latter might retain the fortune.

According to Grote's history of Greece,[b] the Athenian gens in particular was held together by:

1. Common religious. ceremonies, and exclusive right of the priesthood in honour of a definite god, supposed to be the forefather of the gens, and characterised in this capacity by a special surname.

2. A common burial place (cf. Demosthenes' *Eubulides*[103]).

3. Mutual rights of inheritance.

4. Reciprocal obligation to afford help, defence and support against the use of force.

5. Mutual right and obligation to intermarry within the gens in certain cases, especially for orphaned daughters or heiresses.

6. Possession, in some cases at least, of common property, and of an archon (magistrate) and treasurer of its own.

The phratry, binding together several gentes, was less intimate, but here too we find mutual rights and duties of similar character, especially a communion of particular religious rites and the right of prosecution in the event of a phrator being slain. Again, all the phratries of a tribe performed periodically certain common sacred ceremonies under the presidency of a *phylobasileus* (tribal magistrate), selected from among the nobles (*eupatrides*).

Thus Grote. And Marx adds: "In the Grecian gens the savage (for example, the Iroquois) is unmistakably discerned."[c] He becomes still more unmistakable when we investigate somewhat further.

For the Grecian gens has also the following attributes:

7. Descent according to father right.

8. Prohibition of intermarriage within the gens except in the case of heiresses. This exception, and its formulation as an

---

a The 1884 edition has "punaluan family" instead of "group marriage".— *Ed.*
b G. Grote, *A History of Greece,* Vol. III, pp. 54-55.— *Ed.*
c "Marx's Excerpts...", op. cit., p. 198.— *Ed.*

injunction, proves the validity of the old rule. This follows also from the universally accepted rule that when a woman married she renounced the religious rites of her gens and acquired those of her husband, in whose phratry she was enrolled. This, and a famous passage in Dicaearchus,[a] go to prove that marriage outside the gens was the rule. Becker in *Charikles* directly assumes that nobody was permitted to marry in his or her own gens.[b]

9. The right of adoption into the gens; it was practised by adoption into the family, but with public formalities, and only in exceptional cases.

10. The right to elect and depose the chiefs. We know that every gens had its archon; but nowhere is it stated that this office was hereditary in certain families. Until the end of barbarism, the probability is always against strict[c] heredity, which would be totally incompatible with conditions where rich and poor had absolutely equal rights in the gens.

Not only Grote, but also Niebuhr, Mommsen and all other previous historians of classical antiquity, failed with the gens. Although they correctly noted many of its distinguishing features, they always regarded it as a *group of families* and thus made it impossible for themselves to understand the nature and origin of the gens. Under the gentile constitution, the family was never a unit of organisation, nor could it be, for man and wife necessarily belonged to two different gentes. The gens as a whole belonged to the phratry, the phratry to the tribe; but in the case of the family, half of it belonged to the gens of the husband and half to that of the wife. The state, too, does not recognise the family in public law; to this day it exists only in civil law. Nevertheless, all our historiography so far takes as its point of departure the absurd assumption, which became inviolable particularly in the eighteenth century, that the monogamian individual family, which is scarcely older than civilisation, is the nucleus around which society and the state gradually crystallised.

"Mr. Grote will also please note," adds Marx,[104] "that although the Greeks traced their gentes to mythology, the gentes are older than mythology with its gods and demigods, which *they themselves* had created."[d]

Grote is quoted with preference by Morgan as a respected

---

[a] Cited in W. Wachsmuth's *Hellenische Alterthumskunde aus dem Gesichtspunkte des Staates,* Part 1, Section 1, p. 312.— *Ed.*

[b] W. A. Becker, *Charikles, Bilder altgriechischer Sitte,* Part 2, p. 447.— *Ed.*

[c] The word "strict" was added by Engels in the 1891 edition.— *Ed.*

[d] "Marx's Excerpts...", op. cit., p. 200.— *Ed.*

witness beyond suspicion. He further relates that every Athenian gens had a name derived from its supposed forefather; that before Solon's time as a general rule, and afterwards if a man died intestate, his gentiles (*gennêtes*) inherited his property; and that if a man was murdered, first his relatives, next his gentiles, and finally the phrators of the slain had the right and duty to prosecute the criminal in the courts:

"All that we hear of the most ancient Athenian laws is based upon the gentile and phratric divisions." [a]

The descent of the gentes from common ancestors has been a brain-racking puzzle to the "school-taught Philistines" (Marx).[b] Naturally, since they claim that these ancestors are purely mythical, they are at a loss to explain how the gentes developed out of separate and distinct, originally totally unrelated families; yet they must accomplish this somehow, if only to explain the existence of the gentes. So they circle round in a whirlpool of words and do not get beyond the phrase: the genealogy is indeed mythical, but the gens is real. And finally, Grote says—the bracketed remarks being by Marx—:

"We hear of this genealogy but rarely, because it is only brought before the public in certain cases pre-eminent and venerable. But the humbler gentes had their common rites" (rather peculiar, Mr. Grote!) "and common superhuman ancestor and genealogy, as well as the more celebrated" (how very strange this on the part of *humbler* gentes!); "the scheme and ideal (my dear Sir! Not *ideal*, but carnal—*germanice*[c] *fleischlich*!) basis was the same in all." [d]

Marx sums up Morgan's reply to this as follows: "The system of consanguinity which pertained to the gens in its archaic form—and which the Greeks once possessed like other mortals—preserved a knowledge of the relationships of all the members of a gens to each other. They learned this for them decisively important fact by practice from early childhood. This fell into desuetude with the rise of the monogamian family. The gentile name created a pedigree beside which that of the individual family was insignificant. This name was now to preserve the fact of the common descent of those who bore it; but the lineage of the gens went so far back that its members could no longer prove the actual relationship existing between them, except in a limited number of

---

a G. Grote, *A History of Greece,* Vol. III, p. 66. See also "Marx's Excerpts...", op. cit., p. 230.— *Ed.*

b "Marx's Excerpts...", op. cit., p. 201.— *Ed.*

c In plain German.— *Ed.*

d Here and below see "Marx's Excerpts...", op. cit., p. 202, and also G. Grote, *A History of Greece,* Vol. III, p. 60.— *Ed.*

cases through recent common ancestors. The name itself was the
evidence of a common descent, and conclusive proof, except in
cases of adoption. The actual denial of all kinship between gentiles
à la Grote[a] and Niebuhr, which transforms the gens into a purely
fictitious, fanciful creation of the brain, is, on the other hand,
worthy of 'ideal' scientists, that is, of cloistered bookworms.
Because the concatenation of the generations, especially with the
incipience of monogamy, is removed into the distance, and the
reality of the past seems reflected in mythological fantasy, the
good old Philistines concluded, and still conclude, that the fancied
genealogy created real gentes!"[105]

As among the Americans, the *phratry* was a mother gens, split
up into several daughter gentes, and uniting them, often tracing
them all to a common ancestor. Thus, according to Grote,

"all the contemporary members of the phratry of Hekataeus had a common
god for their ancestor at the sixteenth degree".[b]

Hence, all the gentes of this phratry were literally brother
gentes. The phratry still occurs in Homer as a military unit in that
famous passage where Nestor advises Agamemnon: Draw up
people by tribes and by phratries so that phratry may support
phratry, and tribe tribe.[c] Moreover, the phratry has the right and
the duty to prosecute the murderer of a phrator, indicating that at
an earlier stage it had the duty of blood revenge. Furthermore, it
has common shrines and festivals; for the development of all
Greek mythology from the traditional old Aryan cult of nature
was essentially due to the gentes and phratries and took place
within them. The phratry also had a chief (*phratriarchos*) and,
according to de Coulanges, assemblies and binding decisions, a
tribunal and an administration.[d] Even the state of a later period,
while ignoring the gens, left certain public functions to the
phratry.

A number of kindred phratries constituted a tribe. In Attica
there were four tribes of three phratries each, each phratry
consisting of thirty gentes. Such a meticulous demarcation of the
groups presupposes a conscious and planned interference with the
naturally evolved order of things. On how, when and why this
happened Grecian history keeps silent, for the Greeks themselves

---

[a] Like Morgan, Marx has "Pollux", a 2nd-century Greek scholar, to whom Grote
has frequent references.— *Ed.*

[b] G. Grote, op. cit., Vol. III, pp. 58-59. See also "Marx's Excerpts...", op. cit.,
p. 202.— *Ed.*

[c] Homer, *Iliad*, Canto II.— *Ed.*

[d] Fustel de Coulanges, *La cité antique*, p. 146.— *Ed.*

preserved memories reaching back no further than the Heroic Age.

Closely packed in a comparatively small territory as the Greeks were, their dialectal differences were less developed than those in the extensive American forests. Nevertheless, even here we find only tribes of the same main dialect united in a larger whole; and even little Attica had its own dialect, which was later to become dominant as the universal language of prose.

In the epics of Homer we mostly find the Grecian tribes already combined into small peoples, within which, however, the gentes, phratries and tribes still retained their full independence. They already lived in walled cities. The population increased with the growth of the herds, with field agriculture and the beginnings of the handicrafts. With this came increased differences in wealth, which gave rise to an aristocratic element within the old naturally evolved democracy. The separate small peoples engaged in constant warfare for the possession of the best land and also for the sake of loot. The enslavement of prisoners of war was already a recognised institution.

The constitution of these tribes and small peoples was as follows:

1. The permanent authority was the *council* (*boulê*), originally composed, most likely, of the chiefs of the gentes, but later on, when their number became too large, of a selection, which created the opportunity to develop and strengthen the aristocratic element. Dionysius definitely speaks of the council of the Heroic Age as being composed of notables (*kratistoi*).[a] The council had the final decision in important matters. In Aeschylus, the council of Thebes passes a decision definitive in the given case that the body of Eteocles be buried with full honours, and the body of Polynices be thrown out to be devoured by the dogs.[b] Later, with the rise of the state, this council was transformed into a senate.

2. The *popular assembly* (*agora*). Among the Iroquois we saw that the people, men and women, stood in a circle around the council meetings, taking an orderly part in the discussions and thus influencing its decisions. Among the Homeric Greeks, this *Umstand*,[c] to use an old German legal expression, had already developed into a plenary assembly of the people, as was also the case with the ancient Germans. The assembly was convened by the

---

[a] Dionysius of Halicarnassus, *Roman Antiquities*, II, 12.— *Ed.*
[b] Aeschylus, *The Seven Against Thebes*, III, 2.— *Ed.*
[c] *Umstand*: Those standing around.— *Ed.*

council to decide important matters; every man had the right to speak. Decisions were taken by a show of hands (Aeschylus in *The Suppliants*), or by acclamation. They were sovereign and final, for, as Schoemann says in his *Griechische Alterthümer* [Vol. I, p. 27],

"whenever a matter is discussed that requires the co-operation of the people for its execution, Homer gives us no indication of any means by which the people could be forced into it against their will".

At this time, when every adult male member of the tribe was a warrior, there was as yet no public authority separated from the people that could have been set against it. Naturally evolved democracy was still in full bloom, and this must remain the point of departure in judging the power and status of the council and of the *basileus*.

3. The *military commander* (*basileus*). On this point, Marx makes the following comment: "The European savants, most of them born servants of princes, represent the *basileus* as a monarch in the modern sense. The Yankee republican Morgan objects to this. Very ironically, but, truthfully, he says of the oily Gladstone and his *Juventus Mundi*:

"'Mr. Gladstone, who presents to his readers the Grecian chiefs of the Heroic Age as kings and princes, with the superadded qualities of gentlemen, is forced to admit that on the whole we seem to have the custom or law of primogeniture sufficiently, but not oversharply defined.'"[a]

As a matter of fact, Mr. Gladstone himself must realise that such a contingent system of primogeniture, sufficiently but not oversharply defined, is as good as none at all.

What the position as regards heredity was in the case of the offices of chiefs among the Iroquois and other Indians we have already seen. All officials were elected, mostly within the gens, and were, to that extent, hereditary in the gens. Gradually, vacancies came to be filled preferably by the next gentile relative—the brother or the sister's son—unless good reasons existed for passing him over. The fact that in Greece, under father right, the office of *basileus* was generally transmitted to the son, or one of the sons, only indicates that the probability of succession by public election was in favour of the sons; but it by no means implies legally binding succession without public election. What we have here, among the Iroquois and Greeks, are the first rudiments of special aristocratic families within the gentes and, among the Greeks, also the first rudiments of a future hereditary chieftain-

---

[a] L. H. Morgan, *Ancient Society*, p. 248; "Marx's Excerpts...", op. cit., p. 206.— *Ed.*

ship or monarchy. Hence it is to be supposed that among the Greeks the *basileus* was either elected by the people or, at least, had to be confirmed by its recognised organs—the council or the *agora*—as was the case with the Roman "king" (*rex*).

In the *Iliad* the ruler of men, Agamemnon, appears, not as the supreme king of the Greeks, but as supreme commander of a federal army before a besieged city. And when dissension broke out among the Greeks, it is to this quality of his that Odysseus points in the famous passage: the rule of many is not a good thing; let us have one commander, etc. (to which the popular verse about the sceptre was added later).[a] "Odysseus is not here lecturing on the form of government, but is demanding obedience to the supreme commander of the army in the field. For the Greeks, who appear before Troy only as an army, the proceedings in the *agora* are sufficiently democratic. When speaking of gifts, that is, the division of the spoils, Achilles never makes Agamemnon or some other *basileus* the divider, but always the 'sons of the Achaeans', i.e. the people. The attributes 'begotten of Zeus', 'nourished by Zeus', do not prove anything because *every* gens is descended from some god, and the gens of the tribal chief from a 'prominent' god, in this case Zeus. Even personally unfree, such as the swineherd Eumaeus and others, are 'divine' (*dioi* or *theioi*), and this in the *Odyssey,* and hence in a much later period than the *Iliad.* Likewise in the *Odyssey,* we find the name of *heros* given to the herald Mulios as well as to the blind bard Demodocus.[b] In short, the word *basileia,* which the Greek writers apply to Homer's so-called kingship (because military leadership is its chief distinguishing mark), with the council and popular assembly alongside of it, means merely—military democracy." (Marx.)[c]

Besides military functions, the *basileus* also had priestly and judicial functions; the latter were not clearly specified, but the former he exercised in his capacity of supreme representative of the tribe, or of the confederacy of tribes. There is no reference anywhere to civil, administrative functions; but it seems that he was *ex officio* a member of the council. Etymologically, it is quite correct to translate *basileus* as *König* (king), because *König* (*kuning*)

---

[a] Homer, *Iliad,* Canto II.— *Ed.*

[b] In "Marx's Excerpts..." here follows the sentence omitted by Engels: "the term *kairanos* used by Odysseus along with *basileus,* in regard to Agamemnon, also means merely 'commander in the field' ".— *Ed.*

[c] "Marx's Excerpts...", op. cit., p. 207. Marx quotes Morgan (*Ancient Society,* pp. 248-49) with some additions. Engels also makes some abridgements and changes here.— *Ed.*

is derived from *kuni, künne,* and signifies chief of a gens. But the ancient Greek *basileus* in no way corresponds to the modern meaning of the word *König.* Thucydides expressly refers to the old *basileia* as *patrikê,* that is, derived from gentes, and states that it had specified, hence restricted, functions.[a] And Aristotle says that the *basileia* of the Heroic Age was a leadership over freemen, and that the *basileus* was a military chief, judge and high priest.[b] Hence, the *basileus* had no governmental power in the later sense.*

Thus, in the Grecian constitution of the Heroic Age, we still find the old gentile system full of vigour; but we also see the beginning of its decay: father right and the inheritance of property by the children, which favoured the accumulation of wealth in the family and gave the latter power as against the gens; differentiation in wealth affecting in turn the social constitution by creating the first rudiments of a hereditary nobility and monarchy; slavery, first limited to prisoners of war, but already opening up the prospect of the enslavement of fellow members of the tribe and even of the gens; the degeneration of the old intertribal warfare into systematic robbery on land and sea for the purpose of capturing cattle, slaves and treasure, into a regular source of income. In short, wealth is praised and respected as the highest treasure, and the old gentile systems are abused in order to justify forcible robbery of wealth. Only one thing was missing: an institution that would not only safeguard the newly acquired wealth of individuals against the communistic traditions of the gentile system, would not only sanctify private property, formerly held in such low esteem, and pronounce this sanctification the supreme purpose of every human society, but would also stamp the successively developing new forms of acquiring property, and consequently, of constantly accelerating the increase in wealth,

---

* Like the Grecian *basileus,* the Aztec military chief has been wrongly presented as a prince in the modern sense. Morgan was the first to subject to historical criticism the reports of the Spaniards, who at first misunderstood and exaggerated, and later deliberately misrepresented things; he showed that the Mexicans were in the middle stage of barbarism, but on a higher plane than the New Mexican Pueblo Indians,[106] and that their constitution, so far as the garbled accounts enable us to judge, corresponded to the following: a confederacy of three tribes, which had made a number of others tributary, and which was governed by a Federal Council and a federal military chief, whom the Spaniards had made into an "emperor". [See L. H. Morgan, *Ancient Society,* pp. 186-214.— *Ed.*]

---

[a] Thucydides, *The History of the Peloponnesian War,* Book I, Ch. 13.— *Ed.*
[b] Aristotle, *Politics,* Book III, Ch. 10.— *Ed.*

with the seal of general public recognition; an institution that would perpetuate, not only the arising class division of society, but also the right of the possessing class to exploit the non-possessing classes and the rule of the former over the latter.

And this institution arrived. The *state* was invented.

V

THE EMERGENCE OF THE ATHENIAN STATE

How the state developed, with some of the organs of the gentile constitution being transformed, some displaced, by the intrusion of new organs, and, finally, all superseded by real state authorities—while the place of the actual "people in arms" defending themselves through their gentes, phratries and tribes was taken by an armed "public power" at the service of these state authorities and, therefore, also usable against the people—all this can nowhere be better traced, at least in its initial stage, than in ancient Athens. The changes in form are, in the main, described by Morgan; the economic content which gave rise to them I had largely to add myself.

In the Heroic Age, the four tribes of the Athenians were still installed in separate parts of Attica. Even the twelve phratries comprising them seem still to have had separate seats in the twelve towns of Cecrops. The constitution was that of the Heroic Age: a popular assembly, a popular council, a *basileus*. As far back as written history goes we find the land already divided up and transformed into private property, which corresponds with the relatively developed commodity production and the commodity trade that went with it towards the end of the higher stage of barbarism. In addition to cereals, wine and oil were produced. Maritime commerce on the Aegean Sea passed more and more from Phoenician into Attic hands. As a result of the purchase and sale of landed property and the advancing division of labour between agriculture and handicrafts, trade and navigation, the members of gentes, phratries and tribes very soon intermingled. The districts of the phratry and the tribe received inhabitants who, although they were fellow countrymen, did not belong to these bodies and, therefore, were outsiders in their own place of abode. For in times of calm every phratry and every tribe administered its own affairs without consulting the popular council or the *basileus* in Athens. But inhabitants of the area of the phratry or tribe not belonging to either naturally could not take part in this administration.

This disturbed the normal functioning of the organs of the gentile constitution so much that a remedy was needed as far back as the Heroic Age. A constitution, attributed to Theseus, was introduced. The main feature of this change was the institution of a central administration in Athens, i.e., some of the affairs that hitherto had been administered independently by the tribes were declared to be common affairs and transferred to a general council sitting in Athens. Thereby, the Athenians went a step further than any indigenous people in America had ever gone: the simple confederacy of neighbouring tribes was now supplanted by their coalescence into one single people. This gave rise to a general Athenian popular law, which stood above the legal customs of the tribes and gentes. It bestowed on the citizens of Athens, as such, certain rights and additional legal protection even in territory where they were aliens. This, however, was the first step towards undermining the gentile constitution; for it was the first step towards the subsequent admission of citizens who were alien to all the Attic tribes and were and remained entirely outside the pale of the Athenian gentile constitution. A second institution attributed to Theseus was the division of the entire people, irrespective of gentes, phratries and tribes, into three classes: *eupatrides,* or nobles; *geomoroi,* or tillers of the land; and *demiurgi,* or artisans, and the granting to the nobles of the exclusive right to public office. True, apart from reserving for the nobles the right to hold public office, this division had no effect, as it created no other legal distinctions between the classes.[a] It is important, however, because it reveals to us the new social elements that had quietly developed. It shows that the customary holding of office in the gens by certain families had already developed into an entitlement of these families that was little contested; that these families, already powerful owing to their wealth, began to unite outside of their gentes into a privileged class of their own; and that the nascent state sanctified this presumptuousness. It shows, furthermore, that the division of labour between husbandmen and artisans had already become strong enough to call into question, in the social sense, the supremacy of the old division into gentes and tribes. And finally, it proclaimed the irreconcilable antagonism between gentile society and the state. The first attempt to form a state consisted in breaking up the gentes by dividing the members

---

[a] In the 1884 edition the end of the sentence reads: "as the two other classes got no special rights".— *Ed.*

of each into a privileged and an inferior class, and the latter again into two vocational classes, thus setting one against the other.

The ensuing political history of Athens up to the time of Solon is only incompletely known. The office of *basileus* fell into disuse; *archons,* elected from among the nobility, became the heads of the state. The rule of the nobility steadily increased until, round about 600 B.C., it became unbearable. The principal means for stifling common liberty were—money and usury. The nobility lived mainly in and around Athens, where maritime commerce, with occasional piracy still as a sideline, enriched it and concentrated monetary wealth in its hands. From this point the developing money system penetrated like corroding nitric acid into the traditional life of the rural communities founded on the natural economy. The gentile constitution is absolutely incompatible with the money system. The ruin of the Attic small-holding peasants coincided with the loosening of the old gentile bonds that protected them. Creditor's bills and mortgage bonds—for by then the Athenians had also invented the mortgage—respected neither the gens nor the phratry. But the old gentile constitution knew nothing of money, credit and monetary debt. Hence the constantly expanding money rule of the nobility gave rise to a new body of common law to protect the creditor against the debtor and sanction the exploitation of the small peasant by the money owner. All the fields of Attica bristled with mortgage posts bearing the legend that the lot on which they stood was mortgaged to so and so for so and so much. The fields that were not so designated had for the most part been sold on account of overdue mortgages or non-payment of interest and had become the property of the noble-born usurers; the peasant was glad if he was permitted to remain as a tenant and live on *one-sixth* of the product of his labour while paying *five-sixths* to his new master as rent. More than that: if the sum obtained from the sale of the lot did not cover the debt, or if such a debt was not secured by a pledge, the debtor had to sell his children into slavery abroad in order to satisfy the creditor's claim. The sale of his children by the father—such was the first fruit of father right and monogamy! And if the blood-sucker was still unsatisfied, he could sell the debtor himself into slavery. Such was the pleasant dawn of civilisation among the Athenian people.

Previously, when the conditions of life of the people were still in keeping with the gentile constitution, such a revolution would have been impossible; but here it had come about nobody knew how. Let us return for a moment to our Iroquois. Among them a state of affairs like that which had now imposed itself on the Athenians without their own doing, so to say, and certainly against their will, was inconceivable. There the mode of production of the means of subsistence, which, year in and year out, remained unchanged, could never give rise to such conflicts, imposed from without, as it were; to antagonism between rich and poor, between exploiters and exploited. The Iroquois were still far from controlling the forces of nature but within the limits set for them by nature they were masters of their production. Apart from poor harvests in their little gardens, the exhaustion of the fish stocks in their lakes and rivers, or of game in their forests, they knew what the outcome would be of their mode of gaining a livelihood. The outcome would be: means of sustenance, meagre or abundant; but it could never be unpremeditated social upheavals, the severing of gentile bonds, or the splitting of the members of gentes and tribes into antagonistic classes fighting each other. Production was carried on within the most restricted limits, but—the producers exercised control over their own product. This was the immense advantage of barbarian production that was lost with the advent of civilisation; and to win it back on the basis of the enormous control man now exercises over the forces of nature, and of the free association that is now possible, will be the task of the next generations.

Not so among the Greeks. The appearance of private property in herds and articles of luxury led to exchange between individuals, to the transformation of products into *commodities.* Here lies the root of the entire revolution that followed. As soon as producers no longer directly consumed their product, but surrendered it in the course of exchange, they lost control over it. They no longer knew what became of it, and the possibility arose that the product might some day be turned against the producer, used as a means of exploiting and oppressing him. Hence, no society can for long remain master of its own production and continue to control the social effects of its production process, unless it abolishes exchange between individuals.

The Athenians were to learn, however, how quickly after individual exchange is established and products are converted into commodities, the product brings to bear its rule over the producer. With the production of commodities came the tilling of the soil by individual cultivators for their own account, soon followed by individual ownership of the land. There also came money, that universal commodity for which all others could be exchanged. But when men invented money they little suspected that they were creating a new social power, the one universal power to which the whole of society must bow. It was this new power, suddenly sprung into existence without the knowledge or will of its own creators, which, in all the brutality of its youth, exposed the Athenians to its rule.

What was to be done? The old gentile organisation had not only proved impotent against the triumphant march of money; it was also absolutely incapable of even providing a place within its framework for such things as money, creditors, debtors and the forcible collection of debts. But the new social power was there, and neither pious wishes nor a longing for the return of the good old times could drive money and usury out of existence. Moreover, a number of other, minor breaches had been made in the gentile constitution. The indiscriminate mingling of the gentiles and phrators throughout the whole of Attica, and especially in the city of Athens itself, had increased from generation to generation, in spite of the fact that an Athenian, while allowed to sell plots of land out of his gens, was still prohibited from thus selling his dwelling. The division of labour between the different branches of production—agriculture, hand-icrafts, numerous skills within the various crafts, trade, navigation, etc.—had developed more and more fully with the progress of industry and commerce. The population was now divided according to occupation into rather well-established groups, each of which had a number of new, common interests that found no place in the gens or phratry and, therefore, necessitated the creation of new offices to attend to them. The number of slaves had increased considerably and must have far exceeded that of the free Athenians even then. The gentile constitution originally knew no slavery and, therefore, no means of holding this mass of bondsmen in check. And finally, commerce had attracted a great many outsiders to Athens who settled there because it was easier to make money there, and according to the old constitution these outsiders enjoyed neither rights nor the protection of the law. In spite of traditional toleration, they remained a disturbingly alien element among the people.

In short, the gentile constitution was coming to an end. Society was outgrowing it by the day; it was powerless to allay or check even the worst evils that were arising under its very eyes. In the meantime, however, the state had developed. The new groups formed by division of labour, first between town and country, then between the various branches of urban industry, had created new organs to protect their interests. Public offices of every description had been instituted. And then the young state needed, above all, its own fighting forces, which among the seafaring Athenians could at first be only naval forces, to be used for occasional minor wars and to protect merchant vessels. At some uncertain time before Solon, the naucraries were instituted, small territorial districts, twelve in each tribe. Every naucrary had to supply, equip and man a war vessel and, in addition, provided two horsemen. This arrangement was a twofold attack on the gentile constitution. First, it created a public power which was no longer simply identical with the armed people in their totality; secondly, for the first time it divided the people for public purposes, not according to kinship groups, but according to *common domicile*. We shall see what this signified.

As the gentile constitution could not come to the assistance of the exploited people, they could look only to the emerging state. And the state brought help in the form of the constitution of Solon, while at the same time strengthening itself anew at the expense of the old constitution. Solon—the manner in which his reform of 594 B.C. was carried out does not concern us here—started the series of so-called political revolutions by an encroachment on property. All revolutions to date have been revolutions for the protection of one kind of property against another kind of property. They cannot protect one kind without violating another. In the Great French Revolution feudal property was sacrificed in order to save bourgeois property; in Solon's revolution, creditors' property had to suffer for the benefit of debtors' property. The debts were simply annulled. We are not acquainted with the exact details, but Solon boasts in his poems that he removed the mortgage posts from the encumbered lands and enabled all who had been sold or had fled abroad because of debt to return home. This could have been done only by openly violating property rights. And indeed, the object of all so-called political revolutions, from first to last, was to protect *one* kind of property by confiscating—also called stealing—*another* kind of property. This is so true that for 2,500 years it has been possible to maintain private property only by violating property rights.

But now a way had to be found to prevent such re-enslavement of the free Athenians. This was first achieved by general measures; for example, the prohibition of contracts which involved the mortgaging of the debtor's person. Furthermore, a maximum was fixed for the amount of landed property any one individual could own, in order to put some curb, at least, on the voracious craving of the nobility for the peasants' land. Then followed constitutional amendments, of which the most important for us are the following:

The council was increased to four hundred members, one hundred from each tribe. Here, then, the tribe was still the basis. But this was the only side of the old constitution that was incorporated in the new body politic. For the rest, Solon divided the citizens into four classes, according to the amount of land owned and its yield. Five hundred, three hundred and one hundred and fifty medimni of grain (1 medimnus=appr. 41 litres) were the minimum yields for the first three classes; whoever had less land or none at all belonged to the fourth class. Only members of the first three classes could hold office; the highest offices were filled exclusively by the first class. The fourth class had only the right to speak and vote in the popular assembly. But it was here that all officials were elected, here that they had to give account of their actions, here that all the laws were made, and here that the fourth class was in the majority. The aristocratic privileges were partly renewed in the form of privileges of wealth, but the people retained the decisive power. The four classes also formed the basis for the reorganisation of the fighting forces. The first two classes furnished the cavalry; the third had to serve as heavy infantry; the fourth served as light infantry, without armour, or in the navy, in which case they probably were paid.

Thus, an entirely new element was introduced into the constitution: private ownership. The rights and duties of the citizens of the state were graded according to the amount of land they owned; and as the propertied classes gained influence the old consanguine groups were displaced. The gentile constitution suffered another defeat.

The gradation of political rights according to property, however, was not an indispensable institution for the state. Important as it may have been in the constitutional history of states, nevertheless, a good many states, and the most developed at that, did without it. Even in Athens it played only a transient role. From the time of Aristides, all offices were open to all the citizens.[107]

During the next eighty years Athenian society gradually found its way to the path along which it continued to develop in subsequent centuries. Usurious land operations, rampant in the pre-Solon period, were checked, as was the excessive concentration of landed property. Commerce and the arts and crafts conducted on an ever-increasing scale with slave labour became the predominant branches of industry. People became more enlightened. Instead of exploiting their own fellow-citizens in the old brutal manner, the Athenians now exploited mainly the slaves and non-Athenian clients. Movable property, wealth in money, slaves and ships, increased more and more; but instead of being simply a means for acquiring landed property, as in the initial, bigoted period, they became an end in themselves. This, on the one hand, gave rise to the successful competition of the new, wealthy industrial and commercial class against the old power of the nobility, but, on the other hand, it deprived the remnants of the old gentile constitution of their last foothold. The gentes, phratries and tribes, whose members were now scattered all over Attica and lived completely intermingled, thus became quite unsuitable for political bodies. A large number of Athenian citizens did not belong to any gens; they were immigrants who had been adopted into citizenship sure enough but not into any of the old bodies of *consanguinei*. Besides, there was a steadily increasing number of foreign immigrants who only enjoyed protection.[108]

Meanwhile, the struggles of the parties proceeded. The nobility tried to regain its former privileges and for a short time got the upper hand again, until the revolution of Cleisthenes (509 B.C.) brought about its ultimate downfall; and with it fell the last remnants of the gentile constitution.[109]

In his new constitution, Cleisthenes ignored the four old tribes based on the gentes and phratries. Their place was taken by an entirely new organisation based exclusively on the division of the citizens according to place of abode, already attempted in the naucraries. Not membership of a body of *consanguinei*, but place of abode was now the deciding factor. Not people, but territory was now divided; politically, the inhabitants became mere adjuncts of the territory.

The whole of Attica was divided into one hundred self-governing districts, or demes. The citizens of a deme (demots) elected their head (demarch), a treasurer and thirty judges with jurisdiction in minor cases. They also received their own temple and a tutelary god, or *heros*, whose priests they elected. The supreme power in the deme was the assembly of the demots. This, as Morgan correctly remarks, is the prototype of the self-governing American township.[a] The modern state in its highest form ends with the very unit with which the rising state in Athens began.

Ten of these units (demes) formed a tribe, which, however, as distinct from the old kinship tribe, was now called a territorial

---

[a] L. H. Morgan, *Ancient Society*, p. 271.— *Ed.*

tribe. The territorial tribe was not only a self-governing political body, but also a military body. It elected a phylarch or tribal head, who commanded the cavalry, a taxiarch, who commanded the infantry, and a *strategos,* who was in command of the entire contingent levied in the tribal territory. Furthermore, it furnished five war vessels with crews and commander; and it received an Attic *heros,* by whose name it was called, as its patron saint. Finally, it elected fifty councillors to the council of Athens.

The consummation was the Athenian state, governed by a council of five hundred—elected by the ten tribes—and, in the last instance, by the popular assembly, which every Athenian citizen could attend and vote in. Moreover, archons and other officials attended to the different departments of administration and the courts. In Athens there was no official possessing supreme executive authority.

By this new constitution, and by the admission of a very large number of wards, partly immigrants and partly freed slaves, the organs of the gentile constitution were ousted from public affairs. They sank to the position of private societies and religious associations. But their moral influence, the traditional conceptions and views of the old gentile period, were passed on for a long time and expired only gradually. This manifested itself in another state institution.

We have seen that an essential feature of the state is a public power distinct from the mass of the people. At that time Athens possessed only a militia and a navy manned directly by the people. These afforded protection against external enemies and held in check the slaves who at that time already constituted the great majority of the population. For the citizens, this public power at first existed only in the shape of the police force, which is as old as the state, and that is why the naïve Frenchmen of the eighteenth century spoke, not of civilised, but of policed nations (*nations policées*). Thus, simultaneously with their state, the Athenians established a police force, a veritable gendarmerie of bowmen on foot and horseback— *Landjäger,* as they say in South Germany and Switzerland. But this gendarmerie consisted—of *slaves.* The free Athenian regarded this dirty work as being so degrading that he preferred being arrested by an armed slave rather than perform such ignominious acts himself. This was still an expression of the old gentile mentality. The state could not exist without a police force, but it was still young and did not yet command sufficient moral respect to give prestige to an occupation that was bound to appear infamous to the old gentiles.

How well this state, now complete in its main features, suited the new social condition of the Athenians was apparent from the rapid flourishing of wealth, commerce and industry. The class antagonism on which the social and political institutions rested was no longer that between the nobles and the common people, but that between slaves and freemen, wards and citizens. When Athens was in its heyday the total number of free Athenian citizens, women and children included, amounted to about 90,000; the slaves of both sexes numbered 365,000, and the wards— immigrants and freed men—45,000. Thus, for every adult male citizen there were at least eighteen slaves and more than two wards. The large number of slaves is explained by the fact that many of them worked together in manufactories, large rooms, under overseers. But with the development of commerce and industry came the accumulation and concentration of wealth in few hands; the mass of the free citizens were impoverished and had to choose between competing with slave labour by going into handicrafts themselves, which was considered ignoble and base and, moreover, promised little success—and complete pauperisation. Under the prevailing circumstances what inevitably happened was the latter, and, being in the majority, they dragged the whole Athenian state down with them. It was not democracy that caused the downfall of Athens, as the European schoolmasters who fawn upon royalty would have us believe, but slavery, which brought the labour of the free citizen into contempt.

The emergence of the state among the Athenians represents a very typical model of state building in general; because, on the one hand, it took place in an entirely pure form, without the interference of violence, external or internal (the short period of usurpation by Pisistratus left no trace behind it [110]); because, on the other hand, it gave rise to a highly developed form of state, the democratic republic, directly from gentile society; and lastly, because we are sufficiently acquainted with all the essential details.

VI

THE GENS AND THE STATE IN ROME

According to the legend about the foundation of Rome, the first settlement was undertaken by a number of Latin gentes (one hundred, the legend says) united into one tribe. A Sabellian tribe, also said to consist of one hundred gentes, soon followed, and finally a third tribe of various elements, again allegedly of one hundred gentes, joined them. The whole story reveals at the very first glance that there was hardly anything naturally evolved except the gens, and that the gens itself, in some cases, was only an offshoot of a mother gens still existing in the old habitat. The tribes bear the mark of having been artificially constituted; nevertheless, they consisted mostly of kindred elements and were formed on the model of the old, naturally grown, not artificially constituted, tribe; and it is not impossible that an actual old tribe formed the nucleus of each of these three tribes. The middle link, the phratry, contained ten gentes and was called the *curia*. Hence, there were thirty of them.

That the Roman gens was an institution identical with the Grecian gens is a recognised fact; if the Grecian gens was a more advanced form of the social unit the primitive form of which is presented by the American Redskins, then the same, naturally, holds good for the Roman gens. Hence, we can be briefer in its treatment.

At least during the earliest times of the city, the Roman gens had the following constitution:

1. Mutual right of inheritance of the gentiles; the property remained in the gens. Since father right was already in force in the Roman gens, as it was in the Grecian gens, the offspring of female lineage were excluded. According to the law of the Twelve Tables, the oldest written Roman law known to us,[111] the natural children had the first title to the estate; in case no natural children existed, the agnates (kin of *male* lineage) took their place; and in their absence came the gentiles. In all cases the property remained in the gens. Here we observe the gradual infiltration into gentile practice of new legal provisions born of increased wealth and monogamy: the originally equal right of inheritance of the gentiles was first limited in practice to the agnates—probably at an early stage, as mentioned above—and eventually to the children and their offspring in the male line. Of course, in the Twelve Tables this appears in reverse order.

2. Possession of a common burial place. The patrician gens Claudia, on immigrating to Rome from Regili, was allocated a plot, and also a common burial place in the city. Even under Augustus, the head of Varus, who had fallen in the Teutoburg Forest,[112] was brought to Rome and interred in the *gentilitius tumulus*[a]; hence, the gens (Quinctilia) still had a separate burial mound.[b]

---

[a] Burial mound of the gens.— *Ed.*

[b] The end of the sentence from the words "hence, the gens" was added in the 1891 edition.— *Ed.*

3. Common religious celebrations. These, the *sacra gentilitia,* are well known.

4. Obligation not to marry within the gens. In Rome this does not appear to have ever become a written law, but the custom remained. Of the innumerable names of Roman married couples that have come down to our day there is not a single case where husband and wife have the same gentile name. The law of inheritance also proves this rule. A woman by her marriage forfeited her agnatic rights, left her gens, and neither she nor her children could inherit from her father, or his brothers, for otherwise the father's gens would lose part of the inheritance. This rule has a meaning only on the assumption that the woman was not permitted to marry a member of her own gens.

5. Possession of land in common. In primeval times this always existed since the tribal territory was first divided. Among the Latin tribes we find the land partly in the possession of the tribe, partly of the gens, and partly of households that at that time hardly[a] represented single families. Romulus is credited with having been the first to assign land to individuals, about a hectare (two *jugera*) to each. Nevertheless, even later we still find land in the hands of the gentes, not to mention state lands, around which turned the whole internal history of the republic.

6. Obligation of gentiles to protect and assist one another. Written history records only paltry remnants of this; from the outset the Roman state manifested such superior power that the right to redress injury was transferred to it. When Appius Claudius was arrested, his whole gens, even his personal enemies, went into mourning. At the time of the second Punic War[113] the gentes united to ransom their fellow gentiles who were in captivity; the senate *forbade* them to do this.

7. Right to bear the gentile name. This was in force until the time of the emperors. Freed men were permitted to assume the gentile names of their former masters, but without gentile rights.

8. Right of adopting outsiders into the gens. This was done by adoption into a family (as among the American Indians), which brought with it adoption into the gens.

9. The right to elect and depose chiefs is nowhere mentioned. Inasmuch, however, as during the initial period of Rome's existence all offices, from the elective king downward, were filled by election or appointment, and as the *curiae* elected also their own priests, we may assume that the same existed in regard to the

---

[a] The 1884 edition has "not necessarily" instead of "at that time hardly".— *Ed.*

gentile chiefs (*principes*)—no matter how well-established the rule of election from one and the same family in the gens may have already been.

Such were the powers of a Roman gens. With the exception of the already completed transition to father right, they are the faithful image of the rights and duties of an Iroquois gens. Here, too, "the Iroquois is unmistakably discerned".[a]

Of the confusion[b] that still reigns even among our most authoritative historians on the question of the Roman gentile order here only one example: In his treatise on Roman proper names of the Republican and Augustinian eras (*Römische Forschungen*, Berlin, 1864, Vol. I), Mommsen writes:

"The gentile name is not only borne by all male gentiles, including adopted persons and wards, except, of course, the slaves, but also by the women.... The tribe [*Stamm*]" (as Mommsen here translates *gens*) "is ... a community derived from a common—actual, assumed or even invented—ancestor and united by common rites, burial places and inheritance. All personally free individuals, hence women also, may and must be allocated to it. But determining the gentile name of a married woman presents some difficulty. This indeed did not exist as long as women were prohibited from marrying anyone but members of their own gens; and evidently for a long time the women found it much more difficult to marry outside the gens than within it. This right, the *gentis enuptio*,[c] was still bestowed as a personal privilege and reward during the sixth century.... But wherever such outside marriages occurred the woman in primeval times must have been transferred to the tribe of her husband. Nothing is more certain than that by the old religious marriage the woman fully joined the legal and sacral community of her husband and left her own. Who does not know that the married woman forfeits her active and passive right of inheritance in respect to her gentiles, but enters the inheritance group of her husband, her children and his gentiles? And if her husband adopts her as his child and brings her into his family, how can she remain separated from his gens?" (pp. 8-11).

Thus, Mommsen asserts that Roman women belonging to a certain gens were originally free to marry only *within* their gens; the Roman gens, therefore, was endogamous, not exogamous. This opinion, which contradicts all experience among other peoples, is principally, if not exclusively, based on a single, much disputed passage in Livy (Book XXXIX, Ch. 19) according to which the senate decreed in the year of the City 568, that is, 186 B.C.,

uti Feceniae Hispalae datio, deminutio, gentis enuptio, tutoris optio item esset quasi ei vir testamento dedisset; utique ei ingenuo nubere liceret, neu quid ei qui eam duxisset, ob id fraudi ignominiaeve esset—that Fecenia Hispala shall have the right to dispose of her

---

a "Marx's Excerpts...", op. cit., p. 198. The quotation is abridged.— *Ed.*

b The text from here to the words "Almost three hundred years after the foundation of Rome" (see p. 228) was added in the 1891 edition.— *Ed.*

c Of marrying outside the gens.— *Ed.*

property, to diminish it, to marry outside of the gens, to choose a guardian, just as if her (deceased) husband had conferred this right on her by testament; that she shall be permitted to marry a freeman and that for the man who marries her this shall not constitute a misdemeanour or disgrace.[a]

Undoubtedly, Fecenia, a freed woman, here obtained permission to marry outside of the gens. And it is equally doubtless, according to this, that the husband had the right to confer on his wife by testament the right to marry outside the gens after his death. But outside *which* gens?

If a woman had to marry within her gens, as Mommsen assumes, then she remained in this gens after her marriage. In the first place, however, this assertion that the gens was endogamous is the very thing to be proved. In the second place, if the woman had to marry in the gens, then naturally the man had to do the same, otherwise he could never get a wife. Then we arrive at a state where a man could by testament confer on his wife a right which he did not possess himself for his own enjoyment; we arrive at a legal absurdity. Mommsen realises this, and therefore conjectures:

"Marriage outside of the gens most probably required in law not only the consent of the person authorised, but of all members of the gens" (p. 10, note).

First, this is a very bold assumption; and second, it contradicts the clear wording of the passage. The senate gives her this right as her *husband's proxy*; it expressly gives her no more and no less than her husband could have given her; but what it does give is an *absolute* right, not dependent on any other restriction, so that, if she should make use of it, her new husband shall not suffer in consequence. The senate even instructs the present and future consuls and praetors to see that she suffers no hardship from the use of this right. Mommsen's supposition, therefore, appears to be absolutely inadmissible.

Then again: suppose a woman married a man from another gens, but remained in the gens into which she was born. According to the passage quoted above, her husband would then have the right to permit his wife to marry out of her own gens. That is, he would have the right to make provisions in regard to the affairs of a gens to which he did not belong at all. The thing is so utterly absurd that we need say no more about it.

Nothing remains but to assume that in her first marriage the woman wedded a man from another gens and thereby became without more ado a member of her husband's gens, which

---

[a] [Titus Livius] *Titi Livi ab urbe condita libri*, pp. 36-37.— *Ed.*

Mommsen actually admits for such cases. Then the whole matter at once explains itself. The woman, torn from her old gens by her marriage, and adopted into the new gentile group of her husband occupies a quite special position there. She is now a gentile, but not akin by blood; the manner in which she was adopted excludes from the outset all prohibition of her marrying within the gens into which she has entered by marriage. She has, moreover, been adopted into the marriage group of the gens and on her husband's death inherits some of his property, that is to say, the property of a fellow member of the gens. What is more natural than that this property should remain in the gens and that she should be obliged to marry a member of her first husband's gens and no other? If, however, an exception is to be made, who is more competent to authorise this than the man who bequeathed this property to her, her first husband? At the time he bequeathed a part of his property to her and simultaneously gave her permission to transfer this part of property to another gens by marriage, or as a result of marriage, this property still belonged to him; hence he was literally only disposing of his own property. As for the woman and her relation to her husband's gens, it was the husband who, by an act of his own free will—the marriage—introduced her into his gens. Thus, it appears quite natural, too, that he should be the proper person to authorise her to leave this gens by another marriage. In short, the matter appears simple and obvious as soon as we discard the strange conception of an endogamous Roman gens and, with Morgan, regard it as having originally been exogamous.

Finally, there is still another assumption, which has also found its advocates, and probably the most numerous, namely, that the passage only means

"that freed slave girls (*libertae*) cannot, without special permission, *e gente enubere*" (marry outside the gens) "or take any step which, being connected with *capitis deminutio minima*,[a] would result in the *liberta* leaving the gentile group." (Lange, *Römische Alterthümer*, Berlin, 1856, I, p. 195, where the passage we have taken from Livy is commented on in a reference to Huschke.[b])

If this assumption is correct, the passage proves still less as regards the status of free-born Roman women, and there is so much less ground for speaking of their obligation to marry within the gens.

---

[a] Restriction of civil rights.— *Ed.*

[b] Lange refers to Ph. Huschke's *De Privilegiis Feceniae Hispalae senatusconsulto concessis* (XXXIX, 19).— *Ed.*

The expression *enuptio gentis* occurs only in this single passage and is not found anywhere else in the whole of Roman literature. The word *enubere,* to marry outside, is found only three times, also in Livy, and not in reference to the gens. The fantastic idea that Roman women were permitted to marry only within their gens owes its existence solely to this single passage. But it cannot be sustained in the least; for either the passage refers to special restrictions for freed women, in which case it proves nothing for free-born women (*ingenuae*); or it applies also to free-born women, in which case it rather proves that the women as a rule married outside their gens and were by their marriage transferred to their husbands' gentes. Hence it speaks against Mommsen and for Morgan.

Almost three hundred years after the foundation of Rome the gentile bonds were still so strong that a patrician gens, the Fabians, with permission from the senate, was able to undertake off its own back an expedition against the neighbouring town of Veji. Three hundred and six Fabians are said to have set out and to have been killed in an ambush. A single boy, left behind, propagated the gens.

As we have said, ten gentes formed a phratry, which here was called a *curia,* and was endowed with more important social functions than the Grecian phratry. Every *curia* had its own religious practices, sacred relics and priests. The latter in a body formed one of the Roman colleges of priests. Ten *curiae* formed a tribe, which probably had originally its own elected chief—military chief and high priest—like the rest of the Latin tribes. The three tribes together formed the Roman people, the *populus Romanus.*

Thus, only those could belong to the Roman people who were members of a gens, and hence of a *curia* and tribe. The first constitution of this people was as follows. Public affairs were conducted at first by the senate composed, as Niebuhr was the first to state correctly, of the chiefs of the three hundred gentes[a]; precisely for this reason, as the elders of the gentes, they were called fathers, *patres,* and, as a body, senate (council of elders, from *senex,* old). Here too the customary choice of men always from the same family in each gens brought into being the first hereditary nobility. These families called themselves patricians and claimed the exclusive right to the seats in the senate and to all other offices. The fact that in the course of time the people acquiesced this claim so that it became an actual right is expressed

---

[a] B. G. Niebuhr, *Römische Geschichte,* Part 1, p. 352.— *Ed.*

in the legend that Romulus bestowed the rank of patrician and its privileges on the first senators and their descendants. The senate, like the Athenian *boulê,* had power to decide in many affairs and to undertake the preliminary discussion of more important matters, especially of new laws. These were decided by the popular assembly, called *comitia curiata* (assembly of *curiae*). The assembled people were grouped by *curiae,* in each *curia* probably by *gentes,* and in decision-making each of the thirty *curiae* had one vote. The assembly of *curiae* adopted or rejected all laws, elected all higher officials including the *rex* (so-called king), declared war (but the senate concluded peace), and decided as a supreme court, on appeal of the parties, all cases involving capital punishment for Roman citizens.—Finally, by the side of the senate and the popular assembly stood the *rex,* corresponding exactly to the Grecian *basileus,* and by no means such an almost absolute monarch as Mommsen[a] depicts him.* The *rex* also was military commander, high priest and presiding officer of certain courts. He had no civil functions, or any power over life, liberty and property of the citizens whatever, except such as resulted from his disciplinary power as military commander or from his power to execute sentence as presiding officer of the court. The office of *rex* was not hereditary; on the contrary, he was first elected, probably on the nomination of his predecessor, by the assembly of *curiae* and then solemnly invested by a second assembly. That he could also be deposed is proved by the fate of Tarquinius Superbus.

Like the Greeks in the Heroic Age, the Romans at the time of the so-called kings lived in a military democracy based on gentes, phratries and tribes, from which it developed. Even though the *curiae* and tribes may have been partly artificial formations, they were moulded after the genuine and naturally evolved models of the society from which they emerged and which still surrounded them on all sides. And though the naturally evolved patrician

---

* The Latin *rex* is equivalent to the Celtic-Irish *righ* (tribal chief) and the Gothic *reiks.* That this, like our *Fürst* (English *first* and Danish *förste*), originally signified gentile or tribal chief is evident from the fact that the Goths in the fourth century already had a special term for the king of later times, the military chief of a whole people, namely, *thiudans.* In Ulfila's translation of the Bible Artaxerxes and Herod are never called *reiks* but *thiudans,* and the realm of the Emperor Tiberius not *reiki,* but *thiudinassus.* In the name of the Gothic *thiudans,* or, as we inaccurately translate it, king Thiudareiks, Theodorich, that is, Dietrich, the two names merge together.

[a] Th. Mommsen, *Römische Geschichte,* Vol. I, Book 1, Ch. 6.—*Ed.*

nobility had already gained ground, though the *reges* attempted gradually to extend their powers—this does not change the original fundamental character of the constitution, and this alone matters.

Meanwhile, the population of the city of Rome and of the Roman territory, enlarged by conquest, increased, partly by immigration, partly through the inhabitants of the subjugated, mostly Latin, districts. All these new subjects of the state (we leave out the question of the clients) were outside of the old gentes, *curiae* and tribes, and so were not part of the *populus Romanus,* the Roman people proper. They were personally free, could own landed property, had to pay taxes and were liable to military service. But they were not eligible for office and could neither participate in the assembly of *curiae* nor in the distribution of conquered state lands. They constituted the plebs, excluded from all public rights. Owing to their continually increasing numbers, their military training and armament, they became a menace to the old *populus* who had now firmly closed their ranks against any growth from the outside. The landed property, moreover, seems to have been fairly evenly divided between *populus* and plebs, while the mercantile and industrial wealth, though as yet not very developed, may have been mainly in the hands of the plebs.

In view of the large measure of obscurity that enshrouds the whole legendary primeval history of Rome—an obscurity considerably further intensified by the rationalistic-pragmatic attempts at interpretation and reports of later legally trained authors whose works serve us as source material—it is impossible to make any definite statements about the time, the course and the cause of the revolution that put an end to the old gentile constitution. The only thing we are certain of is that its cause lay in the conflicts between the plebs and the *populus.*

The new constitution, attributed to *rex* Servius Tullius and based on the Grecian model, more especially that of Solon, created a new popular assembly including or excluding all, *populus* and plebeians without distinction, according to whether they rendered military service or not. The whole male population liable to military service was divided into six classes, according to wealth. The minimum property qualifications for each of the first five classes were, respectively: I, 100,000 asses; II, 75,000 asses; III, 50,000 asses; IV, 25,000 asses; V, 11,000 asses; which, according to Dureau de la Malle, is equal to about 14,000, 10,500, 7,000, 3,600 and 1,570 marks, respectively.[114] The sixth class, the proletarians, consisted of those who possessed less and were exempt from military service and taxation. In the new popular assembly of *centuriae* (*comitia centuriata*) the citizens formed ranks after the manner of soldiers, in companies of one hundred (*centuria*), and each *centuria* had one vote. The first class placed 80 *centuriae* in the field; the second 22, the third 20, the fourth 22, the fifth 30 and the sixth, for propriety's sake, one. To these one must add 18 *centuriae* of horsemen composed of the wealthiest of all; altogether 193. For a majority 97 votes were required. But the horsemen and the first class alone had together 98 votes, thus being in the majority; when they were agreed, valid decisions were made without even asking the other classes.

Upon this new assembly of *centuriae* there now devolved all the political rights of the former assembly of *curiae* (a few nominal ones excepted); the *curiae* and the gentes composing them were thereby, as was the case in Athens, degraded to the position of mere private societies and religious associations, and as such they continued to vegetate for a long time, while the assembly of *curiae* soon ceased to exist. In order to displace also the three old gentile tribes from the state, four territorial tribes were introduced, each tribe inhabiting one quarter of the city and receiving certain political rights.

Thus, in Rome too, the old social order based on personal blood ties was destroyed even before the abolition of the so-called kingdom, and a new constitution, based on territorial division and differences in wealth, a real state constitution, took its place. Public power here was vested in the citizenry liable to military service, and was directed not only against the slaves, but also against the so-called proletarians, who were excluded from military service and the right to carry arms.

The new constitution was merely further developed upon the expulsion of Tarquinius Superbus, the last *rex,* who had usurped real royal power, and the replacement of the *rex* with two military commanders (consuls) having equal authority (as among the Iroquois). Within this constitution moved the whole history of the Roman republic with all its struggles between patricians and plebeians for access to office and a share in the state lands and the final dissolution of the patrician nobility in the new class of big land and money owners, who gradually absorbed all the land of the peasants ruined by military service, cultivated with the aid of slaves the enormous tracts thus created, depopulated Italy, and thus opened the gates not only to imperial rule, but also to its successors, the German barbarians.

VII

THE GENS AMONG THE CELTS AND GERMANS[115]

Space prevents us from going into the gentile institutions still found, in purer or more adulterated form, among the most diverse savage and barbarian peoples of the present day; or into the traces of such institutions found in the ancient history of civilised nations in Asia.[a] One or the other is encountered everywhere. A few illustrations may suffice: Even before the gens had been recognised its existence was proved and it was described more or less correctly by the man who took the greatest pains to misinterpret it, McLennan, who wrote of this institution among the Kalmucks, the Circassians, the Samoyeds[b] and three peoples in India: the Waralis, the Magars and the Munniporees.[c] Recently it was described by Maxim Kovalevsky, who discovered it among the Pshavs, Khevsurs, Svanetians and other Caucasian tribes.[d] Here we shall confine ourselves to a few brief notes on the occurrence of the gens among Celts and Teutons.

The oldest Celtic laws that have come down to our day show the gens still in full vitality. In Ireland it is alive, at least instinctively in the national consciousness, to this day, now that the English have forcibly torn it apart. It was still in full bloom in Scotland in the middle of the last century, and here, too, it succumbed only to the arms, laws and courts of the English.

The old Welsh laws, written several centuries before the English conquest,[116] not later than the eleventh century, still show communal field agriculture for whole villages, be it only as an exceptional remnant of a former universal custom. Every family had five acres for its own cultivation; another plot was at the same time cultivated in common and its yield divided. Judging by the Irish and Scottish analogies there cannot be any doubt that these village communities represent gentes or subdivisions of gentes, even if a reinvestigation of the Welsh laws, which I cannot undertake for lack of time (my notes are from 1869[117]), may not directly corroborate this. What, however, the Welsh sources, and the Irish with them, do prove directly is that among the Celts

---

[a] The text below, up to the words "Here we shall confine ourselves...", is added in the 1891 edition.— *Ed.*

[b] Nentsi.— *Ed.*

[c] See J. F. McLennan, *Primitive Marriage.*— *Ed.*

[d] M. Kovalevsky, *Tableau des origines et de l'évolution de la famille et de la propriété.*— *Ed.*

pairing marriage had not yet given way by any means to monogamy in the eleventh century. In Wales, marriage did not become indissoluble, or rather did not cease to be subject to notice of dissolution, until after seven years. Even if only three nights were lacking to make up the seven years, a married couple could still separate. Then their property was divided between them; the woman divided, the man made his choice. The furniture was divided according to certain very funny rules. If the marriage was dissolved by the man, he had to return the woman's dowry and a few other articles; if the woman initiated the dissolution, she received less. Of the children the man was given two, the woman one, namely, the middle child. If the woman married again after her divorce, and her first husband fetched her back, she was obliged to follow him, even if she already had *one* foot in the new conjugal bed. But if two people had lived together for seven years, they were considered man and wife, even if they had not previously been formally married. Chastity among girls before marriage was by no means strictly observed, nor was it demanded; the regulations governing this subject are of an extremely frivolous nature and in no way conform to bourgeois morals. If a woman committed adultery, her husband had a right to beat her—this was one of three cases when he could do so without incurring a penalty—but after that he could not demand any other redress, for

"the same offence shall either be atoned for or avenged, but not both".[a]

The reasons that entitled a woman to a divorce without detriment to her rights at the settlement were of a very diverse nature: the man's foul breath was sufficient. The redemption money to be paid to the tribal chief or king for the right of the first night (*gobr merch,* hence the medieval name *marcheta,* French *marquette*) plays a conspicuous part in the legal code. The women had the right to vote at the popular assemblies. Add to this that similar conditions are shown to have existed in Ireland; that temporary marriages were also quite the custom there, and that the women were assured of well-defined generous privileges in case of separation, even to the point of remuneration for domestic services; that a "first wife" existed by the side of others, and in dividing an inheritance no distinction was made between children born in or out of wedlock—and we have a picture of the pairing marriage compared with which the form of marriage valid in

---

[a] *Ancient Laws and Institutes of Wales,* Vol. 1, p. 93.— *Ed.*

North America seems strict; but this is not surprising in the eleventh century for a people which in Caesar's time were still living in group marriage.

The Irish gens (*sept*; the tribe was called *clainne,* clan) is confirmed and described not only by the ancient law-books, but also by the English jurists of the seventeenth century who were sent across for the purpose of transforming the clan lands into domains of the King of England. Up to this time, the land had been the common property of the clan or gens, except where the chiefs had already converted it into their private domains. When a gentile died, and a household thus ceased to exist, the gentile chief (called *caput cognationis* by the English jurists) redistributed the whole land among the remaining households. This distribution must in general have taken place according to rules such as were observed in Germany. We still find a few villages—very numerous forty or fifty years ago—with fields held in so-called rundale. Each of the peasants, individual tenants on the soil that once was the common property of the gens but had been seized by the English conquerors, pays rent for his plot, but all the arable and meadow land is combined and shared out, according to situation and quality, in strips, or "*Gewanne*", as they are called on the Mosel, and each one receives a share of each *Gewann.* Moorland and pastures are used in common. As recently as fifty years ago, redivision was still practised occasionally, sometimes annually. The map of such a rundale village looks exactly like that of a German community of farming households on the Mosel or in the Hochwald. The gens also survives in the "FACTIONS". The Irish peasants often divide into parties that seem to be founded on absolutely absurd and senseless distinctions and are quite incomprehensible to Englishmen and appear to have no other purpose than to rally for the popular sport of solemnly beating the life out of one another. They are artificial reincarnations, later substitutes for the broken-up gentes that in their own peculiar way demonstrate the continuation of the inherited gentile instinct. Incidentally, in some areas members of the same gens still live together on what is practically their old territory. During the thirties, for instance, the great majority of the inhabitants of the county of Monaghan had only four surnames, that is, were descended from four gentes, or clans.*

* During a few days that I spent in Ireland,[118] I again realised to what extent the rural population there is still living in the conceptions of the gentile period. The landlord, whose tenant the peasant is, is still considered by the latter as a sort of clan chief who has to supervise the cultivation of the soil in the interest of

The downfall of the gentile order in Scotland dates from the suppression of the rebellion of 1745.[119] Precisely what link in this order the Scottish clan represents remains to be investigated; no doubt it is a link. Walter Scott's novels bring the clan in the Highlands of Scotland vividly before our eyes. It is, as Morgan says,

"an excellent type of the gens in organisation and in spirit, and an extraordinary illustration of the power of the gentile life over its members.... We find in their feuds and blood revenge, in their localisation by gentes, in their use of lands in common, in the fidelity of the clansman to his chief and of the members of the clan to each other, the usual and persistent features of gentile society.... Descent was in the male line, the children of the males remaining members of the clan, while the children of its female members belonged to the clans of their respective fathers".[a]

That mother right used to be in force in Scotland is proved by the fact that in the royal family of the Picts, according to Beda,[b] inheritance in the female line prevailed. We even see evidence of the punaluan family preserved among the Scots as well as the Welsh until the Middle Ages in the right of the first night, which the chief of the clan or the king, as the last representative of the former common husbands, could claim with every bride, unless redeemed.[c]

all, is entitled to tribute from the peasant in the form of rent, but also has to assist the peasant in emergencies. Likewise, everyone in more comfortable circumstances is considered under obligation to help his poorer neighbours whenever they are in distress. Such assistance is not charity; it is what the poor clansman is entitled to by right from his rich fellow clansman or clan chief. This explains why political economists and jurists complain of the impossibility of inculcating the idea of modern bourgeois property into the minds of the Irish peasants. Property that has only rights, but no duties, is absolutely beyond the ken of the Irishman. No wonder that Irishmen with such naïve gentile conceptions, who are suddenly cast into the great cities of England and America, among a population with entirely different moral and legal standards, easily become utterly confused in their views of morals and justice, lose all hold and often are bound to succumb en masse to demoralisation. [Note to the 1891 edition.]

---

a L. H. Morgan, Ancient Society, pp. 357 and 358.— Ed.

b [Beda Venerabilis] De Venerabilis Baedae Historia ecclesiastica gentis Anglorum, I, 1.— Ed.

c The 1884 edition has here the following passage omitted by Engels in the 1891 edition: "The same right—in North America it occurs frequently in the extreme North-West—also applied among the Russians, where Grand Princess Olga abolished it in the tenth century.

The communistic households which existed up to the time of the revolution among serf families in France, particularly in Nivernais and Franche-Comté, similar to Slavic family communities in Serbo-Croat areas, are likewise remnants of earlier gentile organisations. They have not yet died out completely; in the vicinity of

* * *

That the Germans were organised in gentes up to the time of the migration of peoples [120] is indisputable. Evidently they settled in the area between the Danube, Rhine, Vistula and the northern seas only a few centuries before our era; the Cimbri and Teutons were still in full migration, and the Suebi did not settle down until Caesar's time. Caesar expressly states that they settled down in gentes and kinships (*gentibus cognationibusque*),[a] and in the mouth of a Roman of the Julia gens the word *gentibus* has a definite meaning that cannot possibly be misconstrued. This holds good for all Germans; even the settling of the conquered Roman provinces [b] appears still to have proceeded in gentes. The Alamannian Law confirms that the people settled on the conquered land south of the Danube in gentes (*genealogiae*); *genealogia* is used in exactly the same sense as *Mark* or village community* was used later. Recently Kovalevsky has expressed

---

* *Mark* in German means land originally belonging in common to the inhabitants of a village or district. The fields and meadows were divided among heads of families, but in early times they were subject to further periodic division (this still exists in several villages on the Mosel); each person's portion soon became his own property, but it was still subject to the rules of cultivation for the community. The pastures, woodland and the other uncultivated land remained, and in many cases are still today, common property. The collectivity of the interested parties determines the method of field cultivation and the use of common land. The constitution of the *Mark* is the oldest constitution among the German people and it is the foundation on which all their medieval institutions were built. [*Engels' note to the 1885 Italian edition.*]

Louhans (Saône-et-Loire), for example, one can still find a great deal of strangely built peasant houses with a communal central hall and sleeping rooms all around, which are inhabited by several generations of the same family."— *Ed.*

    a Caesar, *Commentarii de bello Gallico*, VI, 22.— *Ed.*

    b The text below, up to the words "Among the Germans..." (p. 237), was included by Engels in the 1891 edition instead of the following passage in the 1884 edition: "still proceeded in gentes. In the Alamannian law [121] of the eighth century, *genealogia* is used in exactly the same sense as Mark community; so that here we see a German people, once again the Suebi, settled in gentes and each allocated a particular district. Among the Burgundians and the Langobards the gens was called *fara*, and the term for members of a gens (*faramanni*) is used in Burgundian law [122] in exactly the same sense as Burgundian, in contrast to the Roman inhabitants, who are not of course included in the Burgundian gentes. The division of land in Burgundy was thus effected according to gentes. It settled the issue of the *faramanni* about which Germanic jurists had in vain been racking their brains for a hundred years. This name, *fara*, for gens, can hardly have been generally valid among the Germans, although we find it here applied both to a people of Gothic descent and to another of Herminonic (High German) descent. The linguistic roots used in German to denote relationships are extremely numerous and are likewise used for expressions which we may assume refer to the gens."— *Ed.*

the view that these *genealogiae* were large household communities among which the land was divided, and from which the village communities developed only later. The same may be true of the *fara*, the term which the Burgundians and Langobards—a Gothic and a Herminonian, or High German, tribe—applied to nearly, if not exactly, the same thing that in the Alamannian book of laws is called *genealogia*. Whether this really represents the gens or the household community is a matter that must be further investigated.

Linguistic records leave us in doubt as to whether all the Germans had a common term for gens, and if so, what term. Etymologically, the Greek *genos*, the Latin *gens*, corresponds to the Gothic *kuni*, Middle High German *künne*, and is used in the same sense. We are led back to the time of mother right by the fact that the terms for "woman" are derived from the same root: Greek *gynê*, Slav *žena*, Gothic *qvino*, Old Norse *kona*, *kuna*.—Among Langobards and Burgundians we find, as stated, the term *fara*, which Grimm derives from the hypothetical root *fisan*, to beget. I should prefer to trace it to the more obvious root *faran* [*fahren*], to wander, return, a term which designates a certain well-defined section of the nomadic train, composed, it almost, goes without saying, of relatives; a term, which, in the course of centuries of wandering, first to the East and then to the West, was gradually applied to the gentile community itself.—Further, there is the Gothic *sibja*, Anglo-Saxon *sib*, Old High German *sippia*, *sippa*, [*Sippe*], kinsfolk. Old Norse has only the plural *sifjar*, relatives; the singular occurs only as the name of a goddess, Sif.—Finally, another expression occurs in the *Hildebrand Song*[123] where Hildebrand asks Hadubrand,

"who is your father among the men of the people ... or what is your kin?" (*eddo huêlîhhes* cnuosles *du sîs*).

If there was a common German term for gens, it might well have been the Gothic *kuni*; this is not only indicated by its identity with the corresponding term in kindred languages, but also by the fact that the word *kuning*, *König*, which originally signified chief of gens or tribe, is derived from it. *Sibja*, kinsfolk, does not appear worthy of consideration; in Old Norse, at least, *sifjar* signified not only relatives by blood, but also by marriage; hence it comprises the members of at least *two gentes*; thus *sif* cannot have been the term for gens.

Among the Germans, as among the Mexicans and Greeks, the horsemen as well as the wedge-like columns of infantry were grouped in battle array by gentes. If Tacitus says: by families and kinships,[a] the indefinite expression he uses is explained by the fact that in his time the gens had long ceased to be a living association in Rome.

Of decisive significance is a passage in Tacitus where he says: The mother's brother regards his nephew as his son; some even hold that the blood tie between the maternal uncle and the nephew is more sacred and close than that between father and son, so that when hostages are demanded the sister's son is considered a better pledge than the natural son of the man whom they desire to place under bond. Here we have a living survival of the mother-right, and hence original, gens, and it is described as something which particularly distinguishes the Germans.* If a member of such a gens gave his own son as a pledge for a solemn obligation he had undertaken, and if this son became the victim of his father's breach of contract, that was for the father to settle with himself. If the son of a sister was sacrificed, however, then the most sacred gentile law was violated. The next of kin, who was bound above all others to protect the boy or young man, was responsible for his death; he should either have refrained from giving the boy as a pledge, or have kept the contract. If we had no other trace of gentile organisation among the Germans, this one passage would be sufficient proof.[c]

Still more decisive, as it comes about eight hundred years later, is a passage in the Old Norse song about the twilight of the gods and the end of the world, the *Völuspâ*.[124] In this "Vision of the Seeress", in which, as Bang and Bugge have now shown, also

---

* The Greeks know only in the mythology of the Heroic Age the special intimacy of the bond between the maternal uncle and his nephew, originating from the time of mother right and found among many peoples. According to Diodorus (IV, 34), Meleager kills the sons of Thestius, the brothers of his mother Althaea. The latter regards this deed as such a heinous crime that she curses the murderer, her own son, and prays for his death. It is related that "the gods fulfilled her wish and ended Meleager's life". According to the same Diodorus (IV, 44), the Argonauts under Heracles landed in Thracia and there found that Phineus, at the instigation of his second wife, shamefully maltreats his two sons by his first, deserted wife, Cleopatra, the Boreade. But among the Argonauts there are also some Boreadi, the brothers of Cleopatra, the maternal uncles, therefore, of the maltreated boys. They at once come to their nephews' aid, set them free and kill their guards.[b]

---

a Tacitus, *Germania*, 7.— *Ed.*

b Diodorus Siculus, *Bibliothecae historicae quae supersunt.— Ed.*

c The text below, up to the words "For the rest, in Tacitus' time..." (p. 239), was added by Engels in the 1891 edition.— *Ed.*

elements of Christianity are interwoven, the description of the period of universal depravity and corruption preceding the cataclysm contains this passage:

> Broedhr munu berjask ok at bönum verdask, munu *systrungar* sifjum spilla.
> "Brothers will wage war against one another and become each other's slayers, and *sisters' children* will break the bonds of kinship."

Systrungar means son of the mother's sister, and in the poet's eyes, the repudiation by such of blood relationship caps the climax of the crime of fratricide. The climax lies in *systrungar*, which emphasises the kinship on the maternal side. If the term *syskina-börn*, brother's and sister's children, or *syskina-synir*, brother's and sister's sons, had been used, the second line would not have been a crescendo as against the first but a weakening diminuendo. Thus, even in the time of the Vikings, when the *Völuspâ* was composed, the memory of mother right was not yet obliterated in Scandinavia.

For the rest, in Tacitus' time, at least among the Germans with whom he was more familiar,[a] mother right had already given way to father right: the children were the heirs of the father; in the absence of children, the brothers and the paternal and maternal uncles were the heirs. The admission of the mother's brother to inheritance is connected with the preservation of the above-mentioned custom, and also proves how recent father right was among the Germans at that time. We find traces of mother right even well into the Middle Ages. In this period fatherhood seems to have been open to some suspicion, especially among serfs, and when a feudal lord demanded the return of a fugitive serf from a city, it was required, for instance, in Augsburg, Basle and Kaiserslautern, that the fact of his serfdom should be established by the oaths of six of his immediate blood relatives, exclusively on his mother's side (Maurer, *Städteverfassung,* I, p. 381).

Another relic of mother right, then only in its initial stage of decay, was the respect the Germans had for the female sex, from the Roman standpoint almost inexplicable. Virgins of noble family were regarded as the best hostages guaranteeing the keeping of contracts with Germans. In battle, nothing spurred their courage so much as the horrible thought that their wives and daughters might be captured and carried into slavery. They regarded the woman as being holy and a prophetess, and they heeded her advice even in the most important matters. Veleda, the Bructerian

---

[a] The words "at least" and "with whom he was more familiar" were added by Engels in the 1891 edition.— *Ed.*

priestess on the Lippe River, was the moving spirit of the whole Batavian insurrection, in which Civilis, at the head of Germans and Belgians, shook the foundations of Roman rule in Gaul.[125] The women appear to have held undisputed sway in the house. They, with the old men and children, had, of course, to do all the work, for the men went hunting, drank or loafed around. So Tacitus reports; but he does not say who cultivated the fields, and explicitly states that the slaves only paid dues and performed no statute labour, so it would appear that what little agricultural work was required had to be performed by the bulk of the adult men.

As was stated above, the form of marriage was pairing marriage gradually approximating to monogamy. It was not yet strict monogamy, for polygamy was permitted among high society. On the whole (unlike the Celts) they insisted on strict chastity among girls. Tacitus likewise speaks with particular warmth of the inviolability of the matrimonial bond among the Germans. He gives adultery on the part of the woman as the sole reason for divorce. But his report contains many gaps here, and in any case, it excessively holds up the mirror of virtue to the loose Romans. So much is certain: if the Germans in their forests were such exceptional models of virtue, only slight contact with the outer world was required to bring them down to the level of the other, average, Europeans. In the whirl of Roman life the last trace of strict morality disappeared even faster than the German language. It is enough to read Gregory of Tours.[a] It goes without saying that the refined opulence of sensuality could not exist in the primeval forests of Germany as it did in Rome, and so in this respect also the Germans were superior enough to the Roman world, without ascribing to them a continence in carnal matters that has never prevailed among any people as a whole.

From the gentile system arose the obligation to inherit the feuds as well as the friendships of one's father and relatives; and also *wergeld,* the fine paid in atonement for murder or injury, in place of blood revenge. A generation ago this *wergeld* was regarded as a specifically German institution, but it has since been proved that hundreds of peoples practised this milder form of blood revenge which had its origin in the gentile system. Like the obligation to render hospitality, it is found, for instance, among the American Indians. Tacitus' description of the manner in which hospitality was exercised (*Germania,* 21) is almost identical, down to details, with Morgan's relating to his Indians.

---

[a] Gregorius Turonensis, *Historia Francorum.— Ed.*

The heated and ceaseless controversy as to whether or not the Germans in Tacitus' time had definitively divided up the cultivated land and how the pertinent passages should be interpreted is now a thing of the past. Now it has been established that the cultivated land of nearly all peoples was tilled in common by the gens and later on by communistic family communities, which Caesar still found among the Suebi[a]; that later the land was allotted and periodically re-allotted to the individual families; and that this periodical re-allotment of the cultivated land has been preserved in parts of Germany down to this day, no more need be said on the subject. If the Germans in one hundred and fifty years passed from common cultivation, such as Caesar expressly attributes to the Suebi—they have no divided or private tillage whatsoever, he says—to individual cultivation with the annual redistribution of the land in Tacitus' time, it is surely progress enough; a transition from that stage to the complete private ownership of land in such a short period and without any outside intervention was an utter impossibility. Hence I read in Tacitus only what he states in so many words: They change (or redivide) the cultivated land every year, and enough common land is left over in the process.[b] It is the stage of agriculture and appropriation of the soil which exactly tallies with the gentile constitution of the Germans of that time.[c]

I leave the preceding paragraph unchanged, just as it stood in former editions. Meantime the question has assumed another aspect. Since Kovalevsky has demonstrated (see above, p. 44[d]) that the patriarchal household community was widespread, if not universal, as the intermediate stage between the mother-right communistic family and the modern isolated family, the question is no longer whether the land was common or private property, as was still discussed between Maurer and Waitz, but what *form* common property assumed. There is no doubt whatever that in Caesar's time the Suebi not only owned their land in common, but also tilled it in common for common account. The questions whether their economic unit was the gens or the household community or an intermediate communistic kinship group, or whether all three of these groups existed depending on land conditions will remain subjects of controversy for a long time yet. But Kovalevsky maintains that the conditions described by Tacitus

---

[a] Caesar, *Commentarii de bello Gallico,* IV, 1.— *Ed.*
[b] Tacitus, *Germania,* 26.— *Ed.*
[c] The text below, up to the words "While in Caesar..." (p. 242), was added by Engels in the 1891 edition.— *Ed.*
[d] See this volume, p. 167.— *Ed.*

presuppose not the Mark or village community, but the household community; only this latter developed, much later into the village community, owing to the growth of the population.

Hence, it is claimed, the German settlements on the territory they occupied in the time of the Romans, and on the territory they later took from the Romans, must have been not villages, but large family communities comprising several generations, which cultivated a corresponding tract of land and used the surrounding waste land as a common Mark with their neighbours. The passage in Tacitus concerning the change of the cultivated land would then actually have an agronomic sense, namely, that the community cultivated a different tract of land every year, and the land cultivated during the previous year was left fallow or allowed to grow quite wild again. The sparsity of the population would have left enough spare waste land to make all disputes about land unnecessary. Only after the lapse of centuries, when the members of the household had increased in number to such an extent that common housekeeping became no longer possible under prevailing conditions of production, did the household communities dissolve. The former common fields and meadows were then divided in the familiar manner among the individual households now forming, at first for a time, and later once and for all, while forests, pastures and bodies of water remained common property.

As far as Russia is concerned, this course of development appears to have been fully proved historically. As for Germany, and, to a lesser extent, for other Germanic countries, it cannot be denied that, in many respects, this view affords a better interpretation of the sources and an easier solution of difficulties than the former idea of tracing the village community back to the time of Tacitus. The oldest documents, for instance, the *Codex Laureshamensis,*[126] are on the whole more easily explained with the help of the household community than of the village Mark community. On the other hand, it presents new difficulties and new problems that need solution. Here, only further investigation can decide. I cannot deny, however, that it is highly probable the household community was also the intermediate stage in Germany, Scandinavia and England.

While in Caesar the Germans had partly just taken up settled abodes, and partly were still seeking such, they had been settled for a full century in Tacitus' time; correspondingly, the progress in the production of means of subsistence was unmistakable. They lived in log houses; their clothing was still of the primitive forest type, consisting of rough woollen cloaks and animal skins, and linen underclothing for the women and high society. They lived on milk, meat, wild fruit and, as Pliny adds, oatmeal porridge[a] (the Celtic national dish in Ireland and Scotland to this day). Their wealth consisted of livestock, of an inferior breed, however, the animals being small, unsightly and hornless; the horses were small ponies and no racers. Money, Roman only, was little and rarely used. They made no gold- or silverware, nor did they attach any value to them. Iron was scarce and, at least among the tribes on the Rhine and the Danube, was apparently almost wholly imported, not mined by themselves. The runic script (imitations of Greek and Latin letters) was only known as a secret code and used exclusively for religious sorcery. Human sacrifices were still in vogue. In short, they were a people just risen from the middle stage of barbarism to the upper stage. While, however, the tribes immediately bordering on the Romans were prevented by the easy import of Roman industrial products from developing a metal and textile industry of their own, there is not the least doubt that the tribes of the North-East, on the Baltic, did develop these industries. The pieces of armour found in the bogs of Schleswig— a long iron sword, a coat of mail, a silver helmet, etc., together with Roman coins from the close of the second century—and the German metalware spread by the migration of peoples represent a peculiar type of fine workmanship, even where they are modelled on Roman originals. With the exception of England, emigration to the civilised Roman Empire everywhere put an end to this native industry. How uniformly this industry arose and developed is shown, for instance, by the bronze spangles. The specimens found in Burgundy, in Romania and along the Sea of Azov might have been produced in the very same workshop as the English and the Swedish ones, and are likewise of undoubtedly Germanic origin.

Their constitution was also in keeping with the upper stage of barbarism. According to Tacitus,[b] there was commonly a council of chiefs (*principes*) which decided matters of minor importance and prepared more important matters for the decision of the popular assembly. The latter, in the lower stage of barbarism, at least in places where we know it, among the Americans, existed only for the gens, not yet for the tribe or the confederacy of tribes. The chiefs (*principes*) were still sharply distinguished from the war chiefs (*duces*), just as among the Iroquois. The former were already living, in part, on honorary gifts, such as livestock, grain,

---

[a] *Plini Secundi Naturalis historiae libri 37*, XVIII, 17.— *Ed.*
[b] Tacitus, *Germania*, 11.— *Ed.*

etc., from their fellow tribesmen. As in America, they were mostly elected from the same family. The transition to father right favoured, as in Greece and Rome, the gradual transformation of elective office into hereditary office, thus giving rise to a noble family in each gens. Most of this ancient, so-called tribal nobility perished during the migration of peoples,[127] or shortly after. The military leaders were elected solely on their efficiency, irrespective of descent. They had little power and had to rely on force of example. As Tacitus explicitly states, actual disciplinary power in the army was held by the priests.[a] The popular assembly was the real power. The king or tribal chief presided; the people decided: a murmur signified "nay", acclamation and clanging of weapons meant "aye". The popular assembly was also the court of justice. Complaints were brought up here and decided; and death sentences were pronounced, the latter only in cases of cowardice, treason or unnatural lasciviousness. The gentes and other subdivisions also judged in a body, presided over by the chief, who, as in all original German courts, could be only director of the proceedings and questioner. Among the Germans, always and everywhere, sentence was pronounced by the entire community.

Confederacies of tribes came into existence from Caesar's time. Some of them already had kings. The supreme military commander already aspired to tyrannic power, as among the Greeks and Romans, and sometimes succeeded in achieving it. Such successful usurpers were by no means absolute rulers; nevertheless, they began to break the fetters of the gentile constitution. While freed slaves generally occupied an inferior position, because they could not belong to any gens, they often gained rank, wealth and honours as favourites of the new kings. The same occurred after the conquest of the Roman Empire in the case of the military leaders who had now become kings of large lands. Among the Franks, the king's slaves and freedmen played a major role first at court and then in the state; a large part of the new nobility was descended from them.

There was one institution that especially favoured the rise of royalty: the retinue. We have already seen how among the American Redskins private associations were formed alongside the gentile system for the purpose of waging war off their own back. Among the Germans, these private associations had already developed into standing bodies. The military commander, who had earned himself a reputation, gathered around his person a

---

[a] Tacitus, op. cit., 7.— *Ed.*

host of young people, who were eager for booty and pledged personal loyalty to him, as he did to them. He fed them, gave them gifts and organised them on hierarchical principles: a bodyguard and a troop poised for immediate action in short expeditions, a corps of officers ready for larger campaigns. Weak as these retinues must have been, as indeed they proved to be later, for example, under Odoacer in Italy,[128] they, nevertheless, served as the germ of decay of the old popular liberties, and stood the test as such during and after the migration of peoples. Because, first, they created favourable ground for the rise of royal power. Secondly, as Tacitus already observed,[a] they could be held together only by continuous warfare and plundering expeditions. Looting became the main object. If the chieftain found nothing to do in his neighbourhood, he marched his troops to other peoples among whom there was war and the prospect of booty. The German auxiliaries, who under the Roman standard even fought Germans in large numbers, partly consisted of such retinues. They were the first germs of the Landsknecht[b] system, the shame and curse of the Germans. After the conquest of the Roman Empire, these kings' retainers, together with the bonded and the Roman court attendants, formed the second main constituent part of the subsequent nobility.

In general, then, the German tribes, combined into peoples, had the same constitution that had developed among the Greeks of the Heroic Age and among the Romans at the time of the so-called kings: a popular assembly, council of gentile chiefs and military commander who was already aspiring to real royal power. It was the most highly developed constitution the gentile order could actually produce; it was the model constitution of the higher stage of barbarism. As soon as society passed beyond the limits for which this constitution sufficed, the gentile order was finished. It burst asunder and the state took its place.

VIII

THE FORMATION OF THE STATE
AMONG THE GERMANS

According to Tacitus the Germans were a very numerous people. An approximate idea of the strength of individual German

---

[a] Ibid., 14.— *Ed.*
[b] Mercenary.— *Ed.*

peoples we get from Caesar[a]; he puts the number of Usipetes and Tencteri who appeared on the left bank of the Rhine at 180,000, including women and children. Thus, about 100,000 to a single people,* considerably more than, say, the entire number of Iroquois in their heyday, when they, not quite 20,000 strong, became the terror of the whole country, from the Great Lakes to the Ohio and Potomac. If we were to attempt to group on a map the individual peoples settled near the Rhine who are better known to us from reports, we would find that such a people would occupy on the average approximately the area of a Prussian administrative district, about 10,000 square kilometres, or 182 geographical square miles.[b] The *Germania Magna* of the Romans, reaching to the Vistula, comprised, however, roundly 500,000 square kilometres. Counting an average of 100,000 for any single people, the total population of *Germania Magna* would have amounted to five million—a respectable figure for a barbarian group of peoples; by our standards—10 inhabitants to the square kilometre, or 550 to the geographical square mile—very little. But this does not by any means include all the Germans living at that time. We know that German peoples of Gothic origin, Bastarnae, Peucini and others, lived along the Carpathian Mountains all the way down to the mouth of the Danube. They were so numerous that Pliny designated them as the fifth main tribe of the Germans[c]; in 180 B.C. they were already serving as mercenaries of the Macedonian King Perseus, and even in the first years of the reign of Augustus they were pushing their way as far as the vicinity of Adrianople. If we assume that they numbered only one million, then, at the beginning of the Christian era, the Germans numbered probably six million at the least.

After settling in Germany, the population must have grown with increasing rapidity. The industrial progress mentioned above would suffice to prove this. The finds in the bogs of Schleswig, to judge by the Roman coins uncovered with them, date from the third century. Hence at that time the metal and textile industry

---

* The number taken here is confirmed by a passage in Diodorus on the Celts of Gaul: "In Gaul live numerous peoples of unequal strength. The biggest of them number about 200,000, the smallest 50,000." (Diodorus Siculus, V, 25.) That gives an average of 125,000. The individual Gallic peoples, being more highly developed, must certainly have been more numerous than the German ones.

[a] Caesar, *Commentarii de bello Gallico*, IV, 15.— *Ed.*
[b] The German geographical mile is equal to 7.42 km.— *Ed.*
[c] *Plini Secundi Naturalis historiae libri 37*, IV, 14.— *Ed.*

was already well developed on the Baltic, lively trade was carried on with the Roman Empire, and the wealthier class enjoyed a certain luxury—all evidence of a greater population density. At this time, however, the Germans started their general assault along the whole line of the Rhine, the Roman frontier rampart and the Danube, a line stretching from the North Sea to the Black Sea—direct proof of the ever-growing population striving outwards. During the three centuries of battle, the whole main body of the Gothic peoples (with the exception of the Scandinavian Goths and the Burgundians) moved towards the South-East and formed the left wing of the long line of attack; the High Germans (Herminones) pushed forward in the centre of this line, on the Upper Danube, and the Iscaevones, now called Franks, on the right wing, along the Rhine. The conquest of Britain fell to the lot of the Ingaevones. At the end of the fifth century the Roman Empire, exhausted, bloodless and helpless, lay open to the invading Germans.

In preceding chapters we stood at the cradle of ancient Greek and Roman civilisation. Now we are standing at its grave. The levelling plane of Roman world domination had been passing over all countries of the Mediterranean basin, and this for centuries. Where the Greek language offered no resistance all national languages had had to give way to a corrupt Latin. There were no longer any distinctions of nationality, no more Gauls, Iberians, Ligurians, Noricans; all had become Romans. Roman administration and Roman law had everywhere dissolved the old bodies of *consanguinei* and thus crushed the last remnants of local and national self-expression. The new-fangled Romanism offered no compensation; it expressed no nationality, but only lack of nationality. The elements of new nations existed everywhere. The Latin dialects of the different provinces diverged more and more; the natural boundaries that had once made Italy, Gaul, Spain, Africa[129] independent territories still existed and still made themselves felt. Yet nowhere was there a force capable of combining these elements into new nations; nowhere was there the least trace of any capacity for development or any power of resistance, much less of creative capacity. The immense human mass of that enormous territory was held together by one bond alone—the Roman state; and this, in the course of time, had become its worst enemy and oppressor. The provinces had ruined Rome; Rome itself had become a provincial town like all the others, privileged, but no longer ruling, no longer the centre of the world empire, no longer even the seat of the emperors and vice-emperors, who lived in Constantinople, Trier and Milan. The Roman state had become an immense complicated machine, designed exclusively for draining dry its subjects. Taxes, services for the state and levies of all kinds drove the mass of the people deeper and deeper into poverty. The extortionate practices of the governors, tax collectors and soldiers caused the pressure to become intolerable. This is what the Roman state with its world domination had brought things to: it had based its right to existence on the preservation of order within and protection against the barbarians without. But its order was worse than the worst disorder, and the barbarians, against whom the state pretended to protect its citizens, were longed for by them as saviours.

Social conditions were no less desperate. Right from the last period of the republic, Roman rule had been intent on the ruthless exploitation of the conquered provinces. The emperors had not abolished this exploitation; on the contrary, they had regularised it. The more the empire fell into decay, the higher rose the taxes and compulsory services, and the more shamelessly the officials robbed and blackmailed the people. Commerce and industry were never the business of the Romans, who dominated other peoples. Only in usury did they excel all others, before and after them. The commerce that existed and managed to maintain itself for a time was reduced to ruin by official extortion; what survived was carried on in the eastern, Grecian, part of the empire, but this is beyond the scope of our study. Universal impoverishment; decline of commerce, handicrafts, the arts, and of the population; decay of the towns; retrogression of agriculture to a lower stage—this was the ultimate outcome of Roman world domination.

Agriculture, the decisive branch of production in the whole ancient world, now became so more than ever. In Italy, the immense aggregations of estates (*latifundia*) which had covered nearly the whole territory since the end of the republic, had been utilised in two ways: either as pastures, on which the population had been replaced by sheep and oxen, the care of which required only a few slaves; or as villas, on which large-scale horticulture had been pursued with masses of slaves, partly to serve the luxurious needs of the owners and partly for sale at the urban markets. The great pastures had been preserved and even enlarged. But the villa estates and their horticulture had fallen into ruin with the impoverishment of their owners and the decay of the towns. Latifundian economy based on slave labour was no longer profitable; but at that time it was the only possible form of large-scale agriculture. Small-scale farming again became the only profitable form. Villa after villa was parcelled out and leased in small lots to hereditary tenants, who paid a fixed sum, or to *partiarii*,[a] farm managers rather than tenants, who received one-sixth or even only one-ninth of the year's product for their work. Mainly, however, these small plots were distributed to colons, who paid a fixed amount annually, were tied to the land and could be sold together with the plots. Admittedly, they were not slaves, but neither were they free; they could not marry free citizens, and marriages among themselves were not regarded as fully valid marriages, but as mere concubinage (*contubernium*), as in the case of the slaves. They were the forerunners of the medieval serfs.

The slavery of antiquity had outlived itself. Neither in large-scale agriculture in the country, nor in the manufactories of the towns did it any longer bring in a worthwhile return—the market for its products had disappeared. Small-scale agriculture, however, and small handicrafts, to which the gigantic production of the flourishing times of the empire was now reduced, had no room for numerous slaves. Society found room only for the domestic and luxury slaves of the rich. But moribund slavery was still sufficiently virile to make all productive work appear as slave labour, unworthy of a free Roman—and everybody was now a free Roman. On this account, on the one hand, there was an increase in the number of superfluous slaves who, having become a drag, were emancipated; on the other hand, there was an increase in the number of colons and of ruined freemen (similar to the POOR WHITES in the ex-slave states of America). Christianity is perfectly innocent of this gradual dying out of ancient slavery. It had partaken in slavery in the Roman Empire for centuries, and later did nothing to prevent the slave trade of Christians, either of the Germans in the North, or of the Venetians on the Mediterranean, or the Negro slave trade of later years.* Slavery no longer paid, and so it died out; but dying slavery left behind its poisonous sting by outlawing the productive work of the free. This was the blind alley in which the Roman world was caught: slavery

---

* According to Bishop Liutprand of Cremona, the principal industry of Verdun in the tenth century, that is, in the Holy German Empire, was the manufacture of eunuchs, who were exported with great profit to Spain for the harems of the Moors.[b]

---

[a] Sharecroppers.— *Ed.*
[b] Liutprand, *Antapodosis*, VI, 6.— *Ed.*

was economically impossible, while the labour of the free was
morally proscribed. The one could no longer, the other could not
yet, be the basic form of social production. Only a complete
revolution could be of help here.

Things were no better in the provinces. Most of the reports we
have concern Gaul. By the side of the colons, free small peasants
still existed there. In order to protect themselves against the brutal
extortions of the officials, judges and usurers, they frequently
placed themselves under the protection, the patronage, of a man
possessed of power; and they did this not only singly, but in whole
communities, so much so that the emperors of the fourth century
often issued decrees prohibiting this practice. But what use was it
to those who sought this protection? The patron imposed the
condition that they transfer the title of their lands to him, and in
return he ensured them usufruct of their land for life—a trick
which the Holy Church remembered and freely imitated during
the ninth and tenth centuries, for the greater glory of God and
the enlargement of its own landed possessions. At that time, to be
sure, about the year 475, Bishop Salvianus of Marseilles still
vehemently denounced such robbery and related that the oppression of the Roman officials and great landlords had become so
intolerable that many "Romans" fled to the districts already
occupied by the barbarians, and the Roman citizens who had
settled there feared nothing so much as coming under Roman rule
again.[a] That poor parents frequently sold their children into
slavery in those days is proved by a law issued against it.

In return for liberating the Romans from their own state, the
German barbarians appropriated two-thirds of the entire land and
divided it among themselves. The division was made in accordance
with the gentile system; as the conquerors were relatively small in
number, large tracts remained undivided, in the possession partly
of the whole people and partly of individual tribes or gentes.
In each gens fields and pastures were distributed among the
individual households in equal shares by lot. We do not know
whether repeated redivisions took place at that time; at all events,
this practice was soon discarded in the Roman provinces, and the
individual allotment became alienable private property, allodium.
Forests and pastures remained undivided for common use; this
use and the mode of cultivating the divided land were regulated
by ancient custom and the decision of the entire community. The
longer the gens existed in its village, and the more Germans and

---

[a] Salvianus, *De Gubernatione Dei*, V, 8.— *Ed.*

Romans merged in the course of time, the more the consanguineous character of the ties retreated before territorial ties. The gens
disappeared in the Mark community, in which, however, traces of
the original kinship of the members were visible still often enough.
Thus, the gentile constitution, at least in those countries where
Mark communities were preserved—in the North of France, in
England, Germany and Scandinavia—was imperceptibly transformed into a territorial constitution, and thus became capable of
being fitted into the state. Nevertheless, it retained the naturally
evolved democratic character which distinguishes the whole gentile
order, and thus preserved a piece of the gentile constitution even
in its degeneration, forced upon it in later times, thereby leaving a
weapon in the hands of the oppressed, ready to be wielded even
in modern times.

The rapid disappearance of the blood tie in the gens was due to
the fact that its organs in the tribe and the whole people had also
degenerated as a result of the conquest. We know that rule over
subjugated people is incompatible with the gentile constitution.
Here we see it on a large scale. The German peoples, masters of
the Roman provinces, had to organise their conquest; but the mass
of the Romans could neither be absorbed into the gentile bodies
nor ruled by means of the latter. A substitute for the Roman state
had to be placed at the head of the Roman local administrative
bodies, which at first largely continued to function, and this
substitute could only be another state. Thus, the organs of the
gentile constitution had to be transformed into organs of state,
and owing to the pressure of circumstances, this had to be done
very quickly. The first representative of the conquering people
was, however, the military commander. The securing of the
conquered territory internally and externally demanded that his
power be increased. The moment had arrived for transforming
military leadership into kingship. This was done.

Let us take the kingdom of the Franks. Here, not only the wide
dominions of the Roman state, but also all the very large tracts of
land that had not been assigned to the large and small *Gau* and
Mark communities, especially all the large forests, fell into the
hands of the victorious Salian people as their unrestricted
possession. The first thing the king of the Franks, transformed
from an ordinary supreme military commander into a real
monarch, did was to convert this property of the people into a
royal estate, to steal it from the people and to donate or grant it to
his retainers. This retinue, originally composed of his personal
military retainers and the rest of the subcommanders of the army,

was soon augmented not only by Romans, that is, Romanised
Gauls, who quickly became indispensable to him owing to their
knowledge of writing, their education and familiarity with the
Romance vernacular and literary Latin as well as with the laws of
the land, but also by slaves, serfs and freedmen, who constituted
his Court and from among whom he chose his favourites. All
these were granted tracts of public land, first mostly as gifts and
later in the form of benefices—originally in most cases for the
period of the life of the king [130]—and so the basis was laid for a
new nobility at the expense of the people.

But this was not all. The far-flung empire could not be
governed by means of the old gentile constitution. The council of
chiefs, even if it had not long died out, could not have assembled
and was soon replaced by the king's permanent retinue. The old
popular assembly was still ostensibly preserved, but more and
more as an assembly of the subcommanders of the army and the
newly-rising magnates. The free landowning peasants, the mass of
the Frankish people, were exhausted and reduced to penury by
continuous civil war and wars of conquest, the latter particularly
under Charlemagne, just as the Roman peasants had been during
the last period of the republic. These peasants, who originally had
formed the whole army, and after the conquest of the Frankish
lands had been its core, were so impoverished at the beginning of
the ninth century that scarcely one out of five could provide the
accoutrements of war. The army of free peasants, called up
directly by the king, was replaced by an army composed of the
servitors of the newly arisen magnates. Among these servitors
were also villeins, the descendants of the peasants who previously
had known no master but the king, and still earlier had known no
master at all, not even a king. Under Charlemagne's successors the
ruin of the Frankish peasantry was completed by internal wars, the
weakness of royal authority and corresponding encroachments of
the magnates, whose ranks were augmented by the *Gau* counts,[131]
established by Charlemagne and eager to make their office
hereditary, and finally by the incursions of the Normans. Fifty
years after the death of Charlemagne, the Frankish Empire lay as
helpless at the feet of the Normans as four hundred years
previously the Roman Empire had lain at the feet of the Franks.

Not only the external impotence, but the internal order, or
rather disorder, of society, was almost the same. The free Frankish
peasants found themselves in a position similar to that of their
predecessors, the Roman colons.[132] Ruined by war and plunder,
they had to seek the protection of the newly arisen magnates or

the Church, for royal authority was too weak to protect them; but they had to pay dear for this protection. Like the Gallic peasants before them, they had to transfer the ownership of their land to their patrons, and received it back from them as tenants in different and varying forms, but always on condition of performing services and paying dues. Once driven into this form of dependence, they gradually lost their personal freedom; after a few generations most of them became serfs. How rapidly the free peasants were degraded is shown by Irminon's land records of the Abbey Saint-Germain-des-Prés, then near, now in, Paris.[a] Even during the life of Charlemagne, on the vast estates of this abbey, stretching into the surrounding country, there were 2,788 households, almost exclusively Franks with German names; 2,080 of them were colons, 35 lites,[133] 220 slaves and only 8 freeholders! The custom by which the patron had the land of the peasants transferred to himself, giving to them only the usufruct of it for life, the custom denounced as ungodly by Salvianus, was now universally practised by the Church in its dealings with the peasants. Feudal servitude, now coming more and more into vogue, was modelled as much on the lines of the Roman angariae,[134] compulsory services for the state, as on the services rendered by the members of the German Mark in bridge and road building and other work for common purposes. Thus, it looked as if, after four hundred years, the mass of the population had come back to the point it had started from.

This proved only two things, however: First, that the social stratification and the distribution of property in the declining Roman Empire had corresponded entirely to the then prevailing level of production in agriculture and industry, and hence had been inevitable; second, that this level of production had not sunk or risen to any material extent in the course of the ensuing four hundred years, and, therefore, had just as necessarily produced the same distribution of property and the same class division of the population. During the last centuries of the Roman Empire, the town had lost its earlier supremacy over the country, and did not regain it during the first centuries of German rule. This presupposes a low level of development in agriculture, and in industry as well. Such an overall situation necessarily gives rise to big ruling landowners and dependent small peasants. How scarcely

---

[a] Data from Irminon's land records are presumably quoted from P. Roth's *Geschichte des Beneficialwesens von den ältesten Zeiten bis ins zehnte Jahrhundert,* p. 378.— *Ed.*

possible it was to superimpose either the Roman latifundian economy run with slave labour or the newer large-scale farming run with serf labour onto such a society, is proved by Charlemagne's massive experiments with his famous imperial villas,[135] which passed away leaving hardly a trace. These experiments were continued only by the monasteries and were fruitful only for them; but the monasteries were abnormal social bodies founded on celibacy. They could do the exceptional, and for that very reason were bound to remain exceptions.

Nevertheless, progress was made during these four hundred years. Even if in the end we find almost the same main classes as in the beginning, still, the people who constituted these classes had changed. Ancient slavery had disappeared; gone were also the ruined poor freemen, who had despised work as slavish. Between the Roman colonus and the new villein there had been the free Frankish peasant. The "useless reminiscences and vain strife" of decaying Romanism were dead and buried. The social classes of the ninth century had taken shape not in the bog of a declining civilisation, but in the travail of a new one. The new race, masters as well as servants, was a race of men compared with its Roman predecessors. The relation of powerful landlords and serving peasants, which for the latter had been the hopeless form of the decline of the world of antiquity, was now for the former the starting-point of a new development. Moreover, unproductive as these four hundred years appear to have been, they, nevertheless, left *one* great product behind them: the modern nationalities, the refashioning and regrouping of West European humanity for impending history. The Germans, in fact, had infused new life into Europe; and that is why the dissolution of the states in the German period ended, not in Norman-Saracen subjugation, but in the development from the benefices and patronage (commendation[136]) to feudalism, and in such a tremendous increase in the population that the profuse bloodshed caused by the Crusades barely two centuries later could be borne without injury.[a]

But what was the mysterious magic potion with which the Germans infused new vitality into dying Europe? Was it in the innate miraculous power of the German race, as our chauvinistic historians would have it? By no means. The Germans were a highly gifted Aryan tribe, especially at that time, in the process of all-out vigorous development. It was not their specific national

---

[a] The end of the sentence, from the words "and in such a tremendous increase..." was added by Engels in the 1891 edition.— *Ed.*

qualities that rejuvenated Europe, however, but simply—their barbarism, their gentile constitution.

Their personal competence and bravery, their love of liberty, and their democratic instinct, which regarded all public affairs as its own affairs, in short, all those qualities which the Romans had lost and which were alone capable of forming new states and of raising new nationalities out of the muck of the Roman world—what were they but the characteristic features of barbarians in the upper stage, fruits of their gentile constitution?

If they transformed the ancient form of monogamy, moderated male rule in the family and gave a higher status to women than the classical world had ever known, what enabled them to do so if not their barbarism, their gentile customs, their still vital heritage from the time of mother right?

If they were able in at least three of the most important countries—Germany, Northern France and England—to preserve and carry over to the feudal state a piece of the genuine gentile constitution in the form of the Mark communities, and thus give to the oppressed class, the peasants, even under the hardest conditions of medieval serfdom, local cohesion and the means of resistance which neither the slaves of antiquity nor the modern proletarians found ready at hand—to what did they owe this if not to their barbarism, their exclusively barbarian mode of settling in gentes?

And lastly, if they were able to develop and raise to universality the milder form of servitude which they had been practising at home, into which also slavery in the Roman Empire was more and more converted—a form which, as Fourier first emphasised, gave to those subjected to servitude the means of gradual emancipation *as a class* (*fournit aux cultivateurs des moyens d'affranchissement collectif et progressif*[a]) and is therefore far superior to slavery, which permits only of the immediate manumission of the individual without any transitory stage (antiquity did not know any abolition of slavery by a victorious rebellion), whereas in fact the serfs of the Middle Ages, step by step, achieved their emancipation as a class—to what was this due if not their barbarism, thanks to which they had not yet arrived at complete slavery, either in the form of the ancient labour slavery or in that of the Oriental domestic slavery?

All that was vital and life-bringing in what the Germans infused into the Roman world was barbarism. In fact, only barbarians are

---

[a] Furnishes for the cultivators means of *collective and gradual* emancipation (see Ch. Fourier, *Théorie des quatre mouvements et des destinées générales*, p. 220).— *Ed.*

capable of rejuvenating a world labouring in the throes of a dying civilisation. And the highest stage of barbarism, to which and in which the Germans worked their way up previous to the migration of peoples, was precisely the most favourable one for this process. This explains everything.

IX

BARBARISM AND CIVILISATION

We have now traced the dissolution of the gentile order in the three great individual examples: Greek, Roman, and German. We shall investigate, in conclusion, the general economic conditions that had already undermined the gentile organisation of society in the upper stage of barbarism and completely abolished it with the advent of civilisation. For this, Marx's *Capital* will be as necessary as Morgan's book.

Having germinated in the middle stage and developed further in the upper stage of savagery, the gens reached its prime, as far as our sources enable us to judge, in the lower stage of barbarism. With this stage of development, then, we shall begin our investigation.

We find here, where the American Redskins must serve as our example, the gentile system fully developed. A tribe was divided up into several, in most cases two,[a] gentes; with the increase in the population, each of these original gentes again divided into several daughter gentes, in relation to which the mother gens appeared as the phratry; the tribe itself split up into several tribes, in each of which, in most cases, we again find the old gentes. In some cases, at least, a confederacy embraced the kindred tribes. This simple organisation was fully adequate for the social conditions from which it sprang. It was nothing more than a peculiar naturally evolved grouping, capable of smoothing out all internal conflicts that might arise in a society organised on these lines. Externally, conflicts were settled by war, which could end in the annihilation of a tribe, but never in its subjugation. The magnificence, and at the same time the limitation, of the gentile order was that it left no room for domination and servitude. Internally, there was as yet no distinction between rights and duties; the question of whether participation in public affairs, blood revenge or atonement for

---

[a] The words "in most cases two" were added by Engels in the 1891 edition.— *Ed.*

Der Ursprung

der

Familie, des Privateigenthums

und

des Staats.

Im Anschluß an Lewis H. Morgan's Forschungen

von

Friedrich Engels.

Vierte Auflage.

Sechstes und siebentes Tausend.

Stuttgart

Verlag von J. H. W. Dietz

1892.

Title page of the fourth edition
of *The Origin of the Family, Private Property and the State*

injuries was a right or a duty never confronted the Indian; it would have appeared as absurd to him as the question of whether eating, sleeping or hunting was a right or a duty. Nor could any tribe or gens split up into different classes. This leads us to the investigation of the economic basis of those conditions.

The population was very sparse. It was dense only in the habitat of the tribe, surrounded by its extensive hunting grounds and beyond these the neutral protective forest which separated it from other tribes. Division of labour was purely and simply that which had naturally evolved; it existed only between the two sexes. The men went to war, hunted, fished, provided the raw material for food and the implements necessary for these pursuits. The women cared for the house, and prepared food and clothing; they cooked, wove, and sewed. Each of them was master in his or her own field of activity: the men in the forest, the women in the house. Each owned the implements he or she made and used: the men, the weapons and the hunting and fishing tackle, the women, the household utensils. The household was communistic, comprising several, and often many, families.* Whatever was produced and used in common was common property; the house, the garden, the longboat. Here, and only here, then, does the "earned property" exist which jurists and economists have attributed to civilised society—the last mendacious legal pretext on which modern capitalist property still rests.

But man did not remain in this stage everywhere. In Asia he found animals that could be domesticated and bred in captivity. The wild buffalo cow had to be hunted down; the domesticated one gave birth to a calf once a year, and provided milk into the bargain. A number of the most advanced tribes—Aryans, Semites, perhaps also the Turanians—made first the domestication, and later the breeding and tending, of cattle, their principal occupation. Pastoral tribes separated themselves from the remaining mass of the barbarians: *the first great social division of labour.* The pastoral tribes not only produced more means of subsistence, but also a greater variety than the rest of the barbarians. They not only had milk, milk products and meat in greater abundance than the others, but also skins, wool, goat's hair, and more spun and woven fabrics with the increasing quantities of raw material. This, for the first time, made regular exchange possible. In the preceding

---

* Especially on the north-west coast of America; see Bancroft. Among the Haidas of the Queen Charlotte Islands some households gathered as many as seven hundred members under one roof. Among the Nootkas, whole tribes lived under one roof.

stages, exchange could only take place occasionally; exceptional ability in the making of weapons and implements may have led to a temporary division of labour. Thus, unquestionable remains of workshops for stone implements of the Neolithic period have been found in many places. The artificers who developed their skills in those workshops most probably worked for the community, as the permanent handicraftsmen of the gentile communities in India still do. No other exchange than that within the tribe could arise in that stage, and even that was an exception. After the separation of the pastoral tribes, however, we find here all the conditions ready for exchange between members of different tribes, and for its further development and consolidation as a regular institution. Originally, tribe exchanged with tribe through their respective gentile chiefs. When, however, the herds began to be converted into separate property,[a] exchange between individuals predominated more and more, until eventually it became the sole form. The principal article which the pastoral tribes offered their neighbours for exchange was livestock; livestock became the commodity by which all other commodities were appraised, and was everywhere readily taken in exchange for other commodities—in short, livestock assumed the function of money and served as money already at this stage. Such was the necessity and rapidity with which the demand for a money commodity developed right at the very beginning of commodity exchange.

Horticulture, probably unknown to the Asiatic barbarians of the lower stage, arose, among them, no later than at the middle stage, as the forerunner of field agriculture. The climate of the Turanian plateau does not admit of a pastoral life without a supply of fodder for the long and severe winter. Hence, the sowing of meadows and cultivation of grain was indispensable here. The same is true of the steppes north of the Black Sea. Once grown for livestock, grain soon became human food. The cultivated land still remained tribal property and was assigned first to the gens, which, later, in its turn distributed it for use to the household communities, and finally[b] to individuals; these may have had certain rights of possession, but no more.

Of the industrial achievements of this stage two are particularly important. The first is the weaving loom, the second, the smelting of metal ores and metalworking. Copper, tin, and their alloy,

---

[a] The 1884 edition has "private property" instead of "separate property".— Ed.

[b] The words "to the household communities, and finally" were added by Engels in the 1891 edition.— Ed.

bronze, were by far the most important; bronze provided useful implements and weapons, but could not oust stone implements. Only iron could do that, but its production was as yet unknown. Gold and silver began to be used for ornaments and decorations, and must already have been of far higher value than copper and bronze.

The increase of production in all branches—livestock breeding, agriculture, domestic handicrafts—enabled human labour power to produce more than was necessary for its maintenance. It simultaneously increased the amount of work that daily fell to every member of the gens or household community or single family. The attraction of more labour power became desirable. This was provided by war; captives were made slaves. Under the given overall historical conditions, the first great social division of labour, by increasing the productivity of labour, that is, wealth, and enlarging the field of production, necessarily carried slavery in its wake. Out of the first great social division of labour arose the first great division of society into two classes: masters and slaves, exploiters and exploited.

How and when the herds were converted from the common property of the tribe or gens into the property of the individual heads of families we do not know to this day; but it must have occurred, in the main, at this stage. The herds and the other new objects of wealth brought about a revolution in the family. Gaining a livelihood had always been the business of the man; he produced and owned the means to that end. The herds were the new means of gaining a livelihood, and their initial domestication and subsequent tending were his work. Hence, he owned the livestock, and the commodities and slaves obtained in exchange for them. All the surplus now resulting from the task of gaining a livelihood fell to the man; the woman shared in consuming it, but she had no share in owning it. The "savage" warrior and hunter had been content to occupy second place in the house, after the woman. The "gentler" shepherd, insisting on his wealth, pushed forward to first place and forced the woman into second place. And she could not complain. Division of labour in the family had regulated the distribution of property between man and wife. This division of labour remained unchanged, and yet it now turned the former domestic relationship upside down simply because the division of labour outside the family had changed. The very cause that had formerly ensured the woman supremacy in the house, namely, her being confined to domestic work, now ensured supremacy in the house for the man: the woman's housework lost its significance compared with the man's work in obtaining a livelihood; the latter was everything, the former an insignificant addition. Here we see already that the emancipation of women and their equality with men are impossible and must remain so as long as women are excluded from socially productive work and remain restricted to private domestic duties. The emancipation of women becomes possible only when women are enabled to take part in production on a large, social scale, and when domestic duties require their attention only to a minor degree. And this has become possible only as a result of modern large-scale industry, which not only permits of the participation of women in production in large numbers, but actually calls for it and, moreover, strives more and more to reduce private domestic duties to a public industry.

His achievement of actual supremacy in the house threw down the last barrier to the man's autocracy. This autocracy was confirmed and perpetuated by the overthrow of mother right, the introduction of father right and the gradual transition from pairing marriage to monogamy. But this made a breach in the old gentile order: the individual family became a power and rose threateningly against the gens.

The next step brings us to the upper stage of barbarism, the period in which all civilised peoples passed through their Heroic Age: it is the period of the iron sword, but also of the iron ploughshare and axe. Iron came to be utilised by man, the last and most important of all raw materials to play a revolutionary role in history, the last—if we exclude the potato. Iron made possible field agriculture on a larger area and the clearing of extensive forest tracts for cultivation; it gave the craftsman implements of hardness and sharpness that no stone, no other known metal, could withstand. All this came about gradually; the first iron produced was often softer than bronze. Thus, stone weapons disappeared but slowly; stone axes were still used in battle not only in the *Hildebrand Song,* but also in the Battle of Hastings, in 1066.[137] But progress was now irresistible, less interrupted and more rapid. The town, enclosing houses of stone or brick within its turreted and crenellated stone walls, became the headquarters of the tribe or confederacy of tribes. It marked an enormous advance in the art of building; but it was also a sign of increased danger and need for protection. Wealth increased rapidly, but it was the wealth of single individuals. Weaving, metalworking and the other crafts that were becoming more and more specialised displayed growing diversity and skill in their products; agriculture now provided not only cereals, pulse and fruit, but also oil and wine, which people had now learned to make. Such diverse activities could no longer be conducted by any single individual; *the second great division of labour* took place: handicrafts separated from agriculture. The continuing increase in production, and with it the increased productivity of labour, raised the value of human labour power. Slavery, which had been nascent and sporadic in the preceding stage, now became an essential part of the social system. The slaves ceased to be simple assistants; they were now driven in scores to work in the fields and workshops. The division of production into two large main branches, agriculture and handicrafts, gave rise to production directly for exchange, the production of commodities; and with it came trade, not only in the interior and on the tribal boundaries, but also overseas. But all this was still very undeveloped; the precious metals started to become the predominant and universal money commodity, but they were not yet minted and were exchanged merely by bare weight.

The distinction between rich and poor was added to that between freemen and slaves—with the new division of labour came a new division of society into classes. The differences in the property of the individual heads of families caused the old communistic household communities to break up wherever they had survived until then; and this put an end to the common cultivation of the soil for the account of this community. The arable land was assigned for use to the separate families, first for a limited time and later in perpetuity; the transition to complete private ownership took place gradually and parallel to the transition from pairing marriage to monogamy. The individual family started to become the economic unit of society.

The increased population density necessitated firmer cohesion internally and externally. Everywhere the confederacy of kindred tribes became a necessity, and soon after, their amalgamation, and thus the amalgamation of the separate tribal territories into a single territory of the people. The military commander of the people— *rex, basileus, thiudans*—became an indispensable and permanent official. The popular assembly was instituted wherever it did not yet exist. The military commander, the council and the popular assembly formed the organs of the gentile society which had developed into a military democracy. Military—because war and organisation for war were now regular functions of the life of the people. The wealth of their neighbours excited the greed of the peoples to whom the acquisition of wealth appeared one of the main purposes in life. They were barbarians: plunder appeared to them easier and even more honourable than productive work. War, previously waged simply to avenge aggression or as a means of enlarging territory that had become inadequate, was now waged for the sake of plunder alone, and became a regular source of living. It was not for nothing that formidable walls were reared around the new fortified towns: their yawning moats were the graves of the gentile constitution, and their turrets already reached up into civilisation. Internal affairs underwent a similar change. The predatory wars increased the power of the supreme military commander as well as the subcommanders. The customary election of successors from the same families, especially after the introduction of father right, was gradually transformed into hereditary succession, first tolerated, then claimed and finally usurped; the foundation of hereditary royalty and hereditary nobility was laid. In this manner the organs of the gentile constitution were gradually torn away from their roots in the people, in gens, phratry and tribe, and the whole gentile order was transformed into its opposite: from being an organisation of tribes for the free administration of their own affairs, it became an organisation for plundering and oppressing their neighbours; and correspondingly its organs were transformed from instruments of the will of the people into independent organs for ruling and oppressing their own people. But this could not have happened had not the greed for wealth divided the members of the gentes into rich and poor; had not "property differences in the same gens changed the community of interests into antagonism between its members" (Marx)[a]; and had not the growth of slavery already begun to brand working for a living as an activity worthy only of slaves and more ignominious than engaging in plunder.

* * *

This brings us to the threshold of civilisation. This stage is inaugurated by another advance in the division of labour. In the lowest stage men produced only for their own immediate needs; any possible exchange was confined to sporadic cases when a surplus was obtained by chance. In the middle stage of barbarism we find that the pastoral peoples had in their livestock a form of property which, if herds and flocks were of a certain size, regularly

---

[a] "Marx's Excerpts...", op. cit., p. 213.— *Ed.*

provided a surplus over and above their needs; and we also find a division of labour between the pastoral peoples and backward tribes without herds, so that there were two different stages of production side by side, and therefore the conditions for regular exchange. The upper stage of barbarism introduced a further division of labour between agriculture and handicrafts, resulting in the production of a continually increasing portion of products of labour directly for exchange, so that exchange between individual producers reached the point where it became a vital necessity for society. Civilisation consolidated and magnified all these established divisions of labour, particularly by intensifying the contrast between town and country (either the town exercising economic supremacy over the country, as in antiquity, or the country over the town, as in the Middle Ages) and added a third division of labour, peculiar to itself and of decisive importance: it created a class that was no longer engaged in production, but exclusively in exchanging products—the *merchants*. All previous inchoative class formations were exclusively connected with production; they divided those engaged in production into managers and executors, or else into producers on a large scale and producers on a small scale. Here a class appears for the first time which, without taking any part in production, captures the management of production as a whole and economically subordinates the producers to itself; a class that makes itself the indispensable intermediary between any two producers and exploits them both. On the pretext of saving the producers the trouble and risk of exchange, of extending the sale of their products to distant markets, and of thus becoming the most useful class among the population, a class of parasites arises, of genuine social bloodsuckers, which, as a reward for very insignificant real services, skims the cream off production both at home and abroad, rapidly acquires enormous wealth and corresponding social influence, and for this very reason is destined to reap ever new honours and gain increasing control over production during the period of civilisation, until it at last creates a product of its own—periodic commercial crises.

At the stage of development we are discussing, the young merchant class, however, had no inkling as yet of the big things that were in store for it. But it took shape and made itself indispensable, and that was sufficient. With it, however, *metal money,* minted coins, emerged, and with this a new means by which the non-producer could rule the producer and his production. The commodity of commodities, which conceals within itself all other commodities, was discovered; the magic potion that can transform itself at will into anything desirable and desired. Whoever possessed it ruled the world of production; and who had it above all others? The merchant. In his hands the cult of money was safe. He took care to make it plain that all commodities, and hence all commodity producers, must grovel in the dust before money. He proved in practice that all other forms of wealth were mere semblances compared with this incarnation of wealth as such. Never again has the power of money revealed itself with such primitive crudity and violence as it did in this period, its youth. After the purchase of commodities for money came the lending of money, entailing interest and usury. And no legislation of any later period throws the debtor so pitilessly and helplessly at the feet of the usurious creditor as that of ancient Athens and Rome—both sets of law arose spontaneously, as common law, without other than economic compulsion.

Besides wealth in commodities and slaves, besides money wealth, there now came into being wealth in landed property. The entitlement of individuals to own parcels of land originally assigned to them by the gens or tribe had now become so well established that these parcels became their hereditary property. What they had most aspired to just before that time was liberation from the claim of the gentile community to their parcels of land, a claim which had become a fetter for them. They were freed from this fetter—but soon after also from their new landed property. The full, free ownership of land implied not only the possibility of unrestricted and uncurtailed possession, but also the possibility of alienating it. As long as the land belonged to the gens there was no such possibility. But when the new landowner definitively shook off the chains of the paramount title of the gens and tribe, he also tore the bond that had until then tied him inseverably to the soil. What that meant was made plain to him by the money invented simultaneously with the advent of private property. Land could now become a commodity to be sold and mortgaged. Hardly had the private ownership of land been introduced when mortgage was discovered (see Athens). Just as hetaerism and prostitution clung to the heels of monogamy, so from now on mortgage clung to the ownership of land. You wanted full, free, alienable ownership of land. Well, here you have it—*tu l'as voulu*,[a] George Dandin!

---

[a] "You wanted it." This expression is taken from Molière's comedy *George Dandin, ou le mari confondu*, I, 9.—*Ed.*

Commercial expansion, money and usury, landed property and mortgage were thus accompanied by the rapid concentration and centralisation of wealth in the hands of a small class, on the one hand, and by the increasing impoverishment of the masses and a growing mass of paupers, on the other. The new aristocracy of wealth, unless it coincided from the outset with the old tribal nobility, forced the latter definitively into the background (in Athens, in Rome, among the Germans). And this division of freemen into classes according to their wealth was accompanied, especially in Greece, by an enormous increase in the number of slaves,* whose forced labour formed the basis on which the superstructure of the entire society was reared.

Let us now see what became of the gentile constitution as a result of this social revolution. It stood powerless in the face of the new elements that had grown up without its aid. Its precondition was that the members of a gens, or else of a tribe, should live together in the same territory, be its sole inhabitants. This had long ceased to be the case. Gentes and tribes were everywhere intermingled; everywhere slaves, wards and outsiders lived among the citizens. The sedentary state, which had been acquired only towards the end of the middle stage of barbarism, was time and again interrupted by the mobility and changes of abode brought about by commerce, changes of occupation and the transfer of land. The members of the gentile bodies could no longer meet for the purpose of attending to their own common affairs; only matters of minor importance, such as religious ceremonies, were still observed in a rough-and-ready way. Beside the requirements and interests which the gentile bodies were appointed and empowered to take care of, new requirements and interests had arisen from the revolution in the conditions of earning a livelihood and the resulting change in social structure. These new requirements and interests were not only alien to the old gentile order, but thwarted it in every way. The interests of the groups of craftsmen which arose through division of labour, and the special needs of the town as opposed to the country, required new organs; but each of these groups was composed of people from different gentes, phratries and tribes; they even included outsiders. Hence, the new organs necessarily had to take shape outside the gentile constitution, alongside it, and that meant

---

* For the number of slaves in Athens, see above, p. 117 [this volume, p. 222]. In Corinth, at the city's zenith, it was 460,000, and in Aegina 470,000; in both, ten times the number of free citizens.

against it.—And again, in every gentile body the conflict of interests made itself felt and reached its apex by combining rich and poor, usurers and debtors, in the same gens and tribe.—Then there was the mass of new inhabitants, strangers to the gentile associations, which, as in Rome, became a power in the land, and was too numerous to be gradually absorbed by the consanguine gentes and tribes. The gentile associations confronted these masses as exclusive, privileged bodies; what had originally been a naturally evolved democracy was transformed into a hateful aristocracy. Lastly, the gentile constitution had grown out of a society that knew no internal antagonisms, and was suited only to such a society. It had no means of coercion except public opinion. But now a society had come into being that by virtue of all its economic conditions of existence had to split up into freemen and slaves, into exploiting rich and exploited poor; a society that was not only incapable of reconciling these antagonisms, but had to carry them to extremes. Such a society could only exist either in a state of continuous, open struggle of these classes against one another or under the rule of a third power which, while ostensibly standing above the conflicting classes, suppressed their open conflict and permitted a class struggle at most in the economic field, in a so-called legal form. The gentile constitution had outlived itself. It was burst asunder by the division of labour and by its result, the division of society into classes. Its place was taken by the *state*.

*   *   *

Above we discussed in detail each of the three main forms in which the state raised itself up on the ruins of the gentile constitution. Athens represented the purest, most classical form. Here the state derived directly and mainly from the class antagonisms that developed within gentile society. In Rome gentile society became an exclusive aristocracy amidst numerous plebs, standing outside of it, having no rights but only duties. The victory of the plebs burst the old gentile constitution asunder and erected on its ruins the state, into which both the gentile aristocracy and the plebs were soon wholly absorbed. Finally, among the German vanquishers of the Roman Empire, the state derived directly from the conquest of large foreign territories, which the gentile constitution had no means of ruling. As this conquest did not entail either a serious struggle with the old population or a more advanced division of labour, and as conquered and conquerors were almost at the same stage of economic development and thus the economic basis of society remained the same as before, the gentile constitution was able to continue for many centuries in a changed, territorial shape as a Mark constitution, and even rejuvenate itself for a time in enfeebled form in the noble and patrician families of later years, and even in peasant families, as in Dithmarschen.*

The state is, therefore, by no means a power forced on society from without; just as little is it "the reality of the ethical idea", "the image and reality of reason", as Hegel maintains.[a] Rather, it is a product of society at a certain stage of development; it is the admission that this society has become entangled in an insoluble contradiction with itself, that it has split into irreconcilable opposites which it is powerless to dispel. But in order that these opposites, classes with conflicting economic interests, might not consume themselves and society in fruitless struggle, it became necessary to have a power seemingly standing above society which would alleviate the conflict and keep it within the bounds of "order"; and this power, having arisen out of society but placing itself above it, and alienating itself more and more from it, is the state.

As distinct from the old gentile order, the state, first, divides its subjects *according to territory.* As we have seen, the old gentile associations, built upon and held together by ties of blood, became inadequate, largely because they were conditional on the members being bound to a given territory, a bond which had long ceased to exist. The territory remained, but the people had become mobile. Hence, division according to territory was taken as the point of departure, and citizens were allowed to exercise their public rights and duties wherever they settled, irrespective of gens and tribe. This organisation of citizens according to locality is a feature common to all states. That is why it seems natural to us; but we have seen what long and arduous struggles were needed before it replaced, in Athens and Rome, the old organisation according to gentes.

The second distinguishing feature is the establishment of a *public authority* which no longer directly coincides with the population organising itself as an armed force. This special public

---

* The first historian to have at least an approximate idea of the nature of the gens was Niebuhr, thanks to his knowledge of the Dithmarschen families— to which, however, he also owes the errors he mechanically copied from there.[138]

---

a G. W. F. Hegel, *Grundlinien der Philosophie des Rechts,* §§ 257, 360.— *Ed.*

authority is necessary because a self-acting armed organisation of the population has become impossible since the split into classes. The slaves also belong to the population; the 90,000 citizens of Athens formed only a privileged class as against the 365,000 slaves. The people's army of the Athenian democracy was an aristocratic public authority vis-à-vis the slaves, whom it kept in check; however, a gendarmerie also became necessary to keep the citizens in check, as we related above. This public authority exists in every state; it consists not merely of armed men but also of material adjuncts, prisons and institutions of coercion of all kinds, of which gentile society knew nothing. It may be very insignificant, almost infinitesimal, in societies where class antagonisms are still undeveloped and in remote territories as was the case at certain times and in certain regions in the United States of America. It [the public authority] grows stronger, however, to the extent that class antagonisms within the state become exacerbated and adjacent states become larger and more populous. We have only to look at our present-day Europe, where class struggle and competition for conquests have raised the public power to such a level that it threatens to swallow the whole of society and even the state.

In order to maintain this public power, contributions from the citizens are necessary—*taxes*. These were absolutely unknown in gentile society; but we know enough about them today. As civilisation advances, these taxes become inadequate too; the state makes drafts on the future, contracts loans, *public debts*. Old Europe can tell a tale about these, too.

Having public authority and the right to levy taxes, the officials now stand, as organs of society, *above* society. The free, voluntary respect that was accorded to the organs of the gentile constitution does not satisfy them, even if they could gain it; being the vehicles of a power that is becoming alien to society, respect for them must be enforced by means of exceptional laws by virtue of which they enjoy special sanctity and inviolability. The shabbiest police servant in the civilised state has more "authority" than all the organs of gentile society put together; but the most powerful prince and the greatest statesman, or commander, of civilisation may well envy the humblest gentile chief for the unforced and undisputed respect that is paid to him. The one stands in the midst of society, the other is forced to attempt to represent something outside and above it.

Because the state arose from the need to hold class antagonisms in check, but because it arose, at the same time, in the midst of the conflict of these classes, it is, as a rule, the state of the most powerful, economically dominant class, which, through the medium of the state, becomes also the politically dominant class, and thus acquires new means of keeping down and exploiting the oppressed class. Thus, the state of antiquity was above all the state of the slave owners for keeping down the slaves, as the feudal state was the organ of the nobility for keeping down the peasant serfs and villeins, and the modern representative state is an instrument for the exploitation of wage labour by capital. By way of exception, however, periods occur in which the warring classes balance each other so closely that the state authority, as ostensible mediator, acquires, for the moment, a certain degree of independence of both. Such was the absolute monarchy of the seventeenth and eighteenth centuries, which held the balance between the nobility and burghers; such was the Bonapartism of the First, and especially of the Second French Empire, which played off the proletariat against the bourgeoisie and the bourgeoisie against the proletariat. The latest performance of this kind, in which ruler and ruled appear equally ridiculous, is the new German Empire of the Bismarck nation: here capitalists and workers are balanced against each other and equally cheated for the benefit of the impoverished Prussian backwoods Junkers.

In most historical states, the rights granted to citizens are, besides, apportioned according to their wealth, thus directly expressing the fact that the state is an organisation of the possessing class for its protection against the non-possessing class. It was so already in the Athenian and Roman classification according to property. It was so in the medieval feudal state, in which political power was in conformity with the amount of land owned. It is seen in the electoral qualifications of the modern representative states. Yet this political recognition of property distinctions is by no means inherent. On the contrary, it marks a low stage of state development. The highest form of the state, the democratic republic, which under our modern conditions of society is more and more becoming an inevitable necessity, and is the only form of state in which the last decisive struggle between proletariat and bourgeoisie can be fought out—the democratic republic officially knows no more of property distinctions. In it wealth exercises its power indirectly, but all the more surely. On the one hand, in the form of the direct corruption of officials, of which America provides the classical example; on the other hand, in the form of an alliance between government and stock exchange, which becomes the easier to achieve the more the national debt increases and the more joint-stock companies concentrate in their hands not only transport but also production itself, using the stock exchange as their centre. Besides America, the latest French republic is a striking example of this; and even good old Switzerland has contributed its share in this field. But that a democratic republic is not essential for this fraternal alliance between government and stock exchange is proved by England and also by the new German Empire, where one cannot tell who was elevated more by universal suffrage, Bismarck or Bleichröder. And lastly, the possessing class rules directly through the medium of universal suffrage. As long as the oppressed class, in our case, therefore, the proletariat, is not yet ripe to emancipate itself, it will in its majority regard the existing order of society as the only one possible and, politically, will form the tail of the capitalist class, its extreme Left wing. To the extent, however, that this class matures for its self-emancipation, it constitutes itself as a party of its own and elects its own representatives, not those of the capitalists. Thus, universal suffrage is the gauge of the maturity of the working class. It cannot and never will be anything more in the present-day state; but that is sufficient. On the day the thermometer of universal suffrage registers boiling point among the workers, both they and the capitalists will know where they stand.

The state, then, has not existed from eternity. There have been societies that managed without it, that had no idea of the state and state authority. At a certain stage of economic development, which was necessarily bound up with the split of society into classes, the state became a necessity owing to this split. We are now rapidly approaching a stage in the development of production at which the existence of these classes not only will have ceased to be a necessity, but will become a positive hindrance to production. They will fall as inevitably as they arose at an earlier stage. Along with them the state will inevitably fall. Society, which will reorganise production on the basis of a free and equal association of the producers, will put the whole machinery of state where it will then belong: into the museum of antiquities, by the side of the spinning-wheel and the bronze axe.

* * *

Thus, from the foregoing, civilisation is that stage of development of society at which division of labour, the resulting exchange between individuals, and commodity production, which combines the two, reach their full development and revolutionise the whole of hitherto existing society.

Production at all previous stages of society was essentially common production and, likewise, consumption took place by the direct distribution of the products within larger or smaller communistic communities. This production in common was carried on within the narrowest limits, but concomitantly the producers were masters of their process of production and of their product. They knew what became of the product: they consumed it, it did not leave their hands; and as long as production was carried on on this basis, it could not grow beyond the control of the producers, and it could not conjure up any alien, phantom powers against them, as is the case regularly and inevitably under civilisation.

But, slowly, division of labour crept into this process of production. It undermined the communality of production and appropriation, it made appropriation by individuals the predominant rule, and thus gave rise to exchange between individuals— how, we examined above. Gradually, the production of commodities became the dominant form.

With the production of commodities, production no longer for one's own consumption but for exchange, the products necessarily change hands. The producer parts with his product in the course of exchange; he no longer knows what becomes of it. As soon as money, and with it the merchant, steps in as a mediator between the producers, the process of exchange becomes still more complicated, the ultimate fate of the products still more uncertain. The merchants are numerous and none of them knows what the other is doing. Commodities now pass not only from hand to hand, but also from market to market. The producers have lost control of the total production of their life cycle, and the merchants have not acquired it. Products and production fall victim to chance.

But chance is only one pole of an interrelation, the other pole of which is called necessity. In nature, where chance, too, seems to reign, we have long since demonstrated in each particular field the inherent necessity and regularity that asserts itself in this chance. What is true of nature holds good also for society. The more a social activity, a series of social processes, becomes too powerful for conscious human control, grows beyond human reach, the more it seems to have been left to pure chance, the more do its peculiar and innate laws assert themselves in this chance, as if by natural necessity. Such laws also control the fortuities of the production and exchange of commodities; these laws confront the individual producer and exchanger as strange and, in the beginning, even as unknown powers, the nature of which must first be laboriously investigated and ascertained. These economic laws of commodity production are modified at the different stages of development of this form of production; on the whole, however, the entire period of civilisation has been dominated by these laws. To this day, the product is master of the producer; to this day, the total production of society is regulated, not by a plan thought out in common, but by blind laws, which operate with elemental force, in the last resort in the storms of periodic commercial crises.

We saw above how human labour power became able, at a rather early stage of development of production, to deliver considerably more products than were needed for the producer's maintenance, and how this stage, in the main, coincided with that where the division of labour and exchange appeared between individuals. Now, it was not long before the great "truth" was discovered that man, too, may be a commodity; that human power [a] may be exchanged and utilised by converting man into a slave. Men had barely started to engage in exchange when they themselves were exchanged. The active became a passive, whether man wanted it or not.

With slavery, which reached its fullest development under civilisation, came the first great split of society into an exploiting and an exploited class. This split has continued during the whole period of civilisation. Slavery was the first form of exploitation, peculiar to the world of antiquity; it was followed by serfdom in the Middle Ages, and by wage labour in modern times. These are the three great forms of servitude, characteristic of the three great epochs of civilisation; overt, and, latterly, covert slavery, are its constant companions.

The stage of commodity production, with which civilisation began, is marked economically by the introduction of 1) metal money and, thus, of money capital, interest and usury; 2) the merchants acting as mediating class between producers; 3) private ownership of land and mortgage; 4) slave labour as the prevailing form of production. The form of the family corresponding to civilisation and under it becoming the definitively prevailing form is monogamy, the supremacy of the man over the woman, and the individual family as the economic unit of society. The cohesive force of civilised society is the state, which in all typical periods is exclusively the state of the ruling class, and in all cases remains

---

[a] The 1884 edition has "human labour power".— *Ed.*

essentially a machine for keeping down the oppressed, exploited class. Other marks of civilisation are: on the one hand, fixation of the antithesis between town and country as the basis of the entire social division of labour; on the other hand, the introduction of testaments, by which the property holder is able to dispose of his property even after his death. This institution, which was a direct blow in the face of the old gentile constitution, was unknown in Athens until the time of Solon; in Rome it was introduced very early, but we do not know when.* Among the Germans it was introduced by the priests in order that the good honest German might without hindrance bequeath his property to the Church.

With this constitution as its foundation civilisation has accomplished things of which the old gentile society was not remotely capable. But it accomplished them by setting in motion the most sordid instincts and passions of man, and by developing them at the expense of all his other faculties. Naked greed has been the moving spirit of civilisation from its first day to the present time; wealth, wealth and wealth again; wealth, not of society, but of this shabby individual was its sole determining aim. If, in the pursuit of this aim, the increasing development of science and repeated periods of the fullest blooming of art fell into its lap, it was only because without them the ample present-day achievements in the accumulation of wealth would have been impossible.

Since the exploitation of one class by another is the basis of civilisation, its whole development moves in a continuous contradiction. Every advance in production is at the same time a retrogression in the condition of the oppressed class, that is, of the great majority. What is a boon for the one is necessarily a bane for the other; each new emancipation of one class means a new oppression of another class. The most striking proof of this is furnished by the introduction of machinery, the effects of which are today known throughout the world. And while among barbarians, as we have seen, hardly any distinction could be made

* Lassalle's *Das System der erworbenen Rechte* turns, in its second part, mainly on the proposition that the Roman testament is as old as Rome itself, that in Roman history there was never "a time when testaments did not exist"; that the testament arose rather in pre-Roman times out of the cult of the dead. As a confirmed Hegelian of the old school, Lassalle derived the provisions of the Roman law not from the social relations of the Romans, but from the "speculative conception" of the will, and thus arrived at this totally unhistoric assertion. This is not to be wondered at in a book which from the same speculative conception draws the conclusion that the transfer of property was purely a secondary matter in Roman inheritance. Lassalle not only believes in the illusions of Roman jurists, especially of the earlier period, but he even excels them.

between rights and duties, civilisation makes the difference and antithesis between these two plain even to the dullest mind by assigning to one class pretty nearly all the rights, and to the other class pretty nearly all the duties.

But this is not as it ought to be. What is good for the ruling class should be good for the whole of the society with which the ruling class identifies itself. Therefore, the more civilisation advances, the more it is compelled to cover the ills it necessarily creates with the cloak of love, to embellish them, or to deny their existence; in short, to introduce conventional hypocrisy— unknown either in previous forms of society or even in the earliest stages of civilisation—that eventually culminates in the declaration: The exploiting class exploits the oppressed class solely and exclusively in the interest of the exploited class itself; and if the latter fails to appreciate this, and even becomes rebellious, it thereby shows the basest ingratitude to its benefactors, the exploiters.*

And now, in conclusion, Morgan's verdict on civilisation:

"Since the advent of civilisation, the outgrowth of property has been so immense, its forms so diversified, its uses so expanding and its management so intelligent in the interests of its owners that it *has become,* on the part of the people, *an unmanageable power. The human mind stands bewildered in the presence of its own creation.* The time will come, nevertheless, when human intelligence will rise to the mastery over property, and define the relations of the state to the property it protects, as well as [...] the limits of the rights of its owners. The interests of society are paramount to individual interests, and the two must be brought into just and harmonious relation. A mere property career is not the final destiny of mankind, if progress is to be the law of the future as it has been of the past. The time which has passed away since civilisation began is but a fragment of the past duration of man's existence; and but a fragment of the ages yet to come. The dissolution of society bids fair to become the termination of a career of which property is the end and aim, because such a career contains the elements of self-destruction. Democracy in government, brotherhood in society, equality in rights [...], and universal education, foreshadow the next higher plane of society to which experience, intelligence and knowledge are steadily tending. *It will be a revival, in a higher form, of the liberty, equality and fraternity of the ancient gentes.*" (Morgan, *Ancient Society,* p. 552.) [a]

---

* I had intended at the outset to place the brilliant critique of civilisation, scattered through the works of Charles Fourier, by the side of Morgan's and my own. Unfortunately, I cannot spare the time. I only wish to remark that Fourier already considered monogamy and property in land as the main distinguishing features of civilisation, and that he described it as a war of the rich against the poor. We also find already in his works the deep appreciation of the fact that in all imperfect societies, those torn by antagonisms, the individual families (*les familles incohérentes*) are the economic units.

---

[a] Italics by Engels. See also "Marx's Excerpts...", op. cit., p. 139.— *Ed.*

[INTRODUCTORY NOTE
TO THE SEPARATE 1884 EDITION
OF MARX'S *WAGE LABOUR AND CAPITAL*] [139]

The following work appeared as a series of leading articles in the *Neue Rheinische Zeitung* from April 4, 1849 onwards. It is based on the lectures delivered by *Marx* in 1847 at the German Workers' Society in Brussels.[140] The work as printed remained a fragment; the words at the end of No. 269: "To be continued," remained unfulfilled in consequence of the events which just then came crowding one after another: the invasion of Hungary by the Russians, the insurrections in Dresden, Iserlohn, Elberfeld, the Palatinate and Baden, which led to the suppression of the newspaper itself (May 19, 1849).

Written in June 1884

First published in K. Marx, *Lohnarbeit und Kapital*, Hottingen-Zurich, 1884

Printed according to the 1891 edition

MARX AND RODBERTUS

PREFACE TO THE FIRST GERMAN EDITION
OF *THE POVERTY OF PHILOSOPHY* BY KARL MARX[141]

The present work was produced in the winter of 1846-47, at a time when Marx had cleared up for himself the basic features of his new historical and economic outlook. Proudhon's *Système des contradictions économiques, ou Philosophie de la misère,* which had just appeared, gave him the opportunity to develop these basic features, setting them against the views of a man who, from then on, was to occupy the most important place among living French socialists. Since the time in Paris when the two of them had often spent whole nights discussing economic questions, their paths had increasingly diverged: Proudhon's book proved that there was already an unbridgeable gulf between them. To ignore it was at that time impossible, and so Marx put on record the irreparable rupture in this reply of his.

Marx's general opinion of Proudhon is to be found in the article, which is appended to this preface and appeared in the Berlin *Social-Demokrat* Nos 16, 17 and 18 for 1865.[a] It was the only article Marx wrote for that paper; Herr von Schweitzer's attempts to guide it along feudal and government lines, which became evident soon afterwards, compelled us to publicly terminate our collaboration after only a few weeks.[142]

For Germany, the present work has at this precise moment a significance which Marx himself never imagined. How could he have known that, in trouncing Proudhon, he was hitting Rodbertus, the idol of the careerists of today, who was unknown to him even by name at that time?

---

[a] K. Marx, "On Proudhon (Letter to J. B. Schweitzer)."— *Ed.*

This is not the place to deal with relations between Marx and Rodbertus; an opportunity for that is sure to present itself to me very soon.[143] Suffice it to note here that when Rodbertus accuses Marx of having "plundered" him and of having "freely used in his *Capital* without quoting him"[a] his work *Zur Erkenntniß,* he allows himself to indulge in an act of slander which is only explicable by the irksomeness of unrecognised genius and by his remarkable ignorance of things taking place outside Prussia, and especially of socialist and economic literature. Neither these charges, nor the above-mentioned work by Rodbertus ever came to Marx's sight; all he knew of Rodbertus was the three *Sociale Briefe* and even these certainly not before 1858 or 1859.

With greater reason Rodbertus asserts in these letters that he had already discovered "Proudhon's constituted value" *before* Proudhon[b]; but here again it is true he erroneously flatters himself with being the *first* discoverer. In any case, he is thus one of the targets of criticism in the present work, and this compels me to deal briefly with his "fundamental" piece: *Zur Erkenntniß unsrer staatswirthschaftlichen Zustände,* 1842, insofar as this brings forth anticipations of Proudhon as well as the communism of Weitling likewise (again unconsciously) contained in it.

Insofar as modern socialism, no matter of what tendency, starts out from bourgeois political economy, it almost without exception takes up the Ricardian theory of value. The two propositions which Ricardo proclaimed in 1817 right at the beginning of his *Principles,* 1) that the value of any commodity is purely and solely determined by the quantity of labour required for its production, and 2) that the product of the entire social labour is divided among the three classes: landowners (rent), capitalists (profit) and workers (wages)—these two propositions had ever since 1821 been utilised in England for socialist conclusions,[144] and in part with such pointedness and resolution that this literature, which had then almost been forgotten and was to a large extent only rediscovered by Marx, remained unsurpassed until the appearance of *Capital.* About this another time. If, therefore, in 1842, Rodbertus for his part drew socialist conclusions from the above propositions, that was certainly a very considerable step forward

---

[a] See Rodbertus' letters to R. Meyers dated November 29, 1871 (*Briefe und Socialpolitische Aufsätze von Dr. Rodbertus Jagetzow,* Vol. 1, Berlin, p. 134) and to J. Zeller dated March 14, 1875 (*Zeitschrift für die gesammte Staatswissenschaft,* Vol. 35, Tübingen, 1879, p. 219).— *Ed.*

[b] [J. K.] Rodbertus, *Sociale Briefe an von Kirchmann,* Zweiter Brief, p. 54 (Note).— *Ed.*

for a German at that time, but it could rank as a new discovery only for Germany at best. That such an application of the Ricardian theory was far from new was proved by Marx against Proudhon, who suffered from a similar conceit.

"Anyone who is in any way familiar with the trend of political economy in England cannot fail to know that almost all the socialists in that country have, at different periods, proposed the *equalitarian* (i.e. socialist)[a] application of Ricardian theory. We could quote for M. Proudhon: Hodgskin, *Political Economy,* 1827; William Thompson, *An Inquiry into the Principles of the Distribution of Wealth Most Conducive to Human Happiness,* 1824; T. R. Edmonds, *Practical Moral and Political Economy,* 1828, etc., etc., and four pages more of *etc.* We shall content ourselves with listening to an English Communist, Mr. Bray ... in his remarkable work, *Labour's Wrongs and Labour's Remedy,* Leeds, 1839."[b] And the quotations given here from Bray on their own put an end to a good part of the priority claimed by Rodbertus.

At that time Marx had never yet entered the reading room of the British Museum. Apart from the libraries of Paris and Brussels, apart from my books and extracts, he had only examined such books as were obtainable in Manchester during a six-week journey to England we made together in the summer of 1845. The literature in question was, therefore, by no means so inaccesible in the forties as it may be now. If, all the same, it always remained unknown to Rodbertus, that is to be ascribed solely to his Prussian local bigotry. He is the actual founder of specifically Prussian socialism and is now at last recognised as such.

However, even in his beloved Prussia, Rodbertus was not to remain undisturbed. In 1859, Marx's *A Contribution to the Critique of Political Economy,* Part I, was published in Berlin. Therein, among the economists' objections to Ricardo, the following was put forward as the second objection (p. 40):

"If the exchange value of a product equals the labour time contained in the product, then the exchange value of a working day is equal to the product it yields, in other words, wages must be equal to the product of labour. But in fact the opposite is true." On this there was the following note: "This objection, which was advanced against Ricardo by economists,[c] was later taken up by socialists. Assuming that the formula was theoretically sound, they

---

a Italics and words in parentheses by Engels.— *Ed.*
b See present edition, Vol. 6, p. 138.— *Ed.*
c Marx has "bourgeois economists".— *Ed.*

alleged that practice stood in conflict with the theory and demanded that bourgeois society should draw the practical conclusions supposedly arising from its theoretical principles. In this way at least English socialists turned Ricardo's formula of exchange value against political economy."[a] In the same note there was a reference to Marx's *Misère de la philosophie,* which was then obtainable in all the bookshops.

Rodbertus, therefore, had sufficient opportunity of convincing himself whether his discoveries of 1842 were really new. Instead, he proclaims them again and again and regards them as so incomparable that it never occurs to him that Marx might have drawn his conclusions from Ricardo independently, just as well as Rodbertus himself. Absolutely impossible! Marx had "plundered" him—the man whom the same Marx had offered every opportunity to convince himself how long before both of them these conclusions, at least in the crude form which they still have in the case of Rodbertus, had previously been enunciated in England!

The simplest socialist application of the Ricardian theory is indeed that given above. It has led in many cases to insights into the origin and nature of surplus value which go far beyond Ricardo, as in the case of Rodbertus among others. Quite apart from the fact that on this matter he nowhere presents anything which has not already been said at least as well, before him, his presentation suffers like those of his predecessors from the fact that he adopts, uncritically and without examining their content, economic categories—labour, capital, value, etc.—in the crude form, clinging to their external appearance, in which they were handed down to him by the economists. He thereby not only cuts himself off from all further development—in contrast to Marx, who was the first to make something of these propositions so often repeated for the last sixty-four years—but, as will be shown, he opens for himself the road leading straight to utopia.

The above application of the Ricardian theory that the entire social product belongs to the workers as *their* product, because they are the sole real producers, leads directly to communism. But, as Marx indeed indicates in the above-quoted passage, it is incorrect in formal economic terms, for it is simply an application of morality to economics. According to the laws of bourgeois economics, the greatest part of the product does *not* belong to the workers who have produced it. If we now say: that is unjust, that ought not to be so, then that has nothing

---

[a] See present edition, Vol. 29, p. 301.—*Ed.*

immediately to do with economics. We are merely saying that this economic fact is in contradiction to our sense of morality. Marx, therefore, never based his communist demands upon this, but upon the inevitable collapse of the capitalist mode of production which is daily taking place before our eyes to an ever growing degree; he says only that surplus value consists of unpaid labour, which is a simple fact. But what in economic terms may be formally incorrect, may all the same be correct from the point of view of world history. If mass moral consciousness declares an economic fact to be unjust, as it did at one time in the case of slavery and statute labour, that is proof that the fact itself has outlived its day, that other economic facts have made their appearance due to which the former has become unbearable and untenable. Therefore, a very true economic content may be concealed behind the formal economic incorrectness. This is not the place to deal more closely with the significance and history of the theory of surplus value.

At the same time other conclusions can be drawn, and have been drawn, from the Ricardian theory of value. The value of commodities is determined by the labour required for their production. But now it turns out that in this imperfect world commodities are sold sometimes above, sometimes below their value, and indeed not only as a result of ups and downs in competition. The rate of profit tends just as much to balance out at the same level for all capitalists as the price of commodities does to become reduced to the labour value by agency of supply and demand. But the rate of profit is calculated on the total capital invested in an industrial business. Since now the annual products in two different branches of industry may incorporate equal quantities of labour, and, consequently, may represent equal values and also wages may be at an equal level in both, while the capital advanced in one branch may be, and often is, twice or three times as great as in the other, consequently the Ricardian law of value, as Ricardo himself discovered, comes into contradiction here with the law of the equal rate of profit. If the products of both branches of industry are sold at their values, the rates of profit cannot be equal; if, however, the rates of profit are equal, then the products of the two branches of industry cannot always be sold at their values. Thus, we have here a contradiction, the antinomy of two economic laws, the practical resolution of which takes place according to Ricardo (Chapter I, Section 4 and 5 [145]) as a rule in favour of the rate of profit at the cost of value.

But the Ricardian definition of value, in spite of its ominous characteristics, has a feature which makes it dear to the heart of the honest bourgeois. It appeals with irresistible force to his sense of justice. Justice and equality of rights are the cornerstones on which the bourgeois of the eighteenth and nineteenth centuries would like to erect his social edifice over the ruins of feudal injustice, inequality and privilege. And the determination of value of commodities by labour and the free exchange of the products of labour, taking place according to this measure of value between commodity owners with equal rights, these are, as Marx has already proved, the real foundations on which the whole political, juridical and philosophical ideology of the modern bourgeoisie has been built. Once it is recognised that labour is the measure of value of a commodity, the better feelings of the honest bourgeois cannot but be deeply wounded by the wickedness of a world which, while recognising the basic law of justice in name, still in fact appears at every moment to set it aside without compunction. And the petty bourgeois especially, whose honest labour—even if it is only that of his workmen and apprentices—is daily more and more depreciated in value by the competition of large-scale production and machinery, this small-scale producer especially must long for a society in which the exchange of products according to their labour value is at last a complete and invariable truth. In other words, he must long for a society in which a single law of commodity production prevails exclusively and in full, but in which the conditions are abolished in which it can prevail at all, viz., the other laws of commodity production and, later, of capitalist production.

How deeply this utopia has struck roots in the way of thinking of the modern petty bourgeois—real or ideal—is proved by the fact that it was systematically developed by John Gray back in 1831,[a] that it was tried in practice and theoretically propagated in England in the thirties, that it was proclaimed as the latest truth by Rodbertus in Germany in 1842 and by Proudhon in France in 1846, that it was again proclaimed by Rodbertus as late as 1871 as the solution to the social question and, as, so to say, his social testament,[b] and that in 1884 it again finds adherents among the horde of careerists who in the name of Rodbertus set out to exploit Prussian state socialism.[146]

The critique of this utopia has been so exhaustively furnished by Marx both against Proudhon and against Gray[c] (see the appendix

---

[a] J. Gray, *The Social System: A Treatise on the Principle of Exchange.*—*Ed.*
[b] See J. K. Rodbertus, *Der Normal-Arbeitstag.*—*Ed.*
[c] See present edition, Vol. 29, pp. 320-23.—*Ed.*

to this work[a]) that I can confine myself here to a few remarks on the form of substantiating and depicting it peculiar to Rodbertus.

As already noted, Rodbertus adopts the traditional definitions of economic concepts entirely in the form in which they have come down to him from the economists. He does not make the slightest attempt to investigate them. Value is for him

"the valuation of one thing against others according to quantity, this valuation being conceived as measure".[b]

This, to put it mildly, extremely slovenly definition gives us at the best an idea of what value approximately looks like, but says absolutely nothing of what it is. Since this, however, is all that Rodbertus is able to tell us about value, it is understandable that he looks for a measure of value located outside value. After thirty pages in which he mixes up use value and exchange value in higgledypiggledy fashion with that power of abstract thought so infinitely admired by Herr Adolf Wagner,[147] he arrives at the conclusion that there is no real measure of value and that one has to make do with a substitute measure. Labour could serve as such, but only if products of an equal quantity of labour were always exchanged against products of an equal quantity of labour; whether this "is already the case of itself, or whether precautionary measures are adopted" to ensure that it is.[c] Consequently, value and labour remain without any sort of material connection, in spite of the fact that the whole first chapter is taken up to expound to us that commodities "cost labour" and nothing but labour, and why this is so.

Labour, again, is taken uncritically in the form in which it occurs among the economists. And not even that. For, although there is a reference in a couple of words to differences in intensity of labour, labour is still put forward quite generally as something which "costs", hence as something which measures value, quite irrespective of whether it is expended under normal average social conditions or not. Whether the producers take ten days, or only one, to make products which could be made in one day; whether they employ the best or the worst tools; whether they expend their labour time in the production of socially necessary articles and in

---

[a] See this volume, p. 291.— Ed.

[b] [J. K.] Rodbertus, *Zur Erkenntniß unsrer staatswirthschaftlichen Zustände*, p. 61.— Ed

[c] Ibid., p. 62.— Ed.

the socially required quantity, or whether they make quite undesired articles or desired articles in quantities above or below demand—about all this there is not a word: labour is labour, the product of equal labour must be exchanged against the product of equal labour. Rodbertus, who is otherwise always ready, whether rightly or not, to adopt the national standpoint and to survey the relations of individual producers from the high watchtower of general social considerations, is anxious to avoid doing so here. And this, indeed, solely because from the very first line of his book he makes directly for the utopia of labour money, and because any investigation of labour seen from its property of creating value would be bound to put insuperable obstacles in his way. His instinct was here considerably stronger than his power of abstract thought which, by the by, is revealed in Rodbertus only by the most concrete absence of ideas.

The transition to utopia is now made in the turn of a hand. The "measures", which ensure exchange of commodities according to labour value as the invariable rule, cause no difficulty. The other utopians of this tendency, from Gray to Proudhon, rack their brains to invent social institutions which would achieve this aim. They attempt at least to solve the economic question in an economic way through the action of the owners themselves who exchange the commodities. For Rodbertus it is much easier. As a good Prussian he appeals to the state: a decree of the state authority orders the reform.

In this way then, value is happily "constituted", but by no means the priority in this constitution as claimed by Rodbertus. On the contrary, Gray as well as Bray—among many others— before Rodbertus, at length and frequently *ad nauseam,* repeated this idea, viz., the pious desire for measures by means of which products would always and under all circumstances be exchanged only at their labour value.

After the state has thus constituted value—at least for a part of the products, for Rodbertus is also modest—it issues its labour paper money, and gives advances therefrom to the industrial capitalists, with which the latter pay the workers, whereupon the workers buy the products with the labour paper money they have received, and so cause the paper money to flow back to its starting point. How very beautifully this is effected, one must hear from Rodbertus himself:

"In regard to the second condition, the necessary measure that the value certified in the note should be actually present in circulation is realised in that only the person who actually delivers a product receives a note, on which is accurately recorded the quantity of labour by which the product was produced. Whoever delivers a product of two days' labour receives a note marked 'two days'. By the strict observance of this rule in the issue of notes, the second condition too would necessarily be fulfilled. For according to our supposition the real value of the goods always coincides with the quantity of labour which their production has cost and this quantity of labour is measured by the usual units of time, and therefore someone who hands in a product on which two days' labour has been expended and receives a certificate for two days, has received, certified or assigned to him neither more nor less value than that which he has in fact supplied. Further, since *only* the person who has actually put a product into circulation receives such a certificate, it is also certain that the value marked on the note is available for the satisfaction of society. However extensive we imagine the circle of division of labour to be, if this rule is strictly followed *the sum total of available value* must *be exactly equal to the sum total of certified value.*[a] Since, however, the sum total of certified value is exactly equal to the sum total of value assigned, the latter must *necessarily coincide with the available value, all claims will be satisfied and the liquidation correctly brought about*" (pp. 166-67).

If Rodbertus has hitherto always had the misfortune to arrive too late with his new discoveries, this time at least he has the merit of *one* sort of originality: none of his rivals has dared to express the stupidity of the labour money utopia in this childishly naïve, transparent, I might say truly Pomeranian, form. Since for every paper certificate a corresponding object of value has been delivered, and no object of value is supplied except in return for a corresponding paper certificate, the sum total of paper certificates must always be covered by the sum total of objects of value. The calculation works out without the smallest remainder, it is correct down to a second of labour time, and no governmental chief revenue office accountant, however many years of faithful service he may have behind him, could prove the slightest error in calculation. What more could one want?

In present-day capitalist society each industrial capitalist produces off his own bat what, how and as much as he likes. The social demand, however, remains an unknown magnitude to him, both in regard to quality, the kind of objects required, and in regard to quantity. That which today cannot be supplied quickly enough, may tomorrow be offered far in excess of the demand. Nevertheless, demand is finally satisfied in one way or another, good or bad, and, taken as a whole, production is ultimately geared towards the objects required. How is this evening-out of the contradiction effected? By competition. And how does competition bring about this solution? Simply by depreciating below their labour value those commodities which by their kind or

---

[a] Here and below italics by Engels.— *Ed.*

amount are useless for immediate social requirements, and by making the producers feel, through this roundabout means, that they have produced either absolutely useless articles or ostensibly useful articles in unusable, superfluous quantity. Two things follow from this:

First, continual deviations of the prices of commodities from their values are the necessary condition in and through which the value of the commodities as such can come into existence. Only through the fluctuations of competition, and consequently of commodity prices, does the law of value of commodity production assert itself and the determination of the value of the commodity by the socially necessary labour time become a reality. That thereby the form of manifestation of value, the price, as a rule looks somewhat different from the value which it manifests, is a fate which value shares with most social relations. A king usually looks quite different from the monarchy which he represents. To desire, in a society of producers who exchange their commodities, to establish the determination of value by labour time, by forbidding competition to establish this determination of value through pressure on prices in the only way it can be established, is therefore merely to prove that, at least in this sphere, one has adopted the usual utopian disdain of economic laws.

Secondly, competition, by bringing into operation the law of value of commodity production in a society of producers who exchange their commodities, precisely thereby brings about the only organisation and arrangement of social production which is possible in the circumstances. Only through the undervaluation or overvaluation of products is it forcibly brought home to the individual commodity producers what society requires or does not require and in what amounts. But it is precisely this sole regulator that the utopia advocated by Rodbertus among others wishes to abolish. And if we then ask what guarantee we have that necessary quantity and not more of each product will be produced, that we shall not go hungry in regard to corn and meat while we are choked in beet sugar and drowned in potato spirit, that we shall not lack trousers to cover our nakedness while trouser buttons flood us by the million—Rodbertus triumphantly shows us his splendid calculation, according to which the correct certificate has been handed out for every superfluous pound of sugar, for every unsold barrel of spirit, for every unusable trouser button, a calculation which "works out" exactly, and according to which "all claims will be satisfied and the liquidation correctly brought about". And anyone who does not believe this can apply to governmental chief revenue office accountant X in Pomerania, who has checked the calculation and found it correct, and who, as one who has never yet been caught lacking with the accounts, is thoroughly trustworthy.

And now consider the naïveté with which Rodbertus would abolish industrial and commercial crises by means of his utopia. As soon as the production of commodities has assumed world market dimensions, the evening-out between the individual producers who produce for private account and the market for which they produce, which in respect of quantity and quality of demand is more or less unknown to them, is established by means of a storm on the world market, by a commercial crisis.* If now competition is to be forbidden to make the individual producers aware, by a rise or fall in prices, how the world market stands, then they are completely blindfolded. To institute the production of commodities in such a fashion that the producers can no longer learn anything about the state of the market for which they are producing—that indeed is a cure for the crisis disease which could make Dr. Eisenbart envious of Rodbertus.

It is now comprehensible why Rodbertus determines the value of commodities simply by "labour" and at most allows for different degrees of intensity of labour. If he had investigated by what means and how labour creates value and therefore also determines and measures it, he would have arrived at socially necessary labour, necessary for the individual product, both in relation to other products of the same kind and also in relation to society's total demand. He would thereby have been confronted with the question as to how the adjustment of the production of separate commodity producers to the total social demand takes place, and his whole utopia would thereby have been made impossible. This time he preferred in fact to "make an abstraction", namely of precisely that which mattered.

Now at last we come to the point where Rodbertus really offers us something new; something which distinguishes him from all his numerous fellow supporters of the labour money exchange economy. They all demand this exchange organisation for the

---

* At least this was the case until recently. Since England's monopoly of the world market is being increasingly shattered by the participation of France, Germany and, above all, of America in world trade, a new form of evening-out appears to come into operation. The period of general prosperity preceding the crisis still fails to appear. If it should remain absent altogether, then chronic stagnation must necessarily become the normal condition of modern industry, with only insignificant fluctuations.

purpose of abolishing the exploitation of wage labour by capital. Every producer is to receive the full labour value of his product. On this they all agree, from Gray to Proudhon. Not at all, says Rodbertus. Wage labour and its exploitation remain.

In the first place, in no conceivable condition of society can the worker receive the full value of his product for consumption. A series of economically unproductive but necessary functions have to be met from the fund produced, and consequently also the persons connected with them maintained. This is only correct so long as the present-day division of labour applies. In a society in which general productive labour is obligatory, which is also "conceivable" after all, this ceases to apply. But the need for a social reserve and accumulation fund would remain and consequently even in that case, the workers, i.e., *all,* would remain in possession and enjoyment of their total product, but each separate worker would not enjoy the "full returns of his labour". Nor has the maintenance of economically unproductive functions at the expense of the labour product been overlooked by the other labour money utopians. But they leave the workers to tax themselves for this purpose in the usual democratic way, while Rodbertus, whose whole social reform of 1842 is geared to the Prussian state of that time, refers the whole matter to the decision of the bureaucracy, which determines from above the share of the worker in his own product and graciously permits him to have it.

In the second place, however, rent and profit are also to continue undiminished. For the landowners and industrial capitalists also exercise certain socially useful or even necessary functions, even if economically unproductive ones, and they receive in the shape of rent and profit a sort of pay on that account—a conception which was, it will be recalled, not new even in 1842. Actually they get at present far too much for the little that they do, and badly at that, but Rodbertus has need, at least for the next five hundred years, of a privileged class, and so the present rate of surplus value, to express myself correctly, is to remain in existence but is not to be allowed to be increased. This present rate of surplus value Rodbertus takes to be 200 per cent, that is to say, for twelve hours of labour daily the worker is to receive a certificate not for twelve hours but only for four, and the value produced in the remaining eight hours is to be divided between landowner and capitalist. Rodbertus' labour certificates, therefore, are a direct lie. Again, one must be a Pomeranian manor owner in order to imagine that a working class would put up with working twelve hours in order to receive a certificate for four hours of labour. If the hocus-pocus of capitalist production is translated into this naïve language, in which it appears as naked robbery, it is made impossible. Every certificate given to a worker would be a direct instigation to rebellion and would come under § 110 of the German Imperial Criminal Code.[148] One need never have seen any other proletariat than the day-labourer proletariat, still actually in semi-serfdom, of a Pomeranian manor where the rod and the whip reign supreme, and where all the beautiful women in the village belong to his lordship's harem, in order to imagine one can treat the workers in such a shamefaced manner. But, after all, our conservatives are our greatest revolutionaries.

If, however, our workers are sufficiently docile to be taken in that they have in reality only worked four hours during a whole twelve hours of hard work, they are, as a reward, to be guaranteed that for all eternity their share in their own product will never fall below a third. That is indeed pie in the sky of the most infantile kind and not worth wasting a word over. Insofar, therefore, as there is anything novel in the labour money exchange utopia of Rodbertus, this novelty is simply childish and far below the achievements of his numerous comrades both before and after him.

For the time when Rodbertus' *Zur Erkenntniß, etc.,* appeared, it was certainly an important book. His development of Ricardo's theory of value in that one direction was a very promising beginning. Even if it was new only for him and for Germany, still as a whole, it stands on a par with the achievements of the better ones among his English predecessors. But it was only a beginning, from which a real gain for theory could be achieved only by further thorough and critical work. But he cut himself off from further development by also tackling the development of Ricardo's theory from the very beginning in the second direction, in the direction of utopia. Thereby he surrendered the first condition of all criticism—freedom from bias. He worked on towards a goal fixed in advance, he became a *Tendenzökonom.* Once imprisoned by his utopia, he cut himself off from all possibility of scientific advance. From 1842 up to his death, he went round in circles, always repeating the same ideas which he had already expressed or suggested in his first work, feeling himself unappreciated, finding himself plundered, where there was nothing to plunder, and finally refusing, not without intention, to recognise that in essence he had only rediscovered what had already been discovered long before.

* * *

In a few places the translation departs from the printed French original. This is due to handwritten alterations by Marx, which will also be inserted in the new French edition that is now being prepared.[149]

It is hardly necessary to point out that the terminology used in this work does not entirely coincide with that in *Capital.* Thus this work still speaks of *labour* as a commodity, of the purchase and sale of labour, instead of labour *power.*

Also added as a supplement to this edition are:

1) a passage from Marx's work *A Contribution to the Critique of Political Economy,* Berlin, 1859, dealing with the *first* labour money exchange utopia of John Gray, and 2) a translation of Marx's speech on free trade in Brussels (1848),[a] which belongs to the same period of the author's development as the *Misère.*

London, October 23, 1884   *Frederick Engels*

First published in *Die Neue Zeit,* No. 1, 1885 and K. Marx, *Das Elend der Philosophie,* Stuttgart, 1885

Printed according to the 1892 German edition

---

[a] K. Marx, "Speech on the Question of Free Trade".— *Ed.*

REAL IMPERIAL RUSSIAN
PRIVY DYNAMITERS [150]

Everybody knows that the Russian government is using every means at its disposal to arrive at treaties with the West European states for the extradition of Russian revolutionaries who have fled the country.

Everybody also knows that its overriding concern is to obtain such a treaty from England.

And the final thing that everybody knows is that Russian officialdom will shrink at nothing if only it leads to the desired end.

Very well then. On January 13, 1885 Bismarck concludes an agreement with Russia, which provides for the extradition of every Russian political refugee the moment Russia sees fit to accuse him of being a prospective regicide, or prospective dynamiter. [151]

On January 15 Mrs Olga Novikov issued an appeal to England in the *Pall Mall Gazette,* the selfsame Mrs Novikov who in 1877 and 1878, before and during the war against the Turks, so magnificently duped the noble Mr Gladstone in the interests of Russia. [152] In it England is exhorted no longer to tolerate people such as Hartmann, Kropotkin and Stepniak conspiring on English soil *"to murder us in Russia"*, especially now that dynamite has become such a burning issue for the English themselves. And, she remarks, is Russia asking any more of England with respect to Russian revolutionaries than England itself is now obliged to ask of America with respect to Irish dynamiters?

On the morning of January 24 the Prusso-Russian treaty is published in London.[a]

---

[a] See "Extradition by Russia and Prussia", *The Times,* No. 31352, January 24, 1885.— *Ed.*

And on January 24 at 2 o'clock in the afternoon, three dynamite explosions go off in London within the space of a quarter hour, and they cause more damage than all the earlier ones taken together, wounding at least seven people, and according to other sources eighteen.

The timing of these explosions is too opportune not to raise the question—Whose interests do they serve? Who has most to gain from these otherwise pointless shots of terror aimed at nobody in particular, to which not only lower-ranking policemen and bourgeois fall victim but also workers and their wives and children? Who? The few Irishmen who were driven to desperation partially because of the brutality of the English government during their imprisonment, and who are assumed to have planted the dynamite? Or, on the other hand, the Russian government which cannot achieve its end—the extradition treaty—without putting the government and people of England under the most extreme pressure, pressure so great that it whips up public opinion in England into a blind rabid rage against the dynamiters?

When the Polish refugees with very few exceptions, would not lower themselves, at the behest of the Russian diplomatic service and the police, to forge Russian banknotes, the Russian government sent agents abroad, including privy councillor Kamensky, to goad them into doing it, and when this too failed Messrs Kamensky and associates were obliged to forge Russian banknotes themselves. For a further detailed account see the pamphlet *The Counterfeiters or the Agents of the Russian Government,* Geneva, H. Georg, 1875.[a]—The police forces of Switzerland and London, and probably of Paris as well, can tell a tale or two about how, in tracking down the Russian forgers, their inquiries finally led them to people whom the Russian embassies would steadfastly refuse to have prosecuted.

The history of the Balkan peninsula during the past one hundred years sheds enough light on the abilities of Russian officialdom in removing troublesome individuals by means of poison, the dagger, etc. I need refer only to the well-known *Histoire des principautés danubiennes* by Élias Regnault, Paris, 1855. The Russian diplomatic service constantly has at its disposal agents of all kinds, including the kind that are used to commit infamous deeds and then disowned.

I do not hesitate, for the time being to lay the blame for the explosions in London on January 24, 1885 at the door of the

---

[a] Published in Russian.— *Ed.*

Russians. Irish hands may have laid the dynamite, but it is more than probable that a Russian brain and Russian money were behind it.

The means of struggle employed by the Russian revolutionaries are dictated to them by necessity, by the actions of their opponents themselves. They must answer to their people and to history for the means they employ. But the gentlemen who are needlessly parodying this struggle in Western Europe in schoolboy fashion, who are attempting to bring the revolution down to the level of Schinderhannes, who do not even direct their weapons against real enemies but against the public in general, these gentlemen are in no way successors or allies of the Russian revolutionaries, but rather their worst enemies. Since it has become clear that nobody apart from Russian officialdom has any interest in the success of these heroic deeds, the only question that remains to be asked is which of them were coerced and which of them volunteered to become the paid agents of Russian tsarism.

London, January 25, 1885

Frederick Engels

First published in *Der Sozialdemokrat*, No. 5, January 29, 1885

Printed according to the newspaper

Published in English for the first time

The Official Journal of the Socialist League.

VOL. 1.—No. 2.   MARCH, 1885.   ONE PENNY.

ENGLAND IN 1845 AND IN 1885 [153]

Forty years ago England stood face to face with a crisis, solvable
to all appearances by force only. The immense and rapid
development of manufactures had outstripped the extension of
foreign markets and the increase of demand. Every ten years the
march of industry was violently interrupted by a general
commercial crash, followed, after a long period of chronic
depression, by a few short years of prosperity, and always ending
in feverish over-production and consequent renewed collapse. The
capitalist class clamored for Free Trade in corn,[154] and threatened
to enforce it by sending the starving population of the towns back
to the country districts, whence they came: to invade them, as
John Bright said, not as paupers begging for bread, but as an
army quartered upon the enemy.[155] The working masses of the
towns demanded their share of political power—the People's
Charter[156]; they were supported by the majority of the small
trading class, and the only difference between the two was
whether the Charter should be carried by physical or by moral
force.[a] Then came the commercial crash of 1847 and the Irish
famine, and with both the prospect of revolution.

The French Revolution of 1848 saved the English middle class.
The Socialistic pronunciamentoes of the victorious French workmen frightened the small middle class of England and disorganised
the narrower, but more matter-of-fact, movement of the English
working class. At the very moment Chartism was bound to assert
itself in its full strength, it collapsed internally, before even it

---

[a] Instead of "by physical or by moral force" the German translation has
"forcibly or lawfully".— *Ed.*

collapsed externally on the 10th of April, 1848.[157] The action[a] of
the working class was thrust into the background. The capitalist
class triumphed along the whole line.

The Reform Bill of 1831[158] had been the victory of the whole
capitalist class over the landed aristocracy. The repeal of the Corn
Laws[159] was the victory of the manufacturing capitalists not only
over the landed aristocracy, but over those sections of capitalists
too whose interests were more or less[b] bound up with the landed
interest: bankers, stock-jobbers, fundholders, etc. Free Trade
meant the re-adjustment of the whole home and foreign
commercial and financial policy of England in accordance with the
interests of the manufacturing capitalists—the class which now
represented the nation. And they set about this task with a will.
Every obstacle to industrial production was mercilessly removed.
The tariff and the whole system of taxation were revolutionised.
Everything was made subordinate to one end, but that end of the
utmost importance to the manufacturing capitalist: the cheapening
of all raw produce, and especially of the means of living of the
working class; the reduction of the cost of raw material, and the
keeping down—if not as yet the *bringing down*—of wages.
England was to become the "workshop of the world"[160]; all other
countries were to become for England what Ireland already
was—markets for her manufactured goods, supplying her in
return with raw materials and food. England the great manufacturing centre of an agricultural world, with an ever-increasing
number of corn and cotton-growing Irelands,[c] revolving around
her, the industrial sun. What a glorious prospect!

The manufacturing capitalists set about the realisation of this
their great object with that strong common sense and that
contempt for traditional principles which has ever distinguished
them from their more narrow-minded[d] compeers on the Continent. Chartism was dying out. The revival of commercial
prosperity, natural[e] after the revulsion of 1847 had spent itself,
was put down altogether to the credit of Free Trade. Both these
circumstances had turned the English working class, politically,
into the tail of the great Liberal party,[f] the party led by the

---

[a] The German translation has "The political action".— *Ed.*

[b] The German translation has "identical or" instead of "more or less".— *Ed.*

[c] The German translation has "satellites" instead of "Irelands".—*Ed.*

[d] The German translation has "more philistine" instead of "more narrow-
minded".— *Ed.*

[e] The German translation further has "and almost self-evident".— *Ed.*

[f] In the German translation the expression "great Liberal party" is given in
inverted commas.— *Ed.*

manufacturers. This advantage, once gained, had to be perpetuated. And the manufacturing capitalists, from the Chartist opposition[a] not to Free Trade, but to the transformation of Free Trade into the one vital national question, had learnt and were learning more and more that the middle class can never obtain full social and political power over the nation except by the help of the working class. Thus a gradual change came over the relations between both classes. The Factory Acts,[161] once the bugbear of all manufacturers, were not only willingly submitted to, but their expansion into acts regulating almost all trades, was tolerated. Trades' Unions, lately considered inventions of the devil himself, were now petted and patronised as perfectly legitimate institutions and as useful means of spreading sound economical doctrines amongst the workers. Even strikes, than which nothing had been more nefarious up to 1848, were now gradually found out to be occasionally very useful, especially when provoked by the masters themselves, at their own time. Of the legal enactments, placing the workman at a lower level or at a disadvantage with regard to the master, at least the most revolting were repealed. And, practically, that horrid "People's Charter" actually became the political programme of the very manufacturers who had opposed it to the last. "The Abolition of the Property Qualification"[b] and "Vote by Ballot" are now the law of the land. The Reform Acts of 1867 and 1884[162] make a near approach to "universal suffrage," at least such as it now exists in Germany; the Redistribution Bill now before Parliament creates "equal electoral districts"—on the whole not more unequal than those of France or Germany; "payment of members" and shorter, if not actually "annual parliaments" are visibly looming in the distance—and yet there are people who say that Chartism is dead.

The Revolution of 1848, not less than many of its predecessors, has had strange bed-fellows and successors.[c] The very people who put it down, have become, as Karl Marx used to say, its testamentary executors. Louis Napoleon had to create an independent and united Italy, Bismarck had to revolutionise Germany and to restore[d] Hungarian independence and the English manufacturers had[e] to enact the People's Charter.

---

^a The German translation has here "strong Chartist opposition".— *Ed.*

^b Here and below the words in quotes relate the contents of the *People's Charter.—Ed.*

^c The German translation has "a strange fate" instead of "strange bed fellows and successors".— *Ed.*

^d In the German translation here follow the words "a certain".— *Ed.*

^e The German translation has "had nothing better to do than".— *Ed.*

For England, the effects of this domination of the manufacturing capitalists were at first startling. Trade revived and extended to a degree unheard of even in this cradle of modern industry; the previous astounding creations of steam and machinery dwindled into nothing compared with the immense mass of productions of the twenty years from 1850 to 1870, with the overwhelming figures of exports and imports, of wealth accumulated in the hands of capitalists and of human working power concentrated in the large towns. The progress was indeed interrupted, as before, by a crisis every ten years, in 1857 as well as in 1866; but these revulsions were now considered as natural, inevitable events, which must be fatalistically submitted to, and which always set themselves right in the end.

And the condition of the working class during this period? There was temporary improvement even for the great mass. But this improvement always was reduced to the old level by the influx of the great body of the unemployed reserve, by the constant superseding of hands by new machinery, by the immigration of the agricultural population,[a] now, too, more and more superseded by machines.

A permanent improvement can be recognised for two "protected" sections only of the working class. Firstly, the factory hands. The fixing by Act of Parliament of their working day within relatively rational limits,[b] has restored[c] their physical constitution and endowed them with a moral superiority, enhanced by their local concentration. They are undoubtedly better off than before 1848. The best proof is that out of ten strikes they make, nine are provoked by the manufacturers in their own interests, as the only means of securing a reduced production. You can never get the masters to agree to work "short time," let manufactured goods be ever so unsaleable; but get the workpeople to strike, and the masters shut their factories to a man.

Secondly, the great Trades' Unions. They are the organisations of those trades in which the labor of *grown-up men* predominates, or is alone applicable. Here the competition neither of women and children nor of machinery has so far weakened their organised strength. The engineers, the carpenters and joiners, the bricklayers, are each of them a power, to that extent that, as in the case of the bricklayers and bricklayers' labourers, they can even

---

[a] The German translation has "workers" instead of "population".— *Ed.*

[b] The German translation has "a normal working day in their favour" instead of "their working day within relatively rational limits".— *Ed.*

[c] The German translation has "restored to a certain extent".— *Ed.*

successfully resist the introduction of machinery. That their condition has remarkably improved since 1848 there can be no doubt and the best proof of this is in the fact that for more than fifteen years not only have their employers been with them, but they with their employers, upon exceedingly good terms. They form an aristocracy among the working class; they have succeeded in enforcing for themselves a relatively comfortable position, and they accept it as final. They are the model working men of Messrs. Leone Levi and Giffen,[a] and they are very nice people indeed nowadays to deal with, for any sensible capitalist in particular and for the whole capitalist class in general.

But as to the great mass of the working people, the state of misery and insecurity in which they live now is as low as ever, if not lower. The East-end of London is an ever-spreading pool of stagnant misery and desolation, of starvation when out of work, and degradation, physical and moral, when in work. And so in all other large towns—abstraction made of the privileged minority of the workers; and so in the smaller towns and in the agricultural districts. The law which reduces the *value* of labor-power to the value of the necessary means of subsistence, and the other law which reduces its *average price* as a rule to the minimum of those means of subsistence: these laws act upon them with the irresistible force of an automatic engine, which crushes them between its wheels.

This, then, was the position created by the Free Trade policy of 1847, and by twenty years of the rule of the manufacturing capitalists. But then a change came. The crash of 1866 was, indeed, followed by a slight and short revival about 1873; but that did not last. We did not, indeed, pass through the full crisis at the time it was due, in 1877 or 1878; but we have had, ever since 1876, a chronic state of stagnation in all dominant branches of industry. Neither will the full crash come; nor will the period of longed-for prosperity to which we used to be entitled before and after it. A dull depression, a chronic glut of all markets for all trades, that is what we have been living in for nearly ten years. How is this?

The Free Trade theory was based upon one assumption: that England was to be the one great manufacturing centre of an agricultural world. And the actual fact is that this assumption has turned out to be a pure delusion. The conditions of modern

---

[a] The German translation adds here: "(as well as venerable Lujo Brentano)".— *Ed.*

industry, steam-power and machinery, can be established where-ever there is fuel, especially coals. And other countries beside England: France, Belgium, Germany, America, even Russia, have coals. And the people over there did not see the advantage of being turned into Irish pauper farmers merely for the greater wealth and glory of English capitalists. They set resolutely about manufacturing, not only for themselves but for the rest of the world; and the consequence is, that the manufacturing monopoly enjoyed by England for nearly a century is irretrievably broken up.

But the manufacturing monopoly of England is the pivot of the present social system of England. Even while that monopoly lasted the markets could not keep pace with the increasing productivity of English manufacturers; the decennial crises were the conse-quence. And new markets are getting scarcer every day, so much so that even the negroes of the Congo are now to be forced into the civilisation attendant upon Manchester calicoes, Staffordshire pottery, and Birmingham hardware. How will it be when Continental, and especially American goods, flow in in ever increasing quantities—when the predominating share, still held by British manufactures, will become reduced from year to year? Answer, Free Trade, thou universal panacea?

I am not the first to point this out. Already, in 1883, at the Southport meeting of the British Association,[163] Mr. Inglis Palgrave, the President of the Economical section, stated plainly that

"the days of great trade profits in England were over, and there was a pause in the progress of several great branches of industrial labour. *The country might almost be said to be entering the non-progressive state.*" [a]

But what is to be the consequence? Capitalist production *cannot* stop. It must go on increasing and expanding, or it must die. Even now, the mere reduction of England's lion's share in the supply of the world's markets means stagnation, distress, excess of capital here, excess of unemployed work-people there. What will it be when the increase of yearly production is brought to a complete stop?

Here is the vulnerable place, the heel of Achilles, for capitalist production. Its very basis is the necessity of constant expansion, and this constant expansion now becomes impossible. It ends in a

---

[a] "Address by R. H. Inglis Palgrave, F.R.S., F.S.S., President of the Section" in *Report of the Fifty-Third Meeting of the British Association for the Advancement of Science; held at Southport in September 1883*, pp. 608-09.— *Ed.*

deadlock. Every year England is brought nearer face to face with the question: either the country must go to pieces, or capitalist production must. Which is it to be?

And the working class? If even under the unparalleled commercial and industrial expansion, from 1848 to 1868, they have had to undergo such misery; if even then the great bulk of them experienced at best a temporary improvement of their condition, while only a small, privileged, "protected" minority was permanently benefited, what will it be when this dazzling period is brought finally to a close; when the present dreary stagnation shall not only become intensified, but this its intensified condition shall become the permanent and normal state of English trade?

The truth is this: during the period of England's industrial monopoly the English working class have to a certain extent shared in the benefits of the monopoly. These benefits were very unequally parcelled out amongst them; the privileged minority pocketed most, but even the great mass had at least a temporary share now and then. And that is the reason why since the dying-out of Owenism there has been no Socialism in England. With the breakdown of that monopoly the English working class will lose that privileged position; it will find itself generally—the privileged and leading minority not excepted—on a level with its fellow-workers abroad. And that is the reason why there will be Socialism again in England.

Frederick Engels

Written in mid-February 1885

First published in *The Commonweal,* No. 2, March 1885

Reproduced from the magazine collated with the German translation

PREFACE TO THE THIRD GERMAN EDITION
OF *THE EIGHTEENTH BRUMAIRE*
OF LOUIS BONAPARTE BY MARX

The fact that a new edition of the *Eighteenth Brumaire*[a] has become necessary, thirty-three years after its first appearance, proves that even today this little book has lost none of its value.

It was indeed a work of genius. Immediately after the event that struck the whole political world like a thunderbolt from the blue, that was condemned by some with loud cries of moral indignation and accepted by others as a salvation from the revolution and a punishment for its errors, but was only wondered at by all and understood by none—immediately after this event Marx appeared with a concise, epigrammatic exposition that laid bare the whole course of French history since those February days in its inner connection, reduced the miracle of December 2[164] to a natural, necessary result of this connection and, in so doing, did not even need to treat the hero of the *coup d'état* otherwise than with the contempt he so well deserved. And the picture was drawn with such a masterly hand that every fresh disclosure since made has only provided fresh proof of how faithfully it reflects reality. This eminent understanding of the living history of the day, this clear-sighted appreciation of events at the moment they occur, is indeed without parallel.

But this also called for Marx's thorough knowledge of French history. France is the land where, more than anywhere else, historical class struggles were each time fought out to a decision and where, consequently, the changing political forms within which they move and in which their results are condensed have

---

[a] See present edition, Vol. 11, pp. 99-197.— *Ed.*

been stamped in the sharpest outlines. The focus of feudalism in the Middle Ages, the model country of unified estate monarchy since the Renaissance, France demolished feudalism in the Great Revolution and established the unalloyed rule of the bourgeoisie in a classical purity unequalled by any other European land. And the struggle of the rising proletariat against the ruling bourgeoisie manifested itself here in an acute form unknown elsewhere. This was the reason why Marx not only studied the past history of France with particular predilection, but also followed her current history in every detail, collected material for future use and was consequently never surprised by events.

But there was yet another circumstance. It was the very same Marx who had first discovered the great law of motion of history, the law according to which all historical struggles, whether they proceed in the political, religious, philosophical or some other ideological domain, are in fact only the more or less clear expression of struggles between social classes, and that the existence and thereby the collisions, too, of these classes are in turn conditioned by the degree of development of their economic position, by the nature and mode of their production and of their exchange as determined by it. This law, which has the same significance for history as the law of the transformation of energy has for natural science—this law gave him here, too, the key to understanding the history of the Second French Republic. He put his law to the test on these historical events, and even after thirty-three years we must still say that it has stood the test brilliantly.

F. E.

Written in the first half of 1885

First published in Karl Marx, *Der Achtzehnte Brumaire des Louis Bonaparte,* Hamburg, 1885

Printed according to the text of the book

PREFACE [TO THE PAMPHLET
KARL MARX BEFORE THE COLOGNE JURY] [165]

For a better understanding of the proceedings presented here it will suffice to summarise the chief events leading up to them.

The cowardice of the German bourgeoisie had given the feudal, bureaucratic, absolutist reaction a breathing space in which to recover from the shattering blows of March 1848 to such an extent that a second decisive struggle became imminent as early as the end of October. The fall of Vienna,[a] after a long, heroic resistance, emboldened the Prussian camarilla to attempt a coup d'état. The tame Berlin "National Assembly" was still too wild for it. It would have to be dissolved and an end put to the revolution.

On November 8, 1848 the Brandenburg-Manteuffel Ministry was formed. On the 9th it transferred the seat of the Assembly from Berlin to Brandenburg so that it might "freely" deliberate under the protection of bayonets, undisturbed by the revolutionary influences of Berlin. The Assembly refused to leave: the civic militia refused to take action against the Assembly. The Ministry dissolved the civic militia, disarmed it without encountering any resistance and declared Berlin in a state of siege. The Assembly replied on November 13, indicting the Ministry for high treason. The Ministry chased the Assembly from one meeting place in Berlin to the next. On the 15th the Assembly resolved that the Brandenburg Ministry had no right to dispose of government money and to levy taxes as long as it, the Assembly, could not freely continue meeting in Berlin.

This resolution to block taxation could only become effective if the people resisted the collecting of taxes by force of arms. And at that time there was no shortage of arms in the hands of the civic

---

a On October 31, 1848.— *Ed.*

militia. Nevertheless, hardly anyone ventured beyond passive resistance. Only in few places were any preparations made to meet force with force. The boldest call to do just that came from the Committee of the democratic associations of the Rhine Province which had its seat in Cologne and consisted of *Marx, Schapper* and *Schneider.*

The Committee did not delude itself by imagining that the victorious coup d'état in Berlin could be successfully reversed by any campaign on the Rhine. The Rhine Province had five fortresses; about a third of the entire Prussian army including a large number of regiments from the Eastern provinces was stationed in it, in Westphalia, Mainz, Frankfurt and Luxemburg alone. In Cologne and other cities the civic militia had already been disbanded and disarmed. But the intention was not to achieve an immediate victory in Cologne where a state of siege had only been lifted a few weeks before. The point was to set the other provinces an example and thus to rescue the revolutionary honour of the Rhine Province. And that had been done.

The Prussian bourgeoisie had surrendered one stronghold after another to the government for fear of what were at that time the still half-dreaming convulsions of the proletariat. It already long regretted its earlier hankerings for power and ever since March it had been so crazed with fear that it did not know which way to turn, confronted as it was by the double threat of the forces of the old society grouped around the absolute power, on the one side, and the fledgling proletariat with its dawning consciousness of its class position, on the other. The Prussian bourgeoisie did what it always did in moments of decision—it backed down. And the workers were not so stupid as to fight for the bourgeoisie without the aid of the bourgeoisie. Moreover, in their eyes—particularly on the Rhine—Prussian issues were purely local issues; if they were ever to go into the firing line on behalf of the bourgeoisie, then it would have to be in and for Germany as a whole. It was a significant portent that even at that time, the idea of "Prussian leadership"[166] had absolutely no attraction for the workers.

In short, the government was victorious. One month later, on December 5, it was in a position to dissolve once and for all the Berlin Assembly, which had managed to prolong a rather shabby existence until then and to impose a new constitution, which however only became effective once it had been reduced to a mere constitutional farce.

On November 20, the day after the Committee launched its appeal, the three signatories were summoned to appear before the

examining magistrate and proceedings for rebellion were instituted against them. At the time there was no mention of arrests,
even in Cologne. On February 7, the *Neue Rheinische Zeitung* had
to submit to its first press trial; Marx, myself and Korff, the
responsible publisher, appeared before a jury and were acquitted.[167] On the following day the case against the Committee was
heard. The people had already reached its own verdict, having
two weeks previously elected one of the defendants, Schneider,
deputy for Cologne.

Marx's speech for the defence was obviously the highpoint of
the proceedings. It is especially interesting in two respects:

Firstly, because it needed a communist to make clear to the
bourgeois jury that the actions he had taken and for the sake of
which he was now standing accused before them, were of a kind
which in reality it was the duty and obligation of *their* class, of the
bourgeoisie, not simply to perform, but to carry through to their
uttermost implications. This fact alone suffices to throw light on
the attitude of the German, and above all the Prussian,
bourgeoisie during the revolutionary period. At stake was the
question: who was to rule—the forces of society and the state that
rallied around the absolute monarchy: the big feudal landowners,
the army, the bureaucracy, the clergy, or the bourgeoisie? The
only interest of the still emerging proletariat in these struggles lay
in the extent to which the victory of the bourgeoisie would provide
it with enough light and air to further its own development, with
elbow-room on the battlefield where one day it will triumph over
all other classes. But the bourgeoisie, and the petty bourgeoisie
along with it, refused to make a move when the hostile
government attacked the seat of their power, dispersed their
parliament, disarmed their civic militia and even placed them
under a state of siege. It was then that the communists stepped
into the breach and called on them to do their damned duty. Both
of them, the bourgeoisie and the proletariat, constituted the new
society and stood together in one camp against the old feudal
society. Of course, the appeal went unheeded and by an irony of
history this self-same bourgeoisie was now to sit in judgment over
the revolutionary proletarian Communists, on the one hand, and
over the counter-revolutionary government, on the other.

Secondly, however—and this gives the speech its specific
significance, even for our time—in the face of the government's
hypocritical legality it preserves a revolutionary standpoint from
which many could take an example even today.—Did we call on
the people to take up arms against the government? Indeed we

did, and it was our duty to do so. Did we break the law and depart from the foundations of law? Very well, but the laws we broke had already been torn up by the government and trampled upon before the eyes of the people. As for legal foundations, they no longer exist. As vanquished enemies we can be eliminated, but no one has the right to condemn us.

The official parties, from the *Kreuz-Zeitung*[168] to the *Frankfurter*, reproach the Social Democratic Workers' Party with being a revolutionary party, with refusing to recognise the legal foundations established in 1866 and 1871,[169] and thereby—at least this is the refrain of everyone right down to the National Liberals[170]— with putting itself beyond the limits of common law. I shall ignore the monstrous insinuation here that anyone can place himself beyond the bounds of common law simply by expressing an opinion. That is the police state pure and simple, which one should better practise on the quiet, while preaching the constitutional state out loud. But what are then the legal foundations of 1866, if not revolutionary? The Federal Constitution is violated and war declared on the confederates.[171] Not at all, says Bismarck, it was the others who violated the treaty. The answer to which is that a revolutionary party would have to be simple-minded in the extreme if it proved unable to find at least as convincing grounds for any uprising as those put forward by Bismarck for his in 1866.—So a civil war is provoked for that was what the war of 1866 amounted to. But every civil war is a revolutionary war. The war is conducted by revolutionary means. Alliances are concluded with foreign powers against Germans. Italian troops and ships are brought into the battle, Bonaparte is enticed with prospects of acquiring German territory on the Rhine. A Hungarian legion is formed to fight against its hereditary sovereign for revolutionary goals. Reliance is placed on Klapka in Hungary, and Garibaldi in Italy. Victory is won and—three crowns existing by divine right are swallowed up: Hanover, the Electorate of Hesse and Nassau— each of which was just as legitimate, just as "hereditary" and existed just as much "by divine right" as did the crown of Prussia.[172] Finally, a constitution is imposed on the remaining confederates, which in Saxony, for example, was accepted just as freely as Prussia had accepted the Peace of Tilsit at one time.[173]

Do I complain about all this? Not at all. There is no point in complaining about historical events. On the contrary, the problem is to comprehend their causes and hence also their effects, *which are by no means exhausted.* But we do have the right to demand that people who have done all these things should refrain from accusing others of being revolutionaries. The German Empire was created by revolution—admittedly, a revolution of a particular kind, but no less a revolution for all that. What is sauce for the goose is sauce for the gander. A revolution is a revolution, regardless of whether it was made by the Prussian crown or a tinker. If the government of the day makes use of the existing laws to rid itself of its opponents, then it acts like every government. But if it imagines that it can strike them an even more violent blow by thundering the expletive "Revolutionary!" at them—then at best only the philistines will take fright. "Revolutionary yourself!" will be the cry that echoes back from every corner of Europe.

But the preposterous demand that anyone should cast aside his revolutionary nature, a thing which arises inevitably from historical circumstances, becomes utterly comic when it is applied to a party which is first placed outside the confines of common law, i.e. beyond the law itself, and which is then confronted with the demand that it should recognise the foundations of that very law which has been specifically *abolished for it*.[174]

The fact that people have to waste time even discussing such a matter provides yet further evidence of the politically backward state of Germany. In the rest of the world everyone knows that all existing political systems are the product of nothing but revolutions. France, Spain, Switzerland and Italy—there are as many governments existing by right of revolution as there are countries. In England even the Whig Macaulay acknowledges that the present legal order is based on one revolution after another (REVOLUTIONS HEAPED UPON REVOLUTIONS). For the last hundred years America has celebrated its revolution on every 4th of July.[175] In the majority of these countries there are parties which will only continue to abide by the existing legal order as long as the latter can force them to do so. But if anyone in France, for example, were to accuse the Royalists or Bonapartists of being revolutionary, he would simply be laughed to scorn.

Only in Germany, where politically nothing is ever dealt with thoroughly (for otherwise it would not be torn into two parts, Austria and Germany so-called) and where for that very reason the memories of past, but only half digested ages continue to vegetate eternally in people's minds (which is why the Germans call themselves a nation of thinkers)—only in Germany can anyone possibly require a party to be bound by the existing so-called legal order not only in fact but also morally. A party must promise in advance that, come what may, it will not overthrow the legal order it is fighting against, even if it is able to do so. In other words, it must commit itself to upholding the existing political order for all eternity. This and this alone is what is meant when people demand that German Social Democracy should cease to be "revolutionary".

But the German philistine—and his opinion is still German public opinion—is a special sort of person. He has never *made* a revolution. The revolution of 1848 was made for him by the workers—to his horror. But all the more has he had to *suffer* revolutions. For the people who have made revolutions in the last three hundred years in Germany—and they showed it—were the *princes*. Their very rank, and ultimately their sovereignty, was the fruit of rebellions against the Emperor. Prussia set an example to them all. Prussia was only able to become a kingdom after the "Great Elector"[a] had conducted a successful uprising against his feudal overlord, the crown of Poland, thus securing the independence of the Duchy of Prussia from Poland.[176] Ever since Frederick II, Prussia's rebellion against the German Empire had been made into a system; Frederick "spat" upon the Imperial constitution in quite a different manner than our worthy *Bracke* upon the Anti-Socialist Law. Then came the French Revolution[b] and both the princes and the philistines suffered it with tears and sighs. In 1803, by decision of the Imperial Deputation, the German Empire was distributed among the German princes by the French and the Russians in a highly revolutionary manner, because the princes could not agree on how to divide it up themselves.[177] Then came Napoleon and permitted his very special protégés, the rulers of Baden, Bavaria and Württemberg,[c] to take possession of all counties, baronies and cities which had been subject only to the Emperor, and which lay in or between their territories. Immediately after this the same three traitors carried out the last successful rebellion against their Emperor,[d] and, with Napoleon's assistance, they established their own sovereignty and thereby finally tore apart the old German Empire.[178] After that, Napoleon, the de facto German Emperor, redistributed Germany about every three years among his loyal retainers, the German princes and others. Finally, there came the glorious liberation from foreign domination and as a reward Germany was treated as

---

[a] Frederick William, Elector of Brandenburg.— *Ed.*
[b] Of 1789.— *Ed.*
[c] Charles Frederick, Maximilian Joseph, Frederick.— *Ed.*
[d] Franz I.— *Ed.*

a universal source of compensation for princes down on their luck and was divided up and sold off by the Congress of Vienna, i.e. by Russia, France and England. And the German philistines, scattered like so many sheep in around 2,000 separate scraps of territory, were shared out among the various 36 sovereigns, for the majority of whom they would even today "most humbly lay down their lives", as if for their hereditary sovereigns. And none of this is supposed to have been revolutionary—how right Schnapphahnski-Lichnowski was when he exclaimed in the Frankfurt Parliament, "With regard to historical right there does not exist no date!" [179] The fact is that it never had one!

Thus what the German philistine shamefacedly demands from the German Social-Democratic Workers' Party can only have one meaning: that this party should become as philistine as he. It should on no account take part in revolutions, but should *suffer* them instead. And if the government which has come to power by counter-revolution and revolution puts the same preposterous demand, this only means that revolution is good as long as it is made by Bismarck for Bismarck & Co., but reprehensible when it is made against Bismarck & Co.

London, July 1, 1885

Frederick Engels

First published in *Karl Marx vor den Kölner Geschwornen*, Hottingen-Zurich, 1885

Printed according to the pamphlet

[TO THE EDITORS OF THE *SEVERNY VESTNIK*] [180]

Jersey, August 25, 1885

Sir,

Among the papers of my late friend Karl Marx I have found a reply to an article by Mr. Mikhailovsky: "Karl Marx Before the Tribunal of Mr. Zhukovsky". Since this reply, which was not published at the time for reasons unknown to me, may still be of interest to the Russian public, I am putting it at your disposal.

Yours, etc.

First published in: Marx and Engels, *Works,* First Russian Edition, Vol. XXIX, Moscow, 1946

Printed according to the original

Translated from the French

Published in English for the first time

ON THE HISTORY OF THE COMMUNIST LEAGUE [181]

With the sentence of the Cologne Communists in 1852, the curtain falls on the first period of the independent German workers' movement. Today this period is almost forgotten. Yet it lasted from 1836 to 1852 and, with the spread of German workers abroad, the movement developed in almost all civilised countries. Nor is that all. The present-day international workers' movement is in substance a direct continuation of the German movement of that time, which was the *first international workers' movement* ever, and which brought forth many of those who took on the leading role in the International Working Men's Association. And the theoretical principles that the Communist League had inscribed on its banner in the *Communist Manifesto* of 1847 constitute today the strongest international bond of the entire proletarian movement in both Europe and America.

Up to now there has been only one main source for a coherent history of that movement. This is the so-called Black Book, *Die Communisten-Verschwörungen des neunzehnten Jahrhunderts,* by Wermuth and Stieber, Berlin, two parts, 1853 and 1854.[182] This sorry effort fabricated by two of the most contemptible police scoundrels of our century, which bristles with deliberate falsifications, still today serves as the final source for all non-communist writings about that period.[183]

What I am able to give here is only a sketch, and even this only in so far as the League itself is concerned; only what is absolutely necessary to understand the *Revelations.* I hope that some day I shall have the opportunity to work on the rich material collected by Marx and myself on the history of that glorious period of the youth of the international workers' movement.

* * *

In 1836 the most extreme, chiefly proletarian elements of the secret democratic-republican Outlaws' League, which had been founded by German refugees in Paris in 1834, split off and formed the new secret *League of the Just*. The parent League, in which only the most sleepy-headed elements *à la* Jakob Venedey remained soon fell asleep altogether: when in 1840 the police scented out a few sections in Germany, it was hardly a shadow of its former self. The new League, on the contrary, developed comparatively rapidly. Originally it was a German offshoot of the French worker-communism reminiscent of Babouvism [184] that was taking shape in Paris at about the same time; community of goods was demanded as the necessary consequence of "equality". The aims were those of the Parisian secret societies of the time: half propaganda association, half conspiracy, Paris, however, always being regarded as the focus of revolutionary action, although preparation for occasional *putsches* in Germany was by no means excluded. But as Paris remained the decisive battleground, the League was at that time actually not much more than the German branch of the French secret societies, notably the *Société des saisons* led by Blanqui and Barbès, with which close links were maintained. The French went into action on May 12, 1839; the sections of the League marched with them and were thus embroiled in the common defeat. [185]

Of the Germans, *Karl Schapper* and *Heinrich Bauer* were arrested; Louis Philippe's government contented itself with deporting them after a fairly long term of imprisonment. [186] Both went to London. Schapper came from Weilburg in Nassau and while a student of forestry at Giessen in 1832 had joined in the conspiracy organised by Georg Büchner; he had taken part in the storming of the Frankfurt constable station on April 3, 1833, [187] had escaped abroad and in February 1834 joined Mazzini's march on Savoy. [188] Of gigantic stature, resolute and energetic, always ready to risk civil existence and life, he was a model of the professional revolutionary with the role he played in the thirties. In spite of a certain sluggishness of thought, he was by no means incapable of superior theoretical understanding, as is proved by his development from "demagogue" [189] to Communist, and he then held all the more rigidly to what he had once come to recognise. Precisely on that account his revolutionary passion sometimes got the better of his understanding, but he always realised his mistake in hindsight and openly acknowledged it. He was a true man and what he did for the founding of the German workers' movement will not be forgotten.

Heinrich Bauer, from Franconia, was a shoemaker; a lively, alert, witty little fellow, in whose little body, however, also lay hidden much shrewdness and determination.

Having arrived in London, where Schapper, who had been a compositor in Paris, now tried to earn his living as a language teacher, the two of them again joined together the broken threads of alliance and made London the centre of the League. They were joined here, if not already earlier in Paris, by *Joseph Moll*, a watchmaker from Cologne, a medium-sized Hercules—how often did Schapper and he victoriously defend the entrance to a hall against hundreds of onrushing opponents—a man who was at least the equal of his two comrades in energy and determination, and intellectually superior to both of them. Not only was he a born diplomat, as the success of his numerous trips on various missions proved; he was also more capable of theoretical insight. I came to know all three of them in London in 1843. They were the first revolutionary proletarians whom I had seen, and however far apart our views were at that time in details—for I still bore, as against their narrow-minded egalitarian communism,* a goodly dose of just as narrow-minded philosophical arrogance—I shall never forget the deep impression that these three real men made upon me, who was still to become a man at that time.

In London, as to a lesser degree in Switzerland, they had the benefit of freedom of association and assembly. The legally functioning German Workers' Educational Society, which still exists, was founded as early as February 7, 1840.[190] The Society served the League as a recruiting ground for new members, and since, as always, the Communists were the most active and intelligent members of the Society, it was a matter of course that its leadership lay entirely in the hands of the League. The League soon had several communities, or, as they were then still called, "lodges", in London. The same obvious tactics were followed in Switzerland and elsewhere. Where workers' associations could be founded, they were utilised in like manner. Where this was forbidden by law, one joined choral societies, gymnastics societies and the like. Contacts were to a large extent maintained by members who were continually travelling back and forth; they also, when required, served as emissaries. In both respects the

---

* By egalitarian communism I understand, as stated, only that communism which bases itself exclusively or predominantly on the demand for equality.

League obtained lively support through the wisdom of the governments which, by resorting to deportation, converted any objectionable worker—and in nine cases out of ten he was a member of the League—into an emissary.

The spread of the restored League was considerable. Notably in Switzerland, *Weitling, August Becker* (a highly gifted man who, however, like so many Germans, came to grief through his innate instability of character) and others created a strong organisation more or less pledged to Weitling's communist system. This is not the place to criticise the communism of Weitling. But as regards its significance as the first independent theoretical stirring of the German proletariat, I still today subscribe to Marx's words in the Paris *Vorwärts!* of 1844: "Where among the" (German) "bourgeoisie—including its philosophers and learned writers—is to be found a book *about the emancipation of the bourgeoisie—* political emancipation—similar to Weitling's work: *Garantien der Harmonie und Freiheit?* It is enough to compare the petty, faint-hearted mediocrity of German political literature with this vehement and brilliant literary début of the German workers, it is enough to compare these *gigantic infant shoes of the proletariat* with the dwarfish, worn-out political shoes of the bourgeoisie, and one is bound to prophesy that the *German Cinderella* will one day have the figure of an athlete." [a] This athlete's figure confronts us today, although still far from being fully grown.

Numerous sections existed in Germany too; by the nature of things they were of a transient character, but those coming into existence more than made up for those folding up. Only after seven years, in late 1846, did the police discover traces of the League in Berlin (Mentel) and Magdeburg (Beck), without being in a position to follow them further.

In Paris, Weitling, still there in 1840, likewise gathered the scattered elements together again before he left for Switzerland.[191]

The tailors formed the central force of the League. German tailors were everywhere: in Switzerland, in London, in Paris. In the last-named city, German was so much the prevailing tongue in this trade that I was acquainted there in 1846 with a Norwegian tailor who had travelled directly by sea from Drontheim to France and in the space of eighteen months had learned hardly a word of French but had acquired an excellent knowledge of German. Two

---

[a] K. Marx, "Critical Marginal Notes on the Article 'The King of Prussia and Social Reform. By a Prussian'" (see present edition, Vol. 3, pp. 189-206).— *Ed.*

of the Paris communities in 1847 consisted predominantly of tailors, one of cabinet makers.

After the centre of gravity had shifted from Paris to London, a new feature came to the fore: from being German, the League gradually became *international*. In the Workers' Society there were, besides Germans and Swiss, also members of all those nationalities for whom German served as the chief means of communication with foreigners, notably, therefore, Scandinavians, Dutch, Hungarians, Czechs, Southern Slavs, also Russians and Alsatians. In 1847 the regular attendants even included an English grenadier of the Guards in uniform. The Society soon called itself the *Communist* Workers' Educational Society, and the membership cards bore the inscription "All Men are Brothers", in at least twenty languages, though not without mistakes here and there. Like the open Society, so also the secret League soon took on a more international character; at first in a restricted sense, practically through the varied nationalities of its members, theoretically through the realisation that any revolution, to be victorious, must be a European one. It did not go any further as yet; but the foundations were there.

Close contact was maintained with the French revolutionaries through the London refugees, comrades-in-arms of May 12, 1839. Similarly with the more radical Poles. The official Polish *émigrés,* as also Mazzini, were, of course, opponents rather than allies. The English Chartists, on account of the specific English character of their movement, were disregarded as not revolutionary. The London leaders of the League came into contact with them only later, through me.

In other ways, too, the character of the League had altered with events. Although the League still looked upon Paris—and at that time quite rightly—as the mother city of the revolution, it had nevertheless cast off the dependence of the Paris conspirators. The spread of the League raised its self-confidence. There was a feeling that more and more roots were being struck in the German working class and that these German workers were historically destined to be the standard-bearers of the workers of the North and East of Europe. In Weitling there was to be found a communist theoretician who could be boldly placed at the side of his contemporary French rivals. Finally, the experience of May 12 had taught them that for the time being there was nothing more to be gained by attempted *putsches.* And if every event was still explained as a sign of the approaching storm, if the old, semi-conspiratorial rules were still preserved intact, that was mainly the fault of the old revolutionary defiance, which was already beginning to collide with the sounder views that were gaining headway.

However, the social doctrine of the League, no matter how poorly defined it was, contained a very great defect, but one that had its roots in the conditions themselves. The members, insofar as they were workers at all, were almost exclusively real artisans. Even in the big metropolises, the man who exploited them was usually only a small master. The exploitation of tailoring on a large scale, of what is now called the manufacture of off-the-peg clothing, by the conversion of handicraft tailoring into a domestic industry working for a big capitalist, was at that time only just making its appearance even in London. On the one hand, the exploiter of these artisans was a small master; on the other hand, they all hoped ultimately to become small masters themselves. And besides, a host of inherited guild notions still clung to the German artisan at that time. The greatest honour is due to them, in that they, who were themselves not yet full proletarians but only an appendage of the petty bourgeoisie, an appendage which was in the transition to becoming the modern proletariat and which did not yet stand in direct conflict with the bourgeoisie, that is, with big capital—in that these artisans were capable of instinctively anticipating their future development and of constituting them-selves, even if not yet with full consciousness, as the party of the proletariat. But it was also inevitable that their old handicraft prejudices were a stumbling block to them at every moment, whenever it was a question of criticising existing society in detail, that is, of investigating economic facts. And I do not believe there was a single man in the whole League at that time who had ever read a book on political economy. But that mattered little; for the time being "equality", "brotherhood" and "justice" helped them to surmount every theoretical obstacle.

Meanwhile a second, essentially different communism had developed alongside that of the League and of Weitling. In Manchester it had been tangibly brought home to me that the economic facts which have so far played no role or only a contemptible one in historiography are, at least in the modern world, a decisive historical force; that they form the basis for the emergence of the present-day class antagonisms; that these class antagonisms, in the countries where they have become fully developed by dint of large-scale industry, hence especially in England, are in their turn the basis for the formation of political parties, party struggles, and thus of all political history. Marx had not only arrived at the same view, but had already, in the *Deutsch-Französische Jahrbücher* (1844), generalised it to the effect that it is not the state which conditions and regulates civil society at all, but civil society which conditions and regulates the state, and, consequently, that policy and its history are to be explained from the economic relations and their development, and not the other way round. When I visited Marx in Paris in the summer of 1844,[a] our complete agreement in all theoretical fields became evident and our joint work dates from that time. When, in the spring of 1845, we met again in Brussels, Marx had already fully developed his materialist theory of history in its main features from the above-mentioned foundations, and we now applied ourselves to the detailed elaboration of the newly won outlook in the most varied directions.

This discovery, which revolutionised the science of history and, as we have seen, is essentially the work of Marx—a discovery in which I can claim for myself only a very small share—was, however, of immediate importance for the workers' movement of the time. Communism among the French and Germans, Chartism among the English, now no longer appeared as something accidental which could just as well not have occurred. These movements now presented themselves as a movement of the modern oppressed class, the proletariat, as more or less developed forms of its historically necessary struggle against the ruling class, the bourgeoisie; as forms of class struggle, but distinguished from all earlier class struggles by this one thing: that the present-day oppressed class, the proletariat, cannot achieve its emancipation without at the same time emancipating society as a whole from division into classes and, therefore, from class struggles. And communism now no longer meant the concoction, by means of the imagination, of a social ideal as perfect as possible, but insight into the nature, the conditions and the consequent general aims of the struggle waged by the proletariat.

Now, we were by no means of the opinion that the new scientific results should be confided in large tomes exclusively to the "learned" world. Quite the contrary. We were both of us already deeply involved in the political movement and possessed a certain following in the educated world, especially of Western Germany, and abundant contact with the organised proletariat. It was our duty to provide a scientific substantiation for our view, but it was equally important for us to win over the European, and in the first

---

[a] Late August-early September.— *Ed.*

place the German, proletariat to our conviction. As soon as we had become clear in our own minds, we set to work. We founded a German Workers' Society in Brussels [192] and took over the *Deutsche-Brüsseler-Zeitung,* which served us as an organ up to the February Revolution. We kept in touch with the revolutionary section of the English Chartists through Julian Harney, the editor of the movement's central organ, *The Northern Star,* to which I was a contributor. We entered likewise into a sort of cartel with the Brussels democrats (Marx was vice-president of the Democratic Association [193]) and with the French Social-Democrats of the *Réforme,* which I supplied with news of the English and German movements. In short, our connections with the radical and proletarian organisations and press organs were quite what one could wish.

Our relations with the League of the Just were as follows: The existence of the League was, of course, known to us; in 1843 Schapper had suggested that I join it, which I at that time naturally refused to do. However, we not only kept up our continuous correspondence with the Londoners, but remained on still closer terms with Dr. Ewerbeck, the then leader of the Paris communities. Without occupying ourselves with the League's internal affairs, we nevertheless learnt of every important happening. On the other hand, we influenced the theoretical views of the most important members of the League by word of mouth, by letter and through the press. For this purpose we also made use of various lithographed circulars, which we dispatched to our friends and correspondents throughout the world on particular occasions when we were concerned with the internal affairs of the Communist Party that was in the process of formation. In these, the League itself was sometimes involved. Thus, a young Westphalian student, Hermann Kriege, who went to America, posed there as an emissary of the League and associated himself with the crazy Harro Harring for the purpose of using the League to turn South America upside down. He founded a paper[a] in which, in the name of the League, he preached an effusive communism of starry-eyed love, based on "love" and overflowing with love. Against this we let fly with a circular[b] that did not fail to have its effect. Kriege vanished from the League scene.

Later, Weitling came to Brussels. But he was no longer the naïve young journeyman-tailor who, astonished at his own talents, was

---

a *Der Volks-Tribun.—Ed.*
b See K. Marx and F. Engels, "Circular Against Kriege".— *Ed.*

trying to clarify in his own mind just what a communist society would look like. He was now the great man, persecuted by the envious on account of his superiority, who scented rivals, secret enemies and traps everywhere—the prophet, driven from country to country, who carried a prescription for the realisation of heaven on earth ready-made in his pocket, and who imagined that everybody was out to steal it from him. He had already fallen out with the members of the League in London; and even in Brussels, where particularly Marx and his wife treated him with almost superhuman forbearance, he could get along with nobody. So he soon afterwards went to America to try out his role of prophet there.

All these circumstances contributed to the quiet revolution that was taking place in the League, and especially among the leaders in London. The inadequacy of the conception of communism held hitherto, both the simplistic French egalitarian communism and that of Weitling, became more and more clear to them. The tracing of communism back to early Christianity introduced by Weitling—no matter how brilliant certain details to be found in his *Evangelium eines armen Sünders*—had resulted in the movement in Switzerland being delivered to a large extent into the hands, first of fools like Albrecht, and then of exploiting fake prophets like Kuhlmann. The "true socialism" dealt in by a few writers of fiction—a translation of French socialist phraseology into corrupt Hegelian German, and sentimental starry-eyed love (see the section on German or "true", socialism in the *Communist Manifesto*[a])—that Kriege and the study of the said literature introduced in the League was bound to disgust the old revolutionaries of the League, if only because of its slobbering feebleness. In contrast to the untenability of the previous theoretical views, and in contrast to the practical aberrations resulting therefrom, it was realised more and more in London that Marx and I were right in our new theory. This understanding was undoubtedly promoted by the fact that among the London leaders there were now two men who were considerably superior in their capacity for theoretical perception to those previously mentioned: the miniature painter Karl Pfänder from Heilbronn and the tailor Georg Eccarius from Thuringia.*

* Pfänder died about eight years ago in London. He was a man of peculiarly fine intelligence, witty, ironical and dialectical. Eccarius, as we know, was later for many years General Secretary of the International Working Men's Association, in

a See present edition, Vol. 6, pp. 510-13.—*Ed.*

Suffice it to say that in the spring of 1847 Moll visited Marx in Brussels and immediately afterwards myself in Paris, and invited us repeatedly, in the name of his comrades, to join the League. He reported that they were as much convinced of the general correctness of our views as of the need to free the League from the old conspiratorial traditions and forms. Should we join, we would be given an opportunity of expounding our critical communism before a congress of the League in a manifesto, which would then be published as the manifesto of the League; we would likewise be able to contribute our quota towards the replacement of the obsolete League organisation by one in keeping with the new times and aims.

We entertained no doubt that an organisation within the German working class was necessary, if only for propaganda purposes, and that this organisation, in so far as it were not merely local in character, could only be a secret one, even outside Germany. Now, there already existed exactly such an organisation in the shape of the League. What we previously objected to in this League was now relinquished as erroneous by the representatives of the League themselves; we were even invited to cooperate in the work of reorganisation. Could we say no? Certainly not. Therefore, we joined the League; Marx founded a League community in Brussels from among our close friends, while I attended the three Paris communities.

In the summer of 1847, the first League congress took place in London, at which W. Wolff represented the Brussels and I the Paris communities. First of all the congress carried out the reorganisation of the League. Whatever remained of the old mystical names dating back to the conspiratorial period was now also abolished; the League now consisted of communities, circles, leading circles, a Central Authority and a Congress, and henceforth called itself the "Communist League". "The aim of the League is the overthrow of the bourgeoisie, the rule of the proletariat, the abolition of the old bourgeois society which rests on the antagonism of classes, and the foundation of a new society without classes and without private property"—thus ran the first article.[a] The organisation itself was thoroughly democratic, with

the General Council of which the following old League members were to be found, among others: Eccarius, Pfänder, Lessner, Lochner, Marx and myself. Eccarius subsequently devoted himself exclusively to the English trade-union movement.

---

[a] Rules of the Communist League. Art. 1 (see present edition, Vol. 6, p. 633).—*Ed.*

elective and removable authorities. This alone barred all hankering after conspiracy, which requires dictatorship, and the League was converted—for ordinary peacetime at least—into a pure propaganda society. These new Rules were submitted to the communities for discussion—so democratic was the procedure now followed—then once again debated at the Second Congress and finally adopted by the latter on December 8, 1847. They are to be found printed in Wermuth and Stieber, Part I, p. 239, Appendix X.

The Second Congress took place in late November and early December of the same year. Marx too attended this time and expounded the new theory in a lengthy debate—the congress lasted at least ten days. All contradiction and doubt were finally over and done with, the new basic principles were adopted unanimously, and Marx and I were commissioned to draw up the Manifesto. This was done immediately afterwards. A few weeks before the February Revolution it was sent to London to be printed. Since then it has travelled round the world, has been translated into almost all languages and still today serves in numerous countries as a guide for the proletarian movement. In place of the old League motto, "All Men Are Brothers", appeared the new battle cry, "Working Men of All Countries, Unite!" [194] which openly proclaimed the international character of the struggle. Seventeen years later this battle cry resounded throughout the world as the motto of the International Working Men's Association, and today the valiant proletariat of all countries has inscribed it on its banner.

The February Revolution broke out. The London Central Authority functioning hitherto immediately transferred its powers to the Brussels leading circle. But this decision came at a time when an actual state of siege already existed in Brussels, and the Germans in particular could no longer assemble anywhere. We were all of us just on the point of going to Paris, and so the new Central Authority decided likewise to dissolve, to hand over all its powers to Marx and to empower him immediately to constitute a new Central Authority in Paris. Hardly had the five persons who adopted this decision (March 3, 1848) separated, when the police forced their way into Marx's home, arrested him and compelled him to leave for France the following day, which was just where he wanted to go.

In Paris we all soon came together again. It was there that the following document was drawn up and signed by the members of the new Central Authority. It was distributed throughout

Germany and quite a few can still learn something from it even today:

DEMANDS OF THE COMMUNIST PARTY IN GERMANY [195]

1. The whole of Germany shall be declared a single and indivisible republic.

3. Representatives of the people shall receive payment so that workers, too, shall be able to become members of the German parliament.

4. Universal arming of the people.

7. Princely and other feudal estates, together with mines, pits, and so forth, shall become the property of the state. The estates shall be cultivated on a large scale and with the most up-to-date scientific devices in the interests of the whole of society.

8. Mortgages on peasant lands shall be declared the property of the state. Interest on such mortgages shall be paid by the peasants to the state.

9. In localities where the tenant system is developed, the land rent or the quit-rent shall be paid to the state as a tax.

11. All the means of transport, railways, canals, steamships, roads, the posts etc. shall be taken over by the state. They shall become the property of the state and shall be placed free at the disposal of the impecunious classes.

14. The right of inheritance to be curtailed.

15. The introduction of steeply graduated taxes, and the abolition of taxes on articles of consumption.

16. Inauguration of national workshops. The state guarantees a livelihood to all workers and provides for those who are incapacitated for work.

17. Universal and free education of the people.

It is to the interest of the German proletariat, the petty bourgeoisie and the small peasants to support these demands with all possible energy. Only by the realisation of these demands will the millions in Germany, who have hitherto been exploited by a handful of persons and whom the exploiters would like to keep in further subjection, win the rights and attain to that power to which they are entitled as the producers of all wealth.

> *The Committee:*
> *Karl Marx, Karl Schapper, H. Bauer,*
> *F. Engels, J. Moll, W. Wolff*

At that time the craze for revolutionary legions prevailed in Paris. Spaniards, Italians, Belgians, Dutchmen, Poles and Germans flocked together in crowds to liberate their respective fatherlands. The German legion was led by Herwegh, Bornstedt, Börnstein. Since immediately after the revolution all foreign workers not only lost their jobs but in addition were harassed by the public, the influx into these legions was very great. The new government saw in them a means of getting rid of foreign workers and granted them *l'étape du soldat,* that is, quarters along their line of march and a marching allowance of fifty centimes per day up to the frontier, wherupon the eloquent Lamartine, the Foreign Minister who was so readily moved to tears, found an opportunity of betraying them to their respective governments.

We opposed this playing with revolution most decisively. To carry an invasion, which was to import the revolution forcibly from outside, into the midst of the ferment then going on in Germany, meant to undermine the revolution in Germany itself, to strengthen the governments and to deliver the legionaries— Lamartine stood as guarantor for that—defenceless into the hands of the German troops. When subsequently the revolution was victorious in Vienna and Berlin, the legion became all the more pointless; but once begun, the game was continued.

We founded a German communist club [196] in which we advised the workers to keep away from the legion and to return instead to their homelands singly and work there for the movement. Our old friend Flocon, who had a seat in the Provisional Government, obtained for the workers sent by us the same travel concessions as had been granted to the legionaries. In this way we returned three or four hundred workers to Germany, including the great majority of the League members.

As could easily be foreseen, the League proved to be much too weak a lever by comparison with the popular mass movement that had now broken out. Three quarters of the League members who had previously lived abroad had changed their domicile by returning to their homeland; their previous communities were thus to a great extent dissolved and they lost all contact with the League. Some of the more ambitious among them did not even try to resume this contact, but each one began a small separate movement on his own account in his own locality. Finally, the conditions in each separate small state, each province and each town were so different that the League would have been incapable of giving more than the most general directives; such directives were, however, much better disseminated through the press. In

short, from the moment when the causes which had made the
secret League necessary ceased to exist, the secret League lost all
significance as such. But this could least of all surprise the persons
who had just stripped this same secret League of the last vestige of
its conspiratorial character.

That, however, the League had been an excellent school for
revolutionary activity was now demonstrated. On the Rhine, where
the *Neue Rheinische Zeitung* provided a firm centre, in Nassau, in
Rheinish Hesse, etc., everywhere members of the League stood at
the head of the extreme democratic movement. The same was the
case in Hamburg. In Southern Germany the predominance of
petty-bourgeois democracy stood in the way. In Breslau, Wilhelm
Wolff was active with great success until the summer of 1848; in
addition he received a Silesian mandate as an alternate deputy to
the Frankfurt parliament. Finally, the compositor Stephan Born,
who had worked in Brussels and Paris as an active member of the
League, founded a Workers' Fraternity in Berlin which became
fairly widespread and existed until 1850. Born, a very talented
young man, who, however, was a bit too much in a hurry to
become a political figure, "fraternised" with the most motley
Cherethites and Pelethites [a] just to get a crowd together, and was
not at all the man who could bring unity into the conflicting
tendencies, light into the chaos. Consequently, in the official
publications of the association the views represented in the
Communist Manifesto were mingled hodge-podge with guild
recollections and guild aspirations, fragments of Louis Blanc and
Proudhon, protectionism, etc.; in short, they wanted to please
everybody. In particular, strikes, trade unions and producers'
co-operatives were set going and it was forgotten that above all it
was a question of first conquering, by means of political victories,
the field in which alone such things could be realised on a lasting
basis. When, afterwards, the victories of the reactionaries made the
leaders of the Fraternity realise the necessity of taking a direct
part in the revolutionary struggle, they were naturally left in the
lurch by the confused mass which they had grouped around
themselves. Born took part in the Dresden uprising of May
1849 [197] and had a lucky escape. But, in contrast to the great
political movement of the proletariat, the Workers' Fraternity
proved to be a pure *Sonderbund*,[198] which to a large extent existed
only on paper and played such a subordinate role that the
reactionaries did not find it necessary to suppress it until 1850,

---

[a] 2 Samuel 8:18, 15:18, 20:7, 23.— *Ed.*

and its surviving offshoots until several years later.[199] Born, whose
real name was Buttermilch, has become not a big political figure
but an insignificant Swiss professor, who no longer translates Marx
into guild language but the meek Renan into his own fulsome
German.

With June 13, 1849, in Paris,[200] the defeat of the May
insurrections in Germany and the suppression of the Hungarian
revolution by the Russians, a great period of the 1848 Revolution
came to a close. But the victory of the reactionaries was as yet by
no means final. A reorganisation of the scattered revolutionary
forces was required, and hence also of the League. The situation
again forbade, as in 1848, any open organisation of the
proletariat; hence one had to organise again in secret.

In the autumn of 1849 most of the members of the former
central authorities and congresses gathered again in London. The
only ones still missing were Schapper, who was imprisoned in
Wiesbaden but came after his acquittal in the spring of 1850,[a] and
Moll, who, after he had accomplished a series of most dangerous
missions and agitational journeys—eventually he recruited
mounted gunners for the Palatinate artillery right under the noses
of the Prussian army in the Rhine Province—joined the Besançon
workers' company of Willich's corps and was killed by a shot in the
head during the battle at the Murg in front of the Rothenfels
Bridge.[201] On the other hand Willich now entered upon the scene.
Willich was one of those sentimental Communists so common in
Western Germany since 1845, who on that account alone was
instinctively, furtively antagonistic to our critical tendency. More
than that, he was entirely the prophet, convinced of his personal
mission as the predestined liberator of the German proletariat and
as such a direct claimant as much to political as to military
dictatorship. Thus, to the early Christian communism previously
preached by Weitling was added a kind of communist Islam.
However, propaganda for this new religion was for the time being
restricted to the refugee barracks under Willich's command.

Hence, the League was organised afresh; the Address of March
1850, published in an appendix (IX, No. 1), was put into effect
and Heinrich Bauer sent as an emissary to Germany. The
Address, edited by Marx and myself, is still of interest today,
because petty-bourgeois democracy is even now the party which
must certainly be the first to take the helm in Germany as the
saviour of society from the communist workers on the occasion of

---

a February 15, 1850.— *Ed.*

the next European upheaval now soon due (the European revolutions, 1815, 1830, 1848-52, 1870, have occurred at intervals of fifteen to eighteen years in our century). Much of what is said there is, therefore, still applicable today. Heinrich Bauer's mission was crowned with complete success. The jolly little shoemaker was a born diplomat. He brought the former members of the League, some who had become laggards and some who were acting on their own account, back into the active organisation, particularly the then leaders of the Workers' Fraternity. The League began to play the dominant role in the workers', peasants' and gymnastic associations to a far greater extent than before 1848, so that the next quarterly address to the communities, in June 1850, could already report that the student Schurz from Bonn (later on American ex-minister), who was touring Germany in the interest of petty-bourgeois democracy, had "found that the League already controlled all useful forces" (see Appendix IX, No. 2).[a] The League was undoubtedly the only revolutionary organisation that had any significance in Germany.

But what purpose this organisation should serve depended very substantially on whether the prospects of a renewed upsurge of the revolution materialised. And in the course of the year 1850 this became more and more improbable, indeed impossible. The industrial crisis of 1847, which had paved the way for the Revolution of 1848, had been overcome; a new, unprecedented period of industrial prosperity had set in; whoever had eyes to see and used them must have clearly perceived that the revolutionary storm of 1848 was gradually declining.

"With this general prosperity, in which the productive forces of bourgeois society develop as luxuriantly as is at all possible within bourgeois relationships, *there can be no talk of a real revolution*. Such a revolution is only possible in the periods when both these factors, the modern productive forces and the bourgeois forms of production, come in collision with each other. The various quarrels in which the representatives of the individual factions of the Continental Party of Order[202] now indulge and mutually compromise themselves, far from providing the occasion for new revolutions, are, on the contrary, possible only because the basis of the relationships is momentarily so secure and, what the reaction does not know, so *bourgeois*. All reactionary attempts to hold up bourgeois development *will rebound off it just as certainly as all moral indignation and all enthusiastic proclamations of the democrats*." Thus

---

[a] See present edition, Vol. 10, p. 372.— *Ed.*

Marx and I wrote in the "Review. May to October 1850" in the *Neue Rheinische Zeitung. Politisch-ökonomische Revue,* No. V-VI, Hamburg, 1850, p. 153.[a]

This cool estimation of the situation, however, was regarded as heresy by many persons, at a time when Ledru-Rollin, Louis Blanc, Mazzini, Kossuth and, among the lesser German lights, Ruge, Kinkel, Goegg and the rest of them were flocking together in London to form provisional governments of the future not only for their respective fatherlands but for the whole of Europe, and when it only remained a matter of obtaining the requisite money from America as a revolutionary loan to consummate at a moment's notice the European revolution and the various republics which went with it as a matter of course. Can anyone be surprised that a man like Willich was taken in by this, that Schapper, acting on his old revolutionary impulse, also allowed himself to be fooled, and that the majority of the London workers, to a large extent refugees themselves, followed them into the camp of the bourgeois-democratic artificers of revolution? Suffice it to say that the reserve maintained by us was not to the liking of these people; one was to enter into the game of making revolutions. We most decisively refused to do so. A split ensued; more about this is to be read in the *Revelations.*[b] Then came the arrest of Nothjung,[203] followed by that of Haupt, in Hamburg. The latter turned traitor by divulging the names of the Cologne Central Authority and being envisaged as the chief witness in the trial; but his relatives had no desire to be thus disgraced and bundled him off to Rio de Janeiro, where he later established himself as a merchant and in recognition of his services was appointed first Prussian and then German Consul General. He is now back in Europe.*

For a better understanding of what follows, I give the list of the Cologne accused: 1) P. G. Röser, cigarmaker; 2) Heinrich Bürgers, who later died, a Party of Progress deputy to the provincial Diet; 3) Peter Nothjung, tailor, who died a few years ago as a

---

* Schapper died in London at the end of the sixties.[c] Willich took part in the American Civil War with distinction; he became Brigadier-General and was shot in the chest during the battle of Murfreesboro (Tennessee)[204] but recovered and died about ten years ago in America.— Of the other persons mentioned above, I shall only remark that all trace was lost of Heinrich Bauer in Australia, and that Weitling and Ewerbeck died in America.

---

a Ibid., p. 510. Italics by Engels.— *Ed.*
b K. Marx, *Revelations Concerning the Communist Trial in Cologne.— Ed.*
c April 29, 1870.— *Ed.*

photographer in Breslau; 4) W. J. Reiff; 5) Dr. Hermann Becker, now chief burgomaster of Cologne and member of the Upper Chamber; 6) Dr. Roland Daniels, medical practitioner, who died a few years after the trial of tuberculosis contracted in prison; 7) Karl Otto, chemist; 8) Dr. Abraham Jacobi, now medical practitioner in New York; 9) Dr. J. J. Klein, now medical practitioner and town councillor in Cologne; 10) Ferdinand Freiligrath, who, however, was at that time already in London; 11) J. L. Erhard, clerk; 12) Friedrich Lessner, tailor, now in London. Of these, after a public trial before a jury lasting from October 4 to November 12, 1852, the following were sentenced for attempted high treason: Röser, Bürgers and Nothjung to six, Reiff, Otto and Becker to five and Lessner to three years' confinement in a fortress; Daniels, Klein, Jacobi and Erhard were acquitted.

With the Cologne trial this first period of the German communist workers' movement comes to an end. Immediately after the sentence we dissolved our League; a few months later the Willich-Schapper Sonderbund[205] was also laid to eternal rest.

*   *   *

A whole generation lies between then and now. At that time Germany was a country of handicraft and of domestic industry based on manual labour; now it is a big industrial country still undergoing continual industrial transformation. At that time one had to seek out one by one the workers who had an understanding of their position as workers and of their historico-economic antagonism to capital, because this antagonism was itself in the process of taking shape. Today the entire German proletariat has to be placed under exceptional laws,[206] merely in order to slow down a little the process of its development to full consciousness of its position as an oppressed class. At that time the few persons who reached an understanding of the historical role of the proletariat had to gather in secret, to assemble clandestinely in small communities of 3 to 20 persons. Today the German proletariat no longer needs any official organisation, either public or secret. The simple self-evident interconnection of like-minded class comrades suffices, without any rules, authorities, resolutions or other tangible forms, to shake the whole German Empire. Bismarck is the arbiter of Europe beyond the frontiers of Germany, but within them there grows daily more threateningly the athletic figure of the German proletariat that Marx foresaw back in 1844, the giant for whom the cramped imperial edifice designed to fit the philistine is already becoming too small and whose mighty stature and broad shoulders grow until the moment comes when by merely rising from his seat he will blast the whole structure of the imperial constitution to rubble. And still more. The international movement of the European and American proletariat has so grown in strength that not only its first narrow form—the secret League—but even its second, infinitely broader form—the open International Working Men's Association—has become a fetter for it, and that the simple feeling of solidarity based on the understanding of the identity of class position suffices to create and to hold together one and the same great party of the proletariat among the workers of all countries and tongues. The doctrine which the League represented from 1847 to 1852, and which at that time was treated by the wise philistines with a shrug of the shoulders as the hallucinations of utter madcaps, as the secret doctrine of a few scattered sectarians, has now innumerable adherents in all civilised countries of the world, among those condemned to the Siberan mines as much as among the gold diggers of California; and the founder of this doctrine, the most hated, most slandered man of his time, Karl Marx, was when he died, the ever-sought-after and ever-willing counsellor of the proletariat of the old and the new world.

London, October 8, 1885

Frederick Engels

First published in *Karl Marx, Enthüllungen über den Kommunisten-Prozess zu Köln,* Hottingen-Zurich, 1885, and in the newspaper *Der Sozialdemokrat,* Nos. 46-48, November 12, 19 and 26, 1885

Printed according to the book

Première année — N° 8   Samedi 17 Octobre 1885.

LE SOCIALISTE
Organe du Parti ouvrier

| LE NUMERO : 10 CENTIMES
ABONNEMENTS: France, 3 m. 1 fr. 50; 6 m. 3 fr.; Un an, 6 fr.
Etranger, — 2 fr. — 4 fr. — 8 fr. | PARAISSANT LE SAMEDI
Comité de Rédaction :
G. DEVILLE, R. FRÉJAC, J. GUESDE, P. LAVARGUE, A. LE TAILLEUR. | RÉDACTION ET ADMINISTRATION :
17, rue du Croissant, Paris.
ANNONCES : au bureau du Journal |

THE SITUATION [207]

London, 12 October 1885

...I cannot see that the 4 October was a defeat, unless you have been prey to all sorts of illusions. It was a matter of crushing the opportunists [208]; they have been crushed. But in order to crush them pressure from two opposing sides was needed, from the right and from the left. That the pressure from the right was stronger than one might have thought is obvious. But that makes the situation much more revolutionary.

Rather than Orleanists and Bonapartists in disguise, the bourgeois, both big and small, opted for Orleanists and Bonapartists who were open about it; rather than men who seek to get rich at the expense of the nation they opted for those who have already become rich by robbing it; rather than the conservatives of tomorrow, the conservatives of yesterday. That is all.

Monarchy is impossible in France, if only because of the multitude of pretenders. If it were possible, it would be a sign that the Bismarckians are right to speak of the degeneration of France. But this degeneration affects only the bourgeoisie, in Germany and in England as well as in France.

The Republic still remains the government which divides the three monarchist sects [209] the least, permitting them to unite as a conservative party. The moment the possibility of a monarchist restoration becomes a matter for discussion, the conservative party splits up into three sects; whereas the republicans will be forced to group around the only government possible; and, at the moment, it is probably the Clemenceau administration.

Clemenceau is still an advance on Ferry and Wilson. It is most important that he comes to power, not as the bulwark of property against the communists, but as the saviour of the Republic against the monarchy. In this case he will be more or less *forced* to keep his promises; otherwise he would be behaving like the others who thought, like Louis Philippe, that they were "the best of the republics" [210]: we are in power, the Republic can sleep peacefully; our takeover of the ministries is enough, so do not speak to us any more of the promised reforms.

I believe that the men who voted for the monarchists on the 4th are already frightened by their own success and that the 18th will yield results that are more or less in favour of Clemenceau's supporters,[211] with some success, not of esteem but of scorn, for the opportunists. The philistine will say to himself: "After all, with so many Royalists and Bonapartists, I need a few opportunists." Anyway, the 18th will decide the situation; France is the country of the unexpected, and I am wary of expressing a definitive opinion.

But, come what may, there will be radicals [212] and monarchists present. The Republic will run the necessary danger in order to force the petty bourgeois to lean a little more to the extreme left, which he would never have done otherwise. *It is precisely the situation we communists need.* Up till now, I see no reason to believe that there has been any deviation in the exceptionally logical course of political development in France: it is still the logic of 1792-94; only the danger which was caused by the coalition then, is today caused by the coalition of monarchist parties at home. If one examines it closely, it is less dangerous than the other one was...

F. Engels

First published in *Le Socialiste*, No. 8, October 17, 1885

Printed according to the newspaper

Translated from the French

TO THE EDITORIAL COMMITTEE OF *LE SOCIALISTE*

Citizens,

In your issue of the 17th you publish an extract from a private letter[a] which I had addressed to one of you.[b] This letter was written in haste, so much so that in order to catch the post I did not even have time to read through it. Allow me, therefore, to qualify a passage which does not express my thoughts very clearly.

While speaking of M. Clemenceau as the flag-bearer of French radicalism I said: "It is most important that he comes to power, not as the bulwark of property against the communists, but as the saviour of the Republic against the monarchy. In this case he will be more or less *forced* to keep his promises; otherwise he would be behaving (here it is necessary to insert 'perhaps') like the others who thought, like Louis Philippe, that they were 'the best of the republics'[213]: we are in power, the Republic can sleep peacefully; our takeover of the ministries is enough, so do not speak to us any more of the promised reforms."

First of all, I have no right to assert that M. Clemenceau, if he came to power in the routine way of parliamentary governments, would inevitably act "like the others". Secondly, I am not the one who explains the actions of governments as a matter of pure will, whether good or bad; this will itself is determined by independent causes, by the general situation. Thus it is not M. Clemenceau's will, good or bad, which concerns us here. What does concern us, in the interests of the workers' party, is that the radicals come to power in such a situation that the implementation of their

---

a See this volume, pp. 331-32.— *Ed.*

b Paul Lafargue.— *Ed.*

programme is imposed on them as the sole means of holding on. Let us hope that the two hundred monarchists of the Chamber will be sufficient to create this situation.

London, 21 October 1885

F. Engels

First published in *Le Socialiste*, No. 10, October 31, 1885

Printed according to the newspaper

Translated from the French

HOW NOT TO TRANSLATE MARX[214]

The first volume of "Das Kapital" is public property, as far as translation into foreign languages are concerned. Therefore, although it is pretty well known in English Socialist circles that a translation is being prepared and will be published under the responsibility of Marx's literary executors, nobody would have a right to grumble if that translation were anticipated by another, so long as the text was faithfully and equally well rendered.

The first few pages of such a translation by John Broadhouse, are published in the October number of *To-Day*. I say distinctly that it is very far from being a faithful rendering of the text, and that because Mr. Broadhouse is deficient in every quality required in a translator of Marx.

To translate such a book, a fair knowledge of literary German is not enough. Marx uses freely expressions of everyday life and idioms of provincial dialects; he coins new words, he takes his illustrations from every branch of science, his allusions from the literatures of a dozen languages; to understand him, a man must be a master of German indeed, spoken as well as written, and must know something of German life too.

To use an illustration. When some Oxford Undergraduates rowed in a four-oar boat across the straits of Dover, it was stated in the Press reports that one of them "caught a crab." The London correspondent of the *Cologne Gazette*ᵃ took this literally, and faithfully reported to his paper, that "a crab had got entangled in the oar of one of the rowers." If a man who has been living for years in the midst of London is capable of such a

---

ᵃ *Kölnische Zeitung.—Ed.*

ludicrous blunder as soon as he comes across the technical terms
of an art unknown to him, what must we expect from a man who
with a passable knowledge of mere book-German, undertakes to
translate the most untranslatable of German prose writers? And
indeed we shall see that Mr. Broadhouse is an excellent hand at
"catching crabs."

But there is something more required. Marx is one of the most
vigorous and concise writers of the age. To render him
adequately, a man must be a master, not only of German, but of
English too. Mr. Broadhouse, however, though evidently a man of
respectable journalistic accomplishments, commands but that
limited range of English used by and for conventional literary
respectability. Here he moves with ease; but this sort of English is
not a language into which "Das Kapital" can ever be translated.
Powerful German requires powerful English to render it; the best
resources of the language have to be drawn upon; new-coined
German terms require the coining of corresponding new terms in
English. But as soon as Mr. Broadhouse is faced by such a
difficulty, not only his resources fail him, but also his courage.
The slightest extension of his limited stock-in-trade, the slightest
innovation upon the conventional English of everyday literature
frightens him, and rather than risk such a heresy, he renders the
difficult German word by a more or less indefinite term which
does not grate upon his ear but obscures the meaning of the
author; or, worse still, he translates it, as it recurs, by a whole
series of different terms, forgetting that a technical term has to be
rendered always by one and the same equivalent. Thus, in the
very heading of the first section, he translates *Werthgrösse* by
"extent of value," ignoring that *grösse* is a definite mathematical
term, equivalent to magnitude, or determined quantity, while
extent may mean many things besides. Thus even the simple
innovation of "labour-time" for *Arbeitszeit,* is too much for him; he
renders it by (1) "time-labour," which means, if anything, labour
paid by time or labour done by a man "serving" *time* at hard
labour; (2) "time of labour," (3) "labour-time," and (4) "period of
labour", by which term (*Arbeitsperiode*) Marx, in the second
volume, means something quite different.[215] Now as is well known,
the "category" of labour-time is one of the most fundamental of
the whole book, and to translate it by four different terms in less
than ten pages is more than unpardonable.

Marx begins with the analysis of what a commodity is. The first
aspect under which a commodity presents itself, is that of an
object of utility; as such it may be considered with regard either to

its quality or its quantity. "Any such thing is a whole in itself, the sum of many qualities or properties, and may therefore be useful in different ways. To discover these different ways and therefore the various uses to which a thing may be put, is the *act of history*. So, too, is the finding and fixing of *socially recognised standards of measure* for the quantity of useful things. The diversity of the modes of measuring commodities arises partly from the diversity of the nature of the objects to be measured, partly from convention." [a]

This is rendered by Mr. Broadhouse as follows:

"To discover these various ways, and consequently the multifarious modes in which an object may be of use, is *a work of time*. So, *consequently*, is the finding of *the social measure* for the quantity of useful things. The diversity in the *bulk* of commodities arises partly from the different nature," etc.

With Marx, the finding out of the various utilities of things constitutes an essential part of historic progress; with Mr. Broadhouse, it is merely a work of time. With Marx the same qualification applies to the establishment of recognised common standards of measure. With Mr. B., another "work of time" consists in the "finding of the social measure for the quantity of useful things," about which sort of measure Marx certainly never troubled himself. And then he winds up by mistaking *Masse* (*measures*) for *Masse* (*bulk*), and thereby saddling Marx with one of the finest crabs that was ever caught.

Further on, Marx says: "Use values form the material out of which wealth is made up, *whatever may be the social form of that wealth*" (the specific form of appropriation by which it is held and distributed). Mr. Broadhouse has:

"Use values constitute the actual basis of wealth *which is always their social form*"—

which is either a pretentious platitude or sheer nonsense.

The second aspect under which a commodity presents itself, is its exchange-value. That all commodities are exchangeable, in certain varying proportions, one against the other, that they have exchange-values, this fact implies that they contain something which is common to all of them. I pass over the slovenly way in which Mr. Broadhouse here reproduces one of the most delicate analyses in Marx's book, and at once proceed to the passage where Marx says: "This something common to all commodities cannot be a geometrical, physical, chemical or other natural property. In fact their material properties come into consideration only in so far as

---

[a] Here and below italics by Engels.— *Ed.*

they make them useful, that is, in so far as they turn them into use-values." And he continues: "But it is the very act *of making abstraction from their use-values* which *evidently* is the characteristic point of the exchange-*relation* of commodities. *Within this relation,* one use-value is equivalent to any other, so long as it is provided in *sufficient* proportion."

Now Mr. Broadhouse:

"But on the other hand, it is precisely *these Use-values in the abstract* which *apparently* characterise the exchange-*ratio* of the commodities. *In itself,* one Use-value is worth just as much as another if it exists in the *same* proportion."

Thus, leaving minor mistakes aside, Mr. Broadhouse makes Marx say the very reverse of what he does say. With Marx, the characteristic of the exchange-relation of commodities is the fact, that total abstraction is made of their use-values, that they are considered as having no use-values at all. His interpreter makes him say, that the characteristic of the exchange *ratio* (of which there is no question here) is precisely their use-value, only taken "in the abstract"! And then, a few lines further on, he gives the sentence of Marx: "As Use-values, commodities can only be of different quality, as exchange-values they can only be of different quantity, *containing not an atom of Use-value,*" neither abstract nor concrete. We may well ask: "Understandest thou what thou readest?" [a]

To this question it becomes impossible to answer in the affirmative, when we find Mr. Broadhouse repeating the same misconception over and over again. After the sentence just quoted, Marx continues: "Now, if we *leave out of consideration*" (that is, make abstraction from) "the use-values of the commodities, there remains *to them* but one property: that of being the products of labour. But even this product of labour has already undergone a change in our hands. If we make abstraction *from its use-value,* we also make abstraction *from the bodily components* and forms which *make it into* a use-value."

This is Englished by Mr. Broadhouse as follows:

"If we *separate* Use-values *from* the actual material of the commodities, there remains" (where? with the use-values or with the actual material?) "one property only, that of the product of labour. But the product of labour is already transmuted in our hands. If we abstract *from it its* use-value, we *abstract also the stamina and form* which *constitute its* use-value."

Again, Marx: "In the exchange-*relation* of commodities, their exchange-value presented itself to us as something perfectly

---

[a] *The Acts of the Apostles.* VIII. 30.— *Ed.*

independent of their use-values. Now, if we actually make abstraction *from the use-value* of the products of labour, we arrive at their value, as *previously* determined by us." This is made by Mr. Broadhouse to sound as follows:

"In the exchange-*ratio* of commodities their exchange-value appears to us as something altogether independent of their use-value. If we now in effect abstract *the use-value from the labour-products,* we have their value as it is *then* determined."

There is no doubt of it. Mr. Broadhouse has never heard of any other acts and modes of abstraction but bodily ones, such as the abstraction of money from a till or a safe. To identify abstraction and subtraction, will, however, never do for a translator of Marx.

Another specimen of the turning of German sense into English nonsense. One of the finest researches of Marx is that revealing the duplex character of labour. Labour, considered as a producer of use-value, is of a different character, has different qualifications from the same labour, when considered as a producer of value. The one is labour of a specified kind, spinning, weaving, ploughing, etc.; the other is the general character of human productive activity, common to spinning, weaving, ploughing, etc., which comprises them all under the one common term, labour. The one is labour in the concrete, the other is labour in the abstract. The one is technical labour, the other is economical labour. In short—for the English language *has* terms for both—the one is *work,* as distinct from labour; the other is *labour,* as distinct from work. After this analysis, Marx continues: "Originally a commodity presented itself to us as something duplex: Use-value and Exchange-value. Further on we saw that labour, too, as far as it is expressed in value, *does no longer possess the same characteristics* which belong to it in its capacity as a creator of use-value." Mr. Broadhouse insists on proving that he has not understood a word of Marx's analysis, and translates the above passage as follows:

"We saw the commodity as first as a *compound* of Use-value and Exchange-value. Then we saw that labour, so far as it is expressed in value, *only possesses that character so far as* it is a generator of use-value."

When Marx says: White, Mr. Broadhouse sees no reason why he should not translate: Black.

But enough of this. Let us turn to something more amusing. Marx says: "In civil society, the *fictio juris* prevails that everybody, in his capacity as a buyer of commodities, possesses an encyclopaedical knowledge of all such commodities." [216] Now, although the expression, Civil Society, is thoroughly English, and Ferguson's

"History of Civil Society" is more than a hundred years old, this term is too much for Mr. Broadhouse. He renders it "amongst ordinary people," and thus turns the sentence into nonsense. For it is exactly "ordinary people" who are constantly grumbling at being cheated by retailers, etc., in consequence of their ignorance of the nature and values of the commodities they have to buy.

The *production* (*Herstellung*) of a Use-value is rendered by "the *establishing* of a Use-value." When Marx says "If we succeed in transforming, with little labour, *coal* into diamonds, their value may fall below that of bricks," Mr. Broadhouse, apparently not aware that diamond is an allotropic form of carbon, turns *coal* into *coke*. Similarly he transmutes the "total yield of the Brazilian diamond mines" into "the *entire profits* of the whole yield." "The primitive communities of India" in his hands become "*venerable* communities." Marx says: "In the use-value of a commodity is contained" (*steckt*, which had better be translated: For the production of the use-value of a commodity there has been spent) "a *certain productive activity*, adapted to the peculiar purpose, or a certain useful labour." Mr. Broadhouse must say:

"In the use-value of a commodity is contained a certain *quantity of productive power* or useful labour,"

thus turning not only quality into quantity, but productive activity which has been spent, into productive power which is to be spent.

But enough. I could give tenfold this number of instances, to show that Mr. Broadhouse is in every respect *not* a fit and proper man to translate Marx, and especially so because he seems perfectly ignorant of what is really conscientious scientific work.*

Frederick Engels

Written in October 1885   Reproduced from the magazine

First published in *The Commonweal*, No. 10, November 1885

---

* From the above it will be evident that "Das Kapital" is not a book the translation of which can be done by contract. The work of translating it is in excellent hands, but the translators [a] cannot devote all their time to it. This is the reason of the delay. But while the precise time of publication cannot as yet be stated we may safely say that the English edition will be in the hands of the public in the course of next year.

---

[a] E. Aveling and S. Moore.—*Ed.*

ON THE HISTORY OF THE PRUSSIAN PEASANTS

[INTRODUCTION TO WILHELM WOLFF'S PAMPHLET
THE SILESIAN MILLIARD][217]

To aid comprehension of the following work by Wolff, I must preface it with a few words.

Germany east of the Elbe and north of the Erzgebirge and Riesengebirge is a country wrested in the latter half of the Middle Ages from the invading Slavs, and Germanised once again by German colonists. The conquering German knights and barons to whom the land was allotted set themselves up as the "founders" ["Gründer"] of villages, laying out their district in village lands, each of which was divided into a number of smallholdings or hides of equal size. To every hide there belonged a house plot with yard and garden in the village itself. These hides were distributed by lot to the newly arrived Franconian (Rhenish Franconian and Dutch), Saxon and Frisian colonists; in return the colonists had to render very moderate, firmly fixed dues and services to the founder, i.e. the knight or baron. The peasants were hereditary masters of their hides as long as they performed these services. In addition they enjoyed the same rights of usufruct to timber, grazing, pannage, etc., in the forest of the founder (the subsequent landlord) as the West German peasants possessed on their common land. The cultivated village land was subject to compulsory crop rotation, being chiefly cultivated in winter fields, summer fields and fallow fields in accordance with the three-field system; fallow and harvested fields were grazed jointly by the cattle of the peasantry and the founder. All village affairs were settled in the assembly of the manorial inhabitants, i.e. the hide-owners, by majority decision. The rights of the noble founders were restricted to collecting the dues and participating in the fallow grazing and stubble pasture, to the surplus from the

24*

yield of the forests, and to taking the chair at the assembly of manorial inhabitants, who were all personally free men. This was the average condition of the German peasants from the Elbe to East Prussia and Silesia. And this condition was on the whole considerably much better than that of west and south German peasants at the time, who were already then engaged in a violent, continually recurring struggle with the feudal lords for their old hereditary rights, and had to a large extent already succumbed to a form of dependence that was far more oppressive, threatening to or even destructive of their personal freedom.

The feudal lords' increasing need for money in the fourteenth and fifteenth centuries naturally led to attempts to oppress and exploit the peasants in contravention to agreements in the north-east as well. But certainly not on the same scale and with the same success as in South Germany. The population east of the Elbe was still sparse, the wasteland was still extensive; the reclamation of this wasteland, the spread of cultivation and the foundation of new tributary villages here remained the surest means of enrichment for the feudal landlords too. Furthermore, here, on the imperial border with Poland, larger states had already been formed—Pomerania, Brandenburg, the Electorate of Saxony (Silesia was Austrian)—and for this reason the peace of the land was better observed, the feuds and depredations of the nobility were more forcefully suppressed than in the fragmented areas on the Rhine, in Franconia and Swabia. But those who suffered most from the permanent state of war were precisely the peasants.

Only in the neighbourhood of subjugated Polish or Lithuanian-Prussian villages did the nobility more frequently attempt to force the colonists settled there in accordance with German manorial law into the same serfdom as the Polish and Prussian subjects. This occurred in Pomerania and in the Prussian area of the Order,[218] more rarely in Silesia.

As a result of this more favourable position, the peasants east of the Elbe remained almost untouched by the powerful movement of the south and west German peasants in the final quarter of the fifteenth and first quarter of the sixteenth centuries, and when the revolution of 1525 broke out it found in East Prussia only a faint echo, which was suppressed without great difficulty. The peasants east of the Elbe left their rebelling brothers in the lurch, and they received their just deserts. In the regions where the great Peasant War had raged, the peasants were now made serfs without further ado, subjected to unlimited labour services and dues dependent solely on the arbitrary power of the landlord. Their free land was simply turned into seigneurial property, on which they only retained the usufruct accorded to them by the landlord in his bounty. This, the very ideal state of feudal landlordship, to which the German nobility had in vain been aspiring all through the Middle Ages and which it had finally attained now that the feudal system was decaying, was then gradually extended to the lands east of the Elbe as well. Not only were the peasants' contractual rights of usufruct in the seigneurial forest (in so far as they had not previously been curtailed) transformed into revocable concessions bestowed at the grace of the landlord; not only were labour services and tributes unlawfully increased; but new burdens were also introduced, such as the "laudemien" (dues to the landlord on the death of the peasant smallholder) which were considered characteristic of serfdom; or traditional, innocuous services were given the character of services rendered only by serfs, but not by free men. In less than a hundred years the free peasants east of the Elbe were thus turned into serfs, at first in fact, and then also in law.

In the meantime the feudal nobility became more and more bourgeois. To an ever increasing extent it became indebted to the urban money capitalists, and money thus came to be its pressing need. Yet there was no money to be had from the peasant, its serf, but to begin with only labour or arable produce, and the farms, tilled under the most difficult conditions, would only yield a minimum of such produce over and above the most meagre livelihood for the working owners. Alongside, however, lay the lucrative estates of the monasteries, worked by the labour services of dependents or serfs under expert supervision at the expense of the lord. Hitherto the petty nobility had almost never been able to practise this kind of management on their domains, and the larger among them and the princes only in exceptional cases. But now, on the one hand, the restoration of the peace of the land made large-scale cultivation possible everywhere, while, on the other, it was increasingly forced on the nobility by its growing need for money. The running of large estates with the labour services of serf peasants at the expense of the landlord gradually became the source of income which had to compensate the nobility for the loss of the now outmoded robber-knight system. But where could they obtain the necessary land area? True, the noble was landlord of an area large or small, but with few exceptions this was entirely allotted to hereditary copyholders,[219] who had just as much right to their farms and hides, including the land rights, as the noble lord himself, as long as they performed the stipulated services. This had to be remedied, and what was necessary above all was the transformation of the peasants into serfs. For even if the expulsion of serf peasants from house and farm was no less a breach of the law and an act of violence than the expulsion of free copyholders, it was still far easier to extenuate it with the aid of the now habitual Roman law. In short, once the peasants had been successfully turned into serfs, the necessary number of peasants were chased away or resettled on seigneurial land as cottagers, day labourers with a cottage and small garden. While the earlier strongholds of the nobility gave way to their new ones, more or less open manor houses, for this very reason the farms of formerly free peasants gave way to the wretched hovels of bond servants, on a much wider scale.

Once the seigneurial estate—the dominium, as it was called in Silesia—had been established, it was then simply a matter of setting in motion the labour power of the peasants to work it. And this is where the second advantage of serfdom showed itself. The former labour services of the peasants as laid down by contract were by no means appropriate for this end. The vast majority of them were restricted to services in the public interest—road and bridge building, etc.—building work on the seigneurial castle, the labour of the women and girls at the castle in different branches of industry, and personal servants' duties. But as soon as the peasant had been turned into a serf and the latter had been equated with the Roman slave by Roman lawyers, the noble lord changed his tune entirely. With the assent of the lawyers at the bench he now demanded from the peasants unlimited services, as much, whenever and wherever he pleased. The peasant had to do labour service, drive, plough, sow and harvest as soon as he was summoned to do so, even if his own field was neglected and his own harvest ruined by rain. And his corn tribute and money tribute were likewise raised to the extreme limits of what was possible.

But that was not enough. The no less noble reigning prince, who was present everywhere east of the Elbe, also needed money, a lot of money. In return for his permitting the noble to subjugate his peasants, the noble allowed him to impose state taxes on the same peasants—the nobleman himself was of course exempt from taxation! And to cap it all, the same reigning prince sanctioned the spreading transformation of the landlord's former right to preside at the—long since abolished—free manorial court of the peasants into the right of patrimonial jurisdiction and manorial police, according to which the lord of the manor was not only chief of police but also the sole judge over his peasants—even when personally involved in a case—so that the peasant could only indict the lord of the manor through the lord of the manor himself. He was thus legislator, judge and executor in one person, and absolute and supreme lord of his manor.

These notorious conditions, which are not matched even in Russia—for there the peasant still had his self-governing commune—reached their peak in the period between the Thirty Years' War and the redeeming defeat at Jena.[220] The terrible hardships of the Thirty Years' War allowed the nobility to complete the subjugation of the peasants; the devastation of countless peasant farms allowed them to be added without hindrance to the dominium of the manorial estate; the resettlement of the population forcibly driven into vagabondage by war devastation provided the nobility with an excuse to fetter them to the soil as serfs. But that, too, was only short lived. For scarcely had the dreadful wounds of war begun to heal in the following fifty years, the fields again being tilled, the population growing, than the hunger of the noble landlords for peasant land and peasant labour once again made itself felt. The seigneurial dominium was not large enough to absorb all the labour that could still be knocked out of the serfs—"knock" being used here in a highly literal sense. The system of degrading peasants into cottagers, bond day-labourers, had worked magnificently. From the beginning of the eighteenth century it assumes ever greater momentum; it is now called "*peasant expropriation* [*Bauernlegen*]". One "expropriates" as many peasants as possible, according to the circumstances; first one leaves as many as are necessary to perform the draught labour, turning the rest into cottagers (*Dreschgärtner, Häusler, Instleute*[221] or whatever they are called) who have to sweat away on the estate year in, year out in return for a cottage with a tiny potato patch, a wretched day-wage in corn and only very little in cash. Where his lordship is rich enough to provide his own draught-animals, he "expropriates" the other peasants too, adding their hides to the seigneurial estate. In this manner the entire large landed property of the German nobility, but particularly east of the Elbe, is composed of *stolen peasant land,* and even if it is taken away from the robbers again without compensation, they will still not have got their just deserts. Really they should pay compensation as well.

Gradually the reigning sovereigns noticed that this system was by no means to their advantage, however convenient it might be for the nobility. The peasants had paid state taxes before they were "expropriated"; but when their hides were added to the tax-free dominiums the state did not receive a farthing from them and scarcely a penny from the newly-settled cottagers. A proportion of the "expropriated" peasants were quite simply chased away as superfluous for the running of the estate, and thus became free, i.e. outlawed. The population of the plains declined, and since the reigning prince had started complementing his expensive recruited army through the cheaper way of conscripting the peasants, this was by no means a matter of indifference to him. Thus we find throughout the eighteenth century, particularly in Prussia, one decree after another which was supposed to put a stop to "peasant expropriation"; but their fate was the same as ninety-nine percent of the immeasurable amount of waste-paper that has been issued by German governments since the capitularies of Charlemagne.[222] They were only valid on paper; the nobility was not greatly burdened, and the practice of "peasant expropriation" continued.

Even the fearful example which the Great Revolution in France made of the stubborn feudal nobility only frightened them for a moment. Everything remained as before, and what Frederick II had not been able to do,[223] his weak, short-sighted nephew Frederick William III was least of all able to carry out. Then came the vengeance. On October 14, 1806 the entire Prussian state was smashed to smithereens in a single day near Jena and Auerstedt, and the Prussian peasant has every reason to celebrate this day and March 18, 1848 more than all the Prussian victories from Mollwitz to Sedan.[224] Now, finally, it began to dawn dimly on the Prussian government, which had been chased back right to the Russian border, that the free landowning French peasants' sons could not be defeated by the sons of serf peasants who were daily liable to be evicted from house and home; it finally noticed that the peasant was also a human being, so to speak. Now something was to be done.

But no sooner was peace concluded and Court and government back in Berlin than the noble intentions again melted like ice in the March sun. The famous edict of October 9, 1807 had admittedly abolished the *name* of serfdom or hereditary subjection on paper (and even this only from Martinmas 1810), but in reality almost everything had been left as before. That is how things remained; the King, who was as faint-hearted as he was bigoted, allowed himself to be led, as before, by the peasant-plundering nobility—so much so that from 1808 to 1810 four decrees appeared once again permitting the landowners to "expropriate" peasants in a number of cases—in contravention of the edict of 1807.[225] Not until Napoleon's war against Russia was already in sight was it again remembered that the peasants would be needed, and the edict of September 14, 1811 was issued whereby peasants and landlords were *recommended* to come to an amicable arrangement within two years on the redemption of labour service and dues as well as the seigneurial property rights. A royal commission was then to implement this settlement compulsorily in accordance with fixed rules. The main rule was that after relinquishing a third of his landholding (or its value in money), the peasant should become a free proprietor of the part remaining to him. But even this redemption, so immensely advantageous to the nobility, remained illusory. For the nobility held back in order to obtain even more, and after the two years had elapsed Napoleon was back in the country.

No sooner had he been finally expelled from the land—to the frightened King's constant promises of a constitution and popular representation—than all the fine assurances were again forgotten. As early as May 29, 1816—not even a year after the victory at Waterloo[226]—a declaration of the 1811 edict was issued which read quite differently. In it, the redeemability of feudal dues was no longer the rule, but the exception; it was only to apply to those arable estates valued in the land tax rolls (i.e. the larger ones) which had been settled by peasant occupiers back in 1749 in Silesia, 1752 in East Prussia, 1763 in Brandenburg and Pomerania,* and 1774 in West Prussia! In addition, a number of labour services at sowing and harvest time could be retained. And when the redemption commissions finally got down to serious business in 1817, the agrarian legislation regressed much faster than the agrarian commissions progressed. On June 7, 1821 there came a new redemption order, expressly laying down the limitation of redeemability to larger farms, so-called *Acker-nahrungen*,[228] and urging the perpetuation of labour services and other feudal dues for the owners of smaller holdings—cottagers, *Häusler, Dreschgärtner*—in short all settled day-labourers. From now on this remained the rule. Not until 1845, the redemption of

---

* Prussian perfidy is fathomless. Here it shows itself again in the very date. Why was 1763 chosen? Quite simply because in the following year, on July 12, 1764, Frederick II issued a sharp edict ordering the recalcitrant nobles, under pain of punishment, to return the large numbers of farms and smallholdings confiscated since 1740, and particularly since the outbreak of the Seven Years' war,[227] to their rightful occupants within one year. In so far as this edict had any effect, it was thus annulled in 1816 to the advantage of the nobility.

these kinds of dues made possible by way of exception for Saxony[a] and Silesia other than through the joint assent of landlord and peasant[b]—for which, obviously, no law was necessary. Furthermore, the capital sum with which the services, translated into money or corn revenue, could be paid off once and for all, was fixed at twenty-five times the rent, and the instalments could only be made in sums of not less than 100 thalers[229] at once; while as early as 1809 the peasants on the state domains had been permitted to buy redemption at twenty times the amount of the revenue. In short, the much-lauded, enlightened agrarian legislation of the "state of intelligence"[230] had only one ambition: to salvage every bit of feudalism that could still be salvaged.

The practical result was ·in keeping with these lamentable measures. The agrarian commissions understood the benevolent intentions of the government perfectly and, as Wolff drastically depicts in detail, they made sure that the peasant was soundly cheated in favour of the nobility in the matter of these redemptions. From 1816 to 1848 70,582 peasant holdings were redeemed with a total landed property of 5,158,827 Morgen, making up $^6/_7$ of all the larger bond peasants. However, only 289,651 of the smaller occupiers were redeemed (over 228,000 of these being in Silesia, Brandenburg and Saxony). The total number of annual service days redeemed amounted to: draught service, 5,978,295; manual service, 16,869,824. In return the high nobility received compensation as follows: capital payment, 18,544,766 thalers; cash annuities, 1,599,992 thalers; rye revenue, 260,069 Scheffel[c][231] annually; and finally, peasant land relinquished, 1,533,050 Morgen.* Apart from the other forms of compensation, the former landlords thus received a full third of what had been the peasants' land!

1848 finally opened the eyes of the Prussian backwoods Junkers, who were as narrow-minded as they were self-important. The peasants—particularly in Silesia, where the latifundia system and the concomitant downgrading of the population to day-labouring cottagers was furthest developed—stormed the manor houses,

---

* For these statistics, see Meitzen, *Der Boden des Preussischen Staates*, I, p. 432 ff.

[a] A reference to a Prussian province.— *Ed.*

[b] Frederick William IV, "Gesetz, betreffend die Ablösung der Dienste in denjenigen Theilen der Provinz Sachsen, in welchen die Ablösungsordnung vom 7. Juni 1821 gilt. Vom 18. Juli 1845" and "Gesetz, betreffend die Ablösung der Dienste in der Provinz Schlesien. Vom 31. Oktober 1845".— *Ed.*

[c] Bushel.— *Ed.*

burnt the redemption documents that had already been concluded, and forced their lordships to renounce in writing all claim
to any further services. The excesses—wicked even in the eyes of
the bourgeoisie then in power—were, admittedly, suppressed with
military force and severely punished; but now even the most
brainless Junker's skull had realised that labour service had
become impossible. Rather none at all than that from these
rebellious peasants! It was now simply a matter of saving what
could still be saved; and the landowning nobility really did have
the insolence to demand compensation for these services, which
had become impossible. And no sooner was reaction more or less
firmly back in the saddle than it fulfilled this wish.

First, however, there came the law of October 9, 1848, which
adjourned all pending redemption negotiations and the lawsuits
arising out of them, as well as a whole number of other lawsuits
between landlords and peasants. As a result the entire, much-
praised agrarian legislation from 1807 on was condemned. But
then as soon as the so-called National Assembly in Berlin had been
successfully dissolved and the coup d'état was accomplished,[a] the
feudal-bureaucratic ministry of Brandenburg-Manteuffel considered itself strong enough to oblige the nobility with a generous
step. It promulgated the provisional decree of December 20, 1848,
whereby the services, etc., to be performed by the peasants until
further settlement were restored on the old terms, with few
exceptions. It was this decree that prompted our Wolff to deal
with the conditions of the Silesian peasants in the *Neue Rheinische
Zeitung*.

Meanwhile it was over a year before the new, final Redemption
Law of March 2, 1850 was enacted. The agrarian legislation of
1807-47, which even today is still praised to the skies by Prussian
patriots, cannot be more sharply condemned than it was, albeit
reluctantly, in the motives for this law—and it is the Brandenburg-Manteuffel ministry that speaks here.

Enough: a few insignificant dues were simply abolished, the
redemption of the rest was decreed by transforming them into
cash annuities, and their capitalisation set at eighteen times this
sum. To mediate the capital instalments annuity offices were
established, which by means of well-known amortisation operations
were to pay the landlord twenty times the amount of the rent,
while the peasant was relieved of all obligation by fifty-six years of
paying off the amortisation instalments.

---

[a] See this volume, pp. 304-06.— *Ed.*

If the ministry condemned in the motives the entire preceding agrarian legislation, the commission of the Chamber condemned the new law. It was not to apply to the left bank of the Rhine, which had long since been freed of all that rubbish by the French Revolution. The commission concurred in this because at most a single one of the 109 sections of the bill was applicable there anyway:

"While all the other stipulations do not apply there at all, rather they might easily create confusion and needless unrest ... because of legislation on the left bank of the Rhine *having gone much further* with regard to the redemption of real-property dues *than it was at present intended to go*",[a]

and they could not expect the Rhinelanders to allow themselves to be brought down again to the new Prussian ideal state.

Now at last a serious attempt was made to deal with the abolition of feudal forms of labour and exploitation. In a few years the redemption of the peasants was effected. From 1850 to the end of 1865 the following were redeemed: 1. the rest of the larger peasant proprietors; there were by now only 12,706 left with an area of 352,305 Morgen; 2. the smaller proprietors, including the cottagers; but whilst not quite 290,000 had been redeemed up to 1848, in the last fifteen years all of 1,014,341 had bought themselves free. Accordingly the number of redeemed days of draught labour due the larger farms was only 356,274, the number of days of manual service, however, 6,670,507. Similarly the compensation paid in plots of land, and also due only on the larger farms, amounted to only 113,071 Morgen, and the annual annuity to be paid in rye to 55,522 Scheffel. On the other hand the landed nobility received 3,890,136 thalers in new annual cash annuities, and in addition another 19,697,483 thalers in final capital compensation.*

The sum which the entire Prussian landed proprietors, including the state domains, have lifted from the pockets of the peasants for the free return of part of the land previously stolen from the peasants—up to this century—amounts to 213,861,035 thalers according to Meitzen, I, p. 437. But this is far too little. For a Morgen of cultivated land is here "*only*" assessed at 20 thalers, a Morgen of forest land at 10 thalers and a Scheffel of rye at 1 thaler, which is much too low. Furthermore, only "the compensa-

---

* These figures have been arrived at by calculating the difference between the sum totals in the two tables in Meitzen, I, pp. 432 and 434.[232]

---

a Report of the Agrarian Commission of the Prussian Second Chamber on the draft Redemption Law of March 2, 1850. Italics by Engels.— *Ed.*

tion established with certainty" is taken into account, thus making no allowance for at least all the settlements reached privately between the parties involved. As Meitzen himself says, the redeemed services entered here, hence also the compensation paid for them, are only a "minimum".

We may thus assume that the sum paid by the peasants to the nobility and the treasury to be released from unlawfully imposed dues amounted to at least 300,000,000 thalers, perhaps a thousand million marks.

A thousand million marks, to get back free of dues only the smallest part of the land stolen over a period of 400 years! The smallest part, since the nobility and the treasury retained by far the largest part in the form of entailed and other manorial estates and domains!

London, November 24, 1885

Frederick Engels

First published in Wilhelm Wolff, *Die schlesische Milliarde*, Hottingen-Zurich, 1886

Printed according to the book

LUDWIG FEUERBACH AND THE END
OF CLASSICAL GERMAN PHILOSOPHY[233]

Written in early 1886

First published in *Die Neue Zeit*, Nos. 4 and 5, 1886 and as a pamphlet in Stuttgart in 1888

Printed according to the pamphlet

LUDWIG FEUERBACH

UND DER AUSGANG DER

KLASSISCHEN DEUTSCHEN PHILOSOPHIE

VON

FRIEDRICH ENGELS

REVIDIRTER SONDER-ABDRUCK AUS DER „NEUEN ZEIT"

MIT ANHANG:

KARL MARX ÜBER FEUERBACH
VOM JAHRE 1845.

———————

STUTTGART
VERLAG VON J. H. W. DIETZ
1888.

Title page of *Ludwig Feuerbach and the End
of Classical German Philosophy*

357

I

The work* before us takes us back to a period which, although in time no more than a good generation behind us, has become as foreign to the present generation in Germany as if it were already a full century old. Yet it was the period of Germany's preparation for the Revolution of 1848; and all that has happened since then in our country has been merely a continuation of 1848, merely the execution of the testament of the revolution.

Just as in France in the eighteenth century, so in Germany in the nineteenth, a philosophical revolution ushered in the political collapse. But how different the two looked! The French were in open combat against all official science, against the Church and often also against the State; their writings were printed across the frontier, in Holland or England, while they themselves were often in jeopardy of imprisonment in the Bastille. On the other hand, the Germans were professors, State-appointed instructors of youth; their writings were recognised textbooks, and the system that rounded off the whole development—the Hegelian system— was even raised, as it were, to the rank of a royal Prussian philosophy of State! Was it possible that a revolution could hide behind these professors, behind their obscure, pedantic phrases, their ponderous, wearisome periods? Were not precisely those people who were then regarded as the representatives of the revolution, the liberals, the bitterest opponents of this befuddling philosophy? But what neither governments nor liberals saw was seen at least by one man as early as 1833, and this man was none other than Heinrich Heine.[234]

* *Ludwig Feuerbach,* by C. N. Starcke, Ph. D., Stuttgart, Ferd. Encke, 1885.

25*

Let us take an example. No philosophical proposition has earned more gratitude from narrow-minded governments and wrath from equally narrow-minded liberals than Hegel's famous statement:

"All that is real is rational; and all that is rational is real." [235]

That was blatantly a sanctification of the existing order of things, the philosophical benediction upon despotism, the police state, arbitrary justice, and censorship. And so it was understood by Frederick William III, and by his subjects. But according to Hegel certainly not everything that exists is also real, without further qualification. For Hegel the attribute of reality belongs only to that which is at the same time necessary:

"In the course of its development reality proves to be necessity."

Any particular governmental measure—Hegel himself cites the example of "a certain tax regulation"[a]—is therefore for him by no means real without qualification. That which is necessary, however, proves in the last resort to be also rational; and, applied to the Prussian state of that time, the Hegelian proposition, therefore, merely means: this state is rational, corresponds to reason, in so far as it [the state] is necessary; and if it nevertheless appears evil to us, but still, in spite of its evilness, continues to exist, then the evilness of the government is justified and explained by the corresponding evilness of the subjects. The Prussians of that day had the government that they deserved.

Now, according to Hegel, reality is, however, in no way an attribute predicable of any given state of affairs, social or political, in all circumstances and at all times. On the contrary. The Roman Republic was real, but so was the Roman Empire which superseded it. In 1789[b] the French monarchy had become so unreal, that is to say, so robbed of all necessity, so irrational, that it had to be destroyed by the Great Revolution, of which Hegel always speaks with the greatest enthusiasm. In this case, therefore, the monarchy was the unreal and the revolution the real. And so, in the course of development, all that was previously real becomes unreal, loses its necessity, its right of existence, its rationality. And in the place of moribund reality comes a new, viable reality—

---

[a] G. W. F. Hegel, *Encyclopädie der philosophischen Wissenschaften im Grundrisse.* Erster Teil. "Die Logik", §§ 147, 142, Zusatz.— *Ed.*

[b] The words "which superseded it. In 1789" were added by Engels in the 1888 edition.— *Ed.*

peacefully if the old has enough common sense to go to its death without a struggle; forcibly if it resists this necessity. Thus the Hegelian proposition turns into its opposite through Hegelian dialectics itself: All that is real in the sphere of human history becomes irrational in the course of.time, is therefore irrational by its very destination, is encumbered with irrationality from the outset; and everything which is rational in the minds of men is destined to become real, however much it may contradict existing apparent reality. In accordance with all the rules of the Hegelian method of thought, the proposition of the rationality of everything which is real is dissolved to become the other proposition: All that exists deserves to perish.[a]

But precisely therein lay the true significance and the revolutionary character of Hegelian philosophy (to which, as the termination of the whole movement since Kant, we must here confine ourselves), that it once and for all dealt the death blow to the finality of all products of human thought and action. Truth, the cognition of which was the business of philosophy, was in the hands of Hegel no longer a collection of ready-made dogmatic statements, which, once discovered, had merely to be learned by heart. Truth now lay in the process of cognition itself, in the long historical development of science, which ascends from lower to ever higher levels of knowledge without ever reaching, by discovering so-called absolute truth, a point at which it can proceed no further, where it has nothing more to do than to sit back and gaze in wonder at the absolute truth to which it had attained. And what holds good for the realm of philosophical cognition holds good also for that of every other kind of cognition and also for practical action. Just as cognition is unable to reach a definitive conclusion in a perfect, ideal condition of humanity, so is history; a perfect society, a perfect "State", are things which can only exist in the imagination. On the contrary, all successive historical states are only transitory stages in the endless course of development of human society from the lower to the higher. Each stage is necessary, and therefore justified for the time and conditions to which it owes its origin. But in the face of new, higher conditions which gradually develop in its own womb, it loses its validity and justification. It must give way to a higher stage, which will also in its turn decay and perish. Just as the bourgeoisie by large-scale industry, competition and the world

---

[a] A paraphrase of Mephistopheles' words from Goethe's *Faust,* Act I, Scene 3 ("Faust's Study").— *Ed.*

market dissolves in practice all stable time-honoured institutions, so this dialectical philosophy dissolves all conceptions of final, absolute truth and of absolute states of humanity corresponding to it. Against it [dialectical philosophy] nothing is final, absolute, sacred. It reveals the transitory character of everything and in everything; nothing can endure against it except the uninterrupted process of becoming and passing away, of ascending without end from the lower to the higher. And dialectical philosophy itself is nothing more than the mere reflection of this process in the thinking brain. It has, however, also a conservative side: it recognises that definite stages of cognition and society are justified for their time and circumstances; but only so far. The conservatism of this outlook is relative; its revolutionary character is absolute—the only absolute dialectical philosophy admits.

It is not necessary, here, to go into the question of whether this outlook is thoroughly in accord with the present state of natural science, which predicts a possible end for the earth itself and for its habitability a fairly certain one; which therefore recognises that for the history of mankind, too, there is not only an ascending but also a descending branch. At any rate we are still a considerable distance from the turning-point at which the historical course of society becomes one of descent, and we cannot expect Hegelian philosophy to be concerned with a subject which, in its time, natural science had not yet placed on the agenda at all.

But what really must be said here is this: that in Hegel the views developed above are not so sharply defined. They are a necessary conclusion from his method, but one which he himself never drew with such explicitness. And this, indeed, for the simple reason that he was compelled to make a system and, in accordance with traditional requirements, a system of philosophy must conclude with some sort of absolute truth. Therefore, however much Hegel, especially in his *Logik,* emphasises that this eternal truth is nothing but the logical, or, the historical, process itself, he nevertheless finds himself compelled to supply this process with an end, just because he has to bring his system to a termination at some point or other. In his *Logik* he can make this end a beginning again, since here the point of conclusion, the absolute idea—which is only absolute in so far as he has absolutely nothing to say about it—"alienates", that is, transforms itself into nature and comes to itself again later in the mind, that is, in thought and in history. But at the end of the whole philosophy a similar return to the beginning is possible only in one way. Namely, by conceiving the end of history as follows: mankind arrives at the cognition of this selfsame absolute idea, and declares that this cognition of the absolute idea is attained in Hegelian philosophy.[a] In this way, however, the whole dogmatic content of the Hegelian system is declared to be absolute truth, in contradiction to his dialectical method, which dissolves all that is dogmatic. Thus the revolutionary side is smothered beneath the overgrowth of the conservative side. And what applies to philosophical cognition applies also to historical practice. Having, in the person of Hegel, reached the point of working out the absolute idea, mankind must also in practice have advanced so far that it can carry out this absolute idea in reality. Hence the practical political demands of the absolute idea on contemporaries should not be pitched too high. And so we find at the conclusion of the *Rechtsphilosophie*[b] that the absolute idea is to be implemented in that monarchy based on social estates which Frederick William III so persistently promised his subjects to no avail, that is, in a limited and moderate, indirect rule of the possessing classes suited to the petty-bourgeois German conditions of that time; and, moreover, the necessity of the nobility is demonstrated to us in a speculative fashion.

The inner necessities of the system are, therefore, of themselves sufficient to explain why a thoroughly revolutionary method of thinking produced an extremely tame political conclusion. As a matter of fact, the specific form of this conclusion derives from the fact that Hegel was a German, and like his contemporary Goethe, had a bit of the philistine's tail dangling behind. Each of them was an Olympian Zeus in his own sphere, yet neither of them ever quite freed himself from German philistinism.

But all this did not prevent the Hegelian system from covering an incomparably greater domain than any earlier system, nor from developing in this domain a wealth of thought which is astounding even today. The phenomenology of the mind (which one may call a parallel to the embryology and palaeontology of the mind, a development of individual consciousness through its different stages, set in the form of an abbreviated reproduction of the stages through which the consciousness of man has passed in the course of history), logic, philosophy of nature, philosophy of the mind, and the latter in turn elaborated in its separate, historical subdivisions: philosophy of history, of law, of religion, history of

---

philosophy, aesthetics, etc.—in all these different historical fields Hegel worked to discover and demonstrate the pervading thread of development. And as he was not only a creative genius but also a man of encyclopaedic erudition, he played an epoch-making role in every sphere. It is self-evident that owing to the needs of the "system" he very often had to resort to those forced constructions about which his pygmean opponents make such a terrible fuss even today. But these constructions are only the frame and scaffolding of his work. If one does not loiter here needlessly, but presses on farther into the huge edifice, one finds innumerable treasures which still today retain their full value. With all philosophers it is precisely the "system" which is perishable; and for the simple reason that it springs from an imperishable need of the human mind—the need to overcome all contradictions. But if all contradictions are once for all disposed of, we shall have arrived at so-called absolute truth—world history will be at an end. And yet it has to continue, although there is nothing left for it to do—hence, a new, insoluble contradiction. Once we have realised—and in the long run no one has helped us to realise it more than Hegel himself—that the task of philosophy thus stated means nothing but the task that a single philosopher should accomplish that which can only be accomplished by the entire human race in its ongoing development—as soon as we realise that, it is the end of all philosophy in the hitherto accepted sense of the word. One leaves alone "absolute truth", which is unattainable along this path or by any single individual; instead, one pursues attainable relative truths along the path of the positive sciences, and the summation of their results by means of dialectical thinking. With Hegel philosophy comes to an end altogether: on the one hand, because in his system he sums up its whole development in the most splendid fashion; and on the other hand, because, even if unconsciously,[a] he shows us the way out of the labyrinth of systems to real positive cognition of the world.

One can imagine what a tremendous effect this Hegelian system must have produced in the philosophy-tinged atmosphere of Germany. It was a triumphal procession which lasted for decades and which by no means came to a standstill on the death of Hegel. On the contrary, it was precisely from 1830 to 1840 that "Hegelianism" reigned most exclusively, and to a greater or lesser extent infected even its opponents. It was precisely in this period

---

[a] The words "even if unconsciously" were added by Engels in the 1888 edition.— Ed.

that Hegelian views, consciously or unconsciously, most extensively penetrated the most diversified sciences and leavened even popular literature and the daily press, from which the average "educated consciousness" derives its mental pabulum. But this victory along the whole front was only the prelude to an internal struggle.

As we have seen, Hegel's doctrine, taken as a whole, left plenty of room to accommodate the most diverse practical party views. And in the theoretical Germany of that time, two things were practical above all; religion and politics. Whoever placed the emphasis on the Hegelian *system* could be fairly conservative in both spheres; whoever regarded the dialectical *method* as the main thing could belong to the most extreme opposition, both in religion and politics. Hegel himself, despite the fairly frequent outbursts of revolutionary wrath in his works, seemed on the whole to be more inclined to the conservative side. Indeed, his system had cost him much more "hard mental plugging" than his method. Towards the end of the thirties, the cleavage in the school became more and more apparent. The Left wing, the so-called Young Hegelians, in their fight with the pietist orthodox and the feudal reactionaries, abandoned bit by bit that philosophical-genteel reserve in regard to the burning questions of the day which up to that time had secured state toleration and even protection for their teachings. And when, in 1840, orthodox sanctimony and absolutist feudal reaction ascended the throne with Frederick William IV, open partisanship became unavoidable. The fight was still carried on with philosophical weapons, but no longer for abstract philosophical aids. It turned directly on the destruction of traditional religion and the existing state. And while in the *Deutsche Jahrbücher* the practical ends were still predominantly put forward in philosophical disguise, in the *Rheinische Zeitung* of 1842 the Young Hegelian school revealed itself directly as the philosophy of the aspiring radical bourgeoisie and used the meagre cloak of philosophy only to deceive the censors.

At that time, however, politics was a very thorny field, and hence the main fight came to be directed against religion; this fight, particularly since 1840, was indirectly also political. Strauss' *Leben Jesu,* published in 1835, had provided the initial impetus. The theory therein developed of the formation of the gospel myths was combated later by Bruno Bauer with proof that a whole series of evangelical stories had been invented by the authors themselves. The controversy between these two was carried on in the philosophical disguise of a battle between "self-consciousness" and "substance". The question whether the miracle stories of the gospels came into being through unconscious traditional myth-creation within the bosom of the community or whether they were invented by the evangelists themselves was blown up into the question whether, in world history, "substance" or "self-consciousness" was the decisive operative force. Finally came Stirner, the prophet of contemporary anarchism—Bakunin has taken a great deal from him—and surpassed the sovereign "self-consciousness" by his sovereign "ego".[a]

We shall not go further into this aspect of the decomposition process of the Hegelian school. More important for us is the following: the bulk of the most determined Young Hegelians were, by the practical necessities of their fight against positive religion,[236] driven back to Anglo-French materialism. This brought them into conflict with their school system. While materialism conceives nature as the sole reality, nature in the Hegelian system represents merely the "alienation" of the absolute idea, so to say, a degradation of the idea. At all events, thinking and its thought-product, the idea, is here the primary, nature the derivative, which only exists at all by the condescension of the idea. And in this contradiction they floundered as well or as ill as they could.

Then came Feuerbach's *Wesen des Christenthums*. With *one* blow it pulverised the contradiction, by plainly placing materialism on the throne again. Nature exists independently of all philosophy. It is the foundation upon which we human beings, ourselves products of nature, have grown up. Nothing exists outside nature and man, and the higher beings our religious fantasies have created are only the fantastic reflection of our own essence. The spell was broken; the "system" was exploded and cast aside, and the contradiction, shown to exist only in our imagination, was dissolved.—One must have experienced the liberating effect of this book for oneself to get an idea of it. Enthusiasm was universal: we were all Feuerbachians for a moment. How enthusiastically Marx greeted the new conception and how much—in spite of all critical reservations—he was influenced by it,[b] one may read in *The Holy Family*.

Even the shortcomings of the book contributed to its immediate effect. Its literary, sometimes even bombastic, style secured for it a large public and was at any rate refreshing after long years of

---

[a] M. Stirner, *Der Einzige und sein Eigenthum.*—*Ed.*

[b] The words "and how much he was influenced by it" were added by Engels in the 1888 edition.— *Ed.*

abstract and abstruse Hegelianising. The same is true of its extravagant deification of love, which, coming after the now intolerable sovereign rule of "pure reason", had its excuse, if not justification. But what we must not forget is that it was precisely these two weaknesses of Feuerbach that "true socialism",[237] which had been spreading like a plague in "educated" Germany since 1844, took as its starting-point, putting literary phrases in the place of scientific knowledge, the liberation of mankind by means of "love" in place of the emancipation of the proletariat through the economic transformation of production—in short, losing itself in the nauseous fine writing and ecstasies of love typified by Herr Karl Grün.

Another thing we must not forget is this: the Hegelian school had disintegrated, but Hegelian philosophy had not been over-come through criticism; Strauss and Bauer each took one of its sides and set it polemically against the other. Feuerbach broke through the system and simply discarded it. But a philosophy is not disposed of by the mere assertion that it is false. And so mighty a work as Hegelian philosophy, which had exercised so enormous an influence on the intellectual development of the nation, could not be disposed of by simply being ignored. It had to be "transcended" in its own sense, that is, in the sense that while its form had to be annihilated through criticism, the new content which had been won through it had to be saved. How this was brought about we shall see below.

But in the meantime the Revolution of 1848 thrust the whole of philosophy aside as unceremoniously as Feuerbach had thrust aside Hegel. And in the process Feuerbach himself was also pushed into the background.

II

The great basic question of all, especially of latter-day, philosophy, is that concerning the relation of thinking and being. From very early times when men, still completely ignorant of the structure of their own bodies, and prompted by dream apparitions * came to believe that their thinking and sensation were not activities of their

* Among savages and lower barbarians the idea is still universal that the human forms which appear in dreams are souls which have temporarily left their bodies; the real man is, therefore, held responsible for acts committed by his dream apparition against the dreamer. Thus Im Thurn found this belief current, for example, among the Indians of Guiana in 1884.

bodies, but of a distinct soul which inhabits the body and leaves it upon death—from this time men have been driven to reflect about the relation between this soul and the outside world. If upon death it left the body and lived on, there was no occasion to ascribe another distinct death to it. Thus arose the idea of its immortality, which at that stage of development appeared not at all as a consolation but as a fate which it was pointless to fight, and often enough, as among the Greeks, a positive misfortune. Not religious desire for consolation, but the quandary arising from the universal ignorance of what to do with this soul, once its existence had been accepted, after the death of the body, led everywhere to the tedious fancy of personal immortality. In quite a similar manner the first gods arose through the personification of natural forces. And as religions continued to take shape, these gods assumed more and more an extramundane form, until finally by a process of abstraction, I might almost say of distillation, occurring naturally in the course of man's intellectual development, out of the many more or less limited and mutually limiting gods there arose in the minds of men the idea of the one exclusive God of the monotheistic religions.

Thus the question of the relation of thinking to being, of the mind to nature—the paramount question of the whole of philosophy—has, no less than all religion, its roots in the narrow-minded and ignorant notions of savagery. But it was possible to put forward this question for the first time in full clarity to give it its full significance, only after humanity in Europe had awakened from the long hibernation of the Christian Middle Ages. The question of the position of thinking in relation to being, a question which, by the way, had played a great part also in the scholasticism of the Middle Ages, the question: which is primary, mind or nature—that question, in relation to the Church, was sharpened into this: Did God create the world or has the world existed for all time?

Answers to this question split the philosophers into two great camps. Those who asserted the primacy of the mind over nature and, therefore, in the last instance, assumed world creation in some form or other—and among the philosophers, e.g., Hegel, this creation often becomes still more intricate and impossible than in Christianity—comprised the camp of idealism. The others, who regarded nature as primary, belong to the various schools of materialism.

These two expressions, idealism and materialism, originally signify nothing else but this; and here they are not used in any other sense either. What confusion arises when some other meaning is put into them will be seen below.

But the question of the relation of thinking and being has yet another side: in what relation do our thoughts about the world surrounding us stand to this world itself? Is our thinking capable of cognition of the real world? Are we able in our ideas and notions of the real world to produce a correct reflection of reality? In the language of philosophy this question is called the question of the identity of thinking and being, and the overwhelming majority of philosophers answer it in the affirmative. In Hegel, for example, its affirmation is self-evident: for what we cognise in the real world is precisely its thought content—that which makes the world a gradual realisation of the absolute idea, which absolute idea has existed somewhere from eternity, independent of the world and before the world. But it is manifest without further proof that thinking can cognise a content which is from the outset a thought content. It is equally manifest that what is to be proved here is already tacitly contained in the premiss. But that in no way prevents Hegel from drawing the further conclusion from his proof of the identity of thinking and being that his philosophy, because it is correct for his thinking, is therefore the only correct one, and that the identity of thinking and being must prove its validity by mankind immediately translating his philosophy from theory into practice and transforming the whole world according to Hegelian principles. This is an illusion which he shares with well-nigh all philosophers.

In addition there is yet another set of philosophers—those who dispute the possibility of any cognition, or at least of an exhaustive cognition, of the world. Among them, of the more recent ones, we find Hume and Kant, and they have played a very important role in philosophical development. What is decisive in the refutation of this view has already been said by Hegel, as far as this was possible from an idealist standpoint. The materialist additions made by Feuerbach are more quick-witted than profound. The most telling refutation of this as of all other philosophical quirks is practice, namely, experimentation and industry. If we are able to prove the correctness of our conception of a natural phenomenon by bringing it about ourselves, producing it out of its conditions and making it serve our own purposes into the bargain, then the ungraspable Kantian "thing-in-itself" is finished. The chemical substances produced in the bodies of plants and animals remained just such "things-in-themselves" until organic chemistry began to produce them one after another, whereupon the "thing-in-itself" became a thing for us, as, for instance, alizarin, the colouring matter of the madder, which we no longer trouble to grow in the madder roots in the field, but produce much more cheaply and simply from coal tar. For three hundred years the Copernican solar system was a hypothesis with a hundred, a thousand or ten thousand chances to one in its favour, but still always a hypothesis. But when Leverrier, by means of the data provided by this system, not only deduced that an unknown planet must exist, but also calculated the position in the heavens which this planet must necessarily occupy, and when Galle really found this planet,[238] the Copernican system was proved. If, nevertheless, the Neo-Kantians are attempting to resurrect the Kantian conception in Germany and the agnostics that of Hume in England (where it never became extinct), this is, in view of their theoretical and practical refutation accomplished long ago, scientifically a regression and practically merely a shamefaced way of surreptitiously accepting materialism, while denying it before the world.

But during this long period from Descartes to Hegel and from Hobbes to Feuerbach, the philosophers were by no means impelled, as they thought they were, solely by the force of pure reason. On the contrary, what really pushed them forward most was the powerful and ever more rapidly onrushing progress of natural science and industry.[a] Among the materialists this was plain on the surface, but the idealist systems also filled themselves more and more with a materialist content and attempted pantheistically to reconcile the antithesis between mind and matter. Thus, ultimately, the Hegelian system represents merely a materialism idealistically turned upside down in method and content.

It is, therefore, comprehensible that Starcke in his characterisation of Feuerbach first of all investigates the latter's position in regard to this fundamental question of the relation of thinking and being. After a short introduction, in which the views of the preceding philosophers, particularly since Kant, are described in unnecessarily ponderous philosophical language, and in which Hegel, by an all too formalistic adherence to certain passages of his works, gets far less than his due, there follows a detailed description of the course of development of Feuerbach's "metaphysics" itself, in the manner it arises from the sequence of this philosopher's relevant works. This description is industriously and lucidly elaborated; only, like the whole book, it is loaded with

---

[a] The words "and industry" were added by Engels in the 1888 edition.— Ed.

a ballast of philosophical phraseology by no means everywhere unavoidable, which is the more disturbing in its effect the less the author keeps to the manner of expression of one and the same school, or even of Feuerbach himself, and the more he interjects expressions of the most various tendencies, especially of those now rampant and calling themselves philosophical.

Feuerbach's evolution is that of a Hegelian—a never quite orthodox Hegelian, it is true—into a materialist; an evolution which at a certain stage gives rise to a complete break with the idealist system of his predecessor. With irresistible force Feuerbach is finally driven to the realisation that the Hegelian premundane existence of the "absolute idea", the "pre-existence of the logical categories" before the world existed, is nothing more than a fantastic remnant of the belief in the existence of an extramundane creator; that the material sensuously perceptible world to which we ourselves belong is the only reality; and that our consciousness and thinking, however suprasensuous they may seem, are the product of a material, bodily organ, the brain. Matter is not a product of the mind, but the mind itself is merely the highest product of matter. This is, of course, pure materialism. But, having got so far, Feuerbach stops short. He cannot overcome the habitual philosophical prejudice, prejudice not against the thing but against the name materialism. He says:

"To me materialism is the foundation of the edifice of human essence and knowledge; but to me it is not what it is to the physiologist, to the natural scientist in the narrower sense, for example, to Moleschott, and necessarily is from their standpoint and profession, namely, the edifice itself. Backwards I fully agree with the materialists; but not forwards."[239]

Here Feuerbach lumps together the materialism that is a general world outlook resting upon a definite conception of the relation between matter and mind, and the special form in which this world outlook was expressed at a definite historical stage, namely, in the eighteenth century.[a] More than that, he lumps it together with the shallow, vulgarised form in which the materialism of the eighteenth century continues to exist today in the heads of naturalists and doctors, the form in which it was preached on their tours in the fifties by Büchner, Vogt and Moleschott. But just as idealism underwent a series of stages of development, so also did materialism. With each epoch-making discovery even in the sphere of natural science it has to change its form; and history too having

---

[a] The words "namely, in the eighteenth century" were added by Engels in the 1888 edition.— *Ed.*

been subjected to materialistic treatment, a new avenue of development has opened here as well.

The materialism of the last century was predominantly mechanical, because at that time, of all the natural sciences, only mechanics, and indeed only the mechanics of solid bodies—celestial and terrestrial—in short, the mechanics of gravity, had come to any certain conclusion. Chemistry at that time existed only in its infantile, phlogistic form.[240] Biology still lay in swaddling clothes; plant and animal organisms had been only crudely examined and were explained as the result of purely mechanical causes. What the animal was to Descartes, man was to the materialists of the eighteenth century—a machine. This application exclusively of the standards of mechanics to processes of a chemical and organic nature—in which processes the laws of mechanics are, indeed, also valid, but are pushed into the background by other, higher laws—constitutes one specific, but at that time inevitable, limitation of classical French materialism.

The other specific limitation of this materialism lay in its inability to comprehend the world as a process, as matter undergoing uninterrupted historical development. This accorded with the state of the natural science of that time, and with the metaphysical, that is, anti-dialectical manner of philosophising connected with it. Nature, so much was known, was in eternal motion. But according to the ideas of that time, this motion turned just as eternally in a circle and therefore never moved from the spot; it produced the same results over and over again. This conception was at that time inevitable. The Kantian theory of the origin of the solar system had only been put forward and was still regarded merely as an oddity. The history of the evolution of the earth, geology, was still totally unknown, and the idea that the animate natural beings of today are the result of a long sequence of evolution from the simple to the complex could not at that time scientifically be put forward at all. The unhistorical view of nature was therefore inevitable.[a] We have the less reason to reproach the philosophers of the eighteenth century on this account since the same thing is found in Hegel. According to him, nature, as a mere "alienation" of the idea, is incapable of evolution in time—capable only of extending its manifoldness in space, so that it displays simultaneously and side by side all the stages of evolution comprised in it, and is condemned to an eternal repetition of the

---

[a] The text below, up to the end of the paragraph, was added by Engels in the 1888 edition.— Ed.

same processes. This absurdity of evolution in space, but outside of time—the fundamental condition of all evolution—Hegel imposes upon nature just at the very time when geology, embryology, the physiology of plants and animals, and organic chemistry were taking shape, and when everywhere on the basis of these new sciences brilliant presentiments of the subsequent theory of evolution were appearing (for instance, Goethe and Lamarck). But the system demanded it; hence the method, for the sake of the system, had to become untrue to itself.

This same unhistorical conception prevailed also in the domain of history. Here the struggle against the remnants of the Middle Ages captured the limelight. The Middle Ages were regarded as a mere interruption of history by a thousand years of universal barbarism. The great progress made in the Middle Ages—the extension of the domain of European civilisation, the viable great nations taking form there next to each other, and finally the enormous technical advances of the fourteenth and fifteenth centuries—all this was not seen. Thus a rational insight into the great historical coherence was made impossible, and history served at best as a collection of examples and illustrations for the use of philosophers.

The vulgarising pedlars, who dabbled in materialism in the Germany of the fifties in no way overcame this limitation of their teachers. All the advances of natural science which had been made in the meantime served them only as fresh evidence against the existence of a world creator, and, indeed, they did not in the least make it their business to develop the theory any further. Though idealism was stumped and[a] was dealt a death-blow by the Revolution of 1848, it had the satisfaction of seeing that materialism had for the moment sunk to even greater depths. Feuerbach was unquestionably right when he refused to take responsibility for this materialism; only he should not have confounded the doctrines of these itinerant preachers with materialism in general.

Here, however, there are two things to be pointed out. First, even during Feuerbach's lifetime, natural science was still in that process of intense fermentation which has reached a clarifying, relative conclusion only during the last fifteen years. New data for cognition were acquired to a hitherto unheard-of extent, but the establishment of coherence, and thereby of order, in this chaos of

---

[a] The words "was stumped and" were added by Engels in the 1888 edition.— Ed.

discoveries following closely upon each other's heels, has only quite recently become possible. It is true that Feuerbach lived to see all three of the decisive discoveries—that of the cell, the transformation of energy and the theory of evolution named after Darwin. But how was the lonely philosopher in the country to sufficiently follow scientific developments in order to appreciate at their full value discoveries which natural scientists themselves at that time either still contested or did not know how to adequately exploit? The blame for this falls solely upon the wretched conditions in Germany, in consequence of which brooding eclectic flea-crackers had taken possession of the chairs of philosophy, while Feuerbach, who towered above them all, had to rusticate and go to seed in a little village. It is therefore not Feuerbach's fault that the historical conception of nature, which has now become possible and has removed all the one-sidedness of French materialism, remained inaccessible to him.

Secondly, Feuerbach is quite correct in asserting that exclusively natural-scientific materialism is indeed

"the foundation of the edifice of human knowledge, but not the edifice itself".

For we live not only in nature but also in human society, and this also has its evolution and its science no less than nature. It was therefore a question of bringing the science of society, that is, the sum total of the so-called historical and philosophical sciences, into harmony with the materialist foundation, and of reconstructing it thereupon. But it did not fall to Feuerbach's lot to do this. In spite of the "foundation", he remained bound here by the traditional idealist fetters, a fact which he recognises in these words:

"Backwards I agree with the materialists, but not forwards."

But it was Feuerbach himself who did not go "forwards" here, in the social domain, who did not get beyond his standpoint of 1840 or 1844. And this was again chiefly due to his reclusion, which compelled him—of all philosophers the most inclined to social intercourse—to produce thoughts out of his solitary head instead of in amicable and hostile encounters with other men of his calibre. Below we shall see in detail how much he remained an idealist in this sphere.

It need only be added here that Starcke looks for Feuerbach's idealism in the wrong place.

"Feuerbach is an idealist; he believes in the progress of mankind" (p. 19). "The foundation, the substructure of the whole, remains nevertheless idealism. Realism for us is nothing more than a protection against aberrations, while we follow our ideal trends. Are not compassion, love and enthusiasm for truth and justice ideal forces?" (p. VIII).

In the first place, idealism here means nothing but the pursuit of ideal goals. But these necessarily have to do with Kantian idealism at best, and its "categorical imperative"; however, Kant himself called his philosophy "transcendental idealism"; by no means because it dealt also with ethical ideals, but for quite other reasons, as Starcke will remember. The superstition that philosophical idealism revolves around a belief in ethical, that is, social, ideals, arose outside philosophy, among the German philistines, who learned by heart from Schiller's poems the few morsels of philosophical culture they needed. No one has criticised more severely the impotent Kantian "categorical imperative"— impotent because it demands the impossible, and therefore never attains to any reality—no one has more cruelly derided the philistine passion for unrealisable ideals purveyed by Schiller than Hegel of all people, the perfect idealist (see, for example, his *Phänomenologie*).

In the second place, we simply cannot evade the fact that everything which motivates men must pass through their brains— even eating and drinking, which begins as a consequence of the sensation of hunger or thirst transmitted through the brain, and ends as a result of the sensation of satisfaction likewise transmitted through the brain. The influences of the external world upon man express themselves in his brain, are reflected therein as feelings, thoughts, impulses, volitions—in short, as "ideal tendencies", and in this form become "ideal powers". If, then, a man is to be deemed an idealist because he follows "ideal tendencies" and admits that "ideal powers" have an influence over him, then every person who is at all normally developed is a born idealist and how, in that case, can there be any materialists at all?

In the third place, the conviction that humanity, at least at the present moment, is moving on the whole in a progressive direction has absolutely nothing to do with the antagonism between materialism and idealism. The French materialists no less than the deists [241] Voltaire and Rousseau held this conviction to an almost fanatical degree, and often enough made the greatest personal sacrifices to it. If ever anybody dedicated his whole life to "enthusiasm for truth and justice"—using this phrase in the positive sense—it was Diderot, for instance. If, therefore, Starcke declares all this to be idealism, this merely proves that the word materialism, and the whole antagonism between the two trends, has lost all meaning for him here.

The fact is that Starcke, although perhaps unconsciously, makes an unpardonable concession here to the traditional philistine prejudice against the word materialism resulting from its long-continued defamation by the priests. By the word materialism the philistine understands gluttony, drunkenness, lust of the eye, lust of the flesh, arrogance, cupidity, avarice, covetousness, profiteering and stock-exchange swindling—in short, all the filthy vices in which he himself indulges in private. By the word idealism he understands the belief in virtue, universal philanthropy and altogether a "better world", of which he boasts to others but in which he himself believes at best only so long as he is having the blues or going through the bankruptcy consequent upon his customary "materialist" excesses. It is then that he sings his favourite song, What is man?—Half beast half angel.

For the rest, Starcke takes great pains to defend Feuerbach against the attacks and doctrines of the vociferous assistant professors who today go by the name of philosophers in Germany. For people who are interested in this afterbirth of classical German philosophy this is, of course, a matter of importance, for Starcke himself it may have appeared necessary. We will spare the reader this.

III

The real idealism of Feuerbach becomes evident as soon as we come to his philosophy of religion and ethics. He by no means wishes to abolish religion; he wants to perfect it. Philosophy itself must be absorbed in religion.

"The periods of humanity are distinguished only by religious changes. A historical movement is fundamental only when it is rooted in the hearts of men. The heart is not a form of religion, so that the latter should exist also in the heart; the heart is the essence of religion." (Quoted by Starcke, p. 168).[a]

According to Feuerbach, religion is the relation between human beings based on affection, on the heart, which relation until now has sought its truth in a fantastic mirror image of reality—in the mediation of one or many gods, the fantastic mirror images of human qualities—but now finds it directly and without any mediation in the love between "I" and "Thou". Thus, in Feuerbach sex love ultimately becomes one of the highest forms, if not the highest form, of the practice of his new religion.

---

[a] L. Feuerbach, "Grundsätze der Philosophie. Notwendigkeit einer Veränderung".— Ed.

Now relations between human beings, based on affection, and especially between the two sexes, have existed as long as mankind. Sex love in particular has undergone a development and won a place during the last eight hundred years which has made it a compulsory pivot of all poetry during this period. The existing positive religions[242] have limited themselves to the higher consecration of state-regulated sex love, that is, of the marriage laws, and they could all disappear tomorrow without changing in the slightest the practice of love and friendship. Thus the Christian religion in France, as a matter of fact, so completely disappeared in the years 1793-98 that even Napoleon could not re-introduce it without opposition and difficulty; and this without any need for a substitute, in Feuerbach's sense, making itself felt in the interval.

Feuerbach's idealism consists here in this: he does not simply accept people's relations based on reciprocal inclination, such as sex love, friendship, compassion, self-sacrifice, etc., as what they are in themselves—without relating them back to a particular religion which to him, too, belongs to the past; but instead he asserts that they will attain their full value only when consecrated by the name of religion. The chief thing for him is not that these purely human relations exist, but that they shall be conceived of as the new, true religion. They are to have full value only after they have been marked with a religious stamp. Religion is derived from *religare* and meant originally a bond. Therefore, every bond between two people is a religion. Such etymological tricks are the last resort of idealist philosophy. Not what the word means according to the historical development of its actual use, but what it ought to mean according to its derivation, is what counts. And so sex love and sex bonds are apotheosised to a "religion", merely in order that the word religion, which is so dear to idealist memories, may not disappear from the language. The Parisian reformers of the Louis Blanc trend used to speak in precisely the same way in the forties. They likewise were able to conceive of a man without religion only as a monster, and used to say to us: "*Donc, l'athéisme c'est votre religion!*"[a] If Feuerbach wishes to establish a true religion upon the basis of an essentially materialist conception of nature, that is the same as regarding modern chemistry as true alchemy. If religion can exist without its god, then alchemy can exist without its philosopher's stone. By the way, there exists a very close connection between alchemy and religion. The philosopher's stone has many godlike properties and the

a "Well, then atheism is your religion!"—*Ed.*

Egyptian-Greek alchemists of the first two centuries of our era had a hand in the development of Christian doctrines, as the facts given in Kopp and Berthelot have proved.[a]

Decidedly false is Feuerbach's assertion that

"the periods of humanity are distinguished only by religious changes".

Great historical turning-points have been *accompanied* by religious changes only so far as the three world religions which have existed up to the present, Buddhism, Christianity and Islam, are concerned.[b] The old tribal and national religions, which arose spontaneously, did not proselytise and[c] lost all their power of resistance as soon as the independence of the tribe or people was lost. For the Germans it was sufficient simply to have contact with the decaying Roman world empire and with its just adopted Christian world religion that accorded with its economic, political and ideological conditions. Only with these world religions, which arose more or less artificially, particularly Christianity and Islam, do we find that more general historical movements acquire a religious imprint. Even in regard to Christianity[d] the religious stamp in revolutions of really universal significance is restricted to the first stages of the bourgeoisie's struggle for emancipation— from the thirteenth to the seventeenth century—and is to be accounted for not, as Feuerbach thinks, by the hearts of men and their religious needs, but by the entire previous history of the Middle Ages, which knew no other form of ideology than actual religion and theology. But when the bourgeoisie of the eighteenth century had strengthened enough to possess an ideology of its own, suited to its own class standpoint, it made its great and conclusive revolution, the French one, appealing exclusively to juristic and[e] political ideas, and troubled itself with religion only in so far as it stood in its way. But it never occurred to it to put a new religion in place of the old one. Everyone knows how Robespierre failed in that.[f][243]

---

[a] See H. Kopp, *Die Alchemie in älterer und neuerer Zeit* and M. Berthelot, *Les origines de l'alchimie.—Ed.*

[b] In the 1886 edition this sentence reads: "This holds good, even relatively, only so far as the three world religions which have existed up to the present, Buddhism, Christianity and Islam, are concerned—and only between them."—*Ed.*

[c] The words "did not proselytise and" were added by Engels in the 1888 edition.—*Ed.*

[d] The words "in regard to Christianity" were added by Engels in the 1888 edition.—*Ed.*

[e] The words "juristic and" were added by Engels in the 1888 edition.—*Ed.*

[f] This sentence was added by Engels in the 1888 edition.—Ed.

The possibility of purely human sentiments in our intercourse with other human beings has nowadays been sufficiently curtailed by the society in which we must live, which is based upon class antagonism and class rule. We have no reason to curtail it still more by exalting these sentiments to a religion. And similarly the understanding of the great historical class struggles has already been sufficiently obscured by current historiography, particularly in Germany, so that there is also no need for us to make such an understanding totally impossible by transforming the history of these struggles into a mere appendix of ecclesiastical history. Already here it becomes evident how far today we have moved beyond Feuerbach. His "finest passages" in glorification of this new religion of love are totally unreadable today.

The only religion which Feuerbach examines seriously is Christianity, the world religion of the Occident, based upon monotheism. He proves that the Christian God is only a fantastic reflection, a mirror image, of man. Now, this God is, however, himself the product of a protracted process of abstraction, the concentrated quintessence of the numerous earlier tribal and national gods. And accordingly man, whose image this God is, is also not a real man, but likewise the quintessence of the numerous real men, man in the abstract, therefore himself again a mental image. The same Feuerbach, who on every page preaches sensuousness, immersion in the concrete, in actuality, becomes thoroughly abstract as soon as he begins to talk of any other than mere sexual intercourse between human beings.

This intercourse presents him with only one aspect: morality. And here we are again struck by Feuerbach's astonishing poverty when compared with Hegel. The latter's ethics or doctrine of social ethics, is the philosophy of law and embraces: 1) abstract law; 2) morality; 3) social ethics under which again are comprised: the family, civil society and the state. Here the content is as realistic as the form is idealistic. Besides morality the whole sphere of law, economy, politics is included here. With Feuerbach it is just the reverse. In form he is realistic since he takes man as his point of departure; but there is absolutely no mention of the world in which this man lives; hence, this man remains always the same abstract man who occupied the field in the philosophy of religion. For this man is not born of woman; he emerged, as if from a chrysalis, from the god of the monotheistic religions. He therefore does not live in a real world historically come into being and historically determined. True, he has contact with other men; however, each one of them is just as much an abstraction as he himself. In the philosophy of religion we still had men and women at least, but in ethics even this last distinction disappears. Feuerbach, however, at long intervals makes such statements as:

"Man thinks differently in a palace and in a hut." a "If because of hunger, of misery, you have no stuff in your body, you likewise have no stuff for morality in your head, in your mind or heart." b "Politics must become our religion," c etc.

But Feuerbach knows absolutely nothing what to do with these maxims. They remain mere phrases, and even Starcke has to admit that for Feuerbach politics constituted an impassable frontier and the

"science of society, sociology, was *terra incognita* to him." d

He appears just as shallow, in comparison with Hegel, in his treatment of the antithesis of good and evil.

"One believes one is saying something great," Hegel remarks, "if one says that 'man is naturally good'. But one forgets that one says something far greater when one says 'man is naturally evil'." e

In Hegel evil is the form in which the motive force of historical development presents itself. Herein lies the twofold meaning that, on the one hand, each new advance necessarily appears as a heinous deed against what is sacred, as a rebellion against conditions, though old and moribund, yet sanctified by custom; and that, on the other hand, it is precisely the wicked passions of man—greed and lust for power—which, since the emergence of class antagonisms, have become levers of historical development— of which the history of feudalism and of the bourgeoisie, for example, constitutes singular continual proof. f But it does not occur to Feuerbach to investigate the historical role of moral evil. To him history is altogether an uncomfortable, uncanny domain. Even his dictum:

---

a L. Feuerbach, "Wider den Dualismus von Leib und Seele, Fleisch und Geist" in *Ludwig Feuerbach's sämmtliche Werke*, Vol. II, p. 363.— *Ed.*

b L. Feuerbach, "Noth meistert alle Gesetze und hebt sie auf" in *Ludwig Feuerbach in seinem Briefwechsel und Nachlass*, Vol. II, pp. 285-86. Quoted in C. N. Starcke, *Ludwig Feuerbach*, p. 254.— *Ed.*

c L. Feuerbach, "Grundsätze der Philosophie" in *Ludwig Feuerbach in seinem Briefwechsel und Nachlass*, Vol. I, p. 409. Quoted in C. N. Starcke, *Ludwig Feuerbach*, p. 280.— *Ed.*

d C. N. Starcke, *Ludwig Feuerbach*, p. 280.— *Ed.*

e A summary of Hegel's ideas expressed mainly in his *Grundlinien der Philosophie des Rechts.* §§ 18 and 139 and *Vorlesungen über die Philosophie der Religion*, Part 3, II, 3.— *Ed.*

f The 1886 edition has "of which the history of feudalism and of the bourgeoisie provide the classical example".— *Ed.*

"Man as he sprang originally from nature was only a mere creature of nature, not man. Man is a product of man, of culture, of history"[a]—

with him even this dictum remains absolutely sterile. What Feuerbach has to tell us about morality can, therefore, only be extremely meagre. The urge for bliss is innate in man, and must therefore form the basis of all morality. But the urge for bliss is subject to a double correction. First, by the natural consequences of our actions: after the intoxication comes the "hangover", and habitual excess is followed by illness. Second, by their social consequences: if we do not respect the same urge of other people for bliss they will defend themselves, and so interfere with our own urge for bliss. Consequently, in order to satisfy our urge, we must be in a position to correctly appreciate the results of our conduct and must likewise allow others an equal right to seek bliss. Rational self-restraint with regard to ourselves, and love—again and again love!—in our contact with others—these are the basic rules of Feuerbach's morality; from them all others are derived. And neither the wisest utterances of Feuerbach nor the strongest eulogies of Starcke can hide the tenuity and banality of these few propositions.

Only very exceptionally, and by no means to his and other people's profit, can an individual satisfy his urge for bliss by preoccupation with himself. Rather it requires preoccupation with the outside world, means to satisfy his needs, that is to say, food, an individual of the opposite sex, books, conversation, argument, activity, objects to use and work. Feuerbach's morality either presupposes that these means and objects of satisfaction are given to every individual as a matter of course, or else it offers him only impracticable good advice and is, therefore, not worth a brass farthing to people who lack these means. And Feuerbach himself states this in plain terms:

"Man thinks differently in a palace and in a hut." "If because of hunger, of misery, you have no stuff in your body, you likewise have no stuff for morality in your head, in your mind or heart."

Do matters fare any better in regard to the equal right of others to satisfy their urge for bliss? Feuerbach poses this claim as absolute, as holding good for all times and circumstances. But since when has it been valid? Was there ever in antiquity between slaves and masters, or in the Middle Ages between serfs and barons, any talk about an equal right in the urge for bliss? Was not the urge for bliss of the oppressed class sacrificed ruthlessly

---

[a] L. Feuerbach, "Fragmente zur Charakteristik meines philosophischen Curriculum vitae" in *Ludwig Feuerbach's sämmtliche Werke*, Vol. II, p. 411.— *Ed.*

and "by right of law" to that of the ruling class?—Yes, that was
indeed immoral; nowadays, however, equality of rights is recognised.—Recognised in words ever since and inasmuch as the
bourgeoisie, in its fight against feudalism and in the development
of capitalist production, was compelled to abolish all privileges of
estate, that is, personal privileges, and to introduce the equality of
all individuals before the law, first in the sphere of private law,
then gradually also in the sphere of public law. But the urge for
bliss lives only to a trivial extent on idealistic rights. To the
greatest extent of all it lives on material means; and capitalist
production takes care to ensure that the great majority of those
with equal rights shall get only what is essential for bare existence.
It scarcely has, therefore, more respect, if indeed at all, for the
equal right to the urge for bliss of the majority than had slavery
or serfdom. And are we better off in regard to the mental means
of bliss, the educational means? Is not even "the school-master of
Sadowa" [244] a mythical person?

More. According to Feuerbach's theory of morals the Stock
Exchange is the highest temple of social ethics, provided only that
one always speculates right. If my urge for bliss leads me to the
Stock Exchange, and if there I correctly gauge the consequences
of my actions so that only agreeable results and no disadvantages
ensue, that is, if I always win, then I am fulfilling Feuerbach's
precept. Moreover, I do not thereby interfere with the equal right
of another person to pursue his bliss; for that other man went to
the Exchange just as voluntarily as I did and in concluding the
speculative transaction with me he has followed his urge for bliss
as I have followed mine. If he loses his money, his action is *ipso
facto* proved to have been unethical, because it was poorly
calculated, and since I have given him the punishment he
deserves, I can even slap my chest proudly, like a modern
Rhadamanthus. Love, too, rules on the Stock Exchange, in so far
as it is not simply a sentimental figure of speech, for each finds in
others the satisfaction of his own urge for bliss, which is just what
love ought to achieve and how it acts in practice. And if I gamble
with correct prevision of the consequences of my operations, and
therefore with success, I fulfil all the strictest injunctions of
Feuerbachian morality—and become a rich man into the bargain.
In other words, Feuerbach's morality is geared to contemporary
capitalist society, little though Feuerbach himself might desire or
imagine it.[a]

---

[a] This sentence was added by Engels in the 1888 edition.—*Ed.*

But love!—yes, in Feuerbach love is everywhere and at all times the miracle-working god called on to help surmount all difficulties of practical life—and that in a society which is split into classes with diametrically opposite interests. At this point the last relic of its revolutionary character disappears from his philosophy, leaving only the old cant: Love one another—fall into each other's arms without distinction as to sex or estate—a universal orgy of reconciliation!

In short, the Feuerbachian theory of morals fares like all its predecessors. It is designed to suit all times, all peoples and all conditions, and precisely for that reason it is never and nowhere applicable. Vis-à-vis the real world it remains as powerless as Kant's categorical imperative. In reality every class, even every profession, has its own morality, and even this it violates whenever it can do so with impunity. And love, which is to unite all, manifests itself in wars, altercations, lawsuits, domestic broils, divorces and every possible exploitation of one by another.

Now how was it possible that the powerful impetus given by Feuerbach turned out to be so unfruitful for himself? For the simple reason that Feuerbach himself cannot find the way out of the realm of abstraction—for which he has a deadly hatred—into that of living reality. He clings fiercely to nature and man; but nature and man remain mere words to him. He is incapable of telling us anything definite either about real nature or real men. But from the abstract man of Feuerbach one arrives at real living men only when one considers them as participants in history. And that is what Feuerbach resisted, and therefore the year 1848, which he did not understand, meant to him merely the final break with the real world, withdrawal into solitude. The blame for this again falls chiefly on the conditions then obtaining in Germany, which condemned him to rot away miserably.

But the step which Feuerbach did not take had nevertheless to be taken. The cult of abstract man, which formed the kernel of Feuerbach's new religion, had to be replaced by the science of real men and of their historical development. This further development of Feuerbach's standpoint beyond Feuerbach was inaugurated by Marx in 1845 in *The Holy Family*.

IV

Strauss, Bauer, Stirner, Feuerbach—these were the offshoots of Hegelian philosophy, in so far as they did not abandon the field of philosophy. Strauss, after his *Leben Jesu* and *Dogmatik*,[a] produced only literary studies in philosophy and ecclesiastical history à la Renan. Bauer worked only in the field of the history of the origin of Christianity, though what he did here was important. Stirner remained an oddity, even after Bakunin blended him with Proudhon and labelled the blend "anarchism". Feuerbach alone was of significance as a philosopher. But not only did philosophy—claimed to soar above all individual sciences and to be the science of sciences, connecting them—remain to him an impassable barrier, an inviolable sacrament, but as a philosopher, too, he stopped halfway, was a materialist below and an idealist above. He could not cope with Hegel through criticism; he simply cast him aside as useless, while he himself, compared with the encyclopaedic wealth of the Hegelian system, achieved nothing positive beyond a bombastic religion of love and a meagre, impotent morality.

Out of the dissolution of the Hegelian school, however, there emerged still another tendency, the only one which has borne real fruit. And this tendency is essentially connected with the name of Marx.*

The departure from Hegelian philosophy was here too the result of a return to the materialist standpoint. That means it was resolved to comprehend the real world—nature and history—just as it presents itself to everyone who approaches it free from preconceived idealist quirks. It was decided mercilessly to sacrifice every idealist quirk which could not be brought into harmony with the facts conceived in their own, and not in a fantastic,

---

* Here I may be permitted to make a personal explanation. Lately repeated reference has been made to my share in this theory, and so I can hardly avoid saying a few words here to settle this point. I cannot deny that both before and during my forty years' collaboration with Marx I had a certain independent share in laying the foundations of the theory, and more particularly in its elaboration. But the greater part of its leading basic principles, especially in the realm of economics and history, and, above all, their final trenchant formulation, belongs to Marx. What I contributed—at any rate with the exception of my work in a few special fields—Marx could very well have done without me. What Marx accomplished I would not have achieved. Marx stood higher, saw further, and took a wider and quicker view than all the rest of us. Marx was a genius; we others were at best talented.[b] Without him the theory would not be by far what it is today. It therefore rightly bears his name.

---

a A reference to the second part of D. Strauss' *Die christliche Glaubenslehre...* entitled *Der materiale Inbegriff der christlichen Glaubenslehre (Dogmatik).—Ed.*

b This sentence was added by Engels in the 1888 edition.—Ed.

interconnection. And materialism means nothing more than this. But here the materialistic world outlook was taken really seriously for the first time and was carried through consistently—at least in its basic features—in all relevant domains of knowledge.

Hegel was not simply put aside. On the contrary, his revolutionary side, described above, the dialectical method was taken up. But in its Hegelian form this method was no use. According to Hegel, dialectics is the self-development of the concept. The absolute concept does not only exist—unknown where—from eternity, it is also the actual living soul of the whole existing world. It develops into itself through all the preliminary stages which are treated at length in *Logik* and which are all included in it. Then it "alienates" itself by changing itself into nature, where, without consciousness of itself, disguised as the necessity of nature, it goes through a new development and finally comes again to self-consciousness in man. This self-consciousness then elaborates itself again in history from the crude form until finally the absolute concept again comes to itself completely in Hegelian philosophy. According to Hegel, therefore, the dialectical development apparent in nature and history, that is, the causal interconnection of the progressive movement from the lower to the higher, which asserts itself through all zigzag movements and temporary retrogressions, is only a copy of the self-movement of the concept going on from eternity, no one knows where, but at all events independently of any thinking human brain. This ideological perversion had to be done away with. We comprehended the concepts in our heads once more materialistically—as images of real things instead of regarding the real things as images of some or other stage of the absolute concept. Thus dialectics reduced itself to the science of the general laws of motion, both of the external world and of human thinking—two sets of laws which are identical in substance, but differ in their expression in so far as the human mind can apply them consciously, while in nature and also up to now for the most part in human history, these laws assert themselves unconsciously, in the form of external necessity, in the midst of an endless series of apparent accidents. Thereby the dialectic of concepts itself became merely the conscious reflection of the dialectical motion of the real world and thus the Hegelian dialectic was placed upon its head; or rather, turned off its head, on which it was standing, and placed upon its feet. And this materialist dialectic, which for years was our best means of labour and our sharpest weapon, was, remarkably enough, rediscovered not only

by us but also, independently of us and even of Hegel, by a
German worker, Joseph Dietzgen.*

In this way, however, the revolutionary side of Hegelian
philosophy was again taken up and at the same time freed from
the idealist trimmings which with Hegel had prevented its
consistent execution. The great basic thought that the world is not
to be comprehended as a complex of ready-made *things,* but as a
complex of *processes,* in which the apparently stable things, no less
than their mental images in our heads, the concepts, go through
uninterrupted change of coming into being and passing away, in
which, for all apparent accidentality and despite all temporary
retrogression, a progressive development asserts itself in the
end—this great fundamental thought has, especially since the time
of Hegel, so thoroughly permeated ordinary consciousness that in
this generality it is now scarcely ever contradicted. But to
acknowledge this fundamental thought in words and to apply it in
reality in detail to each domain of investigation are two different
things. If, however, investigation always proceeds from this
standpoint, the demand for final solutions and eternal truth ceases
once and for all; one is always conscious of the necessary limitation
of all acquired knowledge, of the fact that it is conditioned by the
circumstances in which it was acquired. On the other hand, one no
longer permits oneself to be impressed by the antitheses,
unsuperable for the still common old metaphysics, between true
and false, good and bad, identical and different, necessary and
accidental. One knows that these antitheses have only a relative
validity; that that which is now recognised as true has also its
hidden false side which will later manifest itself, just as that which
is now recognised as false has also its true side by virtue of which
it was previously regarded as true. One knows that what is
maintained to be necessary is composed of sheer accidents and
that the allegedly accidental is the form behind which necessity
hides itself—and so on.

The old method of investigation and thinking which Hegel calls
"metaphysical", which preferred to investigate *things* as given, as
fixed and stable, a method the relics of which still strongly haunt
people's minds, had a great deal of historical justification in its
day. It was necessary first to examine things before it was possible
to examine processes. One had first to know what any particular
thing was before one could observe the changes it was undergoing.
And such was the case with natural science. The old metaphysics,

* See *Das Wesen der Kopfarbeit, von einem Handarbeiter,* Hamburg, Meißner.

which accepted things as *faits accomplis,* arose from a natural science which investigated dead and living things as *faits accomplis.* But when this investigation had progressed so far that it became possible to take the decisive step forward, that is, to pass on to the systematic investigation of the changes which these things undergo in nature itself, then the death knell of the old metaphysics struck in the realm of philosophy too. And in fact, while natural science up to the end of the last century was predominantly a *collecting* science, a science of *faits accomplis,* in our century it is essentially a *systematising* science, a science of the processes, of the origin and development of these things and of the interconnection which binds all these natural processes into one great whole. Physiology, which investigates the processes occurring in plant and animal organisms; embryology, which deals with the development of individual organisms from germ to maturity; geology, which traces the gradual formation of the earth's surface—all these are the offspring of our century.

But, above all, there are three great discoveries which have advanced our knowledge of the interconnection of natural processes by leaps and bounds:

First, the discovery of the cell as the unit from whose multiplication and differentiation the whole plant and animal body develops, so that not only is the development and growth of all higher organisms recognised to proceed according to a single general law,[a] but also, in the capacity of the cell to change, the way is pointed out by which organisms can change their species and thus go through a more than individual development.

Second, the transformation of energy, which has demonstrated to us that all the so-called forces operative in the first instance in inorganic nature—mechanical force and its complement, so-called potential energy, heat, radiation (light, or radiant heat), electricity, magnetism and chemical energy—are different forms of manifestation of universal motion, which pass into one another in definite proportions so that in place of a certain quantity of one which disappears, a certain quantity of another makes its appearance and thus the whole motion of nature[b] is reduced to this incessant process of transformation from one form into another. Finally, the proof which Darwin first developed in coherent form that the stock of organic products of nature surrounding us today,

---

[a] The words "and differentiation", "not only", "general", and the rest of the sentence were added by Engels in the 1888 edition.— *Ed.*

[b] The 1886 edition has "inanimate nature".— *Ed.*

including man, is the product of a long process of evolution from a few originally unicellular germs, and that these in turn arose from protoplasm or albumen, which came into existence by chemical means.

Thanks to these three great discoveries and the other immense advances in natural science, we have now arrived at the point where we can demonstrate the interconnection between the processes in nature not only in particular spheres but also the interconnection of these particular spheres as a whole, and so can present in an approximately systematic form a clear picture of the coherence in nature by means of the facts provided by empirical natural science itself. To furnish this overall picture was formerly the task of so-called philosophy of nature. It could do this only by putting in place of the real but as yet unknown interconnections ideational, fancied ones, filling in the missing facts by mental images and bridging the actual gaps merely in imagination. In the course of this procedure it conceived many brilliant ideas and foreshadowed many later discoveries, but it also produced a considerable amount of nonsense, which indeed could not have been otherwise. Today, when one needs to comprehend the results of natural science only dialectically, that is, in the sense of their own interconnection, in order to arrive at a "system of nature" sufficient for our time; when the dialectical character of this interconnection is forcing itself against their will even into the metaphysically trained minds of the natural scientists, today the philosophy of nature is definitively discarded. Every attempt at resurrecting it would be not only superfluous but a *step backwards.*

But what is true of nature, which is hereby recognised also as a historical process of development, is likewise true of the history of society in all its branches and of the totality of all sciences which occupy themselves with things human (and divine). Here, too, the philosophy of history, of law, of religion, etc., has consisted in the substitution of an interconnection fabricated in the mind of the philosopher for the real interconnection demonstrable in events; has consisted in the comprehension of history as a whole, as well as in its separate parts, as the gradual implementation of ideas—and naturally always only the pet ideas of the philosopher himself. According to this, history worked unconsciously but of necessity towards a certain ideal goal set in advance—as, for example, in Hegel, towards the implementation of his absolute idea—and the unshakeable trend towards this absolute idea formed the inner interconnection of the events in history. A new mysterious providence—unconscious or gradually coming into consciousness—was thus put in the place of the real, still unknown interconnection. Here, therefore, just as in the realm of nature, it was necessary to do away with these fabricated, artificial interconnections by the discovery of the real ones—a task which ultimately amounts to the discovery of the general laws of motion which assert themselves as the ruling ones in the history of human society.

In one point, however, the history of the development of society turns out to be essentially different from that of nature. In nature—in so far as we ignore man's reverse action upon nature—there are only blind, unconscious agencies acting upon one another, out of whose interplay the general law comes into operation. Of all that happens—whether in the innumerable apparent accidents observable upon the surface, or in the ultimate results which confirm the regularity inherent in these accidents—nothing happens as a consciously desired aim. In the history of society, on the contrary, the actors are all endowed with consciousness, are men acting with deliberation or passion, working towards definite goals; nothing happens without a deliberate intention, without a desired aim. But this distinction, important as it is for historical investigation, particularly of individual epochs and events, cannot alter the fact that the course of history is governed by innate general laws. For here, too, on the whole, in spite of the consciously desired aims of all individuals, accident apparently reigns on the surface. What is desired happens but rarely; in the majority of instances the numerous desired ends cross and conflict with one another, or these ends themselves are from the outset impracticable or the means of attaining them are insufficient. Thus the conflicts of innumerable individual wills and individual actions in the domain of history lead to a state of affairs quite similar to that prevailing in the realm of unconscious nature. The ends of the actions are desired, but the results which actually follow from these actions are not desired; or when they do seem to correspond to the desired end, they ultimately have consequences quite other than those desired. Historical events thus appear on the whole to be likewise governed by chance. But wherever on the surface chance holds sway, it is always governed by inner, hidden laws and these laws only have to be discovered.

Men make their own history, whatever its outcome may be, in that each person follows his own consciously desired end, and it is precisely the result of these many wills operating in different directions and of their manifold effects upon the world outside that constitutes history. Thus it is also a question of what the many individuals desire. The will is determined by passion or deliberation. But the levers which immediately determine passion or deliberation are of very different kinds. In part they may be external objects, in part ideal motives, ambition, "enthusiasm for truth and justice", personal hatred or even purely individual whims of all kinds. But, on the one hand, we have seen that the many individual wills active in history for the most part produce results quite other than those desired—often quite the opposite; that their motives, therefore, in relation to the total result are likewise of only secondary importance. On the other hand, the question also arises: What driving forces in turn stand behind these motives? What are the historical causes which transform themselves into these motives in the minds of the actors?

The old materialism never asked itself this question. Its conception of history, as far as it has one at all, is therefore essentially pragmatic; it judges everything according to the motives of the action; it divides men who act in history into noble and ignoble and then finds that as a rule the noble are defrauded and the ignoble are victorious. Hence, it follows for the old materialism that nothing very edifying is to be got from the study of history, and for us that in the realm of history the old materialism becomes untrue to itself because it takes the ideal driving forces which operate there as ultimate causes, instead of investigating what is behind them, what are the driving forces of these driving forces. The inconsistency does not lie in the fact that *ideal* driving forces are recognised, but in the investigation not being carried further back from these into their motive causes. On the other hand, the philosophy of history, particularly as represented by Hegel, recognises that the ostensible and also the actually operating motives of men who act in history are by no means the ultimate causes of historical events; that behind these motives are other motive powers, which have to be explored. But it does not seek these powers in history itself, it imports them rather from outside, from philosophical ideology, into history. Hegel, for example, instead of explaining the history of Ancient Greece out of its own inner coherence, simply maintains that it is nothing more than the bringing out of "forms of beautiful individuality", the realisation of a "work of art" as such.[a] He says much in this connection about the Ancient Greeks that is fine and profound,

---

[a] G. W. F. Hegel, *Vorlesungen über die Philosophie der Geschichte*, Zweiter Teil, Zweiter Abschnitt.— *Ed.*

but that does not prevent us today from refusing to be palmed off with such an explanation, which is mere empty talk.

When, therefore, it is a question of investigating the driving powers which—consciously or unconsciously, and indeed very often unconsciously—lie behind the motives of men who act in history and which constitute the real ultimate driving forces of history, then it is not a question so much of the motives of single individuals, however eminent, as of those motives which set in motion great masses, whole peoples, and again whole classes of the people in each people; and even this, not momentarily, giving rise to the transient flaring up of a straw-fire which quickly dies down, but to lasting action resulting in a great historical transformation. Ascertaining the driving causes which in this context, in the minds of the acting masses and their leaders—the so-called great men—are reflected as conscious motives, clearly or unclearly, directly or in ideological, even sanctified form—that is the only way which can put us on the track of the laws holding sway in history as a whole, as well as in particular periods and in particular countries. Everything which sets men in motion must pass through their minds; but what form it takes in the mind depends very much upon the circumstances. The workers have by no means become reconciled to capitalist machine industry now that they no longer simply break the machines to pieces, as they did as recently as 1848 on the Rhine.

But while in all earlier periods the investigation of these driving causes of history was almost impossible—on account of the complicated and concealed interconnections with their effects—our present period has so far simplified these interconnections that it has been possible to solve the riddle. Since the establishment of large-scale industry, that is, at least since the European peace of 1815, it has been no longer a secret to any man in England that the whole political struggle there turned on the claims to supremacy of two classes: the LANDED ARISTOCRACY[a] and the bourgeoisie (MIDDLE CLASS). In France, with the return of the Bourbons, the same fact was perceived, the historians of the Restoration period, from Thierry to Guizot, Mignet and Thiers, speak of it everywhere as the key to the understanding of French history since the Middle Ages. And since 1830 the working class, the proletariat, has been recognised in both countries as a third competitor for power. Conditions had become so simplified that

---

[a] In the original this English term is given in parentheses after its German equivalent.— *Ed.*

one would have had to close one's eyes deliberately not to see in the fight of these three great classes and in the conflict of their interests the driving force of modern history—at least in the two most advanced countries.

But how had these classes come into existence? If it was possible at first glance still to ascribe the origin of the large, formerly feudal landed property—at least in the first instance—to political causes, to seizure by force, this could not be done in regard to the bourgeoisie and the proletariat. Here the origin and development of two great classes was seen to lie clearly and palpably in purely economic causes. And it was just as clear that in the struggle between landed proprietors and the bourgeoisie, no less than in the struggle between the bourgeoisie and the proletariat, the matter at issue was, first and foremost, economic interests, which were to be secured using political power merely as a means. Bourgeoisie and proletariat both arose in consequence of a change in the economic conditions, more precisely, in the mode of production. The transition, first from guild handicrafts to manufacture, and then from manufacture to large-scale industry with steam and mechanical power, had caused the development of these two classes. At a certain stage the new forces of production set in motion by the bourgeoisie—in the first place the division of labour and the combination of many workers performing individual operations in one manufactory handling all stages of production—and the conditions and requirements of exchange, developed through these forces of production, became incompatible with the existing order[a] of production handed down through history and sanctified by law, that is to say, incompatible with the privileges of the guild and the numerous other personal and local privileges (which were just as numerous fetters for the unprivileged estates) of the feudal order of society. The forces of production represented by the bourgeoisie rebelled against the order[a] of production represented by the feudal landlords and the guild-masters. The result is well known: the feudal fetters were smashed, gradually in England, at one blow in France. In Germany the process is not yet finished. But just as, at a definite stage of its development, manufacture came into conflict with the feudal order[a] of production, so large-scale industry has even now come into conflict with the bourgeois order of production established in its place. Tied down by this order, by the narrow limits of the capitalist mode of production, this industry produces,

_____

[a] The 1886 edition has "relations".— *Ed.*

on the one hand, an ever-increasing proletarianisation of the great mass of the people, and on the other hand, an ever greater volume of unsaleable products. Overproduction and mass destitution, each the cause of the other—that is the absurd contradiction which is its outcome, and which of necessity calls for the productive forces to be unfettered by means of a change in the mode of production.

In modern history at least it is, therefore, proved that all political struggles are class struggles, and all struggles by classes for emancipation, despite their necessarily political form—for every class struggle is a political struggle[a]—turn ultimately on the question of *economic* emancipation. Therefore, here at least, the state—the political order—is the subordinate factor and civil society—the realm of economic relations—the decisive element. The traditional conception, to which Hegel, too, pays homage, saw in the state the determining element, and in civil society the element determined by it. Appearances correspond to this. As all the driving forces of the actions of any individual person must pass through his brain, and transform themselves into motives of his will in order to set him into action, so also all the needs of civil society—no matter which class happens to be the ruling one—must pass through the will of the state in order to attain general validity in the form of laws. That is the formal aspect of the matter which is self-evident. The question arises, however, as to the content of this merely formal will—of the individual as well as of the state—and whence this content is derived. Why is just this willed and not something else? If we enquire into this, we discover that in modern history the will of the state is, on the whole, determined by the changing needs of civil society, by the supremacy of this or that class, in the last resort, by the development of the productive forces and relations of exchange.

But if even in our modern era, with its gigantic means of production and communication, the state is not an independent domain with independent development, but one whose existence as well as development is to be explained in the last resort by the economic conditions of life of society, then this must be still more true of all earlier times when the production of the material life of man was not yet carried on with these abundant auxiliary aids, and when, therefore, the necessity of such production must have exercised a still greater rule over men. If the state even today, in the era of large-scale industry and railways, is on the whole only

---

a The words in dashes were added by Engels in the 1888 edition.— *Ed.*

the reflection, in concentrated form, of the economic needs of the class controlling production, then this must have been much more the case in an epoch when each generation of men had to spend a far greater part of its aggregate lifetime satisfying its material needs, and was therefore much more dependent on them than we are today. An examination of the history of earlier periods, as soon as it deals seriously with this aspect, most abundantly confirms this. But, of course, this cannot be gone into here.

If the state and public law are determined by economic relations, so, too, of course is private law, which indeed in essence only sanctions the existing economic relations between individuals which are normal in the given circumstances.[a] The form in which this occurs can, however, vary considerably. It is possible, as happened in England, in harmony with the whole of national development, to retain to a large extent the forms of the old feudal laws and give them a bourgeois content; in fact, directly reading a bourgeois meaning into the feudal name. But, also, as happened in continental Western Europe, Roman Law, the first world law of a commodity-producing society, with its unsurpassably fine elaboration of all the essential legal relations of simple commodity owners (of buyers and sellers, creditors and debtors, contracts, obligations, etc.), can be taken as the foundation. In which case, for the benefit of a still petty-bourgeois and semi-feudal society it can either be reduced to the level of such a society simply through judicial practice (common law) or else, with the help of allegedly enlightened, moralising jurists, it can be worked into a special code of law to correspond with such a social level—a code which in these circumstances will be a bad one even from the legal standpoint (for instance, Prussian common law). In which case, however, after a great bourgeois revolution, it is also possible to work out upon the basis of this same Roman Law such a classic legal code of bourgeois society as the French *Code civile.* If, therefore, bourgeois legal rules merely express the economic conditions of life in society in legal form, then they can do so well or badly according to circumstances.

The state presents itself to us as the first ideological power over man. Society creates for itself an organ for the safeguarding of its common interests against internal and external attacks. This organ is the state power. Hardly come into being, this organ makes itself independent vis-à-vis society; and, indeed, all the more so, the

---

[a] The words "which are normal in the given circumstances" were added by Engels in the 1888 edition.— *Ed.*

more it becomes the organ of a particular class, the more it directly enforces the rule of that class. The fight of the oppressed class against the ruling class necessarily becomes a political fight, a fight first of all against the political rule of this class. Consciousness of the connection between this political struggle and its economic foundation becomes dulled and can be lost altogether. While this is not wholly the case with the participants, it almost always happens with the historians. Of the ancient sources on the struggles within the Roman Republic only Appian tells us clearly and distinctly what was ultimately at issue—namely, landed property.[a]

But once the state has become an independent power vis-à-vis society, it immediately produces a further[b] ideology. It is among professional politicians, theorists of public law and jurists of private law that the connection with economic facts gets well and truly lost. Since in each particular case the economic facts must assume the form of juristic motives in order to receive legal sanction; and since, in so doing, consideration has, of course, to be given to the whole legal system already in operation, the juristic form is, in consequence, made everything and the economic content nothing. Public law and private law are treated as separate spheres, each having its own independent historical development, each being capable of, and needing, a systematic presentation by the consistent elimination of all innate contradictions.

Still higher ideologies, that is, such as are still further removed from the material, economic basis, take the form of philosophy and religion. Here the connection between conceptions and their material conditions of existence becomes more and more complicated, more and more obscured by intermediate links. But the connection exists. Just as the whole Renaissance period, from the middle of the fifteenth century, was an essential product of the towns and, therefore, of the burghers, so also was the subsequently newly awakened philosophy. Its content was in essence only the philosophical expression of the thoughts corresponding to the development of the small and middle burghers into a big bourgeoisie. Among the last century's Englishmen and Frenchmen who in many cases were just as much political economists as philosophers, this is clearly evident; and we have proved it above in regard to the Hegelian school.

Let us now in addition deal only briefly with religion, since this

---

a See Appian of Alexandria, *The Roman History*, Books 13-17.— *Ed.*
b The 1886 edition has "another".— *Ed.*

stands furthest away from material life and seems to be most alien to it. Religion arose in very primitive times from erroneous, primitive conceptions by men about their own nature and external nature surrounding them. Every ideology, however, once it has arisen, develops in connection with the given concept-material, and develops this material further; otherwise it would not be an ideology, that is, occupation with thoughts as with independent entities, developing independently and subject only to their own laws. That the material conditions of life of the persons inside whose heads this thought process goes on in the last resort determine the course of this process remains of necessity unknown to these persons, for otherwise all ideology would be finished. These original religious notions, therefore, which in the main are common to each group of kindred peoples, develop, after the group separates, in a manner peculiar to each people, according to the conditions of life falling to their lot. For a number of groups of peoples, and particularly for the Aryans (so-called Indo-Europeans), this process has been demonstrated in detail by comparative mythology. The gods thus fashioned among each people were national gods, whose domain extended no farther than the national territory which they were to protect; on the other side of its frontiers other gods held undisputed sway. They could continue to exist, in the imagination, only as long as the nation existed; they fell with its fall. The Roman world empire, the economic conditions of whose origin we do not need to examine here, brought about this downfall of the old nationalities. The old national gods declined, even those of the Romans, which also were geared to suit only the narrow confines of the city of Rome. The need to complement the world empire by means of a world religion was clearly revealed in the attempts made to provide in Rome recognition and altars for all the foreign gods that were to the slightest degree respectable, alongside the indigenous ones. But a new world religion is not to be made in this fashion, by imperial decrees. The new world religion, Christianity, had already quietly come into being, out of a mixture of generalised Oriental, particularly Jewish, theology, and vulgarised Greek, particularly Stoic, philosophy. What it originally looked like has yet to be laboriously discovered, since its official form, as it has been handed down to us, is merely that in which it became the state religion, to which purpose it was adapted by the Council of Nicaea.[245] The fact that it became the state religion in as little as 250 years suffices to show that it was the religion corresponding to the conditions of the time. In the Middle Ages, in the same measure as feudalism developed, Christianity grew into its religious counterpart, with a corresponding feudal hierarchy. And when the burghers began to thrive, there developed, in opposition to feudal Catholicism, the Protestant heresy, which first appeared in Southern France, among the Albigenses,[246] at the time the cities there were in their heyday. The Middle Ages had attached to theology all the other forms of ideology—philosophy, politics, jurisprudence—and made them subdivisions of theology. It thereby constrained every social and political movement to take on a theological form. The sentiments of the masses, fed exclusively on religion, had to have their own interests presented to them in a religious guise in order to create a great turbulence. And just as the burghers from the beginning produced an appendage of propertyless urban plebeians, day labourers and servants of all kinds, belonging to no recognised social estate, precursors of the later proletariat, so likewise[a] heresy soon became divided into a moderate burgher heresy and a revolutionary plebeian one, the latter an abomination even to the burgher heretics.

The ineradicableness of the Protestant heresy corresponded to the invincibility of the rising burghers. When these burghers had become sufficiently strengthened, their struggle against the feudal nobility, which till then had been predominantly local, began to assume national dimensions. The first great campaign occurred in Germany—the so-called Reformation. The burghers were neither powerful enough nor sufficiently developed to be able to unite under their banner the remaining rebellious estates—the plebeians of the towns, the lower nobility and the peasants in the countryside. The nobles were the first to be defeated; the peasants rose in a revolt which formed the climax of the whole revolutionary movement; the cities left them in the lurch, and thus the revolution succumbed to the armies of the sovereigns, who swept the board. Thenceforward Germany disappears for three centuries from among the countries playing an independent active part in history. But beside the German Luther there had appeared the Frenchman Calvin. With true French acuity he put the bourgeois character of the Reformation in the forefront, republicanised and democratised the Church. While the Lutheran Reformation in Germany degenerated and reduced the country to rack and ruin, the Calvinist Reformation served as a banner for the republicans in Geneva, in Holland and in Scotland, freed

---

[a] This part of the sentence was added by Engels in the 1888 edition.— *Ed.*

Holland from Spain and from the German Empire and provided the ideological costume for the second act of the bourgeois revolution, which was taking place in England. Here Calvinism stood the test as the true religious disguise of the interests of the contemporary bourgeoisie and on this account did not attain full recognition when the revolution ended in 1689 in a compromise between part of the nobility and the bourgeoisie.[247] The English Established Church was reconstituted; but not in its earlier form, as a Catholicism with the king for its pope, being, instead, strongly Calvinised. The old Established Church had celebrated the merry Catholic Sunday and had fought against the dull Calvinist one. The new, bourgeois Church introduced the latter, which adorns England to this day.

In France, the Calvinist minority was suppressed in 1685 and either Catholicised or driven out of the country.[248] But what was the good? Already at that time the freethinker Pierre Bayle was hard at work, and in 1694 Voltaire was born. The forcible measures of Louis XIV only made it easier for the French bourgeoisie to carry through its revolution in the irreligious, exclusively political form which alone was suited to a developed bourgeoisie. Instead of Protestants, freethinkers took their seats in the national assemblies. Christianity had thus entered into its final stage. It had become incapable of continuing to serve any progressive class as the ideological garb of its aspirations. It became more and more the exclusive possession of the ruling classes and they use it as a mere means of government, to keep the lower classes within certain bounds. Moreover, each of the different classes uses its own appropriate religion: the landed Junkers—Catholic Jesuitism or Protestant orthodoxy; the liberal and radical bourgeoisie—rationalism; and it makes no difference whether these gentlemen themselves believe in their respective religions or not.

We see, therefore: religion, once formed, always contains traditional material, just as in all ideological domains tradition constitutes a great conservative force. But the changes which this material undergoes spring from class relations, that is to say, from the economic relations of the people who carry out these changes. And here that is sufficient.

In the above it could only be a question of giving a general outline of the Marxian conception of history, at most with a few illustrations as well. The proof must be derived from history itself; and in this regard I may be permitted to say that it has been sufficiently provided in other writings. This conception, however, puts an end to philosophy in the realm of history, just as the dialectical conception of nature makes all philosophy of nature as unnecessary as it is impossible. It is no longer a question anywhere of inventing interconnections from out of our brains, but of discovering them in the facts. For philosophy, having been expelled from nature and history, there remains only the realm of pure thought, so far as anything is left of it: the theory of the laws of the thought process itself, logic and dialectics.

* * *

With the revolution of 1848, "educated" Germany said farewell to theory and went over to the field of practice. Small-scale production and manufacture, based upon manual labour, were superseded by real large-scale industry. Germany again appeared on the world market. The new little German Empire [249] abolished at least the most flagrant of the abuses with which this development had been obstructed by the system of petty states, the relics of feudalism, and bureaucratic management. But to the same degree that speculation abandoned the philosopher's study in order to erect its temple in the Stock Exchange, educated Germany lost the great aptitude for theory which had been the glory of Germany in the days of its deepest political humiliation — the aptitude for purely scientific investigation, irrespective of whether the result obtained was applicable in practice or not, adverse to the police or not. Official German natural science, it is true, kept abreast of the times, particularly in the field of specialised research. But even the American journal *Science* rightly remarks that the decisive advances in the sphere of the comprehensive correlation of particular facts and their generalisation into laws are now being made much more in England, instead of in Germany, as used to be the case. And in the sphere of the historical sciences, philosophy included, the old reckless zeal for theory has now well and truly disappeared, along with classical philosophy. Inane eclecticism and an obsessive concern for career and income, down to the most vulgar tuft-hunting, have taken its place. The official representatives of these sciences have become the undisguised ideologists of the bourgeoisie and the existing state — but at a time when both stand in open antagonism to the working class.

Only among the working class does the German aptitude for theory remain unimpaired. Here it cannot be exterminated. Here there is no concern for careers, for profiteering, or for gracious patronage from above. On the contrary, the more ruthlessly and disinterestedly science proceeds the more it finds itself in harmony with the interests and aspirations of the workers. The new tendency, which recognised that the key to the understanding of the whole history of society lies in the history of the development of labour, from the outset addressed itself preferentially to the working class and here found the response which it neither sought nor expected from official science. The German working-class movement is the heir to German classical philosophy.

APPENDIX [TO THE AMERICAN EDITION
OF *THE CONDITION OF THE WORKING CLASS
IN ENGLAND*][250]

The book which is herewith submitted to the English-speaking public in its own language, was written rather more than forty years ago. The author, at the time, was young, twenty-four years of age, and his production bears the stamp of his youth with its good and its faulty features, of neither of which he feels ashamed. That it is now translated into English, is not in any way due to his initiative. Still he may be allowed to say a few words, "to show cause" why this translation should not be prevented from seeing the light of day.

The state of things described in this book belongs to-day in many respects to the past, as far as England is concerned. Though not expressly stated in our recognized treatises, it is still a law of modern Political Economy that the larger the scale on which Capitalistic Production is carried on, the less can it support the petty devices of swindling and pilfering which characterize its early stages. The pettifogging business-tricks of the Polish Jew, the representative in Europe of commerce in its lowest stage, those tricks that serve him so well in his own country, and are generally practiced there, he finds to be out of date and out of place when he comes to Hamburg or Berlin; and again the Commission Agent, who hails from Berlin or Hamburg, Jew or Christian, after frequenting the Manchester Exchange for a few months, finds out that in order to buy cotton-yarn or cloth cheap, he, too, had better drop those slightly more refined but still miserable wiles and subterfuges which are considered the acme of cleverness in his native country. The fact is, those tricks do not pay any longer in a

large market, where time is money, and where a certain standard
of commercial morality is unavoidably developed, purely as a
means of saving time and trouble. And it is the same with the
relation between the manufacturer and his "hands." The repeal of
the Corn-laws,[251] the discovery of the Californian and Australian
gold-fields,[252] the almost complete crushing-out of domestic
handweaving in India, the increasing access to the Chinese market,
the rapid multiplication of railways and steam-ships all over the
world, and other minor causes have given to English manufacturing industry such a colossal development, that the status of 1844
now appears to us as comparatively primitive and insignificant.
And in proportion as this increase took place, in the same
proportion did manufacturing industry become apparently moral-
ized. The competition of manufacturer against manufacturer by
means of petty thefts upon the workpeople did no longer pay.
Trade had outgrown such low means of making money; they were
not worth while practicing for the manufacturing millionaire, and
served merely to keep alive the competition of smaller traders,
thankful to pick up a penny wherever they could. Thus the
truck-system was suppressed; the Ten Hours' Bill[253] was enacted,
and a number of other secondary reforms introduced—much
against the spirit of Free Trade and unbridled competition, but
quite as much in favor of the giant-capitalist in his competition
with his less favored brother. Moreover, the larger the concern,
and with it the number of hands, the greater the loss and
inconvenience caused by every conflict between master and men;
and thus a new spirit came over the masters, especially the large
ones, which taught them to avoid unnecessary squabbles, to
acquiesce in the existence and power of Trades Unions, and
finally even to discover in strikes—at opportune times—a
powerful means to serve their own ends. The largest manufacturers, formerly the leaders of the war against the working-class, were
now the foremost to preach peace and harmony. And for a very
good reason. The fact is, that all these concessions to justice and
philanthropy were nothing else but means to accelerate the
concentration of capital in the hands of the few, for whom the
niggardly extra extortions of former years had lost all importance
and had become actual nuisances; and to crush all the quicker and
all the safer their smaller competitors who could not make both
ends meet without such perquisites. Thus the development of
production on the basis of the capitalistic system has of itself
sufficed—at least in the leading industries, for in the more
unimportant branches this is far from being the case—to do away

with all those minor grievances which aggravated the workman's fate during its earlier stages. And thus it renders more and more evident the great central fact, that the cause of the miserable condition of the working class is to be sought, not in these minor grievances, but in the Capitalistic System itself. The wage-worker sells to the capitalist his labor-force for a certain daily sum. After a few hours' work he has reproduced the value of that sum; but the substance of his contract is, that he has to work another series of hours to complete his working day; and the value he produces during these additional hours of surplus labor is surplus value which costs the capitalist nothing but yet goes into his pocket. That is the basis of the system which tends more and more to split up civilized society into a few Vanderbilts, the owners of all the means of production and subsistence, on the one hand, and an immense number of wage-workers, the owners of nothing but their labor-force, on the other. And that this result is caused, not by this or that secondary grievance, but by the system itself—this fact has been brought out in bold relief by the development of Capitalism in England since 1847.

Again, the repeated visitations of cholera, typhus, small-pox and other epidemics have shown the British bourgeois the urgent necessity of sanitation in his towns and cities, if he wishes to save himself and family from falling victims to such diseases. Accordingly, the most crying abuses described in this book have either disappeared or have been made less conspicuous. Drainage has been introduced or improved, wide avenues have been opened out athwart many of the worst "slums" I had to describe. "Little Ireland" has disappeared and the "Seven Dials" [254] are next on the list for sweeping away. But what of that? Whole districts which in 1844 I could describe as almost idyllic have now, with the growth of the towns, fallen into the same state of dilapidation, discomfort and misery. Only the pigs and the heaps of refuse are no longer tolerated. The bourgeoisie have made further progress in the art of hiding the distress of the working class. But that, in regard to their dwellings, no substantial improvement has taken place, is amply proved by the Report of the Royal Commission "on the Housing of the Poor," 1885.[a] And this is the case, too, in other respects. Police regulations have been plentiful as blackberries; but they can only hedge in the distress of the workers, they cannot remove it.

---

a See *Report of the Royal Commission on the Housing of the Working Classes. England and Wales. 1885.—Ed.*

But while England has thus outgrown the juvenile state of capitalist exploitation described by me, other countries have only just attained it. France, Germany, and especially America, are the formidable competitors who at this moment—as foreseen by me in 1844[a]—are more and more breaking up England's industrial monopoly. Their manufactures are young as compared with those of England, but increasing at a far more rapid rate than the latter; but curious enough, they have at this moment arrived at about the same phase of development as English manufacture in 1844. With regard to America, the parallel is indeed most striking. True, the external surroundings in which the working class is placed in America are very different, but the same economical laws are at work, and the results, if not identical in every respect, must still be of the same order. Hence we find in America the same struggles for a shorter working-day, for a legal limitation of the working time, especially of women and children in factories; we find the truck system in full blossom, and the cottage-system, in rural districts,[255] made use of by the "bosses" as a means of domination over the workers. At this very moment I am receiving the American papers with accounts of the great strike of 12,000 Pennsylvanian coal-miners in the Connellsville district, and I seem but to read my own description of the North of England colliers' strike of 1844.[256] The same cheating of the work-people by false measure; the same truck system; the same attempt to break the miners' resistance by the Capitalists' last, but crushing, resource, the eviction of the men out of their dwellings, the cottages owned by the companies.

There were two circumstances which for a long time prevented the unavoidable consequences of the Capitalist system from showing themselves in the full glare of day in America. These were the easy access to the ownership of cheap land, and the influx of immigration. They allowed, for many years, the great mass of the native American population to "retire" in early manhood from wage-labor and to become farmers, dealers, or employers of labor, while the hard work for wages, the position of a proletarian for life, mostly fell to the lot of immigrants. But America has outgrown this early stage. The boundless backwoods have disappeared, and the still more boundless prairies are fast and faster passing from the hands of the Nation and the States into those of private owners. The great safety-valve against the

---

[a] See present edition, Vol. 4, pp. 579-80.— *Ed.*

formation of a permanent proletarian class has practically ceased
to act. A class of life-long and even hereditary proletarians exists
at this hour in America. A nation of sixty millions striving hard to
become—and with every chance of success, too—the leading
manufacturing nation of the world—such a nation cannot
permanently import its own wage-working class; not even if
immigrants pour in at the rate of half a million a year. The
tendency of the Capitalist system towards the ultimate splitting-up
of society into two classes, a few millionaires on the one hand, and
a great mass of mere wage-workers on the other, this tendency,
though constantly crossed and counteracted by other social
agencies, works nowhere with greater force than in America; and
the result has been the production of a class of native American
wage-workers, who form, indeed, the aristocracy of the wage-
working class as compared with the immigrants, but who become
conscious more and more every day of their solidarity with the
latter and who feel all the more acutely their present condemnation to life-long wage-toil, because they still remember the bygone
days, when it was comparatively easy to rise to a higher social
level. Accordingly the working class movement, in America, has
started with truly American vigor, and as on that side of the
Atlantic things march with at least double the European speed,
we may yet live to see America take the lead in this respect
too.

I have not attempted, in this translation, to bring the book up to
date, to point out in detail all the changes that have taken place
since 1844. And for two reasons: Firstly, to do this properly, the
size of the book must be about doubled, and the translation came
upon me too suddenly to admit of my undertaking such a work.
And secondly, the first volume of "Das Kapital", by Karl Marx, an
English translation of which is about to appear, contains a very
ample description of the state of the British working class, as it
was about 1865, that is to say, at the time when British industrial
prosperity reached its culminating point. I should, then, have been
obliged again to go over the ground already covered by Marx's
celebrated work.

It will be hardly necessary to point out that the general
theoretical standpoint of this book—philosophical, economical,
political—does not exactly coincide with my standpoint of to-day.
Modern international Socialism, since fully developed as a science,
chiefly and almost exclusively through the efforts of Marx, did not
as yet exist in 1844. My book represents one of the phases of its
embryonic development; and as the human embryo, in its early

stages, still reproduces the gill-arches of our fish ancestors, so this book exhibits everywhere the traces of the descent of Modern Socialism from one of its ancestors, German philosophy. Thus great stress is laid on the dictum that Communism is not a mere party doctrine of the working class, but a theory compassing the emancipation of society at large, including the Capitalist class, from its present narrow conditions. This is true enough in the abstract, but absolutely useless, and worse, in practice. So long as the wealthy classes not only do not feel the want of any emancipation, but strenuously oppose the self-emancipation of the working class, so long the social revolution will have to be prepared and fought out by the working class alone. The French bourgeois of 1789, too, declared the emancipation of the bourgeoisie to be the emancipation of the whole human race; but the nobility and clergy would not see it; the proposition—though for the time being, with respect to feudalism, an abstract historical truth—soon became a mere sentimentalism, and disappeared from view altogether in the fire of the revolutionary struggle. And to-day, the very people who, from the impartiality of their "superior stand-point" preach to the workers a Socialism soaring high above their class interests and class struggles, and tending to reconcile in a higher humanity the interests of both the contending classes—these people are either neophytes, who have still to learn a great deal, or they are the worst enemies of the workers—wolves in sheeps' clothing.

The recurring period of the great industrial crises is stated in the text as five years. This was the period apparently indicated by the course of events from 1825 to 1842. But the industrial history from 1842 to 1868 has shown that the real period is one of ten years; that the intermediate revolutions were secondary and tended more and more to disappear. Since 1868 the state of things has changed again, of which more anon.

I have taken care not to strike out of the text the many prophecies, amongst others that of an imminent social revolution in England, which my youthful ardor induced me to venture upon. The wonder is, not that a good many of them proved wrong, but that so many of them have proved right, and that the critical state of English trade, to be brought on by German and especially American competition, which I then foresaw—though in too short a period—has now actually come to pass. In this respect I can, and am bound to, bring the book up to date, by placing here an article which I published in the London "Commonweal" of March 1, 1885, under the heading: "England in 1845 and in

1885."[a] It gives at the same time a short outline of the history of the English working class during these forty years.

London, February 25, 1886

Frederick Engels

First published in F. Engels, *The Condition of the Working Class in England in 1844,* New York, 1887

Reproduced from the book

---

[a] See this volume, pp. 295-301.— *Ed.*

28*

[ON THE ANNIVERSARY OF THE PARIS COMMUNE]²⁵⁷

This evening, at the same time as you, and with you, the workers of the Two Worlds celebrate the anniversary of the most glorious and most tragic stage of proletarian evolution. In 1871, for the first time in its history, the working class seized political power in a major capital. It was, alas! but a dream. Caught between the mercenaries of the former French Empire on one side and the Prussians on the other, the Commune was soon strangled in an unparalleled massacre which will never be forgotten. Victorious, reaction knew no bounds; socialism seemed to have been drowned in blood, and the proletariat doomed to slavery forever.

Fifteen years have elapsed since that defeat. In all this time, in every country, the powers-that-be, in the service of the owners of land and capital, have not shunned any means to eradicate the last remaining intentions of working class revolt. And what have they achieved?

Look around you. Revolutionary working-class socialism, more alive than ever, is today a force before which governments everywhere tremble, the French radicals as well as Bismarck, the stock-exchange kings of America just as the Tsar of all the Russias.

That is not all.

We have arrived at the point where all our adversaries, whatever they do, are working for us in spite of themselves.

They believed they had killed the International. Yet at the present moment the international union of the proletariat, the revolutionary brotherhood between the workers of different countries, is a thousand times stronger, more widespread than it was before the Commune. The International no longer needs an organisation in the proper sense; it lives and grows through the spontaneous and heartfelt cooperation of the workers of Europe and America.

In Germany Bismarck has exhausted every means, even the foulest, in order to crush the working-class movement. Result: before the Commune he was faced with four socialist deputies; his persecutions have led to the election of twenty-five today.[258] And the German proletariat is laughing at the Grand Chancellor who could not have made better revolutionary propaganda if he were paid for it.

In France they have imposed on you voting by list,[259] this bourgeois election method *par excellence,* deliberately invented to ensure the election of lawyers, journalists and other political adventurers, the spokesmen of capital. And what has it done for the bourgeoisie, this poll of the rich? It has created in the heart of the French parliament a revolutionary socialist workers' party whose mere appearance on the scene was sufficient to throw the ranks of all the bourgeois parties into disarray.[260]

This is where we are now. Every event turns out in our favour. The most calculated measures to arrest the progress of the proletariat serve only to speed its victorious march. The enemy itself is fighting for us, is condemned to fight for us. And it has done so much and done it so well that on this day, the 18 March 1886, the same cry emerges from thousands of workers' throats, from the proletarian miners of California and Aveyron to the convict miners of Siberia:

"Long live the Commune! Long live the international union of workers!"

Written on March 15, 1886

First published in *Le Socialiste,* No. 31, March 27, 1886

Printed according to the newspaper

Translated from the French

A STATEMENT TO THE EDITORIAL BOARD OF THE *NEW YORKER VOLKSZEITUNG*[261]

As a report of an interview with me by one of its correspondents has appeared in the *Missouri Republican,* I have the following remarks to make:

It is true that a Mr. McEnnis visited me as representative of this newspaper and put various questions to me, but promising on his *honour* not to send a line of it for print without first submitting it to me. Instead of doing that he never turned up again. I therefore declare herewith that I must refuse each and every responsibility for his publication, all the more so as I had the opportunity to satisfy myself that, because he lacked the necessary background knowledge, Mr. McEnnis, even with the best of wills, is hardly in a position to understand my statements correctly.

London

Frederick Engels

Written on April 29, 1886

First published in the *New Yorker Volkszeitung,* No. 162, July 8, 1886

Printed according to the newspaper

Published in English for the first time

[ON THE STRIKE AT A GLASS-WORKS IN LYONS]

The French Republican Government[262] seem resolved to show in every possible way that they are quite as much the Government of the capitalists as any of their predecessors. Not content with siding with the Mining Company in Decazeville,[263] they now come out even stronger in Lyons. There is a strike at a glass-works there; a few knobsticks continue working, and are lodged inside the works for safety's sake. When the furniture of one of them—a German anarchist of the name of Litner—was removed to the works, the strikers followed it, hooting. No sooner was the cart with the furniture inside and the gates closed, than shots were fired from the windows upon the people outside—revolver-bullets, and buckshot flying about in every direction, and wounding about thirty people. The crowd of course dispersed. Now the police and the judicial authorities interfered. But not to arrest the capitalist and his retainers who had fired—oh no! they arrested a number of the strikers for interfering with the freedom of labour! This affair coming on at this very moment, has caused immense excitement in Paris. Decazeville has swelled the Socialist votes in Paris from 30,000 to above 100,000,[264] and the effect of this murderous affair on the La Malotier[a] Gray at Lyons will be greater still.

F. E.

Written between May 8 and 14, 1886

First published in *The Commonweal,*
No. 18, May 15, 1886

Reproduced from the magazine

---

[a] Should read "La Mulatier".— *Ed.*

THE POLITICAL SITUATION IN EUROPE [265]

In March 1879[a] Disraeli sent four armour-plated ships into the Bosporus; their presence alone was sufficient to halt the Russians' triumphal march on Constantinople and to break the Treaty of San Stefano. The Peace of Berlin regulated the situation in the Orient for some time.[266] Bismarck managed to bring about an accord between the Russian Government and Austrian Government. Austria was to dominate behind the scenes in Serbia, whereas Bulgaria and Rumelia were to be abandoned to the overwhelming influence of Russia. This allowed one to predict that if, later on, Bismarck permitted the Russians to take Constantinople, he was reserving Salonica and Macedonia for Austria.

But what is more, Austria was given Bosnia too, just as in 1794 Russia had abandoned the greater part of Poland proper to the Prussians and Austrians, only to take it back in 1814.[267] Bosnia was a permanent drain on Austria, a bone of contention between Hungary and Western Austria, and above all it was *proof to Turkey* that the Austrians, just like the Russians, were preparing for it the same fate that Poland had suffered. Henceforth Turkey could have no confidence in Austria: an important victory for Russian government policy.

Serbia had Slavophile, and hence Russophile, tendencies; but since its emancipation it has drawn all its means of bourgeois development from Austria. Young people go to study in the

---

[a] Engels' letter has "winter of 1879". The erroneous date was preserved in the article. The English squadron entered the Sea of Marmara (not the Bosporus) in February 1878.— *Ed.*

Austrian universities; the bureaucratic system, the code, the court procedure, the schools—everything has been copied from the Austrian models. It was natural. But Russia had to prevent this imitation in Bulgaria; it did not wish to pull Austria's chestnuts out of the fire. So Bulgaria was organised as a Russian satrapy. The administration, the officers and the non-commissioned officers, the staff, in fact the entire system were Russian: the Battenberg who was bestowed on it was the cousin of Alexander III.

The domination of the Russian Government, at first direct and then indirect, was sufficient to stifle in less than four years all Bulgarian sympathy for Russia, though it had been great and enthusiastic. The population grew increasingly fractious in the face of the insolence of their "liberators"; and even Battenberg, a man without any political ideas, with a pliant character, who sought merely to serve the Tsar but clamoured for esteem, became more and more intractable.

Meanwhile, things were developing in Russia: by taking severe action the government was able to disperse the Nihilists and break up their organisation for a time.[268] But that was not enough, it needed some support in public opinion, it needed to turn minds away from the contemplation of the growing social and political ills at home; finally, what it needed was a little patriotic phantasmagoria. Under Napoleon III the left bank of the Rhine had served to deflect revolutionary passions towards the exterior; similarly, the Russian Government showed a troubled and restless people the conquest of Constantinople, the "deliverance" of Slavs oppressed by the Turks and their unification into one great federation under Russian tutelage. But it was not sufficient to evoke this phantasmagoria—it was necessary to do something to translate it into the sphere of reality.

Circumstances were favourable. The annexation of Alsace and Lorraine had sown seeds of discord between France and Germany which seemed bound to neutralise these two powers. Austria on her own could not stand up to Russia, because its most effective weapon, the appeal to the Poles, would always be held in the scabbard by Prussia. And the occupation, the theft, of Bosnia was an Alsace between Austria and Turkey. Italy was offered most, that is with regard to Russia, who offered it Trentino and Istria, along with Dalmatia and Tripoli. And England? The peace-loving Russophile Gladstone had listened to the tempting words of Russia; *he had occupied Egypt,* in a time of peace,[269] which guaranteed England a perpetual quarrel with France and, in addition, ensured the *impossibility of an alliance between the Turks and the English, who had just robbed them* by appropriating a Turkish fief, Egypt. Moreover, the Russian preparations in Asia were sufficiently far advanced to give the English plenty of trouble in the Indies in the event of war. Never before had the Russians been presented with so many chances: their diplomacy was triumphing all along the line.

The rebellion of the Bulgarians against Russian despotism provided the opportunity to enter into the fray. In the summer of 1885 they dangled before the eyes of the Bulgarians and the Rumelians the possibility of this union promised by the peace of San Stefano and destroyed by the Treaty of Berlin. They were told that if they threw themselves once again into the arms of Russia the liberator the Russian Government would fulfil its mission by bringing about this union; but to achieve this the Bulgarians had to start by chasing out Battenberg. The latter was warned in time; unusually for him he acted promptly and vigorously; he brought about, for his own ends, this union which Russia hoped to make against him.[270] From this moment there was relentless warfare between him and the Tsar.

To begin with, this war was waged slyly and indirectly. Louis Bonaparte's splendid doctrine, whereby when a hitherto scattered people such as Italy or Germany was united and attained nationhood, the other states such as France were entitled to territorial compensation, was revived for the small states of the Balkans. Serbia swallowed the bait and declared war on the Bulgarians; Russia triumphed by making this war, instigated in its own interests, appear in the eyes of the world to be under the auspices of Austria, who dared not prevent it for fear of seeing the Russian side coming to power in Serbia. For its part, Russia threw the Bulgarian army into confusion by recalling all the Russian officers, that is to say the entire general staff and all the senior officers, including the battalion commanders.

But contrary to all expectations the Bulgarians, without their Russian officers, and fighting two against three, beat the Serbs hands down and won the respect and admiration of an astonished Europe. These victories were due to two things. Firstly, Alexander of Battenberg, although a weak politician, is a good soldier; he waged the war as he had learnt from the Prussian school, while the Serbs followed the strategy and tactics of their Austrian models. So it was a second edition of the 1866 campaign in Bohemia.[271] Moreover, the Serbs had lived for sixty years under a bureaucratic Austrian regime which, without giving them a powerful bourgeoisie and an independent peasantry (the peasants are already all mortgaged), had ruined and disorganised the remains of collectivism of the *gens* which had been their strength in their battles with the Turks. Amongst the Bulgarians, on the other hand, these primitive institutions had been left intact by the Turks—which explains their superior gallantry.

So, a further setback for the Russians; they had to begin from scratch. Slavophile chauvinism, stoked up as a counter-weight to the revolutionary element, was growing day by day and already becoming a threat to the government. The Tsar goes off to Crimea; and the Russian newspapers announce that he is about to do something great; he tries to attract the Sultan by showing him his old allies (Austria and England) betraying and despoiling him, with France following suit and at the mercy of Russia. But the Sultan turns a deaf ear and the enormous armaments of Western and Southern Russia remain idle for the time being.

The Tsar returns from Crimea (last June). But meanwhile the chauvinist tide rises, and the government, unable to repress this aggressive movement, is increasingly dragged along behind it; so much so that it is necessary to allow the mayor of Moscow[a] to speak publicly about the conquest of Constantinople *in his address to the Tsar.*[b] [272] The press, under the influence and the *protection* of the generals, says openly that it expects from the Tsar an energetic operation against Austria and Germany, who are hindering him, and the government lacks the courage to silence it. Slavophile chauvinism is more powerful than the Tsar, he will have to give way[c] for fear of revolution, the Slavophiles would ally with the constitutionalists, with the nihilists,[273] and finally with all malcontents.

The dire financial plight complicates the situation. Nobody is willing to lend to this government which, from 1870 to 1875, borrowed 1 billion 750,000 francs from London and which threatens the peace of Europe. Two or three years ago Bismarck facilitated a loan of 375 million francs in Germany; but this has long since been swallowed up; and without Bismarck's signature the Germans will not hand over a farthing. But this signature cannot be obtained without humiliating conditions. The manufacture of warrants at home has produced too much, the silver rouble

---

[a] N. A. Alexeyev.— *Ed.*

[b] See "Morning Post. Wednesday, May 14", *Novoye Vremya,* No. 3666, May 15 (27), 1886.— *Ed.*

[c] The rest of the paragraph is missing in Engels' letter; instead it says: "or else—the Slavophiles would rebel".— *Ed.*

is worth 4 frs, the paper rouble 2 frs 20. Armaments cost no end of money.

In the end it is necessary to act.— Success in the direction of Constantinople, or revolution.— Giers goes to see Bismarck and explains the situation to him; he understands it very well. Out of consideration for Austria he would have liked to hold back the government of the Tsar, whose insatiability worries him. *But revolution in Russia means the fall of the Bismarck regime.* Without Russia, the great reserve army of reaction, the domination by the Prussian squirearchy, would not last a single day. Revolution in Russia would change the situation in Germany immediately; it would destroy at a stroke this blind faith in Bismarck's omnipotence which secures him the cooperation of the ruling classes; it would bring revolution in Germany to a head.

Bismarck, who knows that the existence of Tsarism is the basis of his whole system, would hurry to Vienna to inform his friends that in the face of such danger it is no longer the time to dwell on questions of *amour-propre*; that it is necessary to allow the Tsar some semblance of triumph, and that it is in the interests of Austria and Germany, as they well realise, that they should bow before Russia. Moreover, if the Austrians insist on meddling in Bulgaria's affairs he would wash his hands of them; they would see what would happen. Kalnoky gives way, Alexander Battenberg is sacrificed, and Bismarck runs off to carry the news to Giers in person.

Unfortunately the Bulgarians display unexpected political skill and energy, intolerable in a Slav nation "delivered by holy Russia". Battenberg is arrested by night, but the Bulgarians arrest the conspirators, appoint a government that is capable, energetic and incorruptible, qualities completely intolerable in a nation that is scarcely liberated; they recall Battenberg; the latter displays all his spinelessness and takes flight. But the Bulgarians are incorrigible. With or without Battenberg they resist the sovereign orders of the Tsar and compel the heroic Kaulbars to make a fool of himself in front of the whole of Europe.[274]

Imagine the fury of the Tsar. Having forced Bismarck to submit, broken the Austrian resistance, he sees himself pulled up short by this tiny people of yesteryear which owes its "independence" to him or his father,[a] and refuses to realise that this independence means nothing more than blind obedience to the orders of the "liberator". The Greeks and the Serbs were

---

[a] Alexander II.— *Ed.*

ungrateful; but the Bulgarians are really overdoing it. Fancy taking their independence seriously! What a crime!

To save himself from revolution the poor Tsar is obliged to take another step forward. But every step becomes more dangerous, because it is only taken at the risk of a European war, which Russian diplomacy has always sought to avoid. It is certain that if there is direct intervention by the Russian government in Bulgaria and if it leads to further complications, the moment will come when the hostility between Russian and Austrian interests will break out into the open. It will then be impossible to localise the war—it will become general. Given the honesty of the rogues who govern Europe, it is impossible to predict how the two camps will form up. Bismarck is quite capable of siding with the Russians against the Austrians if he can see no other way of delaying the revolution in Russia. But it is more likely that if war breaks out between Russia and Austria, Germany will come to the aid of the latter in order to prevent its complete annihilation.

While waiting for spring, for the Russians will not be able to mount a major winter campaign on the Danube before April, the Tsar is working to lure the Turks into his net, and the treason of Austria and England towards Turkey are making the task easier for him. His goal is to occupy the Dardanelles and thus to transform the Black Sea into a Russian lake; to turn it into an inaccessible shelter for the organisation of powerful fleets which would emerge to dominate what Napoleon called a "French lake", the Mediterranean. But he has not managed it yet, although his supporters in Sofia have betrayed his secret thought.

This is the situation. In order to escape a revolution in Russia the Tsar needs Constantinople; Bismarck hesitates, he would like to find the means to avoid one eventuality as well as the other.

* * *

And France?

The patriotic French, who have been dreaming of revenge for sixteen years, believe there is nothing more natural than to grasp any opportunity which may present itself. But for our party the matter is not so simple; nor is it any simpler for Messieurs the chauvinists. A war of revenge, conducted with the alliance and under the aegis of Russia, could lead to a revolution or a counter-revolution in France. In the eventuality of a revolution which brought the socialists to power, the Russian alliance would collapse. First, *the Russians would immediately make peace with Bismarck to fling themselves with the Germans on revolutionary France.* Then France would not bring the socialists to power in order to prevent by a war a revolution in Russia. But this eventuality is hardly likely; the *monarchist counter-revolution* is more so. The Tsar wants the restoration of the Orléans, his intimate friends, the only government which offers him the conditions of a good and solid alliance. Once the war was under way, good use would be made of the monarchist officers to prepare it. At the slightest partial defeat, and there would be some, the cry would go up that it is the fault of the Republic, that in order to win victories and to obtain the full cooperation of Russia, a stable, monarchist government is needed, in other words Philippe VII[a]; the monarchist generals would act feebly so as to be able to blame their lack of success on the Republican government; and there you are—the monarchy is back. With Philippe VII restored, the kings and emperors will reach immediate agreement and instead of devouring one another they will divide Europe up, swallowing the small states. With the French Republic dead, a new congress of Vienna would be held where, perhaps, the sins of the French republicans and socialists would be used as a pretext to deny France Alsace-Lorraine, either in part or entirely; and the princes would mock the republicans for having been so naive as to believe in the possibility of a true alliance between Tsarism and the Republic.

Moreover, is it true that General Boulanger is saying to anyone who will listen to him, "*A war is necessary to prevent the social revolution*"? If it is true, may it serve as a warning to the socialist party. This fine Boulanger has boastful airs, for which as a soldier he may be forgiven, but they give a poor idea of his political sense. He is not the one who will save the Republic. Between the socialists and the Orleanists[275] it is possible that he will reach an arrangement with the latter if they assure him of the Russian alliance. In any case, *the bourgeois republicans in France are in the same position as the Tsar; they see the spectre of social revolution looming up ahead of them, and they know but one means of salvation: war.*

In France, Russia and Germany events are turning out so well for us that, for the time being, we can only desire the continuation of the *status quo.* If revolution broke out in Russia it would create a set of most favourable conditions. A general war would, on the other hand, propel us into the realm of the unforeseen. Revolution in Russia and Germany would be delayed; our party in

---

[a] Louis Philippe Albert d'Orléans, count of Paris.— *Ed.*

Germany would meet the fate of the Commune of 1871. Without a doubt events will finish by turning in our favour; but what a waste of time, what sacrifices, what new obstacles to surmount.

The forces in Europe which are pushing towards a war are powerful. The Prussian military system, adopted everywhere, requires twelve to sixteen years for its complete development; after this interval the reserve lists are filled with men who are experienced in handling arms. These twelve to sixteen years have elapsed everywhere; everywhere there are twelve to sixteen year groups which have passed through the army. So everywhere people are ready, and the Germans have no special advantage on their side. That is to say: this war which is threatening us would throw ten million soldiers into the field of battle. And old William is probably going to die. Bismarck will see his position shaken, more or less, and *perhaps he will push for war as a means of hanging on.* Indeed, the Stock Exchange everywhere believes in war as soon as the old man has breathed his last.

If there is a war, it will be with the sole aim of preventing revolution: in Russia to forestall the common action of all the malcontents, Slavophiles, constitutionalists, nihilists, peasants; in Germany to keep Bismarck in office; in France to drive back the victorious movement of the socialists and restore the monarchy.

Between French socialists and German socialists there is no Alsace question. The German socialists know only too well that the annexations of 1871, against which they have always protested, have been the main focus of Bismarck's reactionary politics, both at home and abroad. The socialists of the two countries have an equal interest in preserving the peace; it is they who will pay all the costs of the war.

F. Engels

Written on October 25, 1886

First published in *Le Socialiste*, No. 63, November 6, 1886

Printed according to the newspaper

Translated from the French

Published in English for the first time

JOHANN PHILIPP BECKER[276]

Death has torn another hole in the ranks of the champions of the proletarian revolution. *Johann Philipp Becker* died in Geneva on December 7.

Born at Frankenthal in the Bavarian Palatinate in 1809, he took part in the political movement of his native region back in the 1820s, when little more than a child. When this movement became republican in character in the early 1830s, after the July Revolution, Becker was one of its most active and stalwart supporters. Several times arrested, brought before a jury and acquitted, when reaction triumphed he eventually had to flee. He went to Switzerland, settled in Biel and took Swiss citizenship. He did not remain idle there, either. He was involved not only in the affairs of the German workingmen's associations and the revolutionary endeavours of the German, Italian and European refugees in general, but also in the struggle of the Swiss democrats for control of the individual cantons. It will be recalled that this struggle was waged by means of a series of armed raids on the aristocratic and clerical cantons, particularly in the early 1840s. Becker was implicated to a greater or lesser extent in most of these "coups" and was finally sentenced to ten years' banishment from his home canton of Berne on this account. These minor campaigns eventually culminated in the Sonderbund War of 1847. Becker, who was an officer in the Swiss Army, took up his post and, during the march on Lucerne, led the advance guard of the division to which he was assigned.

The February Revolution of 1848 broke out; there ensued attempts to republicanise Baden by means of campaigns by volunteer corps. When Hecker launched his campaign,[277] Becker formed a refugees legion but was not able to get to the border until Hecker had already been pushed back. This legion, most members of which were subsequently interned in France, provided the nucleus for some of the best units in the armies of the Palatinate and Baden in 1849.

When the republic was proclaimed in Rome in the spring of 1849,[278] Becker sought to form an auxiliary corps from this legion to fight on the side of Rome. He went to Marseilles, set up the officer cadre and took steps to gather together the troops. But, as we well know, the French Government was preparing to suppress the Roman republic and bring back the Pope.[a] It went without saying that the French Government prevented the auxiliaries from coming to the aid of its Roman adversaries. Becker, who had already hired a ship, was informed in no uncertain terms that she would be sent to the bottom as soon as she made any move to leave harbour.

Revolution then broke out in Germany.[279] Becker immediately hurried to Karlsruhe; the legion followed, and later took part in the struggle under Böning's leadership, while another section of the old legion of 1848, trained by Willich in Besançon, formed the nucleus of Willich's voluntary corps. Becker was appointed head of the entire Baden people's militia, that is to say, all troops except troops of the line, and at once set about organising it. He immediately came up against the government, which was dominated by the reactionary bourgeoisie, and its leader, Brentano. His orders were countermanded, his requests for arms and equipment left unheeded or turned down flat. The attempt on June 6 to intimidate the government by a show of revolutionary armed strength, an attempt in which Becker was a major participant, proved indecisive[280]; but Becker and his troops were then sent post-haste from Karlsruhe to the Neckar to face the enemy.

There the battle had already started in a small way, and the decisive moment was rapidly approaching. With his volunteers and militiamen, Becker occupied the Odenwald forest. Without artillery and cavalry he was obliged to waste his few troops holding this extensive and awkward area, and not enough was left at his disposal to mount an attack. Nonetheless, on June 15 he relieved, in a brilliantly fought action, his Hanau Gymnasts,[281] who had been surrounded in Hirschhorn Castle by Peucker's imperial troops.

---

[a] Pius IX.— Ed.

When Mieroslawski became commander-in-chief of the revolutionary army, Becker was given command of the 5th
Division—nothing but militiamen and infantry—with orders to
resist Peucker's corps, which outnumbered Becker's division by at
least 6 to 1. But shortly afterwards came the crossing of the Rhine
by the first Prussian corps at Germersheim, Mieroslawski's
countermove and the defeat at Waghäusel on June 21. Becker
occupied Heidelberg; the second Prussian corps under Gröben
advanced from the north, from the northeast came Peucker's
corps, each more than 20,000 strong, while to the southwest were
Hirschfeld's Prussians, likewise more than 20,000 strong. And
then the refugees from Waghäusel—the entire Baden army, both
troops of the line and militiamen—poured into Heidelberg to
make an enormous detour through the mountains and rejoin the
road to Karlsruhe and Rastatt, which was blocked to them in the
plain.

Becker was supposed to cover this retreat—with his newly
recruited, untrained troops and as usual without cavalry or
artillery. At 8 p.m. on the 22nd, after allowing the refugees an
adequate start, he marched from Heidelberg to Neckargemünd,
where he rested for a few hours. Arriving on the 23rd at
Sinsheim, where he again gave his troops a few hours' rest in
battle formation in the face of the enemy, he reached Eppingen
the same evening, and on the 24th he marched via Bretten to
Durlach, arriving at 8 p.m. only to become tangled up again in the
disorderly retreat of the now united Palatinate-Baden army. Here
Becker was also given command of the remnants of the Palatinate
troops, and was now expected not only to cover Mieroslawski's
retreat but also to hold Durlach long enough for Karlsruhe to be
evacuated. As always, he was again left without any artillery, since
the artillery assigned to him had already marched off.

Becker hastily fortified Durlach as well as he could, and was
attacked the very next morning (June 25) on three sides by two
Prussian divisions and Peucker's imperial troops. He not only
repulsed all the attacks but also launched several counter-attacks,
although he had only small arms to pit against the enemy's
artillery fire, and after four hours' fighting withdrew in perfect
order, unchecked by the columns despatched to outflank him,
after receiving word that Karlsruhe had been evacuated and his
mission accomplished.

This must be the most brilliant episode in the entire Baden-
Palatinate campaign. With men most of whom had only been in
the army for 2-3 weeks and who as completely raw recruits had

been given a perfunctory training by improvised officers and NCOs and hardly had a trace of discipline, Becker carried out, as the rearguard of the beaten and half-dispersed armies, a march of more than 80 kilometres (or 11 German miles[a]) in 48 hours, starting straight away with a night march, bringing them right through the enemy to Durlach in a fit state to offer the Prussians, the next morning, one of the few engagements of the campaign in which the battle objective of the revolutionary army was achieved in full. It was an achievement that would do credit to experienced troops and in the case of such young soldiers is extremely rare and praiseworthy.

Having reached the Murg, Becker came to a halt with his division east of Rastatt and played an honourable part in the battles of June 29 and 30. The outcome is well known: the enemy, six times superior in strength, marched round the position through the territory of Württemberg and then rolled it back from the right flank. The campaign was now formally settled and ended of necessity with the withdrawal of the revolutionary army to Swiss territory.

Until then Becker had acted basically as an ordinary democratic republican; but from now on he went considerably further. Closer acquaintance with the German "pure republicans", particularly the south German ones, and his experience in the 1849 revolution demonstrated to him that the matter would have to be tackled differently in future. The strong proletarian sympathies that Becker had entertained since his youth now assumed a more tangible form; he had realised that while the bourgeoisie always formed the core of the reactionary parties, only the proletariat could form the core of a genuinely revolutionary force. The communist by sentiment became a conscious communist.

Once again he attempted to set up a voluntary corps; it was in 1860, after Garibaldi's victorious march on Sicily. He travelled from Geneva to Genoa to make the preparations in collaboration with Garibaldi. But Garibaldi's rapid progress and the intervention of the Italian Army, which was to secure the fruits of victory for the monarchy, brought the campaign to an end. Meanwhile, there were widespread expectations of another war with Austria next year. It is common knowledge that Russia sought to use Louis Napoleon and Italy to consummate the Russian revenge on Austria, which had remained incomplete in 1859. The Italian Government sent a high-ranking officer from the general staff to

---

[a] The German geographical mile≈7.42 km.— Ed.

see Becker in Genoa, offering him the rank of colonel in the
Italian Army, a splendid salary and an allowance, and command
over a legion to be formed by him in the war that was expected,
provided he agreed to make propaganda in Germany for Italy
and against Austria. But the proletarian Becker turned the offer
down; the service of princes was not for him.

That was his last attempt as a volunteer. Soon after, the
International Workingmen's Association was established, and
Becker was among its founders; he was present at the famous
meeting in St. Martin's Hall that saw the birth of the International.[282] He organised the German and native workers of Romance
Switzerland, founded the *Vorbote* as the group's journal, attended
all the congresses of the International and was in the vanguard
of the struggle against the Bakuninist anarchists of the
Alliance de la Démocratie socialiste[283] and the Swiss Jura.

After the disintegration of the International there was less
opportunity for Becker to play a public role. But he always
remained, nevertheless, in the midst of the working-class movement and continued to exert his influence on its development
through his extensive correspondence and by virtue of the many
visits he received in Geneva. In 1882 he played host to Marx for a
day, and as recently as this September the 77-year-old undertook a
journey through the Palatinate and Belgium to London and Paris,
during which I had the pleasure of having him to stay for a
fortnight and talking over old times and new with him. And
scarcely two months later the telegraph brings news of his death!

Becker was a rare kind of man. He can be epitomised in a
nutshell: *hale and hearty.* In body and mind he was hale and hearty
to the end. A giant of a man, of tremendous physical strength and
handsome with it, he had developed his untutored, but far from
uncultivated mind, thanks to a fortunate disposition and healthy
activity, as harmoniously as his body. He was one of the few men
who, to do the right thing, only need to follow their own instinct.
That was why it was so easy for him to keep pace with every
development in the revolutionary movement and to stand in the
front rank in his seventy-eighth year as fresh as when he was
eighteen. The boy who had played with cossacks passing through
in 1814 and seen Sand (who stabbed Kotzebue to death) executed
in 1820, advanced further and further from the vague oppositional figure of the 1820s and was still fully abreast of the movement
in 1886. Yet he was no gloomy timeserver like most of the
"serrrious" republicans of 1848, but a true son of the gay
Palatinate, full of life and as fond of wine, women and song as the

next man. Having grown up in the land of the *Nibelungenlied*[284] around Worms, he still looked like one of the figures from our old epic, even in old age: light-hearted yet sardonic, calling to his opponent between sword blows, composing popular ballads if there was no one to beat—this, and no other ways, is how Volker the Fiddler must have looked!

But his greatest talent was undoubtedly military. In Baden he accomplished much more than anyone else. While the other officers, raised in the school of standing armies, found outlandish, almost unmanageable soldier material here, Becker had learned all his organisational skill, tactics and strategy in the outrageous school of the Swiss militia. A people's army was nothing strange to him, its inevitable shortcomings nothing new. Where others despaired or raged, Becker remained calm and found one solution after another; he knew how to handle his men, cheering them up with a jest, and finally had them in his hand. Many a Prussian general of 1870 might envy him the march from Heidelberg to Durlach with a division of almost nothing but untrained recruits, who still remained capable of going straight into battle and giving a good account of themselves. And in the same engagement he threw into battle the hitherto intractable Palatinate troops that had been assigned to him, and even got them to attack in open country. In Becker we have lost the only German revolutionary general we had.

He was a man who took part, with distinction, in the freedom struggles of three generations.

But the workers will honour his memory as one of their best!

London, December 9, 1886

Frederick Engels

First published in *Der Sozialdemokrat,* No. 51, December 17, 1886

Printed according to the newspaper

Published in English in full for the first time

PREFACE
[TO THE SECOND EDITION
OF *THE HOUSING QUESTION*[a]]

The following work is a reprint of three articles which I wrote in 1872 for the Leipzig *Volksstaat*. Just at that time the French milliards came pouring down on Germany[285]; public debts were paid off, fortresses and barracks built, stocks of weapons and war matériel renewed; the available capital no less than the volume of money in circulation was suddenly enormously increased, and all this just at a time when Germany was entering the world arena not only as a "united empire", but also as a great industrial country. These milliards lent young large-scale industry a powerful upswing, and it was they above all that brought about the short period of prosperity, rich in illusions, which followed the war, and immediately afterwards, in 1873-74 the great crash by which Germany proved itself to be an industrial country capable of holding its own on the world market.

The period in which an old civilised country makes such a transition from manufacture and small-scale production to large-scale industry, a transition, moreover, accelerated by such favourable circumstances, is at the same time predominantly a period of "housing shortage". On the one hand, masses of rural workers are suddenly drawn into the big towns, which develop into industrial centres; on the other hand, the concept applied in building these older towns no longer accords with the conditions needed for the new large-scale industry and the corresponding traffic; streets are widened and new ones cut through, and railways are run right across them. At the very time when workers are streaming into the towns in masses, workers' dwellings are pulled down wholesale.

---

[a] See present edition, Vol. 23, pp. 317-91.— *Ed.*

Hence the sudden housing shortage for the workers and for the small traders and small manufacturing businesses, which depend on the workers for their custom. In towns which grew up from the outset as industrial centres, this housing shortage is as good as unknown; for instance, Manchester, Leeds, Bradford, Barmen-Elberfeld. On the other hand, in London, Paris, Berlin, Vienna it took on an acute form at the time, and has, for the most part, continued to exist in a chronic form.

It was therefore precisely this acute housing shortage, this symptom of the industrial revolution taking place in Germany, which filled the press of the day with treatises on the "housing question" and gave rise to all sorts of social quackery. A series of such articles also found their way into the *Volksstaat*. The anonymous author, who revealed himself later on as A. Mülberger, M. D. of Württemberg, considered the opportunity a favourable one for enlightening the German workers, by means of this question, on the miraculous effects of Proudhon's social panacea.[a] When I expressed my astonishment to the editors at the acceptance of these peculiar articles, I was challenged to answer them, and this I did (see Part I: How Proudhon Solves the Housing Question). This series of articles was soon followed by a second series, in which I examined the philanthropic bourgeois view of the question, on the basis of a work by Dr. Emil Sax[b] (Part II: How the Bourgeoisie Solves the Housing Question). After a rather long pause Dr. Mülberger did me the honour of replying to my articles,[c] and this compelled me to make a rejoinder (Part III: Supplement on Proudhon and the Housing Question), whereby both the polemic and also my special occupation with this question came to an end. That is the genesis of these three series of articles, which have also appeared as a separate reprint in pamphlet form. The fact that a new reprint has now become necessary I owe undoubtedly to the benevolent solicitude of the German imperial government which, by prohibiting the work, tremendously increased its sale, as usual, and I hereby take this opportunity of expressing my respectful thanks to it.[286]

I have revised the text for this new edition, inserted a few additions and notes, and have corrected a small economic error in

a [A. Mülberger,] "Die Wohnungsfrage", *Der Volksstaat*, Nos 10-13, 15, 19, February 3, 7, 10, 14, 21 and March 6, 1872.— *Ed.*

b E. Sax, *Die Wohnungszustände der arbeitenden Classen und ihre Reform*, Vienna, 1869.— *Ed.*

c A. Mülberger, "Zur Wohnungsfrage (Antwort an Friedrich Engels von A. Mülberger)", *Der Volksstaat*, No. 86, October 26, 1872.— *Ed.*

the first part,[a] as my opponent, Dr. Mülberger, unfortunately failed to discover it.

During this revision it came home to me what gigantic progress the international working-class movement has made during the past fourteen years. At that time it was still a fact that "for twenty years the workers speaking Romance languages have had no other mental pabulum than the works of Proudhon",[b] and at a pinch, the still more one-sided version of Proudhonism presented by the father of "anarchism", Bakunin, who regarded Proudhon as "the schoolmaster of us all", *notre maître à nous tous*. Although the Proudhonists in France were only a small sect among the workers, they were still the only ones who had a definitely formulated programme and who under the Commune were able to take over the leadership in the economic field. In Belgium, Proudhonism reigned unchallenged among the Walloon workers, and in Spain and Italy, with a few isolated exceptions, everything in the working-class movement which was not anarchist was decidedly Proudhonist. And today? In France, Proudhon has been completely discarded among the workers and retains supporters only among the radical bourgeois and petty bourgeois, who as Proudhonists also call themselves "socialists", but against whom the most energetic fight is carried on by the socialist workers. In Belgium, the Flemings have ousted the Walloons from the leadership of the movement, deposed Proudhonism and greatly raised the level of the movement. In Spain, as in Italy, the anarchist high tide of the seventies has receded and washed away with it the remnants of Proudhonism. While in Italy the new party is still in process of clarification and formation, in Spain the small nucleus, which as the Nueva Federación Madrileña [287] remained loyal to the General Council of the International, has developed into a strong party, which—as can be seen from the republican press itself—is destroying the influence of the bourgeois republicans on the workers far more effectively than its noisy anarchist predecessors were ever able to do. Among Latin workers the forgotten works of Proudhon have been replaced by *Capital,* the *Communist Manifesto* and a number of other works of the Marxian school, and Marx's main demand—the seizure of all the means of production in the name of society by a proletariat risen to absolute political power—is now the demand of the whole revolutionary working class in the Latin countries as well.

---

[a] See present edition, Vol. 23, p. 334.— *Ed.*
[b] Ibid., p. 369.— *Ed.*

If therefore Proudhonism has been finally supplanted among the workers of the Latin countries as well, if it—in accordance with its real destination—only serves French, Spanish, Italian and Belgian bourgeois radicals as an expression of their bourgeois and petty-bourgeois cravings, why then return to it today? Why combat anew a dead opponent by reprinting these articles?

First of all, because these articles do not confine themselves to a mere polemic against Proudhon and his German deputies. As a consequence of the division of labour that existed between Marx and myself, it fell to me to present our views in the periodical press, and, therefore, particularly in the fight against opposing views, in order that Marx should have time for the elaboration of his great main work. This made it necessary for me to present our views for the most part in a polemical form, in opposition to other views. Here too. Parts One and Three contain not only a critique of the Proudhonist conception of the question, but also a presentation of our own conception.

Secondly, Proudhon played much too significant a role in the history of the European working-class movement for him to fall into oblivion without more ado. Refuted theoretically and discarded practically, he remains of historical interest. Anyone who occupies himself in any detail with modern socialism must also acquaint himself with the "surmounted standpoints" of the movement. Marx's *Poverty of Philosophy* appeared several years before Proudhon put forward his practical proposals for social reform.[288] Here Marx could only discover in embryo and criticise Proudhon's exchange bank. From this angle, therefore, his work is supplemented by the present one, imperfectly enough, sad to say. Marx would have done it all much better and far more convincingly.

And finally, bourgeois and petty-bourgeois socialism is strongly represented in Germany down to this very hour. On the one hand, by armchair socialists[289] and philanthropists of all sorts, among whom the wish to turn the workers into owners of their dwellings still plays a great role and with regard to whom, therefore, my work is still appropriate. On the other hand, a certain petty-bourgeois socialism finds representation in the Social-Democratic Party itself, and even in the ranks of the Reichstag group. This is done in the following way: while the fundamental views of modern socialism and the demand for the transformation of all the means of production into social property are recognised as justified, their accomplishment is declared possible only in the distant, and for all practical purposes, unforeseeable future. Thus, for the present one has to rely on mere social patchwork, and sympathy can be shown, according to circumstances, even with the most reactionary efforts for what is known as the "uplifting of the labouring class". The existence of such a tendency is quite inevitable in Germany, the land of philistinism *par excellence,* particularly at a time when industrial development is uprooting this deeply rooted philistinism forcibly and on a mass scale. The tendency is quite harmless to the movement, in view of the wonderful common sense of our workers, which has stood the test so magnificently precisely during the past eight years of struggle against the Anti-Socialist Law,[290] the police and the judges. But it is necessary clearly to realise that such a tendency exists. And if this tendency subsequently takes on a firmer shape and more defined contours, as is necessary and even desirable, it will have to go back to its predecessors for the formulation of its programme, and in doing so it will hardly be able to overlook Proudhon.

The essence of both the big-bourgeois and petty-bourgeois solutions of the "housing question" is that the worker should own his dwelling. However, this is a point which has been shown in a very peculiar light by the industrial development of Germany during the past twenty years. In no other country do there exist so many wage labourers who own not only their dwellings but also a garden or field as well. Besides these there are numerous others who hold house and garden or field as tenants, having in fact fairly secure possession. Rural domestic industry combined with gardening or small-scale agriculture forms the broad basis of Germany's new large-scale industry. In the West the workers are for the most part owners, in the East chiefly tenants, of their homesteads. We find this combination of domestic industry with gardening and agriculture, and therefore with a secure dwelling, not only wherever hand weaving still fights against the mechanical loom: in the Lower Rhineland and in Westphalia, in the Saxon Erzgebirge and in Silesia, but also wherever domestic industry of any sort has established itself as a rural occupation, as, for instance, in the Thuringian Forest and in the Rhön area. At the time of the discussion of the tobacco monopoly, it was revealed to what great extent cigar making too was being carried on as a rural domestic industry. Wherever distress spreads among the small peasants, as for instance a few years ago in the Eifel area,[291] the bourgeois press immediately raises a call for the introduction of a suitable domestic industry as the only remedy. And in fact both the growing plight of the German allotment peasants and the general situation of German industry urge a continual extension of rural domestic industry. This is a phenomenon peculiar to Germany. Only very exceptionally do we find anything similar in France; for instance, in the regions of silk cultivation. In England, where there are no small peasants, rural domestic industry rests on the work of the wives and children of the agricultural day-labourers. Only in Ireland can we observe the rural domestic industry of garment making being carried on, as in Germany, by real peasant families. We are not, of course, concerned here with Russia and other countries not represented on the industrial world market.

Thus, as regards industry there exists today a state of affairs in large parts of Germany which appears at first glance to resemble that which prevailed generally before the introduction of machinery. However, this is so only at first glance. The rural domestic industry of earlier times, combined with gardening and agriculture, was, at least in the countries in which industry was developing, the basis of a tolerable and, here and there, even comfortable material situation for the working class, but at the same time the basis of its intellectual and political insignificance. The hand-made product and its cost determined the market price, and owing to the infinitesimal labour productivity compared with the present day, the sales markets as a rule grew faster than the supply. This held good at about the middle of the last century for England, and partly for France, particularly in the textile industry. In Germany which was at that time only just recovering from the devastation of the Thirty Years' War [292] and working its way up under most unfavourable circumstances, the situation was, however, quite different. The only domestic industry producing for the world market there, linen weaving, was so oppressed by taxes and feudal dues that it did not raise the peasant weavers above the very low level of the rest of the peasantry. Nevertheless, at that time the rural industrial worker enjoyed a certain guaranteed existence.

With the introduction of machinery all this changed. Prices were now determined by the machine-made product, and the wage of the domestic industrial worker fell with this price. However, the worker had to accept it or look for other work, and he could not do that without becoming a proletarian, that is, without giving up his little house, garden and field, whether owned or rented. Only in the rarest cases was he ready to do this. And thus the gardening and agriculture of the old rural hand weavers became the cause by virtue of which the struggle of the hand loom against the mechanical loom was everywhere so protracted and has not yet been fought to conclusion in Germany. In this struggle it was demonstrated for the first time, especially in England, that the same circumstance which had previously served as a basis of comparative prosperity for the worker—the fact that he owned his means of production—had now become a hindrance and a misfortune for him. In industry the mechanical loom defeated his hand loom, and in agriculture large-scale cultivation got the better of his small-scale cultivation. However, while the collective labour of many and the application of machinery and science became the social rule in both fields of production, he was chained to the antiquated method of individual production and hand labour by his little house, garden, field and hand loom. The possession of house and garden was now worth much less than complete freedom of movement. No factory worker would have changed places with the slowly but surely starving rural hand weaver.

Germany appeared late on the world market. Our large-scale industry dates from the forties; it owed its first upswing to the revolution of 1848, and was able to develop fully only after the revolutions of 1866 and 1870 [293] had cleared at least the worst political obstacles out of its way. But it found the world market occupied to a large extent. The articles of mass consumption were supplied by England and the elegant luxury articles by France. Germany could not beat the former in price or the latter in quality. For the moment, therefore, nothing else remained but, following the beaten path of German production up to that time, to wedge its way into the world market with articles which were too petty for the English and too shoddy for the French. However, the favourite German custom of cheating, by first sending good samples and afterwards inferior articles, soon met with sufficiently severe punishment on the world market and was pretty well abandoned. On the other hand, the competition of overproduction gradually forced even the respectable English onto the downward path of quality deterioration and so gave an advantage to the Germans, who are matchless in this sphere. And thus we finally came to possess a large-scale industry and to play a role on the world market. But our *large-scale* industry works almost exclusively for the home market (with the exception of the iron industry, which produces far beyond the limits of home demand), and our mass export consists of a tremendous number of small articles, for which large-scale industry provides at most the necessary semi-manufactures, while the small articles themselves are supplied chiefly by rural domestic industry.

And here is seen in all its glory the "blessing" of house and landownership for the modern worker. Nowhere, hardly excepting even the Irish domestic industries, are such infamously low wages paid as in the German domestic industries. Competition permits the capitalist to deduct from the price of labour power that which the family earns from its own little garden or field. The workers are compelled to accept any piece rates offered them, because otherwise they would get nothing at all and they could not live from the products of their agriculture alone, and because, on the other hand, it is precisely this agriculture and landownership which chains them to the spot and prevents them from looking around for other employment. This is the reason which maintains Germany's capacity to compete on the world market in a whole number of small articles. *The whole profit is derived from a deduction from normal wages and the whole surplus value can be presented to the purchaser.* That is the secret of the extraordinary cheapness of most German export articles.

It is this circumstance more than any other which keeps the wages and the living conditions of the German workers also in other industrial fields below the level of the West European countries. The dead weight of such prices for labour, kept traditionally far below the value of labour power, depresses also the wages of the urban workers, and even of the workers in the cities, below the value of labour power; and this all the more so as poorly paid domestic industry has taken the place of the old handicrafts in the towns as well, and here too depresses the general level of wages.

Here we see clearly that what at an earlier historical stage was the basis of relative well-being for the workers, namely, the combination of agriculture and industry, the ownership of house, garden and field, and guarantee of a dwelling place, is becoming today, under the rule of large-scale industry, not only the most terrible shackle to the worker, but the greatest misfortune for the whole working class, the basis for an unprecedented depression of wages below their normal level, and that not only for separate branches of enterprise and districts, but for the whole country. No wonder the big and petty bourgeoisie, who live and grow rich on these abnormal deductions from wages, are enthusiastic over rural industry and home-owning workers, and they regard the introduction of new domestic industries as the sole remedy for all rural distress!

That is one side of the matter, but it also has its reverse side. Domestic industry has become the broad basis of the German export trade and therefore of the whole of large-scale industry. Due to this it is spread over wide areas of Germany and is extending still further by the day. The ruin of the small peasant, inevitable ever since his industrial domestic labour for his own use was destroyed by cheap ready-made clothing and machined products, as was his animal husbandry, and hence his manure production, by the dissolution of the mark system, the common mark and compulsory crop rotation—this ruin forcibly drives the small peasant, having fallen victim to the usurer, into the arms of modern domestic industry. Like the ground rent of the landowner in Ireland, the interest of the mortgage usurer in Germany cannot be paid from the yield of the soil but only from the wages of the industrial peasant. However, with the expansion of domestic industry one peasant area after another is being dragged into the present-day industrial movement. It is this revolutionising of the rural districts by domestic industry which is spreading the industrial revolution in Germany over a far wider territory than was the case in England and France. It is the comparatively low level of our industry which makes its extension in area all the more necessary. This explains why in Germany, in contrast to England and France, the revolutionary working-class movement has spread so tremendously over the greater part of the country instead of being confined exclusively to urban centres. And this in turn explains the tranquil, certain and irresistible progress of the movement. In Germany it is perfectly clear that a victorious rising in the capital and in the other big cities will be possible only when the majority of the smaller towns and a great part of the rural districts as well have become ripe for revolutionary change. Given anything like normal development, we shall never be in a position to win working-class victories like those of the Parisians in 1848 and 1871, but for just that reason we shall also not suffer defeats of the revolutionary capital by the reactionary province, such as Paris suffered in both cases. In France the movement always originated in the capital; in Germany it originated in the areas of large-scale industry, of manufacture and of domestic industry; the capital was conquered only later. Therefore, perhaps in future too, the initiative will continue to rest with the French, but the decisive struggle can be fought out only in Germany.

Now, this rural domestic industry and manufacture, which due to its expanse has become the decisive branch of German production and is thus revolutionising the German peasantry more and more, is itself, however, only the preliminary stage of a further revolutionary change. As Marx has already proved

(*Capital,* Vol. I, 3rd edition, pp. 484-95[a]), at a certain stage of development the hour of downfall owing to machinery and factory production will sound for it also. And this hour would appear to be at hand. But the destruction of rural domestic industry and manufacture by machinery and factory production means in Germany the destruction of the livelihood of millions of rural producers, the expropriation of almost half the German small peasantry; the transformation, not only of domestic industry into factory production, but also of peasant farming into large-scale capitalist agriculture, and of small landed property into big estates—an industrial and agricultural revolution in favour of capital and big landownership at the cost of the peasants. Should it be Germany's fate to undergo also this transformation while still under the old social conditions, it will unquestionably be the turning point. If the working class of no other country has taken the initiative by that time, Germany will certainly strike first, and the peasant sons of the "glorious army" will bravely lend assistance.

And with this the bourgeois and petty-bourgeois utopia, which would give each worker the ownership of his little house and thus chain him in semi-feudal fashion to his particular capitalist, takes on a very different complexion. As its materialisation there appears the transformation of all the small rural house-owners into industrial domestic workers; the destruction of the old isolation and, with it, of the political insignificance of the small peasants, who are dragged into the "social turmoil"; the expansion of the industrial revolution over the rural areas and thus the transformation of the most stable and conservative class of the population into a nursery for revolutionaries; and, as the culmination of it all, the expropriation of the peasants engaged in home industry by machinery, which drives them forcibly into insurrection.

We can readily allow the bourgeois-socialist philanthropists the private enjoyment of their ideal so long as they continue in their public function as capitalists to implement it in this inverted fashion, for the greater good of the social revolution.

London, January 10, 1887

Frederick Engels

First published in *Der Sozialdemokrat*, Nos. 3 and 4, January 15 and 22, 1887 and in the book: F. Engels, *Zur Wohnungsfrage*, Hottingen-Zurich, 1887

Printed according to the book

---

[a] See present edition, Vol. 35, Ch. XIII, 8 (e).—*Ed.*

THE LABOR MOVEMENT IN AMERICA

PREFACE TO THE AMERICAN EDITION
OF *THE CONDITION OF THE WORKING CLASS IN ENGLAND*[294]

Ten months have elapsed since, at the translator's[a] wish, I wrote the Appendix[b] to this book; and during these ten months, a revolution has been accomplished in American society such as, in any other country, would have taken at least ten years. In February 1886,[c] American public opinion was almost unanimous on this one point; that there was no working class, in the European sense of the word, in America;* that consequently no class struggle between workmen and capitalists, such as tore European society to pieces, was possible in the American Republic; and that, therefore, Socialism was a thing of foreign importation which could never take root on American soil. And yet, at that moment, the coming class struggle was casting its gigantic shadow before it in the strikes of the Pennsylvania coal miners,[296] and of many other trades, and especially in the preparations, all over the country, for the great Eight Hours' movement which was to come

---

* An English translation of the book I had written in 1844 was justified precisely by the fact that industrial conditions in present-day America coincide almost entirely with those in the England of the forties, that is those described by myself. How much this is the case is evinced by the articles on "The Labor Movement in America" by Edward and Eleanor Marx-Aveling in the London monthly *Time* of March, April, May and June. I take all the greater pleasure in referring to these excellent articles in that it gives me an opportunity to simultaneously rebuff the miserable slander about Aveling which the Executive of the Socialist Labor Party of America has so foolishly transmitted around the world.[295] [*Note by Engels for the 1887 offprint.*]

---

a Florence Kelley-Wischnewetzky.— *Ed.*
b See this volume, pp. 399-405.— *Ed.*
c In the original mistakenly "1885".— *Ed.*

off, and did come off, in the May following.[297] That I then duly appreciated these symptoms, that I anticipated a working class movement on a national scale, my "Appendix" shows; but no one could then foresee that in such a short time the movement would burst out with such irresistible force, would spread with the rapidity of a prairie-fire, would shake[a] American society to its very foundations.

The fact is there, stubborn and indisputable. To what an extent it had struck with terror the American ruling classes, was revealed to me, in an amusing way, by American journalists who did me the honor of calling on me last summer; the "new departure" had put them into a state of helpless fright and perplexity.[298] But at that time the movement was only just on the start; there was but a series of confused and apparently disconnected upheavals of that class which, by the suppression of negro slavery and the rapid development of manufactures, had become the lowest stratum of American society. Before the year closed, these bewildering social convulsions began to take a definite direction. The spontaneous, instinctive movements of these vast masses of working people, over a vast extent of country, the simultaneous outburst of their common discontent with a miserable social condition, the same everywhere and due to the same causes, made them conscious of the fact, that they formed a new and distinct class of American society; a class of—practically speaking—more or less hereditary wage-workers, proletarians. And with true American instinct this consciousness led them at once to take the next step towards their deliverance: the formation of a political workingmen's party, with a platform of its own, and with the conquest of the Capitol and the White House for its goal. In May the struggle for the Eight Hours' working-day, the troubles in Chicago, Milwaukee, etc., the attempts of the ruling class to crush the nascent uprising of Labor by brute force and brutal class-justice; in November the new Labor Party organized in all great centres, and the New York, Chicago and Milwaukee elections.[299] May and November have hitherto reminded the American bourgeoisie only of the payment of coupons of U.S. bonds; henceforth May and November will remind them, too, of the dates on which the American working class presented *their* coupons for payment.

In European countries, it took the working class years and years before they fully realized the fact that they formed a distinct and,

---

[a] The German has: "...would even now shake American society to its foundations".— *Ed.*

under the existing social conditions, a permanent class of modern society; and it took years again until this class-consciousness led them to form themselves into a distinct political party, independent of, and opposed to,[a] all the old political parties formed by the various sections of the ruling classes. On the more favored soil of America, where no mediaeval ruins bar the way, where history begins with the elements of modern bourgeois society as evolved in the seventeenth century, the working class passed through these two stages of its development within ten months.

Still, all this is but a beginning. That the laboring masses should feel their community of grievances and of interests, their solidarity as a class in opposition to all other classes; that in order to give expression and effect to this feeling, they should set in motion the political machinery provided for that purpose in every free country—that is the first step only. The next step is to find the common remedy for these common grievances, and to embody it in the platform of the new Labor Party. And this—the most important and the most difficult step in the movement—has yet to be taken in America.

A new party must have a distinct positive platform; a platform which may vary in details as circumstances vary and as the party itself develops, but still one upon which the party, for the time being, is agreed. So long as such a platform has not been worked out, or exists but in a rudimentary form, so long the new party, too, will have but a rudimentary existence; it may exist locally but not yet nationally; it will be a party potentially but not actually.

That platform, whatever may be its first initial shape, must develop in a direction which may be determined beforehand. The causes that brought into existence the abyss between the working class and the Capitalist class are the same in America as in Europe; the means of filling up that abyss, are equally the same everywhere. Consequently, the platform of the American proletariat will in the long run[b] coincide as to the ultimate end to be attained, with the one which, after sixty years of dissensions and discussions, has become the adopted platform of the great mass of the European militant proletariat. It will proclaim, as the ultimate end, the conquest of political supremacy by the working class, in order to effect the direct appropriation of all means of production—land, railways, mines, machinery, etc.—by society at large, to be worked in common by all for the account and benefit of all.

---

[a] Instead of "opposed to", we find in the German edition "hostile to".— *Ed.*

[b] Instead of "in the long run", the German edition has "as the movement continues to develop".— *Ed.*

But if the new American party, like all political parties everywhere, by the very fact of its formation aspires to the conquest of political power, it is as yet far from agreed upon what to do with that power when once attained.[a] In New York and the other great cities of the East, the organization of the working class has proceeded upon the lines of Trades' Societies, forming in each city a powerful Central Labor Union. In New York the Central Labor Union, last November, chose for its standard bearer Henry George, and consequently its temporary electoral platform has been largely imbued with his principles. In the great cities of the North West the electoral battle was fought upon a rather indefinite labor platform, and the influence of Henry George's theories was scarcely, if at all, visible. And while in these great centres of population and of industry the new class movement came to a political head, we find all over the country two wide spread labor organizations: the "Knights of Labor"[300] and the "Socialist Labor Party," of which only the latter has a platform in harmony with the modern European standpoint as summarized above.

Of the three more or less definite forms under which the American labor movement thus presents itself, the first, the Henry George movement in New York, is for the moment of a chiefly local significance. No doubt New York is by far the most important city of the States; but New York is not Paris and the United States are not France. And it seems to me that the Henry George platform, in its present shape, is too narrow to form the basis for anything but a local movement, or at best for a short-lived phase of the general movement. To Henry George, the expropriation of the mass of the people from the land is the great and universal cause of the splitting up of the people into Rich and Poor. Now this is not quite correct historically. In Asiatic and classical antiquity, the predominant form of class-oppression was slavery, that is to say, not so much the expropriation of the masses from the land as the appropriation of their persons. When, in the decline of the Roman Republic, the free Italian peasants were expropriated from their farms, they formed a class of "poor whites" similar to that of the Southern Slave States before 1861; and between slaves and poor whites,[b] two classes equally unfit for self-emancipation, the old world went to pieces. In the middle

---

a In the German edition the words "when once attained" are omitted.— *Ed.*

b Instead of "poor whites", the German edition has "free men gone to the dogs".— *Ed.*

ages, it was not the expropriation of the people *from,* but on the contrary, their appropriation *to* the land which became the source of feudal oppression. The peasant retained his land, but was attached to it as a serf or villein, and made liable to tribute to the lord in labor and in produce. It was only at the dawn of modern times, towards the end of the fifteenth century, that the expropriation of the peasantry on a large scale laid the foundation for the modern class of wage-workers[a] who possess nothing but their labor-power and can live only by the selling of that labour power to others. But if the expropriation from the land brought this class into existence, it was the development of capitalist production, of modern industry and agriculture on a large scale which perpetuated it, increased it, and shaped it into a distinct class with distinct interests and a distinct historical mission. All this has been fully expounded by Marx ("Capital," Part VIII: "The so-called primitive Accumulation.") According to Marx, the cause of the present antagonism of the classes and of the social degradation[b] of the working class is their expropriation from *all* means of production, in which the land is of course included.

If Henry George declares land-monopolization to be the sole cause of poverty and misery, he naturally finds the remedy in the resumption of the land by society at large. Now, the Socialists of the school of Marx, too, demand the resumption, by society, of the land, and not only of the land but of all other means of production likewise. But even if we leave these out of the question, there is another difference. What is to be done with the land? Modern Socialists, as represented by Marx, demand that it should be held and worked in common and for common account, and the same with all other means of social production, mines, railways, factories, etc.; Henry George would confine himself to letting it out to individuals as at present, merely regulating its distribution and applying the rents for public, instead of, as at present, for private purposes. What the Socialists demand, implies a total revolution of the whole system of social production; what Henry George demands, leaves the present mode of social production untouched, and has, in fact,[c] been anticipated by the extreme

---

a Instead of "the expropriation of the peasantry on a large scale laid the foundation for the modern class of wage-workers", the German edition has: "the expropriation of the peasants was carried out on a grand scale, and this time under historical conditions which gradually turned the peasants who had become propertyless into the modern class of wage-workers, into people...".— *Ed.*

b The German has "current humiliation" instead of "social degradation".— *Ed.*

c In the German edition, the words "in fact" are followed by "years ago".— *Ed.*

section of Ricardian bourgeois economists who, too, demanded the confiscation of the rent of land by the State.

It would of course be unfair to suppose that Henry George has said his last word once for all. But I am bound to take his theory as I find it.

The second great section of the American movement is formed by the Knights of Labor. And that seems to be the section most typical of the present state of the movement, as it is undoubtedly by far the strongest. An immense association spread over an immense extent of country in innumerable "assemblies," representing all shades of individual and local opinion within the working class; the whole of them sheltered under a platform of corresponding indistinctness and held together much less by their impracticable constitution than by the instinctive feeling that the very fact of their clubbing together for their common aspiration makes them a great power in the country; a truly American paradox clothing the most modern tendencies in the most mediaeval mummeries, and hiding the most democratic and even rebellious spirit behind an apparent, but really powerless despotism—such is the picture the Knights of Labor offer to a European observer. But if we are not arrested by mere outside whimsicalities, we cannot help seeing in this vast agglomeration an immense amount of potential energy evolving slowly but surely into actual force. The Knights of Labor are the first national organization created by the American Working Class as a whole; whatever be their origin and history, whatever their shortcomings and little absurdities, whatever their platform and their constitution, here they are, the work of practically the whole class of American wage-workers, the only national bond that holds them together, that makes their strength felt to themselves not less than to their enemies, and that fills them with the proud hope of future victories. For it would not be exact to say that the Knights of Labor are liable to development. They are constantly in full process of development and revolution; a heaving, fermenting mass of plastic material seeking the shape and form appropriate to its inherent nature. That form will be attained as surely as historical evolution has, like natural evolution, its own immanent laws. Whether the Knights of Labor will then retain their present name or not, makes no difference, but to an outsider it appears evident that here is the raw material out of which the future of the American working class movement, and along with it, the future of American society at large, has to be shaped.

The third section consists of the Socialist Labor Party. This section is a party but in name, for nowhere in America has it, up to now, been able actually to take its stand as a political party. It is, moreover, to a certain extent foreign to America, having until lately been made up almost exclusively by German immigrants, using their own language and for the most part little conversant with the common language of the country. But if it came from a foreign stock, it came, at the same time, armed with the experience earned during long years of class-struggle in Europe, and with an insight into the general conditions of working class emancipation,[a] far superior to that hitherto gained by American workingmen. This is a fortunate circumstance for the American proletarians who thus are enabled to appropriate, and to take advantage of, the intellectual and moral fruits of the forty years' struggle of their European classmates, and thus to hasten on the time of their own victory. For, as I said before, there cannot be any doubt that the ultimate platform of the American working class must and will be essentially the same as that now adopted by the whole militant working class of Europe, the same as that of the German-American Socialist Labor Party. In so far this party is called upon to play a very important part in the movement. But in order to do so they will have to doff every remnant of their foreign garb. They will have to become out and out American. They cannot expect the Americans to come to them; they, the minority and the immigrants, must go to the Americans, who are the vast majority and the natives. And to do that, they must above all things learn English.

The process of fusing together these various elements of the vast moving mass—elements not really discordant, but indeed mutually isolated by their various starting-points—will take some time and will not come off without a deal of friction, such as is visible at different points even now. The Knights of Labor, for instance, are here and there, in the Eastern cities, locally at war with the organized Trades Unions. But then this same friction exists within the Knights of Labor themselves, where there is anything but peace and harmony. These are not symptoms of decay, for capitalists to crow over. They are merely signs that the innumerable hosts of workers, for the first time[b] set in motion in a common direction, have as yet found out neither the adequate expression for their common interests, nor the form of organiza-

---

[a] In the German edition the end of the sentence reads: "as found only exceptionally hitherto in American workers".—Ed.

[b] Instead of "for the first time", the German edition has "now at last".—Ed.

tion best adapted to the struggle, nor the discipline required to insure victory.[a] They are as yet the first levies *en masse* of the great revolutionary war, raised and equipped locally and independently, all converging to form one common army, but as yet without regular organization and common plan of campaign. The converging columns cross each other here and there; confusion, angry disputes, even threats of conflict arise. But the community of ultimate purpose in the end overcomes all minor troubles; ere long the straggling and squabbling battalions will be formed in a long line of battle array, presenting to the enemy a well-ordered front, ominously silent under their glittering arms, supported by bold skirmishers in front and by unshakeable reserves in the rear.

To bring about this result, the unification of the various independent bodies into one national Labor Army, with no matter how inadequate a provisional[b] platform, provided it be a truly working class platform—that is the next great step to be accomplished in America. To effect this, and to make that platform worthy of the cause, the Socialist Labor Party can contribute a great deal, if they will only act in the same way as the European Socialists have acted at the time when they were but a small minority of the working class. That line of action was first laid down in the "Communist Manifesto" of 1847 in the following words:

"The Communists"—that was the name we took at the time and which even now we are far from repudiating—"the Communists do not form a separate party opposed to other working class parties.

"They have no interests separate and apart from the interests of the whole working class.

"They do not set up any sectarian principles of their own, by which to shape and model the proletarian movement.

"The Communists are distinguished from the other working class parties by this only: 1. In the national struggles of the proletarians of the different countries they point out, and bring to the front, the common interests of the whole proletariat, interests independent of all nationality; 2. In the various stages of development which the struggle of the working class against the capitalist class has to pass through, they always and everywhere represent the interests of the movement as a whole.

---

[a] In the German edition the end of the sentence from the words "nor the discipline..." is omitted.— *Ed.*

[b] The German has "general" instead of "provisional".— *Ed.*

"The Communists, therefore, are on the one hand, practically, the most advanced and resolute section of the working class parties of all countries, that section which ever pushes forward all others; on the other hand, theoretically, they have, over the great mass of the proletarians, the advantage of clearly understanding the line of march, the conditions, and the ultimate general results of the proletarian movement.

"Thus they fight for the attainment of the immediate ends, for the enforcement of the momentary interests of the working class; but in the movement of the present, they represent and take care of the future of the movement." [a]

That is the line of action which the great founder of Modern Socialism, Karl Marx, and with him, I and the Socialists of all nations who worked along with us, have followed for more than forty years, with the result that it has led to victory everywhere, and that at this moment the mass of European Socialists, in Germany and in France, in Belgium, Holland and Switzerland, in Denmark and Sweden as well as in Spain and Portugal, are fighting as one common [b] army under one and the same flag.

London, January 26, 1887

Frederick Engels

First published in F. Engels, *The Condition of the Working Class in England in 1844*, New York, 1887 and, in the author's translation into German, in *Der Sozialdemokrat*, Nos. 24 and 25, June 10 and 17, 1887

Reproduced from the book collated with the German translation

---

[a] Cf. present edition, Vol. 6, pp. 497, 518.— *Ed.*
[b] The German edition follows "common" with "great".— *Ed.*

443

[LETTER TO THE ORGANISING COMMITTEE OF THE INTERNATIONAL FESTIVAL IN PARIS]

Citizens,

We find ourselves face to face with a terrible danger. We are threatened by a war in which those who loathe it and have only common interests—the French proletariat and the German proletariat—will be forced to butcher each other.

What is the real cause of this state of things?

It is militarism, it is the introduction of the Prussian military system in all the major countries of the Continent.

This system claims to arm the whole nation for the defence of its territory and its rights. That is a lie.

The Prussian system ousted the system of limited conscription and substitution bought by the wealthy, because it placed at the disposal of rulers all the resources of their countries, both manpower and materials. But it has not been able to create a popular army.

The Prussian system divides the citizens who are called up into two categories. The first are drafted into the army of the line, while the second are straightway assigned to the reserve or to the territorial army. The men in this second category receive no military instruction at all, or almost none; but the first serve with the colours for two or three years, sufficient time to turn them into an obedient army, accustomed to discipline, in other words an army ever ready to embark on foreign conquests and to suppress by violence any popular movements at home. For let us not forget that all the governments which have adopted this system are much more frightened of the working people within their frontiers than of rival governments beyond them.

Thanks to its flexibility this system is capable of enormous expansion. For as long as there remains a single young man who has not been drafted into the army, the available resources have not been exhausted. Hence the frantic competition between the states as to which of them possesses the largest and strongest army. Every addition to the military force of one state prompts the other states to do the same, if not more. And all this costs an enormous amount of money. The peoples are crushed by the burden of military expenditure. Peace becomes almost more expensive than war, so that eventually war no longer seems like a terrible scourge, but like a salutary crisis which will put an end to an impossible situation.

This is what has allowed intriguers of all countries keen to fish in troubled waters to press for war.

And the remedy?

Abolish the Prussian system, replace it with a truly popular army, an ordinary school into which any citizen capable of bearing arms will be drafted for the time strictly necessary in order to learn the soldier's job; group the men graduating from this school into a reserve list, firmly organised by districts, so that every town, every canton has its own battalion, made up of men who know one another, united, armed, equipped, ready to march at twenty-four hours' notice if necessary. This means that every man will keep his rifle and equipment at home, as they do in Switzerland.

The first nation to adopt this system will double its real military strength while halving its war budget. It will prove its love of peace by the very fact of arming all its citizens. For this army, which is the nation itself, is as ill suited to conquest abroad as it is invincible in the defence of its own territory. *And what government would dare lay a finger on civil liberties, if every citizen has at home his rifle and fifty rounds of ammunition?*

London, February 13, 1887

Frederick Engels

First published in *Le Socialiste*, No. 79,
February 26, 1887

Printed according to the newspaper collated with the manuscript

Translated from the French

TO THE FEDERATION OF THE CENTRE OF THE FRENCH WORKERS' PARTY[302]

IN PARIS

London, 18 March, 1887

Citizens,

I am with you in my heart to celebrate the 18 March.

F. Engels

First published in *Le Socialiste*, No. 83, March 26, 1887

Printed according to the newspaper

Translated from the French

INTRODUCTION
[TO SIGISMUND BORKHEIM'S PAMPHLET,
*IN MEMORY OF THE GERMAN BLOOD-AND-THUNDER
PATRIOTS. 1806-1807]*[303]

Sigismund Borkheim, the author of the following pamphlet, was born in Glogau on March 29, 1825. After completing his grammar-school education in Berlin in 1844, he studied in turn in Breslau, Greifswald and Berlin. Since he was too poor to bear the costs of the one-year military service, he satisfied his obligations to the army by joining in 1847 the artillery in Glogau as a three-year volunteer. After the 1848 revolution he took part in democratic meetings and this led to his being investigated by a court martial, from which he escaped by fleeing to Berlin. Here, safe from pursuit for the moment, he remained active in the movement and played an outstanding role in the storm on the Arsenal.[304] A further flight to Switzerland became necessary to evade the new threat of arrest arising from this. In September 1848, when Struve organised the march of his volunteer corps to the Black Forest in Baden,[305] Borkheim joined his force, was captured and remained in gaol until the Baden Revolution of May 1849[306] liberated the prisoners.

Borkheim went to Karlsruhe to offer his services as a soldier to the revolution. When Johann Philipp Becker was appointed colonel in command of the entire people's militia, he gave Borkheim the task of forming a battery for which the government initially supplied only the unharnessed guns. The horse teams had still not arrived when the movement of June 6 broke out.[307] This was an attempt by the more resolute elements to induce the inert provisional government, which consisted in part of outright traitors, to bestir itself to greater efforts. Along with Becker, Borkheim had taken part in the demonstration whose only immediate effect, however, was that Becker, together with all his volunteers and militiamen, was sent away from Karlsruhe to join the front on the Neckar. Borkheim could not follow him with his battery until he had been provided with horses for his cannons. By the time he was finally issued with these—Herr Brentano, the head of the government, found it was very much in his interest to get rid of the revolutionary battery—the Prussians had already conquered the Palatinate and the first act of Borkheim's battery was to take position on the Knieling Bridge and cover the withdrawal of the Palatinate army to Baden territory.

Together with the troops from the Palatinate and those from Baden still stationed around Karlsruhe, Borkheim's battery now advanced in a northerly direction. On June 21 it saw action at Blankenloch and played an honourable part in the encounter at Ubstadt (June 25). As part of the reorganisation of the army for its new positions on the River Murg, Borkheim and his artillery were assigned to the Oborski Division and distinguished himself in the fighting around Kuppenheim.

After the withdrawal of the revolutionary army to Swiss territory, Borkheim went to Geneva. Here he found his old commander and friend, J. Ph. Becker, and some younger comrades-in-arms, and they all banded together to form as cheerful a society as possible amidst the privations of refugee life. I myself spent several enjoyable days with them when I passed through there in autumn 1849. This was the same society that under the name of the "Brimstone Gang" acquired a highly undeserved posthumous notoriety thanks to the colossal lies of Herr Karl Vogt.[308]

However, the fun was not to last long. In the summer of 1850 the arm of the stern Federal Council reached also the harmless "Brimstone Gang", and the majority of its happy-go-lucky members were forced to leave Switzerland, since they were among the categories of refugees to be expelled. Borkheim went to Paris and subsequently to Strasbourg. But here too his stay was cut short. In February 1851 he was arrested and taken under police escort to Calais for deportation to England. For a whole three months he was dragged from place to place, for the most part in chains, through 25 different prisons. But wherever he came, the republicans had been notified in advance, and they went out to meet the prisoner, made sure he was well-provided for, did deals with and bribed the police and officials, and provided transport whenever possible. In this way he finally arrived in England.

Of course, he found the condition of the refugees in London far more wretched than in Geneva or even in France, but even here his resilience did not desert him. He looked around for work and found it at first in a Liverpool emigration firm which needed German clerks to act as interpreters for the numerous German emigrants bidding farewell to their old fatherland in which peace and quiet had at last been restored. At the same time, he looked around for other business contacts and was so successful that after the outbreak of the Crimean War, he managed to despatch a steamship laden with all sorts of goods to Balaclava and, once there, to sell the cargo at fantastic prices, partly to the army authorities and partly to the English officers. On his return he had made a net profit of £15,000 (300,000 marks). But this success only spurred him on to further speculation. He made an agreement with the English Government to arrange for a further shipment. However, since by this time peace negotiations were already underway, the government stipulated in the contract that it could refuse to take delivery of the goods if the peace preliminaries had been settled by the time they arrived. Borkheim agreed to this. When he arrived in the Bosporus with his steamship, peace was already a fact. Since the ship had only been hired for the outward voyage and since any amount of lucrative cargoes could be obtained for the return journey, the captain insisted on unloading without delay. The harbour was full to bursting point and as Borkheim was unable to find anywhere to store the cargo which was now left on his hands, the captain simply unloaded everything on the nearest beach. So Borkheim was stuck there in the middle of his useless crates and bales and barrels and had to helplessly watch his wares being plundered by the rabble that had come to the Bosporus from all corners of Turkey and the whole of Europe. When he returned to England he found himself a pauper again—the £15,000 were all gone. His irrepressible resilience, however, was still there. He had lost all his money through speculation, but had gained a knowledge of business and made contacts in the world of commerce. He now discovered that he had an extremely fine palate for wine and became a successful representative for various Bordeaux exporters.

At the same time, however, he remained as active as he could in the political movement. He had known Liebknecht from Karlsruhe and Geneva. He came into contact with Marx through the Vogt scandal and in this way I renewed my acquaintance with him. Without committing himself to any specific programme, Borkheim always sided with the most extreme revolutionary party. His principal political activity was combating the great bulwark of

European reaction, Russian absolutism. So as to be better able to follow the Russian intrigues designed to subjugate the Balkans and indirectly increase its influence in Western Europe, he learnt Russian and spent many years studying the Russian daily press and émigré writings. Among other things, he translated Serno-Solovyevich's pamphlet *Our Russian Affairs* which denounced the hypocrisies fabricated by Herzen (and continued subsequently by Bakunin) as a result of which the Russian refugees in Western Europe propagated not the truth they knew about Russia, but a conventional legend which fitted in with their nationalist and Pan-Slavist twaddle. He also wrote many essays on Russia for the Berlin *Zukunft,* the *Volksstaat* and so on.

In the summer of 1876, while on a visit to Germany, he suffered a stroke in Badenweiler which left him paralysed to his last day on the left side of his body. He was forced to give up his business. His wife died some years later. Since he had a weak chest, he had to move to Hastings so as to enjoy the mild sea air of the South English coast. Neither paralysis, nor illness, nor his straitened and far from assured means of subsistence were able to break his irrepressible mental powers. His letters were always cheerful to the point of exuberance, and when you visited him you had to help him laugh. His favourite reading matter was the Zurich *Sozialdemokrat.* He died after an attack of pneumonia on December 16, 1885.

The *Blood-and-Thunder Patriots* appeared straight after the war against France in the *Volksstaat* and soon after in an off-print. It proved to be a highly effective antidote to the mood of super-patriotic intoxication which overcame and which still affects both the German authorities and the German bourgeois. And, indeed, there could have been no better aid to sobering down than to recall the time when the same Prussia which was now praised to the skies had collapsed ignominiously before the onslaught of the same Frenchmen who were now being derided as the vanquished foe. And the medicine had to be all the more effective since the facts it recounted were drawn from a book in which a Prussian general, who was moreover the director of the general Academy of War, had used official Prussian documents to portray the moment of humiliation—and it should be admitted, in an impartial and dispassionate manner.[a] Like any other large social

---

[a] E. Höpfner, *Der Krieg von 1806 und 1807.—Ed.*

organisation, a great army is never better than when it turns in upon itself after a major defeat and does penance for its past sins. This was the fate of the Prussians after Jena, and again after 1850. In the latter case, even though they had not suffered a major defeat, their total military decline became palpably clear both to themselves and to the whole world in a series of minor campaigns—in Denmark and South Germany—and in the first large-scale mobilisation of 1850, when they only averted a real defeat by the political humiliations of Warsaw and Olmütz.[309] They were forced to subject their own past to ruthless criticism in order to learn how to repair the damage. Their military literature, which in Clausewitz had brought forth a star of the first magnitude, but which had since sunk to unbelievable depths, arose once more under the necessity for this self-examination. And one of the fruits of this self-examination was Höpfner's book from which Borkheim culled the material for his pamphlet.

Even today it will be essential to recall again and again that age of arrogance and defeat, of the incapacity of the monarch, of the naive cunning of the Prussian diplomats ensnared in their own double-dealing, of the aristocratic officer-class whose loud-mouthed swaggering outlived their cowardly betrayals, and of the total collapse of a state-authority estranged from the people and based on lies and deception. The German philistine (and that includes the nobility and the princes) is, if possible, even more conceited and chauvinistic than he was then; diplomatic practice has become significantly more insolent, but it is as two-faced as ever; the aristocratic officer-class has grown sufficiently, both by natural and by artificial means, to enable it more or less to regain its old control over the army; the state is becoming more and more estranged from the masses of the people and is now well on the way to transforming itself into a consortium of landowners, stockbrokers and big industrialists for the exploitation of the people. True enough, if another war breaks out the Prussian-German army will have significant advantages over its opponents as well as its allies, if only because it was the model they all imitated. But these advantages will never again be as great as in the last two wars.[310] The unity of the supreme command, for example, such as existed then, thanks to particularly fortunate circumstances, and the corresponding unconditional obedience of the lower echelons, is unlikely to recur in the same way. The business clique which now occupies a dominant position between the agrarian and military nobility—right up to the Emperor's entourage—and the stockjobbers, can easily prove fatal for the provision of the army in the field. Germany will have allies, but it will leave them in the lurch, and they Germany, at the first opportunity. And, finally, the only war left for Prussia-Germany to wage will be a world war, a world war, moreover, of an extent and violence hitherto unimagined. Eight to ten million soldiers will be at each other's throats and in the process they will strip Europe barer than a swarm of locusts. The depredations of the Thirty Years' War [311] compressed into three to four years and extended over the entire continent; famine, disease, the universal lapse into barbarism, both of the armies and the people, in the wake of acute misery; irretrievable dislocation of our artificial system of trade, industry and credit, ending in universal bankruptcy; collapse of the old states and their conventional political wisdom to the point where crowns will roll into the gutters by the dozen, and no one will be around to pick them up; the absolute impossibility of foreseeing how it will all end and who will emerge as victor from the battle. Only one consequence is absolutely certain: universal exhaustion and the creation of the conditions for the ultimate victory of the working class.

That is the prospect for the moment when the systematic development of mutual oneupmanship in armaments reaches its climax and finally brings forth its inevitable fruits. This is the pass, my worthy princes and statesmen, to which you in your wisdom have brought our ancient Europe. And when no alternative is left to you but to strike up the last dance of war—that will be no skin off our noses. The war may push us into the background for a while, it may wrest many a conquered base from our hands. But once you have unleashed the forces you will be unable to restrain, things can take their course: by the end of the tragedy you will be ruined and the victory of the proletariat will either have already been achieved or else inevitable.

London, December 15, 1887

Frederick Engels

First published in S. Borkheim, *Zur Erinnerung fur die deutschen Mordspatrioten. 1806-1807,* Hottingen-Zurich, 1888

Printed according to the book

Published in English in full for the first time

THE ROLE OF FORCE IN HISTORY [312]

Written between the end of December 1887 and March 1888

First published in *Die Neue Zeit*, Vol. 1, Nos. 22-26, 1895-96

Printed according to the manuscript, and the text of the journal where the manuscript has not been preserved

Let us now apply our theory to contemporary German history and its use of force, its policy of blood and iron. We shall clearly see from this why the policy of blood and iron was bound to be successful for a time and why it was bound to collapse in the end.

In 1815, the Vienna Congress had partitioned and sold off Europe in a manner which revealed to the whole world the complete ineptitude of the potentates and statesmen. The universal war of the peoples against Napoleon was the reaction of the national feeling of all the peoples which Napoleon had trampled on. In gratitude for this, the princes and diplomats at the Vienna Congress trampled still more contemptuously on that national feeling. The smallest dynasty was more esteemed than the largest nation. Germany and Italy were once again split up into small states, Poland partitioned for the fourth time and Hungary remained enslaved. It cannot even be said that an injustice was committed against the peoples; why did they tolerate it, and why did they greet the Russian Tsar[a] as their liberator?

But this could not go on for long. Since the end of the Middle Ages, history has been working towards a Europe composed of large national states. Only such states are the normal political constitution of the ruling European bourgeoisie and, at the same time, an indispensable precondition for the establishment of harmonious international co-operation between peoples, without which the rule of the proletariat is impossible. To ensure international peace, all avoidable national friction must first be done away with, each people must be independent and master in their own house. With the

---

[a] Alexander I.— *Ed.*

advance of commerce, agriculture, industry and thereby of the social position of power enjoyed by the bourgeoisie, national feeling rose everywhere and partitioned and oppressed nations demanded unity and independence.

Hence the 1848 revolution was aimed everywhere except in France at satisfying national demands just as much as the demand for freedom. But behind the bourgeoisie, which had been victorious at the first attempt, there already arose everywhere the menacing figure of the proletariat, which had actually won the victory, and which drove the bourgeoisie into the arms of the just defeated enemy—monarchistic, bureaucratic, semi-feudal and military reaction to which the revolution succumbed in 1849. In Hungary, where this was not the case, the Russians invaded and crushed the revolution. Not content with this, the Russian Tsar[a] went to Warsaw, where he sat in judgment as the arbiter of Europe. He appointed his obedient creature Christian of Glücksburg heir to the Danish throne. He humiliated Prussia as it had never been humiliated before, prohibiting it even the slightest craving to exploit the German aspirations for unity and forcing it to re-establish the Federal Diet and submit to Austria.[313] At first sight it seemed that the whole result of the revolution was the establishment in Austria and Prussia of a system of government, constitutional in form, but in the old spirit, and that the Russian Tsar was master of Europe more than ever before.

In reality, however, the revolution had vigorously jostled the bourgeoisie even in the dismembered countries, notably in Germany, out of its old traditional rut. The bourgeoisie had received a share, however modest, of political power, and every political success of the bourgeoisie is used for industrial advance. The "crazy year",[314] which had fortunately passed, tangibly demonstrated to the bourgeoisie that it now had to put an end to the old lethargy and doziness once and for all. As a result of the Californian and Australian gold rush[315] and other circumstances, an expansion of world trade contacts and a business boom set in as never before—it was a matter of seizing the opportunity and making sure of one's share. The large-scale industry which had appeared since 1830, and particularly since 1840, on the Rhine, in Saxony, in Silesia, in Berlin and some towns in the south, was now rapidly developed and expanded, cottage industry in rural districts became increasingly widespread, railway construction was accelerated, while the rapidly increasing flow of emigrants which

---

[a] Nicholas I.— Ed.

accompanied all this gave rise to a German transatlantic steamship service which required no subsidies. German merchants settled in all overseas trade centres on a wider scale than ever before, handled an ever growing share of world trade and gradually began to offer their services for the sale not only of English, but also of German industrial products.

But the German system of small states with their numerous and varied trade and industrial laws inevitably soon became an unbearable fetter on vigorously growing industry and the trade associated with it. Every few miles a different law governed bills of exchange, there were different trade conditions; everywhere, literally everywhere, there were different sorts of chicanery, bureaucratic and fiscal traps, and often also guild barriers against which even licences were powerless. In addition there were many different local settlement laws [316] and residence restrictions which made it impossible for the capitalists to move the labour force at their disposal in sufficient numbers to places where the availability of ore, coal, water power and other favourable natural conditions called for the siting of industrial enterprises. The ability to exploit the massive labour force of the Fatherland without hindrance was the first condition for industrial development, but wherever the patriotic manufacturer gathered workers from all parts, the police and the poor administration opposed the settlement of the new arrivals. All-German civic rights and full freedom of movement for all citizens of the Empire, a uniform body of commercial and industrial law were no longer patriotic fantasies of eccentric students, they had now become vital conditions for industry.

Besides, there were different currencies, different weights and measures in every state, no matter how small, and often there were two or three in a single state. And not a single one of these innumerable kinds of coins, weights and measures was recognised on the world market. [It is] hardly surprising, therefore, that merchants and manufacturers who traded on the world market or had to compete against imported articles, had, in addition to the many coins, weights and measures, to use also foreign ones; that cotton yarn was reeled in English pounds, silk cloth was produced in metres, foreign bills were issued in pounds sterling, dollars and francs. And how could large credit institutions be set up in these limited currency zones with banknotes here in gulden, there in Prussian talers, next to them in gold talers, "new two-third" talers, bank marks, current marks, the twenty-gulden system, the twenty-four-gulden system, with endless exchange computations and rate fluctuations? [317]

And even if all this was finally overcome, how much effort had been spent on all this friction, how much money and time had been wasted! Finally, in Germany too, people became aware that nowadays time is money.

The fledgling German industry had to stand the test on the world market, it could grow only through export. For this it had to enjoy abroad the protection of international law. The English, French, American merchant could still take somewhat greater liberties abroad than at home. His legation intervened on his behalf, and, if need be, even a few men-of-war. But the German! In the Levant the Austrian at least could rely to some extent on his legation, elsewhere it did not help him much either. But whenever a Prussian merchant in a foreign land complained to his ambassador about an injustice he had suffered, he was almost always told: "Serves you right, what do you want here, why don't you stay well at home?" The subject of a small state was well and truly deprived of all rights everywhere. Wherever one went, German merchants were under foreign—French, English or American—protection, or else had quickly got themselves naturalised in their new country.[a] Even if their ambassadors had wished to intervene on their behalf, what would have been the use? German ambassadors themselves were treated no better than boot-blacks overseas.

This shows that the call for a united "Fatherland" had a very material background. It was no longer the obscure urge of a member of a *Burschenschaft* at the Wartburg festival,[318] "where courage and power burned bright in German souls", and where, as in the song set to a French tune, "the young man was carried away by a tempestuous striving to go and die fighting for the Fatherland"[b] in order to restore the romantic imperial grandeur of the Middle Ages,— while in his older days the tempestuous youth became a common sanctimonious and absolutist vassal of his prince. Neither was it any longer the considerably more down-to-earth call for unity of the lawyers and other bourgeois ideologists of the Hambach festival,[319] who thought they loved freedom and unity for their own sake and did not at all notice that the turning of Germany into a cantonal republic after the Swiss pattern, which the ideal of the least muddled among them amounted to, was just as impossible as the Hohenstaufen Empire[320] of the students mentioned above. No, it was the desire of the practical merchant

---

[a] Here Engels wrote "Weerth" in pencil in the margin.— *Ed.*
[b] K. Hinkel, "Jugend-Muth und -Kraft".— *Ed.*

and industrialist arising out of immediate business needs to sweep away all the historically inherited small state junk which was obstructing the free development of commerce and industry, to abolish all the unnecessary friction the German businessman first had to overcome at home if he wished to enter the world market, and to which all his competitors were superior. German unity had become an economic necessity. And the people who now demanded it knew what they wanted. They had been educated in commerce and for commerce, knew how to drive a bargain and were willing to bargain. They knew that it was necessary to demand a high price but also that it was necessary to reduce it liberally. They sang of the "German Fatherland" including in it Styria, the Tyrol and "Austria rich in honours and victories",[a] and

> From the Maas to the Memel,
> From the River Adige to the Belt
> Deutschland, Deutschland über alles,
> Over everything in the world—[b]

but for a payment in cash they were prepared to grant a considerable discount—from 25 to 30 per cent—on that Fatherland that was to become ever greater.[321] Their plan for unification was ready and immediately practicable.

German unity, however, was not a purely German question. Since the Thirty Years' War,[322] not a single all-German issue had been decided without very perceptible foreign interference.[c] Frederick II had conquered Silesia in 1740 with the help of the French.[324] The reorganisation of the Holy Roman Empire by decision of the Imperial Deputation in 1803 had literally been dictated by France and Russia.[325] After that, Napoleon had organised Germany to suit his convenience. And finally, at the Vienna Congress,[d] it was again mainly owing to Russia and in the second place to England and France that it was shattered into thirty-six states with over two hundred separate large and small patches of land, and, just as at the 1802-03 Imperial Diet in Regensburg,[326] the German dynasties had veritably assisted in this and made the fragmentation still worse. In addition, some parts of Germany had been handed over to foreign sovereigns. Thus, Germany was not only powerless and helpless, torn by internal

---

a E. M. Arndt, "Des Teutschen Vaterland".— *Ed.*

b [A. H. Hoffmann von Fallersleben,] "Das Lied der Deutschen".— *Ed.*

c Here Engels wrote in the margin in pencil: "Westphalian and Teschen Peace." [323]— *Ed.*

d Here Engels wrote between the lines: "Germany—Poland."— *Ed.*

strife, condemned to political, military and even industrial insignificance. What was much worse, France and Russia had by repeated usage acquired a right to the fragmentation of Germany, just as France and Austria arrogated the right to see that Italy remained dismembered. This alleged right was invoked in 1850 by Tsar Nicholas when, refusing in the coarsest manner to allow any change in the constitution without authorisation, he endorsed the restoration of that expression of Germany's impotence, the Federal Diet.[327]

Germany's unity therefore had to be won in struggle not only against the princes and other internal enemies, but also against foreign countries. Or else—with help from abroad. What was the situation abroad at that time?

In France, Louis Bonaparte had utilised the struggle between the bourgeoisie and the working class to raise himself with the help of the peasants into the office of President and with the help of the army to the imperial throne. But a new Emperor Napoleon, one placed on the throne by the army within the borders of the France of 1815, was a still-born chimera. The resurrected Napoleonic empire meant the extension of France to the Rhine, the realisation of the hereditary dream of French chauvinism. At first, however, the Rhine was beyond Louis Bonaparte's reach; every attempt in that direction would have led to a European coalition against France. On the other hand, there was an opportunity to enhance France's position of power and to win fresh laurels for the army by waging in agreement with almost the whole of Europe a war against Russia, which had made use of the revolutionary period in Western Europe to occupy on the quiet the Danubian principalities and to prepare for a new war of conquest against Turkey. England entered into alliance with France, Austria showed good will towards both, only heroic Prussia kissed the Russian rod which had chastised it only but yesterday, and continued to maintain a pro-Russian neutrality. But neither England nor France wished a serious defeat of the enemy, and the war thus ended in very mild humiliation for Russia and a Russo-French alliance against Austria.*

---

* The Crimean War was an unparalleled, colossal comedy of errors, where one wondered at every new scene: who will be cheated this time? But that comedy took a toll of uncountable wealth and over a million human lives. No sooner had the war begun than Austria invaded the Danubian principalities; the Russians retreated before them. This made a war against Turkey on Russia's land frontier impossible so long as Austria remained neutral. However, Austria was willing to become an ally in a war on this frontier on condition that the war was waged in all seriousness

The Crimean War made France Europe's leading power and the adventurer Louis Napoleon the greatest man of the day, which, to be sure, does not mean much. However, the Crimean War had not brought France any territorial expansion and was therefore pregnant with a new war, in which Louis Napoleon was to fulfil his true mission, that of "aggrandiser of the empire".[328] This new war had already been planned during the first one, since Sardinia was allowed to join the alliance of the Western powers as a satellite of imperial France and especially as its outpost against Austria; further preparations were made during the conclusion of peace by Louis Napoleon's agreement with Russia,[329] who wanted nothing more than to chastise Austria.

Louis Napoleon was now the idol of the European bourgeoisie. Not only because he had "saved society" on December 2, 1851,[330] when he destroyed the political rule of the bourgeoisie, it is true, but only to save its social rule. Not only because he showed that, under favourable circumstances, universal suffrage could be turned into an instrument for the oppression of the masses. Not only because, under his rule, industry and trade and notably speculation and stock exchange machinations advanced to a degree previously unknown. But, first and foremost, because the bourgeoisie saw in him the first "great statesman", who was flesh of their flesh, and bone of their bone. He was an upstart like every true bourgeois. "A dyed in the wool" Carbonari

to restore Poland and permanently push back Russia's western border. This would also have brought in Prussia, through which Russia was still getting all imports; Russia would have been blockaded by land and by sea and would soon have been defeated. This, however, did not enter the plans of the allies. On the contrary, they were glad to have escaped the danger of a serious war. Palmerston proposed that the theatre of war be transferred to the Crimea—which was what Russia desired—and Louis Napoleon gladly agreed. Here the war could only be a sham one, and so all the protagonists were satisfied. However, Tsar Nicholas took it into his head to wage a serious war and forgot at the same time that this was most favourable country for a sham war but most unfavourable for a serious war. What is Russia's strength in defence—the immense extent of its territory, sparsely populated, roadless and poor in auxiliary resources—in the event of any Russian offensive war turns against Russia itself, and nowhere more than in the Crimean direction. The South Russian steppes, which were to become the graves of the invaders, became the graves of the Russian armies, whom Nicholas, with brutal and stupid ruthlessness, drove one after another—finally in mid-winter—into Sebastopol. When the last hurriedly recruited, haphazardly equipped and miserably provisioned army lost about two-thirds of its number (whole battalions perished in snowstorms) and the rest was unable to drive the enemy from Russian soil, arrogant, empty-headed Nicholas miserably broke down and poisoned himself. From then on, the war once again became a sham war and peace was soon concluded.

conspirator in Italy, an artillery officer in Switzerland, a debt-burdened tramp of distinction and special constable in England,[331] yet constantly and everywhere a pretender to the throne, he had prepared himself by his adventurous past and moral failings in all countries for the role of Emperor of the French and ruler of the destinies of Europe, as the exemplary bourgeois, the American, prepares himself by a series of bankruptcies, genuine and fraudulent, for the role of millionaire. As Emperor he not only made politics serve the interests of capitalist profits and stock exchange machinations, but also pursued politics entirely according to the rules of the stock exchange and speculated on the "nationalities principle".[332] In France's previous policy the fragmentation of Germany and Italy had been an inalienable fundamental right of France; Louis Napoleon immediately began to sell off that fundamental right bit by bit for so-called compensations. He was ready to help Italy and Germany do away with their fragmentation, provided Germany and Italy paid him for every step towards national union by ceding territory. This not only satisfied French chauvinism and gradually expanded the empire to its 1801 borders[333] but, in addition, restored to France the exclusive role of enlightened power and the liberator of the peoples, and depicted Louis Napoleon as the protector of oppressed nationalities. And the whole enlightened bourgeoisie, enthusiastic for national ideas—because it was deeply interested in the removal of all obstacles to business on the world market—unanimously exulted in this world-liberating enlightenment.

The beginning was made in Italy.[a] Austria had exercised absolute rule there since 1849, and Austria was then the scapegoat for the whole of Europe. The meagre results of the Crimean War were not ascribed to the indecision of the Western powers, which had only wanted a sham war, but to Austria's irresolute attitude, for which no one had been more to blame than the Western powers themselves. But the advance of the Austrians to the Pruth—in gratitude for Russia's assistance in Hungary in 1849[335]—aggrieved Russia so much (although it was precisely that advance which had saved Russia), that it looked with joy upon every attack on Austria. Prussia no longer counted and had already been treated en canaille[b] at the Paris Peace Congress. Thus, the war for the liberation of Italy "up to the Adriatic" was

---

[a] Here Engels wrote "Orsini"[334] in pencil in the margin.— Ed.
[b] Ungraciously.— Ed.

contrived with Russia's participation, launched in the spring of 1859 and completed in the summer on the Mincio. Austria was not driven out of Italy, Italy was not "free up to the Adriatic" and not united, Sardinia had extended its territory, but France had acquired Savoy and Nice and thus re-established its 1801 frontier with Italy.[336]

However, the Italians were not satisfied with this state of affairs. At that time, manufacture proper was still predominant in Italy, large-scale industry being as yet in its infancy. The working class was far from fully expropriated and proletarianised; in the towns, it still had its own means of production, in rural areas, industrial labour was a side-line occupation of small peasant owners or tenants. The energy of the bourgeoisie had therefore not yet been broken by opposition to a modern class-conscious proletariat. And since the fragmentation of Italy was preserved only as a result of foreign rule by the Austrians, under whose protection the princes carried their misgovernment to the extreme, the big landed nobility and the mass of the townspeople sided with the bourgeoisie as the champion of national independence. However, foreign rule was thrown off, except in Venetia, in 1859; Austria's further intervention in Italy was made impossible by France and Russia and nobody was afraid of it any longer. In Garibaldi, Italy had a hero of ancient dignity, who was able to work wonders and did work wonders. With a thousand volunteers, he overthrew the entire Kingdom of Naples, in fact united Italy, and tore to pieces the ingenious web of Bonapartist politics. Italy was free and essentially united—though not by Louis Napoleon's intrigues, but by the revolution.

Since the Italian war, the foreign policy of the Second French Empire was no longer a secret to anybody. The conquerors of the great Napoleon were to be punished—but *l'un après l'autre,* one after another. Russia and Austria had received their share, Prussia was next in turn. And Prussia was despised more than ever before; its policy during the Italian war had been cowardly and wretched, just as at the time of the Basle Peace in 1795.[337] With its "free-hand policy"[338] it had reached a point when it stood absolutely isolated in Europe, and its neighbours, big and small, anticipated with pleasure the spectacle of its being given a thrashing; its hands were free for one thing only—to cede the left bank of the Rhine to France.

Indeed, in the years immediately following 1859, the conviction grew everywhere, and nowhere more than on the Rhine, that the left bank would irretrievably be lost to France. Not that this was particularly desired, but it was regarded as an inescapable fate, and, to tell the truth, it was not particularly feared. Old memories of French times, which had really brought liberty, were aroused in the peasant and petty bourgeois; among the bourgeoisie, the finance aristocracy, especially in Cologne, was already deeply involved in the machinations of the Parisian Crédit Mobilier [339] and other fraudulent Bonapartist companies and loudly demanded annexation.*

However, the loss of the left bank of the Rhine would weaken not only Prussia, but Germany too. And Germany was more divided than ever before. There was greater estrangement than ever between Austria and Prussia owing to Prussia's neutrality in the Italian war; the brood of small princes cast half scared, half longing looks at Louis Napoleon as protector of a renewed Confederation of the Rhine [340]—such was the position of official Germany. And that at a time when only the united forces of the entire nation were capable of averting the danger of dismemberment.

But how could the forces of the entire nation be united? After the attempts of 1848—almost all of them hazy—had failed and some of the haze was dispelled precisely because of this, three roads lay open.

The first road was that of genuine unification through the abolition of all individual states, that is, the openly revolutionary road. This road had just led Italy to its goal; the Savoy dynasty had joined the revolution and thereby walked off with the Italian crown. However, our German Savoyans, the Hohenzollerns, and even their most daring Cavours à la Bismarck, were altogether unable to take such a courageous step. The people would have had to do everything themselves—and in a war over the left bank of the Rhine they would have probably been able to do the necessary. The inevitable retreat of the Prussians beyond the Rhine, a protracted war at the fortifications on the Rhine, and the betrayal by the South German princes that would undoubtedly ensue, would have been sufficient to fan up a national movement which would have swept away the entire dynastic system. In that case, Louis Napoleon would have been the first to sheathe the sword. The Second Empire could afford to have opponents only among reactionary states against which it appeared as the

---

* Marx and I repeatedly saw on the spot that this was the general mood on the Rhine at that time. Industrialists on the left bank asked me, inter alia, how their industry would fare under the French customs tariff.

continuer of the French revolution, the liberator of the peoples. It was powerless against a people themselves embroiled in revolution, in fact, a victorious German revolution could have provided the impetus for the overthrow of the entire French Empire. That was at best; at worst, if the dynastic princes got the better of the movement, the left bank of the Rhine would be temporarily lost to France, the active and passive betrayal of the dynastic princes would be revealed to the whole world and would create a predicament in which there would be no way out for Germany but that of revolution, the eviction of all the princes, the establishment of a united German republic.

As things stood, this road to the union of Germany could be taken only if Louis Napoleon began a war over the border on the Rhine. But, for reasons we shall soon explain, this war did not take place. As a result, however, the issue of national union also ceased to be a vital question, one that had to be settled immediately under pain of destruction. For the time being, the nation could wait.

The second road was that of a union under Austrian supremacy. In 1815, Austria had willingly retained the position of a state with a compact, rounded-off territory, which had been imposed on it by the Napoleonic wars. It laid no claim to the former possessions in South Germany which it had ceded. It was content with annexing old and new territories which could be matched geographically and strategically with the remaining nucleus of the monarchy. The separation of German Austria from the rest of Germany, begun by the protective tariffs of Joseph II, aggravated by the police regime of Francis I in Italy, and carried to the extreme by the disintegration of the German Empire [341] and by the Confederation of the Rhine, continued for all practical purposes ever after 1815. Metternich built a veritable Chinese Wall between his state and Germany. Tariffs kept out the material, censorship the intellectual products of Germany, the most incredible chicanery with regard to passports limited personal contacts to the barest minimum. The country was protected domestically against any, even the mildest, political stirring by an absolutist tyranny unique even in Germany. Thus, Austria had remained absolutely aloof from Germany's entire bourgeois-liberal movement. By 1848, at least the intellectual barrier was torn down to a large extent, but the events of that year and their consequences were hardly fitted to bring Austria closer to the rest of Germany. On the contrary, Austria more and more insisted on its independent position as a great power. And thus it happened that, although the Austrian soldiers in the fortresses of the Confederation[342] were liked, while the Prussians were hated and derided, and although Austria was still popular and respected throughout the predominantly Catholic South and West, no one thought seriously of German unification under Austrian supremacy, except perhaps a few princes from the small and medium German states.

Nor could it be otherwise. Austria itself had not wanted it any other way, even though it continued on the quiet to cherish romantic dreams of an empire. The Austrian customs barrier had in time become the only remaining material partition within Germany, and was therefore felt all the more acutely. There was no sense in the independent great power policy if it did not mean a sacrifice of German interests to specifically Austrian, that is, Italian, Hungarian, etc., interests. After, as before the revolution, Austria continued to be the most reactionary state in Germany, the most reluctant to follow modern trends, and, besides, the only remaining specifically Catholic great power. The more the post-March government[343] strove to re-establish the old management of priests and Jesuits, the more impossible became its hegemony over a country which was one to two-thirds Protestant. And, finally, a unification of Germany under Austria was only possible through the breaking-up of Prussia. Although this in itself would have been no calamity for Germany, the breaking-up of Prussia by Austria would have been just as harmful as the breaking-up of Austria by Prussia before the imminent triumph of the revolution in Russia (after which it would become superfluous, because the now redundant Austria would disintegrate of itself).

In short, German unity under Austria's wing was a romantic dream and proved such when the German princes of the small and medium states assembled in Frankfurt in 1863 to proclaim Francis Joseph of Austria emperor of Germany. The King of Prussia[a] simply did not show up and the emperor comedy was a flop.[344]

There remained the third road: unification under Prussia's supremacy. And because this road was actually taken, it leads us from the field of speculation onto the more solid, even if rather filthy, ground of practical "Realpolitik".[345]

Since Frederick II, Prussia had regarded Germany, as also Poland, merely as territory to be conquered, from which one took what one could get, on the understanding, however, that one had

---

[a] William I.— *Ed.*

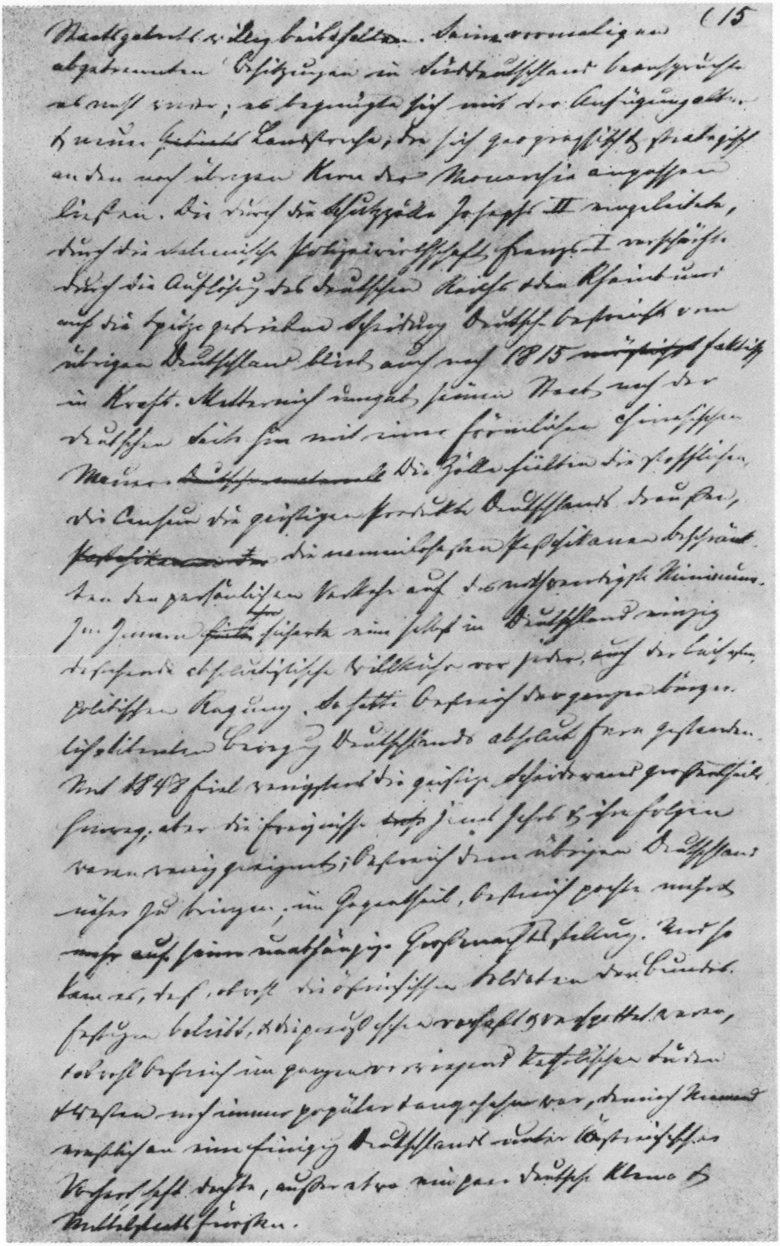

A page of the manuscript
of *The Role of Force in History*

to share with others. The division of Germany with foreign countries, notably with France, had been Prussia's "German mission" since 1740. "*Je vais, je crois, jouer votre jeu; si les as me viennent, nous partagerons*" (I think I am going to play your game; if I am dealt the aces, we shall share them)—such were Frederick's parting words to the French ambassador,[a] when he went off to his first war.[346] True to this "German mission", Prussia betrayed Germany in 1795 when the peace was signed in Basle, agreed in advance (in the Treaty of August 5, 1796) to cede the left bank of the Rhine to France in return for a promise of territorial expansion, and actually collected the reward for its treason against the Empire under a decision of the imperial deputation dictated by Russia and France.[347] Again in 1805, it betrayed Russia and Austria, its allies, when Napoleon held up Hanover to it—a bait it was always willing to swallow, but became so entangled in its own stupid cunning that it was drawn into war with Napoleon after all and received a well-deserved thrashing at Jena.[348] Still under the impression of these blows, Frederick William III was willing, even after the victories of 1813 and 1814, to forego all West German outposts, to confine himself to the possession of North-East Germany, to withdraw, like Austria, as much as possible from Germany—which would have transformed the whole of West Germany into a new Confederation of the Rhine under Russian or French protection. The plan failed: Westphalia and the Rhine Province were forced upon the King against his will, and with them a new "German mission".

For the time being, it was over with annexations—except for the purchase of some tiny patches of land. At home, the old bureaucratic Junker system gradually began to flourish again; the constitutional promises made to the people in times of great distress were persistently broken. Yet in spite of all that, the bourgeoisie was increasingly in the ascendant in Prussia too, because without industry and trade even the haughty Prussian state was now nothing. Slowly, unwillingly, in homeopathic doses, economic concessions had to be made to the bourgeoisie. In a way, these concessions offered a prospect of support for Prussia's "German mission": since Prussia, to remove the foreign customs barriers between its two parts, invited the neighbouring German states to form a customs union. Thus came into existence the Customs Union which, up to 1830, had been no more than a pious wish (only Hesse-Darmstadt had joined), but later, as a result of

---

[a] L. Ch. Beauvau.— *Ed.*

the somewhat quicker rate of political and economic development, joined the greater part of inner Germany economically to Prussia.[349] The non-Prussian coastal regions remained outside the Union even after 1848.

The Customs Union was a major success for Prussia. The fact that it meant a victory over Austrian influence was hardly the crux of the matter. The main thing was that it won over the entire bourgeoisie of the medium and small states to Prussia's side. With the exception of Saxony, there was no German state whose industry had developed to a degree even approaching Prussia's, and this was due not only to natural and historical preconditions, but also to its bigger customs area and internal market. The more the Customs Union expanded, and the more it drew small states into this internal market, the more the rising bourgeoisie of these states became used to regarding Prussia as its economic and later also political leader, and the professors danced to the tune of the bourgeoisie. What the Hegelians construed philosophically in Berlin—namely that Prussia was called upon to assume leadership in Germany, Schlosser's pupils, notably Häusser and Gervinus, demonstrated historically in Heidelberg. This naturally presupposed that Prussia would change its entire political system, that it would fulfil the demands of the ideologists of the bourgeoisie.*

All this, however, happened not because there was any special bias in favour of the Prussian state, as was the case, for example, when the Italian bourgeoisie accepted Piedmont as the leading state after it had openly placed itself at the head of the national and constitutional movement. No, it was done reluctantly, the bourgeoisie chose Prussia as the lesser evil, because Austria barred them from its market and because, compared with Austria, Prussia still had a certain bourgeois nature, if only because of its meanness in financial matters. Prussia had two good institutions ahead of other large states: universal conscription and universal compulsory education. It had introduced them in times of desperate need, and in better days had been content with emptying them of their content—dangerous under certain circumstances—by negligently enforcing them and deliberately distorting them. But they continued to exist on paper, and this gave Prussia the possibility some day to unfold the latent potential energy of the masses to a

---

* The *Rheinische Zeitung* of 1842 discussed the question of Prussia's hegemony from this viewpoint. Gervinus told me as early as the summer of 1843 in Ostend: Prussia must assume leadership in Germany, but this presupposes three conditions: Prussia must provide a constitution, grant freedom of the press and pursue a more definite foreign policy.

degree unattainable in any other place with the same population. The bourgeoisie reconciled itself to these two institutions: around 1840 it was easy and comparatively cheap for the one-year conscripts, that is, for the sons of the bourgeois, to evade service by bribery, especially as the army itself attached little value to *Landwehr*[350] officers recruited from merchant and industrial circles. The undoubtedly larger number of people with a certain amount of elementary knowledge still available in Prussia as a result of compulsory education was highly useful for the bourgeoisie; with the advance of large-scale industry it ultimately even became insufficient.* The complaints over the high cost of the two institutions,[a] expressed in heavy taxation, were made predominantly by the petty bourgeoisie; the ascendant bourgeoisie calculated that the annoying, to be sure, but unavoidable expenditure connected with the country's future position as a great power would be amply compensated by higher profits.

In short, the German bourgeois had no illusions about Prussian kindness. If the idea of Prussian hegemony had become popular with them since 1840, it was only because and insofar as the Prussian bourgeoisie, owing to its quicker economic development, assumed the economic and political leadership of the German bourgeoisie, only because and insofar as the Rottecks and Welckers of the old constitutional South were eclipsed by the Camphausens, Hansemanns and Mildes of the Prussian North, and the lawyers and professors were eclipsed by the merchants and manufacturers. Indeed, in the years just preceding 1848, there had developed among Prussian liberals, especially on the Rhine, a quite different revolutionary atmosphere from that of the cantonalist liberals of the South.[352] At that time there appeared the two best political folk songs since the 16th century, the song about Burgomaster Tschech and the one about the Baroness von Droste-Fischering,[353] whose wantonness appals the now aged people who in 1846 gaily sang:

> Has ever man had such hard luck
> As our poor Burgomaster Tschech,
> He shot at Fatty two paces away
> And yet his bullet went astray!

---

* Even during the *Kulturkampf*[351] days, Rhenish industrialists complained to me that they could not promote otherwise excellent workers to the job of supervisor because of the insufficiency of their knowledge acquired at school. This was particularly true in Catholic regions.

---

a Engels wrote in the margin: "Secondary schools for the bourgeoisie."—*Ed.*

But all this was soon to change. The February revolution was followed by the March days in Vienna and the Berlin revolution of March 18. The bourgeoisie triumphed without having to put up a serious fight, it did not even want the serious fight when it came. The bourgeoisie, which shortly before had flirted with the socialism and communism of the time (notably on the Rhine), suddenly noticed that it had reared not only individual workers, but a working *class,* a still half-dreaming, it is true, but gradually awakening and, by its innate nature, revolutionary proletariat. This proletariat, which had everywhere won the victory for the bourgeoisie, was already advancing demands, particularly in France, which were incompatible with the entire bourgeois system; in Paris the first terrible struggle between the two classes took place on June 23, 1848, and after a four-day battle the proletariat was defeated. From then on, the mass of the bourgeoisie in the whole of Europe went over to the side of reaction and allied itself with the absolutist bureaucrats, feudals and priests, whom it had just overthrown with the help of the workers, against the enemies of society, those very same workers.

The form this took in Prussia was that the bourgeoisie left in the lurch the representatives it had itself elected and, with concealed or overt glee, sat by and watched them being dispersed by the government in November 1848. True, the Junker-bureaucratic ministry, which now asserted itself in Prussia for nigh on a decade, had to rule according to constitutional forms, but it avenged itself by resorting to a system of petty vexations and obstructions, unprecedented even in Prussia, under which no one suffered more than the bourgeoisie.[354] But the latter had retired penitently into its shell and meekly submitted to the blows and kicks raining down on it as a punishment for its former revolutionary cravings, and gradually learned to think what it later was to express aloud: Yes, to be sure, we are dogs!

Then came the regency. To prove his loyalty to the throne Manteuffel surrounded the heir apparent,[a] the present emperor, with spies, just at Puttkamer now does the editorial office of the *Sozialdemokrat.* When the heir apparent became regent, Manteuffel, of course, was immediately kicked out and the New Era set in.[355] It was only a change of scenery. The prince regent deigned to allow the bourgeoisie to be liberal again. The bourgeoisie gladly availed themselves of this permission, but they deluded themselves that they were now in full control of the situation and that the

---

[a] Prince William, later Emperor William I.— *Ed.*

Prussian state would have to dance to their tune. That was by no means what was intended by the "authoritative circles", as they are servilely called. The reorganisation of the army was to be the price the liberal bourgeoisie had to pay for the New Era. The government demanded only the implementation of universal conscription to the extent to which it had been practised around 1816. From the viewpoint of the liberal opposition, absolutely nothing could be said against it that would not at the same time have flown in the face of its own talk about Prussia's authority and its German mission. But the liberal opposition demanded as a condition for its consent that the term of service be limited by law to two years. In itself this was quite rational, the question was whether it could be enforced, whether the liberal bourgeoisie of the country were prepared to insist on this condition to the end, to risk their property and their lives. The government firmly insisted on a three years' term of service, the Chamber on two, and a conflict broke out.[356] And with the conflict over the military question, foreign policy once again became decisive for domestic policy too.

We have seen how Prussia, by its stance in the Crimean and Italian wars, forfeited the last remnants of respect it had still enjoyed. That miserable policy could be partially justified by the poor state of its army. Since even before 1848, new taxes could not be imposed or new loans taken out without the consent of the estates, and since no one was willing to assemble the estates for this purpose, there never was enough money for the army, which went to ruin as a result of this boundless niggardliness. The spirit of parade and military drill that had prevailed under Frederick William III did the rest. How helpless this parade army showed itself in 1848 on the battlefields in Denmark can be read in the writings of Count Waldersee.[a] The mobilisation of 1850 was a complete fiasco; there was a shortage of everything, and what was available was mostly useless.[357] True, the voting of funds by the Chambers helped in this respect, the army was shaken out of the old rut, field service replaced parades, at least in most cases. But the numerical strength of the army was still the same as it had been around 1820, while all other great powers, notably France, which now presented the main danger, had substantially increased their armed forces. And yet there was universal conscription in Prussia, on paper every Prussian was a soldier, and while the

---

[a] See F. G. Waldersee, *Die Methode zur kriegsgemäßen Ausbildung der Infanterie für das zerstreute Gefecht.—Ed.*

population had grown from $10^1/_2$ million (1817) to $17^3/_4$ million (1858), the scale of the army was insufficient to accommodate and train more than a third of all the men fit for service. The government now demanded an increase in the army's strength corresponding almost exactly to the population growth since 1817. But the same liberal deputies who had been continually insisting on the government assuming the leadership of Germany, safeguarding its external power, and restoring its prestige among the nations — these same people higgled and haggled and refused to grant anything except on the basis of a two-year term of service. Did they possess the power to accomplish their will, on which they so stubbornly insisted? Did the people, or at least the bourgeoisie, back them, ready for action?

Quite the reverse. The bourgeoisie exulted in their verbal battles with Bismarck but actually organised a movement which, even if unconsciously, was in fact directed against the policy of the majority in the Prussian Chamber. Denmark's encroachments upon the Holstein constitution and the attempts at a forcible Danification of Schleswig made the German bourgeois indignant.[358] He was used to being bullied by the great powers; but to be kicked by little Denmark, that roused his ire. The National Association[359] was formed; it was precisely the bourgeoisie of the small states that constituted its strength. And the National Association, liberal to the bone as it was, demanded first and foremost national unification under Prussia's leadership, a liberal Prussia if possible, a Prussia the same as ever if it came to the worst. Getting a move on at long last, doing away with the wretched position of second-rank people the Germans held on the world market, chastising Denmark, showing their teeth to the great powers in Schleswig-Holstein, those were the main demands of the National Association. The demand for Prussian leadership was now free of the vagueness and haziness which had still characterised it up to 1850. It was now known for sure that it meant Austria's expulsion from Germany, the actual abolition of the sovereignty of small states, and that neither could be achieved without civil war and the division of Germany. But there was no longer any fear of civil war and the division was no more than the conclusion drawn from the Austrian customs restrictions. Germany's industry and trade had advanced to such a height, the network of German trading firms that spanned the world market had become so extensive and dense, that the proliferation of small states at home and the lack of rights and protection abroad had become intolerable. And while the strongest political organisation the

German bourgeoisie had ever had practically gave a vote of no confidence in the Berlin deputies, the latter continued to haggle over the term of service.

Such was the state of affairs when Bismarck decided to intervene actively in foreign politics.

Bismarck is Louis Napoleon translated from the adventurous French pretender to the throne into the Prussian backwoods Junker and member of the German students' association. Just like Louis Napoleon, Bismarck is a man of great practical judgment and great cunning, a born and sharp businessman, who in different circumstances would have competed on the New York stock exchange with the Vanderbilts and Jay Goulds; indeed, he has not badly succeeded in feathering his nest. But this advanced sense of the practical often goes hand in hand with a corresponding narrowness of outlook, and in this respect Bismarck excels his French predecessor. The latter had himself worked out his "Napoleonic ideas"[a] during his vagabond years—of which they bore the stamp—while Bismarck, as we shall see, never managed to produce even a hint of any political ideas of his own but always combined the ready-made ideas of others to suit his own purposes. However, precisely this narrow-mindedness was his good fortune. Without it he would never have been able to regard the entire history of the world from a specific Prussian point of view; and if in this typically Prussian world outlook of his there had been a rent through which daylight could penetrate, he would have bungled his entire mission and it would have been the end of his glory. True, he was stumped when he had fulfilled, in his own way, his special mission dictated to him from outside, and we shall see what leaps he was forced to make because of his absolute lack of rational ideas and his inability to understand the historical situation he himself had created.

If Louis Napoleon's past had taught him to show little consideration in the choice of methods, Bismarck learned from the history of Prussian politics, notably from those of the so-called Great Elector[b] and of Frederick II, to have even less regard for scruples, though here he could retain the exalting awareness of having remained true to the traditions of the Fatherland. His business sense taught him to repress his Junker appetites when this was necessary; when no longer necessary, they once again came sharply to the fore; this was, of course, a sign of his decline.

---

[a] An allusion to N. L. Bonaparte's *Des idées napoléoniennes.—Ed.*
[b] Frederick William.—*Ed.*

His political method was that of the students' association, the
comically literal interpretation of the students' beer drinking code
designed to get them out of a scrape in their pub, and he used it
unceremoniously in the Chamber in respect of the Prussian
constitution; all innovations he introduced in diplomacy were
borrowed from the students' association. But if Louis Napoleon
often hesitated in decisive moments, as, for example, during the *coup
d'état* in 1851, when Morny positively had to force him to complete
what he had begun, or on the eve of the 1870 war, when his
uncertainty spoiled his whole position, it must be admitted that this
never happened with Bismarck. His willpower never abandoned
him, it was much more likely to turn into open brutality. And this,
more than anything else, was the secret of his success. All the
ruling classes in Germany, the Junkers and the bourgeoisie, had so
much lost the last remnants of energy, it had become so much the
custom in "educated" Germany to have no will, that the only man
among them who really still possessed one became, precisely
because of this, the greatest man among them and a tyrant over
them all, at whose bidding they were ready to "jump over the
stick", as they themselves call it, against their better judgment and
their conscience. True, in the "uneducated" Germany things have
not yet reached such a pass; the working people have shown that
they possess a will against which even Bismarck's strong will is
unable to prevail.

A brilliant career lay before our Brandenburg Junker, if only he
had the courage and sense to help himself to it. Had not Louis
Napoleon become the idol of the bourgeoisie precisely because he
dispersed their parliament while raising their profits? And did not
Bismarck possess the same business talents which the bourgeois
admired so much in the false Napoleon? Was he not attracted to
his Bleichröder as much as Louis Napoleon to his Fould? Was
there not in 1864 a contradiction in Germany between the
bourgeois representatives in the Chamber, who, out of stinginess,
wanted to reduce the service term, and the bourgeois outside, in
the National Association, who demanded national action at any
cost, action for which an army was essential? Was it not a
contradiction quite similar to the one that existed in France in
1851 between the bourgeois in the Chamber who wanted to keep
the power of the President in check and the bourgeois outside
who wanted peace and quiet and a strong government, peace and
quiet at any cost—a contradiction which Louis Napoleon solved by
dispersing the brawlers in parliament and giving peace and quiet
to the mass of the bourgeois? Were not things in Germany much

more assuredly in favour of a bold move? Had not the plan for the reorganisation been supplied ready-made by the bourgeoisie, and were not the latter themselves calling loudly for an energetic Prussian statesman who would carry out their plan, expel Austria from Germany and unite the small states under Prussia's supremacy? And if this demanded that the Prussian constitution be treated a bit roughly, that the ideologists in and outside the Chamber be pushed aside according to their deserts, was it not possible to rely on universal suffrage, just as Louis Bonaparte had done? What could be more democratic than to introduce universal suffrage? Had not Louis Napoleon proved that it was absolutely safe—if properly handled? And did not precisely this universal suffrage. offer the means to appeal to the broad mass of the people, to flirt a bit with the emerging social movement, should the bourgeoisie prove refractory?

Bismarck took action. What had to be done was to repeat Louis Napoleon's *coup d'état,* to make the real balance of power tangibly clear to the German bourgeoisie, forcibly to dispel their liberal self-delusion, but to carry out their national demands which coincided with Prussia's aspirations. It was Schleswig-Holstein that first provided a lever for action. As regards foreign policy, the field had been prepared. The Russian Tsar[a] had been won over to Bismarck's side by the latter's dirty work against the Polish insurgents in 1863[360]; Louis Napoleon had also been worked on and could justify his indifference, if not his silent abetment, of Bismarck's plans, with his favourite "nationalities principle"[361]; Palmerston was Prime Minister in England, but he had placed the little Lord John Russell in the Foreign Office only for the purpose of having him make a laughing-stock of himself. But Austria was Prussia's rival for supremacy in Germany and precisely in this matter it could not afford to let Prussia outdo it, especially since it had in 1850 and 1851 acted in Schleswig-Holstein as Emperor Nicholas' henchman more vilely even than Prussia.[362] The situation was therefore extremely favourable. No matter how much Bismarck hated Austria, and how gladly Austria would once again have taken it out of Prussia, there was nothing they could do after the death of Frederick VII of Denmark but take joint action against Denmark—with the tacit consent of Russia and France. Success was assured in advance, so long as Europe remained neutral; it did, the duchies were conquered and ceded under the peace treaty.[363]

---

[a] Alexander II.— *Ed.*

In this war, Prussia had pursued an additional purpose—that of testing before the enemy the army it had been training according to new principles since 1850 and had reorganised and strengthened in 1860. It had stood the test beyond all expectations and that in all manner of military situations. The battle at Lyngby in Jutland proved that the needle-gun was far superior to the muzzle-loader and that the Prussians knew how to use it properly, since the rapid firing of 80 Prussians from behind hedgerows turned three times as many Danes to flight. At the same time it had been noticed that the only lesson the Austrians had drawn from the Italian war[a] and French fighting tactics was that shooting was no good, that a true soldier had to repulse the enemy immediately with his bayonet, and this was borne in mind, for no more welcome enemy tactics could even be desired against the muzzles of the breech-loaders. To give the Austrians the chance of convincing themselves of this in practice at the earliest possible moment, the peace treaty gave over the duchies to the joint sovereignty of Austria and Prussia, thereby creating a purely temporary situation, which was bound to breed conflict after conflict, and which thus left it entirely to Bismarck to decide when he should choose to use such a conflict for his big blow at Austria. Since it was a Prussian political tradition to exploit a favourable situation "ruthlessly to extreme", in Herr von Sybel's words, it was self-evident that under the pretext of freeing the Germans from Danish oppression about 200,000 Danes of North Schleswig were annexed to Germany. The one who got nothing was the Duke of Augustenburg, the candidate of the small states and of the German bourgeoisie for the Schleswig-Holstein throne.

Thus Bismarck had carried out the will of the German bourgeoisie in the duchies against their will. He had expelled the Danes and defied the foreign countries, and the latter had not made a move. But no sooner were they liberated than the duchies were treated as conquered territory, not consulted about their wishes and simply temporarily shared out between Austria and Prussia. Prussia had once again become a great power, was no longer the fifth wheel on the European coach, there was good progress in the fulfilment of the bourgeoisie's national aspirations, but the way chosen was not the liberal way of the bourgeoisie. Thus the Prussian military conflict continued; it even became ever

---

[a] Austro-Italo-French war of 1859.— *Ed.*

more insoluble. The second scene of Bismarck's principal state action[364] had to be ushered in.

* * *

The Danish war had fulfilled part of the national aspirations. Schleswig-Holstein was "liberated", the Warsaw and London Protocols, in which the great powers had put their seal to Germany's humiliation by Denmark,[365] had been torn to pieces and thrown at their feet, and they had not uttered a sound. Austria and Prussia were together again, their armies had been victorious shoulder to shoulder, and no potentate any longer thought of encroaching upon German territory. Louis Napoleon's cravings for the Rhine, which hitherto had been pushed into the background by other business—the Italian revolution, the Polish insurrection, the Danish complications, and finally the Mexican campaign,[366] had no longer any chance of being satisfied. For a conservative Prussian statesman, the world situation left nothing to be desired from the foreign policy point of view. But up to 1871 Bismarck had never been conservative, and was less so now than ever, and the German bourgeoisie was not at all satisfied.

The German bourgeoisie continued to labour under the familiar contradiction. On the one hand, it demanded exclusive political power for itself, i.e., for a ministry elected from among the liberal majority in the Chamber; and such a ministry would have had to wage a ten-year struggle against the old system represented by the crown before its new position of power was finally recognised; hence ten years of internal weakness. On the other hand, it demanded a revolutionary transformation of Germany, which could be effected only by force, that is, only by an actual dictatorship. At the same time, however, the bourgeoisie since 1848 had demonstrated again and again, at every decisive moment, that it did not possess even a trace of the energy needed to accomplish either of these demands, let alone both. In politics there are only two decisive powers: organised state power, the army, and the unorganised, elemental power of the popular masses. Since 1848, the bourgeoisie had forgotten how to appeal to the masses; it feared them even more than it did absolutism. The bourgeoisie by no means had the army at its disposal. But Bismarck had.

In the continuing conflict over the constitution, Bismarck fought the parliamentary demands of the bourgeoisie to the uttermost.

But he burned with the desire to carry out its national demands, since they coincided with the innermost strivings of Prussian policy. If he now once more carried out the will of the bourgeoisie against its will, if he made the unification of Germany, in the way it had been formulated by the bourgeoisie, a reality, the conflict would be resolved of itself, and Bismarck would inevitably become the idol of the bourgeoisie as Louis Napoleon, his model, before him.

The bourgeoisie supplied him with the aim, Louis Napoleon with the method of achieving the aim; only the implementation was left to Bismarck.

To place Prussia at the head of Germany, it was necessary not only to expel Austria forcibly from the German Confederation[367] but also to subjugate the small states. In Prussian politics, such a refreshing jolly war[368] of Germans against Germans had been the principal means of territorial expansion since the year dot, no worthy Prussian feared such a thing. Just as little misgiving could be caused by the other principal means: alliance with foreign countries against Germans. The out-and-out support of sentimental Alexander of Russia was certain. Louis Napoleon had never denied Prussia's Piedmont mission in Germany and was quite willing to make a deal with Bismarck. If he could get what he wanted peacefully, in the form of compensation, so much the better. Besides, he did not need to get the entire left bank of the Rhine at one go, if he received it piecemeal, a strip for every new advance by Prussia, it would be less conspicuous, and yet lead to his goal. In the eyes of the French chauvinists, a square mile on the Rhine was worth the whole of Savoy and Nice. Negotiations were therefore held with Louis Napoleon, and his permission was obtained for Prussia's expansion and the establishment of a North German Confederation.[369] That he was offered in return a strip of German territory on the Rhine is beyond doubt[a]; in the negotiations with Govone, Bismarck mentioned Rhenish Bavaria and Rhenish Hesse.[370] This he subsequently denied, to be sure. But a diplomat, particularly a Prussian diplomat, has his own views of the limits within which one is justified, and even obliged, to do a little violence to the truth. After all, truth is a woman and therefore, according to Junker ideas, actually likes it. Louis Napoleon was not so stupid as to allow Prussian expansion without a Prussian promise of compensation; Bleichröder would sooner

---

[a] Engels' note in pencil in the margin: "Division — the Main line" (see p. 484 of this volume).— Ed.

have lent money without interest. But he did not know his Prussians well enough and was anyway cheated in the end. In short, after he had been assured, an alliance was formed with Italy for the "stab in the heart".

The philistines in various countries were highly indignant over this expression. But quite wrongly. *À la guerre comme à la guerre.*[a] The expression only proves that Bismarck recognised the German civil war of 1866 for what it was, namely, a *revolution,* and that he was willing to carry out that revolution with revolutionary methods. And he did. His treatment of the Federal Diet was revolutionary. Instead of submitting to the constitutional decision of the federal authorities, he accused them of violating the federal treaty—a pure pretext—broke up the Confederation, proclaimed a new constitution with a Reichstag elected by revolutionary universal suffrage and finally expelled the Federal Diet from Frankfurt.[371] In Upper Silesia he formed a Hungarian legion under revolutionary General Klapka and other revolutionary officers whose soldiers, Hungarian deserters and prisoners of war, were to fight against their own legitimate commander-in-chief.[b] After the conquest of Bohemia, Bismarck issued a proclamation "To the Population of the Glorious Kingdom of Bohemia", whose content was likewise a hard slap in the face for legitimist traditions.[c] After peace had already been established, he seized for Prussia all the possessions of three legitimate German federal monarchs and a free city[372] without the slightest qualms of his Christian and legitimist conscience over the fact that these princes who had been expelled were no less rulers "by the grace of God" than the King of Prussia. In short, it was a complete revolution, carried out with revolutionary means. We are naturally the last to reproach him for this. On the contrary, what we reproach him with is that he was not revolutionary enough, that he was no more than a Prussian revolutionary from above, that he began a whole revolution in a position where he was able to carry through only half a revolution, that, once having set out on the course of annexations, he was content with four miserable small states.

And then Napoleon the Little[373] came limping up behind and demanded his reward. During the war he could have taken whatever he wanted on the Rhine, for not only the land, but also

---

a That's how it is in wartime.— *Ed.*

b Engels' note in pencil in the margin: "Oath!"— *Ed.*

c O. Bismarck, "Ansprache an die Einwohner des glorreichen Königreichs Böhmen".— *Ed.*

the fortresses, were exposed. He hesitated; he expected a protracted war that would wear out both sides; instead, there was a series of quick blows, and Austria was crushed in eight days. At first he demanded what Bismarck had named to General Govone as a possible compensation—Rhenish Bavaria and Rhenish Hesse, including Mainz. But Bismarck could not give that up now, even if he had wanted to. The enormous successes of the war had imposed new obligations on him. At a time when Prussia set itself up as the protector of Germany, it could not sell off Mainz, the key to the Middle Rhine, to a foreign country. Bismarck refused. Louis Napoleon was willing to bargain; he now demanded only Luxemburg, Landau, Saarlouis and the Saarbrücken coal basin. But this too Bismarck no longer could relinquish, the more so as Prussian territory too was claimed. Why had Louis Napoleon not seized it himself at the right moment, when the Prussians were stuck in Bohemia? In short, nothing came of the compensation to France. Bismarck knew this meant a future war with France, but that was exactly what he wanted.

In the peace treaties, Prussia did not exploit the favourable situation as ruthlessly this time as it had usually done in moments of success. There were sound reasons for it. Saxony and Hesse-Darmstadt were included in the new North German Confederation and, if only for this reason, were spared. Bavaria, Württemberg and Baden had to be treated with indulgence, because Bismarck had to sign secret offensive and defensive agreements with them. And Austria—had not Bismarck rendered it a service by smashing the traditional entanglement that tied it to Germany and Italy? Had he not just now secured for it the long-sought position of an independent great power? Had he not actually known better than Austria itself what was good for it when he had defeated it in Bohemia? Did not Austria, if properly handled, have to realise that the geographical position, the mutual entanglement of the two countries made the Germany united by Prussia its essential and natural ally?

Thus it came about that, for the first time in its existence, Prussia was able to surround itself with a halo of generosity, and this because it threw a sprat to catch a salmon.

Not only Austria had been beaten on the Bohemian bat-tlefields—the German bourgeoisie had been beaten as well. Bismarck had shown it that he knew better what was good for it than it knew itself. A continuation of the conflict by the Chamber was out of the question. The liberal pretensions of the bourgeoisie had been buried for a long time to come, but its national demands

were receiving fuller satisfaction with every passing day. Bismarck
fulfilled its national programme with a speed and accuracy that
surprised the bourgeoisie itself, and having proved to it palpably,
in corpore vili—on its own vile body—its limpness and listlessness,
and thus its complete inability to implement its own programme,
he also played the magnanimous towards it and applied to the
now actually disarmed Chamber to exempt the government from
indemnity for its anti-constitutional rule during the conflict.
Touched to tears, it agreed to this now harmless step forward.[374]

Nevertheless, the bourgeoisie was reminded that it too had been
defeated at Königgrätz.[375] The constitution of the North German
Confederation was modelled on the pattern of the Prussian
constitution as authentically interpreted during the conflict.
Refusal of taxes was prohibited. The federal Chancellor and his
ministers were appointed by the King of Prussia, independently of
any parliamentary majority. The army's independence of parliament, secured by the conflict, was stressed also in respect of the
Reichstag. But the members of this Reichstag had the exalting
awareness that they had been elected by universal suffrage. They
were also reminded of this, and most unpleasantly, by the sight of
the two socialists[a] sitting among them. For the first time socialist
deputies, representatives of the proletariat, appeared in a parliamentary body. This was an ominous sign.

At first all this was unimportant. The thing now was to advance
and exploit the new unity of the Empire, at least that of the
North, in the interests of the bourgeoisie and thereby to lure the
South German bourgeois too into the new Confederation. The
constitution of the Confederation took the economically most
important legislative relations away from the competency of the
individual states and transferred them to the Confederation:
common civil law and freedom of movement within the entire
Confederation, right of residence, legislation on the crafts, trade,
customs tariffs, navigation, coins, weights and measures, railways,
waterways, post and telegraphs, patents, banks, all foreign policy,
consulates, commercial protection abroad, sanitary police, the
penal code, judicial proceedings, etc. Most of these questions were
now regulated quickly, and in general liberally, by law. And
then,—at long last!—the ugliest abuses of the small state system
were abolished, those that, on the one hand, most obstructed
capitalist development, and, on the other, the Prussian craving for
power. But that was no world-historic achievement, as the

---

[a] August Bebel and Wilhelm Liebknecht.— *Ed.*

bourgeoisie, now turning chauvinistic, trumpeted forth, but a very, very long overdue and imperfect imitation of what the French Revolution had already done seventy years before, and what all other civilised states had introduced long ago. Instead of boasting, it would have been more appropriate to feel ashamed that "highly educated" Germany was the last to do it.

Throughout all this period of the North German Confederation, Bismarck willingly obliged the German bourgeoisie in the economic field and, even in questions affecting the competency of parliament, showed the iron fist only in a velvet glove. This was his best period; at times one could entertain doubts about his peculiarly Prussian narrow-mindedness, his inability to realise that there are in world history other and more powerful forces than armies and diplomatic intrigues relying on them.

Bismarck not only knew that the peace with Austria was pregnant with war with France, he also desired it. This war was to provide the means of perfecting the Prusso-German Empire demanded of him by the German bourgeoisie.* The attempts gradually to transform the Customs Parliament[376] into a Reichstag and thus to draw the southern states little by little into the North German Confederation were wrecked by the loud call of the South German deputies: No extension of competence! The mood of the governments, which had only recently been defeated on the field of battle, was no more favourable. Only fresh, palpable proof that the Prussians were not only much more powerful than these governments, but also powerful enough to protect them, that is, a new all-German war, could rapidly bring the moment of surrender. Besides, after the victories, it seemed as though the dividing line on the Main,[377] upon which Bismarck and Louis Napoleon had secretly agreed beforehand, had after all been imposed on the Prussians by the latter; in that case, a union with South Germany was a violation of the formally recognised right of the French this time to the fragmentation of Germany, was a *casus belli.*

In the meantime, Louis Napoleon had to search for a patch of

---

* Even before the Austrian war, when Bismarck was interpellated by a minister from a central German state on his demagogic German policy, he replied that, despite all the rhetoric, he would expel Austria from Germany and break up the Confederation.—"And the central states, do you think they will quietly look on?"—"You, the central states, you will do nothing."—"And what is to become of the Germans then?"—"I shall then lead them to Paris and unite them there." (Told in Paris before the Austr[ian] war by the said minister from the central state and published during that war in the *Manchester Guardian* by Mrs. Crawford, its Paris correspondent.)

land somewhere near the German border which he could pocket as compensation for Sadowa. When the new North German Confederation was formed, it did not include Luxemburg, now a state in personal union with Holland, but otherwise completely independent. Besides, it was approximately as much Frenchified as Alsace and was far more attracted to France than to Prussia, which it positively hated.

Luxemburg is a striking example of what Germany's political wretchedness since the Middle Ages had made of the German-French borderlands, the more striking because Luxemburg had until 1866 nominally belonged to Germany. Up to 1830, it had been composed of a French and a German part, but the German part had already at this early stage submitted to superior French culture. The German Emperors of Luxemburg were French in both language and education. Since its incorporation in the Burgundy lands (1440), Luxemburg, like all the other Low Countries, had remained in a purely nominal union with Germany; even admission to the German Confederation in 1815 changed nothing. After 1830, the French part and a substantial portion of the German part were annexed to Belgium. However, in what remained of German Luxemburg, everything continued on a French footing: the courts, the authorities, the Chamber, everything was conducted in French, all public and private documents, all business accounts were kept in French, in secondary schools the teaching was in French, French was and remained the language of the educated—naturally a French that groaned and panted with the High German sound shift. In short, two languages were spoken in Luxemburg: a Rhenish Franconian popular dialect, and French, while High German remained a foreign tongue. The Prussian garrison in the capital made things worse rather than better. This may be shameful for Germany but it is true. And this voluntary Frenchification of Luxemburg showed the similar processes in Alsace and German Lorraine in their true light.

The King of Holland,[a] the sovereign Duke of Luxemburg, who could well use hard cash, was willing to sell the duchy to Louis Napoleon. The people of Luxemburg would have undoubtedly approved their incorporation into France—the proof was their attitude in the war of 1870. From the standpoint of international law, Prussia could not object, since it had itself brought about

---

[a] William III.— Ed.

33*

Luxemburg's exclusion from Germany. Its troops were stationed in the capital as the federal garrison of a federal German fortress; as soon as Luxemburg ceased to be a federal fortress, they no longer had any right to be there. Why did they not go home, why could Bismarck not agree to Luxemburg's annexation?

Simply, because the contradictions in which he had become entangled were now becoming evident. As far as Prussia was concerned, *before* 1866 Germany was simply territory for annexation, which had to be shared with foreign countries. *After* 1866, Germany became a Prussian *protectorate,* which had to be defended against foreign claws. True, in the interests of Prussia, whole parts of Germany had been excluded from the newly founded so-called Germany. But the right of the German nation to its own territory now imposed on the Prussian Crown the duty of preventing the incorporation of these parts of the former federal territory into foreign states, of leaving the door open for their future union with the new Prussian-German state. It was for this reason that Italy had stopped at the Tyrolean border,[378] and that Luxemburg could not be allowed to go over to Louis Napoleon. A truly revolutionary government could declare this openly. Not so the royal Prussian revolutionary, who had finally succeeded in transforming Germany into a "geographic concept" in Metternich's sense.[379] From the point of view of international law, he had placed himself in the wrong, and the only way he could get out of the difficulty was to use his favourite students' beerhouse interpretation of international law.

If in so doing he was not simply laughed to scorn, it was only because, in the spring of 1867, Louis Napoleon was not at all ready for a big war. Agreement was reached at the London Conference. The Prussians evacuated Luxemburg, the fortress was demolished, the duchy was declared neutral.[380] The war was again postponed.

Louis Napoleon could not rest content with this. He was willing to tolerate the aggrandisement of Prussia only if he received corresponding compensation on the Rhine. He was willing to content himself with little, he had even reduced that, but he had received nothing, had been cheated of everything. However, a Bonapartist Empire in France could exist only if it shifted the border gradually towards the Rhine and if France—in fact or at least in imagination—remained the arbiter of Europe. The border shift had failed, France's position as arbiter was already threatened, the Bonapartist press loudly called for revenge for Sadowa—if Louis Napoleon wanted to keep his throne, he had to remain true to his role and to obtain by force what he had not obtained amicably, in spite of services rendered.

So eager war preparations, both diplomatic and military, were begun by both sides. And then the following diplomatic event occurred:

Spain was looking for a candidate for the throne. In March[a] Benedetti, the French ambassador in Berlin, picked up rumours about claims for the throne advanced by Prince Leopold of Hohenzollern; he was charged by Paris to investigate the matter. Under-Secretary of State von Thile gave him his word of honour that the Prussian Government knew nothing about it. During a visit to Paris, Benedetti learned the Emperor's opinion: "This candidature is essentially anti-national, the country will not tolerate it, it must be prevented."

Incidentally, Louis Napoleon showed thereby that he was already down at heel. Indeed, what could have been a better "revenge for Sadowa" than a Prussian Prince on the Spanish throne, the unavoidable annoyances resulting therefrom, Prussian involvement in the internal relations between the Spanish parties, perhaps even a war, a defeat of the dwarfish Prussian navy, in any case a Prussia looking quite grotesque in the eyes of Europe? But Louis Bonaparte could no longer afford this spectacle. His credit was already so much shaken that he was committed to the traditional point of view according to which a German sovereign on the Spanish throne would place France between two fires and was therefore intolerable—a childish point of view after 1830.

So Benedetti visited Bismarck to receive further information and to make France's point of view clear to him (May 11, 1869). He did not learn anything particularly conclusive from Bismarck. Bismarck, however, did learn from Benedetti what he wanted to find out: that Leopold's nomination as candidate would mean an immediate war with France. This gave Bismarck the opportunity to have the war break out when it suited him.

In actual fact, Leopold's candidature emerged once again in July 1870 and immediately led to war, no matter how much Louis Napoleon resisted it. He not only saw that he had walked into a trap, he also knew that his emperorship was at stake, and he had little confidence in the faithfulness of his Bonapartist Brimstone gang,[381] who assured him that everything was ready, up to the last button on the men's spats, and even less confidence in their military and administrative skill. But the logical consequences of

---

his own past drove him towards destruction; his hesitation itself hastened his doom.

Bismarck, on the other hand, was not only quite ready for action militarily, but this time he actually had the people behind him, who saw only one fact behind the diplomatic lies spread by both sides: namely, that this was a war not only for the Rhine, but for national existence. For the first time since 1813, reserves and the *Landwehr*[382] once again flocked to the colours, eager and keen to fight. It did not matter how all this had come about, did not matter what piece of the two-thousand-year-old national heritage Bismarck had, off his own back, promised or not promised to Louis Napoleon: the thing was to teach foreign countries once and for all that they were not to interfere in German internal affairs and that it was not Germany's mission to support Louis Napoleon's shaky throne by ceding German territory. All class differences vanished in the face of this national upsurge, all cravings of the South German courts for a Confederation of the Rhine, all attempts at a restoration of the expelled monarchs melted away.

Both sides had sought allies. Louis Napoleon had Austria and Denmark for sure, and was pretty certain of Italy. Bismarck had Russia. But Austria, as always, was not ready and could not participate effectively before September 2—and on September 2 Louis Napoleon was a prisoner of war of the Germans, and Russia had informed Austria that it would attack Austria the moment Austria attacked Prussia. In Italy, however, Louis Napoleon's double-dealing policy wrought vengeance upon him: he had sought to set national unity in motion, but at the same time to protect the Pope from that same national unity; he had kept Rome occupied with troops he now needed at home but which he could not withdraw without obliging Italy to respect the sovereignty of Rome and the Pope; this in turn prevented Italy from supporting him. Denmark finally got the order from Russia to behave itself.

The rapid blows of the German armies from Spicheren and Wörth to Sedan[383] were more decisive in localising the war than all diplomatic negotiations. Louis Napoleon's army was defeated in every battle and finally three-quarters of it went to Germany as prisoners of war. This was not the fault of the soldiers, who had fought bravely enough, but of the leaders and the administration. But if, like Louis Napoleon, one had created an empire with the help of a gang of rascals, if this empire had been maintained for eighteen years merely by abandoning France to the exploitation of that gang, if all decisive posts in the state had been filled with people belonging to that very gang and all subordinate posts with their accomplices, then one should not engage in a life-and-death battle if one does not wish to be left in the lurch. The entire edifice of the empire that had been the admiration of European philistines for years crashed in less than five weeks; the revolution of September 4 [384] simply cleared away the rubble, and Bismarck, who had gone to war to found a small German empire, turned out one fine morning to be the founder of a French republic.

According to Bismarck's own proclamation,[385] the war was waged not against the French people, but against Louis Napoleon. With his fall, all the reasons to wage war thus disappeared. The government of September 4, which was not so naïve in other matters, also deluded itself to this effect, and was greatly surprised when Bismarck suddenly showed himself a Prussian Junker.

No one in the world hates the French as much as the Prussian Junkers do. For not only had the hitherto tax-exempled Junker suffered heavily during the chastisement by the French (from 1806 to 1813), which he had brought about by his own arrogance; but, what was much worse, the godless French had so confused the people by their outrageous revolution that the old grandeur of the Junkers had for the most part been laid to rest even in old Prussia, so that year in and year out the poor Junkers had to struggle hard to keep what was left of it, and many of them were already debased to a shabby sponging nobility. For this, revenge had to be taken on France, and the Junker officers in the army under Bismarck's leadership took care of that. Lists of war contributions exacted by France from Prussia were drawn up and the size of the war contributions imposed on the various towns and departments was calculated accordingly, but naturally taking into account France's much greater wealth. Foodstuffs, forage, clothes, footwear, etc., were requisitioned with demonstrative ruthlessness. A mayor in the Ardennes who said that he would be unable to make the deliveries was given twenty-five strokes of the cane without further ado, as the Paris government officially proved. The francs-tireurs, who acted in such strict accordance with the Prussian Landsturm Statute of 1813 [386] as if they had made a special study of it, were shot without mercy on the spot. The stories about clocks being sent home are also true, even the *Kölnische Zeitung* reported it. Only, according to Prussian views, those clocks were not stolen but were ownerless, having been found in abandoned villas near Paris and confiscated for the dear ones at home. Thus, the Junkers under Bismarck's leadership saw to it that, despite the irreproachable behaviour of the men and many of the officers, the specifically Prussian character of the war was preserved, and that this was driven home to the French, who held the entire army responsible for the mean spitefulness of the Junkers.

And yet it fell to the lot of these same Junkers to render to the French people an honour unequalled in history. When all attempts to make the enemy relieve the siege of Paris had failed, all the French armies had been beaten back. Bourbaki's last great counter-attack on the German lines of communication had proved abortive, when all Europe's diplomats had abandoned France to its fate without stirring a finger, emaciated Paris finally had to surrender.[387] The hearts of the Junkers beat faster when they were finally able to enter the godless nest in triumph and take complete vengeance upon the Paris arch-rebels—the complete vengeance which had been denied to them by Alexander of Russia in 1814 and Wellington in 1815; now they could chastise the seat and homeland of the revolution to their hearts' content.

Paris surrendered, it paid a contribution of 200 millions; the forts were handed over to the Prussians; the garrison laid down its arms before the victors and delivered up its field guns; the cannons on the wall around Paris were taken off their gun-carriages; all means of resistance belonging to the state were handed over piece by piece. But the actual defenders of Paris, the National Guard, the armed Parisians, remained untouched, for nobody expected them to give up their arms, either their rifles or their cannons*; and so that it would be known to the whole world that the victorious German army had respectfully stopped before the armed people of Paris, the victors did not enter Paris, but were content to be allowed to occupy for three days the Champs Élysées, a public park, protected, guarded and enclosed on all sides by the sentries of the Parisians! No German soldier set foot in Paris City Hall or stepped on the boulevards, and the few that were admitted to the Louvre to admire the art treasures there had to ask for permission, otherwise it would have been a violation of the surrender. France was defeated, Paris starved, but the Parisian people had by their glorious past ensured respect for themselves, so that no victor dared to demand their disarmament, no one had the courage to enter their homes or to desecrate by a triumphal march those streets which had been the battle-ground of so many

---

* It was these cannons, which belonged to the National Guard and not to the state, and had therefore not been handed over to the Prussians, that Thiers ordered on March 18, 1871, to be *stolen* from the Parisians, thereby bringing about the rebellion that gave rise to the Commune.

revolutions. It was as if the upstart German Emperor[a] was taking off his hat before the living revolutionaries of Paris, as once his brother[b] had before the dead March fighters of Berlin,[388] and as if the entire German army stood behind him presenting arms.

But that was the only sacrifice Bismarck had to make. Under the pretext that there was no government in France which could sign a peace treaty with him—which was just as true as it was false both on September 4 and on January 28—he had exploited his successes in the truly Prussian manner, to the very last drop, and declared himself ready for peace only after France had been completely crushed. In the peace treaty itself, once again according to the good old Prussian custom, he "ruthlessly exploited the favourable situation". Not only was the unheard-of sum of 5,000 millions in war reparations extorted, but also two provinces, Alsace and German Lorraine, with Metz and Strasbourg were torn away from France and incorporated into Germany.[389] With this annexation, Bismarck appeared for the first time as an independent politician, who was no longer implementing in his own way a programme dictated from outside, but translating into action the products of his own brain, thereby committing his first enormous blunder.[c]

Alsace had been conquered in the main by France during the Thirty Years' War.[390] Richelieu had thereby abandoned Henry IV's sound principle:

"Let the Spanish language belong to the Spaniard, the German to the German, but where French is spoken, that belongs to me."

In so doing, Richelieu relied on the principle of the natural border on the Rhine, the historical border of old Gaul. This was folly; but the German Empire, which incorporated the French-speaking parts of Lorraine and Belgium and even of the Franche-Comté, had no right to reproach France with annexing German-speaking lands. And even if, in 1681, in peacetime, Louis XIV had seized Strassburg with the help of a pro-French party in the city,[391] it is not for Prussia to be indignant over it, having raped the Free Imperial town of Nuremberg in exactly the

---

a William I.—Ed.
b Frederick William IV.—Ed.
c The text below, up to the words "Bismarck had reached his objective" (see this volume, p. 497), is printed according to the Neue Zeit, Vol. I, No. 25, 1895-96, pp. 772-76, because the relative manuscript pages are missing.—Ed.

same way in 1796, although, to be sure, without having been called by a Prussian party, and without success.*

Lorraine was sold off to France in 1735 by Austria under the Peace of Vienna,[394] and in 1766 it definitively became a French possession. For centuries it had belonged to the German Empire only nominally, its dukes were French in every respect and had almost always been allied with France.

Before the French Revolution, there were a great many small domains in the Vosges which behaved in respect to Germany like estates of the empire subject immediately to the emperor, but recognised the sovereignty of France. They derived benefits from this hermaphroditic position, and if the German Empire tolerated it instead of calling these sovereigns to account, it could not complain when France, by virtue of its sovereignty, extended protection to the people of these territories against the expelled princes.

On the whole, before the Revolution, this German territory was practically not Frenchified at all. German remained the school and official language internally, at least in Alsace. The French Government patronised the German provinces, which now, after many years of war devastation, had seen no more enemies on their lands since the early 18th century. The German Empire, perpetually torn by internal wars, was really not in a state to attract the Alsatians back to the maternal bosom; at least they now

---

* Louis XIV is reproached with having set loose his "reunion chambers"[392] in times of peace on German areas which did not belong to him. This is something that could not be said of the Prussians even by those who had the most malicious envy of them. On the contrary. After they had signed a separate peace with France in 1795[393] in direct violation of the imperial constitution and had rallied their equally renegade small neighbours behind the demarcation line around themselves in the first North German Confederation, they utilised, for attempts to annex territory in Franconia, the tight spot the South German estates of the empire found themselves in as a result of continuing the war alone in alliance with Austria. They set up reunion chambers according to Louis' pattern in Ansbach and Bayreuth (which were then Prussian), raised claims to a series of neighbouring areas, in comparison with which Louis' legal pretexts were absolutely convincing; and when the Germans then retreated after a beating and the French moved into Franconia, the Prussian saviours occupied the Nuremberg area, including the suburbs up to the city wall, and tricked the Nuremberg philistines, who were trembling with fear, into signing a treaty (September 2, 1796) which subjected the city to Prussian rule on the condition that Jews would never be allowed within the city walls. Immediately after that, Archduke Charles took the offensive again, beat the French at Würzburg on September 3 and 4, 1796, and the attempt to knock the idea of Prussia's German mission into the heads of the Nurembergers thus went up in smoke.

had peace and quiet, knew how things stood, and the philistines who set the tone accepted the inscrutable ways of the Lord; after all, their fate was not unprecedented: the people of Holstein were also under foreign, Danish, rule.

Then came the French Revolution. What Alsace and Lorraine never dared hope to receive from Germany was given to them by France as a gift. The feudal fetters were smashed. The serf, the peasant liable to statute labour, became a free man, in many cases the free owner of his farmstead and field. In the towns, patrician rule and guild privileges disappeared. The nobility was driven out. In the lands of the small princes and lords, the peasants followed the example of their neighbours and expelled the sovereigns, government chambers and nobility, and declared themselves free French citizens. In no other part of France did the people join the revolution with greater enthusiasm than in the German-speaking part. And when the German Empire now declared war on the revolution, when the Germans, who not only continued to carry their own chains submissively, but also allowed themselves to be used once again to force the old servitude upon the French and to re-impose on the Alsatian peasants the feudal lords they had only just expelled, now it was all over with the Germanism of the people of Alsace and Lorraine, it was then that they learned to hate and despise the Germans; it was then that the *Marseillaise* was written in Strasbourg, set to music and first sung by the Alsatians, and that the German French, despite their language and their past, fused on hundreds of battlefields in the struggle for the revolution into a single nation with the native French.

Did not the great revolution work the same miracle with the Flemings of Dunkirk, the Celts of Brittany, the Italians of Corsica? And if we complain that this happened also with Germans, does it not show that we have forgotten our entire history, which made this possible? Have we forgotten that the whole left bank of the Rhine, which took only a passive part in the revolution, was pro-French when the Germans again moved in in 1814, and continued to be pro-French up to 1848, when the revolution rehabilitated the Germans in the eyes of the people on the Rhine? Have we forgotten that Heine's enthusiasm for the French and even his Bonapartism were but the echo of general public feeling on the left bank of the Rhine?

When the allies invaded in 1814 it was precisely in Alsace and German Lorraine that they encountered the most resolute hostility, the most vehement resistance on the part of the people themselves; because here the danger was felt of having to become

German again. And yet, at that time, practically only German was spoken there. But when the danger of being torn from France had passed, when an end had been put to the annexationist appetites of the romantic Germanophile chauvinists, the awareness appeared that a closer fusion with France was needed also in respect of the language, and then the Frenchification of schools was introduced, similar to that voluntarily established by the Luxemburgers in their land. Yet the transformation proceeded very slowly; only the present generation of the bourgeoisie is really Frenchified, while the peasants and workers speak German. The position is approximately the same as in Luxemburg: literary German has been ousted by French (except partially in the pulpit), but the German folk dialect has lost ground only at the language border and is used as the popular language to a much greater extent than in most parts of Germany.

Such was the land that Bismarck and the Prussian Junkers, backed by the revival of chauvinistic romanticism which seems inseparable from all German problems, undertook to make German again. The wish to make Strasbourg, the homeland of the *Marseillaise,* German, was just as absurd as to make Nice, the homeland of Garibaldi, French. But in Nice, Louis Napoleon at least observed decency and put the question of annexation to the vote—and the manoeuvre succeeded. Quite apart from the fact that for very good reasons the Prussians detest such revolutionary measures—never and nowhere has there been an instance when the mass of the people wanted to be annexed to Prussia—it was known only too well that precisely here the entire population was more closely attached to France than were the native French themselves. And thus this arbitrary act was performed by brute force. It was an act of revenge against the French Revolution; one of the parts which had been fused with France precisely as a result of the revolution was torn away.

It is true that militarily there was a purpose behind this annexation. Metz and Strasbourg gave Germany an enormously strong line of defence. So long as Belgium and Switzerland remain neutral a massive French offensive can be begun only on the narrow strip of land between Metz and the Vosges; and besides, Koblenz, Metz, Strasbourg and Mainz form the strongest and biggest quadrangle of fortresses in the world. However, half of this quadrangle of fortresses, as is the case also with the Austrian fortresses in Lombardy,[395] lies in enemy territory and forms citadels there to keep the population down. Moreover, to complete the quadrangle, it was necessary to seize areas beyond the

German-language border and to annex a quarter of a million of native Frenchmen as well.

The great strategic advantage is thus the only reason that can justify the annexation. However, can this gain in any way be compared with the harm it wrought?

The Prussian Junker refused to reckon with the great moral disadvantage at which the young German Empire had placed itself by openly and frankly declaring brutal force its guiding principle. Quite the reverse, refractory subjects forcibly kept in check are a necessity for him; they are proof of increased Prussian might; and essentially he has never any others. But he was obliged to reckon with the political consequences of the annexation. And these were clearly apparent. Even before the annexation came into force, Marx loudly drew the world's attention to it in a circular of the International: *The annexation of Alsace and Lorraine makes Russia the arbiter of Europe.*[a] And this has been repeated often enough by the Social-Democrats from the rostrum of the Reichstag until the truth of this statement was finally acknowledged by Bismarck himself in his Reichstag speech of February 6, 1888, by his whimpering before the almighty Tsar,[b] the lord of war and peace.[396]

Actually, the situation was clear as daylight. To tear from France two of its fanatically patriotic provinces, meant to push it into the arms of anybody who held out hope for their return and to make it an eternal enemy. However, Bismarck, in this respect a worthy and conscientious representative of the German philistines, demanded that the French renounce Alsace and Lorraine not only constitutionally but also morally, and in addition wanted them to be downright glad that these two parts of revolutionary France "had been returned to the old Fatherland", of which they simply would not hear. Unfortunately, however, the French did not do so, any more than the Germans morally renounced the left bank of the Rhine during the Napoleonic wars, even though this area had not the slightest longing to return to them at that time. As long as the people of Alsace and Lorraine wish to return to France, it must and will strive to regain them and look for means and, hence, also for allies, to achieve this. And the natural ally against Germany is Russia.

If the two biggest and strongest nations of the Western

---

a See K. Marx, *Second Address of the General Council of the International Working Men's Association on the Franco-Prussian War* (present edition, Vol. 22, pp. 266-68).— *Ed.*

b Alexander III.— *Ed.*

continent neutralise each other by their hostility, if there is just one bone of contention between them which incites them to fight each other, the advantage lies only with Russia, whose hands are so much the freer; Russia who is all the less hampered by Germany in its cravings for conquest, the more it can count on unconditional support from France. And was it not Bismarck who placed France in a position where it has to beg for Russia's alliance, where it must willingly abandon Constantinople to Russia, if only the latter promises the return of France's lost provinces? And if in spite of all that the peace has been kept for seventeen years, is there any other reason than that the *Landwehr* system introduced in France and Russia requires at least sixteen, and after the most recent German improvements even twenty-five years, to provide the full number of trained age groups? And now that the annexation has for seventeen years been the dominant factor in all European politics, is it not at this moment the main cause of the crisis threatening the continent with war? Remove this single fact and peace is assured!

The Alsatian bourgeois who speaks French with an Upper German accent, that hybrid fop who puts on greater French airs than a Frenchman through and through, who looks down on Goethe and goes into raptures over Racine, who still cannot rid himself of his bad conscience over his secret Germanness and exactly for that reason has to run down everything German, so that he does not even suit the role of a mediator between Germany and France, this Alsatian bourgeois is indeed a despicable fellow, be he a Mulhouse industrialist or a Paris journalist. But what has made him what he is if not the history of Germany over the past three hundred years? And were not until quite recently almost all Germans abroad, especially the merchants, genuine Alsatians, who denied their German origin, who masochistically imposed on themselves the alien nationality of their new homeland and thus voluntarily made themselves certainly no less ridiculous than the Alsatians, who at least are more or less compelled by circumstances to do so? In England, for example, the German merchants who immigrated between 1815 and 1840 had almost without exception become Anglicised, spoke almost exclusively English among themselves, and even today, for example, at the Manchester Stock Exchange, there are old German philistines running around who would give half their wealth if they could pass for true Englishmen. Only in 1848 did a change set in, and since 1870, when even lieutenants of the reserve have been coming to England and Berlin has been sending its contingents here, the former servility is being ousted by a Prussian arrogance which makes us no less ridiculous abroad.

Perhaps the union with Germany has been made more palatable to the Alsatians since 1871? On the contrary. They have been placed under a dictatorship, whereas next door, in France, there was a republic. A pedantical and obtrusive Prussian Landrat system has been introduced, in comparison with which the interference of the notorious French system of prefects, regulated by strict laws, is solid gold. An end has been rapidly put to the last remnants of freedom of the press, right of assembly and association, refractory town councils have been dissolved and German bureaucrats appointed mayors. On the other hand, however, there has been flattery of the "notables", that is, the thoroughly Frenchified nobles and bourgeois, and their exploiter interests have been protected against the peasants and workers, who, although not well disposed towards Germany, at least spoke German, and formed the only element with which an attempt at reconciliation was possible. And what has been the result? That in February 1887, when the whole of Germany allowed itself to be intimidated and put a majority of the Bismarck cartel[397] in the Reichstag, Alsace and Lorraine elected nothing but staunch Frenchmen and rejected everyone who was suspected of even the mildest pro-German sympathies.

Now, if the Alsatians are as they are, have we the right to be angry over that? Not at all. Their opposition to the annexation is an historical fact, which should not be deleted but explained. And this is the time for us to ask ourselves: how numerous and how colossal were the historical sins Germany committed before such a feeling could assert itself in Alsace? And how must our new German Empire look from the outside if, after seventeen years of re-Germanisation attempts, the Alsatians unanimously tell us: Spare us that? Have we the right to imagine that two successful campaigns and seventeen years of Bismarckian dictatorship suffice to do away with all the effects of three hundred years of ignominious history?

Bismarck had reached his objective. His new Prussian-German Empire had been publicly proclaimed at Versailles, in Louis XIV's splendid state hall.[398] France lay defenceless at his feet; defiant Paris, which he himself had not dared touch, had been incited to the Commune uprising by Thiers and then crushed by the soldiers of the former imperial army returning from captivity. All European philistines admired Bismarck as they had admired Louis Napoleon, Bismarck's model, in the fifties. With Russian help

Germany had become the first power in Europe, and all power in Germany was concentrated in the hands of dictator Bismarck. Everything depended now on what he could do with that power. If he had so far carried out the unification plans of the bourgeoisie, even if not by bourgeois, but by Bonapartist methods, this matter was pretty well settled, and he now had to make his own plans, to show what ideas his own head could produce, and these had to find expression in the internal consolidation of the new empire.

German society is composed of big landowners, peasants, bourgeois, petty bourgeois and workers; these can in turn be grouped into three major classes.

Big landed property is in the hands of a few magnates (notably in Silesia) and a large number of middle landowners, most highly concentrated in the old Prussian provinces east of the Elbe. It is these Prussian Junkers who more or less dominate the entire class. They are farmers themselves, inasmuch as they entrust the cultivation of their estates for the most part to managers, and in addition they often own distilleries and beet-sugar refineries. Wherever possible, their landed property is entailed upon the family by right of primogeniture. The younger sons join the army or the civil service, so that an even less wealthy petty nobility made up of officers and civil servants clings to this petty landowning gentry and is supplemented over and above this through the intensive promotion of nobles from among the higher officers and civil servants of bourgeois origin. On the lower fringes of all this bunch of nobles, there naturally emerges a numerically parasitic nobility, a noble Lumpenproletariat, which lives on debts, dubious gambling, pushiness, begging and political espionage. This society in its totality forms the Prussian Junkers and is one of the main pillars of the old Prussian state. However, the landowning core of the Junkers themselves has feet of clay. The duty to live up to its status becomes more and more expensive every day; the support for the younger sons through the lieutenant and assessor stage, the marrying off of daughters, all costs money; and since all these are duties which push all other considerations into the background, it is no wonder that incomes are insufficient, that IOUs have to be signed or even mortgages have to be taken out. In short, Junkers stand always on the brink of the abyss; every misfortune, be it a war, a bad harvest or a commercial crisis, threatens to push them over the brink; and it is therefore no wonder that for well over a hundred years now they have been saved from ruin only by all sorts of state assistance and, in fact, continue to exist only thanks to state assistance. This artificially preserved class is doomed to extinction and no state assistance can keep it alive in the long run. But with it disappears also the old Prussian state.

The *peasant* is an element that is little active politically. In so far as he himself is a proprietor, he is going ever more to ruin because of the unfavourable production conditions of the allotment peasants, who cannot engage in stock-breeding, having been deprived of the old common Mark or community pasture. As a tenant, his position is even worse. Petty peasant production presupposes a predominantly subsistence economy, the money economy seals its doom. Hence the growing indebtedness, the massive expropriation by mortgage creditors, the recourse to domestic industry, so as just not to be evicted from his native soil. Politically, the peasantry is mainly indifferent or reactionary: on the Rhine it is ultramontane because of its old hatred for the Prussians, in other areas it is particularist or protestant-conservative. Religious feeling still serves this class as an expression of social or political interests.

We have already spoken about the *bourgeoisie.* From 1848 it experienced an unprecedented economic advance. Germany had increasingly participated in the vast expansion of industry following the 1847 commercial crisis, an expansion brought about by the establishment during that period of ocean steam navigation, the enormous extension of the railways and the discovery of gold in California and Australia.[399] It was precisely the bourgeoisie's striving for the abolition of the obstructions to trade caused by the system of small states and for a position on the world market equal to that of its foreign competitors that gave the impetus to Bismarck's revolution. Now that French milliards were flooding Germany, a new period of feverish enterprise opened up before the bourgeoisie, during which it—by a crash on a national German scale[400]—proved for the first time that it had become a big industrial nation. The bourgeoisie was even then the economically most powerful class among the population; the state had to obey its economic interests; the revolution of 1848 had given the state an external constitutional form within which the bourgeoisie could rule also politically and develop its domination. Yet it was still far from actual political domination. In the conflict it had not triumphed over Bismarck; the resolution of the conflict through the revolutionising of Germany from above had also taught it that, for the time being, the executive power was dependent on it, at best, in a very indirect form, that it could neither appoint nor dismiss ministers, nor dispose of the army. Besides, it was cowardly and limp in the face of an energetic executive power, but so were the Junkers, though this was more excusable in the case of the bourgeoisie because of the direct economic antagonism between it and the revolutionary industrial working class. There was no doubt, however, that it gradually had to destroy the Junkers economically, that it was the only propertied class which retained any prospect of a future.

The petty bourgeoisie consisted first of all of remnants of the medieval craftsmen, who had been represented on a larger scale in backward Germany than in the rest of Western Europe; secondly, of the down-and-out bourgeois; and thirdly, of elements of the propertyless population who had risen to be small merchants. With the expansion of large-scale industry, the existence of the entire petty bourgeoisie lost the last remnants of stability; changes of occupation and periodic bankruptcies became the rule. This once so stable class which had been the nucleus of the German philistines fell from its previous contentment, docility, servility, piety and respectability into wild decadence and dissatisfaction with the fate allotted to it by God. The remnants of the craftsmen loudly demanded the restoration of guild privileges, some of the others became mildly democratic men of Progress,[401] some even grew closer to the Social-Democrats and in some instances directly joined the working-class movement.

Finally the workers. The agricultural workers, at least those in the east, still lived in semi-serfdom and could not be taken into account. On the other hand, Social-Democracy had made enormous progress among the urban workers and grew to the extent that large-scale industry proletarianised the mass of the people and thereby exacerbated the class antagonism between the capitalists and the workers. Even if the Social-Democratic workers were for the time being still divided into two parties fighting each other,[402] since the publication of Marx's *Capital,* the fundamental differences between them had nevertheless as good as disappeared. Orthodox Lassalleanism, with its exclusive demand for "producer associations assisted by the state", was gradually dying away and proved less and less capable of forming the nucleus of a Bonapartist state socialist workers' party. The harm wrought in this respect by individual leaders was rectified by the common sense of the masses. The union of the two Social-Democratic tendencies, which was delayed almost exclusively because of questions of personalities, was certain to take place in the near future. But even during the split and despite it, the movement was strong enough to strike fear into the industrial bourgeoisie and to paralyse it in its struggle against the government, which was still independent of it; and after 1848 the German bourgeoisie never rid itself of the Red spectre again.

The class structure underlay the party structure in parliament and in the provincial diets. The large landed estate owners and part of the peasantry formed the mass of the conservatives[403]; the industrial bourgeoisie provided the Right wing of the bourgeois liberals—the National Liberals,[404] while the Left wing comprised the weakened democratic party or so-called Party of Progress, which consisted of petty bourgeois supported by a section of the bourgeoisie and the workers. Finally, the workers had their independent party, the Social-Democrats, which included also some petty bourgeois.

A person in Bismarck's position and with Bismarck's past, having a certain understanding of the state of affairs, could not but realise that the Junkers, such as they were, were not a viable class, and that of all the propertied classes only the bourgeoisie could lay claim to a future, and that therefore (disregarding the working class, an understanding of whose historical mission we cannot expect of him) his new empire promised to be all the stabler, the more he succeeded in laying the groundwork for its gradual transition to a modern bourgeois state. Let us not expect of him what was impossible under the circumstances. An immediate transition to a parliamentary government with the decisive power vested in the Reichstag (as in the British House of Commons) was neither possible nor even advisable at that moment; Bismarck's dictatorship in parliamentary forms must have seemed to him still necessary for the time being; and we do not in the least blame him for allowing it to survive for the moment, we only ask what good it was. And there can be hardly any doubt that paving the way for a system corresponding to the British constitution was the only way which offered the prospect of ensuring a sound basis and quiet internal development for the new empire. By leaving the larger part of the Junkers, who were beyond salvation anyway, to their inevitable doom, it still seemed possible to forge what remained of them with new elements into a class of independent big landowners, which would become only the ornamental élite of the bourgeoisie; a class to which the bourgeoisie, even at the height of its power, would have to grant state representation and with it the most lucrative positions and enormous influence. By granting the bourgeoisie political concessions, which anyway could not be withheld for any length of time (such at least should have been the argument from the standpoint of the propertied classes), by granting it these concessions gradually, and even in small and rare doses, the new empire would at least be steered onto a course which would enable it to catch up with the other, politically far more advanced West-European states, to shake off the last remnants of feudalism and philistine traditions which still held a firm grip on the bureaucracy, and, above all, to stand on its own feet by the time its by no means youthful founders departed this life.

This was not even difficult. Neither the Junkers nor the bourgeoisie possessed even average energy. The Junkers had proved this in the past sixty years, during which the state had constantly done what was best for them despite the opposition of these Don Quixotes. The bourgeoisie, also made malleable by its long prehistory, was still licking the wounds left by the conflict; Bismarck's successes since then had further broken its power of resistance, and fear of the dangerously growing working-class movement did the rest. Under these circumstances, it would not have been difficult for the man who had put the national aspirations of the bourgeoisie into practice to keep any pace he desired in implementing its political demands, which were in any case very modest on the whole. It was only necessary for him to be clear about the objective.

From the point of view of the propertied classes, this was the only rational way. From the standpoint of the working class, it was obvious that it was already too late to set up bourgeois rule on a lasting basis. Large-scale industry, and with it the bourgeoisie and the proletariat, took shape in Germany at a time when the proletariat could enter the political scene as an independent force almost simultaneously with the bourgeoisie, that is, at a time when the struggle of the two classes has already begun, before the bourgeoisie has conquered exclusive or predominant political power. But even if the time for quiet and firmly founded rule by the bourgeoisie had already passed in Germany, it was still the best policy in 1870, in the interests of the propertied classes in general, to steer towards this bourgeois rule. For only in this way was it possible to abolish the abundant remnants of the times of decaying feudalism which continued to flourish in legislation and administration; only thus was it possible gradually to transplant all the achievements of the Great French Revolution to Germany, in short, to cut off Germany's overlong old pigtail, and to place it deliberately and irrevocably on the road of modern development, to adapt its political system to its industrial development. When ultimately the unavoidable struggle between the bourgeoisie and the proletariat set in, it would at least proceed under normal circumstances, in which everyone would realise what was at stake, and not in the state of disorder, obscurity, conflicting interests and perplexity we saw in Germany in 1848. The only difference being that this time the perplexity would be exclusively on the side of the propertied classes; the working class knows what it wants.

As things stood in Germany in 1871, a man like Bismarck was indeed compelled to pursue a policy of manoeuvring between the various classes. And to that extent he is not open to reproach. It is only a question of what aim that policy pursued. If, irrespective of the pace, it was aimed consciously and resolutely at the ultimate rule of the bourgeoisie, it was in harmony with historical development as far as this could be possible at all from the standpoint of the propertied classes. If it aimed at preserving the old Prussian state, at gradually Prussianising Germany, it was reactionary and doomed to ultimate failure. But if it only pursued the aim of preserving Bismarck's rule, it was Bonapartist and bound to meet the same end as all Bonapartism.

* * *

The immediate task was the imperial constitution. The material available was the constitution of the North German Confederation, on the one hand, and the treaties with the South German states,[405] on the other. The factors which were to help Bismarck draw up the imperial constitution were, on the one hand, the dynasties represented in the Federal Council[406] and, on the other, the people represented in the Reichstag. The North German constitution and treaties limited the claims of the dynasties. The people, on the other hand, were entitled to a considerable increase in their share of political power. They had won independence from foreign interference and unification—as far as there could be any talk of unification—on the battlefield; they were also above all called upon to decide what use this independence was to be put to, how this unification would be implemented in detail and how it would be used. And even if the people recognised the legal grounds underlying the North German constitution and treaties, that in no way prevented them from being granted a greater share of power in the new constitution than they had in the old one. The Reichstag was the only body which in reality represented the new "unity". The greater the voice of the Reichstag and the freer the imperial constitution as compared with the constitutions of the individual provinces, the more the new Empire would have to fuse into one, the more the Bavarian, Saxon and Prussian would have to dissolve into the German.

To anyone who could see further than his nose this should have been obvious. But Bismarck held quite a different opinion. On the contrary, he used the patriotic frenzy unleashed after the war precisely to persuade the majority in the Reichstag to renounce not only an extension but even a clear definition of the rights of the people and to confine itself to a simple reproduction in the imperial constitution of the legal basis underlying the North German constitution and the treaties. All attempts of the small parties to give expression in it to the freedoms of the people were dismissed, including even the proposal of the Catholic Centre to incorporate in it the articles of the Prussian constitution guaranteeing the freedom of the press, of assembly and association and the independence of the Church. The Prussian constitution, twice and thrice pruned as it was, was still more liberal than the imperial constitution. Taxes were voted not yearly, but once and for all, "by law", so that any refusal of taxes by the Reichstag was out of the question. Thus there was applied to Germany the Prussian doctrine, inconceivable to the non-German constitutional world, according to which the elected assembly had only the right on paper to refuse expenditure, while the government pocketed the revenue in hard cash. While the Reichstag was thus robbed of the most effective means of power and reduced to the humble position of the Prussian chamber smashed up by the revisions of 1849 and 1850, by Manteuffelism, by conflict and by Sadowa,[407] the Federal Council, in effect, enjoyed full power, which the old Federal Diet possessed nominally, and enjoyed it in reality, for it had been freed of the fetters that paralysed the Federal Diet. The Federal Council had a decisive voice not only in legislation, alongside the Reichstag; it was also the supreme administrative body, inasmuch as it issued instructions on the implementation of imperial laws, and in addition decides "on shortcomings, which emerge during the implementation of imperial laws...", i.e., on shortcomings, which in other civilised countries can be remedied only by a new law (Article 7, Para. 3, which greatly resembles a legal trap).[a]

Thus, Bismarck sought his main support not in the Reichstag,

---

[a] Verfassung des Deutschen Reichs in Reichs-Gesetzblatt, 1871, p. 68.— Ed.

which represented national union, but in the Federal Council, which represented particularistic disunion. He lacked the courage—he, who set himself up as champion of the national idea—to place himself genuinely at the head of the nation or of its representatives; democracy was to serve him and not he democracy; rather than rely on the people, he relied on underhand dealings behind the scenes, on his ability to scrape together a majority, even if a refractory one, in the Federal Council by means of diplomacy, the stick and the carrot. The pettiness of his conception, the baseness of his view point that is revealed to us here is quite in keeping with the man's character as we have got to know him so far. Yet, it is suprising that his great successes were unable to make him rise above himself even for a moment.

However, in the prevailing situation, the point was to provide a single firm pivot for the entire imperial constitution, namely, the imperial chancellor. The Federal Council had to be put in a position in which there could be no other responsible executive authority than that of the imperial chancellor and which would exclude the admissibility of responsible imperial ministers. Indeed, every attempt to normalise the imperial administration by setting up a responsible ministry was regarded as an encroachment upon the rights of the Federal Council and encountered insurmountable resistance. As was soon discovered, the constitution was "made to measure" for Bismarck. It was a further step on the road to his absolute personal dictatorship by balancing the parties in the Reichstag and the particularist states in the Federal Council—a further step on the road to Bonapartism.

By the way, it cannot be said that the new imperial constitution—except for certain concessions to Bavaria and Württemberg—was a direct step back. But that is the best that can be said of it. The economic requirements of the bourgeoisie were in the main satisfied, its political claims—inasmuch as it still made any—encountered the same obstructions as during the conflict.

Inasmuch as it still made political claims! For it cannot be denied that with the National Liberals these claims had shrunk to a very modest size and continued to shrink with every passing day. These gentlemen, far from demanding that Bismarck should facilitate their collaboration with himself, were much more concerned with doing his will wherever possible, and quite often also where it was impossible, or should have been impossible. Bismarck despised them and no one can blame him for that—but were his Junkers one iota better or braver?

The next field in which unity of the Empire had to be introduced, the monetary system, was normalised by the currency and banking laws passed between 1873 and 1875. The introduction of gold currency was a considerable step forward; but it was introduced only hesitantly and waveringly and is not firmly established even today. The monetary system adopted—the third of a taler under the name of "mark", a unit with a decimal division—had been suggested by von Soetbeer at the close of the thirties; the actual unit was the gold twenty-mark piece. By a barely noticeable change in value it could have been made absolutely equivalent either to the British sovereign, or the gold twenty-five franc coin, or the gold U.S. five-dollar piece, and linked to one of the three great currency systems on the world market. Preference was given to a separate currency system, thereby needlessly complicating trade and exchange calculations. The laws on imperial treasury notes and banks [408] limited the fraudulent transactions in securities of small states and their banks and, taking into consideration the crash which had in the meantime occurred, they were marked by a definite timidity, which well became Germany, still inexperienced in this field. But here, too, the economic interests of the bourgeoisie were on the whole adequately looked after.

Finally there came an agreement on uniform laws. The resistance of the central German states to the extension of imperial competency to the material civil law was overcome, but the civil code is still in the making, while the penal code, criminal and civil procedural law, trade laws, the regulations concerning insolvency and the judicial system have been unified everywhere. The abolition of the motley formal and material legal standards in force in the small states was in itself an urgent requirement for ongoing bourgeois development, and this abolition is the chief merit of the new laws—a far greater one than their content.

The English jurist relies on a legal heritage that has preserved a good part of the old German freedoms through the Middle Ages, that does not know the police state, which was nipped in the bud by the two revolutions of the 17th century and has attained its apex in two centuries of uninterrupted development of civic freedom. The French jurist relies on the Great Revolution, which, after the total destruction of feudalism and absolutist police tyranny, translated the economic conditions of life in the newly created modern society into the language of legal standards in the classical code of law proclaimed by Napoleon. But on what legal basis do our German jurists rely? Nothing but the several-century-long process of disintegration of medieval survivals, a passive process mostly spurred on by blows from the outside, and not complete to this day; an economically backward society, which the feudal Junker and the guild master haunt as ghosts looking for a new body; a legal order in which police tyranny—even though the arbitrary justice of the princes disappeared in 1848—is daily tearing new holes. The fathers of the new imperial legal codes have come from this worst of all bad schools, and their work is quite in keeping with it. Apart from the purely legal aspect, political freedom has fared pretty badly in these codes of law. If the Schöffen courts[409] provide the bourgeoisie and petty bourgeoisie with a means of collaborating in repressing the working class, the state insures itself as much as possible against the danger of renewed bourgeois opposition by curtailing the rights of the jury. The political paragraphs of the penal code are frequently enough as vague and elastic as if they were made to measure for the present imperial court, and the latter for them. That the new legal codes are a step forward in comparison with Prussian common law[410]—today even Stoecker would be unable to concoct something as horrible as that code, even if he were to allow himself to be cut back. But the provinces which had until now lived under French law feel very acutely the difference between the blurred copy and the classic original. It was the defection of the National Liberals from their programme that made possible this strengthening of state power at the expense of civic freedoms, this first actual retrogression.

Mention should also be made of the imperial press law.[411] The penal code had essentially already regulated the material law pertaining to it; the elaboration of identical formal stipulations for the whole Empire and the abolition of the security and stamp duties existing here and there were therefore the main content of the law and at the same time the only progress it achieved.

To enable Prussia once again to prove itself a model state, so-called self-government was introduced there. The aim was to abolish the most objectionable survivals of feudalism and yet, actually, to leave, as far as possible, everything as before. The District Ordinance[412] served this purpose. The manorial police power of the Junkers had become an anachronism. In name—as a feudal privilege—it was abolished, but actually it was reinstituted by the establishment of independent rural districts [Gutsbezirke], within which the landowner either himself acts as rural superintendent [Gutsvorsteher] with the powers of the head of the rural community [Gemeindevorsteher] or appoints this rural superintendent, and was also reinstituted by transferring the entire police power and police jurisdiction of the administrative district [*Amtsbezirk*] to a district head [*Amtsvorsteher*], a position held in rural areas almost exclusively by big landowners, of course, who in this way got the rural community under their thumb. The feudal privileges of individuals were abolished, but the absolute power connected with these privileges was handed over to the entire class. By similar conjuring the English big landowners turned into justices of the peace and the masters of the rural administration, the police and the lower courts of justice and thereby secured for themselves under a new, modernised title further enjoyment of all essential positions of authority, which they could not continue to hold under the old feudal form. That, however, is the only similarity between the English and the German "self-government". I should like to see the British Minister who would dare to propose in Parliament that elected local officials should be approved and that in case an undesired person is elected he be forcibly replaced by an appointee of the state, to propose that there be civil servants vested with the authority of the Prussian Landrats, heads of administrative districts and *Oberpräsidents,* to propose that the administrative bodies of the state be given the right provided for in the District Ordinance to intervene in the internal affairs of communities, small administrative units and districts and to exclude recourse to law, a thing unheard of in English-speaking countries and in English law, but which we see on almost every page of the District Ordinance. And while the district diets [*Kreistag*] as well as the provincial diets are still composed in the old feudal manner of representatives of the three estates: the big landowners, towns and rural communities, in England even a highly conservative ministry moves a bill transferring the whole county administration to authorities elected by almost universal suffrage.[413]

The draft of the District Ordinance for the six Eastern provinces (1871) was the first indication that Bismarck did not even think of allowing Prussia to dissolve into Germany, but that, on the contrary, he sought to further strengthen these six provinces—the stronghold of the old Prussianism. Under changed names, the Junkers retained all essential positions of power, while the helots of Germany, the rural workers of these areas—such as farmhands and day labourers—remained in their former *de facto* serfdom and were admitted to only two public functions: to become soldiers and to serve the Junkers as voting stock during the elections to the Reichstag. The service Bismarck rendered thereby to the revolutionary socialist party is indescribable and deserves the warmest gratitude.

What can be said about the mindlessness of the Junker gentlemen, who, like spoiled children, kicked against the District Ordinance which had been drawn up exclusively in their interest, in the interest of perpetuating their feudal privileges, under a somewhat modernised name? The Prussian House of Lords, or, to be more exact, of Junkers, at first rejected the draft, which had already been delayed for a whole year, and adopted it only after 24 new "Lords" had been nominated peers. Once again the Prussian Junkers proved that they were petty, obdurate, incorrigible reactionaries, unable to form the nucleus of a large independent party which could play an historical role in the life of the nation, as the English big landowners actually do. Thereby they proved their complete lack of sense; Bismarck had only to reveal to the world their equally complete lack of character, and a little pressure, pertinently applied, would transform them into a Bismarck Party *sans phrase*.

The Kulturkampf[414] was to serve this purpose.

The implementation of the Prussian-German imperial plan should have evoked a counterblow—the amalgamation into a single party of all anti-Prussian elements, which had previously relied on separate development. These motley elements found a common banner in Ultramontanism.[415] The rebellion of sound common sense even among the numerous orthodox Catholics against the new dogma of Papal infallibility, on the one hand, the destruction of the Papal States, and the so-called imprisonment of the Pope in Rome,[416] on the other, forced all the pugnacious forces of Catholicism to rally closer together. Thus even during the war, in the autumn of 1870, the specifically Catholic Party of the Centre was formed in the Prussian Provincial Diet; in the first German Reichstag of 1871 it had only 57 seats, but it grew stronger with every new election until it had over 100 representatives. It was composed of very heterogeneous elements. In Prussia its main strength consisted of the Rhenish small peasants, who still regarded themselves as "Prussians under duress", then of the Catholic big landowners and peasants of the Westphalian bishoprics of Münster and Paderborn, and of the Catholic Silesians. The second great contingent was provided by the South German Catholics, notably the Bavarians. It was not so much the Catholic religion that formed the Centre Party's strength, but the fact that it represented the antipathies of the popular masses against everything specifically Prussian, now laying claim to domination over Germany. These antipathies were particularly strong in the Catholic areas; and then there were sympathies with Austria, now expelled from Germany. In harmony with these two popular trends, the Centre was decidedly particularist and federalist.

This essentially anti-Prussian character of the Centre was immediately recognised by the other small Reichstag factions, which were anti-Prussian for local reasons, not, as the Social-Democrats, for national and general reasons. Not only the Catholic Poles and Alsatians, but even the Protestant Guelphs[417] allied themselves closely with the Centre. And even though the bourgeois liberal factions could never fully understand the actual character of the so-called Ultramontanes, they did have an inkling of the true state of affairs when they styled the Centre "unpatriotic" and "hostile to the Empire"....[a]

---

[a] The manuscript breaks off here.— *Ed.*

[ROUGH DRAFT OF THE PREFACE
TO *THE ROLE OF FORCE IN HISTORY*][418]

The following piece of writing is an off-print of part of my work *Herr Eugen Dühring's Revolution in Science,* and contains three chapters that bear the title "The Force Theory".[419] They have already appeared separately in Russian translation, namely as the appendix to the Russian edition of my *Socialism: Utopian and Scientific.*[a] Only the most necessary changes and addenda have been made in the present edition. But an off-print requires a special addendum.

If I publish in German a pamphlet on "the role of force in history", the German reader has every right to expect me not to conceal my views on the very important part played by force precisely in his own history over the past thirty years. For this reason I have added a fourth section, which naturally covers only the main points. Perhaps I shall be granted the opportunity one day to deal with the subject in more detail.

Written between the end of December 1887 and March 1888

First published in *Die Neue Zeit,* Vol. 1, No. 22, 1895

Printed according to the manuscript

Published in English for the first time

---

[a] Ф. Энгельс, *Развитіе научнаго соціализма,* Женева, 1884.— *Ed.*

PREFACE TO THE 1888 ENGLISH EDITION
OF THE *MANIFESTO OF THE COMMUNIST PARTY*

The "Manifesto" was published as the platform of the "Communist League", a working-men's association, first exclusively German, later on international, and, under the political conditions of the Continent before 1848, unavoidably a secret society. At a Congress of the League, held in London in November, 1847, Marx and Engels were commissioned to prepare for publication a complete theoretical and practical party programme. Drawn up in German, in January, 1848, the manuscript was sent to the printer in London a few weeks before the French revolution of February 24th. A French translation was brought out in Paris, shortly before the insurrection of June, 1848. The first English translation, by Miss Helen Macfarlane, appeared in George Julian Harney's "Red Republican," London, 1850. A Danish and a Polish edition had also been published.

The defeat of the Parisian insurrection of June, 1848,—the first great battle between Proletariat and Bourgeoisie—drove again into the background, for a time, the social and political aspirations of the European working-class. Thenceforth, the struggle for supremacy was again, as it had been before the revolution of February, solely between different sections of the propertied class; the working class was reduced to a fight for political elbow-room, and to the position of extreme wing of the Middle-class Radicals. Wherever independent proletarian movements continued to show signs of life, they were ruthlessly hunted down. Thus the Prussian police hunted out the Central Board of the Communist League, then located in Cologne. The members were arrested, and, after eighteen months' imprisonment, they were tried in October, 1852. This celebrated "Cologne Communist trial" lasted from October 4th till November 12th; seven of the prisoners were sentenced to terms of imprisonment in a fortress, varying from three to six

PRICE TWOPENCE.

MANIFESTO

OF THE

COMMUNIST PARTY,

By KARL MARX, and FREDERICK ENGELS.

Authorized English Translation.

EDITED AND ANNOTATED BY FREDERICK ENGELS,
1888.

London:

WILLIAM REEVES, 185, FLEET STREET, E.C.

Title page of the English edition
of the *Manifesto of the Communist Party*

years. Immediately after the sentence, the League was formally dissolved by the remaining members.[a] As to the "Manifesto," it seemed thenceforth to be doomed to oblivion.

When the European working-class had recovered sufficient strength for another attack on the ruling classes, the International Working Men's Association sprang up. But this association, formed with the express aim of welding into one body the whole militant proletariat of Europe and America, could not at once proclaim the principles laid down in the "Manifesto." The International was bound to have a programme broad enough to be acceptable to the English Trades' Unions, to the followers of Proudhon in France, Belgium, Italy, and Spain, and to the Lassalleans* in Germany. Marx, who drew up this programme to the satisfaction of all parties, entirely trusted to the intellectual development of the working-class, which was sure to result from combined action and mutual discussion. The very events and vicissitudes of the struggle against Capital, the defeats even more than the victories, could not help bringing home to men's minds the insufficiency of their various favourite nostrums, and preparing the way for a more complete insight into the true conditions of working-class emancipation. And Marx was right. The International, on its breaking up in 1874, left the workers quite different men from what it had found them in 1864. Proudhonism in France, Lassalleanism in Germany were dying out, and even the Conservative English Trades' Unions, though most of them had long since severed their connexion with the International, were gradually advancing towards that point at which, last year at Swansea, their President[b] could say in their name "Continental Socialism has lost its terrors for us."[c] In fact: the principles of the "Manifesto" had made considerable headway among the working men of all countries.

The Manifesto itself thus came to the front again. The German text had been, since 1850, reprinted several times in Switzerland,

---

* Lassalle personally, to us, always acknowledged himself to be a disciple of Marx, and, as such, stood on the ground of the "Manifesto". But in his public agitation, 1862-64, he did not go beyond demanding co-operative workshops supported by State credit.

---

[a] See this volume, p. 329.— *Ed.*

[b] W. Bevan.— *Ed.*

[c] [W. Bevan's speech at the Twentieth Annual Trades' Union Congress at Swansea on September 6, 1887.] In: W. Binning, "The Trades' Union Congress", *The Commonweal*, No. 88, September 17, 1887.— *Ed.*

England and America. In 1872, it was translated into English in New York, where the translation was published in *Woodhull and Claflin's Weekly.*[420] From this English version, a French one was made in "Le Socialiste" of New York. Since then at least two more English translations, more or less mutilated, have been brought out in America, and one of them has been reprinted in England. The first Russian translation, made by Bakounine, was published at Herzen's "Kolokol" office in Geneva, about 1863[421]; a second one, by the heroic Vera Zasulitch, also in Geneva, 1882.[422] A new Danish edition is to be found in "Socialdemokratisk Bibliothek," Copenhagen, 1885; a fresh French translation in "Le Socialiste," Paris, 1886. From this latter a Spanish version was prepared and published in Madrid, 1886.[423] The German reprints are not to be counted, there have been twelve altogether at the least. An Armenian translation, which was to be published in Constantinople some months ago, did not see the light, I am told, because the publisher was afraid of bringing out a book with the name of Marx on it, while the translator declined to call it his own production. Of further translations into other languages I have heard, but have not seen them. Thus the history of the Manifesto reflects, to a great extent, the history of the modern working-class movement; at present it is undoubtedly the most wide-spread, the most international production of all Socialist Literature, the common platform acknowledged by millions of working men from Siberia to California.

Yet, when it was written, we could not have called it a *Socialist* Manifesto. By Socialists, in 1847, were understood, on the one hand, the adherents of the various Utopian systems: Owenites in England, Fourierists in France,[424] both of them already reduced to the position of mere sects, and gradually dying out; on the other hand, the most multifarious social quacks, who, by all manners of tinkering, professed to redress, without any danger to capital and profit, all sorts of social grievances in both cases men outside the working class movement, and looking rather to the "educated" classes for support. Whatever portion of the working class had become convinced of the insufficiency of mere political revolutions, and had proclaimed the necessity of a total social change, that portion, then, called itself Communist. It was a crude, rough-hewn, purely instinctive sort of Communism; still, it touched the cardinal point and was powerful enough amongst the working class to produce the Utopian Communism, in France, of Cabet, and in Germany, of Weitling. Thus, Socialism was, in 1847, a middle-class movement, Communism a working class movement.

Socialism was, on the Continent at least, "respectable"; Communism was the very opposite. And as our notion, from the very beginning, was that "the emancipation of the working class must be the act of the working class itself," [a] there could be no doubt as to which of the two names we must take. Moreover, we have, ever since, been far from repudiating it.

The "Manifesto" being our joint production, I consider myself bound to state that the fundamental proposition which forms its nucleus, belongs to Marx. That proposition is: that in every historical epoch, the prevailing mode of economic production and exchange, and the social organisation necessarily following from it, form the basis upon which is built up, and from which alone can be explained, the political and intellectual history of that epoch; that consequently the whole history of mankind (since the dissolution of primitive tribal society, holding land in common ownership) has been a history of class struggles, contests between exploiting and exploited, ruling and oppressed classes; that the history of these class struggles form a series of evolution in which, nowadays, a stage has been reached where the exploited and oppressed class—the proletariat—cannot attain its emancipation from the sway of the exploiting and ruling class—the bourgeoisie—without, at the same time, and once and for all emancipating society at large from all exploitation, oppression, class-distinctions and class-struggles.

This proposition which, in my opinion, is destined to do for history what Darwin's theory has done for biology, we, both of us, had been gradually approaching for some years before 1845. How far I had independently progressed towards it, is best shown by my "Condition of the Working Class in England." * But when I again met Marx at Brussels, in spring, 1845, he had it ready worked out, and put it before me, in terms almost as clear as those in which I have stated it here.

From our joint preface to the German edition of 1872, I quote the following:—

"However much the state of things may have altered during the last 25 years, the general principles laid down in this Manifesto are, on the whole, as correct to-day as ever. Here and there some

---

* *The Condition of the Working Class in England in 1844.* By Frederick Engels. Translated by Florence K. Wischnewetzky, New York, Lovell—London. W. Reeves. 1888.

---

[a] K. Marx, "Provisional Rules of the Association" (present edition, Vol. 20, p. 14; see also Vol. 23, p. 3.).—*Ed.*

detail might be improved. The practical application of the principles will depend, as the manifesto itself states, everywhere and at all times, on the historical conditions for the time being existing, and, for that reason, no special stress is laid on the revolutionary measures proposed at the end of Section II. That passage would, in many respects, be very differently worded to-day. In view of the gigantic strides of Modern Industry since 1848,[a] and of the accompanying improved and extended[b] organisation of the working-class, in view of the practical experience gained, first in the February revolution, and then, still more, in the Paris Commune, where the proletariat for the first time held political power for two whole months, this programme has in some details become antiquated. One thing especially was proved by the Commune, viz., that 'the working-class cannot simply lay hold of the ready-made State machinery, and wield it for its own purposes.' (See "The Civil War in France; Address of the General Council of the International Working-men's Association," London, Truelove, 1871, p. 15, where this point is further developed.)[c] Further, it is self-evident, that the criticism of socialist literature is deficient in relation to the present time, because it comes down only to 1847; also, that the remarks on the relation of the Communists to the various opposition-parties (Section IV.), although in principle still correct, yet in practice are antiquated, because the political situation has been entirely changed, and the progress of history has swept from off the earth the greater portion of the political parties there enumerated.

"But then, the Manifesto has become a historical document which we have no longer any right to alter."[d]

The present translation is by Mr. Samuel Moore, the translator of the greater portion of Marx's *Capital.* We have revised it in common, and I have added a few notes explanatory of historical allusions.

London, 30th January, 1888   *Frederick Engels*

First published in K. Marx and F. Engels,   Reproduced from the book
Manifesto of the Communist Party, London,
1888

---

[a] Instead of "since 1848", the 1872 edition has "in the past twenty-five years".— *Ed.*

[b] Instead of "of the accompanying improved and extended", the 1872 edition has "with its advancing party".— *Ed.*

[c] See present edition, Vol. 22, p. 328.— *Ed.*

[d] K. Marx and F. Engels, "Preface to the 1872 German Edition of the *Manifesto of the Communist Party*" (present edition, Vol. 23, pp. 174-75).— *Ed.*

519

[PREFACE TO THE PAMPHLET
*LUDWIG FEUERBACH AND THE END
OF CLASSICAL GERMAN PHILOSOPHY*[a]]

In the preface to *A Contribution to the Critique of Political Economy*, Berlin, 1859, Karl Marx relates how the two of us in Brussels in the year 1845 decided "to set forth together our conception"—the materialist conception of history which was elaborated mainly by Marx—"as opposed to the ideological one of German philosophy, in fact to settle accounts with our former philosophical conscience. The intention was carried out in the form of a critique of post-Hegelian philosophy. The manuscript,[b] two large octavo volumes, had long ago reached the publishers in Westphalia when we were informed that owing to changed circumstances it could not be printed. We abandoned the manuscript to the gnawing criticism of the mice all the more willingly since we had achieved our main purpose—self-clarification."[c]

Since then more than forty years have elapsed and Marx died without either of us having had an opportunity of returning to the subject. We have expressed ourselves in various places regarding our relation to Hegel, but nowhere in a comprehensive, coherent account. To Feuerbach, who after all in some respects forms an intermediate link between Hegelian philosophy and our conception, we never returned.

In the meantime the Marxian world outlook has found adherents far beyond the boundaries of Germany and Europe and

---

[a] See this volume, pp. 353-98.— *Ed.*
    [b] K. Marx and F. Engels, *The German Ideology.—Ed.*
    [c] K. Marx, *A Contribution to the Critique of Political Economy* (present edition, Vol. 29, p. 264).— *Ed.*

in all the literary languages of the world. On the other hand, classical German philosophy is experiencing a kind of rebirth abroad, especially in England and Scandinavia, and even in Germany itself people appear to be getting tired of the pauper's broth of eclecticism which is ladled out in the universities there under the name of philosophy.

In these circumstances a short, coherent account of our relation to Hegelian philosophy, of how we proceeded, as well as of how we departed, from it, appeared to me to be increasingly necessary. Equally, a full acknowledgement of the influence which Feuerbach, more than any other post-Hegelian philosopher, had upon us during our *Sturm und Drang* period,[425] appeared to me to be an undischarged debt of honour. I therefore willingly seized the opportunity when the editors of the *Neue Zeit* asked me for a critical review of Starcke's book on Feuerbach. My contribution was published in that journal in the fourth and fifth numbers of 1886 and appears here in revised form as a separate publication.

Before sending these lines to press I have once again ferreted out and looked over the old manuscript of 1845-46. The section dealing with Feuerbach is not completed. The finished portion consists of an exposition of the materialist conception of history which proves only how incomplete our knowledge of economic history still was at that time. It contains no criticism of Feuerbach's doctrine itself; for the present purpose, therefore, it was useless. On the other hand, in an old notebook of Marx's I have found the eleven theses on Feuerbach printed here as an appendix.[a] These are notes hurriedly scribbled down for later elaboration, absolutely not intended for publication, but invaluable as the first document in which is deposited the brilliant germ of the new world outlook.

London, February 21, 1888

Frederick Engels

First published in F. Engels, *Ludwig Feuerbach und der Ausgang der klassischen deutschen Philosophie*, Stuttgart, 1888

Printed according to the book

---

[a] K. Marx, "Theses on Feuerbach".— *Ed.*

PROTECTION AND FREE TRADE *
PREFACE TO THE PAMPHLET: KARL MARX, *SPEECH ON THE QUESTION OF FREE TRADE* [426]

Towards the end of 1847, a Free Trade Congress was held at Brussels.[427] It was a strategic move in the Free Trade campaign then carried on by the English manufacturers. Victorious at home, by the repeal of the Corn Laws in 1846,[428] they now invaded the continent in order to demand, in return for the free admission of continental corn into England, the free admission of English manufactured goods to the continental markets. At this Congress, Marx inscribed himself on the list of speakers; but, as might have been expected, things were so managed that before his turn came on, the Congress was closed. Thus, what Marx had to say on the Free Trade question, he was compelled to say before the Democratic Association of Brussels, an international body of which he was one of the vice-presidents.[429]

The question of Free Trade or Protection being at present on the order of the day in America, it has been thought useful to publish an English translation of Marx' speech, to which I have been asked to write an introductory preface.

"The system of protection," says Marx, "was an artificial means of manufacturing manufacturers, of expropriating independent laborers, of capitalizing the national means of production and subsistence, and of forcibly abbreviating the transition from the

---

* Preface (translated by the author) to the English edition of Marx's speech on the question of free trade, being published in New York (German by E. Bernstein and K. Kautsky, Appendix II to Marx's *Poverty of Philosophy*, Stuttgart, Dietz, p. 188 ff.). Since this preface is intended primarily for an American audience, the German policy on protective tariffs could be mentioned only in passing. However, the author will doubtless soon find an occasion to deal with the question specifically with respect to Germany. [*Engels' note to the German translation.*]

medieval to the modern mode of production."* Such was
protection at its origin in the seventeenth century, such it
remained well into the nineteenth century. It was then held to be
the normal policy of every civilized state in Western Europe. The
only exceptions were the smaller states of Germany and Switzerland—not from dislike of the system, but from the impossibility of
applying it to such small territories.

It was under the fostering wing of protection that the system of
modern industry—production by steam-moved machinery—was
hatched and developed in England during the last third of the
eighteenth century. And, as if tariff-protection was not sufficient,
the wars against the French Revolution helped to secure to
England the monopoly of the new industrial methods. For more
than twenty years English men-of-war cut off the industrial rivals
of England from their respective colonial markets, while they
forcibly opened these markets to English commerce. The secession
of the South American colonies from the rule of their European
mother-countries, the conquest by England of all French and
Dutch colonies worth having, the progressive subjugation of India,
turned the people of all these immense territories[a] into customers
for English goods. England thus supplemented the protection she
practised at home, by the Free Trade she forced upon her possible
customers abroad; and, thanks to this happy mixture of both
systems, at the end of the wars,[b] in 1815, she found herself, with
regard to all important branches of industry, in possession of the
virtual monopoly of the trade of the world.

This monopoly was further extended and strengthened during
the ensuing years of peace. The start which England had obtained
during the war, was increased from year to year; she seemed to
distance more and more all her possible rivals. The exports of
manufactured goods in ever growing quantities became indeed a
question of life and death to that country. And there seemed but
two obstacles in the way: the prohibitive or protective legislation of
other countries, and the taxes upon the import of raw materials
and articles of food in England.

Then the Free Trade doctrines of classical political economy—
of the French physiocrats[430] and their English successors, Adam
Smith and Ricardo—became popular in the land of John Bull.

---

* Karl Marx, *Capital*. London: Swan Sonnenschein Co., 1886 [1887], p. 782.

---

a In the German translation: "turned all these countries".—*Ed.*
b The reference is to the Napoleonic Wars of 1796-1814.—*Ed.*

Protection at home was needless to manufacturers who beat all their foreign rivals, and whose very existence was staked on the expansion of their exports. Protection at home was of advantage to none but the producers of articles of food and other raw materials, to the agricultural interest, which, under then existing circumstances in England, meant the receivers of rent, the landed aristocracy. And this kind of protection was hurtful to the manufacturers. By taxing raw materials it raised the price of the articles manufactured from them; by taxing food, it raised the price of labor; in both ways, it placed the British manufacturer at a disadvantage as compared with his foreign competitor. And, as all other countries sent to England chiefly agricultural products, and drew from England chiefly manufactured goods, repeal of the English protective duties on corn and raw materials generally, was at the same time an appeal to foreign countries, to do away with, or at least, to reduce, in return, the import duties levied by them on English manufactures.

After a long and violent struggle, the English industrial capitalists, already in reality the leading class of the nation, that class whose interests were then the chief national interests, were victorious. The landed aristocracy had to give in. The duties on corn and other raw materials were repealed. Free Trade became the watchword of the day. To convert all other countries to the gospel of Free Trade, and thus to create a world in which England was the great manufacturing centre, with all other countries for its dependent agricultural districts, that was the next task before the English manufacturers and their mouthpieces, the political economists.

That was the time of the Brussels Congress, the time when Marx prepared the speech in question. While recognizing that protection may still, under certain circumstances, for instance in the Germany of 1847, be of advantage to the manufacturing capitalists; while proving that Free Trade was not the panacea for all the evils under which the working class suffered, and might even aggravate them; he pronounces, ultimately and on principle, in favor of Free Trade. To him, Free Trade is the normal condition of modern capitalistic production. Only under Free Trade can the immense productive powers of steam, of electricity, of machinery, be fully developed; and the quicker the pace of this development, the sooner and the more fully will be realized its inevitable results: society splits up into two classes, capitalists here, wage-laborers there; hereditary wealth on one side, hereditary poverty on the other; supply outstripping demand, the markets being unable to absorb the ever growing mass of the productions of industry; an ever recurring cycle of prosperity, glut, crisis, panic, chronic depression and gradual revival of trade, the harbinger not of permanent improvement but of renewed overproduction and crisis; in short, productive forces expanding to such a degree that they rebel, as against unbearable fetters, against the social institutions under which they are put in motion; the only possible solution: a social revolution,[a] freeing the social productive forces from the fetters of an antiquated social order, and the actual producers, the great mass of the people, from wage-slavery. And because Free Trade is the natural, the normal atmosphere for this historical evolution, the economic medium in which the conditions for the inevitable social revolution[b] will be the soonest created,—for this reason, and for this alone, did Marx declare in favor of Free Trade.

Anyhow, the years immediately following the victory of Free Trade in England seemed to verify the most extravagant expectations of prosperity founded upon that event. British commerce rose to a fabulous amount; the industrial monopoly of England on the market of the world seemed more firmly established than ever; new iron works, new textile factories arose by wholesale; new branches of industry grew up on every side. There was, indeed, a severe crisis in 1857, but that was overcome, and the onward movement in trade and manufactures soon was in full swing again, until in 1866 a fresh panic occurred, a panic, this time, which seems to mark a new departure in the economic history of the world.

The unparalleled expansion of British manufactures and commerce between 1848 and 1866 was no doubt due, to a great extent, to the removal of the protective duties on food and raw materials. But not entirely. Other important changes took place simultaneously and helped it on. The above years comprise the discovery and working of the Californian and Australian gold fields[431] which increased so immensely the circulating medium of the world; they mark the final victory of steam over all other means of transport[c]; on the ocean, steamers now superseded sailing vessels; on land, in all civilized countries, the railroad took

---

[a] The German translation has "social transformation" instead of "social revolution".— Ed.

[b] The German translation has here "this inevitable solution".— Ed.

[c] Instead of the last phrase the German translation has: "they represent a general transformation of the means of transport".— Ed.

the first place, the macadamized road the second; transport now became four times quicker and four times cheaper. No wonder that under such favorable circumstances British manufactures worked by steam should extend their sway at the expense of foreign domestic industries based upon manual labor. But were the other countries to sit still and to submit in humility to this change, which degraded them to be mere agricultural appendages of England, the "workshop of the world"?

The foreign countries did nothing of the kind. France, for nearly two hundred years, had screened her manufactures behind a perfect Chinese wall of protection and prohibition, and had attained in all articles of luxury and of taste a supremacy which England did not even pretend to dispute. Switzerland, under perfect Free Trade, possessed relatively important manufactures which English competition could not touch. Germany, with a tariff far more liberal than that of any other large continental country, was developing its manufactures at a rate relatively more rapid than even England. And America was, by the civil war of 1861,[432] all at once thrown upon her own resources, had to find means how to meet a sudden demand for manufactured goods of all sorts, and could only do so by creating manufactures of her own at home. The war demand ceased with the war; but the new manufactures were there, and had to meet British competition. And the war had ripened, in America, the insight that a nation of thirty-five millions, doubling its numbers in forty years at most, with such immense resources, and surrounded by neighbors that must be for years to come chiefly agriculturalists, that such a nation had the "manifest destiny"[433] to be independent of foreign manufactures for its chief articles of consumption, and to be so in time of peace as well as in time of war. And then America turned protectionist.

It may now be fifteen years ago, I travelled in a railway carriage with an intelligent Glasgow merchant, interested, probably, in the iron trade. Talking about America, he treated me to the old Free Trade lucubrations: "Was it not inconceivable that a nation of sharp business men like the Americans should pay tribute to indigenous iron masters and manufacturers, when they could buy the same, if not a better article, ever so much cheaper in this country?" And then he gave me examples as to how much the Americans taxed themselves in order to enrich a few greedy iron masters. "Well," I replied, "I think there is another side to the question. You know that in coal, water-power, iron and other ores, cheap food, home-grown cotton and other raw materials, America has resources and advantages unequalled by any 'European country; and that these resources cannot be fully developed except by America becoming a manufacturing country. You will admit, too, that nowadays a great nation like the Americans cannot exist on agriculture alone; that that would be tantamount to a condemnation to permanent barbarism and inferiority; no great nation can live, in our age, without manufactures of her own. Well, then, if America must become a manufacturing country, and if she has every chance of not only succeeding, but even outstripping her rivals, there are two ways open to her: either to carry on, for let us say fifty years, under Free Trade an extremely expensive competitive war against English manufactures that have got nearly a hundred years' start; or else to shut out, by protective duties, English manufactures, for say twenty-five years, with the almost absolute certainty that at the end of the twenty-five years she will be able to hold her own in the open market of the world. Which of the two will be the cheapest and the shortest? That is the question. If you want to go from Glasgow to London, you can take the parliamentary train [434] at a penny a mile and travel at the rate of twelve miles an hour. But you do not; your time is too valuable, you take the express, pay twopence a mile and do forty miles an hour. Very well, the Americans prefer to pay express fare and to go express speed." My Scotch Free Trader had not a word in reply.

Protection, being a means of artificially manufacturing manufacturers, may, therefore, appear useful not only to an incompletely developed capitalist class still struggling with feudalism; it may also give a lift to the rising capitalist class of a country which, like America, has never known feudalism, but which has arrived at that stage of development where the passage from agriculture to manufactures becomes a necessity. America, placed in that situation, decided in favor of protection. Since that decision was carried out, the five and twenty years of which I spoke to my fellow-traveller have about passed, and, if I was not wrong, protection ought to have done its task for America, and ought to be now becoming a nuisance.

That has been my opinion for some time. Nearly two years ago, I said to a protectionist American: "I am convinced that if America goes in for Free Trade she will in ten years have beaten England in the market of the world."

Protection is at best an endless screw, and you never know when you have done with it. By protecting one industry, you directly or indirectly hurt all others, and have therefore to protect them too.

By so doing you again damage the industry that you first protected, and have to compensate it; but this compensation reacts, as before, on all other trades, and entitles them to redress, and so on *in infinitum*. America, in this respect, offers us a striking example of the best way to kill an important industry by protection. In 1856, the total imports and exports by sea of the United States amounted to $641,604,850, of this amount, 75.2 per cent. were carried in American, and only 24.8 per cent. in foreign vessels. British ocean-steamers were already then encroaching upon American sailing vessels; yet, in 1860, of a total sea-going trade of $762,288,550, American vessels still carried 66.5 per cent. The civil war came on, and protection to American ship-building; and the latter plan was so successful that it has nearly completely driven the American flag from the high seas. In 1887 the total sea-going trade of the United States amounted to $1,408,502,979, but of this total only 13.8 per cent. were carried in American, and 86.2 per cent. in foreign bottoms. The goods carried by American ships amounted, in 1856, to $482,268,274; in 1860 to $507,247,757. In 1887 they had sunk to $194,356,746.* Forty years ago, the American flag was the most dangerous rival of the British flag, and bade fair to outstrip it on the ocean; now it is nowhere. Protection to ship-building has killed both shipping and ship-building.

Another point. Improvements in the methods of production nowadays follow each other so rapidly, and change the character of entire branches of industry so suddenly and so completely, that what may have been yesterday a fairly balanced protective tariff is no longer so to-day. Let us take another example from the Report of the Secretary of the Treasury for 1887:

"Improvement in recent years in the machinery employed in combing wool has so changed the character of what are commercially known as worsted cloths that the latter have largely superseded woollen cloths for use as men's wearing apparel. This change ... has operated to the serious injury of our domestic manufacturers of these (worsted) goods, because the duty on the wool which they must use is the same as that upon wool used in making woollen cloths, while the rates of duty imposed upon the latter when valued at not exceeding 80 cents per pound are 35 cents per pound and 35 per cent. ad valorem,[a] whereas the duty on worsted cloths valued at not exceeding 80 cents ranges from 10 to 24 cents per pound and 35 per cent. ad valorem. In some cases the duty on the wool used in making worsted cloths *exceeds the duty imposed on the finished article.*"

* *Annual Report of the Secretary of the Treasury etc., for the Year 1887*, Washington, 1887, pp. XXVIII, XXIX.

---

[a] In proportion to estimated value of goods.— *Ed.*

Thus what was protection to home industry yesterday, turns out to-day to be a premium to the foreign importer; and well may the Secretary of the Treasury[a] say:

"There is much reason to believe that the manufacture of worsted cloths must soon cease in this country unless the tariff law in this regard is amended" (p. XIX).

But to amend it, you will have to fight the manufacturers of woollen cloths who profit by this state of things; you will have to open a regular campaign to bring the majority of both Houses of Congress, and eventually the public opinion of the country, round to your views, and the question is, Will that pay?

But the worst of protection is, that when you once have got it you cannot easily get rid of it. Difficult as is the process of adjustment of an equitable tariff, the return to Free Trade is immensely more difficult. The circumstances which permitted England to accomplish the change in a few years, will not occur again. And even there the struggle dated from 1823 (Huskisson), commenced to be successful in 1842 (Peel's tariff),[435] and was continued for several years after the repeal of the Corn Laws. Thus protection to the silk manufacture (the only one which had still to fear foreign competition) was prolonged for a series of years and then granted in another, positively infamous form; while the other textile industries were subjected to the Factory Act, which limited the hours of labor of women, young persons and children,[436] the silk trade was favored with considerable exceptions to the general rule, enabling them to work younger children, and to work the children and young persons longer hours, than the other textile trades. The monopoly that the hypocritical Free Traders repealed with regard to the foreign competitors, that monopoly they created anew at the expense of the health and lives of English children.

But no country will again be able to pass from Protection to Free Trade at a time when all, or nearly all branches of its manufactures can defy foreign competition in the open market. The necessity of the change will come long before such a happy state may be even hoped for. That necessity will make itself evident in different trades at different times; and from the conflicting interests of these trades, the most edifying squabbles, lobby intrigues, and parliamentary conspiracies will arise. The machinist, engineer, and ship-builder may find that the protection granted to the iron master raises the price of his goods so much that his export trade is thereby, and thereby alone, prevented; the

---

[a] Charles Fairchild.— Ed.

cotton-cloth manufacturer might see his way to driving English cloth out of the Chinese and Indian markets, but for the high price he has to pay for the yarn, on account of protection to spinners; and so forth. The moment a branch of national industry has completely conquered the home market, that moment exportation becomes a necessity to it. Under capitalistic conditions, an industry either expands or wanes. A trade cannot remain stationary; stoppage of expansion is incipient ruin; the progress of mechanical and chemical invention, by constantly superseding human labor, and ever more rapidly increasing and concentrating capital, creates in every stagnant industry a glut both of workers and of capital, a glut which finds no vent everywhere, because the same process is taking place in all other industries. Thus the passage from a home to an export trade becomes a question of life and death for the industries concerned; but they are met by the established rights, the vested interests of others who as yet find protection either safer or more profitable than Free Trade. Then ensues a long and obstinate fight between Free Traders and Protectionists; a fight where, on both sides, the leadership soon passes out of the hands of the people directly interested into those of professional politicians, the wire-pullers of the traditional political parties, whose interest is, not a settlement of the question, but its being kept open forever; and the result of an immense loss of time, energy, and money is a series of compromises, favoring now one, now the other side, and drifting slowly though not majestically in the direction of Free Trade—unless Protection manages, in the meantime, to make itself utterly insupportable to the nation, which is just now likely to be the case in America.

There is, however, another kind of protection, the worst of all, and that is exhibited in Germany. Germany, too, began to feel, soon after 1815, the necessity of a quicker development of her manufactures. But the first condition of that was the creation of a home market by the removal of the innumerable customs lines and varieties of fiscal legislation formed by the small German states, in other words, the formation of a German Customs Union or Zollverein.[437] That could only be done on the basis of a liberal tariff, calculated rather to raise a common revenue than to protect home production. On no other condition could the small states have been induced to join. Thus the new German tariff, though slightly protective to some trades, was, at the time of its introduction, a model of Free Trade legislation; and it remained so, although, ever since 1830, the majority of German manufacturers kept clamoring for protection. Yet, under this extremely liberal tariff, and in spite of German domestic industries based on hand-labor being mercilessly crushed out by the competition of English factories worked by steam, the transition from manual labor to machinery was gradually accomplished in Germany too, and is now nearly complete; the transformation of Germany from an agricultural to a manufacturing country went on at the same pace, and was, since 1866, assisted by favorable political events: the establishment of a strong central government, and federal legislature, ensuring uniformity in the laws regulating trade, as well as in currency, weights and measures, and, finally, the flood of the French milliards. Thus, about 1874, German trade on the market of the world ranked next to that of Great Britain,* and Germany employed more steam power in manufactures and locomotion than any European Continental country. The proof has thus been furnished that even nowadays, in spite of the enormous start that English industry has got, a large country can work its way up to successful competition, in the open market, with England.

Then, all at once, a change of front was made: Germany turned protectionist, at a moment when more than ever Free Trade seemed a necessity for her. The change was no doubt absurd; but it may be explained. While Germany had been a corn-exporting country, the whole agricultural interest, not less than the whole shipping trade, had been ardent Free Traders. But in 1874, instead of exporting, Germany required large supplies of corn from abroad. About that time, America began to flood Europe with enormous supplies of cheap corn; wherever they went, they brought down the money revenue yielded by the land, and consequently its rent; and from that moment, the agricultural interest, all over Europe, began to clamor for protection. At the same time, manufacturers in Germany were suffering from the effect of the reckless overtrading[b] brought on by the influx of the French milliards, while England, whose trade, ever since the crisis of 1866, had been in a state of chronic depression, inundated all accessible markets with goods unsalable at home and offered abroad at ruinously low prices. Thus it happened that German

---

* General Trade of Exports and Imports added in 1874, in millions of dollars: Great Britain — 3300; Germany — 2325; France — 1665; United States — 1245 millions of dollars. (Kolb, *Statistik*, 7th edit., Leipsic, 1875, p. 790.)[a]

---

[a] In the pamphlet the figures are given in millions of thaler, and in the German translation, in millions of marks.— *Ed.*

[b] The German translation adds here "and excessive speculation".— *Ed.*

manufacturers, though depending, above all, upon export, began to see in protection a means of securing to themselves the exclusive supply of the home market. And the government, entirely in the hands of the landed aristocracy and squirearchy, was only too glad to profit by this circumstance, in order to benefit the receivers of the rent of land, by offering protective duties to both landlords and manufacturers. In 1878, a highly protective tariff was enacted both for agricultural products and for manufactured goods.[438]

The consequence was that henceforth the exportation of German manufactures was carried on at the direct cost of the home consumers. Wherever possible, "rings" or "trusts"[a] were formed to regulate the export trade and even production itself. The German iron trade is in the hands of a few large firms, mostly joint stock companies, who, betwixt them, can produce about four times as much iron as the average consumption of the country can absorb. To avoid unnecessary competition with one another, these firms have formed a trust which divides amongst them all foreign contracts, and determines in each case the firm that is to make the real tender. This "trust," some years ago, had even come to an agreement with the English iron masters, but this no longer subsists. Similarly, the Westphalian coal mines (producing about thirty million tons annually) had formed a trust to regulate production, tenders for contracts, and prices. And, altogether, any German manufacturer will tell you that the only thing the protective duties do for him is to enable him to recoup himself in the home market for the ruinous prices he has to take abroad. And this is not all. This absurd system of protection to manufacturers is nothing but the sop thrown to industrial capitalists to induce them to support a still more outrageous monopoly given to the landed interest. Not only is all agricultural produce subjected to heavy import duties which are increased from year to year, but certain rural industries, carried on on large estates for account of the proprietor, are positively endowed out of the public purse. The beet-root sugar manufacture is not only protected, but receives enormous sums in the shape of export premiums. One who ought to know is of opinion that if the exported sugar was all thrown into the sea, the manufacturer would still clear a profit out of the government premium. Similarly, the potato-spirit distilleries receive, in consequence of

---

[a] Here and below the German translation has "cartels" instead of "rings" and "trusts".— Ed.

recent legislation, a present, out of the pockets of the public, of about nine million dollars[a] a year. And as almost every large land-owner in Northeastern Germany is either a beet-root sugar manufacturer or a potato-spirit distiller, or both, no wonder the world is literally deluged with their productions.

This policy, ruinous under any circumstances, is doubly so in a country whose manufactures keep up their standing in neutral markets chiefly through the cheapness of labor. Wages in Germany, kept near starvation point at the best of times, through redundancy of population (which increases rapidly, in spite of emigration), must rise in consequence of the rise in all necessaries caused by protection; the German manufacturer will, then, no longer be able, as he too often is now, to make up for a ruinous price of his articles by a deduction from the normal wages of his hands, and will be driven out of the market.[b] Protection, in Germany, is killing the goose that lays the golden eggs.

France, too, suffers from the consequences of protection. The system, in that country, has become, by its two centuries of undisputed sway, almost part and parcel of the life of the nation. Nevertheless, it is more and more becoming an obstacle. Constant changes in the methods of manufacture are the order of the day[c]; but protection bars the road. Silk velvets have their backs nowadays made of fine cotton thread; the French manufacturer has either to pay protection price for that, or to submit to such interminable official chicanery as fully makes up for the difference between that price and the government drawback on exportation; and so the velvet trade goes from Lyons to Crefeld, where the protection price for fine cotton thread is considerably lower. French exports, as said before, consist chiefly of articles of luxury, where French taste cannot, as yet, be beaten; but the chief consumers, all over the world, of such articles are our modern upstart capitalists who have no education and no taste, and who are suited quite as well by cheap and clumsy German or English imitations, and often have these foisted upon them for the real French article at more than fancy prices. The market for those specialties which cannot be made out of France is constantly getting narrower, French exports of manufactures are barely kept up, and must soon decline; by what new articles can France

---

[a] The German translation has "thirty-six million marks".— Ed.

[b] The German translation has "will lose its competitiveness" instead of "will be driven out of the market".— Ed.

[c] In the German translation the sentence begins as follows: "Large-scale industry calls for constant changes in the methods of production".— Ed.

replace those whose export is dying out? If anything can help here, it is a bold measure of Free Trade, taking the French manufacturer out of his accustomed hothouse atmosphere and placing him once more in the open air of competition with foreign rivals.[a] Indeed, French general trade would have long since begun shrinking, were it not for the slight and vacillating step in the direction of Free Trade made by the Cobden treaty of 1860,[439] but that has well-nigh exhausted itself and a stronger dose of the same tonic is wanted.

It is hardly worth while to speak of Russia. There, the protective tariff—the duties having to be paid in gold, instead of in the depreciated paper currency of the country—serves above all things to supply the pauper government with the hard cash indispensable for transactions with foreign creditors; on the very day on which that tariff fulfils its protective mission by totally excluding foreign goods, on that day the Russian government is bankrupt. And yet that same government amuses its subjects[b] by dangling before their eyes the prospect of making Russia, by means of this tariff, an entirely self-supplying country, requiring from the foreigner neither food, nor raw material, nor manufactured articles, nor works of art. The people who believe in this vision of a Russian Empire, secluded and isolated from the rest of the world, are on a level with the patriotic Prussian lieutenant who went into a shop and asked for a globe, not a terrestrial or a celestial one, but a globe of Prussia.

To return to America. There are plenty of symptoms that Protection has done all it could for the United States, and[c] that the sooner it receives notice to quit, the better for all parties. One of these symptoms is the formation of "rings" and "trusts" within the protected industries for the more thorough exploitation of the monopoly granted to them. Now, "rings" and "trusts" are truly American institutions, and, where they exploit natural advantages, they are generally, though grumblingly, submitted to. The transformation of the Pennsylvanian oil supply into a monopoly by the Standard Oil Company[440] is a proceeding entirely in keeping with the rules of capitalist production. But if the sugar-refiners attempt to transform the protection granted them, by the nation, against foreign competition, into a monopoly against the home consumer, that is to say against the same nation that granted the

---

[a] The last three words are omitted in the German translation.—*Ed.*

[b] The German translation has "faithful subjects".—*Ed.*

[c] In the German translation the end of the sentence reads: "it is time to finish with it".—*Ed.*

protection, that is quite a different thing. Yet the large sugar-refiners have formed a "trust" which aims at nothing else.[441] And the sugar trust is not the only one of its kind. Now, the formation of such trusts in protected industries is the surest sign that protection has done its work, and is changing its character; that it protects the manufacturer no longer against the foreign importer, but against the home consumer; that it has manufactured, at least in the special branch concerned, quite enough, if not too many manufacturers; that the money it puts into the purse of these manufacturers[a] is money thrown away, exactly as in Germany.

In America, as elsewhere, Protection is bolstered up by the argument that Free Trade will only benefit England. The best proof to the contrary is that in England not only the agriculturists and landlords but even the manufacturers are turning protectionists. In the home of the "Manchester school" of Free Traders,[442] on Nov. 1, 1886, the Manchester chamber of commerce discussed a resolution

"that, having waited in vain forty years for other nations to follow the Free Trade example of England, the chamber thinks the time has arrived to reconsider that position."

The resolution was indeed rejected, but by 22 votes against 21! And that happened in the centre of the cotton manufacture, i.e., the only branch of English manufacture whose superiority in the open market seems still undisputed! But, then, even in that special branch inventive genius has passed from England to America. The latest improvements in machinery for spinning and weaving cotton have come, almost all, from America, and Manchester has to adopt them. In industrial inventions of all kinds, America has distinctly taken the lead, while Germany runs England very close for second place. The consciousness is gaining ground in England that that country's industrial monopoly is irretrievably lost, that she is still relatively losing ground, while her rivals are making progress, and that she is drifting into a position where she will have to be content with being one manufacturing nation among many, instead of, as she once dreamt, "the workshop of the world." It is to stave off this impending fate that Protection, scarcely disguised under the veil of "fair trade" and retaliatory tariffs, is now invoked with such fervor by the sons of the very men who, forty years ago, knew no salvation but in Free Trade. And when English manufacturers begin to find that Free Trade is ruining them, and ask the government to protect them against their foreign

---

[a] The German translation has here "through the protective tariffs".— *Ed.*

competitors, then, surely, the moment has come for these competitors to retaliate by throwing overboard a protective system henceforth useless, to fight the fading industrial monopoly of England with its own weapon, Free Trade.

But, as I said before, you may easily introduce Protection, but you cannot get rid of it again so easily. The legislature, by adopting the protective plan, has created vast interests, for which it is responsible. And not every one of these interests—the various branches of industry—is equally ready, at a given moment, to face open competition. Some will be lagging behind, while others have no longer need of protective nursing. This difference of position will give rise to the usual lobby-plotting, and is in itself a sure guarantee that the protected industries, if Free Trade is resolved upon, will be let down very easy indeed, as was the silk manufacture in England after 1846. That is unavoidable under present circumstances, and will have to be submitted to by the Free Trade party so long as the change is resolved upon in principle.

The question of Free Trade or Protection moves entirely within the bounds of the present system of capitalist production, and has, therefore, no direct interest for us Socialists who want to do away with that system. Indirectly, however, it interests us, inasmuch as we must desire the present system of production to develop and expand as freely and as quickly as possible; because along with it will develop also those economic phenomena which are its necessary consequences, and which must destroy the whole system [a]: misery of the great mass of the people, in consequence of overproduction; this overproduction engendering either periodical gluts and revulsions, accompanied by panic, or else a chronic stagnation of trade; division of society into a small class of large capitalists, and a large one of practically hereditary wage-slaves, proletarians, who, while their numbers increase constantly, are at the same time constantly being superseded by new labor-saving machinery; in short, society brought to a deadlock, out of which there is no escaping but by a complete remodelling of the economic structure which forms its basis. From this point of view, forty years ago, Marx pronounced, in principle, in favor of Free Trade as the more progressive plan, and, therefore, the plan which would soonest bring capitalist society to that deadlock. But if Marx declared in favor of Free Trade on that ground, is that

---

[a] In the German translation the words "and which must destroy the whole system" are absent.— Ed.

not a reason for every supporter of the present order of society to declare against Free Trade? If Free Trade is stated to be revolutionary, must not all good citizens vote for Protection as a conservative plan?

If a country nowadays accept Free Trade, it will certainly not do so to please the Socialists. It will do so because Free Trade has become a necessity for the industrial capitalists. But if it should reject Free Trade, and stick to Protection, in order to cheat the Socialists out of the expected social catastrophe, that will not hurt the prospects of Socialism in the least.[a] Protection is a plan for artificially manufacturing manufacturers, and therefore also a plan for artificially manufacturing wage-laborers. You cannot breed the one without breeding the other. The wage-laborer everywhere follows in the footsteps of the manufacturer; he is like the "gloomy care" of Horace, that sits behind the rider, and that he cannot shake off wherever he go.[b] You cannot escape fate; in other words you cannot escape the necessary consequences of your own actions. A system of production based upon the exploitation of wage-labor, in which wealth increases in proportion to the number of laborers employed and exploited, such a system is bound to increase the class of wage-laborers,[c] that is to say, the class which is fated one day to destroy the system itself. In the meantime, there is no help for it: you must go on developing the capitalist system, you must accelerate the production, accumulation, and centralization of capitalist wealth, and, along with it, the production of a revolutionary class of laborers.[d] Whether you try the Protectionist or the Free Trade plan will make no difference in the end, and hardly any in the length of the respite left to you until the day when that end will come. For long before that day will protection have become an unbearable shackle to any country aspiring, with a chance of success, to hold its own in the world market.

Written in April and early May 1888

First published in *Die Neue Zeit*, No. 7, July 1888 and also in the pamphlet K. Marx, *Free Trade*, Boston, 1888

Reproduced from the pamphlet collated with *Die Neue Zeit*

---

[a] The German translation has "then nobody will be cheated more than itself" instead of "that will not hurt the prospects of Socialism in the least".— *Ed.*

[b] Horace, *Carminum*. III. 1.— *Ed.*

[c] In the German translation the end of the sentence reads: "and thus to exacerbate a class antagonism which will one day destroy the entire system".— *Ed.*

[d] In the German translation the word "revolutionary" is absent, and the sentence ends as follows: "located outside official society".— *Ed.*

[LETTER TO THE EDITORS OF *THE LABOUR ELECTOR*] [443]

Seeing the constant interest you take in the questions raised with regard to the coming International Working Men's Congress, I hope you will allow a Frenchman and a Member of the so-called Marxist Organisation of France (Agglomération Parisienne), to say a few words in reply to a circular published in the Bulletin of the Paris Labour Exchange and reproduced in English, in *Justice* of April 27th.

Now the Paris Labour Exchange is an out and out Possibilist institution. They have got hold of it with the help of the Opportunist and Radical Members [444] of the Paris Town Council, and every trades union which dares openly oppose Possibilist principles and tactics, is at once excluded. This above mentioned circular, though issued in the name of 78 Paris Trades Unions, is therefore quite as much a Possibilist production as if issued by the Possibilist Committee themselves.

This circular calls upon "all the working class organisations of France, without distinction of the shades of Republican or Socialist opinion," to join in the Possibilist Congress. Now this seems fair enough. And as our section of the French Socialists has driven the Possibilists entirely out of the provinces, so much so that they dared not attend their own Congress at Troyes, as soon they heard that we were to be admitted, and as our organisations in the provinces are by far more numerous than all the Possibilist organisations in France put together, no doubt we should have the majority of French delegates even in this Possibilist Congress, if a fair basis of representation was secured. But there's the rub. The Possibilist Committee have made heaps of regulations for their Congress, but this most important point is never mentioned.

Nobody knows whether each group is to send one, two, or more delegates, or whether the number of delegates is to be regulated by the number of members in each group. Now, as the Possibilists are acknowledged to be strongest in Paris, they might send two or three delegates for each group, where we, in our simplicity, send only one. They may manufacture as many delegates as they like. They have them ready at hand in Paris, and need merely nominate them. And thus, with all this apparent fairness, the French section of the Congress may be turned into a packed set of Possibilists, who might treat us as they liked, unless we had an appeal to the Congress.

For this reason alone we could not give up the sovereignty of the Congress with regard to all its internal concerns, if, indeed, that first and fundamental principle could be given up. It is not quite forgotten in London yet, I believe, that the Parliamentary Committee,[445] last November, made it pretty clearly understood that they had hired the room, and that the Congress[446] was there at their sufferance—and we do not want to have that repeated in Paris.

Written in late April 1889

First published in *The Labour Elector*, vol. I, No. 18, May 4, 1889

Reproduced from the newspaper

[THE RUHR MINERS' STRIKE OF 1889][447]

The German miners' strike is an immense event for us. Like the miners in England in the Chartist times, the colliers of Germany are the last to join the movement, and this is their first start. The movement began in the Westfalian coalfield in the North—a district producing 45 million tons annually, and not yet half-developed, coal having been bored at a depth of 500 yards. These miners—hitherto good subjects, patriotic, obedient, and religious, and furnishing some of the finest infantry for the VII. army corps (I know them well, my native place is only 6 or 7 miles south of the coalfields), have now been thoroughly aroused by the oppression of their capitalists. While the mines—almost all joint stock concerns—paid enormous dividends, the *real* wages of the men were constantly being reduced, the nominal weekly wages were kept up, in some cases even raised in appearance, by forcing the men to work enormous overtime—in place of single shifts of 8 hours they worked from 12 to 16 hours, thus making from 9 to 12 shifts weekly. Truck shops,[448] disguised under the name of "Co-operative" shops, prevailed. Cheating, on the quantity of coal got by rejecting whole truckfuls of coal as being bad or not properly filled, was the rule. Well, since last winter, the men have given notice several times that they would strike unless this was remedied, but to no purpose, and at last they did strike, after having given due notice of their intention, and the owners lie when they maintain the contrary. In a week 70,000 men were out, and the *masters had to feed the strike,* for they paid wages once a month only, and always kept one month's wages in hand *which they now had to fork out to the strikers.* The masters were thus caught in their own net. Well, the men sent that celebrated deputation to the

Emperor[a]—a snobby, conceited coxcomb of a boy—who received them with a threatening speech; if they turned towards the social democrat and reviled the authorities, he would have them shot down without mercy.[449] (That had in fact been tried already at Bochum, where a sublieutenant, *a lad of 19,* ordered his men to fire on the strikers, most of them fired in the air.) But all the same, the whole empire trembled before these men on strike. The military commander of the district[b] went to the spot, so did the Home Secretary,[c] and everything was tried to bring the masters round to make concession. The Emperor even told them to open their pockets, and said in a council of ministers "My soldiers are there to keep order, but not to provide big profits to the mine-owners."

Well, by the intervention of the Liberal Opposition (who have lost one seat in Parliament after another by the workmen passing over to us) a compromise was effected, and the men returned to work. But no sooner were they in than the masters broke their word, discharged some of the ringleaders (though they had agreed not to do so), refused arranging for overtime by agreement with the men, as agreed upon, etc. The strike threatened to break out again, but the matter is still in suspense, and, I am sure, the Government, who are in a devil of a funk, will make them give in at least for a time. Then the strike spread to Coalfield No. II. and III. This district has been kept, so far, free from Socialist contagion, as every man who went there to agitate, when caught in the meshes of the law, got as many years' imprisonment as he would have got months' anywhere else in Germany. The Government alone made concessions to the men, but whether these will suffice remains to be seen. Then the men in the Saxon Coalfield, and in the two Siberian[d] Coalfields, still further east, took up the tune, so that in the last three weeks there have been at least 120,000 colliers on strike in Germany, and from them the Belgian and Bohemian miners caught the infection, while in Germany a number of other trades who had prepared strikes for this spring season, have also left work.[450] Thus there is no doubt the German colliers have joined their brethren in the struggle against capital, and as they are a splendid body of men, and almost all have passed through the army, they form an important addition to our ranks. Their belief in emperor and priest has been

---

[a] William II.— *Ed.*
[b] E. Albedyll.— *Ed.*
[c] E. Herrfurth.— *Ed.*
[d] Should read: "Silesian".— *Ed.*

shattered, and whatever the Government may do, no Government can give satisfaction to the men without upsetting the capitalist system—and that the German Government neither can nor will attempt. It is the first time that the Government had to pretend to observe an impartial position in a strike in Germany: so its virginity in that respect has gone for ever, and both William and Bismarck had to bow before the array of 100,000 working men on strike. That alone is a glorious result.

Written in late May 1889   Reproduced from the magazine

First published in *The Labour Leader,*
vol. I, No. 5, June 1889

POSSIBILIST CREDENTIALS[451]

The partisans of the Possibilist Paris Congress—the unmistakeable Mr. Smith Hedingley in the *Star,* Mr. H. Burrows and Mrs. Besant in the weekly Press—are repeating over and over again that their Congress was a really representative one, while the Marxist Congress contained people who represented only themselves, and for that reason dared not accept the challenge of the Possibilists to show them their credentials. The English delegates to the Marxist Congress will no doubt seek, and find, an opportunity to prove the untruth of the charges brought against them; so we may for the present dismiss that part of the subject, and merely observe that the Possibilists could hardly offer a greater insult to the Marxist Congress than to ask it to ignore the process of the verification of its own credentials, completed as far back as the second (or third?) day, and to submit their credentials to a fresh examination; while the Possibilists, in their resolution on the subject, carefully avoided engaging themselves to an examination of their credentials by the Marxists.

That the above is the correct view of the matter, and that the Possibilists, much more than the Marxists, had reason to show their credentials to none but friends, was proved by the observations of Dr. Adler, in the Marxist Congress, of what he had learnt about the "Austrian" Possibilist delegates. As the thing is characteristic of the way in which the Possibilists manufactured truly representative delegates, it deserves reproduction.

In the Possibilist list of delegates we find under "Austria" the following bodies represented:—"Bakers Union of Vienna," "Federation of Upper Austria and Salzburg," "Federation of Workingmen of Bohemia-Moravia, and Silesia." Now Dr. Adler, who has during the last three years, with wonderful energy, tact, and perseverance, reorganised the Socialist movement in Austria, and who knows every workmen's society in every town in Austria, told the Congress that these various societies, whatever may be their other merits, have one fatal defect: *they do not exist.*

When it became known in Paris that the Marxist Congress had met on the Sunday, and that there were delegates from Austria, there came to it on the Monday two Austrians and saw Dr. Adler. They told him they were bakers, for some time past working in Paris; that a Hungarian baker, of the name of Dobosy, had engaged them as "delegates" for a workingmen's congress; was this the same congress? Adler questioned them and found out that they were engaged for the Possibilist Congress, for which they had cards of membership; that they had told the people who had engaged them that they represented absolutely nobody but themselves, that they were told that did not matter, Austria being a despotic country, regular credentials were not required; that they now found the true Austrian delegates were at the other Congress; what were they to do? The Austrian delegates told them they had no business to play at delegates at any Congress. Well, they arranged for another interview. They came again a day or two after, assisted at the meeting of the Marxist Congress, and then declared they saw themselves they must get out of this false position, but how? They were told to return their credentials. They had none. Then return your cards of membership. This they promised to do, and returned to say they had done so.

This is a sample of what the Possibilists and their English partisans call "strictly representative." And the imposing list of Hungarian societies with names so well hidden under misprints that only with a few of them is the pretended locality recognizable, are, according to the true Hungarian delegates at the Marxist Congress, equally non-existent outside the wonderland of Possibilist fancy. Indeed, the concoction here is too flagrant. "Circles of Social Study and Federation of Croatia, Slavonia, Dalmatia, Trieste, and Fiume"—this pompous title bears the stamp of its Parisian origin too conspicuously. And to think that behind all this there are not even the—three tailors of Tooley Street![452]

We are further told that it is absolutely false that the Possibilist Congress was a mere Trades Unions Congress. Mr. Herbert Burrows is quite indignant at such a calumny; with the exception of a few English Trades Unionists "the whole of the delegates" were revolutionary Socialists, and as such represented their respective societies. Well, to give but one example, what does *El*

Socialista, of Madrid (26th July) say of the Spanish Possibilist delegates? That "they say they represent 20,000 Socialists, when they are but delegates of societies in which there is room for the Carlist[453] as well as for the revolutionary Socialist"—entirely non-political clubs, in fact, what is called, in England, Trades Unions.

Written in early August 1889   Reproduced from the newspaper

First published in *The Labour Elector,* vol. II, No. 32, August 10, 1889

[APROPOS OF THE LONDON DOCKERS' STRIKE] [454]

I envy you your work in the Dock Strike. It is the movement of the greatest promise we have had for years, and I am proud and glad to have lived to see it. If Marx had lived to witness this! If these poor down-trodden men, the dregs of the proletariat, these odds and ends of all trades, fighting every morning at the dock gates for an engagement, if *they* can combine, and terrify by their resolution the mighty Dock Companies, truly then we need not despair of any section of the working class. This is the beginning of real life in the East End, and if successful will transform the whole character of the East End. There—for want of self-confidence, and of organisation among the poor devils grovelling in stagnant misery—*lasciate ogni speranza.*[a] ... If the dockers get organised, all other sections will follow... It is a glorious movement and again I envy those that can share in the work.

Written between August 20 and 26, 1889   Reproduced from the newspaper

First published in *The Labour Elector*, vol. II, No. 35, August 31, 1889

---

a "All hope abandon..." (Dante, *Divine Comedy, Inferno*, c. III, v. 5).— *Ed.*

THE ABDICATION OF THE BOURGEOISIE [455]

Of all the national bourgeoisies, it is undoubtedly the English one that has up to now preserved the keenest sense of class, i.e., sense of politics. Our German bourgeoisie is stupid and cowardly; it has not even been able to seize and hold onto the political power the working class won for it in 1848; in Germany the working class must first sweep away the remnants of feudalism and of patriarchal absolutism, which our bourgeoisie was duty-bound to eradicate long ago. The French bourgeoisie, the most mercenary and pleasure-seeking of all, is blinded to its future interests by its own greed for money; it lives only by the day; in its frenzied thirst for profit it plunges itself into the most ignominious corruption, declares that income tax is socialist high treason, can find no way of countering any strike other than with infantry salvoes, and thus manages to bring about a situation where in a republic with universal suffrage the workers are left with hardly any other means of victory than violent revolution. The English bourgeoisie is neither as greedily stupid as the French, nor as pusillanimously stupid as the German. During the period of its greatest triumphs it has constantly made concessions to the workers; even its most dyed-in-the-wool contingent, the conservative landowning and finance aristocracy, was not afraid to give the urban workers suffrage on such a scale that it is purely the fault of the workers themselves that they have not had 40 to 50 representatives of their own in Parliament since 1868. And since then the entire bourgeoisie—the Conservatives and the Liberals combined—has extended this wider suffrage to the rural areas as well, has roughly equalled out the size of the constituencies and thereby placed at least another thirty constituencies at the disposal of the working class. Whereas the German bourgeoisie has never had the ability to lead and represent the nation as its ruling class, whereas the French proves daily—and just again at the elections[456]—that it has completely lost this ability—and yet there was a time when it possessed that ability to a higher degree than any other middle class—the English bourgeoisie (into which the so-called aristocracy has been absorbed and assimilated) exhibited until recently a certain talent for doing justice to its position as leading class at least to some degree.

This now seems to be changing more and more.

Everything connected with the old government of the City of London—the constitution and the administration of the City proper—is still downright medieval. And this includes also the Port of London, the leading port in the world. The WHARFINGERS, the LIGHTERMEN and the WATERMEN[a] form regular guilds with exclusive privileges and in part still don medieval costumes. These antiquated guild privileges have in the past seventy years been crowned with the monopoly of the dock companies, and thereby the whole huge Port of London has been handed over for ruthless exploitation to a small number of privileged corporations. And this whole privileged monstrosity is being perpetuated and, as it were, made inviolable through an endless series of intricate and contradictory Acts of Parliament through which it was born and raised, and in such a manner that this legal labyrinth has become its best rampart. But while these corporations presume on their medieval privileges in dealing with ordinary traders and make London the most expensive port in the world, their members have become regular bourgeois, who besides fleecing their customers, exploit their workers in the most despicable manner and thus profit simultaneously from the advantages of medieval guild and modern capitalist society.

Since, however, this exploitation took place within the framework of modern capitalist society, it was, despite its medieval cloak, subject to the laws of that society. The big swallowed the small or at least chained them to their triumphal chariot. The big dock companies became the masters of the guilds of the wharfingers, the lightermen and the watermen, and thereby of the whole Port of London, thus opening up the prospect of unlimited profits for themselves. This prospect blinded them. They squandered millions on stupid installations; and since there were several

---

[a] In the original these English words are given in parentheses after their German equivalents.— *Ed.*

such companies, they engaged in a competitive war, which cost further millions, produced more senseless structures and pushed the companies to the brink of bankruptcy, until finally they came to terms two years ago.

In the meantime the London trade had passed its peak. Le Havre, Antwerp, Hamburg and, since the new sea canal had been built, also Amsterdam, drew a growing share of the traffic that had formerly centred on London. Liverpool, Hull and Glasgow also took their share. The newly built docks remained empty, dividends dwindled and partly disappeared altogether, shares dropped, and the dock managers, arrogant, purse-proud snobs, stubborn and spoilt by the good old times, were at their wits' end. They did not want to admit the true reasons for the relative and absolute decline in the traffic of the Port of London. And these reasons, insofar as they are of a local character, are purely and simply their own arrogant perversity and its cause, the privileged position, the medieval, long outdated constitution of the City and Port of London, which by right should be in the British Museum, next to the Egyptian mummies and the Assyrian stone monsters.

Nowhere else in the world would such folly be tolerated. In Liverpool, where similar conditions were taking shape, they were nipped in the bud and the entire port constitution was modernised. But in London traders suffer because of it, grumble and—submit to it. The bourgeoisie, the bulk of whom have to pay the costs of these fatuities, yield to this monopoly, even if unwillingly, but yield just the same. They no longer have the energy to shake off this demon that in time threatens to stifle the living conditions of all of London.

Then the dock workers' strike breaks out.[457] It is not the bourgeoisie robbed by the dock companies that rebel, it is the workers exploited by them, the poorest of the poor, the lowest layer of the East End proletarians, who fling down the gauntlet to the dock magnates. And then, at last, the bourgeoisie realise that they too have an enemy in the dock magnates, that the striking workers have taken up the struggle not only in their own interests, but indirectly also in the interests of the bourgeois class. That is the secret of the public sympathy for the strike and of the unprecedentedly generous money contributions from bourgeois circles. But thus far and no further. The workers went into action to the accompaniment of acclamation and applause from the bourgeoisie; the workers fought the battle to the end and proved not only that the proud dock magnates could be defeated but by their struggle and victory also stirred up public opinion to such an extent that the dock monopoly and the feudal port constitution are no longer tenable and will soon really have to move to the British Museum.

The job should have been done by the bourgeoisie long ago. They were unable or unwilling to do it. Now the workers have taken it in hand and now it will be done. In other words, in this case the bourgeoisie have renounced their own part in favour of the workers.

Now a different picture. From the medieval Port of London we move on to the modern cotton spinneries of Lancashire. We presently find ourselves at a juncture where the cotton harvest of 1888 is exhausted and that of 1889 has not yet come onto the market, that is, speculation in raw materials has the best prospects at present. A rich Dutchman called Steenstrand has, with other cronies, formed a "ring" to buy up all the available cotton and to boost prices accordingly. The cotton spinners can retaliate only by cutting consumption, that is, by shutting down their mills for several days a week or altogether, until the new cotton is in sight. They have been trying to do this for six weeks. But now as on previous occasions it refuses to work. This is because many of the spinners are so heavily indebted that a partial or complete standstill would push them to the brink of ruin. Others even want the majority to stop and thereby to boost the price of cotton yarn; while they themselves intend to continue operating and to profit from the higher yarn prices. A good ten years' experience has shown that there is only one way to enforce a shut-down of all cotton mills—no matter for what ultimate purpose—namely, by introducing a wage cut of, say, 5 per cent. Then there is a strike, or a lockout by the mill-owners themselves, and then, in the struggle against the workers, absolute unity prevails among the mill-owners, and the machines are brought to a standstill even by those who do not know whether they will ever be able to set them going again.

As things stand, a wage cut is not advisable today. But how otherwise can a general closure of the mills be brought about, without which the spinners will for about six weeks be delivered, bound hand and foot, to the speculators? By a step which is unique in the history of modern industry.

The mill-owners, through their central committee, "semi-officially" approach the Central Committee of the Workers' Trade Unions with a request that the organised workers in the common interest, *force* the obstinate mill-owners to shut down by organising strikes. Messrs mill-owners, admitting their own inability to take concerted action, ask the once so hated workers' trade unions kindly to use coercion against them, the mill-owners, so that the mill-owners, induced by bitter necessity, should finally act in concert, as a class, in the interests of their own class. They have to be forced to do so by the workers, for they themselves are unable to bring this about!

The workers consented. And the workers' threat alone sufficed. In 24 hours the "ring" of cotton speculators was smashed. This shows what can be done by the mill-owners, and what by the workers.

Thus, here, in the most modern of all modern large-scale industries, the bourgeoisie proves to be just as incapable of asserting its own class interests as in medieval London. And what is more, it openly admits it, and by turning to the organised workers with the request that they force through a major class interest of the mill-owners against the will of mill-owners themselves, it not only abdicates, but recognises in the organised working class its successor, which is called upon to rule and is capable of doing so. It proclaims itself that even if every single mill-owner is able to manage his own mill, it is the organised workers alone who are now able to take the management of the entire cotton industry into their own hands. And this means, in plain language, that the only occupation left to the mill-owners is to become paid business managers in the service of the organised workers.

F. Engels

Written between late September and early October 1889

First published in *Der Sozialdemokrat*, No. 40, October 5, 1889

Printed according to the newspaper

FROM THE PREPARATORY MATERIALS

[ON THE ASSOCIATION OF THE FUTURE][458]

In essence, associations—whether naturally evolved or created—have hitherto existed for economic ends, but these ends have been concealed and buried beneath ideological matters of secondary importance. The ancient polis,[459] the medieval town or guild, the feudal confederacy of landowning nobility—all had secondary ideological aims which they hallowed and which in the case of the patrician body of consanguinity and the guild arose from the memories, traditions and models of gentile society no less than in that of the ancient polis. The capitalist commercial companies are the first to be wholly rational and objective—but vulgar. The association of the future will combine the rationality of the latter with the old ones' concern for the social welfare of all, and thus fulfil its purpose.

Written in 1884

First published in: Marx and Engels, *Works*, First Russian Edition, Vol. XVI, Part 1, Moscow, 1937

Printed according to the manuscript

Published in English for the first time

ON THE PEASANT WAR [460]

Reformation—Lutheran and Calvinist—bourgeoisie's revolution No. 1, in which Peasant War is the critical episode. Dissolution of feudalism, along with the development of towns, both decentralising, absolute monarchy therefore a virtual necessity for holding together the nationalities. *Had* to be absolute, precisely because of the centrifugal nature of all the elements. Absolute not to be understood in the vulgar sense, however: constantly at odds partly with the Estates, partly with rebellious feudal lords and towns; the Estates nowhere abolished; thus better described as an *Estate* monarchy (still feudal, decaying feudal and embryonic bourgeois).

Victory of revolution No. 1, which was much more European than the English one, and became European much more quickly than the French one, in Switzerland, Holland, Scotland, England—to a certain extent in Sweden, too, already [under] G[ustavus] Vasa, and Denmark, here not until 1660 in orthodox, absolutist form.

I.[a] Causes in Germany. History from beginning. Germany broken after the heroic age of the migration of peoples. Only restored from France, by Charlemagne. Hence Roman empire

---

[a] In the manuscript the text marked "I" by Engels is placed after that marked "II".— *Ed.*

idea. Renewed by Otto. More non-Germans than Germans. Ruin of Germany by this policy—of pillaging the Italian cities—under the Hohenstaufens. Thus fragmentation confirmed—*excepto casu revolutionis*.[a] Development from interregnum [461] to 15th century. Rise of the towns. Decay of feudalism never perfected in Germany under pressure from the princes (the emperor as sovereign *against,* as emperor *for* the imperial knights). Gradual emancipation of the peasants, until setback in 15th century. Germany materially on a par with the other countries of the day.—Crucial that in Germany because of provincial fragmentation *and long-term freedom from invasion* the need for national unity not so strong as in France (the Hundred Years' War), Spain, which had just been reconquered from the Moors, Russia, which had just driven out the Tatars, England (Wars of the Roses),[462] and that even the emperors of the day so shabby.

II. With the Renaissance in its European guise based on general decay of feudalism and rise of the towns. Then absolutist national monarchies—everywhere except in Germany and Italy.

III. Character of the Reformation as sole possible, *popular* expression of universal aspirations, etc.

Written at the end of 1884

First published, in Russian, in *Marx-Engels Archives,* Vol. X, Moscow, 1948

Printed according to the manuscript

Published in English for the first time

---

[a] Save in the case of revolution.—*Ed.*

[ON THE DECLINE OF FEUDALISM
AND THE EMERGENCE OF NATIONAL STATES] [463]

While the wild battles of the ruling feudal nobility filled the Middle Ages with their clamour, the quiet work of the oppressed classes had undermined the feudal system throughout Western Europe, had created conditions in which less and less room remained for the feudal lord. To be sure, the noble lords still carried on their mischievous ways in the country, tormenting the serfs, living high on their sweat, demolishing their crops under horses' hooves, raping their wives and daughters. But towns had sprung up all around; in Italy, Southern France, on the Rhine, old Roman municipia [464] had risen from their ashes; elsewhere, particularly in the heart of Germany, new creations; always ringed by protective walls and ditches, fortresses far stronger than the nobility's castles, because pregnable only by a large army. Behind these walls and ditches evolved the medieval handicrafts (burgher guild and pretty small), the first capitals accumulated, the need arose for traffic between the towns themselves and with the rest of the world, and, with this need, gradually the means to protect this traffic.

In the fifteenth century the burghers of the towns had already become more indispensable to society than the feudal nobility. True, agriculture was still the occupation of the vast majority of the population, and thus the main branch of production. But the few isolated free peasants who here and there withstood the arrogant behaviour of the nobility were sufficient proof that the main ingredient in farming was not the nobles' indolence and extortion, but the peasant's labour. And then the needs of the nobles, too, had increased and changed to such an extent that the towns had become indispensable even to them; after all, they procured their only instrument of production, their armour and weapons, from the towns! Native cloth, furniture and jewellery, Italian silks, Brabant lace, Nordic furs, Arabian perfumes, fruit from the Levant, Indian spices—everything apart from soap—they bought from the town dwellers. International trade of a kind had developed; the Italians travelled the Mediterranean and, beyond that, the Atlantic coasts as far as Flanders; the Hanseatic merchants still controlled the North Sea and the Baltic in the face of mounting competition from the Dutch and the English. Communication was maintained by land between the northern and southern centres of the maritime traffic; the routes along which this communication took place passed through Germany. While the nobility became increasingly superfluous and an ever greater obstacle to development, the burghers of the towns became the class that embodied the further development of production and trade, of culture and of the social and political institutions.

All these advances in production and exchange were, in point of fact, by today's standards, of a very limited nature. Production remained enthralled in the form of pure guild crafts, thus itself still retaining a feudal character; trade remained within the limits of European waters, and did not extend any further than the coastal towns of the Levant, where the products of the Far East were acquired by exchange. But small-scale and limited though the trades—and hence the trading burghers—remained, they were sufficient to overthrow feudal society, and at least they continued to move forward, whereas the nobility stagnated.

But then the burghers of the towns had a mighty weapon with which to oppose feudalism: *money.* Money had scarcely found any place in the archetype feudal economy of the early Middle Ages. The feudal lord obtained from his serfs everything that he needed; either in the form of labour or in finished products; the women spun and wove the flax and wool and made the clothes; the men sowed the fields; the children minded the lord's livestock, collected for him wild fruits, birds' nests and straw; besides that, the whole family had to supply corn, fruit, eggs, butter, cheese, poultry, young livestock and much else. Every feudal form was self-sufficient; even military services were exacted in products; trade and exchange did not exist, money was superfluous. Europe had been reduced to such a low level, had begun all over again to such an extent that at that time money had much less of a social function than a purely political one: it was a means of *paying taxes,* and was chiefly acquired through *robbery.*

All this had now changed. Money had again become a universal means of exchange, and consequently its volume had increased considerably; the noble could no longer do without it either, and having little or nothing to sell, since robbery was also not quite so easy now, he eventually had to make up his mind to borrow from the usurer among the burghers. Long before the castles of the knights were breached by the new artillery they had been undermined by money; in fact, gunpowder was merely a bailiff, as it were, in the service of money. Money was the burghers' greatest political leveller. Wherever a personal relationship was superseded by a money relationship, a payment in kind by payment in money, a bourgeois relationship took the place of a feudal one. Admittedly, in the countryside the old brutal natural economy continued to exist in the great majority of cases; but there were already whole districts where, as in Holland, in Belgium, on the Lower Rhine, the peasants paid the lord money instead of labour service and tributes in kind, where lords and bondsmen had already taken the first decisive step towards becoming landowners and tenants, where even in the countryside the political institutions of feudalism were thus losing their social basis.

The extent to which the feudal system had, by the end of the fifteenth century, already been undermined and eaten away on the inside by money is strikingly illustrated by the thirst for gold that seized Western Europe at this time. It was *gold* the Portuguese sought on the African coast, in India, throughout the Far East; *gold* was the magic word which drove the Spaniards across the Atlantic Ocean to America; *gold* was the first thing the white man enquired about the moment he set foot on a newly discovered shore. But this urge to set off on adventures to far-off places in search of gold, no matter how much it manifested itself in feudal and semi-feudal forms at the beginning, was nevertheless in its very roots incompatible with feudalism, whose foundation was agriculture and whose campaigns of conquest were essentially aimed at the *acquisition of land.* Moreover, shipping was a decidedly *bourgeois* trade which has stamped its anti-feudal character on all modern navies too.

In the fifteenth century the feudal system was thus in utter decline throughout Western Europe; everywhere towns with anti-feudal interests, with their own laws and with an armed citizenry had wedged their way into feudal areas, bringing the feudal lords under their sway, in part already socially, through money, and here and there also politically; even in country areas where agriculture had flourished because of particularly favourable conditions the old feudal ties began to dissolve under the influence of money; only in newly conquered lands such as Germany east of the Elbe, or in otherwise backward tracts far from the trade routes, did the old rule of the nobility continue to prosper. But everywhere—in the towns and in the country alike—there had been an increase in the elements among the population whose chief demand was to put an end to the constant, senseless warring, to the feuds between the feudal lords which made internal war permanent even when there was a foreign enemy on their native soil, to that state of incessant, utterly pointless devastation that had persisted throughout the Middle Ages. Still too weak themselves to impose their will, these elements found strong support at the apex of the whole feudal system—in the monarchy. And this is the point where the consideration of social relations leads us to those of the state, where we make the transition from economics to politics.

Out of the confusion of peoples that characterised the earliest Middle Ages, there gradually developed the new nationalities, a process whereby, it will be recalled, in most of the former Roman provinces the vanquished assimilated the victor, the peasant and townsman assimilated the Germanic lord. Modern nationalities are thus also the product of the oppressed classes. Menke's district map of central Lorraine* gives a clear picture of the ways in which fusion took place here, boundary demarcation there. One need only follow the boundary line between Romance and German placenames on this map to be convinced that this linguistic boundary between Belgium and Lower Lorraine coincides in the main with that which existed between French and German as recently as a hundred years ago. Here and there one finds a narrow, disputed area where the two languages are struggling for predominance; but on the whole it is clear what is to remain German and what is to remain Romance. The Old Low Franconian and Old High German form of most placenames on the map shows, however, that they belong to the ninth century, to the tenth at the latest, and hence that the boundary had already been essentially drawn towards the end of the Carolingian age. On the Romance side, particularly close to the linguistic boundary, there are now mixed names, made up of a German personal name and a Romance placename, e.g. west of the Maas near Verdun:

---

* Spruner-Menke, *Hand-Atlas für die Geschichte des Mittelalters und der neueren Zeit*, 3rd ed., Gotha, 1874, Map No. 32.

Eppone curtis, Rotfridi curtis, Ingolini curtis, Teudegisilo-villa, today Ippécourt, Récourt la Creux, Amblaincourt-sur-Aire, Thierville. These were Franconian manor houses, small German colonies on Romance soil, which sooner or later succumbed to Romanisation. In the towns and in scattered rural areas there were stronger German colonies that retained their language for some time to come; it was from one of these, for example, that *The Lay of Ludwig*[465] originated at the end of the ninth century; but the fact that prior to this a large proportion of the Franconian lords had been Romanised is proved by the oath formulas of the kings and magnates of 842, in which Romance already appears as the official language of France.[466]

Once their boundaries had been fixed (disregarding subsequent wars of conquest and annihilation, such as those against the Slavs of the Elbe[467]) it was natural for the linguistic groups to serve as the existent basis for the formation of states; for the nationalities to start developing into nations. The rapid collapse of the mixed state of Lotharingia[468] shows how powerful this element was as early as the ninth century. True, linguistic boundaries and national frontiers were far from coincident throughout the Middle Ages; but every nationality except perhaps Italy was represented by a separate big state in Europe, and the tendency to form national states, which becomes increasingly clear and deliberate, constitutes one of the Middle Ages' most considerable levers of progress.

In each of these medieval states the king now constituted the head of the entire feudal hierarchy, a head with whom the vassals were unable to dispense and against whom they were at the same time in a state of permanent rebellion. The basic relation of the whole feudal system—the granting of land in return for the delivery of certain personal services and dues—provided, even in its original and simplest form, plenty of material for strife, especially when so many people had an interest in picking quarrels. So what was to be expected in the later Middle Ages, when the conditions of vassalage in every country formed an inextricable tangle of rights and duties that had been granted, withdrawn, renewed once more, forfeited, amended or subjected to new conditions? For part of his lands, Charles the Bold, for instance, was the Emperor's vassal, for others the King of France's vassal; on the other hand, the King of France, his liege lord, was simultaneously in certain areas the vassal of Charles the Bold, his own vassal; how were conflicts to be avoided? Hence these centuries of alternation between the vassals' attraction towards the royal centre, which alone could protect them from outsiders and from one another, and the repulsion away from the centre into which that attraction was continually and inevitably transformed; hence the incessant struggle between kings and vassals, whose desolate din drowned out all else during this long period when robbery was held to be the only source of income worthy of a free man; hence that endless, constantly regenerated cycle of betrayal, assassination, poisoning, treachery and every conceivable vileness that, concealed behind the poetical name of chivalry, never ceased to speak of honour and loyalty.

That in this general turmoil the monarchy was the progressive element is perfectly obvious. It stood for order amid disorder, the nation in the process of formation as opposed to disintegration into rebellious vassal states. Any revolutionary elements that formed beneath the surface of feudalism were as dependent on the monarchy as the monarchy on them. The alliance between the monarchy and the burghers dates from the tenth century; often interrupted by conflicts, just as nothing else followed a steady course during the Middle Ages, it was renewed, becoming firmer and more powerful each time, until it helped the monarchy to ultimate victory, and to show its gratitude the monarchy subjugated and plundered its ally.

Kings and burghers alike found a powerful support in the rising estate of *lawyers*. With the rediscovery of Roman law came the division of labour between the priests, the legal advisers of the feudal age, and the non-clerical law scholars. These new lawyers were from the very outset essentially a bourgeois estate; but the law they studied, purveyed and practised was by its nature essentially anti-feudal and in certain respects bourgeois. Roman law is the classic legal expression of the day-to-day relations and conflicts of a society in which pure private property dominates, so much so that no subsequent legislation has ever been able to improve on it in any major respect. But the bourgeois property of the Middle Ages still had a heavy admixture of feudal restrictions, and consisted, for example, very largely of privileges; to that extent, then, Roman law was a long way ahead of the bourgeois conditions of the time. Subsequent historical development of bourgeois property could proceed, however, only in one way: it was bound to turn into pure private property, and this is what happened. But this development was bound to find a powerful lever in Roman law, which already contained in a finished form all that the bourgeoisie of the later Middle Ages aspired to, albeit unconsciously as yet.

Though Roman law in many individual cases provided a pretext for even greater oppression of the peasants by the nobility, for instance when the peasants were unable to adduce any written proof of their exemption from otherwise customary burdens, it does not alter the matter. Even without Roman law, the nobility would have found such pretexts, and indeed found them daily. At any rate, it was a tremendous advance when a legal system came into force that knew absolutely nothing of feudal relations and fully anticipated modern private property.

We have seen how the feudal nobility started to become superfluous in economic terms, indeed a hindrance, in the society of the later Middle Ages—how it already stood in the way, politically, of the development of the towns and the national state which was then only possible in a monarchist form. In spite of all this, it had been sustained by the fact that it had hitherto possessed a monopoly over the bearing of arms: without it no wars could be waged, no battles fought. This, too, was to change; the last step would be taken to make it clear to the feudal nobles that the period in which they had ruled society and the state was now over, that they were no longer of any use in their capacity as knights—not even on the battlefield.

Opposing the feudal economy with an army that was itself feudal, in which the soldiers were bound by closer ties to their immediate liege lord than to the command of the royal army—this obviously meant going round in a vicious circle, without achieving any advance. From the beginning of the fourteenth century the kings strove to free themselves of this feudal army and create an army of their own. From this time on we find in the armies of the kings a constantly growing proportion of recruited or hired troops. At first they were chiefly infantry, comprising the scum of the towns and runaway serfs, Lombards, Genoese, Germans, Belgians, etc., who were employed for occupying towns and for siege duties, but in the beginning could scarcely be used on the battlefield. But towards the end of the Middle Ages we also find knights entering the service of foreign princes as mercenaries with their retinues gathered together the devil knows how, thus demonstrating the irrevocable collapse of feudal warfare.

The fundamental condition for an efficient infantry arose simultaneously in the towns and in the free peasants, wherever the latter were still to be found or had re-formed. Until then the knights with their retinue, likewise mounted, had been not so much the core of the army as the army itself; the baggage-train of attendant, serf infantrymen did not count, appearing in the open field merely in order to run away or to loot. As long as the golden age of feudalism lasted, until the end of the thirteenth century, the cavalry fought and decided every battle. From that time on things changed, and moreover in various points simultaneously. The gradual disappearance of serfdom in England created a sizeable class of free farmers, either landowners (yeomen) or tenants, and thus the raw material for a new type of infantry, skilled in the use of the bow, the English national weapon at the time. The introduction of these archers, who always fought on foot whether they travelled on horseback or not, gave rise to a major change in the tactics of English armies. From the fourteenth century onwards the English knights preferred to fight on foot where the terrain or other circumstances rendered this appropriate. Behind the archers, who started the battle and softened up the enemy, the massed array of dismounted knights awaited the enemy attack or the right moment to advance, while only part of them remained on horseback in order to facilitate the decisive encounter by attacks on the flanks. The then unbroken series of English victories in France [469] were largely due to the restoration of a defensive element in the army, and were for the most part just as much defensive battles with offensive retaliation as Wellington's in Spain and Belgium. [470] With the adoption of new tactics by the French—possible since Italian mercenary crossbowmen had assumed the functions of the English archers in their case—the triumphant progress of the English was at an end. Also at the beginning of the fourteenth century, the infantrymen of the Flemish towns had dared—often successfully—to confront the French knights in open battle, and Emperor Albrecht, by his attempt to betray the autonomous Swiss peasants to the Archduke of Austria, who was he himself, had provided the impetus for the formation of the first modern infantry with a European reputation. [471] In the victories of the Swiss over the Austrians, and particularly over the Burgundians, heavily armed cavalry—mounted and dismounted—succumbed once and for all to the infantry, the feudal army to the beginnings of the modern army, the knight to the burgher and free peasant. And the Swiss, to establish from the outset the bourgeois character of their republic, the first independent republic in Europe, immediately *turned* their fame as warriors *to cash*. All political considerations faded away: the cantons turned into recruiting offices to drum up mercenaries for the highest bidder. The recruitment drive also made its way around other places, in Germany in particular; but the cynicism of a government which only seemed to exist in order to sell off its native people remained unequalled until surpassed by German princes in the years of greatest national humiliation.

Then, also in the fourteenth century, gunpowder and artillery were brought over to Europe via Spain by the Arabs. Until the end of the Middle Ages hand guns remained unimportant, which is understandable, since the bows of the English archers at Crécy had as great a range as the smoothbore rifles of the infantry at Waterloo and were perhaps more accurate—though lacking the same effect.[472] Field guns were also still in their infancy; on the other hand, heavy guns had already breached the free-standing walls of the knights' castles on many occasions, demonstrating to the feudal nobility that gunpowder marked the end of their rule.

The spread of book printing, the revival of the study of classical literature, the entire cultural movement which had been gathering strength and becoming more widespread ever since 1450[473]—all these factors aided the bourgeoisie and the monarchy in their fight against feudalism.

The combined action of all these causes, strengthened year after year by their increasing interaction on one another, which tended more and more in the same direction, was crucial to the victory over feudalism in the second half of the fifteenth century, not yet for the bourgeoisie, but certainly for the monarchy. All at once the monarchy gained the upper hand throughout Europe, as far as the distant lands adjoining it that had not passed through the feudal state. On the Iberian peninsula two of the Romance language peoples there united to form the Kingdom of Spain, and the Provençal-speaking Aragonese empire submitted to standard Castilian[a]; the third people joined its linguistic area (with the exception of Galicia) with the Kingdom of Portugal, the Iberian Holland, turning their back on the interior and demonstrating their right to a separate existence through its activity at sea.

In France Louis XI finally managed, after the demise of the Burgundian middle kingdom,[474] to establish national unity represented by the monarchy on the then much curtailed French territory to such an extent that his successor[b] was already able to interfere in Italian quarrels[475] and this unity was only once called into question for a short time, by the Reformation.[476]

England had at last given up its quixotic wars of conquest in France, which in the long run would have bled it dry; the feudal

[a] Aragon and Castile united in 1479.—Ed.
[b] Charles VIII.—Ed.

nobility sought recompense in the Wars of the Roses,[477] and got more than they had bargained for: they wiped each other out, and brought the House of Tudor to the throne, whose royal power exceeded that of all its predecessors and successors. The Scandinavian countries had long since achieved unity; after its unification with Lithuania,[478] Poland was approaching its heyday, with the power of its monarchy as yet undiminished; even in Russia the subjugation of the princelings and the shedding of the Tatar yoke, had gone hand in hand and were finally sealed by Ivan III.[a] In the whole of Europe there were only two countries in which the monarchy, and the national unity that was then impossible without it, either did not exist at all or existed only on paper: Italy and Germany.

Written at the end of 1884

First published, in Russian, in the journal *Proletarskaya Revolutsia*, No. 6, 1935

Printed according to the manuscript

Published in English for the first time

---

[a] In 1480.— *Ed.*

38*

[CHARTIST AGITATION][479]

CHRONOLOGICAL TABLE

Melbourne—September '41, Whig[a]

1838. August 6.	Meeting in Birmingham (speakers: Attwood, Scholefield, F. O'Connor) to petition the House of Commons to make the *People's Charter* law.[b]
September 17.	Chartist meeting in New Palace Yard, Westminster.[c]
December 13.	Royal proclamation that torchlight meetings and armed assemblies illegal.
" 20.	Meeting of the ANTI-CORN LAW LEAGUE in Manchester.
1839. January 15.	ANTI-CORN LAW meeting in Birmingham: Chartist resolution CARRIED, that universal suffrage takes priority.—In Leeds UNSUCCESSFUL.
" 21, 22.	ANTI-CORN LAW meetings [in] Manchester and Edinburgh.
February 5.	In the Queen's Speech Chartists threatened with the law.
March 16.	Chartist CONVENTION AT CROWN AND ANCHOR. PHYSICAL FORCE PROCLAIMED BY O'Connor AND Harney.
April 1.	Meeting in Edinburgh TO SUPPORT ministers. The Chartists won and threw the

---

[a] The date when the Melbourne Whig Cabinet fell.— *Ed.*
[b] In the manuscript this sentence is crossed out by a vertical line.— *Ed.*
[c] In the next three dates in the manuscript some of the words are crossed out.— *Ed.*

LORD PROVOST out of the CHAIR AND CARRIED THEIR RESOLUTION.

April 29. Chartist RIOTS in Llanidloes.—The Chartists in control of the town for a while. (In Newport shortly before, John Frost removed from the MAGISTRACY.)

May 8. H. Vincent arrested FOR INCITING TO RIOT at Newport. (Ministerial crisis—*replâtrage*.[a])

” 13. The rest of the Chartist CONVENTION (thus the petty bourgeois out) removed to Birmingham. 50,000 men received and led through the city. Manifesto passed immediately at the first session: TO WITHDRAW ALL THEIR MONEY FROM BANKS, TO DEAL EXCLUSIVELY WITH CHARTISTS AND TO HAVE A SACRED MONTH[480] AND TO ARM.—F. O'Connor demands that the petition to the Queen[b] to appoint a Chartist ministry should be presented peacefully by 500,000 men armed with rifles.

May 25. Meeting in Kersal Moor. F. O'Connor says he came *because* the meeting had been declared illegal by the magistracy.

June 14. Attwood presents the Chartist Petition, 1,280,000 signatures. URGENCY REFUSED BY 235:46.

” 18. Grote's MOTION ON BALLOT rejected 333:216.

July 4. Chartist RIOTS in Birmingham, Bull Ring meeting broken up by police and army. Secretary of the CONVENTION[c] arrested. The CONVENTION protests.

” 15. Bull Ring riots again, procession through the town, looting, several shops burnt down. Army called out, NO LOSS OF LIFE.

” 18. Llanidloes RIOTERS SENTENCED TO IMPRISONMENT.

” 20. RIOTS [in] Newcastle.

August 2. Vincent & Co. sentenced to imprisonment AT Monmouth.

” 3. Birmingham RIOTERS TRIED, 3 sentenced to death, but REPRIEVED.

---

[a] Here: patching up.— *Ed.*
[b] Victoria.— *Ed.*
[c] William Lovett.— *Ed.*

August 6.   Chartist CONVENTION, now in Arundel Coffee House, London, decides to postpone the SACRED MONTH set for August 12 owing to lack of preparation, but on the 12th the TRADES which can are to take 2-3 days off and to hold processions and meetings ON THE PRESENT AWFUL STATE OF THE COUNTRY.

"   11.   St. Paul's Church [in London] and the Manchester OLD CHURCH occupied by Chartists during the sermon, which did not lead to anything.

"   12.   Manchester, Macclesfield, Bolton, etc. Attempt to go through with the three-day SACRED MONTH. Feeble and unsuccessful.

"   15.   Chester ASSIZES. J. R. *Stephens'* TRIAL for UNLAWFUL MEETING AND EXCITING TO RIOT AT *Cotton Tree,* Hyde. That was the meeting where the volleys were fired.— 18 MONTHS Knutsford.

"   27.   PARLIAMENT PROROGUED.

"   30.   *Nouveau replâtrage ministeriel.*[a]

September 14.   DISSOLUTION OF CHARTIST NATIONAL CONVENTION.

"   20.   F. O'Connor ARRESTED, Manchester, SEDITION.

"   23.   Ebenezer Elliott accuses the Chartists of being Tory agents (Sheffield).

November 4.   *Newport RIOTS.* The HILL MEN under Frost and Williams march on the town, meet up at Tredegar Park with Jones' column (from Pontypool) and attack the soldiers, who had already been summoned (to protect the assembled magistrates). Skirmish. 9 dead are left lying there, others ... and the wounded carried off. Frost arrested the next morning. The soldiers commanded by a lieutenant! Williams apprehended soon after.—TRIAL December 31-January 8. According to one witness the *Welsh Mail* to Birmingham was to be stopped, and its non-arrival was to be the signal to strike in the Midlands

---

[a] New ministerial patch-up.— *Ed.*

and the North. Frost, Williams and Jones sentenced to death, TRANSPORTED FOR LIFE.

1840. January 13.	Resumption of ANTI-CORN LAW agitation with BANQUET and meeting in Manchester.
" 16.	Parliament opened.
March .	The ministry twice defeated in the HOUSE OF COMMONS. Start of the BLASPHEMY PROSECUTIONS by HOME SECRETARY'S COMMITTEE.
" 17.	F. O'Connor TRIED at York ASSIZE. Now DEFERRED.
" 25.	Meeting of the ANTI-CORN LAW LEAGUE. Palace Yard. Resolution PASSED.
" 31.	To date total of ANTI-CORN LAW petition signatures only 980,352.
April 8.	Bronterre O'Brien, Liverpool ASSIZES, 18 MONTHS IMPRISONMENT FOR SEDITION.
" 11.	F. O'Connor 18 MONTHS IN York Castle FOR LIBEL, treated like a common criminal (F. O'Connor's letter April 20).
August 4.	Lord Ashley CARRIES ADDRESS TO CROWN [a] on child labour (thus only because of LIBERALS' weakness!)
" 11.	Parliament closed.
November 6.	Hetherington condemned for BLASPHEMY, SENTENCE DEFERRED.
1841. January 21.	RADICAL MEETING AT Leeds for unity with the Chartists. But only agreed on UNIVERSAL SUFFRAGE, not on the other points of the Charter.
" 26.	Parliament opened.
February 16.	MINISTRY DEFEATED BY 31 OUT OF 223.
April 29.	ANTI-CORN LAW MEETINGS in Deptford, in vain, in Leeds actually broken up by Chartists. Russell wishes to tinker with CORN LAWS.
May 7.	MINISTRY DEFEATED 36 OUT OF 598.
" 25.	Duncombe presents Chartists' petition (amnesty), 1,300,000 signatures, the ANTI-CORN LAW only 474,448.

---

[a] Queen Victoria.— *Ed.*

June 2.   Anti-Corn Law meeting [in] Manchester attacked in vain by Chartists.

"   4.   Peel's no confidence in Ministry: 312 for, 311 against dissolution.

"   23.   Hetherington versus Moxon. Blasphemy against Shelley. Guilty.

August 19. Parliament opened after the elections. Tory majority.

"   28.   Melbourne ministry brought down, majority—91 out of 629. *Peel*.
Peel Ministry—until July 1846.

October 7. Parliament closed.
Great distress in manufacturing districts Leeds, Paisley, Glasgow, Bradford, Nottingham, etc.

November 10. Trade Convention in Derby, for Free Trade.

December 29. Bankruptcies in Glasgow.

1842. January 7. Chartist Convention in Glasgow, F. O'Connor there.

February 1. Anti-Corn Law Meeting broken up by Chartists in Southampton with Tory help?

"   2.   Anti-Corn Law Bazar in Manchester.

"   3.   Parliament opened.

"   9.   Peel proposes the sliding scale 20/- at 51/- corn price, 1/- at 73/- corn price.[a]

March 11. Peel's budget—tariffs of £1,200,000 abolished, particularly on raw materials and semi-manufactures. Income tax. The sliding scale becomes law (Royal ascent) April 29.

May 2.   Chartist Petition with 3,317,702 signatures carried to Parliament in procession from Lincoln's Inn Fields. Had to be taken to pieces because the door too small. Duncombs demands that the Petition should be heard by Council at the bar. 49:287.

---

[a] From the maximum duty of 20s. at the price of 51s. and lower per quarter to the minimum duty of 1s. at the price of 73s. and higher per quarter.—*Ed.*

May 25.   Meeting in Stockport ON DISTRESS. POOR RATES risen from £2,628 in 1836/37 to £7,120; over $^1/_2$ the spinners ruined; over 3,000 houses empty (Stockport TO LET); in Heaton Norris $^1/_4$ of the houses empty and 1,000 OCCUPANTS RELIEVED BY PARISH.

June 1.   STRIKE OF COLLIERS in Dudley DISTRICT.

" 3.   Large meeting of UNEMPLOYED in Glasgow, ending in a BEGGING PROCESSION through the town.

In Ireland PROVISION RIOTS, in Ennis a ship carrying flour looted, in Cork futile assault on the POTATO MARKET.

" 7.   Ashley introduces a FACTORY BILL, RESTRICTING WOMEN'S AND CHILDREN'S LABOUR IN MINES AND FACTORIES.

June 25.   *Leeds Mercury* says 4,025 FAMILIES,$=^1/_5$ of the town's population receiving POOR RELIEF. Great "DISTRESS" everywhere.

" 28.   Peel's tariff through the Commons. July 4 through the Lords 2ND READING.

July 1.   DEBATE ON DISTRESS. No result, as usual. In Ireland AGRARIAN OUTRAGES all the time.

" 2.   FOOD RIOTS [in] Dumfries, several mealmongers' shops looted.

" 5.   ANTI-CORN LAW CONFERENCE in London. Bright's threatening speech. Reports that in Sheffield 10,000 PEOPLE IN EXTREME DISTRESS, in Wolverhampton 62 blast furnaces idle, in Stockport the POOR RATE of 2/- in the £ produces only £3,600, whereas in 1839 1/8d. had produced £5,000. More POOR RATE 3/4d. in the £ and almost daily meetings of workers and SHOPKEEPERS TO SEE WHAT TO DO. Burslem great agitation, MILITARY CALLED OUT.

" 5.   FREETRADE CONFERENCE [in] Sheffield. REVEREND W. Bailey: IT WAS NOT WORDS WHICH WOULD MOVE PARLIAMENT, BUT FORCE, a GENTLEMAN is reported to have spoken of Peel's assassination, etc.

" 11.   Villiers' MOTION FOR COMMITTEE OF WHOLE HOUSE TO CONSIDER CORN LAWS rejected, 117:231.

	At the same time several attempts on the Queen's life and Peel's protective law against causing a nuisance to the Queen: transportation and the [colonies].
July 18.	Meetings in Liverpool, Manchester, Leeds ON DISTRESS, deputation to Peel to do something before the closing of Parliament.
August 1.	STRIKE of the COAL and IRON MINERS, Airdrie and Coatbridge, immediately followed by the Glaswegians, FOR ADVANCING WAGES.
" 4.	Ashton AND Oldham STRIKE—Manchester RIOTS.
" 12.	Parliament closed.
" 15.	Delegate Trades Meeting [in] Manchester—peaceful.
" 17.	Proclamation by the Chartist NATIONAL EXECUTIVE (in contrast)—warlike.
" 18.	"THE PACIFICATION OF THE NORTH IS COMPLETED."
" 24.	White (George) in Birmingham despite the police, despite warrant goes with guard to meetings and speaks.
September 5.	York AND Lancaster SPECIAL ASSIZES, some 156 RIOTERS TRIED.
" 30.	Stafford SPECIAL ASSIZES FOR RIOTERS. F. O'Connor arrested FOR EXCITING TO SEDITION in Manchester, etc., at meetings in August.
October 6.	Cobden announces at Manchester meeting that the League intends to raise £50,000.
December 9.	The quaint city COMMON COUNCIL votes for FREE TRADE IN CORN.
" 31.	REVENUE FOR QUARTER SHOWS DECREASE £940,062.
1843. January 9.	O'Connell announces REPEAL[481] for this year—hence renewed agitation.
" 26.	ANTI-CORN LAW WEEKLY MEETING, Wilson announces renewed agitation, 400,000 TRACTS SENT OUT LAST WEEK, 3 TONS MORE TO-MORROW.
February 11.	Parliament opened.

February 13.   Ld. Howick's motion for COMMITTEE OF WHOLE HOUSE ON DISTRESS. Debate till 17, then defeated, 301:191. Cobden threatening towards Peel.

" 23.   Walter's motion for easing the POOR LAW, during which it emerged that the Government has been implementing the new POOR LAW with increasing severity.

March 1.   TRIAL OF F. O'Connor and Co. in Lancaster. O'Connor guilty and many others, now RESERVED ON POINT OF LAW.

" 15.   From today weekly MEETINGS of the ANTI-CORN LAW LEAGUE in Drury Lane Theatre resumed.

March 24.   FACTORY BILL READ 2ND TIME.[482]

" 31.   Revenue a/c rising, but still below last year (EXCEPT NEW INCOME TAX).

April 27.   Irish Arms Bill,[483] as many arms bought up there.

May 9.   Villiers' CORN LAW Motion, after 5 evening debates, defeated 381:125.
Peel declares that he intends to oppose REPEAL absolutely.

" 24.   Richard Arkwright's WILL PROVED— £8,000,000.

June 8.   MONSTER REPEAL MEETING [in] Kilkenny— 300,000 men.

" 10.   Rebecca RIOTS in Wales[484] BEGAN: ABOLITION OF TURNPIKES, OF TITHES AND COMMUTED RENT CHARGES, CHURCH RATE AND NEW POOR LAW.

" 15.   REPEAL MEETING [in] Ennis—500,000 MEN. EDUCATIONAL CLAUSES[485]—IN FACT BILL ABANDONED on account of opposition of the DISSENTERS[486] (petition over 2,000,000 signatures).
(All REPEAL MAGISTRATES in Ireland dismissed up to now.)

July 19.   Still over a week's debate Smith O'Brien's MOTION FOR INQUIRY INTO DISTRESS in Ireland defeated 243:164.

" 25.   Bright M.P. FOR Durham City.

August 15.   MONSTER REPEAL MEETING [at] Tara Hill.

" 24.   Parliament closed.

	Rebecca in Wales continuing.—OUTRAGES in Ireland.—Threat to withhold rent payment, CUTTING CROPS, etc.
September 28.	ANTI-CORN-LAW agitation in London resumed with meeting in Covent Garden Theatre. 9,000,000 TRACTS distributed in previous year.
October 1.	REPEAL MONSTER MEETING in Mullaghmust.
" 7.	" " " [in] Clontarf banned BY PROCLAMATION.
" 10.	ROYAL COMMISSION TO INQUIRE INTO Rebecca CAUSES.
" 14.	O'Connell accused—still no point formulated, but QUIT UNDER BAIL TO APPEAR NEXT TERM TO ANSWER ANY CHARGE BY ATTORNEY GENERAL.
" 21.	ANTI-CORN-LAW VICTORY AT CITY LONDON ELECTION: Pattison OVER Baring.
" 23.	COUNCIL AT HALL in Dublin opened.— O'Connell now "PEACEFUL"!
" 26.	TRIALS OF Rebecca—heavy sentences (Cardiff).
November 8.	O'Connell finally charged.
1844. January 1.	Marquis [of] Westminster goes over to the ANTI-CORN LAW LEAGUE. Many ANTI-CORN LAW and PRO-CORN LAW MEETINGS held throughout the country.
January 15.	O'Connell's TRIAL. Sentenced, confirmed on May 24 by QUEEN'S BENCH.[487] 12 MONTHS.
February 1.	Parliament opened.
" 6.	New FACTORY BILL (not passed previous year).
" 12.	REVEREND Oastler freed after 3 years in debtors gaol.
1845. June 6.	FACTORY ACT, LAW. Railway speculation and autumn potato blight.

July '46-February '62. *Russell*

1847. July 28.	Elections. F. O'Connor and Walter elected in Nottingham.

December 7.   F. O'Connor's motion to investigate how the Union with Ireland had been made and what it had achieved, 23:255.

1848. March 13.   Chartist Demonstration [on] Kennington Common. Jones spoke forcefully. In Ireland Young Ireland[488] revolutionary, demanding arms. At Trafalgar Square meeting, March 6, ostensibly about INCOME TAX, police knocked down, strengthened to 500 men, new ROW in the evening.—On the 6th RIOT in Glasgow by UNEMPLOYED, some looting, military called out, but the mass dispersed without shooting.
Similar in Edinburgh and Liverpool.

April 1.   RIFLE CLUBS formed in Ireland.

"   4.   NATIONAL CHARTIST CONVENTION in London, demonstration for the 10th. E. Jones for FIGHTING. B. O'Brien for waiting until the people stronger than the law.

"   6.   F. O'Connor's motion to pardon Frost, Williams and Jones defeated 91:23.

"   7.   A GAGGING ACT[489] against inflammatory speeches introduced by Grey.

"   10.   Kennington Common. The Chartists in processions to Kennington Common to assemble there and thence on to the HOUSE OF COMMONS with the MONSTER petition. 250,000 SPECIAL CONSTABLES.—4,300 soldiers to Kennington.—On Saturday evening SPLIT over arming: B. O'Brien for, F. O'Connor against. B. O'Brien withdraws with his LOT. The demonstration fell FLAT, the march to Westminster abandoned, and F. O'Connor handed over the petition that evening in the usual way.

"   13.   Debate on the petition, instead of 5,706,000 signatures, said to be only 1,975,496, including much nonsense.

May 16.   CHARTIST NATIONAL CONVENTION BREAKS UP.

"   27.   John Mitchel 14 YEARS TRANSPORTATION.— RIOTS in Clarkenwell Green and Bethnal

Green, nothing significant, because of this CONVICTION of Chartists and Repealers.[490]

June GOLD EXCITEMENT IN CALIFORNIA.

" 6. Jones and 3 others COMMITTED FOR SEDITION.

" " O'Connell's REPEAL ASSOCIATION BROKEN UP.

" 11. Great precautions in London against Chartist insurrection: bank, mint, government offices, Thames steamers full of soldiers. Parliament moreover provisioned.

" 12. Chartist demonstration a failure it seems, very pitiful.
June. Insurrection.[a]

July 7. Jones and 5 others 2 years and BOUND OVER AFTERWARDS.

" 22. Russell demands suspension OF habeas corpus[491] in Ireland, BILL introduced.

" 25. Smith O'Brien's attempt at insurrection.—[On the] 29th Smith O'Brien apprehended.

August 8. Berkeley's BALLOT MOTION CARRIED AGAINST GOVERNMENT 86:81.

" 14. Chartists' rising [in] Ashton under Lyne. MIDNIGHT ATTACK AGAINST TOWN HALL with pistols and lances—one POLICEMAN shot—broken up.

" 15. 14 Chartist leaders arrested in Manchester for INCITING TO RISE IN ARMS.

" 16. 18 Chartist leaders arrested in London, Orange Street, *armed*; others in Moor Street. Allegedly they were due to strike during the night. Lot of ammunition seized.

" 25. TRIAL of the London Chartists, 26th, TRIAL of Manchester Chartists. Condemned to 2 YEARS HARD LABOUR.

" 26. TRIAL of those arrested on August 16 in London—TRANSPORTATION FOR LIFE.

---

[a] Of the Paris workers on June 22-25, 1848.—*Ed.*

1852. June 8.   F. O'Connor gets up to silly tricks in HOUSE OF COMMONS, arrested by SERGEANT AT ARMS, taken to madhouse.

1855. August 30.   †F. O'Connor in Notting Hill.

1856. May 3.   Amnesty for Frost, Williams and Jones and the other transported Irish prisoners.

1869. January 26.   †Ernest Jones, 50.

Written in August 1886

First published, in Russian, in *Marx-Engels Archives*, Vol. X, Moscow, 1948

Printed according to the manuscript

Published in English for the first time

[PLAN OF CHAPTER FOUR OF THE PAMPHLET
THE ROLE OF FORCE IN HISTORY]

1. 1848. Postulate of national states. Italy, Germany, Poland, Hungary.
2. Bonaparte's enlightened policy of conquest: nationhood in exchange for compensation. Italy.
3. Against this, [Prussian] army reorganisation. Conflict. Bismarck. Policy not original.
4. Position in Germany. Unity: 1. through revolution, 2. through Austria, 3. through Prussia (Customs' Union).
5. War [of] 1864 and 1866. Revolutionary means.
6. Bismarck's best years—until 1870.
7. French War.[a] Empire. Annexation of Alsace-Lorraine. Russia the arbitrator.
8. Bismarck at the end—turns reactionary, feeble-minded. Kulturkampf [492] (civil marriage). Protective tariffs and agrarian alliance with bourgeois.—Colonial swindles. Slandering of Bismarck.—Anti-Socialist Law.[493]—Suppression of coalition.—Social reform.—Militarism because of annexation of Alsace.—The Junker [in Bismarck] comes to the fore for the lack of other ideas.

Written between the end of 1887 and March 1888

Printed according to the manuscript

First published, in Russian, in *Marx-Engels Archives*, Vol. X, Moscow, 1948

Published in English for the first time

---

[a] This point also includes the notes written on the same sheet and crossed out by Engels presumably after he had used them in his work, "1. Methods of warfare. Contribution, franc-tireurs, [Thefts of] clock, thrashing. Severity of Junkers' revenge from above. 2. Overthrow of the Empire. 3. Hats off to Paris! 4. Milliards and Alsace-Lorraine."—*Ed.*

PLAN OF THE FINAL SECTION
OF CHAPTER FOUR OF THE PAMPHLET
THE ROLE OF FORCE IN HISTORY

I. 3 classes: two lousy, one of them decaying, the other on the
ascent, and workers who only want bourgeois FAIR PLAY.
Manoeuvring between the latter two therefore the only
proper way—perish the thought! Policy: To strengthen state
power in general and to make it financially independent
in particular (nationalisation of the railways, monopolies),
police state and regional principles of justice.

"Liberal" and "National", the dual nature of 1848, still in
evidence in Germany of 1870-88.

Bismarck had to rely on the Reichstag and the people, and
this called for complete freedom of the press, speech,
association and assembly, just for orientation.

II. 1. Structure [of the Empire]

  a) Economic—ill-conceived currency law main achievement already.

  b) Political—restoration of the police state, and anti-bourgeois judicial laws (1876), poor copy of the French version.—Legal uncertainty.—Culminated in the Imperial Court. 1879.

  2. Lack of ideas proved by playing around and slandering Bismarck. Bismarck's party *sans phrase.*

  a) Kulturkampf. The Catholic priest is no gendarme or policeman. Jubilation by the bourgeoisie—hopelessness—going to Canossa.[494] Only rational result—civil marriage!

3. Swindles and crash. His involvement. Wretchedness of conservative Junkers, who are just as dishonourable as the bourgeoisie.

4. [Bismarck's] complete transformation into a Junker.

        a) Protective tariffs, etc., coalition of bourgeois and Junkers, with the latter taking the lion's share.

        b) Attempts at a tobacco monopoly defeated in 1882.

        c) Colonial swindles.

5. Social policy à *la* Bonaparte.

        a) Anti-Socialist Law and crushing of workers' associations and funds.

        b) Social reform crap.

III. 6. Foreign policy. Threat of war, effect of annexation. Increase in strength of army. Septennate.[495] In due course, a return to the pre-1870 year group to maintain superiority for a few more years.

IV. Result: a) A domestic situation which collapses with the death of those two[a]: no empire without emperor! Proletariat driven to revolution; an unprecedented growth in social-democracy on the repeal of the Anti-Socialist Law—chaos.

        b) Overall outcome—a peace worse than war at best; or else a world war.

Written between late December 1887 and March 1888

Printed according to the manuscript

First published in *Die Neue Zeit*, Vol. 1, No. 26, 1895-96

Published in English for the first time

---

[a] Bismarck and William I.—*Ed.*

[NOTES ON MY JOURNEY
THROUGH AMERICA AND CANADA][496]

Primitiveness. "CIVILISED COUNTRY." [a]

Furniture.—Manners—Boston cabs. Hotel organisation, STAGE COACHES, 17th-century travel. Alongside hypermodern features—even in rooms. Window fastenings—roller blinds—keys—double locks.

Country of unexpected contrasts: more railways than roads and the latter appalling—GOOD PLANK ROAD—ELEVATED RAILWAYS above and dreadful pavement below—log cabins but carpets and pianos inside—indeed, even the bourgeois Yankees and the feudal Canadians alongside them—the idyllic Hoboken and insects close to New York.

Publicness of life, in contrast to England. Only bedrooms private, and even these scarcely so (fanlights, ventilation).—HALL, OFFICE, WRITING ROOM, LADIES' PARLORS; heaters make it unnecessary to keep rooms closed even in winter, and so it does not exist. LOAFING ABOUT in the hotels.

Greeks in Rome in the last days of the republic.

Religion—*their* theory, to be grasped historically. GO-AHEAD NATION—pushing past, not being able to see anyone walking or standing in front of them. Even in Boston, and worst there on account of the narrow streets—women too.

Spitting—privies—hypocrisy about drink not only in PROHIBITION STATES—nobody drinks in public—prudery—ROOSTER and ROACHES.

Opposite to Canada.—French Canadians really detached from France by the Revolution and have preserved the feudalism guaranteed by the conquest—they are going to ruin—Falls opposite Niagara [497]—empty houses, bridges, etc.—Emigration to

---

[a] The words in English are written in the margin.—*Ed.*

New England, where they replace the Chinese.—English Canadians also slow, even in Toronto much dilapidation.

The Americans *unable to enjoy.*

The Americans unable to walk—either rush or loaf.

Provincials.[a]

Foundation the old solid petty bourgeois, small townsman and small peasant of the 17th-18th centuries. He is everywhere unmistakable with his wooden fashion, but also forms the solid foundation amidst wild speculation, just like the Swiss, to whom a certain resemblance.

Obtrusiveness of American manners: Doctor, *City of Berlin.*[b]

Get up early.

New York—harbour—beauty.—Natural setting for the centre of capitalist production—and how this destiny is fulfilled. First evening impression, dazzling, pavements, dirt, noise, horrible. By day even more ugliness—telegraph poles, overhead railways, signs crossways, company signs, architecture hidden, throngs of people, carriages, TRAMS and ELEVATED far above London, ugly, disfigured, everywhere *advertisements,* obtrusiveness. Croupier type. Haggard appearance of the people, even the women. Shops dazzling compared with London, and in greater numbers. This the *gateway* to the promised land. Ghastly noises at sea and on land. Noise from the carts, one makes more than ten in Europe. All aesthetics trampled underfoot as soon as momentary profit comes in view.

Horses like the people: elements of a good stock, not yet ready. Mostly lighter than in England—in Canada, on the other hand, thoroughly English type.

Résumé: capitalist production is overexploitation. Adirondacks forest devastation—nowhere else timber forest either (Isle of Gnats perhaps excepted).

Railways poor, slow, stopping train, delay and wait in Buffalo, incomprehensibly long halt at the stations; *few* trains per day; long bends, hence the long carriages (cf. street corner tracks in New York—ELEVATED), rolling, due to elasticity of the beams and the trembling, sea-sickness.

---

[a] This word is written in the margin.— *Ed.*

[b] The name of the steamer in which Engels travelled to America.— *Ed.*

Americans no nation. 5-6 different types, held together by the need for cohesion forged in the Civil War,[498] and the feeling that they have in them the making *of the greatest nation of the 20th century.*

Genuinely capitalist[a]:

Business is concluded in a strictly businesslike manner. No tips. Anyone who gives them in situations where we would consider them unavoidable is then thoroughly exploited as a GREENHORN.

The parvenu—national character.

Educated persons commonly display great self-possession, others at least show confidence and ASSURANCE to the point of importunity.

Written in the latter half of September 1888

First published in: Marx and Engels, *Works,* Second Russian Edition, Vol. 50, Moscow, 1981

Printed according to the manuscript

Published in English for the first time

---

a These words are written in the margin.— *Ed.*

[IMPRESSIONS OF A JOURNEY ROUND AMERICA][499]

We generally imagine America to be a new world—new not merely with regard to the time of its discovery, but also in all its institutions, far ahead of us olde-worlde sleepy Europeans in its scorn for everything hereditary and traditional, a world, newly built from scratch on virgin soil, by modern men on purely modern, practical, rational principles. And the Americans do their part in strengthening this view of ours. They look down with contempt on us as dubious, impractical people, enmeshed in all sorts of received prejudices, who go in fear of everything new, whereas they, THE MOST GO-AHEAD NATION,[a] examine every new proposal for improvement simply for its practical utility and, having once recognised it as possible, introduce it immediately, indeed almost overnight. But in America everything ought to be new, rational, practical—that is, everything ought to be different from what it is with us.

I first met a large number of Americans on the steamer *City of Berlin.* They were mostly very nice people, ladies and gentlemen, more accessible than the English, at times somewhat blunt in their speech, but otherwise rather like the better dressed people anywhere else. What, however, set them apart was a strangely petty-bourgeois bearing—not that of the timid, uncertain German petty bourgeois, nor that of the English; a bearing which, by virtue of the great assurance with which it presented itself as if it were quite natural, showed itself to be an inherited quality. The younger ladies, in particular, left the impression of a certain

---

[a] In the manuscript this English phrase is given in parentheses after its German equivalent.— *Ed.*

naivety such as is found in Europe only in smaller towns; when striding resolutely, almost fiercely across the deck, arm in arm, or on the arm of a man, they had the very same springy gait and held down their skirts when threatened by the wind with the same demure grip as innocent young things from the country back home. They reminded me mostly of Swedish girls—they were big and robust like them, too—and I expected them to curtsey at any moment, as Swedish women do. My American fellow travellers had also received their share of the physical and intellectual clumsiness which is the universal hereditary trait of the Germanic race and had not shaken it off at all. In short, my initial impression of the Americans was by no means one of national superiority over the Europeans, by no means that of a totally new, modern national type, but on the contrary that they were people who still clung on to inherited petty-bourgeois habits which are considered outdated in Europe, that we Europeans contrast with them in this connection as the Parisians with the provincials.

When I entered my first bedroom in New York, what did I find? Furniture of the quaintest old style imaginable, chests of drawers with brass rings or hoops as handles on the drawers, such as was the fashion in the early years of the century, and in Europe are still found only in the country; alongside them, more recent styles after the English or French pattern, but even these were also dated enough and mostly in the wrong place; nothing new since the huge rocking chair, which described an arc of 240 degrees, went out of fashion again. And thus everywhere, the chairs, tables and cupboards mostly look like the heirlooms of past generations. The carriages on the New York streets have such an outdated appearance that at first glance one believes no European farm would still have in its possession a hand-cart of such a model. True, on closer observation one finds that these carriages are much improved and most expediently equipped, furnished with excellent suspension and extremely lightly built out of very strong wood; but for all these improvements the old-fashioned model remained intact. In London, right up to the early 40s, there were cabs which people boarded from the rear and where they sat on the right and the left opposite one another, as in an omnibus; since 1850 they have disappeared; yet in Boston, as far as I know the only American city where cabs are in common use, these boneshakers still flourish to this day. The American inns of today, with their luxurious furnishings and their hundreds of rooms, show in their entire AMERICAN PLAN that they have grown out of the remote farmhouses in sparsely populated areas, which even today occasionally offer travellers board and lodging for payment—I shall return to this point—and hence display peculiarities which appear to us to be not simply strange, but downright quaint. And so on.

But anyone who wishes to savour the pleasure of a journey such as one had to endure in Europe at the time of the Thirty Years' War[500] should head for an American mountain district and travel to the end of the last railway line and take the stagecoach further out into the wilderness. The four of us made such a trip to the Adirondacks and have seldom laughed as much as we did on the roof of that coach. An old boneshaker of an indescribable model, compared with which the famous Prussian carriages from the year dot seem the height of splendour, with seats—quite in keeping— for six to nine people up on the roof and the box, that was the conveyance. As for the road, I beg your pardon, it wasn't a road, one could hardly even call it a path; two deeply rutted tracks in the sandy soil, uphill, downhill.[a]

Written in late September 1888

First published in: Marx and Engels, *Works*, First Russian Edition, Vol. XXVIII, Moscow, 1940

Printed according to the manuscript

Published in English for the first time

---

[a] The manuscript breaks off here.— *Ed.*

APPENDICES

[TO THE EDITORS OF *TO-DAY*] [501]

[Draft] [a]

To the British Publishing Co.

Sir (or Gentn)

In reply to your letter of the — I beg to say that since my last I have compared your article with the original *Le Capital*.

I find that it is a very imperfect translation of Ch. XXIII (23) *Réproduction simple,* and that the translator has made very important mistakes in consequence of want of sufficient acquaintance, partly with the leading ideas of *Le Capital,* partly with French grammar.

It must appear to me very unfair that a single chapter should be taken out of the middle of a closely-reasoned scientific work and without a word of introduction be presented to the public.

When it comes to the publishing of translations of entire chapters of my father's works, the question of copyright crops up. Please do not forget that I am responsible for their share of that copyright to other people and to my father's memory for the way his works are done into English. Upon this point I reserve all my rights.

However I will permit you to publish another chapter in your next issue, on condition that you head it with a few lines stating

1) That the last was Ch. 23 and the present is Ch. so and so, out of *Le Capital,* published in Paris 1872. [502]

2) That the translation is yours; and

3) That you inform me which further chapters you intend to translate after which I shall consider whether I can give you my

---

[a] The draft was written in Engels' hand on behalf of Eleanor Marx-Aveling.— *Ed.*

permission to do so, which will very materially depend upon the character of the translation itself.

Your allusion to a poem of V. Hugo is entirely irrelevant, considering that it is well known that V. Hugo could not write a line of English and that my father has been an English author for more than thirty years.

Written in the latter half of April 1883

First published in: Marx and Engels, *Works*, Second Russian Edition, Vol. 50, Moscow, 1980

Reproduced from the manuscript

Published in English for the first time

FROM HERMANN LOPATIN'S LETTER
TO MARIA OSHANINA [503]

London, September 20, 1883

...I must let you know the result of my first meeting with Engels, because I think some of his opinions will be pleasing for you.

We talked a great deal about Russian matters, about how the cause of our political and social revival is likely to proceed. As was to be expected, our views were in total agreement; each of us kept finishing off the ideas and phrases of the other. He too believes (like both Marx and myself) that the task of a *revolutionary* party or a party of *action* in Russia at the present time lies not in propagating the new socialist ideal and not even in striving to realise this by no means fully elaborated ideal with the help of a provisional government composed of our comrades, but in directing all forces towards 1) either forcing the Tsar to convene a Zemsky Sobor, [504] 2) or by means of intimidating the Tsar, etc., causing profound disorder that would result in the convening of the Sobor or something similar. He believes, as I do, that such a Sobor would *inevitably* lead to a radical, not only political but also social reorganisation. He believes in the tremendous significance of the electoral period, in the sense of incomparably more successful propaganda than all books and whispered communications. He regards a purely liberal constitution without profound economic restructuring as impossible, and therefore does not fear this danger. He believes that enough material for the restructuring of society on new principles has accumulated in the *real* conditions of the people's life. Of course, he does not believe in the instantaneous realisation of communism or anything like that, but only of that which has already matured in the life and heart of the people. He believes that the people will find themselves eloquent spokesmen to express their needs and aspirations, etc. He believes that no forces will be capable of halting this reorganisation, or revolution, once it has begun. Thus one thing only is important: to smash the fatal force of stagnation, to knock the people and society for a moment out of the state of inertness and immobility, to cause disorder which will force the government and the people to set about internal restructuring, which will stir up the calm popular sea and arouse the attention and *enthusiasm* of the whole people for the cause of a full social reorganisation. And the results will show themselves, precisely those results which are possible, desirable and practicable for the time in question.

All this is devilishly brief, but I cannot write in any more detail at the moment. Moreover all this may not be entirely to your liking, so I will hasten to convey to you with literal accuracy other opinions of his which are most flattering to the Russian revolutionary party. They are as follows:

"Everything now depends on what is done in the immediate future in St. Petersburg, to which the eyes of all thinking, far-seeing and perspicacious people in the whole of Europe are now turned."

"Russia is the France of the present century. The revolutionary initiative of a *new* social reorganisation legally and rightly belongs to it."

"...The collapse of Tsarism, which will destroy the last bastion of monarchism in Europe and put an end to Russia's 'aggressiveness', Poland's hatred of it and a great deal more, will lead to a completely different combination of powers, smash Austria to smithereens and arouse in all countries a powerful impetus for internal reorganisation."

"...It is unlikely that Germany will decide to take advantage of the Russian disorders and move its forces into Russia to support the Tsar. But if it did do so, all the better. It would mean the end of its present government and the beginning of a new era. Annexation by it of the Baltic provinces is pointless and impracticable. Such seizures of opposite (?) or adjoining narrow littorals and bits of land, and the resultant ludicrous configurations of states, were possible only in the sixteenth and seventeenth centuries, but not now. Moreover it is no secret to anyone that the Germans constitute an insignificant reactionary minority there." (I am adding this point for Y.P.[a] in view of her ultra-patriotic opinions on this point.)

---

[a] Yulia Petrovna—the pseudonym of Galina Chernyavskaya-Bokhanovskaya.—Ed.

"Both Marx and I find that the Committee's letter to Alexander III [505] is positively excellent in its political essence and calm tone. It shows that there are people with a statesmanlike cast of mind in the ranks of the revolutionaries."

May I hope that all this is sufficiently flattering and pleasing for you and that you will thank me for these lines? Do you remember that I said Marx himself had never been a Marxist? Engels told me that during the struggle of Brousse, Malon and Co. with the others, Marx used to joke: "All I know is that *I am not a Marxist*!"... [506]

First published in *Osnovy teoreticheskogo sotsializma i ikh prilozheniye k Rossii*, Geneva, March 1893

Printed according to the book

Translated from the Russian

Published in English for the first time

THE INSURRECTION OF MAY 1849[507]

The insurrection of May 1849, which roused the Rhenish provinces and South Germany to revolt, was provoked by the refusal of most of the governments of the small states to accept the constitution approved by the National Assembly at Frankfurt. This Assembly never had any real power and, to make matters worse, had neglected to take the necessary steps to acquire some; once it had finished its constitution on paper it lost the last remains of its moral power. Although rather romantic, the constitution was the sole banner to rally around to try to launch a new movement, even if it meant not implementing it after the victory.

The rising started in Dresden on 3 May; a few days later it spread to the Bavarian Palatinate and the Grand Duchy of Baden. The Grand Duke[a] hastened to flee as soon as he had seen the troops fraternising with the people.

The Prussian Government, which had crushed the revolutionary movement in November 1848, disarmed Berlin and placed Prussia under a state of siege, became the protector of all the governments of the other states. It immediately sent troops to Dresden who, after four days of fighting and heroic resistance, defeated the insurgents.

But to subdue the Palatinate and the Duchy of Baden an army was needed: in order to form it, Prussia had to call the *Landwehr*[508] to arms. At Iserlohn (Westphalia) and Elberfeld (Rhenish Prussia) men refused to march. Troops were sent. The towns

---

[a] Leopold.— *Ed.*

barricaded themselves and repulsed them. Iserlohn was taken after two days of fighting. Elberfeld offering no opportunities for resistance, the insurgents, about a thousand in number, resolved to force a way through the troops surrounding them and to reach the south in full revolt. They were cut to pieces, and their commander, Mirbach, was taken prisoner; nevertheless, a large number of insurgents, aided by the populace of the countryside, did manage to get through to the south. Engels was Mirbach's aide-de-camp; but the latter, before putting his plan into action, sent him on a mission to Cologne, which was in the hands of the Prussian army. The truth is that Mirbach did not want to have this known communist in his corps, lest he should scare the bourgeois of the country which he intended to pass through.

In the meantime the rising spread throughout the south of Germany; but as in Paris in 1871 the revolutionaries committed the fatal blunder of not attacking. The troops of the surrounding small states were demoralised and looking for an excuse to join the insurrection: at that time they were determined not to fight against the people. The insurgents could have got the population to rise up and join them by announcing that they were going to the rescue of the Frankfurt Assembly, surrounded by Prussian and Austrian troops. Engels and Marx, after the suppression of the *Neue Rheinische Zeitung,* went to Mannheim to propose to the leaders of the movement that they should march on Frankfurt. They refused to listen to them. They pleaded as an excuse that the troops were disorganised by the flight of their former officers, that they were short of ammunition, etc.

Whereas the insurgents remained with shouldered arms, the Prussians, united with the Bavarians and reinforced by the troops of the small states, which the insurgents could have won over with greater daring, advanced in forced marches on the rebellious areas. The reactionary army, 36,000 men strong, cleared the Palatinate in a week of the 8-9,000 insurgents who were occupying it: it must be said that the two fortresses of the country had remained in the hands of reaction. The revolutionary army fell back on the Baden troops comprising roughly 10,000 men of the line and 12,000 irregulars. There were four general engagements: the reactionary forces were only victorious thanks to their numerical superiority and to the violation of Württemberg territory, which allowed them to turn the revolutionary army's flank at the decisive moment. After six weeks of fighting in the open country the remains of the rebel army had to take refuge in Switzerland.

During this last campaign Engels was aide-de-camp to Colonel Willich, commander of a corps of communist irregulars. He took part in three engagements and in the final decisive battle of the Murg. Colonel Willich, having fled to the United States, died with the rank of general, which he won during the war of secession.[509]

This stubborn resistance in open country, mounted by a few thousand insurgents with no organisation and almost without artillery against a skilfully disciplined Prussian army, shows what our friends, the socialists beyond the Rhine, will be able to achieve the day the revolutionary clarion call rings out in Europe.

Written in mid-November 1885

First published in *Le Socialiste*, November 21, 1885

Printed according to the newspaper

Translated from the French

Published in English in full for the first time

LAWYERS' SOCIALISM [510]

The medieval world view was essentially theological. The unity of the European world, though actually non-existent on the inside, was established against outside forces, the common Saracen enemy, by Christianity. The unity of the West European world, which comprised a group of nations developing in constant interaction, was epitomised by Catholicism. This theological epitome was not merely an idea. It really existed, not only in the Pope, its monarchical focus, but above all in the Church. The Church was organised on feudal and hierarchical lines and, owning about a third of the land in each country, occupied a position of tremendous power within the feudal system. With its feudal landholdings, the Church was the actual link between the different countries, and the Church's feudal organisation gave a religious blessing to the secular feudal system of government. Besides, the clergy was the only educated class. It was therefore natural that Church dogma formed the starting-point and basis of all thought. Everything—jurisprudence, science, philosophy—was pursued in accordance with it, from the angle of whether or not the contents were in keeping with Church doctrine.

But in the bosom of the feudal system there developed the power of the bourgeoisie. A new class emerged to oppose the big landowners. Above all, the burghers were exclusively producers of, and traders in, commodities, while the feudal mode of production essentially rested on the direct consumption of products produced within a limited circle—consumption partly by the producers themselves, partly by the recipients of feudal tributes. The Catholic world view, tailored as it was to feudalism, was no longer adequate for this new class and its conditions of production and exchange. Nevertheless, it, too, continued for some time to be ensnared in the toils of the prevailing omnipotent theology. From the thirteenth to the seventeenth century, all the reformations and the ensuing struggles waged in the name of religion were, theoretically speaking, no more than repeated attempts by the bourgeoisie, the urban plebeians and the peasantry that rose in rebellion together with them, to adapt the old, theological world view to the changed economic conditions and position of the new class. But this did not work. The religious banner was raised for the last time in England in the seventeenth century, and scarcely fifty years later the new world view that was to become the classical one of the bourgeoisie emerged undisguised in France: *the legal world view.*

It was a secularisation of the theological world view. Dogma, divine law, was supplanted by human law, the Church by the State. The economic and social relations, which people previously believed to have been created by the Church and its dogma—because sanctioned by the Church—were now seen as being founded on the law and created by the State. Because the exchange of commodities on the level of society and in its fully developed form, i.e. based on the granting of advances and credit, results in complex contractual relations and thus requires universally valid regulations, which can only be provided by the community—legal norms laid down by the State—people imagined that these legal norms did not arise from the economic facts of life but from their formal stipulation by the State. And because competition, the basic form of intercourse between free commodity producers, is the greatest equaliser, equality before the law became the bourgeoisie's main battlecry. The fact that the struggle of this new rising class against the feudal lords and the absolute monarchy, which then protected them, had to be, like any class struggle, a political struggle, a struggle for control over the State, and had to be waged for the sake of *legal demands,* helped to consolidate the legal world view.

But the bourgeoisie produced its negative complement, the proletariat, and with it a new class struggle, which broke out even before the bourgeoisie had completely won political power. Just as the bourgeoisie, in its day, in the struggle against the nobility, continued for a time to labour under the burden of the theological world view, which had been handed down to it, so the proletariat initially adopted the legal outlook from its adversary and sought weapons therein to use against the bourgeoisie. Like their theoretical champions, the first proletarian parties remained firmly on the juridical "legal foundation"—only they constructed a legal foundation different from that of the bourgeoisie. On the one hand, the demand for equality was extended to include social as well as legal equality; on the other hand, from Adam Smith's propositions that labour is the source of all wealth, but that the product of labour must be shared by the worker with the landowner and the capitalist, the conclusion was drawn that this division was unjust and should either be abolished altogether or at least modified in favour of the workers. But the feeling that leaving the matter on the purely juridical "legal foundation" would not at all make it possible to eliminate the evils created by the bourgeois capitalist mode of production, notably that based on modern, large-scale industry, led the greatest thinkers among even the early socialists—Saint-Simon, Fourier and Owen—to abandon the juridical and political domain altogether and declare all political struggle fruitless.

The two views were equally incapable of precisely and fully expressing the striving of the working class for emancipation, a striving stemming from the obtaining economic situation. The demand for equality, just like that for the full fruits of one's labour, became entangled in insoluble contradictions as soon as they were to be legally formulated in detail, leaving the heart of the matter, the transformation of the mode of production, more or less untouched. The rejection of political struggle by the great utopians was simultaneously a rejection of class struggle, i.e. of the only course of action open to the class whose interests they championed. Both views overlooked the historical background to which they owed their existence; both appealed to the emotions— one to the sense of justice, and the other to the sense of humanity. Both clothed their demands in pious wishes that left unanswered the question as to why they had to be implemented at this precise moment, and not a thousand years earlier or later.

Stripped of all property in the means of production as a result of the transformation of the feudal into the capitalist mode of production and constantly reproduced by the mechanism of the capitalist mode of production in this hereditary state of property-lessness, the working class cannot adequately express its condition in terms of the legal illusion of the bourgeoisie. It can only fully perceive this condition itself if it views things as they really are, without legally tinted spectacles. And it was enabled to do this by Marx with his materialist conception of history, with the proof that all of people's legal, political, philosophical, religious, etc., ideas ultimately derive from their economic conditions, from the way in which they produce and exchange products. This set out the world view corresponding to the conditions of proletarian life and struggle; the workers' lack of property could only be matched by a corresponding lack of illusions. And this proletarian world view is now spreading throughout the world.

Understandably, the struggle between the two world views continues; not only between proletariat and bourgeoisie, but also between free-thinking workers and those still dominated by the old tradition. On the whole, ordinary politicians here use the customary arguments to defend the old view. But there are also so-called scholarly lawyers, who have made legal sophistry a profession of their own.*

Until now these gentlemen have considered themselves too refined to deal with the theoretical aspect of the labour movement. We should therefore be extremely grateful that a real professor of law, Dr. Anton Menger, at last deigns to give a "closer dogmatic elucidation" of the history of socialism from the viewpoint of the "philosophy of law".**

In fact the socialists have hitherto been barking up the wrong tree. They have neglected the very thing that mattered most.

"Not until socialist ideas are detached from the interminable *economic* and philanthropic discussions ... and transformed into down-to-earth legal terms" (p. III), not until all the "politico-economic frippery" (p. 37) is done away with, can the "legal treatment of socialism ... the most important task of the contemporary philosophy of law" [p. III] be taken in hand.

Now, "socialist ideas" are concerned precisely with economic relations, above all the relation between wage labour and capital, and, this being so, these economic discussions would appear, after all, to amount to more than mere detachable "frippery". Moreover, political economy is a science, so called, and a somewhat more scientific one than the philosophy of law at that,

---

* See the article by *Fr. Engels* on "*Ludwig Feuerbach*" in the *Neue Zeit* IV, p. 206 [see this volume, p. 393]: "It is among professional politicians, theorists of public law and jurists of private law that the connection with economic facts gets well and truly lost. Since in each particular case the economic facts must assume the form of juristic motives in order to receive legal sanction; and since, in so doing, consideration has, of course, to be given to the whole legal system already in operation, the juristic form is, in consequence, made everything and the economic content nothing. Public law and private law are treated as separate spheres, each having its own independent historical development, each being capable of, and needing, a systematic presentation by the consistent elimination of all innate contradictions."

** Dr. Anton Menger, *Das Recht auf den vollen Arbeitsertrag in geschichtlicher Darstellung*, Stuttgart, Cotta, 1886, X, p. 171.

being concerned with facts and not with mere ideas, like the latter. But this is a matter of total indifference to the professional lawyer. For him, economic research stands on a par with philanthropic rhetoric. *Fiat justitia, pereat mundus.*[a]

Furthermore, the "politico-economic frippery" in Marx—and this is what our lawyer finds hardest to swallow—is not simply economic research. It is essentially historical. It demonstrates the course of social development, from the feudal mode of production of the Middle Ages to the advanced capitalism of today, the demise of earlier classes and class antagonisms and the formation of new classes with new conflicts of interest manifesting themselves, inter alia, in new legal demands. Even our lawyer seems to have a faint glimmering of this, discovering on p. 37 that today's

"philosophy of law ... is essentially nothing more than a replica of the state of the law as handed down by history", which could be "termed the *bourgeois philosophy of law*" and "alongside which a *philosophy of law of unpropertied classes of the people* has emerged in the shape of socialism".

But if this is so, what is the cause? Where do the "bourgeois" and the "unpropertied classes of the people" come from, each possessing a specific philosophy of law corresponding to its class position? From the law, or from economic development? What else does Marx tell us but that the views of law held by each of the large social classes conform with their respective class positions? How did Menger get in among the Marxists?

Yet this is but an oversight, an inadvertent acknowledgement of the strength of the new theory which the stern lawyer let slip, and which we shall therefore simply record. On the contrary, when our man of law is on his home, legal ground, he scorns economic history. The declining Roman Empire is his favourite example.

"The means of production were never so centralised," he tells us, "as when half the African province was in the possession of six people ... never were the sufferings of the working classes greater than when almost every productive worker was a slave. Neither was there at that time any lack of fierce criticism of the existing social order—particularly from the Church Fathers—which could rival the best socialist writings of the present; nevertheless, the fall of the Western Roman Empire was not followed by socialism, for instance, but—by the medieval legal system" (p. 108).

And why did this happen? Because

"the nation did not have a clear picture of the future order, one free of all effusiveness".

---

[a] Let justice be done, though the world perish (a dictum attributed to Emperor Ferdinand I of Austria (1556-64). See J. Manlius, *Loci Communes,* II, p. 290).— *Ed.*

Mr. Menger is of the opinion that during the decline of the Roman Empire the *economic* preconditions for modern socialism were in existence; it was simply its legal formulation that was lacking. Because of this, it was feudalism, and not socialism, that took over, making a nonsense of the materialist conception of history!

What the lawyers of the declining Roman Empire had formed so neatly into a system was not *feudal* law but Roman law, the law of a society of commodity producers. Since Mr. Menger operates on the assumption that the legal idea is the driving force of history, he now makes the quite preposterous demand on the Roman lawyers that, instead of the legal system of existing Roman society, they should have delivered the very opposite—"a clear picture, free of all effusiveness", of an imaginary social system. So that is Menger's philosophy of law, applied to *Roman* law! But Menger's claim that the economic conditions had never been so favourable to socialism as under the Roman Emperors is downright horrendous. The socialists that Menger seeks to disprove see the guarantee of socialism's success in the development of production itself. On the one hand, the development of large-scale machine-based enterprises in industry and agriculture makes production increasingly social, and the productivity of labour enormous; this necessitates the abolition of class distinctions and the transfer of commodity production in private enterprises into direct production for and by society. On the other hand, the modern mode of production gives rise to the class which increasingly gains the power for, and interest in, actually carrying through this development: a free, working proletariat.

Now compare the conditions in imperial Rome, where there was no question of large-scale machine-based production, either in industry or in agriculture. True, we find a concentration of land*ownership,* but one would have to be a lawyer to equate this with the development of labour performed socially in large enterprises. For the sake of argument, let us present Mr. Menger with three examples of landownership. Firstly, an Irish landlord who owns 50,000 acres tilled by 5,000 tenants in smallholdings averaging 10 acres; secondly, a Scottish landlord who has turned 50,000 acres into hunting grounds; and thirdly, an immense American farm of 10,000 acres, growing wheat on a large industrial scale. No doubt he will declare that in the first two cases the concentration of the means of production has advanced five times as far as in the last.

The development of Roman agriculture during the imperial age led, on the one hand, to the extension of pastoral farming over vast areas and the depopulation of the land; on the other, to the fragmentation of the estates into smallholdings which were handed over to *colons* and became miniature enterprises run by dependent small farmers, the forerunners of the serfs, thus establishing a mode of production that already contained the germ of the medieval one. And it was for this reason among others, esteemed Mr. Menger, that the Roman world was superseded by the "medieval legal system". No doubt there were, at various times, large-scale agricultural enterprises in individual provinces, but there was no machine production with free workers—it was a *plantation* economy that used *slaves,* barbarians of widely differing nationalities, who often could not understand one another. Then there were the free proletarians: not *working* proletarians but the *Lumpen*proletarians. Nowadays society increasingly depends on the labour of the proletarians and they are becoming increasingly essential to its continued survival; the Roman Lumpenproletarians were parasites who were not merely useless but even harmful to society, and hence lacked any effective power.

But to Mr. Menger's way of thinking, the mode of production and the people were apparently never so ripe for socialism as they were in the imperial age! The advantage of steering well clear of economic "fripperies" is obvious.

We shall allow him the Church Fathers, since he says nothing as to wherein their "criticism of the existing social order ... could rival the best socialist writings of the present". We are indebted to the Church Fathers for not a little interesting information about Roman society in decline, but as a rule they never engaged in *criticism,* being content simply to *condemn* it, and they often did it in such strong terms that the fiercest language of the modern socialists, and even the clamour of the anarchists, seem tame in comparison. Is this the "superiority" to which Mr. Menger refers?

With the same contempt for historical fact that we have just observed, Menger states on p. 2 that the privileged classes receive their income *without personal services to society* in return. So the fact that ruling classes in the ascendant phase of their development have very definite social functions to perform, and for this very reason become ruling classes, is quite unknown to him. While socialists recognise the temporary historical justification for these classes, Menger here declares their appropriation of surplus product to be theft. Therefore, it must come as a surprise to him to find on pp. 122 and 123 that these classes are daily losing more and more of the *power* to protect their right to this income. That this power consists in the performance of social functions and vanishes at a later stage of development with the demise of these functions is a complete enigma to this great thinker.

Enough. The worthy professor then proceeds to deal with socialism from the point of view of the philosophy of law, in other words, to reduce it to a few brief legal formulas, to socialist "basic rights", a new edition of human rights for the nineteenth century. Such basic rights have, of course,

"little practical effect", but they are "not without their uses in the scientific sphere" as "*slogans*" (pp. 5, 6).

So we have already sunk to the point where we are only dealing with *slogans*. First the historical context and content of this mighty movement are eliminated to make way for mere "philosophy of law", and then this philosophy of law is reduced to slogans which, it is admitted, are not worth a rap in practice! It was certainly worth the trouble.

The worthy professor now discovers that the *whole of socialism* can be reduced, legally speaking, to *three* such slogans, three basic rights. These are:

1. the right to the full proceeds of one's labour,
2. the right to a livelihood,
3. the right to work.

The right to work is only a provisional demand, "the first clumsy formula wherein the revolutionary demands of the proletariat are summarised" (Marx),[a] and thus does not belong here. Yet he overlooks the demand for *equality,* which dominated all of French revolutionary socialism, from Babeuf to Cabet and Proudhon, but which Mr. Menger will hardly be able to formulate legally, although (or perhaps because) it is the most legalistic of all the demands mentioned. We are thus left with a quintessence consisting of the meagre propositions 1 and 2, which, to cap it all, are mutually contradictory. Menger finally realises this on p. 27, but it in no way prevents every socialist system from having to live with them (p. 6). But it is quite evident that cramming widely differing socialist doctrines from widely differing countries and stages of development into these two "slogans" is bound to adulterate the entire exposé. The peculiarity of each individual doctrine—what actually constitutes its historical importance—is not merely cast aside as a matter of secondary importance; it is

---

[a] K. Marx, *The Class Struggles in France, 1848 to 1850,* present edition, Vol. 10, pp. 77-78.— *Ed.*

actually rejected as quite wrong because it diverges from the slogan and contradicts it.

The work we discuss deals only with No. 1, the right to the full proceeds of one's labour.

The worker's right to the full proceeds of his labour, that is, each individual worker's right to *his* specific proceeds, is only found in this strict sense in the doctrine of Proudhon. To demand that the means of production and the products should belong to the workers as a whole is quite a different matter. This demand is communist and, as Menger discovers on p. 48, goes *beyond* demand No. 1, which causes him a good deal of embarrassment. Consequently, one moment he has to place the communists under No. 2, and the next he has to twist and turn basic right No. 1 until he can fit them in there. This occurs on p. 7. Here it is assumed that even after commodity production has been abolished it nevertheless continues to exist. It seems quite natural to Mr. Menger that even in a socialist society *exchange values,* i.e. commodities for sale, are produced and the *prices of labour* continue to exist—in other words, that labour power continues to be sold as a commodity. The only point which concerns him is whether the historically inherited prices of labour will be maintained in a socialist society with a surcharge, or whether there ought to be

"a completely new method of determining the prices of labour".

The latter would, in his opinion, shake society even more severely than the introduction of the socialist social system itself. This confusion of concepts is understandable as on p. 94 our scholar talks about a *socialist theory of value,* imagining, as others have done before him, that Marx's theory of value is supposed to provide a yardstick for distribution in the society of the future. Indeed, on p. 56 it is stated that the full proceeds of labour are nothing definite, as they can be calculated according to at least *three* different standards, and eventually, on pp. 161, 162, we are told that the full proceeds of labour constitute the "natural principle of distribution" and are only possible in a society with common property but individual use—that is, a society not today proposed as an ultimate goal by a single socialist anywhere! What an excellent basic right! And what an excellent philosopher of the law for the working class!

In this way Menger has made it easy for himself to give a "critical" presentation of the history of socialism. Three words I'll tell you of import great, and even though they are not on everyone's lips,[a] they are quite sufficient for the matriculation examination that is being carried out with the socialists here. So step this way, Saint-Simon, over here, Proudhon, come on, Marx and whatever you are called: Do you swear by No. 1, or No. 2, or No. 3? Now quick into my Procrustean bed, and if anything overhangs, I'll chop it off, as economic and philanthropic fripperies!

The point at issue is simply in whom the three basic rights foisted onto socialism by Menger are first to be found: whoever is the first to come up with one of these formulas is the great man. Understandably enough, it is impossible to do such a thing without dropping a few ridiculous clangers, the would-be learned apparatus notwithstanding. He believes, for example, that to the Saint-Simonists the *oisifs* denote the owning classes and the *travailleurs,* the working classes (p. 67), in the title of Saint-Simon's work *Les oisifs et les travailleurs.— Fermages, loyers, intérêts, salaires* (The Idle and the Workers.— Farm Rents, Rents, Interest, Wages),[b] where the absence of *profit* alone should have taught him better. On the same page Menger himself quotes a key passage from the *Globe,* the organ of Saint-Simonism, which, alongside the scholars and the artists, lavishes praise on the *industriels,* i.e. the *manufacturers,* (as opposed to the *oisifs*) as mankind's benefactors and which simply demands the abolition of the tribute to the *oisifs,* that is, the *rentiers,* those who are in receipt of farm rent, rent and interest. In this list, *profit* is again excluded. In the Saint-Simonist system the manufacturer occupies a prominent position as a powerful and well-paid agent of society, and Mr. Menger would do well to study this position more closely before continuing his treatment of it from the point of view of the philosophy of law.

On page 73 we are told that in the *Contradictions économiques* Proudhon had, *"albeit rather obscurely"*, promised "a new solution of the social problem", while retaining commodity production and competition. What the worthy professor still finds *rather obscure* in 1886, Marx saw through as early as in 1847, demonstrating that it was actually an old idea, and predicting the bankruptcy that Proudhon in fact suffered in 1849.[511]

But enough of this. Everything we have discussed up to now is only of secondary concern to Mr. Menger, and also to his audience. If he had only written a history of right No. 1, his book

---

[a] Paraphrase of two lines from Schiller's poem "Die Worte des Glaubens".— *Ed.*

[b] Headline of an article by B. P. Enfantin published in *Le Globe,* No. 66, March 7, 1831.— *Ed.*

would have disappeared without a trace. The history is only a
pretext for writing the book; the purpose of that book is to *drag
Marx down.* And it is only read because it deals with Marx. For a
long time now it has not been so easy to criticise him—ever since
an understanding of his system has gained wider currency and the
critic has no longer been able to count on the ignorance of his
audience. There is only one option: in order to drag Marx down,
his achievements are attributed to other socialists in whom no one
is interested, who have vanished from the scene and who have no
political or scientific importance any longer. In this way they hope
to dispose of the founder of the proletarian world view, and
indeed the world view itself. Mr. Menger undertook the task.
People are not professors for nothing. They want to make their
mark, too.

The matter becomes quite simple.

The present social order gives landowners and capitalists a
"right" to part—the bulk—of the product produced by the
worker. Basic right No. 1 says that this right is a wrong and the
worker should have the whole proceeds of his labour. This takes
care of the entire content of socialism, unless basic right No. 2
comes into the picture. So whoever first said that the present right
of those who own the soil and the other means of production to
part of the proceeds of labour is a *wrong* is the great man, the
founder of "scientific" socialism! And these men were *Godwin, Hall*
and *Thompson.* Leaving out all the interminable economic fripperies and getting to the legal residue, Menger finds nothing but
the same assertion in Marx. Consequently Marx simply copied
these old Englishmen, particularly Thompson, and took care to
keep quiet about his source. The proof has been adduced.

We give up any attempt to make this hidebound lawyer
understand *that nowhere does Marx demand the "right to the full
proceeds of labour",* that he makes no legal demands of any kind at
all in his theoretical works. Even our lawyer seems to have a faint
inkling of this when he reproaches Marx for nowhere giving

"a thorough presentation of the right to the full proceeds of labour" (p. 98).

In Marx's theoretical studies legal right, which always merely
reflects the economic conditions prevalent in a specific society, is
only considered as a matter of purely secondary importance; his
main concern is the historical justification for certain conditions,
modes of appropriation and social classes in specific ages, the
investigation of which is of prime importance to anyone who sees
in history a coherent, though often disrupted, course of develop-

ment rather than, as the eighteenth century did, a mere muddle of folly and brutality. Marx views the historical inevitability of, and hence the justification for, the slave-owners of classical times, the feudal lords of the Middle Ages, etc., as the lever of human development for a limited historical period. He thereby also recognises the temporary historical justification for exploitation, for the appropriation of the product of labour by others. Yet at the same time he demonstrates that not only has this historical justification disappeared, but that the continued existence of exploitation in any form, far from furthering social development, is daily impeding it more and more and involving it in increasingly violent collisions. Menger's attempt to force these epoch-making historical investigations into his narrow, legalistic Procrustean bed only goes to show his total inability to understand things that go beyond the narrowest legal horizon. Basic right No. 1, as formulated by him, does not exist for Marx at all.

But here it comes!

Mr. Menger has discovered the term "SURPLUS VALUE" in Thompson. No doubt about it—Thompson is the discoverer of surplus value, and Marx a wretched plagiarist:

"In Thompson's views one immediately recognises the mode of thinking, indeed even the forms of expression, that are later found in so many socialists, particularly *Marx* and *Rodbertus*" (p. 53).

Thompson is therefore undeniably the "foremost founder of scientific socialism" (p. 49). And what does this scientific socialism consist in?

The view "that rent and profits on capital are deductions which the owners of land and capital make from the full proceeds of labour, is by no means *peculiar to socialism*, as many representatives of bourgeois political economy, e.g. Adam Smith, *proceed from the same opinion*. Thompson and his followers are *original only in so far* as they regard rent and profit on capital as *wrongful* deductions that conflict with the worker's right to the full proceeds of his labour" (pp. 53-54).

Thus scientific socialism does not consist in discovering an economic fact—according to Menger, this had already been done by earlier economists—but simply in declaring this fact *wrongful*. That is Mr. Menger's view of the matter. If the socialists had really made it so easy for themselves, they could have packed up long ago, and Mr. Menger would have been spared his legal-philosophical clanger. But that's what happens when you reduce a movement in world history to legal slogans that fit in your waistcoat pocket.

But what about the surplus value stolen from Thompson? The facts of the matter are as follows:

In his *Inquiry into the Principles of Distribution of Wealth etc.* (Chapter 1, section 15), Thompson considers

"what proportion of the products of their labour ought the labourers to pay" ("OUGHT", literally "are obliged", hence "ought to pay under the law") "for the use of the articles, called capital, to the possessors of them, called capitalists". The capitalists say that "without this capital, in the shape of machinery, materials, etc., mere labour would be unproductive; and therefore it is but just that the labourer should pay for the use of that". And Thompson continues: "Doubtless, the labourer must pay for the use of these, when so unfortunate as not himself to possess them; the question is, how much of the products of his labour OUGHT[a] to be subtracted for their use" (p. 128 of the Pare edition of 1850).

This certainly does not sound at all like the "right to the full proceeds of labour". On the contrary, Thompson finds it quite acceptable that the worker should forfeit part of the proceeds of his labour for the use of the borrowed capital. The question for him is simply how much. Here there are "two measures, the worker's and the capitalist's". And what is the worker's measure? It is

"the contribution of such sums as would replace the waste and value of the capital, by the time it would be consumed, with such *added compensation* to the owner and SUPERINTENDENT of it, as would support him *in equal comfort* with the MORE ACTIVELY EMPLOYED[b] productive labourers".

Thus, then, is the *worker*'s demand, according to Thompson, and anyone who does not "immediately recognise the mode of thinking, indeed even the forms of expression" from "Marx" would be mercilessly failed in Mr. Menger's philosophy-of-law examination.

But surplus value—what about surplus value? Patience, dear reader, we are almost there.

"The measure of the capitalist would be the *additional value produced* by the same quantity of labour, *in consequence of the use of the machinery* or other capital; *the whole of such surplus value* to be enjoyed by the capitalist for his superior intelligence and skill in accumulating and advancing to the labourers his capital, or the use of it" (Thompson, p. 128).

This passage, taken literally, is utterly incomprehensible. No production is possible without the means of production. But the means of production are here assumed to be in the form of capital, i.e. in the possession of capitalists. So if the worker

---

[a] The English word "ought" is given after the quotation, which is in German.— *Ed.*

[b] The English words "superintendent" and "more actively employed" are given after their German equivalents in the text.— *Ed.*

produces without the "use of machinery or other capital", he is attempting the impossible; he does not in fact produce anything at all. But if he does produce *with* the use of capital, then his *entire* product would be what is called surplus value here. So let's read on. On p. 130 Thompson has the same capitalist say:

"Before the invention of machinery, before the accommodation of workshops, or factories, what was the amount of produce which the unaided powers of the labourer produced? Whatever that was, let him still enjoy... To the maker of the buildings or the machinery, or to him who by voluntary exchange acquired them, let all the *surplus value* of the manufactured article go, as a reward", etc.

Here Thompson's capitalist is simply expressing the manufacturers' everyday illusion that the working hour of the worker producing with the aid of machinery, etc., produces a greater *value* than the working hour of the simple artisan before the invention of machinery. This notion is fostered by the *extraordinary* "surplus value" pocketed by the capitalist who breaks into a field hitherto held by manual labour, with a newly invented machine on which he and perhaps a few other capitalists have a monopoly. In this case, the price of the hand-made product determines the market price of the entire output of this sector of industry; the machine-made product might cost a mere quarter of the labour, thus leaving the manufacturer with a "surplus value" of 300 per cent of his cost price.

Naturally, the general spread of the new machine soon puts paid to this sort of "surplus value"; but then the capitalist notices that as the machine-made product comes to determine the market price and this price progressively falls to the real value of the machine-made product, the price of the hand-made product also falls and is thus forced down below its previous value, so that machine labour still produces a certain "surplus value" compared with manual labour. Thompson places this fairly common self-deception in the mouth of his manufacturer. How little he shares it himself, however, he expressly states immediately before this, on p. 127:

"The materials, the buildings, the wages, can add nothing to their own value. The *additional value* proceeds from labour alone."

We must beg our reader's indulgence when we point out especially for Mr. Menger's edification that this "additional value" of Thompson's is by no means the same as Marx's surplus value but the *entire* value added to the raw material by labour, that is, the sum total of the value of the labour power and surplus value in the Marxian sense.

Only now, after this indispensable "economic frippery", can we fully appreciate the audacity with which Mr. Menger says on p. 53:

"In Thompson's view ... the capitalists consider ... *the* difference between *the worker's necessities of life* and the real proceeds of their labour, rendered more productive by machinery and other capital expenditure, to be SURPLUS (or ADDITIONAL) VALUE,[a] which must fall to the owners of land and capital."

This purports to be the "free" German rendering of the passage that we quoted above from Thompson, p. 128. But all that Thompson's capitalist is referring to is the difference between the product of THE SAME QUANTITY OF LABOUR,[a] according to whether the work is performed with or without the use of capital: the difference between the product of the same quantity of labour performed manually or with the help of machines. Mr. Menger can only smuggle in "the worker's necessities of life" by totally falsifying Thompson.

To sum up: The "surplus value" of Thompson's capitalist is not Thompson's "surplus" or "additional value"; much less is either of them Mr. Menger's "surplus value"; and least of all is any of the three Marx's "surplus value".

But that does not bother Mr. Menger in the slightest. On p. 53 he continues:

"Rent and profit on capital are therefore nothing but deductions which the owners of land and capital are able to make from the full proceeds of labour, to the detriment of the worker, by virtue of their legal position of power"—the whole substance of this sentence is already found in Adam Smith—and then he triumphantly exclaims: "In *Thompson*'s views one immediately recognises the mode of thinking, indeed even the forms of expression, that are later found in so many socialists, particularly Marx and Rodbertus."

In other words, Mr. Menger came across the term SURPLUS (or ADDITIONAL) VALUE in Thompson, only managing to conceal by means of an outright misrepresentation that in Thompson the term is used in two totally different senses, which again are both totally different from the sense in which Marx uses the term surplus value [*Mehrwert*].

This is the entire substance of his momentous discovery! What a pitiful result when set against the grandiose proclamation in the preface:

"In this work I shall *present proof* that *Marx* and *Rodbertus* borrowed their principal socialist theories from older English and French theorists, without giving the sources of their views."

---

[a] The English words are given after their German equivalents in the text.— *Ed.*

41–1243

How miserable the comparison that precedes this sentence now seems:

"If anyone had 'discovered' the theory of the division of labour thirty years after the publication of Adam Smith's work on the wealth of nations, or if a writer today sought to present Darwin's theory of evolution as his own intellectual property, he would be considered either an *ignoramus* or a *charlatan.* Only in the social sciences, which almost entirely lack an historical tradition, are successful attempts of this kind conceivable."

We shall disregard the fact that Menger still believes Adam Smith "discovered" the division of labour, while Petty had fully developed this point as long as eighty years before Adam Smith. What Menger says about Darwin, however, now rather rebounds on him. Back in the sixth century B. C., the Ionian philosopher Anaximander put forward the view that man had evolved out of a fish, and this, it will be recalled, is also the view of modern evolutionary science. Now if someone were to stand up and maintain that the mode of thinking and indeed the forms of expression of Darwin could be recognised in Anaximander and that Darwin had done nothing more than plagiarise Anaximander carefully concealing his source, he would be adopting exactly the same approach to Darwin and Anaximander as Mr. Menger adopts to Marx and Thompson. The worthy professor is right: "only in the social sciences" can one count on the ignorance that makes "successful attempts of this kind conceivable".

But as he places so much emphasis on the term "surplus value", regardless of the concept associated with it, let us divulge a secret to this great expert on the literature of socialism and political economy: not only does the term "SURPLUS PRODUCE" occur in Ricardo (in the chapter on wages),[a] but the expression "*plus-value*", alongside the "*mieux-value*" employed by Sismondi, is commonly used in business circles in France, and has been used as far back as anyone can remember, to designate any increase in value that does not cost the owner of the commodities anything. This would seem to make it doubtful whether Menger's discovery of Thompson's discovery (or rather Thompson's capitalist's discovery) of surplus value will be recognised even by the philosophy of law.

However, Mr. Menger is not finished with Marx yet, by any means. Just listen:

"It is characteristic that Marx and Engels have been *misquoting* this *fundamental work* of English socialism" (viz. Thompson) "for forty years" (p. 50).

---

[a] D. Ricardo, *On the Principles of Political Economy, and Taxation,* pp. 90-115.— Ed.

So Marx—not content with hushing up his secret Egeria for forty years—also has to go and misquote her! And not just once, but for forty years. And not only Marx, but Engels too! What an accumulation of premeditated villainy! Poor Lujo Brentano, who has been hunting in vain for twenty years for just one single misquotation by Marx, and during this witch-hunt has not only burnt his own fingers but has brought ruin upon his gullible friend Sedley-Taylor of Cambridge[512]—kick yourself, Lujo, for not finding it! And in what does it consist, this horrendous falsification that has been stubbornly pursued for forty years, is "characteristic" into the bargain, and, to cap it all, is given the character of a treacherous plot by Engels' malicious forty-year-long complicity?

"...misquoting for forty years by giving its year of publication as 1827!"

When the book had appeared as early as 1824! "Characteristic", indeed—of Mr. Menger. But that is far from being the only—listen here, Lujo!—the only misquotation by Marx and Engels, who seem to practise misquotation professionally—perhaps even on the move? In the *Misère de la philosophie* (1847) Marx got *Hodgskin* mixed up with *Hopkins,* and forty years later (nothing less than forty years will satisfy these wicked men) Engels commits the same offence in his preface to the German translation of the *Misère.*[513] With his eagle eye for printer's errors and slips of the pen it really is a loss to mankind that the good professor did not become a printer's proofreader. But no—we must take back this compliment. Mr. Menger is no good at reading proofs, either; for he, too, commits slips of the pen, that is to say, he misquotes. This happens not only with English titles but also with German ones. He refers, for instance, to "Engels' translation of this work", i.e. the *Misère.* According to the title page of the work the translation was not by Engels. In the preface in question Engels quotes the passage from Marx mentioning Hopkins *verbatim*: he was thus obliged to reproduce the error in his quotation in order not to misquote Marx. But these people simply cannot do anything right for Mr. Menger.

But enough of these trivia in which our philosopher of law takes such delight. It is "characteristic" of the man and the likes of him that he feels obliged to show he has read two or three more books than Marx had "forty years ago", in 1847, even though he became familiar with the entire literature on the subject through Marx in the first place—nowhere does he quote a single English author not already quoted by Marx, apart from perhaps Hall and

world-famous people like Godwin, Shelley's father-in-law. A man
who has the titles of all the books quoted by Marx in his pocket
and all the present facilities and amenities of the British Museum
at his disposal and is unable to make any discovery in this field
apart from the fact that Thompson's DISTRIBUTION appeared in
1824, and not 1827, really should not brag about his bibliographi-
cal erudition.

The same applies to Mr. Menger as to many other social
reformers of our day: grand words and negligible deeds, if any.
He promises to demonstrate that Marx is a plagiarist—and shows
that one *word,* "Mehrwert" [surplus value], had been used before
Marx, though in a different sense!

The same holds for Mr. Menger's legal socialism. In his preface,
Mr. Menger declares that in the

"legal treatment of socialism" he sees the "most important task of the
philosophy of law *of our time....* Its correct handling will substantially contribute
to ensuring that the indispensable amendments of our legal system are effected by
way of a peaceful reform. Only when the ideas of socialism are transformed into
sober legal concepts will the practical politicians be able to acknowledge how far the
existing legal system needs reforming in the interests of the suffering masses." [a]

He intends to set about this transformation by presenting
socialism as a legal system.

And what does this legal treatment of socialism amount to? In
the "Concluding Remarks" he says:

"There can surely be no doubt that the formation of a legal system that is fully
dominated by these fundamental legal concepts" (basic rights 1 and 2) "can only be
a matter of the distant future" (p. 163).

What appears to be the most important task of "our time" in
the preface is assigned to the "distant future" at the end.

"The necessary changes" (in the existing legal system) "will take place by way of
prolonged historical development, just as our present social system eroded and
destroyed the feudal system over the centuries, *until all that was needed was one blow
to completely eliminate it"* (p. 164).

Fine words, but what place is there for the philosophy of law if
society's "historical development" brings about the necessary
changes? In the preface it is the lawyers who determine the course
taken by social development; now that the lawyer is about to be
taken at his word, his pluck deserts him and he mutters something
about historical development, which does everything on its own.

"But does our social development advance towards realising the right to the full
proceeds of one's labour or the right to work?"

---

[a] A. Menger, *Das Recht auf den vollen Arbeitsertrag...,* p. III.— *Ed.*

Mr. Menger declares that he does not know. How ignominiously he now abandons his socialist "basic rights". But if these basic rights cannot coax a dog away from the hearth, if they do not determine and realise social development but are determined and realised by it, why go to all the trouble of reducing socialism to the basic rights? Why all the bother of stripping socialism of its economic and historical "fripperies", if we are to find out in hindsight that these "fripperies" are its real substance? Why only tell us at the end that the whole study is utterly pointless, since the objective of the socialist movement cannot be perceived by turning the ideas of socialism into sober legal concepts but only by studying social development and its motive forces?

Mr. Menger's wisdom ultimately amounts to declaring that he cannot say which direction social development will take, but he is sure of one thing: "the weaknesses of our present social system should not be *artificially* exacerbated" (p. 166) and, to make it possible to preserve these "weaknesses", he recommends—*free trade* and the avoidance of further *indebtedness* on the part of the State and the local communities!

This advice is the sole tangible result of Mr. Menger's philosophy of law, which presents itself with such fuss and self-praise. What a pity that the worthy professor does not let us into the secret of how modern states and local communities are supposed to manage without "contracting national and local debts". If he should happen to know the secret, let him not keep it to himself forever. It would certainly pave his way "to the top" and a ministerial portfolio a good deal faster than his achievements in the "philosophy of law" ever will.

Whatever reception these achievements may find in "high places", we believe we can safely say that the socialists of the present and the future will make Mr. Menger a gift of all his basic rights, or at any rate will refrain from disputing his right to the "full proceeds of his labour".

This does not mean to say, of course, that the socialists will refrain from making *specific legal demands*. An active socialist party is impossible without such demands, like any political party. The demands that derive from the common interests of a class can only be put into effect by this class taking over political power and securing universal validity for its demands by making them law. Every class in struggle must therefore set forth its demands in the form of *legal demands* in a programme. But the demands of every class change in the course of social and political transformations, they differ from country to country according to the country's distinctive features and level of social development. For this reason, too, the legal demands of the individual parties, for all their agreement on ultimate goals, are not entirely the same at all times and for every nation. They are an element subject to change and are revised from time to time, as may be observed among the socialist parties of different countries. When such revisions are made, it is the *actual conditions* that have to be taken into account, it has not, however, occurred to any of the existing socialist parties to construct a new philosophy of law out of its programme, nor is this likely ever to happen in the future. At any rate, Mr. Menger's achievements in this field can only have a deterrent effect.

That is the only useful thing about his little book.

Written November-beginning of December 1886

First published in *Die Neue Zeit*, No. 2, 1887

Printed according to the journal

Published in English in full for the first time

TO THE EDITORS
OF THE *NEW YORKER VOLKSZEITUNG*[514]

In your article concerning me[a] in the *Volkszeitung* of March 2 [b] you maintain

"that Aveling is said to have submitted a bill which contained items that a labour agitator, who must know that the donations[c] raised to finance agitation come almost entirely out of the pockets of hard-working labourers, really should not present".

Passing over all the minor points and restricting my reply to the one main point, I wish to state:

The weekly bills submitted by me to the Executive contained all my expenses, that is to say both those chargeable to the Party and others to be met by me personally. I had made it clear to the Executive in advance and in the most unambiguous way—first in a verbal agreement with the treasurer, R. Meyer, and then in several letters—that all the purely personal expenses were to be defrayed by me in return for the $366.00 ($3 per day) guaranteed to me by the Executive, and that I left it entirely up to the Executive to decide which items of expenditure should be passed on to the party, and which items should be charged to me personally.

I never expected—even less demanded—that any of these personal items of expenditure should be paid for "out of the pockets of hard-working labourers", and indeed none of them have been. For further information about this I refer you to my

---

[a] Edward Aveling, on behalf of whom this letter was written.— *Ed.*

[b] "Affaire Aveling noch einmal", *New Yorker Volkszeitung*, No. 52, March 2, 1887.— *Ed.*

[c] The *New Yorker Volkszeitung* has "money".— *Ed.*

enclosed circular of February 26 to the sections,[515] to the publication of which I can no longer object after what has occurred.

In addition I would point out that a printing error has crept into your article. My reply to your article of January 12 [a] was dated not "Feb. 1887" but January 26, 1887, and was sent off to you on the same day that article came to my notice.

With social-democratic greetings.[b]

Edward Aveling

London, March 16, 1887

First published in the *New Yorker Volks-zeitung*, No. 76, March 30, 1887

Printed according to the manu-scrpit collated with the newspaper text

Published in English for the first time

---

[a] "Aveling und die Sozialisten", *New Yorker Volkszeitung*, No. 10, January 12, 1887.— *Ed.*

[b] This phrase is omitted in the text published in the newspaper.— *Ed.*

ENGELS' AMENDMENTS
TO THE PROGRAMME OF THE NORTH OF ENGLAND
SOCIALIST FEDERATION[516]

Wage-workers of all Countries — Unite!

THE NORTH OF ENGLAND SOCIALIST FEDERATION

(FOUNDED IN NORTHUMBERLAND, MAY, 1887)

PRINCIPLES[a]

The North of England Socialist Federation has been formed to educate and organize the people to achieve the economic emancipation of labour.

While fully sympathising with and helping every effort of the wage-earners to win better conditions of life under the present system, the Socialist Federation aims at abolishing the Capitalist and Landlord class, *as well as the wage-working class,* and forming //the workers of society// *all members of society* into a Co-operative Commonwealth.

An employing class monopolising all the means of getting and making wealth, and a wage-earning class compelled to work //primarily// for the profit of these employers, is a system of tyranny and slavery.

The antagonism of these two classes //brings about// *manifests itself in* fierce competition—for employment amongst the workers and for markets amongst the capitalists. This //gives rise to class hatred and class strife// *divides the nation against itself, forms it into two hostile camps,* and destroys real independence, liberty, and happiness.

The present system gives ease and luxury to the idlers, toil and poverty to the workers, and degradation to all; it is essentially unjust and should be abolished. *And it can be abolished, now that the productiveness of labour has become so vast that no extension of markets can absorb its overflowing produce, the very superabundance of the means*

---

[a] The words crossed out by Engels are given in double oblique lines, and the text added by him is printed in italics.—*Ed.*

of life and of enjoyment thus becoming the cause of stagnation of trade,
want of employment and consequent misery of the toiling millions.

Our aim is to bring about a Socialist System which will give
healthy and useful labour to all, ample wealth and leisure to all,
and the truest and fullest freedom to all.

All are invited to help the Socialist Federation in this great
cause. Adherents shall acknowledge truth, justice, and morality as
the basis of their conduct towards each other and towards all men.
They shall acknowledge *no rights without duties: no duties
without rights.*

Written between June 14 and 23, 1887

First published in: Marx and Engels,
Works, First Russian Edition, Vol. XVI,
Part 1, Moscow, 1937

Reproduced from the *Principles*
with amendments in Engels' hand

Published in English for the first
time

Wage-workers of all Countries—Unite!

THE NORTH OF ENGLAND
SOCIALIST FEDERATION.

(FOUNDED IN NORTHUMBERLAND, MAY, 1887.)

PRINCIPLES.

The North of England Socialist Federation has been formed to educate and organize the people to achieve the economic emancipation of labour.

While fully sympathising with and helping every effort of the wage-earners to win better conditions of life under the present system, the Socialist Federation aims at abolishing the Capitalist and Landlord class, and forming the workers of society into a Co-operative Commonwealth.

An employing class monopolising all the means of getting and making wealth, and a wage-earning class compelled to work primarily for the profit of these employers, is a system of tyranny and slavery.

The antagonism of these two classes brings about fierce competition—for employment amongst the workers and for markets amongst the capitalists. This gives rise to class hatred and class strife, and destroys real independence, liberty and happiness.

The present system gives ease and luxury to the idlers, toil and poverty to the workers, and degradation to all; it is essentially unjust and should be abolished.

Our aim is to bring about a Socialist System which will give healthy and useful labour to all, ample wealth and leisure to all, and the truest and fullest freedom to all.

All are invited to help the Socialist Federation in this great cause, Adherents shall acknowledge truth, justice, and morality as the basis of their conduct towards each other and towards all men. They shall acknowledge no RIGHTS WITHOUT DUTIES; NO DUTIES WITHOUT RIGHTS.

PROGRAMME.

The Socialist Federation seeks to gain its ends by working on the following lines:—

(1) Forming and helping other Socialist bodies to form a National and International Socialist Labour Party.

(2) Striving to conquer political power by promoting the election of Socialists to Parliament, Local governments, School Boards, and other, administrative bodies.

(3) Helping Trade Unions, Co-operation, and every genuine movement for the good of the workers.

(4) Promoting scheme for the National and International Federation of Labour.

All who agree with these objects are invited to become members.
For Rules see other side.

Programme of the North of England Socialist Federation with Engels' amendments

TO THE EDITOR OF *JUSTICE*[517]

Dear Comrade.—The Press has already announced that four German Socialists—Bernstein, Motteler, Schlueter and Tauscher, editors and publishers of the Zurich *Sozial Demokrat,*—have been expelled from Switzerland by the Federal Council of that country for "having abused the hospitality extended to them." This severe measure must appear all the more surprising, as the paper in question, during the eight years of its existence, has always carefully refrained from attacks upon Switzerland and Swiss institutions, and as its language generally has never been more moderate than during the last few months.

The official text of the order of expulsion giving the reasons upon which the Federal Council bases it, is now before us, and these reasons are surprising indeed. The Federal Council would make us believe that its attention was first called to the *Sozial Demokrat,* not by anything published by that paper itself, but by a comic paper, printed in the same office in January, 1887, of which only one number was bought! And yet the *Sozial Demokrat* from the first day of its publication had been watched with the greatest and most constant attention by the German authorities, and, at their request by the Swiss authorities.

The Federal Council having thus become aware of the necessity of watching the *Sozial Demokrat,* now found out, as it tells us, that this paper "was written in a generally violent language offensive to the authorities of the German Empire." That is to say, the paper did not proclaim actual and forcible resistance against the State power in Germany, much less in Switzerland. It merely stigmatised as such and called by their proper names, the infamies committed in Germany by the authors of the Anti-Socialist Law and their executive tools. That, however, is "abuse of hospitality" in a republic, which itself celebrates year by year in hundreds of commemorative festivals the homicidal act of William Tell, and brags of the asylum it offers to refugees of all nations.

In consequence of this violent language, we are further informed, an official warning was administered to the *Sozial Demokrat,* which, however, had not the desired effect. "Certainly the editors henceforth took care to avoid coarsely offensive expressions." But they declined "to change anything in the fundamental programme of the paper," and moreover they "reproduced articles which appeal to force, though accompanied by commentaries intended to make people believe in the moderation of the paper itself." To prove this latter grave offence, the Federal Council states that on April 7th, 1888, the *Sozial Demokrat* reprinted certain resolutions passed in 1866—twenty-two years ago!—by 500 Germans in Zurich, resolutions calling upon the German people of that day to rise in arms against their government. In 1866 not one of the 500 Germans present at that meeting in Zurich was molested by the Federal Council on account of these resolutions. But if in 1888 the *Sozial Demokrat* merely states these facts, that is sufficient to expel from Switzerland four men connected with that paper.

Altogether the reasons given are ridiculous. But the fact is the Federal Council dared not state the real reasons for its actions: that Bismarck and Puttkamer, his home secretary, are furious at the German Social-Democrats in Switzerland having succeeded in unmasking a set of spies and agents provocateurs sent out by the German police in order to manufacture evidence to enable the government to demand the prolongation, and with increased stringency, of this Socialist Coercion Bill. The expulsion is Puttkamer's revenge for the defeat inflicted upon him by the Socialist members in the Reichstag and by the *Sozial Demokrat,* and the Federal Council acts as Puttkamer's humble servant. The expulsion of our comrades means the extension of the German Socialist Coercion Act to Switzerland; it means that the dynamitards of the Russian police will henceforth enjoy in Zurich the same official protection that is extended to them in Berlin.

The only country in Europe where a right of asylum may still be said to exist is England. No doubt Bismarck will try, as he has done before now, to draw England within the nets of his international political police and to place German Socialists, in England too, under his "petty state of siege." Will there be English statesmen prepared to meet him half way? If so, let us hope that English working men will know how to stop their government from playing the same abject and cowardly part now played by the Swiss Federal Council.

I am, dear comrade, yours fraternally,

Karl Kautsky

Written on April 25 or 26, 1888

Reproduced from the newspaper

First published in the newspaper *Justice*, No. 224, April 28, 1888

INTERVIEW GIVEN BY FREDERICK ENGELS
TO THE *NEW YORKER VOLKSZEITUNG*[518]

Question: Is socialism in England moving forward—that is, do the English working men's organisations accept the socialist critique of economic development more readily than they used to, and do they aspire—to any extent worth mentioning—to the "ultimate aims" of socialism?

Engels: I am quite satisfied with the progress of socialism and the workers' movement in England; but this progress mainly consists in the development of the proletarian consciousness of the *masses*. The official workers' organisations, the trade unions, which were threatening in places to become reactionary, are obliged to limp along behind, like the Austrian *Landsturm*.[519]

Question: What is the position in this respect in Ireland? Is there anything there—apart from the national question—that could arouse hope among socialists?

Engels: *A pure socialist movement cannot be expected from Ireland for quite a long time yet.* First people want to become small landowning farmers, and when they are, along comes the mortgage and ruins them all over again. Meanwhile that is no reason why we shouldn't help them to free themselves from their landlords—that is, to make the transition from a semi-feudal to a capitalist condition.

Question: What is the attitude of the English workers to the Irish movement?

Engels: The masses are *for* the Irish. The organisations, like the workers' aristocracy in general, follow Gladstone and the liberal bourgeois, and go no further than they.

Question: What do you think about Russia? That is, how far have you modified your view—which you and Marx expressed some six years ago when I a was in

---

a Theodor Cuno, the representative of the *New Yorker Volkszeitung*.—*Ed.*

London—that because of the nihilist, terrorist successes of the day the impulse for a European revolutionary movement would probably come from Russia?[a]

Engels: On the whole I am still of the opinion that a revolution or even just the convocation of some kind of national assembly in Russia would revolutionise the whole European political situation. But today this is no longer the most obvious possibility. To make up for it, we have a new William.[b]

To the question of how he would characterise the present European situation, Engels answered: "I have not seen a European paper for seven weeks now, so I am in no position to characterise anything that is going on over there."

This concluded the discussion.

First published in the *New Yorker Volks-zeitung*, No. 226, September 20, 1888

Printed according to the newspaper

---

[a] Marx and Engels expressed this idea in the "Preface to the Second Russian Edition of the *Manifesto of the Communist Party*" (see present edition, Vol. 24).— *Ed.*

[b] William II.— *Ed.*

NOTES
AND
INDEXES

NOTES

[1] Engels' works on the early history of the Germans relate to his study of the early stages in the development of society. They laid the basis for the historical materialist explanation of the origin of classes and the state and made a major contribution to the research into the history of the formation of European peoples.

These manuscripts were not published during the author's lifetime. Engels used part of the material he had collected in the essay "The Mark" (see present edition, Vol. 24, pp. 439-56).

During his work on the manuscript Engels may have changed his initial plan. The material relating to point 2 ("The District and Army Structure") of the draft plan, published here, is missing in the manuscript *On the Early History of the Germans* and is evidently used in the second chapter of *The Frankish Period* directly linked with the first manuscript. That Engels departed from his initial plan is also proved by the fact that *The Franconian Dialect* (see this volume, pp. 81-107), originally planned as a note, was transferred to *The Frankish Period* and elaborated as its component part.

The headings of the first three chapters of Engels' manuscript *On the Early History of the Germans* ("Caesar and Tacitus", "The First Battles Against Rome" and "Progress Until the Migration Period") were supplied by the editors according to Engels' draft plan; the heading of the fourth chapter ("Note: The German Peoples") is given in the manuscript by Engels himself.

On the Early History of the Germans was first published in Marx and Engels, *Works,* First Russian Edition, Vol. XVI, Part I, Moscow, 1937 and in the language of the original in Friedrich Engels, *Zur Geschichte und Sprache der deutschen Frühzeit. Ein Sammelband.* Besorgt vom Marx-Engels-Lenin Institut beim ZK des SED, Berlin, 1952, S. 37-94.

Passages from this work were published in English for the first time in: Marx, Engels, *On Literature and Art,* Progress Publishers, Moscow, 1976, pp. 187-88 and 212-14 and in full in Marx, Engels, *Pre-Capitalist Socio-Economic Formations.* A Collection, Progress Publishers, Moscow, 1979, pp. 298-360.

The dating of the draft plan, as of the works themselves, is given according to *MEGA*2, Abt. I, Bd. 25, S. 988-89.

In this volume, these works have been arranged according to the dates on which Engels completed them. p. 3

[2] In the nineteenth century the term *Aryans* referred to the peoples using Indo-European languages. Nowadays the term is applied to the tribes and peoples speaking Indo-Iranian languages.   p. 8

[3] Herodotus Halicarnassensis, *Historiae*, Book II, Chapter 33 and Book IV, Chapter 49. Most of the Greek and Latin sources are quoted by Engels from *Die Geschichtschreiber der deutschen Vorzeit*, published by v. G. H. Pertz, J. Grimm, etc., Vol. 1: *Die Urzeit*. Berlin, 1849.   p. 9

[4] *Periodos oder Über den Ozean*, a work by Pytheas of Massilia, has not been preserved and is only known from references by other ancient authors. p. 10

[5] The *great migration of peoples* (Völkerwanderung)—a conventional name for mass intrusions of the Germanic, Slavic, Sarmatian and other peoples into the territory of the Roman Empire in the 4th-7th centuries, which led to the collapse of the Western Roman Empire and the transition from slavery to feudalism throughout the Roman Empire.   p. 11

[6] See Note 1.   p. 19

[7] *Proconsul*—an office introduced in Ancient Rome in 327 B.C. Originally the proconsul discharged military duties outside Rome, but after the provinces were formed he acted as governor and military commander there (propraetor in minor provinces).   p. 24

[8] Germany received Roman law in the 15th and 16th centuries. Here, as in the rest of Europe, Roman law originated from Digests (or Pandects), the main part of the Byzantine codification of Roman law promulgated under Emperor Justinian in 533 (*Corpus iuris civilis*). Digests mainly cover private law regulating property, family, hereditary and liability relations, as well as criminal and procedural law.   p. 25

[9] *Lictor*—a minor official in Ancient Rome.   p. 25

[10] General Yorck, who in 1812 commanded a Prussian auxiliary corps of the Napoleonic army in Russia, concluded the Tauroggen Convention with the Russian Command on December 30, 1812, pledging to take no part in the fighting against the Russian army for two months.
In the Battle of Leipzig between the allied Russian, Austrian, Prussian and Swedish forces and the army of Napoleon I (October 16-19, 1813), the Saxon Corps, which fought in the ranks of Napoleon's army, at a crucial moment suddenly went over to the other side and turned its guns against the French.
                                          p. 29

[11] This refers to the mutiny in the mercenary army of the Spanish King Philip II, which occupied the Netherlands, in the summer and autumn of 1576. The soldiers revolted because they had not been paid for a number of years.
                                          p. 30

[12] The reference is to the insurrection of the Illyrian tribes (A.D. 6-9) sparked off by oppression on the part of the Roman administration, and unbearable taxes. It swept over Dalmatia and Pannonia, that is the whole of Illyricum. The insurgents killed Roman soldiers and merchants, attacked Macedonia and threatened Italy. Fifteen Roman legions were brought together to suppress the insurrection which was not quelled until the August of A.D. 9, following three military expeditions under the command of Tiberius and Germanicus. p. 30

13 The reference is to the Roman fortification which owes its name to the Germanic tribe of Angrivarians who lived on both banks of the Weser, north of the Cherusci and south of the Saxons.   p. 31

14 This refers to the ancient burial place which was discovered near the town of Hallstatt in Southwest Austria in 1846 and gave the name to the archaeological culture of the tribes inhabiting the southern part of Central Europe in the period of the early Iron Age (c. 900-400 B.C.).   p. 33

15 The reference is to the *Agri Decumates* (tithe lands). These lands, lying between the right bank of the Upper Rhine and the Danube, were annexed to the Roman Empire in A.D. 83 under Domitian and distributed among the Roman veterans and Gauls.   p. 34

16 The events described by Engels are mentioned in: Carl Fredrik Wiberg, *Der Einfluß der klassischen Völker auf den Norden durch den Handelsverkehr*, Hamburg, 1867, p. 115 and Hans Hildebrand, *Das heidnische Zeitalter in Schweden*, Hamburg, 1873, p. 182.   p. 38

17 This refers to *Leges barbarorum* (laws of the barbarians)—codes of law which originated between the 5th and 9th centuries and were, in the main, a written record of the customary or prescriptive law of the various Germanic tribes.
                                                                              p. 42

18 Alamannic law (*Lex Alamannorum*)—a code of common law of the Alamanni, one of the ancient Germanic tribes. It dates back to the period between the end of the 6th and 8th centuries and reflects the transition from the gentile and tribal system to early feudalism. Smiths are mentioned in Chapter LXXIV, 5.
                                                                              p. 42

19 Bavarian law (*Lex Baiuvariorum*)—a code of common law of the Bavarians, a Germanic tribe. It dates back to the mid-8th century and, distinct from Alamannic law, reflects a later stage in the development of the Germanic tribes, when the Mark community was disintegrating and feudalism just emerging. Punishment for theft is mentioned in Chapter IX, 2.   p. 42

20 Frisian law (*Lex Frisionum*)—a code of common law of the ancient Germanic tribe of Frisians (8th cent.). It contains passages borrowed from Alamannic law and certain revised enactments of the Frankish kings.   p. 42

21 Salic law (*Lex Salica*)—a code of common law of the Salian Franks, used by the greater part of the population of the Frankish state. Compiled in the early 6th century on the orders of King Clovis (481-511), it was supplemented and revised under his successors. Salic law reproduces various stages of ancient judicial procedure and is an important historical document showing the evolution of Frankish society from the primitive communal system to the emergence of feudal relations.   p. 42

22 The *grand army* (*grande armée*)—the name given in 1805 to the group of the armed forces of the French Empire operating in the main theatres of the Napoleonic wars. Besides French troops, it included contingents from various countries conquered by Napoleon (Italy, Holland, the German states and Poland).   p. 46

23 Pliny's work *Bellorum Germaniae libri* is not extant.   p. 46

24 The *Carolingians*—the dynasty of kings and emperors (from 800) in the Frankish state (751-10th cent.), which got its name from Charlemagne. The

policy pursued by the Carolingians was conducive to the growth of feudalism in Western Europe, accelerated the enserfment of the peasantry, strengthened the economic and political position of big landowners and led to the consolidation of central authority.

p. 48

25 In the first book of his *Natural History* Pliny lists the works by Roman and Greek authors whom he quotes, Strabo and Plutarch among them.   p. 56

26 Engels' manuscript *The Frankish Period* was not published during his lifetime.
The manuscript has two parts; the first part includes two chapters: "The Radical Transformation of the Relations of Landownership under the Merovingians and Carolingians" and "The District and Army Structure". The second part of the manuscript bears the title "Note: The Franconian Dialect". Each part is a complete whole. All headings are given in conformity with Engels' manuscript.

The Frankish Period was first published in full ("The Franconian Dialect" was published earlier, see Note 47) in: Marx and Engels, *Works*, First Russian Edition, Vol. XVI, Part I, Moscow, 1937, and in the language of the original in: Friedrich Engels, *Zur Geschichte und Sprache der deutschen Frühzeit. Ein Sammelband.* Berlin, 1952, S. 97-152.

The Frankish Period (without "Note: The Franconian Dialect") was published in English for the first time in: Marx, Engels, *Pre-Capitalist Socio-Economic Formations.* A Collection, Progress Publishers, Moscow, 1979.

p. 58

27 The *Merovingians*—the first royal dynasty in the Frankish state (457-751), which got its name from its legendary founder Merovaeus. The policy pursued by the Merovingians promoted the rise of feudal relations among the Franks. For the *Carolingians,* see Note 24.

p. 58

28 The terms the "Mark system" and "Mark" are explained in G. L. von Maurer, *Einleitung zur Geschichte der Mark-, Hof-, Dorf- und Stadt-Verfassung der öffentlichen Gewalt,* Munich, 1854, pp. 5 and 40.
For more details about the "Mark", see present edition, Vol. 24, pp. 439-56.

p. 58

29 See Note 17.

p. 59

30 *Antrustions*—warriors under the early Merovingians (see Note 27); evidently descendants of the gentile nobility.

p. 61

31 *Major-domo* (Lat. *major domus*)—the highest official in the Frankish state under the Merovingians (see Note 27). Originally the major-domo was appointed by the king and was in charge of the palace. As feudalism advanced and royal power was weakened the functions of major-domos were extended; they became the biggest landowners and concentrated state power in their hands. Most powerful of all were the major-domos from the Pepinide clan—Pepin of Heristal (687-712), Charles Martel (715-741) and Pepin the Short (741-751) who became the first king (751-768) of the Carolingian dynasty (see Note 24).

p. 61

32 The Saxons defeated the Frankish army at Mount Süntel on the right bank of the Weser (782).
For more than two centuries, from around 560, the Avars made innumerable raids on the territory of the Frankish state. In 796 the joint forces of the Franks and the southern Slavs destroyed the Avars' central fortification in Pusta-Ebene.

The Arabs, who conquered Spain at the beginning of the 8th century, invaded Southern Gaul in 720. In the Battle of Poitiers (732) Charles Martel defeated the Arabs and put an end to their incursions into Europe.   p. 62

[33] See Note 24.   p. 62

[34] The Franks were converted to Christianity in 496 during the reign of Clovis I (481-511). The adoption of Christianity and alliance with the Catholic episcopate secured Clovis the support of the clergy and goodwill towards the Franks on the part of the Catholic Gauls and Romans.   p. 62

[35] *Capitularies*—royal legislative acts and ordinances of the early Middle Ages (the Carolingian dynasty—8th-10th cent.). The Aachen Capitulary (*Capitulare duplex Aquisgranense a. 811*), which noted the wholesale seizure of peasant lands by ecclesiastical and secular feudal lords, is a major source on the history of the Frankish state. The full Latin text of the Aachen Capitulary is quoted by Paul Roth in *Geschichte des Beneficialwesens von den ältesten Zeiten bis ins zehnte Jahrhundert,* Erlangen, 1850, p. 253, Note 31.   p. 63

[36] The information quoted by Engels is taken from the 9th-century polyptych (record of landed property, population and incomes) of Saint-Germain-des-Prés Monastery. For the first time this record was published with commentaries by the French historian Guérard, under the title *Polyptique de l'abbé Irminon,* vols I-II, Paris, 1844. Engels is quoting from Paul Roth's book *Geschichte des Beneficialwesens...,* Erlangen, 1850, p. 251.

Details on the landed property of the monasteries of St. Denis, Luxeuil and St. Martin de Tours are also taken from Roth's book.   p. 64

[37] *Colons* were bondsmen of the Carolingian feudal lord on whose land they lived; colons had no right to abandon their plots which were in their hereditary use.

Lites—a semi-free stratum among the Franks and Saxons. They occupied an intermediate position between free-holders and slaves.   p. 64

[38] In response to an appeal by Pope Stephen II, Pepin the Short undertook two campaigns to Italy (in 754 and 756) against the Langobardian King Aistulf. Part of the lands he conquered Pepin ceded to the Pope and this laid the foundation of the Papal States (756).   p. 66

[39] This refers to the second synod in Lestines (743) which endorsed the secularisation of Church lands in favour of the state as effected under Charles Martel.   p. 66

[40] The risings of the Alamanni were suppressed by Pepin the Short (in 744) and Carloman (in 746), and after this their duchy was destroyed. The Thuringians won independence in 640.

Charlemagne's wars against Saxony, which was conquered and annexed to the Frankish state, lasted for more than 30 years (from 772 to 804). During this period the Saxons twice (in 782 and 792) rose in revolt against their conquerors.   p. 67

[41] The growing discord in the family forced Louis the Pious, Charlemagne's son and successor, to divide the empire among his heirs on three occasions (in 817, 829 and 837); this led to the internal wars that continued till his death and ended in the political disintegration of the empire. In 843, following Louis' death, his sons concluded in Werden a treaty on a new division of the empire. The Werden treaty virtually laid the foundation of France, Germany and Italy—three modern states of Western and Central Europe.   p. 67

636   Notes

[42] *Formulas* were models for drawing up legal deeds and transactions relating to property and other matters in the Frankish state between the end of the 6th and the end of the 9th centuries. Several collections of such formulas have survived to this day. That quoted by Engels is included in the collection *Formulae Turonenses vulgo Sirmondicae dictae.* Engels may have taken it from Roth's book *Geschichte des Beneficialwesens...,* p. 379, Note 51.   p. 73

[43] In his description of Charlemagne's Capitularies (*Capitulare a. 847, Capitulare a. 813, Capitulare a. 816*) Engels makes use of the material in Paul Roth's *Geschichte des Beneficialwesens...,* pp. 380-81, notes 58 and 61.   p. 74

[44] The reference is to the *Annales Bertiniani,* an important source on the history of the Carolingian empire. The *Annales,* which owe their name to St. Bertin Monastery in France, are a chronicle covering the period from 741 to 882 and consisting of three parts written by different authors. The *Annales* advocate the interests of the French Carolingians and support their claim to the territory of the East Frankish kingdom. The *Annales Bertiniani* were published in the well-known series *Monumenta Germaniae historica.*

Engels' description of the *Annales Bertiniani* is based on Roth's *Geschichte des Beneficialwesens...,* p. 385, Note 81.   p. 75

[45] This refers to the rising of free and semi-free Saxon peasants-freelings and lites or the *Stellinga* (from *Stellinger*—Sons of the Old Law), which took place in 841-843 and was directed against the feudal order in Saxony.   p. 81

[46] Charlemagne was crowned Roman Emperor in 800.   p. 81

[47] Engels' manuscript *The Franconian Dialect* remained unfinished and was not printed during the author's lifetime. It was first published by the Institute of Marxism-Leninism in Friedrich Engels, *Der fränkische Dialekt,* Moskau, 1935 (Фридрих Энгельс, *Франкский диалект,* Москва, 1935), the German and Russian given parallel.

Here it is published in English for the first time.   p. 81

[48] *Hêliand,* a literary monument of the ancient Saxon language dating back to the 9th century, is an abridged version of the Gospel. Its author was presumably a monk from the Werden Monastery on the Ruhr.

Two manuscripts of the *Hêliand* are extant: one originating in Munich (dating back to the 9th century); the other named after Cotton, an English collector of antiquities, dates back to the 10th and 11th centuries. The title of the manuscript, which literally means Saviour, was provided by the German linguist Johann Schmeller in 1830. The *Hêliand* was first published by Moritz Heyne in 1866 in *Bibliothek der ältesten deutschen Litteratur-Denkmäler.* Vol. II. *Altniederdeutsche Denkmäler,* Part I.   p. 81

[49] The *Werden tax registers* (*Die Freckenhorster Heberolle*) got their name from the monastery in Freckenhorst, a town to the southeast of Münster. They were published by Moritz Heyne in *Kleinere altniederdeutsche Denkmäler,* Paderborn, 1867, pp. 65-82.   p. 84

[50] The reference is to the glosses, i.e. explanation of obscure and unusual words, which the Dutch philologist Justus Lipsius copied in 1599 from the 9th-century manuscript of the psalms. The Lipsius Glosses (*Glossae Lipsianae*) were published by Moritz Heyne in *Kleinere altniederdeutsche Denkmäler,* Paderborn, 1867, pp. 41-58.   p. 84

51 The *Paderborn records*, relics of local law relating to the 10th and 11th centuries, were published in 1831-32 by the German historian Paul Wigand in *Archiv für Geschichte und Alterthumskunde Westphalens*, Vol. 5, Lemgo, 1831, and in *Die Provinzialrechte der Fürstenthümer Paderborn und Corvey in Westphalen*, vols 2 and 3, Leipzig, 1832.   p. 85

52 This refers to the rendering of the *Gospel* made by Otfrid, a monk from Weissenburg, between 863 and 871. Otfrid's *Gospel* (*Liber Evangeliorum domini gratia theotisce conscriptus*) is one of the first relics of ancient German literature. Its language is regarded as a southern variety of the Rhenish Franconian dialect.

Engels quotes Otfrid's *Gospel* according to Jacob Grimm's *Deutsche Grammatik*, Part 1, 2nd ed., Göttingen, 1822, pp. 874-76 and 894.   p. 86

53 The reference is to the manuscript dating back to the end of the 8th or the beginning of the 9th century and expressing a formula of the baptismal vow (*Taufgelöbnis*). Engels quotes this manuscript according to *Kleinere altniederdeutsche Denkmäler*, published by Moritz Heyne. Paderborn, 1867, p. 85.

p. 86

54 In 1234, in the battle of Altenesch, the combined forces of the Count of Oldenburg, other princes and of Archbishop of Bremen defeated the Eastern Frisians, who lived between the Weser and the Jade, and annexed their lands to Oldenburg.   p. 87

55 The reference is to the bourgeois revolution of 1566-1609 in the Netherlands. It combined the national liberation war against absolutist Spain with the anti-feudal struggle and ended in victory in the north of the country (now the territory of the Netherlands) where the first bourgeois republic in Europe was formed.   p. 87

56 *Manneken-Pis*—a statue of the boy crowning the ancient fountain in Brussels, the work of Jérôme Duquesnoy, a Flemish sculptor of the 17th century.   p. 90

57 A reference to the *Topographische Special-Karte von Deutschland*, published by Gottlob Daniel Reymann, continued by C. W. von Oesfeld and F. Handtke, Glogau, n.d. Engels made use of separate sheets designated by the name of the principal town and the number of the corresponding square or section of the map.
p. 96

58 *Hand-Atlas für die Geschichte des Mittelalters und der neueren Zeit*, 3. Aufl. von Dr. K. v. Spruner's Hand-Atlas, neu bearbeitet von Dr. Th. Menke. Gotha, 1880.

The geographical data which Engels refers to at various points in his work are taken mainly from Map 32 (Deutschland's Gaue. II. Mittleres Lothringen).
p. 96

59 On September 27, 1856, soon after Georg Weerth's death, Engels wrote to Marx about his firm intention to write an obituary and have it published in one of the Berlin newspapers (see present edition, Vol. 40, p. 72). However, this proved impossible in the reactionary situation of the 1850s.

Engels fulfilled his intention 27 years later. The essay about the revolutionary poet that appeared in the newspaper *Sozialdemokrat* on June 7, 1883 was entitled "*Song of the Apprentices*" *by Georg Weerth* (*1846*). In the Second Russian Edition of the *Works* and in the editions in other languages that followed the title of the article was changed in conformity with its subject-matter.

The essay was published in English for the first time in K. Marx and F. Engels, *Literature and Art*, International Publishers, New York, 1947.
p. 108

[60] Between December 1843 and April 1846 Weerth was a clerk at the Bradford branch of the textile firm Passavant and Co.

From April 1846 Weerth was employed by the Hamburg trade firm Emanuel und Sohn with offices in England (Bradford), France, the Netherlands and Belgium.   p. 109

[61] In this article devoted to an historical and linguistic analysis of the last book of the New Testament, *The Revelation of St. John the Divine* or *The Apocalypse*, Engels examines questions relating to the history of early Christianity. He had dealt with some of the same problems previously in the article "Bruno Bauer and Early Christianity" (see present edition, Vol. 24); later, in 1894, Engels analysed them more thoroughly in the article "On the History of Early Christianity" (present edition, Vol. 27).   p. 112

[62] The *Tübingen school,* comprising a group of liberal German Protestant theologians, was founded in 1830 by Ferdinand Christian Baur, a professor at Tübingen University. (As distinct from the group of Tübingen theologians that existed in the last quarter of the 18th century, it is sometimes called the neo-Tübingen school.) Its adherents engaged in a critical study of ancient Christian literature, notably the New Testament. Without essentially abandoning the confines of Christian theology, they were the first to inquire into the sources of the New Testament. At the beginning of his philosophical career David Strauss also belonged to the Tübingen school, but subsequently his criticism became much more radical. The school disintegrated by the 1860s.

Engels gave a detailed description of this school in his article "On the History of Early Christianity" (present edition, Vol. 27).   p. 112

[63] The *Stoics*—disciples of philosopher Zeno of Citium, who taught at the Stoa (Painted Porch) in Athens. Hence the name of this one of the principal schools of Hellenistic and Roman philosophy founded in the late 4th and early 3rd centuries B.C. Among its followers were such ancient philosophers as Seneca (1st cent. A.D.), Philo of Alexandria (1st cent. A.D.) and Marcus Aurelius (2nd cent. A.D.).

The Stoics sought to corroborate the inner independence of human personality, yet at the same time they displayed an extreme sense of resignation towards the surrounding world and made no attempts to change it. Stoicism introduced a strict division of philosophy into logic, physics and ethics. It exerted a considerable influence on the formation of the Christian religion.   p. 113

[64] Ferdinand Benary gave a course of lectures in Berlin University and simultaneously published them in the *Jahrbücher für wissenschaftliche Kritik* that appeared in Berlin (Nos. 17-20 and 30-32 for 1841).   p. 115

[65] See also Engels' article "On the History of Early Christianity" (present edition, Vol. 27).   p. 116

[66] This Preface to the *Manifesto of the Communist Party* (see present edition, Vol. 6, pp. 477-519) was written for the third German authorised edition, the first to appear after Marx's death.

It was published in English for the first time in Marx K. and Engels F., *Manifesto of the Communist Party,* Modern Books, London, 1929.   p. 118

[67] Engels wrote this article for the newspaper *Der Sozialdemokrat* on the first anniversary of Marx's death.

This article was published in English for the first time in Marx K. and

Engels F., *Selected Works*, Vol. 2, Co-operative Publishing Society of Foreign Workers in the USSR, Moscow-Leningrad, 1936.   p. 120

68 Referring here and below to the *Code Napoléon*, Engels meant the entire system of bourgeois law as represented by five codes (civil, civil procedure, commercial, criminal and criminal procedure) promulgated in 1804-10 during Napoleon's reign. These codes were introduced into the regions of Western and South-Western Germany conquered by France and remained in force in the Rhine Province even after its incorporation into Prussia in 1815.   p. 123

69 The *Prussian Law* (*Das Allgemeine Landrecht für die Preussischen Staaten*) was promulgated in 1794. It included civil, commercial, credit, maritime and insurance law as well as criminal, ecclesiastical, state and administrative law, and endorsed the obsolete legal standards of semi-feudal Prussia. To a large extent the Prussian Law remained in force until the introduction of the civil code in 1900.   p. 123

70 After the March 1848 Revolution Gustav Adolph Schlöffel, a German democratic student, began to publish the *Volksfreund* newspaper in Berlin. On April 19, in its issue No. 5, the newspaper carried two of his articles in which he attacked private property and defended the rights of the working people. For this Schlöffel was brought before a court of law and sentenced to six months' imprisonment in a fortress on a charge of incitement to revolt.
                                                                              p. 123

71 The reference is to the Camphausen-Hansemann liberal ministry formed in Prussia on March 29, 1848.   p. 124

72 Engels is referring to the articles in the *Neue Rheinische Zeitung* devoted to a critique of the French and Berlin National Assemblies. Some of these articles were written by Marx (see present edition, vols 7, 8); Engels summarised this critique in his work *Revolution and Counter-Revolution in Germany* (see present edition, Vol. 11, p. 79).   p. 125

73 On *February 24*, 1848 Louis Philippe was overthrown in France.
     On *February 24* (March 7), 1848, having received news of the victory of the February Revolution in France, Nicholas I ordered a partial mobilisation in Russia in preparation for the struggle against the revolution in Europe.
                                                                              p. 126

74 A series of articles "Die schlesische Milliarde" written by Wilhelm Wolff, a friend and associate of Marx and Engels, appeared in the *Neue Rheinische Zeitung*, Nos. 252, 255, 256, 258, 264, 270-72 and 281 between March 22 and April 25, 1849. In 1886 these articles with some changes were published as a separate pamphlet with Engels' Introduction (see this volume, pp. 341-51). A detailed analysis of these articles is given by Engels in his work "Wilhelm Wolff" (see present edition, Vol. 24).   p. 127

75 On June 13, 1849, the Party of the Mountain organised in Paris a peaceful protest demonstration against the despatch of French troops to Italy to restore the power of the Pope in Rome and consolidate French influence in that country. The proposed troop despatch was a violation of the French constitution which prohibited the use of the army against the freedom and independence of other nations.
     The vacillations and indecision of its leaders led to the demonstration's failure, and it was dispersed by government troops. Many leaders of the Mountain were arrested and deported or were forced to emigrate from France.

The Legislative Assembly adopted a number of laws suppressing democratic rights. p. 128

76 Concerning Engels' part in the Baden-Palatinate uprising of 1849, see *The Campaign for the German Imperial Constitution* (present edition, Vol. 10, pp. 147-239). p. 128

77 *The Origin of the Family, Private Property and the State* is one of Engels' most important works. It is based on a detailed synopsis made by Marx in 1880-81 of Lewis H. Morgan's book, *Ancient Society or Researches in the Lines of Human Progress from Savagery, Through Barbarism to Civilization*, London, 1877. Marx's synopsis contained his critical notes, his own propositions and also some factual material taken from other sources. Engels assumed that Marx had planned to write a special work on the history of mankind in the early period of its development using Morgan's book as a basis. Having acquainted himself with Marx's synopsis and Morgan's book, Engels deemed it necessary to write such a work, regarding it as the fulfilment of Marx's behest. On March 24, 1884 Engels wrote to Karl Kautsky: "Actually I am indebted to Marx for it and can incorporate his notes" (see present edition, Vol. 47). In his work on the book, Engels made use of almost all Marx's notes, pointing this out in every case, and also of the structure of Marx's synopsis, which differed from that of Morgan's book. Engels relied, particularly in the first three chapters, on the factual material from Morgan's observations of the life of the North American Indians and in several cases on his arguments and conclusions; he also employed information provided by other scholars about peoples at the same stage of development. In chapters IV-VI, in addition to the information from Morgan's book, Engels used a number of specialised works on ancient history. Chapters VII and VIII are based exclusively on Engels' own studies of the early history of the Germans (see this volume, pp. 6-107). Chapter IX, the last one, contains conclusions drawn by Engels himself.

The first edition of *The Origin of the Family* appeared early in October 1884 in Zurich, since it was impossible to publish the book in Germany given the Anti-Socialist Law. The two editions that followed (in 1886 and 1889) were published in Stuttgart without any changes. Polish, Romanian, Italian, Danish and Serbian translations were issued in the latter half of the 1880s.

The fourth edition of the book, with considerable addenda and certain changes made by Engels on the basis of the latest findings in the field of archaeology, ethnography and anthropology, appeared in 1891. In this volume all the essential differences in reading occurring in the 1884 and 1891 editions are given in footnotes.

The first English edition of the book appeared in 1902. p. 129

78 Marx's synopsis of Morgan's book was first published in Russian translation in: *Marx-Engels Archives*, Vol. IX, Moscow, 1941, and later in Marx and Engels, *Works*, Second Russian Edition, Vol. 45, Moscow, 1975. The first publication in the languages of the original appeared in *The Ethnological Notebooks of Karl Marx*. Translated and edited, with an introduction by Lawrence Krader, Assen, 1972.

All references in the text of the present volume are given according to this edition. p. 131

79 *Pueblo* (Sp.—people, population) is the name of the four linguistic groups of Indian tribes who lived on the territory of New Mexico (now the South-Western part of the USA). Originally the Spanish conquerors applied this name to five-

or six-storey fortress-like houses inhabited by Indian communities; later this name was also applied to the inhabitants of these unusual villages. The Pueblo culture had its heyday in the 12th and 13th centuries. p. 137

80 This letter of Marx's is not extant. Engels mentions it in his letter to Karl Kautsky of April 11, 1884 (see present edition, Vol. 47). p. 147

81 The reference is to the libretto of the operatic tetralogy *Ring of the Nibelungs* (*Der Ring des Nibelungen*) composed by Richard Wagner, the subject of which was taken from the Scandinavian epic *Edda* and the German epic *Nibelungenlied*.

The *Nibelungenlied* is the ancient German heroic epic based on myths and lays. Written versions of the song appeared only in the 13th-16th centuries. The *Nibelungenlied* penetrated into Scandinavia (6th-8th cent.) where it found reflection in the songs of *Edda*.

The events that accompanied the great migration of peoples (see Note 5), notably the invasion of Europe by the Huns (5th cent.), served as the historical basis of the *Nibelungenlied,* though its final character owed more to the conditions of life in Germany in the 12th century. p. 147

82 The *Ögisdrekka* (Lokasenna) is a song from the first part of *The Elder Edda,* known as *Songs about Gods.* The *Ögisdrekka* describes the quarrel between Loki, the god of fire, and other gods at a feast given by the sea giant Ogir.

The *Elder Edda* is a collection of epic poems and songs about the lives and deeds of the Scandinavian gods and heroes. It has come down to us in a manuscript dating back to the 13th century, discovered in 1643 by the Icelandic Bishop B. Sveinsson. p. 147

83 *Asa* and *Vana*—gods in Scandinavian mythology.

The *Ynglinga Saga* is the first of the 16 sagas in the book about Norwegian kings (from ancient times to the 12th century) entitled *Heimskringla.* It was written by Snorri Sturluson, an Icelandic poet and chronicler, in the first half of the 13th century. p. 148

84 According to this system each tribe was divided into two or four marriage classes (sections). Marriage was allowed only between certain specified pairs of these classes. Children born of this marriage belonged to the third marriage class which was part of the tribe including either a maternal or a paternal marriage class. Such a division restricted marriages between close relatives. p. 151

85 Wright's letters found in Morgan's archives were published in the magazine *American Anthropologist.* New Series, Vol. 35, No. 1, 1933. p. 158

86 *Saturnalian feasts* were held annually in Ancient Rome in honour of Saturn, the god of agriculture. They began on December 17, after the harvest, and were accompanied by carnivals and festivals, with the entire population taking part, including slaves who were allowed to sit at the table alongside free citizens. The cult of fertility presupposed the freedom of sexual intercourse during Saturnalian feasts. p. 159

87 This refers to the decision which King Ferdinand V of Spain, acting as mediator between peasants and seigniors, took under the pressure of the insurgent peasants of Northern Catalonia in 1484.

The decision is known as the Guadalupe decree after the name of the monastery in Estremadura, where, on April 21, 1486, the King met authorised representatives of the peasants and the landlords. The decree granted the peasants personal freedom, but for the right to keep land holdings they had to pay their landlords high redemption fees. The decree abolished the jurisdiction of the landlords and several humiliating feudal practices. A number of burdensome duties had to be redeemed.

p. 161

88 The *Pravda of Yaroslav*, or the *Ancient Pravda*, is the first part of the *Russian Pravda*, the code of laws of ancient Rus. It appeared in the first half of the 11th century and is associated with the name of Prince Yaroslav the Wise of Kiev. The *Pravda* is based on the common law of the Eastern Slavs in the period of early feudalism and reflects the social and economic relations of the 11th and 12th centuries.

p. 167

89 The *Dalmatian Laws*, or the *Poljica Statute*, were in force in Poljica, a historical part of Dalmatia, up to the beginning of the 19th century. The first articles of the Statute were drawn up in the first half of the 15th century. The document reflects the norms of the criminal, civil and procedural law as well as the social and economic relations existing in the communities of Poljica in the 15th-18th centuries.

p. 167

90 Engels may have taken the information on family communities in France from M. M. Kovalevsky's book *Tableau des origines et de l'évolution de la famille et de la propriété*, Stockholm, 1890.

p. 168

91 *Calpullis*—a territorial community of the Aztecs (ancient Mexico) based on the common ownership of land. Part of the land was assigned to individual families each of which embraced several generations inhabiting a common dwelling and constituted a household community.

p. 168

92 The *Helots*, part of the agricultural population of Ancient Sparta subjugated by the Dorians, belonged to the state and were attached to the land owned by the *Spartiates*—a class of citizens of Ancient Sparta enjoying full civil rights. Helots could be neither sold nor killed; they owned the means of production and worked on their plots of land.

p. 172

93 The *hierodules*—temple slaves and attendants in Ancient Greece and the Greek colonies. In many places, including Asia Minor and Corinth, the female temple slaves were engaged in prostitution.

p. 174

94 This refers to the troubadour poetry of Provence (Southern France) between the end of the 11th and the beginning of the 13th centuries.

p. 177

95 Engels is referring to the nine poems that have survived from the lyrical cycle attributed to Wolfram von Eschenbach and written in the *Tagelieder* genre, as well as his epic poem *Parzival* and two unfinished poems *Titurel* and *Willehalm*.

p. 178

96 *Daphnis* and *Chloe*—heroes of the ancient Greek novel (2nd-3rd century); no information concerning its author, Longus, is extant.

p. 184

97 *Gutrun (Kudrun)*—a German epic poem of the 13th century. It has survived in a manuscript dating back to the 16th century and was not discovered until the beginning of the 19th century.

p. 185

98 The reference is to the conquest of Mexico by Spanish conquistadors in 1519-21.

p. 196

99 New Mexicans—see Note 79.

p. 200

100 The main works written by Georg Ludwig Maurer are: *Einleitung zur Geschichte der Mark-, Hof-, Dorf- und Stadt-Verfassung und der öffentlichen Gewalt*, Munich,

1854; *Geschichte der Markenverfassung in Deutschland,* Erlangen, 1856; *Geschichte der Fronhöfe, der Bauernhöfe und der Hofverfassung in Deutschland,* vols I-IV, Erlangen, 1862-63; *Geschichte der Dorfverfassung in Deutschland,* vols I-II, Erlangen, 1865-66; *Geschichte der Städteverfassung in Deutschland,* vols I-IV, Erlangen, 1869-71.   p. 202

101 The *"Neutral Nations"* was the name of a 17th-century tribe related to the Iroquois which lived on the northern shore of Lake Erie. It was given this name by the French colonists because it remained neutral in the war between the Iroquois proper and the Hurons. The war ended in victory for the Iroquois in 1651.   p. 203

102 In January 1879, the British troops invaded Zululand (South Africa) with the aim of conquering this country. On January 22, the Zulu army under Cetschwayo (Cetywayo) defeated the colonialist troops near Isandhlwana, inflicting heavy losses. It was only after the arrival of fresh reinforcements that the British troops succeeded in finally defeating the Zulus in the summer of 1879.

In 1881, the Nubians, Arabs and other nationalities of the Sudan rose up against the British colonialists, Turkish and Egyptian authorities and native feudal lords. The uprising was led by Mohammed Ahmed, who proclaimed himself "Mahdi" (saviour). On November 5, 1883, the ten-thousand-strong expeditionary corps under General Hicks was defeated and routed by the insurgents near the town of El Obeid. The uprising lasted till 1898-99.

p. 203

103 The reference is to Demosthenes' speech in court, *Against Eubulides* (LVII), in which he mentions the ancient custom of laying to rest only persons of the given gens in gentile burial places.   p. 205

104 This passage written in Marx's synopsis in German is a concise summary of Morgan's following argument:

"Although these [Grote's] observations seem to imply that they [the Grecian gentes] are no older than the then existing mythology ... in the light of the facts presented, the gentes are seen to have existed long before this mythology was developed—before Jupiter or Neptune, Mars or Venus were conceived in the human mind" (Lewis H. Morgan, *Ancient Society,* London, 1877, p. 228).

p. 206

105 In the passage which Engels quotes from Marx's synopsis, part of the quotation (from the words "The system of consanguinity" to "the relationships of all the members of a gens to each other" and from the words "This fell into desuetude" to "a purely fictitious, fanciful creation of the brain") is a slightly abridged version of Morgan's text (Lewis H. Morgan, *Ancient Society,* pp. 233-34).

p. 208

106 See Note 79.   p. 212

107 *Thetes,* the fourth, and lowest, class of Athenian citizens, were admitted to civil offices by the law on lower electoral qualifications adopted in 477 B.C.

p. 219

108 The reference is to the *metoikos,* or aliens who settled in a Greek city state (polis). Being personally free, they were denied political rights, could not marry Athenian citizens and, as a rule, could not own real estate and land on the territory of the city state where they settled. The *metoikos* were obliged to have "patrons" from among the Athenian citizens, to pay a special tax to the state and serve in the army.

In the 5th-4th centuries B.C. the *metoikos* formed a considerable part of the urban population in Attica and played an important role in its economic life, particularly in trade.   p. 220

109 The reference is to the reforms carried out by Cleisthenes in 510-509 B.C. They deprived the gentile nobility of its supremacy in governing Athens and abolished the last remnants of the gentile constitution, since the population was now divided according to the territorial principle, and not according to the gentile principle as before. The reforms increased the importance of the urban population; many *metoikos* (see Note 108) and freedmen who engaged in trade and handicrafts received civic rights.   p. 220

110 Pisistratus, who belonged to an impoverished aristocratic family, usurped power in Athens in 560 B.C. and established a dictatorial regime, becoming a tyrant. This regime existed with intervals (Pisistratus was twice driven out of Athens and returned again) until his death in 527 B.C., and then up to 510 B.C. when his son Hippius was banished and the slave-owning democracy headed by Cleisthenes won the day in Athens. Pisistratus' efforts to defend the interests of small and medium landowners and penalise the gentile aristocracy did not give rise to any serious changes in the political structure of the Athenian state.
                                                                              p. 222

111 The *Laws of the Twelve Tables* (*Leges duodecim tabularum*) were enacted in 451-450 B.C. by the Committee of Decemvirs. Originally the laws were carved on ten tables, later two more tables were added. The laws preserved remnants of the gentile system and reflected the social relations of Ancient Rome, referring mainly to civil and criminal law and legal procedure. They were used as the basis for the further development of Roman civil law.   p. 223

112 The reference is to the battle in Teutoburg Forest (A.D. 9) fought between the Germanic tribes led by the Cherusci chief Arminius in revolt against Rome and the Roman legions commanded by Quintilius Varus. The Roman troops were routed and their general killed.   p. 223

113 This refers to the end of the rule of Appius Claudius, head of the Committee of Decemvirs which enacted the Laws of the Twelve Tables in 451-450 B.C. (see Note 111). However, abuses of power on the part of Appius Claudius led to an insurrection by the plebeians; he was arrested and died in prison.

The *Second Punic War* (218-201 B.C.) was one of the three wars between Rome and Carthage, the two largest slave-owning states of antiquity. Rome sought to abolish Carthage's domination of trade in the Western Mediterranean and indeed defeated it.   p. 224

114 The reference is to the comparative tables of ancient and modern measures and also of monetary units, given at the end of A. Dureau de la Malle's *Économie politique des Romains*, Vol. I.   p. 230

115 At several points in this and the next chapters Engels makes use of his unfinished works "On the Early History of the Germans" and "The Frankish Period" (see this volume, pp. 6-107) and the article "The Mark" (see present edition, Vol. 24, pp. 439-56).   p. 232

116 The conquest of Wales by the English was completed in 1283. However, Wales retained its autonomy and was united with England in the mid-16th century.
                                                                              p. 232

117 In 1869-70 Engels devoted himself to a major work on the history of Ireland,

but failed to complete it (see present edition, Vol. 21, pp. 145-85 and 283-314 and also Marx and Engels, *Ireland and the Irish Question,* Progress Publishers, Moscow, 1978, pp. 306-56, and *Marx-Engels Archives,* Russian edition, Vol. X, Moscow, 1948, pp. 157-248). Simultaneously with the study of Celtic history Engels analysed the old Welsh laws.   p. 232

118 In September 1891 Engels toured Scotland and Ireland.   p. 234

119 A reference to the rebellion of the Scottish highlanders in 1745 caused by oppression and eviction from the land carried out in the interests of the Anglo-Scottish landed aristocracy and bourgeoisie. Part of the nobility in the Scottish Highlands, who supported the claims of the overthrown House of Stuart to the English Crown (the official aim of the insurgents was to enthrone Charles Edward, the grandson of James II), took advantage of the discontent among the highlanders. The suppression of the rebellion put an end to the clan system in the Scottish Highlands and resulted in further evictions.
        p. 235

120 See Note 5.   p. 236

121 See Note 18.   p. 236

122 *Burgundian law (Lex Burgundionum)*—a code of legislative acts promulgated by the Burgundian kings in the second half of the 5th and the beginning of the 6th century. It regulated the major aspects of the life of Burgundian society and its relations with the Gallic and Roman population.   p. 236

123 The *Hildebrand Song (Hildebrandslied)*—an 8th-century German epic poem, of which only a few passages have survived.   p. 237

124 The *Völuspá (Vision of the Seeress)*—the best-known song from *The Elder Edda* (see Note 82), depicting the history of the world from its creation to the final desctruction—the "Twilight of the Gods"—and its second birth—the triumph of peace and justice.   p. 238

125 In 69-70, Claudius Julius Civilis, chief of the Batavians, who lived at the Rhine estuary and were allied with the Romans, led an insurrection against Rome. It was joined by other Germanic peoples and some of the Gauls. The insurrection was sparked off by the growing taxes, increased levies to the army and the abuse of power by Roman officials. Initially the insurgents achieved considerable success. The Gaulish aristocracy, however, continued to support Rome, and this spelled defeat for the insurgents. The insurrection was quelled, but the Batavians were freed from taxes.   p. 240

126 *Codex Laureshamensis (Lorch Capitulary)*—a collection of the copies of letters patent and privileges belonging to the Lorch Monastery which was founded in the latter half of the 8th century in the Frankish state. A large feudal estate in South-Western Germany, it was located close to the town of Worms. The collection was compiled in the 12th century and is an important historical document on the system of peasant and feudal landownership in the 8th-9th centuries.   p. 242

127 See Note 5.   p. 244

128 The reference may have been to the defeats which the retinues of Odoacer, the founder of the first barbarian kingdom on the territory of Italy, suffered from the Ostgoth leader Theodoric in the battles of Aquileja and Verona in 489. As a result of these defeats Odoacer lost power in Italy and was killed. p. 245

[129] The reference is to the provinces which were part of the Roman state.

p. 247

[130] *Benefices*—plots of land bestowed as rewards—were a transitional form of holding, on the road to feudal ownership. This form of remuneration became common practice in the Frankish state following Charles Martel's reform on benefices in the 730s. Gradually the beneficiaries succeeded in turning these life-long grants into fiefs, or hereditary feudal estates. A detailed description of the role which the system of benefices played in the development of feudalism is given by Engels in his unfinished work *The Frankish Period* (see this volume, pp. 58-81).

p. 252

[131] *Gau counts* (Gaugrafen)—royal officers appointed to administer districts or counties in the Frankish state. They were invested with judicial power, collected taxes and led the troops during military campaigns. For their service they received one-third of the royal income collected in the given county and were rewarded with landed estates. Gradually the counts became feudal seigneurs endowed with sovereign powers, particularly after 877, when the office was formally proclaimed hereditary.

p. 252

[132] See Note 37.

p. 252

[133] See Note 37.

p. 253

[134] *Angariae*—compulsory services performed by residents of the Roman Empire, who were obliged to supply carriers and horses for state transports.   p. 253

[135] The reference is to the economic organisation of vast estates owned by Charlemagne. It was established by the so-called *Capitulary on Royal Estates* (*capitulare de villis*) promulgated in about 800. Special attention was given to more effective control over the fulfilment of numerous obligations imposed on the peasants working on such estates, as well as to the preservation of the estates themselves and of profits received from them. All this testified to the growth of feudalism in Frankish society.

p. 254

[136] *Commendation*—an act by which a peasant commended himself to the "patronage" of a small landowner or a small landowner to the "patronage" of a powerful feudal lord in accordance with the established practice (military and other services for the benefit of the "patron", the transfer to him of a plot of land in return for a conventional holding). This meant the loss of personal freedom for the peasants and made small landowners vassals of the powerful feudal lords. This practice, widespread in Europe from the 8th and 9th centuries onwards, led, on the one hand, to the transformation of the peasants into serfs and, on the other, to the consolidation of the feudal hierarchy.

p. 254

[137] The *Hildebrand Song*—see Note 123.

The *Battle of Hastings* took place on October 14, 1066 between the troops of William, Duke of Normandy, which invaded England, and the Anglo-Saxon army of King Harold. The poorly armed Anglo-Saxons were defeated and King Harold killed. In December 1066 William took London, was crowned King of England and came to be known as William the Conqueror. p. 262

[138] *Dithmarschen*—a district in the south-west of present-day Schleswig-Holstein. It was remarkable for its peculiar historical development; in particular, up to the second half of the 19th century there were still survivals of patriarchal customs

and the communal system was preserved among the peasants even after the conquest by Danish and Holstein feudal lords in the 16th century.   p. 269

139 Engels wrote this introductory note for the 1884 edition of Marx's *Wage Labour and Capital* (see present edition, Vol. 9, pp. 197-228); in 1891 Engels incorporated it into his Introduction to the new edition of this work by Marx (see present edition, Vol. 27).
     This note was published in English for the first time in K. Marx, *Wage Labour and Capital*, Modern Press, London, 1885.   p. 277

140 The *German Workers' Society* was founded by Marx and Engels in Brussels at the end of August 1847, its aim being the political education of the German workers who lived in Belgium and dissemination of the ideas of scientific communism among them. With Marx, Engels and their followers at its head, the Society became the legal centre of the revolutionary proletarian forces in Belgium. Its most active members belonged to the Communist League. The Society played an important part in founding the Brussels Democratic Association (see Note 193). After the February 1848 revolution in France, the Belgian authorities arrested and banished many of its members.   p. 277

141 Engels' letters written between August and October 1884 show that he did a great deal of work in preparing Marx's *Poverty of Philosophy* for publication in German. (The book was written and published in French in 1847 and was not republished in full during Marx's lifetime.) Engels edited the translation made by Eduard Bernstein and Karl Kautsky and supplied a number of notes to it.
     The first German edition of Marx's book appeared in the second half of January 1885 and, a little earlier, at the beginning of January, Engels published his Preface in the magazine *Die Neue Zeit* under the title "Marx und Rodbertus". It was also included in the second German edition of the book which appeared in 1892 with a special preface written by Engels (see present edition, Vol. 27).   p. 278

142 Marx wrote the statement about the break with *Der Social-Demokrat* on February 18, 1865 and sent it to Engels, who fully endorsed it and returned it to Marx with his signature; on February 23, 1865 Marx sent the statement to the editors of the newspaper. This was occasioned by Schweitzer's series of articles *Das Ministerium Bismarck* in which he expressed overt support for Bismarck's policy of unifying Germany under Prussian supremacy. Marx took measures to make Schweitzer publish the statement. It was published in many papers, among them the *Barmer Zeitung* and *Elberfelder Zeitung* on February 26. Schweitzer was forced to publish this statement in *Der Social-Demokrat*, No. 29, March 3, 1865 (see present edition, Vol. 20, p. 80). p. 278

143 The reference is to Engels' Preface to the first German edition of Vol. II of Marx's *Capital*, which Engels completed on May 5, 1885 (see present edition, Vol. 36).   p. 279

144 See the anonymous pamphlet: *The Source and Remedy of the National Difficulties, deduced from principles of political economy, in a letter to Lord John Russell*, London, 1821.
     For more details about the pamphlet see Engels' Preface to Vol. II of Marx's *Capital* (present edition, Vol. 36).   p. 279

145 Engels is referring to the second edition of Ricardo's book *On the Principles of Political Economy, and Taxation*, London, 1819, pp. 32-46, where the author divided the text into sections.   p. 282

[146] The reference is to the people who took part in publishing the literary legacy of Rodbertus-Jagetzow, in particular his work *Das Kapital. Vierter socialer Brief an von Kirchmann,* Berlin, 1884; the publisher of this work and the author of the introduction to it was Theophil Kozak; the preface was written by the German vulgar economist Adolf Wagner.   p. 283

[147] Engels is referring to the preface to K. Rodbertus-Jagetzow's work, *Das Kapital. Vierter socialer Brief an von Kirchmann,* Berlin, 1884, pp. VII-VIII, in which Adolf Wagner wrote: "Rodbertus evinces here such a power of abstract thinking as is possessed only by the greatest masters."   p. 284

[148] § 110 of the German Imperial Criminal Code promulgated in 1871 stipulated a fine of up to 600 marks or imprisonment for a term of up to 2 years for a public appeal in writing to disobey the laws and decrees operating in the German Empire.   p. 290

[149] The second French edition of *The Poverty of Philosophy,* which was being prepared by Marx's daughter Laura Lafargue, appeared in Paris only after Engels' death, in 1896.   p. 291

[150] Engels wrote this article on January 25, 1885 for *Der Sozialdemokrat.* About the same time he sent a letter to Paul Lafargue describing the same facts and expressing the same ideas more concisely and in somewhat different terms (see present edition, Vol. 47). Lafargue passed this letter on to Jules Guesde who drew on it in writing his article published as a leader in *Cri du Peuple,* No. 461 on January 31, 1885. Guesde quoted a long passage from Engels' letter without naming him, just saying that he had received this letter from London from "one of the veterans of our great social battles". The article was reprinted in the Polish socialist press and in the USA.   p. 292

[151] On January 13 (1), 1885, Russia and Prussia exchanged notes on extradition of persons accused of criminal offences against the monarchs of the contracting parties or members of their families, as well as of persons found guilty of manufacturing or storing explosives.   p. 292

[152] Olga Novikova, a Russian journalist who lived in London in 1876 and 1877, took an active part in the campaign against the attempts by Disraeli's Conservative government to involve Britain in the war against Russia on the side of Turkey. She had contacts with the ruling circles of Russia and support among the members of the British Liberal Party, Gladstone in particular. The campaign, which swept both Britain and Russia, helped to prevent Britain entering the war. Engels is referring to Olga Novikova's article "The Russianization of England".   p. 292

[153] Engels wrote this article for the magazine *The Commonweal*; later he translated it into German and had it published in *Die Neue Zeit* (June 1885). Subsequently he incorporated it into the Appendix to the 1887 American edition of *The Condition of the Working-Class in England* (see this volume, pp. 399-405) and in 1892 into the prefaces to the English and the second German editions of this work (see present edition, Vol. 27).   p. 295

[154] The reference is to the movement for the repeal of the Corn Laws introduced in the interests of the English landed aristocracy as far back as the 15th century. The maintenance of high import tariffs on corn in order to maintain high prices on the home market prevented the growth of capitalist profit.

In 1838 the Manchester factory owners Cobden and Bright founded the Anti-Corn Law League, which demanded lower corn tariffs and unlimited freedom of trade for the purpose of weakening the economic and political power of the landed aristocracy and reducing agricultural workers' wages. The battle over the Corn Laws ended with their repeal in 1846.   p. 295

155 Evidently, it was not John Bright who said this but his followers. See: "Anti-Corn-Law Agitation" in *The Quarterly Review*, Vol. 71, No. 141, London, 1843, p. 273.   p. 295

156 The *People's Charter* containing the demands of the Chartists was published on May 8, 1838 in the form of a Bill to be submitted to Parliament. It consisted of six points: universal suffrage (for men of 21 years of age and over), annual elections to Parliament, secret ballots, equal constituencies, abolition of property qualifications for parliamentary candidates, and salaries for M.P.s. In 1839 and 1842, petitions for the Charter were rejected by Parliament.   p. 295

157 The reference is to the Chartists' peaceful march to Parliament planned for April 10, 1848, in order to hand in the third petition concerning the People's Charter. The government, however, prohibited the demonstration and took steps to prevent it by concentrating military units in the capital and mobilising a whole army of "special constables" from among the bourgeoisie. Many of the Chartist leaders wavered, abandoned their intention of staging the march and persuaded those who had assembled to disperse.   p. 296

158 The reference is to the *Reform Bill* which was finally passed by the British Parliament in June 1832. The Reform Act of 1832 consisted of three acts adopted for England and Wales on June 7, for Scotland on July 17, and for Ireland on August 17, 1832. It was directed against the political monopoly of the landed and finance aristocracy and enabled the industrial bourgeoisie to be duly represented in Parliament. The proletariat and the petty bourgeoisie, the main forces in the struggle for the reform, remained disfranchised.   p. 296

159 See Note 154.   p. 296

160 The expression the "workshop of the world", first used with regard to England by Benjamin Disraeli in his speech to the House of Commons on March 15, 1838, was current in the 19th century.   p. 296

161 The reference is to the factory legislation that appeared in England in the first third of the 19th century in connection with the factory system of the capitalist mode of production and the struggle of the proletariat for legislative regulation of working conditions. The first Factory Acts (1802, 1819, 1833, 1844) limited the employment of child labour in the textile industry. The Act of 1833 introduced a special office of factory inspectors who had the right to supervise the operation of factory legislation and the right to penalise manufacturers violating the Factory Acts. Of great importance was the Act of 1847 which limited the working day of women and children employed in the textile industry to ten hours.   p. 297

162 The *Reform of 1867* granted the franchise in towns to all house-owners, lease-holders and tenants residing in the same place not less than a year and paying a rent of not less than £10. The property qualification for voters in the counties was lowered to £12 rent per year. Voting rights were also granted to a section of the industrial workers.

The *Reform of 1884* extended the provisions of the 1867 Reform to rural areas, and voting rights were granted to a section of rural population. As a result of the two reforms, the number of electors, however, comprised just 13 per cent of the country's total population. The rural and urban poor and women were still deprived of voting rights.   p. 297

[163] The *British Association for the Advancement of Science* was founded in 1831 and continues to exist to this day. It publishes accounts of its annual meetings in the quarterly magazine *The Advancement of Science*.   p. 300

[164] On December 2, 1851 Louis Bonaparte carried out a coup d'état by dissolving the Legislative Assembly.

On January 14, 1852 a new constitution was introduced which conferred all state power upon the President, elected for ten years; the composition and legislative functions of the Council of State, the Legislative Corps and the Senate were placed under his direct control. This constitution in fact restored the regime of the empire in France. On December 2, 1852 the Second Republic was abolished and the Prince-President was formally proclaimed Emperor of the French under the name of Napoleon III. Thus the coup d'état of December 2, 1851 had led to the establishment of the Bonapartist Second Empire in France.   p. 302

[165] The pamphlet, *Karl Marx vor den Kölner Geschwornen. Prozeß gegen den Ausschuß der rheinischen Demokraten wegen Aufrufs zum bewaffneten Widerstand,* appeared early in October 1885 as the second instalment of the "Social-Democratic Library" published in German, first in Zurich, and later in London (1885-90). The pamphlet reprinted the newspaper reports on the trial from the *Neue Rheinische Zeitung,* Nos. 226 and 231-33 of February 19, 25, 27 and 28, 1849.
                                    p. 304

[166] This expression was used in the royal proclamation of March 21, 1848, in which Frederick William IV declared his readiness to stand "at the head [an die Spitze] of the whole fatherland in order to save Germany". During the campaign for the unification of Germany this expression was used to describe Prussia's intention to unite the country under its supremacy.   p. 305.

[167] The trial of the *Neue Rheinische Zeitung* began on February 7, 1849. Karl Marx, editor-in-chief, Frederick Engels, co-editor, and Hermann Korff, responsible publisher, were tried by a Cologne jury court. They were accused of slandering Chief Public Prosecutor Zweiffel and calumniating the police officers who had arrested Gottschalk and Anneke, in the article "Arrests" published in the *Neue Rheinische Zeitung,* No. 35, July 5, 1848 (see present edition, Vol. 7, pp. 177-79). Marx's and Engels' defence counsel at the trial of February 7 was Karl Schneider II. The jury acquitted the defendants. For Marx's and Engels' speeches at this trial see present edition, Vol. 8, pp. 304-22.   p. 306

[168] The *Kreuz-Zeitung's* party—a name given from 1851 to the end of the 19th century to the extreme Right wing of the Prussian Conservative Party grouped round the *Neue Preussische (Kreuz-) Zeitung.*   p. 307

[169] The reference is to the formation of the North German Confederation under Prussian supremacy. As a result of the Austro-Prussian War of 1866, Austria and the South-German states remained outside the Confederation (see Note 171). The victory of Prussia in the Franco-Prussian War led to the national unification of Germany and the foundation of a German Empire in which the Prussian monarchy played the leading role.   p. 307

[170] The *National Liberal Party,* formed in the autumn of 1866 after a split in the

Party of Progress (see Note 401), was the mainstay of an alliance between the Junkers and the bourgeoisie and advocated struggle for civil equality and bourgeois-democratic freedoms.

The policy of the National Liberals showed that the German liberal bourgeoisie had capitulated to Bismarck's government. Following the introduction of Bismarck's half-hearted reforms, the National Liberal Party actively supported the policy of colonial expansion, the military build-up and suppression of the working-class movement. It continued its existence until the November 1918 Revolution in Germany.   p. 307

171 Engels is referring to the steps taken by Prussia on the eve of the Austro-Prussian War of 1866: on June 8, Prussian troops invaded the Duchy of Holstein which, according to the treaty between Prussia and Austria, was under Austrian jurisdiction and belonged to the German Confederation. Following a decision by the member-states of the German Confederation, initiated by Austria, to mobilise the federal army, Prussia declared its withdrawal from the Confederation and on June 16 began hostilities against Saxony, Hanover, the Electorate of Hesse, and Nassau, all members of the Confederation. On June 17, Austria declared war on Prussia.

The *German Confederation* (Deutscher Bund) was an ephemeral union of German states formed by decision of the Congress of Vienna in June 1815 and originally comprised 35 absolutist feudal states and 4 free cities. The central body of the German Confederation was the Federal Diet which consisted of representatives of the German states. Though it had no real power, it was nevertheless a vehicle of feudal and monarchical reaction. For all practical purposes the Confederation sealed Germany's political and economic fragmentation and retarded its development.

The German Confederation ceased to exist during the Austro-Prussian War of 1866.   p. 307

172 The reference is to the military and diplomatic steps which Bismarck's government took in connection with the Austro-Prussian War of 1866.

In October 1865, Bismarck conducted unofficial negotiations with Napoleon III in Biarritz, seeking to secure France's neutrality in the war he was planning. Questions under discussion concerned a possible return to Italy of Venetia, then belonging to Austria, as well as territorial concessions to France at the expense of the Rhine provinces and other territories. These talks resulted in the conclusion on April 8, 1866 of a treaty on an offensive and defensive alliance between Prussia and Italy. The treaty provided for Italy to attack Austria only after Prussia had started the war. If Prussia's attack did not follow within three months, the treaty was to be invalid.

In July 1866, on Bismarck's initiative, a Hungarian legion was formed in Silesia under the command of General Klapka. The aim of the legion, which consisted of Hungarian émigrés and prisoners-of-war, was to invade Hungary during the war. However, Klapka's legion, soon after crossing the frontier early in August 1866, was recalled and disbanded in connection with the end of the war.

After the conclusion of the Prague Peace Treaty on August 23, 1866, Prussia annexed (on September 20) the Kingdom of Hanover, the Electorate of Hesse-Kassel, the Duchy of Nassau and the city of Frankfurt am Main, which had fought on Austria's side.   p. 307

173 The Constitution of the North German Confederation (the Confederation included 19 states and 3 free cities) was approved on April 17, 1867 by the

Constituent Reichstag of the Confederation (it held sessions between February 24 and April 17, 1867) and reaffirmed Prussia's de facto domination. The Prussian King was proclaimed President of the Confederation and Commander-in-Chief of the federal armed forces; he was also put in charge of foreign policy. The legislative powers of the Confederation's Reichstag, which was elected by universal suffrage, were extremely limited: the laws it adopted became valid only after approval by the Federal Council and endorsement by the President. This constitution later became the basis for the Constitution of the German Empire. Saxony, which fought on Austria's side in the Austro-Prussian War of 1866, was forced after the war to become a member of the North German Confederation and then submit to this constitution.

The *treaties of Tilsit* were signed on July 7 and 9, 1807 by Napoleonic France and Russia and Prussia, members of the fourth anti-French coalition. The treaty imposed harsh terms on Prussia, which lost nearly half its territory to the German states dependent on France, was made to pay indemnities, and had its army reduced. p. 307

[174] A reference to the *Anti-Socialist Law,* or *Exceptional Law against the Socialists* (*Gesetz gegen die gemeingefährlischen Bestrebungen der Sozialdemokrate*), introduced by Bismarck's government with the support of a majority in the Reichstag on October 21, 1878 for the purpose of combatting the socialist and working-class movement. The law deprived the Social-Democratic Party of Germany of its legal status; it prohibited all its organisations, workers' mass organisations and the socialist and workers' press, decreed confiscation of socialist literature, and subjected Social-Democrats to repression. The Social-Democratic Party, however, with the active assistance of Marx and Engels, managed to gain the upper hand over both the opportunist and "ultra-left" elements within its ranks. By correctly combining illegal work with utilising all legal possibilities the Party considerably increased and extended its influence among the masses while the Anti-Socialist Law was in force. The law was abrogated on October 1, 1890. For Engels' appraisal of it see his article "Bismarck and the German Working Men's Party" (present edition, Vol. 24, pp. 407-09). p. 308

[175] The reference is to the American War of Independence (1775-83). On July 4, 1776 the Declaration of Independence was passed by the delegates of 13 North American colonies at a Congress in Philadelphia. The Declaration proclaimed secession from England and the formation of an independent republic—the United States of America. It formulated such bourgeois-democratic principles as freedom of the individual, equality before the law, sovereignty of the people, and exerted a major influence on the European revolutionary movement and the French Revolution in particular. However, the democratic rights proclaimed were from the very start violated by the American bourgeoisie and plantation owners, who excluded the common people from political life and preserved slavery. p. 308

[176] In 1611, the Polish Diet adopted a decision on the unification of the Duchy of Prussia with Brandenburg under Hohenzollern rule. This was done despite the opposition of a group of deputies who supported Poland's rights to East Prussia. However, the Duchy of Prussia remained a territory held in fee by Poland. This decision was implemented in 1618 when the Elector of Brandenburg, Johann Sigismund, received the Duchy of Prussia in fee from the Polish King in return for his promise to take part in the war against Sweden. Under the Wielawa-Bydgoszcz Treaty of 1657 Poland finally renounced its supreme rights to the Duchy of Prussia in favour of Brandenburg. p. 309

177 On October 8-10, 1801, France and Russia signed a secret convention on the regulation of territorial issues in Rhenish Germany in favour of Napoleonic France, using as a pretext the need to compensate those German states whose possessions on the left bank of the Rhine had been seized by France during its wars against the first and second coalitions. This convention found reflection in the Russo-French declaration of June 3, 1802, under which 112 German states (nearly all ecclesiastical possessions and imperial towns) with a total population of three million were handed over to Bavaria, Württemberg and Baden, which were dependent on Napoleonic France, and also to Prussia. Formally this was done under the terms of a resolution adopted by what was known as the Imperial Deputation, a commission made up of representatives of the states incorporated in the German Empire and elected by the Imperial Diet in October 1801. The resolution was adopted on February 25, 1803 after long discussions and under pressure from France and Russia. p. 309

178 Under the ·terms of the Peace Treaty signed by France and Austria at Pressburg (Bratislava) on December 26, 1805, Bavaria and Württemberg, which took part in the war waged by Napoleonic France against the third coalition, were granted the status of independent kingdoms. Baden, which also fought on France's side, became an independent grand duchy in 1806 after the Holy Roman Empire ceased to exist. p. 309

179 Engels is quoting the Prussian officer, Prince Felix Lichnowski, who spoke on the Polish question in the Frankfurt National Assembly on July 26, 1848 (see also present edition, Vol. 7, p. 369). p. 310

180 Engels wrote this letter on the advice of Nikolai Danielson who had informed him of the opportunity to have Marx's unpublished letter to the editors of the *Otechestvenniye Zapiski* printed in the magazine *Severny Vestnik* (see present edition, Vol. 24, pp. 196-201). However, Marx's letter did not appear in that magazine either and was first published in Russian in 1886 in Geneva in *Vestnik Narodnoi Voli*, No. 5 and in the Russian legal journal *Yuridichesky Vestnik* in October 1888. p. 311

181 Engels wrote this work as an introduction to the third German edition of Marx's pamphlet *Revelations Concerning the Communist Trial in Cologne* (see present edition, Vol. 11, pp. 395-457) and had it published first in the newspaper *Sozialdemokrat*, Nos. 46, 47 and 48 of November 12, 19 and 26, 1885, and also in the book K. Marx, *Enthüllungen über den Kommunisten-Prozess zu Köln. Neuer Abdruck mit Einleitung von Friedrich Engels und Dokumenten*, that appeared late in November 1885. Besides Marx's pamphlet, the book also contained *The Communist Trial in Cologne*, the fourth appendix to Marx's *Herr Vogt* (see present edition, Vol. 17, pp. 305-11), Marx's Epilogue to the second German edition of the pamphlet (see present edition, Vol. 24, pp. 51-54) and Addresses of the Central Authority to the League, March and June 1850 (see present edition, Vol. 10, pp. 277-87 and 371-77). p. 312

182 Wermuth, Stieber, *Die Communisten-Verschwörungen des 19. Jahrhunderts*, Berlin, Part I, 1853, Part II, 1854. The appendices to Part I of the book which expounded the "history" of the workers' movement in the form of instructions for the police carried several documents of the Communist League which had fallen into the hands of the police. Part II (the "Black List") contained detailed information about people connected with the working-class and democratic movement. p. 312

183 Engels may have had in mind the book by G. Adler, *Die Geschichte der ersten*

sozialpolitischen Arbeiterbewegung in Deutschland, Breslau, 1885. In his letter to August Bebel, dated October 28, 1885, Engels writes the following: "Kautsky has given me Adler's very superficial book which is largely based on Stieber; I shall help him write a review" (see present edition, Vol. 47). The critical analysis of this book, which Karl Kautsky wrote on the basis of Engels' comments, was published in the magazine *Die Neue Zeit* in February 1886. Engels' remarks on Adler's book are to be found in *Marx-Engels-Jahrbuch,* 2., Berlin, 1979.

p. 312

[184] *Babouvism*—one of the trends of utopian egalitarian communism based on the ideas of natural right. Founded at the close of the 18th century by François Noël Babeuf (Gracchus). Babouvism played a very important role in shaping the socialist views of secret revolutionary societies in the 1830s and 1840s.

p. 313

[185] *Société des saisons (Society of the Seasons)*—a secret revolutionary organisation that existed in Paris between 1837 and 1839. It was founded by Auguste Blanqui, Armand Barbès and Martin Bernard with the aim of overthrowing the bourgeois monarchy of Louis Philippe, proclaiming a republic and implementing revolutionary egalitarian ideas. An uprising on *May 12, 1839* in Paris, in which revolutionary workers played the leading part, had been planned by the Society of the Seasons; it was suppressed by troops and the National Guard.

p. 313

[186] Karl Schapper was arrested immediately after the uprising of May 12, 1839 and deported from France after serving seven months in prison; Heinrich Bauer continued his revolutionary activity in Paris, was arrested in December 1841 and also deported.

p. 313

[187] The reference is to the *Frankfurter Attentat* (the Frankfurt Attempt). On April 3, 1833, in response to the police measures undertaken by the Federal Diet, a group of conspirators, mainly students, attempted to seize Frankfurt am Main, overthrow the Diet and proclaim a republic. But the conspirators only managed to take possession of the guard house for a short time, following which they were dispersed by troops.

p. 313

[188] The reference is to the march by revolutionary émigrés and members of the "Young Italy" society, organised by Mazzini in February 1834 with a view to inciting a republican uprising in Piedmont. A detachment of insurgent émigrés of various nationalities under the command of Ramorino invaded Savoy from Switzerland but was defeated by Piedmontese troops.

p. 313

[189] *Demagogues* in Germany were the participants in the students' opposition movement after the liberation of the country from Napoleonic rule. The name became current after the Karlsbad Conference of Ministers of the German States in August 1819, which adopted a special resolution on the persecution of the demagogues.

p. 313

[190] The *German Workers' Educational Society* in London was founded in February 1840 by Karl Schapper, Joseph Moll and other leaders of the League of the Just (in the 1850s the Society had its premises in Windmill Street, Soho). After the reorganisation of the League of the Just in the summer of 1847 and the founding of the Communist League, the latter's local communities played a leading role in the Society. In 1847 and 1849-50 Marx and Engels took an active part in the Society's work, but on September 17, 1850 they and a

number of their followers withdrew because the Willich-Schapper sectarian and adventurist faction had temporarily increased its influence in the Society and caused a split in the Communist League. Later Schapper realised the errors of his ways and took steps towards a reconciliation with Marx. The resultant weakening of sectarian influence made it possible for Marx and Engels to resume their work in the Educational Society in late 1850. In 1918, the Society was closed down by the British Government. p. 314

191 The reference is to the latter half of 1840 when Weitling returned to Paris after a propaganda trip to Germany begun in the spring of 1839. He made a short visit to Geneva in the summer of 1840 and again came back to Paris. In May 1841 Weitling settled in Switzerland for good. p. 315

192 See Note 140. p. 319

193 The *Democratic Association*, founded on September 27, 1847 in Brussels, united proletarian revolutionaries, mainly German refugees and advanced bourgeois and petty-bourgeois democrats. Marx and Engels took an active part in its establishment. On November 15, 1847 Marx was elected its Vice-President (the President was Lucien Jottrand, a Belgian democrat) and under his influence it becamè a centre of the international democratic movement. During the February 1848 revolution in France, the proletarian wing of the Brussels Democratic Association sought to arm the Belgian workers and to intensify the struggle for a democratic republic. However, when Marx was expelled from Brussels in March 1848 and the most revolutionary elements were repressed by the Belgian authorities, its activity assumed a narrow, purely local character and in 1849 the Association ceased to exist. p. 319

194 The motto was changed at the First Congress of the Communist League in June 1847. p. 322

195 Engels reproduces the main points of the "Demands of the Communist Party in Germany" (see present edition, Vol. 7, pp. 3-7) which were written by Marx and himself in Paris between March 21 and 24, 1848. This document was discussed by members of the Central Authority, who approved and signed it as the political programme of the Communist League in the revolution that broke out in Germany. In March it was printed as a leaflet, for distribution among revolutionary German émigré workers who were about to return home. The leaflet soon reached members of the Communist League in other countries, notably German émigré workers in London.

Early in April, the "Demands" were published in several democratic German papers. p. 323

196 The reference is to the *German Workers' Club*, founded in Paris on March 8-9, 1848, on the initiative of the Communist League leaders. The leading role in it belonged to Marx. The Club's aim was to unite the German émigré workers in Paris, explain to them the tactics of the proletariat in a bourgeois-democratic revolution and also to counter the attempts of the bourgeois and petty-bourgeois democrats to stir up the German workers by nationalist propaganda and make them join the adventurist march of volunteer legions into Germany. The Club was successful in arranging the return of German workers one by one to their own country to take part in the revolutionary struggle there.

p. 324

197. From May 3 to 9, 1849 Dresden, the capital of Saxony, was the scene of an armed uprising caused by the refusal of the King of Saxony to approve the

Imperial Constitution drafted by the Frankfurt National Assembly. The insurgents, among whom the workers played a prominent part in fighting on the barricades, gained control of a considerable section of the city and formed a provisional government headed by the radical democrat Samuel Tzschirner. An active part in the uprising was played by Mikhail Bakunin, the Russian revolutionary, Stephan Born and Richard Wagner, the composer. The uprising was suppressed by Saxon and Prussian troops.   p. 325

198 The *Sonderbund*—a separatist union of the seven economically backward Catholic cantons of Switzerland formed in 1843 to resist progressive bourgeois reforms and to defend the privileges of the Church and the Jesuits.

p. 325

199 The *Workers' Fraternity* was suppressed in all the states belonging to the German Confederation in mid-1850. But some of its groups in North and South Germany existed until 1852.

Following the defeat of the Dresden uprising Born fled to Switzerland.

p. 326

200 See Note 75.   p. 326

201 Joseph Moll was mortally wounded in the stomach (not in the head) during the encounter at the Rothenfels Bridge on the River Murg on June 29, 1849.

p. 326

202 The French Party of Order formed in 1848 was a coalition of monarchist groups: the Legitimists (supporters of the Bourbon dynasty), the Orleanists (supporters of the Orleans dynasty) and the Bonapartists. It was the party of the conservative big bourgeoisie. From 1849 until the coup d'état of December 2, 1851 it held sway in the Legislative Assembly of the Second Republic.   p. 327

203 Early in May 1851 Peter Nothjung was sent on a tour of Germany as an emissary of the Cologne Central Authority of the Communist League. On May 10 he was arrested in Leipzig. The documents seized from him enabled the authorities of Prussia and other German states to arrest more League members.

p. 328

204 The *Battle of Murfreesboro*, on the Stone River (Tennessee), took place between December 31, 1862 and January 2, 1863, and ended in the defeat of the Confederate army. This was one of the first victories won by the North over the slave-owning states.   p. 328

205 The reference is to the Willich-Schapper sectarian group that seceded from the Communist League after the split of September 15, 1850 and formed an independent organisation with its own Central Committee. By its activities it helped the Prussian police uncover the illegal communities of the Communist League in Germany and gave it a pretext for fabricating evidence in a trial against the prominent leaders of the Communist League in Cologne in 1852.

On the *Sonderbund* see Note 198.   p. 329

206 See Note 174.   p. 329

207 This is an extract from Engels' letter to Paul Lafargue. The complete text of the letter has not been traced.

Engels wrote this letter in connection with the first ballot to the French Chamber of Deputies, held on October 4, 1885 amidst general discontent with the home and foreign policy pursued by the party of moderate bourgeois republicans (the so-called opportunists, see Note 208) who had been in power since 1879.

During this period the country's economic situation had deteriorated (state budget deficit, growing taxes and increased borrowing, etc.); the promises given during the election campaign, such as the abolition of the Senate, separation of the Church from the state, introduction of progressive income tax, and others, were not kept; colonial adventures caused discontent among the popular masses; many of the party's leaders were exposed as corrupt. All this brought victory to the monarchists in the first ballot. The French Socialists regarded this as their own defeat and Lafargue wrote about it to Engels on October 7 and 11. Engels deemed it necessary to explain the situation to them and did so in his letter of which an extract was published in the newspaper of the French Workers' Party.

Similar ideas expressed by Engels in his letter to Eduard Bernstein of October 8, 1885 (see present edition, Vol. 47) were utilised in the leading article of the *Sozialdemokrat*, No. 42, October 15, 1885.

The letter was published in English for the first time in: Frederick Engels, Paul and Laura Lafargue, *Correspondence*, Vol. I, Foreign Languages Publishing House, Moscow, 1959, pp. 310-11.   p. 331

208 The *opportunists*—this name was applied to the party of moderate bourgeois republicans in France after its Left wing split away from it in 1881 to form the Radical Party headed by Georges Clemenceau.

The name, proposed by the journalist Henri Rochefort, derived from the words of Party leader Léon Gambetta that reforms should be carried out "at an opportune time".   p. 331

209 The reference is to the Orleanists, the Bonapartists and the Legitimists. See also Note 202.   p. 331

210 The expression "the best of the republics" ("Voici la meilleure de république") is attributed to La Fayette, who used it on July 31, 1830 when the members of the Paris Municipal Commission fulfilling the functions of the Provisional Government after the overthrow of Charles X had a meeting with Louis Philippe, the Duke of Orleans, who had been proclaimed King of France.   p. 332

211 Since at the elections of October 4, 1885, most of the candidates did not receive the required number of votes, a second ballot was fixed for October 18. It brought victory to the deputies from the party of moderate republicans (opportunists) (see Note 208) and the Radical Party (see Note 212). The Chamber of Deputies numbered 382 republicans, among them 180 radicals and 202 monarchists.   p. 332

212 The *radicals*—a parliamentary group that emerged from the party of moderate republicans (opportunists, see Note 208) in the 1880s-90s. The radicals relied mainly on the petty bourgeoisie and partly on the middle bourgeoisie and championed such bourgeois-democratic demands as a single-chamber parliamentary system, separation of the Church from the state, introduction of progressive income tax, limitation of the working day and solution of some other social problems. In 1901 the group acquired official status as the Republican Party of Radicals and Radical Socialists (*Parti républicain radical et radicalsocialiste*).   p. 332

213 See Note 210.   p. 333

[214] In this article Engels is making a critical analysis of the English translation of the first and part of the second sections of Chapter I, Vol. I of Marx's *Capital* (see present edition, Vol. 35), printed in the magazine *To-day,* Vol. 4, No. 22, October 1885, pp. 429-36. The translation was the work of Henry Hyndman, leader of the Social-Democratic Federation, who wrote under the pseudonym John Broadhouse. After the appearance of Engels' article, Hyndman continued to publish his translation; altogether seven chapters and the greater part of the eighth chapter of Vol. I were printed in *To-day* up to May 1889. The full English translation of Vol. I of *Capital,* done by Samuel Moore and edited by Engels, appeared in 1887.   p. 335

[215] Engels is referring to *Capital,* Vol. II, Chapter XII (see present edition, Vol. 36).   p. 336

[216] See present edition, Vol. 35 (Chapter I). Here Engels translates the expression "in der bürgerlichen Gesellschaft" as "in civil society"; in the French authorised edition of 1872-75 and in the 1887 English edition edited by Engels this expression is translated differently: "in the bourgeois society".   p. 339

[217] Engels wrote this article as part two of his Introduction to the separate edition of Wilhelm Wolff's series of articles on the condition of the Silesian peasants (see Note 74) published on his (Engels') initiative. Part one of the Introduction comprised a considerably abridged version of Engels' article "Wilhelm Wolff" printed in 1876 (see present edition, Vol. 24, pp. 129-71).   p. 341

[218] The reference is to the *Teutonic Order*—a German Catholic Order of Knights founded in 1190 during the Crusades. The Order had vast possessions in Germany, and in the 13th-14th centuries it conquered extensive territories between the Lower Vistula and the Niemen (East Prussia). During the 15th century the Order gradually declined and lost a considerable part of its possessions; in 1525 the Order ceased to exist as a state. Only small areas scattered throughout Germany remained in its possession until the beginning of the 19th century.   p. 342

[219] *Hereditary copyholders*—dependent peasants living in Germany, Bohemia and the Kingdom of Poland in the 13th-15th centuries. They enjoyed personal freedom, and had to pay quit-rent (in money or in kind) to the landlord for using their plots of land.   p. 343

[220] The *Thirty Years' War* (1618-48)—a European war, in which the Pope, the Spanish and Austrian Habsburgs and the Catholic German princes rallied under the banner of Catholicism and fought the Protestant countries Bohemia, Denmark, Sweden, the Republic of the Netherlands and a number of Protestant German states. The rulers of Catholic France—rivals of the Habsburgs—supported the Protestant camp. Germany was the main battle arena and the object of plunder and territorial claims. The Peace of Westphalia (1648) sealed the political dismemberment of Germany.

At the *Battle of Jena* (October 14, 1806) the French army, commanded by Napoleon, routed the Prussian army, thus forcing Prussia to surrender.

p. 345

[221] *Dreschgärtner, Häusler, Instleute*—categories of landless peasants in Germany, who, in their status, were close to day-labourers. These peasants were obliged to render the landlord all kinds of services in return for a roof over their heads, a tiny plot of land and, sometimes, meagre remuneration in kind and money.   p. 345

222 See Note 35 and also this volume, p. 74.   p. 346

223 To supply the Prussian state with material resources and ensure the recruitment of soldiers Frederick II of Prussia promulgated a number of laws, among them the Statute on the Peasants of 1764, which proscribed the eviction of the peasants from their plots of land. However, these laws were implemented only to a very small extent.   p. 346

224 At *Mollwitz* (Małujowice, Silesia) Frederick II's army defeated the Austrians on April 10, 1741, during the War of the Austrian Succession (1740-48).

On September 1-2, 1870, the Châlon Army of the French was routed by the Germans near Sedan. The Franco-Prussian War of 1870-71 brought about the collapse of the Second Empire in France.   p. 346

225 The reference is to the decrees of February 14, 1808, of March 27 and April 8, 1809 and of January 9, 1810. The decree of April 8, 1809 stated that abolition of personal hereditary dependence should not be interpreted as releasing the peasants from their feudal obligations.   p. 347

226 In the *Battle of Waterloo* fought on June 18, 1815, the Anglo-Dutch and Prussian forces commanded by the Duke of Wellington and Blücher defeated Napoleon's army.   p. 347

227 The *Seven Years' War* (1756-63)—a war between the Anglo-Prussian and the Franco-Russo-Austrian coalition. The war was caused by the conflict of interests among the feudal absolutist powers (Prussia, Austria, Russia and France) and the colonial rivalry between France and Britain. It resulted in the expansion of the British colonial empire at the expense of the French possessions and in the growth of Russia's might; Austria and Prussia more or less retained their pre-war frontiers.   p. 347

228 *Ackernahrung*—a plot of land sufficient to maintain a peasant family.
                                                                    p. 347

229 *Thaler*—a silver coin equal to about three marks; it appeared in the 16th century in Bohemia and circulated in the 19th century in all North German states as well as in Prussia and Saxony.   p. 348

230 The expression *state of intelligence,* often used in an ironical sense, originates from a phrase in Hegel's opening lecture in Heidelberg University in October 1816.   p. 348

231 *Scheffel*—dry measure used in different German states. Its size varied up to 1872.   p. 348

232 Engels is referring to the two tables from August Meitzen's book *Der Boden und die landwirthschaftlichen Verhältnisse des Preußischen Staates nach dem Gebietsumfange vor 1866,* Vol. I, Berlin, 1868. The first table sums up the results of the redemption operations from 1816 to 1848; the second table those from 1816 to the end of 1865.   p. 350

233 This is one of the fundamental works of Marxism. It reveals the relationship between Marxism and its philosophical predecessors as represented by Hegel and Feuerbach, the prominent exponents of German classical philosophy, and provides a systematic exposition of the fundamentals of dialectical and historical materialism. The work was originally published in *Die Neue Zeit,* the theoretical journal of the German Social-Democratic Party; in 1888 it appeared as a pamphlet for which Engels wrote a special preface (see this volume, pp. 519-20). The supplement to this edition contained Marx's *Theses on*

Feuerbach, published for the first time. In 1889, the St. Petersburg journal *Severny Vestnik,* Nos 3 and 4, carried a Russian translation of Engels' work entitled *The Crisis of the Philosophy of Classical Idealism in Germany.* The author's name was not mentioned, and the text contained many additions and digressions. It was signed G. L. (the initials of the translator—G. Lvovich). In 1890 Engels' work was translated into Polish. In 1892 the Emancipation of Labour group in Geneva published the full Russian translation of this work by Georgy Plekhanov; the same year it was translated into Bulgarian. In 1894 the Paris journal *Ère nouvelle,* Nos 4 and 5 published the French translation by Laura Lafargue edited by the author. The second (stereotype) German edition appeared in 1895. There were no other editions of this work during Engels' lifetime.

The work was published in English for the first time in 1903 by Kerr Publishers, USA, under the title *The Roots of Socialist Philosophy.*   p. 353

234 The reference is to Heinrich Heine's *Zur Geschichte der Religion und Philosophie in Deutschland,* originally published in French translation in the Paris *Revue des deux mondes* in March-December 1834.

In his work Heine draws a parallel between the development of German philosophy and the events of the French Revolution of 1789. In conclusion he says: "Our philosophical revolution is concluded. Hegel has closed its great circle.... Such methodical people as we are had to begin with the Reformation; only after that could we occupy ourselves with philosophy, and only after its consummation could we pass on to political revolution."   p. 357

235 Engels is quoting here, in a slightly changed form, a passage from Hegel's preface to *Grundlinien der Philosophie des Rechts* (p. XIX), which reads: "What is rational is real and what is real is rational."   p. 358

236 The term *positive religion* was used by Hegel in his *Philosophy of Religion* where he says: "that it is revealed, is *positive* religion in the sense that it has come to man from without, has been given to him" ("daß sie geoffenbart ist, *positive* Religion sei, in dem Sinne, daß sie dem Menschen von Außen gekommen, gegeben worden" (See Hegel, *Vorlesungen über die Philosophie der Religion,* Vol. II, Part 3, 2nd ed., Stuttgart, 1928, p. 198.)   p. 364

237 The reference is to German, or "true", socialism which was widespread in Germany in the 1840s, mostly among petty-bourgeois intellectuals. The "true socialists"—Karl Grün, Moses Hess, Hermann Kriege—substituted the sentimental preaching of love and brotherhood for the ideas of socialism and denied the need for a bourgeois-democratic revolution in Germany. Marx and Engels criticised this trend in *The German Ideology* (see present edition, Vol. 5), *Circular Against Kriege, German Socialism in Verse and Prose* and *Manifesto of the Communist Party* (ibid., Vol. 6).   p. 365

238 The planet referred to is Neptune, discovered on September 23, 1846 by the German astronomer Johann Galle.   p. 368

239 This passage is quoted in C. N. Starcke, *Ludwig Feuerbach,* Stuttgart, 1885, p. 166. The quotation was taken from K. Grün, *Ludwig Feuerbach in seinem Briefwechsel und Nachlaß sowie in seiner Philosophischen Charakterentwicklung,* Vol. II, Leipzig and Heidelberg, 1874, p. 308.   p. 369

240 The *phlogiston theory* was formulated in 1703 by Georg Stahl, a German

physician and chemist, who asserted that all combustible materials and base metals contained a substance called phlogiston which was emitted during combustion. Towards the end of the 18th century this hypothesis was disproved by Antoine Lavoisier, but it played a considerable role in the development of chemistry as a science.   p. 370

241 The *deists* recognise the idea of God as the rational creator of the universe, but deny God's interference in nature and social life.   p. 373

242 See Note 236.   p. 375

243 The state religion—*Culte de l'Etre suprême*—was decreed by the Convention on May 7, 1794 during the Jacobine dictatorship. Its creed was a powerful supreme being and the immortality of the soul. The new religion was needed, on the one hand, to stop the de-Christianisation of the population connected with the dissemination of the cult of reason rejected by believers, and, on the other, to strengthen the ideological influence of the authorities upon the masses. The cult disappeared together with the Jacobine dictatorship. p. 376

244 "The school-master of Sadowa"—an expression first used by Oskar Peschel, editor of the Augsburg journal *Ausland,* in his article "Die Lehren der jüngsten Kriegsgeschichte", published in No. 29 of that journal on July 17, 1866, and then widely employed by German journalists, especially after the Prussian victory at Königgrätz in the Austro-Prussian War of 1866 (the Battle of Sadowa), the implication being that the Prussian victory was to be attributed to the superiority of the Prussian system of public education.   p. 380

245 The *Council of Nicaea*—the first ecumenical council of the Christian Bishops of the Roman Empire, convened by Emperor Constantine I in the town of Nicaea (Asia Minor) in 325. The Council formulated the Nicene Creed and made it obligatory for all Christians. Non-recognition of it was punishable as a state offence.   p. 394

246 The *Albigenses*—a religious sect that existed in the 12th and 13th centuries in Southern France (notably in Provence and Toulouse) and in Northern Italy. This movement took the form of a "heresy", being directed against the power and doctrine of the Catholic Church, and against the secular power of the feudal state. Its adherents were called Albigenses because the city of Albi was one of the sect's main centres.   p. 395

247 The reference is to the revolution of 1688 (the overthrow of the House of Stuart and the enthronement of William III of Orange), following which (1689) the constitutional monarchy was consolidated in England on the basis of a compromise between the landed aristocracy and the bourgeoisie.   p. 396

248 From the 1620s political and religious repressions of Huguenots (Calvinist Protestants) intensified, and in 1685 Louis XIV revoked the Edict of Nantes which had been enacted by Henry IV in 1598 and granted Huguenots religious freedom and considerable political independence. After the revocation of the Edict of Nantes several hundred thousand Huguenots left France.   p. 396.

249 The reference is to the German Empire which was founded in January 1871 under the supremacy of Prussia and did not include Austria.   p. 397

250 This article was occasioned by the first English edition of Engels' work *The Condition of the Working-Class in England* (see present edition, Vol. 4, pp. 295-596), then in preparation in the USA. Originally Engels intended to

use it as a Preface or Afterword to this edition, but the publication of the book was considerably delayed because Engels could not find a publisher at the time. He therefore deemed it necessary to write a new preface (see this volume, pp. 434-42) and use this article as an Appendix. In 1892 Engels included almost the whole of this article in the Prefaces to the English and second German editions of his work (see present edition, Vol. 27).   p. 399

251 See Note 154.   p. 400

252 The discovery of rich gold deposits in California in 1848 and in Australia in 1851 greatly influenced the economic development of Europe and America.
                                                                                  p. 400

253 The *truck-system*—the payment of workers in goods. Engels described this system in his work *The Condition of the Working-Class in England* (see present edition, Vol. 4, pp. 470-71). The *Truck-Act* prohibiting the truck-system was adopted in 1831, but many factory owners violated it.
    The *Ten Hours' Bill*, which applied to women and children only, was passed by the British Parliament on June 8, 1847.   p. 400

254 "*Little Ireland*"—a district in the southern suburbs of Manchester, inhabited mainly by Irish workers; a detailed description of it is given by Engels in *The Condition of the Working-Class in England* (present edition, Vol. 4, pp. 360-62).
    The "*Seven Dials*"—seven radial streets in the heart of London at that time inhabited mainly by workers.   p. 401

255 Under the *cottage-system* the factory owners leased dwellings to the workers on harsh conditions: rent was deducted from wages (for details see present edition, Vol. 4, pp. 471-72).   p. 402

256 The reference is to a strike of over 10,000 coal-miners in Pennsylvania (USA) between January 22 and February 26, 1886. Blast and coke furnace workers demanding higher wages and better working conditions managed to secure some of their demands.
    On the colliers' strike of 1844 in Northern England see present edition, Vol. 4, pp. 541-47.   p. 402

257 Engels wrote this letter in response to a request by the French Socialists that he express publicly his solidarity with them on the occasion of the 15th anniversary of the Paris Commune. The letter was read out at a meeting in commemoration of the Commune on March 18, 1886 and published in *Le Socialiste* on March 27, 1886 under the title "Lèttre d'Engels".
    This letter was published in English for the first time in Frederick Engels, Paul and Laura Lafargue, *Correspondence*, Vol. I, Foreign Languages Publishing House, Moscow, 1959, pp. 406-07.   p. 406

258 The reference is to the 1884 elections to the Reichstag, when, under the conditions of the Anti-Socialist Law (see Note 174), the German Social-Democratic Party polled about 550,000 votes, and doubled its representation to 24 members.   p. 407

259 Until 1885 France was divided into "small constituencies", each sending one representative to the Chamber of Deputies. In June 1885, on the initiative of moderate bourgeois republicans, a system of voting by department lists was introduced. Under this system, which operated until 1889, small constituencies were combined to form larger ones each corresponding to a department. Now a voter received a ballot paper with the names of candidates from different

parties, but he was obliged to vote for a total number of candidates to be elected, one deputy from 70,000 people. A deputy was considered elected in the first ballot provided he had received an absolute majority of votes; a relative majority was sufficient in the second ballot. p. 407

260 On February 11, 1886, the workers' deputies in the French Parliament made an interpellation concerning the government's actions against the miners' strike in Decazeville (see Note 263). Engels regarded this as the formation of the socialist group in the Chamber of Deputies. p. 407

261 Engels wrote this Statement because he feared McEnnis would not be able to interpret his words correctly. He asked Sorge to have it published in one of the American socialist papers if the interview should appear in the press (see Engels' letter to Friedrich Sorge dated April 29, 1886, present edition, Vol. 47). p. 408

262 The reference is to the Freycinet Government (January 7-December 3, 1886) consisting mostly of radicals and moderate republicans, as distinct from the majority of the previous cabinets, to which, as a rule, radicals were in opposition. p. 409

263 In late January 1886 more than 3,000 workers of Decazeville (south of France) went on strike. The reason was their cruel exploitation by the capitalists of the Aveyron Company of coal-mines and foundries; the government despatched troops to Decazeville. The strike continued till mid-June and evoked a broad response throughout the country; under its impact a small workers' group was formed in the Chamber of Deputies which came out in defence of the workers' economic demands. p. 409

264 The reference is to the by-election to the Chamber of Deputies in Paris on May 2, 1886, when the socialist candidate Ernest Roche received 100,795 votes. p. 409

265 This article is a letter written by Engels to Paul Lafargue on October 25, 1886 (see present edition, Vol. 47), with slight abridgements and editorial changes. Engels wrote this letter in reply to Lafargue's request for his opinion on the situation in the Balkans and the course the foreign policy of the European powers would take in connection with the growing rivalry between Tsarist Russia and the Austro-Hungarian monarchy. This article is the only one Engels wrote for the press in the 1880s on questions of foreign policy. The German translation of the article was published in the New York paper *Sozialist* on November 20 and 27 and December 4, 1886. It was also translated into Romanian and printed in the magazine *Revista Sociala*, No. 2, December 1886; an abridged version of the article was published in German translation in the newspaper *Sozialdemokrat* on December 12, 1886. p. 410

266 The *Preliminary Peace Treaty* between Russia and Turkey, which put an end to the Russo-Turkish War of 1877-78, was concluded on March 3 (February 19), 1878 in San Stefano (near Constantinople). The Treaty envisaged the creation of an autonomous Bulgarian principality nominally dependent on Turkey, state independence for Serbia, Montenegro and Romania as well as their territorial expansion, etc. The Treaty considerably strengthened the position of Russia in the Balkans which caused a sharp reaction on the part of Great Britain and Austria-Hungary, including a show of military force (e.g. the despatch of English warships to the Sea of Marmara and other measures). This forced Russia to agree to the convocation of an international congress for the purpose

of revising the treaty, since it affected "general European" problems. The representatives of Russia, Great Britain, Austria-Hungary, Turkey, Germany, France and Italy took part in the congress which was held in Berlin between June 13 (1) and July 13 (1), 1878. The Berlin Treaty signed at this Congress radically changed the provisions of the San Stefano Treaty to the detriment of Russia and the Slavs of the Balkan Peninsula. The territory of self-governing Bulgaria, stipulated by the San Stefano Treaty, was cut more than twice; an autonomous province known as "Eastern Rumelia", which remained under the power of the sultan, was formed at the expense of Bulgarian regions lying south of the Balkan Ridge; the territory of Montenegro was substantially curtailed. The Berlin Treaty endorsed the return to Russia of the part of Bessarabia severed from it in 1856, and at the same time sanctioned the occupation of Bosnia and Herzegovina by Austria-Hungary. The decisions of the Berlin Congress turned the Balkans into the hotbed of conflict which led to the outbreak of the First World War.   p. 410

[267] The suppression of the Polish national insurrection was followed, in 1795, by the third partition of Poland between Austria, Prussia and Russia, and the final abolition of the Polish state. By decision of the Vienna Congress (1814-15) the Kingdom of Poland was formed within the Russian Empire. It incorporated the greater part of lands seized by Prussia and Austria during the third partition of Poland.   p. 410

[268] Engels is referring to the reprisals instituted by the Tsarist government against the members of the Narodnaya Volya (People's Will) organisation in the early 1880s, which practically destroyed it.

Nihilism—a system of views held in the 1860s by the progressive-minded Russian intellectuals of different social estates. The Nihilists refused to recognise the dominant ideology and morality, rejected religion and demanded freedom of the personality. In West European writing, the term was applied to participants in the Russian revolutionary movement of the 1870s and 1880s, notably the Narodnaya Volya members.   p. 411

[269] The reference is to the occupation of Egypt by Great Britain as a result of the Anglo-Egyptian War of 1882.

In the 1870s, capitalising on the financial difficulties facing the Egyptian government, above all, its considerable foreign debt, England and France, its principal creditors, established financial control over the country. This led to the growth of the national liberation movement and attempts to shake off foreign dependence in the early 1880s. In the summer of 1882, Great Britain provoked a conflict with Egypt and launched military operations which terminated in September 1882. To all intents and purposes, Egypt was turned into a British colony, although on paper it was still part of the Ottoman Empire. As a result of Britain's actions, its relations with France deteriorated.
                                                                          p. 411

[270] In September 1885, an uprising of Bulgarian patriots took place in Eastern Rumelia. The Turkish governor was overthrown. Rumelia was reunited with Bulgaria.   p. 412

[271] The reference is to the Austro-Prussian War of 1866, which ended in victory for Prussia (see also notes 171 and 172). The principal theatre of operations was Bohemia (Čechy).

Engels compares this campaign with the military operations conducted by Bulgaria in the war against Serbia, which began on November 14 (2), 1885.

The war was triggered off by the attempt of Serbia, instigated by Austria-Hungary, to reverse the results of the unification of Eastern Rumelia and the Bulgarian Principality that had taken place in September 1885. In the first month of the war, Bulgarian troops defeated the Serbian army and soon entered Serbia. Under pressure from Austria-Hungary, Bulgaria called a halt to the advance of its troops. The frontiers of the united Bulgaria were confirmed by the Bucharest Peace Treaty of 1886.   p. 412

272 Greeting Alexander III on May 13 (25), 1886, on his return to Moscow from the Crimea, the city mayor Alexeyev said, "Our faith is strengthening that the cross of Christ will shine on St. Sophia" (he meant St. Sophia's Cathedral in Constantinople).   p. 413

273 *Slavophilism*—a trend in Russian social thought in the 1840s-60s, which advocated a special path of historical development for Russia, one differing fundamentally from that of Western Europe.

Engels is referring here to those representatives of Russian society who in the 1880s championed active use of the slogan of Slavic unity in the foreign policy pursued by the Tsarist autocracy.

On the *Nihilists*, see Note 268.   p. 413

274 The reference is to the political crisis of 1886-87 in Bulgaria. After the deposition of the Prince of Battenberg and the establishment of the Regency in August 1886, the Russian government sent General Kaulbars to Burgaria on a special mission to prepare the ground for the election of a Russian candidate to the Bulgarian throne. The mission failed, however, partly because of the stand taken on the Bulgarian issue by West European powers headed by Britain. Kaulbars was recalled, and diplomatic relations between Russia and Bulgaria were broken off in November 1886.   p. 414

275 The *Orleanists* were supporters of the Orleans dynasty which held power in France during the July monarchy (1830-48). They upheld the interests of the financial aristocracy and the big industrial bourgeoisie and were members of the so-called Party of Order (see Note 202).   p. 416

276 Part of this article was published in English for the first time in K. Marx and F. Engels, *On Literature and Art*, Progress Publishers, Moscow, 1978, pp. 406-07.   p. 418

277 The reference is to the republican insurrection in Baden, led by the petty-bourgeois democrats Friedrich Hecker and Gustav Struve, which was crushed in April 1848.   p. 418

278 On February 9, 1849, the Constituent Assembly in Rome abolished the secular power of the Pope and proclaimed a republic. The Roman Republic had to repulse attacks by the counter-revolutionary Neapolitan and Austrian troops and the French expeditionary corps sent to Italy in April 1849 by decision of President Louis Bonaparte to restore Papal power. The republic only survived until July 3, 1849.   p. 419

279 The reference is to the campaign for the Imperial Constitution adopted by the Frankfurt National Assembly on March 27, 1849 but rejected by the majority of German governments. In May 1849, popular uprisings in support of the Constitution broke out in Saxony, Rhenish Prussia, Baden and the Palatinate. The insurgents received no support from the Frankfurt National Assembly and the movement was suppressed in July 1849. Engels devoted his work *The

Campaign for the German Imperial Constitution to these events (see present edition, Vol. 10).

p. 419

280 This refers to the events of June 5-6, 1849 in Karlsruhe, the capital of Baden. The radical wing of the democrats, who were discontented with the capitulatory policy of the Baden Provisional Government headed by Brentano, founded the *Club of Resolute Progress* in Karlsruhe on June 5, 1849. The Club suggested that Brentano extend the revolution beyond Baden and the Palatinate and introduce radicals into his government. When Brentano refused, the Club tried, on June 6, to force the government to comply by threatening an armed demonstration. But the government, supported by the civil militia and other armed units, proved the stronger party in the conflict. The Club of Resolute Progress was disbanded.

p. 419

281 The reference is to the volunteer unit of the Gymnastics Society of Hanau (in the vicinity of Frankfurt am Main) which took part in the Baden-Palatinate uprising of 1849.

p. 419

282 On September 28, 1864, an international meeting was held at St. Martin's Hall, Long Acre, London. It was organised by the London trade union leaders and a group of Paris Proudhonist workers jointly with representatives of German, Italian and other foreign workers then living in London, and a number of prominent European democratic émigrés. The meeting resolved to found an International Working Men's Association (later known as the First International) and elected a Provisional Committee, which shortly afterwards constituted itself as the leading body of the Association.

p. 422

283 *L'Alliance internationale de la démocratie socialiste* (The International Alliance of Socialist Democracy) was founded by Mikhail Bakunin in Geneva in September 1868. Alongside Bakunin, its Provisional Committee comprised Brosset, Duval, Guétat, Perron, Zagorsky and Johann Philipp Becker. In 1868, the Alliance published in Geneva leaflets in French and German containing its Programme and Rules. Shortly afterwards, Becker broke with Bakunin.

The Alliance incorporated a secret conspiratorial union that Bakunin had set up previously.

In December 1868, the Alliance applied to the General Council requesting admission to the First International. The Central Bureau of the Alliance joined the International as its Geneva section under the name *Alliance de la démocratie socialiste*.

In the International, the Bakuninists formed a bloc with anti-Marxian elements and openly campaigned against Marx and Engels, seeking to establish their supremacy over the international working-class movement. The Alliance fell apart soon after Bakunin's expulsion from the International in 1872.

p. 422

284 See Note 81.

p. 423

285 The reference is to the five-milliard-franc contribution imposed on France under the Frankfurt Peace Treaty of 1871 signed after the Franco-Prussian War.

p. 424

286 The reference is to the ban on the printing and distribution of socialist literature in Germany (Engels' work *The Housing Question* included). It was introduced under the Anti-Socialist Law passed in October 1878 (see Note 174).

p. 425

287 The *Nueva Federación Madrileña* (*New Madrid Federation*) was formed on

July 8, 1872 by the members of *La Emancipacion* editorial board expelled from the Madrid Federation by the anarchist majority for the paper's exposure of the activities of the secret Alliance of Socialist Democracy (see Note 283) in Spain. A major part in its foundation was played by Paul Lafargue. On August 15, 1872, the General Council admitted the New Madrid Federation to the First International.

The New Madrid Federation fought against the spread of anarchist influence in Spain, popularised ideas of scientific socialism, and helped establish the Spanish Socialist Workers' Party in 1879. p. 426

288 During the revolution of 1848, Proudhon advanced several concrete projects of social and economic reforms. In very general terms, they were expounded in the book: P. J. Proudhon, *Idée générale de la Révolution au XIX-e siècle*, Paris, 1851. p. 427

289 *Armchair socialism* (Kathedersozialismus), a trend in the German bourgeois political economy that emerged in the last third of the 19th century as a reaction to the growth of the workers' movement and the spread of scientific socialism in it. Its representatives advocated bourgeois reformism from university rostrums under the pretence of commitment to socialism. They asserted, among other things, that the state, specifically the German Empire, had a supra-class character and could be used to improve the position of the working class through social reforms. p. 427

290 See Note 174. p. 428

291 *Eifel* (the Rhine Province of Prussia), a mountainous area with vast swamps and wastelands, had a harsh climate and barren soil. Engels refers to the events of 1882, when, following a series of crop failures and the earlier drop in prices for agricultural produce, the area was struck by famine. p. 428

292 See Note 220. p. 429

293 The reference is to the Austro-Prussian War of 1866 and the Franco-Prussian War of 1870-71. See also Note 169. p. 430

294 This article was printed as a Preface to the American edition of Engels' work *The Condition of the Working-Class in England* which appeared in New York in May 1887 (see Note 250). In the same year, it was published in the author's German translation in *Der Sozialdemokrat* (June 10 and 17) under the title "Die Arbeiterbewegung in Amerika", as separate offprints in German and English in New York in July and in French translation in the *Socialiste* (July 9, 16 and 23). Even before the book appeared, the article had been translated into German without the author's knowledge or permission and printed in the *New Yorker Volkszeitung* in April 1887. Engels launched an official protest against this because he was not satisfied with the quality of the translation (see Engels to Friedrich Sorge, April 23, 1887, present edition, Vol. 48). p. 434

295 The reference is to the conflict between Edward Aveling and the Executive of the Socialist Labor Party of North America, which accused Aveling of overspending when touring the USA together with Eleanor Marx-Aveling and Wilhelm Liebknecht for the purpose of propaganda. The conflict, which lasted for several months, was resolved with Engels' active participation. For more details, see this volume, pp. 617-18.

The *Socialist Labor Party of North America* was formed in 1876 at the Unity Congress in Philadelphia by the members of the American sections of the First International and other socialist organisations in the USA. Most of its members were immigrants (chiefly Germans), who had little contact with American-born workers. There was a struggle inside the Party between the reformist leaders, who were mostly Lassalleans, and the Marxist wing headed by Marx's and Engels' comrade-in-arms Friedrich Adolph Sorge. The Party proclaimed as its programme the fight for socialism but did not become a truly revolutionary Marxist mass organisation owing to the sectarian policy of its leaders, who disregarded the need for work in the mass organisations of the American proletariat.   p. 434

[296] See Note 256.   p. 434

[297] The reference is to the general strike in the USA for an eight-hour working day which began on May 1, 1886 and continued for several days. The strike spread to the chief industrial centres, New York, Philadelphia, Chicago, Louisville, Saint Louis, Milwaukee and Baltimore, and ended with nearly 200,000 workers winning shorter hours. The employers, however, soon launched a counter-attack. On May 4, a bomb exploded at a police station in Chicago, and the police seized this opportunity to use arms against workers and make several hundred arrests. Court proceedings were instituted and harsh sentences meted out to the leaders of the Chicago working-class movement. Four of them were hanged in November 1887.   p. 435

[298] The reference is probably to John McEnnis, a reporter on the *Missouri Republican,* who visited Engels in April 1886.   p. 435

[299] During the preparations for the municipal elections in New York in the autumn of 1886, a *United Labor Party* was founded to rally the workers for political action. The initiative was taken by the *New York Central Workers' Union,* an association of New York trade unions formed in 1882. Similar parties were set up in many other cities. Led by the new parties, the working class achieved substantial success in the elections in New York, Chicago, and Milwaukee: Henry George, the United Labor Party candidate for Mayor of New York, received 31 per cent of the vote; in Chicago, the adherents of the Labor Party succeeded in getting ten Party members elected to the Legislative Assembly of the State: one senator and nine members of the Lower Chamber. The Labor Party candidate to the US Congress lost by just 64 votes. In Milwaukee, the Labor Party's candidate was elected Mayor of the city, one candidate was elected to the Senate, six to the Lower Chamber of the Legislative Assembly of this State, and one to the US Congress.   p. 435

[300] The *Knights of Labor* (the *Noble Order of the Knights of Labor*), an American workers' organisation founded in Philadelphia in 1869. It was a secret society up to 1878. Its members were mostly unskilled workers. Its aim was the establishment of cooperatives and organisation of mutual aid; it took part in a number of working-class campaigns. But its leaders in fact opposed the workers' participation in the political struggle and stood for class collaboration. They opposed the 1886 general strike, forbidding the organisation's members to take part in it; however, the rank and file joined in the strike. After those events, it began to lose its influence among the workers and disintegrated by the end of the 1890s.   p. 437

[301] Engels wrote this letter on the occasion of the international festival of brotherhood held in Paris on February 19, 1887 on the initiative of a number of organisations of foreign socialists in France. Taking part in it were German, Scandinavian, Polish and Russian socialist émigrés. The purpose of the festival was to voice protest against the military build-up and war preparations in

Europe. Engels' letter was read out at the festival and printed in the *Socialiste* on February 26. A German translation was carried by *Der Sozialdemokrat* on March 11, by the Austrian paper *Gleichheit* on March 5, and by the New York *Sozialist* on March 19.   p. 443

302 Engels addressed this message of greetings to the meeting organised by the Federation of the Centre of the French Workers' Party on the occasion of the 16th anniversary of the Paris Commune. It was read out at the meeting.
                                                                        p. 445

303 The pamphlet was published on Engels' initiative as issue XXIV of *The Social-Democratic Library*. Even before the pamphlet appeared the second half of the introduction was published in *Der Sozialdemokrat* on January 15, 1888 under the heading "Was Europa bevorsteht".   p. 446

304 On June 14, 1848, Berlin workers and craftsmen, outraged by the National Assembly's disavowal of the March revolution, took the arsenal by storm in an attempt to uphold the revolutionary gains. This action was, however, spontaneous and unorganised, and army reinforcements and units of the bourgeois civil militia were soon able to push back and disarm the people.
                                                                        p. 446

305 The reference is to the invasion of Baden from Swiss territory by detachments of German republican refugees led by Gustav Struve on September 21, 1848. Supported by the local republicans, Struve proclaimed a German Republic and formed a provisional government. The insurgent detachments, however, were shortly afterwards scattered by the troops. Struve and other leaders of the uprising were imprisoned by decision of a court martial. They were released during another republican uprising in Baden in May 1849.   p. 446

306 See Note 279.   p. 446

307 See Note 280.   p. 446

308 The *Brimstone Gang* (Schwefelbande), the name of a students' association at Jena University in the 1770s whose members were notorious for their brawls; subsequently, the expression gained wide currency.
    In 1859, Karl Vogt published a pamphlet *Mein Prozess gegen die Allgemeine Zeitung* (Geneva, 1859) spearheaded against Marx and his associates in the Communist League. Distorting the facts, Vogt referred to Marx and his associates as the Brimstone Gang, which he depicted as a society engaged in unseemly political machinations. In actual fact, a group of German refugees in Geneva in 1849-50, including Borkheim among its members, was jokingly known under the name of Brimstone Gang. Marx and his associates had no connection with the group, which, incidentally, was far removed from political activity being a harmless circle of revellers.
    In February 1860, Marx requested Borkheim to give him some information about the Geneva Brimstone Gang and used the latter's reply of February 12 (see present edition, Vol. 17, pp. 29-32) to expose Vogt and his allegations concerning the Brimstone Gang in his pamphlet *Herr Vogt* (see ibid., pp. 21-329).
                                                                        p. 447

309 Engels is referring to the final stage of the Danish-Prussian War of 1848-50 for the duchies of Schleswig and Holstein. Prussia entered the war on the side of the duchies, seeking to use the national liberation movement there to promote its own ends. However, the war ended in the restoration of Danish rule in Schleswig-Holstein.

In the autumn of 1850, the struggle between Austria and Prussia for supremacy in Germany was aggravated as a result of the conflict over Hesse-Cassel. Revolutionary actions there were used by Austria and Prussia as a pretext for interfering in the electorate's internal affairs, with each party claiming the right to suppress them. The Prussian government reacted to the entry of Austrian troops into Hesse-Cassel by mobilising and sending its own troops there in November 1850. In October 1850, Warsaw hosted a peace conference, as a result of which Austria and Prussia signed an agreement in Olmütz on November 29. Prussia yielded on the issues of Schleswig-Holstein and Hesse-Cassel.   p. 450

310 See Note 293.
                                                                    p. 450

311 See Note 220.
                                                                    p. 451

312 *The Role of Force in History* was intended for a pamphlet of the same title that Engels planned to write but did not complete. It was to become Chapter 4, a sequel to the three chapters of *Anti-Dühring* devoted to a critique of the theory of force. Engels planned to elaborate the main ideas of the three chapters mentioned above using German history between 1848 and 1888 as an example and to make a critical analysis of Bismarck's policies. The work was begun late in 1887 and continued into the first months of 1888 (see Engels' correspondence with Hermann Schlüter, head of a social-democratic publishing house, present edition, vols 47-48). Engels interrupted work in March 1888 and, most probably, never resumed it.

After Engels' death, an envelope inscribed "The Theory of Force" was found in his archive. It contained the three chapters from *Anti-Dühring*, an unfinished manuscript of the fourth chapter of the planned pamphlet, a draft preface to it, a plan of the fourth chapter as a whole and one of its last part, which remained unwritten, as well as chronological notes on the history of Germany of the 1870s and 1880s, specifically excerpts from the book by C. Bulle, *Geschichte der neuesten Zeit, 1815-1885*, 2 ed., vols I-IV, Berlin, 1888.

The manuscript of the unfinished chapter, the rough draft of the preface and part of the preparatory materials were published by Eduard Bernstein in the *Neue Zeit* magazine, Vol. 1, Nos. 22-26, 1895-96 under the heading "Gewalt und Oekonomie bei der Herstellung des neuen Deutschen Reichs". Preparing the manuscript for publication, Bernstein divided it into sections in his own hand, supplying each with a subtitle invented by himself, marking the notes and actually making his own insertions in Engels' text. Until recently, several pages (from the words "Alsace had been conquered", this volume, p. 491 and up to the phrase "Bismark had reached his objective", this volume, p. 497) were printed according to the *Neue Zeit* publication. Not long ago, when preparing Vol. 1/31 of MEGA, researchers in the GDR discovered the missing pages in the archive of the International Institute of Social History (Amsterdam). In the present edition, this text is for the first time published according to the manuscript, which has made possible a number of corrections (this volume, pp. 493 and 494). In 1896, the work was translated into French and appeared in the *Devenir Social*, Nos. 6-9, together with the three pertinent chapters from *Anti-Dühring*. In 1898, this work was published in Russian, in an incomplete form, in St. Petersburg by the *Nauchnoye Obozreniye* (*Scientific Review*), No. 5. In 1899, it appeared in Rome in Italian as a separate edition, which completely followed the *Neue Zeit*.

The work was published in English for the first time in: F. Engels, *The Role of Force in History*. A study of Bismarck's policy of blood and iron. Lawrence & Wishart, London, 1967.

Alongside of the manuscript of the fourth chapter of the pamphlet *The Role of Force in History*. this volume also features the rough draft of its preface and, in the section "From the Preparatory Materials" the plan of Chapter 4 as a whole and the plan of its final section which throws light on the content of the part of the work that remained unfinished.   p. 453

313 The reference is to the meeting of the emperors of Russia and Austria and the King of Prussia in Warsaw in October 1850. It was called on the initiative of Emperor Nicholas I of Russia to regulate the relations between Austria and Prussia (see also Note 309).

On the Federal Diet, see Note 171.   p. 456

314 The expression the "crazy year" ("das tolle Jahr") was first used by Johann Heinrich von Falkenstein in a chronicle published in 1739 to describe the popular unrest in Erfurt in 1509. Later, it was widely applied to the revolutionary year 1848.   p. 456.

315 See Note 252.   p. 456

316 The *local settlement laws* (*Heimatgesetzgebung*) established the right of citizens to permanently reside in a certain locality, as well as the right of impoverished families to receive material aid from the communities to which they belonged.
     p. 457

317 The *Prussian taler* was equal to $1/14$ Mark of sterling silver; had currency in Prussia between 1750 and 1857. It was also recognised by North German and some other states.

The *gold taler*, a monetary unit of the free city of Bremen which retained the gold standard up to 1872, as distinct from other German monetary systems. See also Note 229.

The "*new two-third*" *taler*, a silver coin that had currency in North German states.

Bank Mark (*Mark Banko*), a coin introduced by the Hamburg Bank and used in settling international accounts.

Current Mark (*Mark Kurant*), a silver coin; from the 17th century, this was the name of silver money with a value of up to half a mark, as distinct from gold coins, small change and paper money. The *20 gulden piece* and the *24 gulden piece* (Zwanzig-Guldenfuss; Vierundzwanzig-Guldenfuss), a system under which one Mark of sterling silver was used to mint either 20 or 24 gulden. It was introduced in 1748 in Austria and later in the Electorate of Saxony and the states of Western and Southern Germany.   p. 457

318 The *Wartburg festival* was held on the initiative of Jena University students on October 18, 1817 to commemorate the tercentenary of the Reformation and the fourth anniversary of the Battle of Leipzig. The festival was a demonstration of the students' opposition to the Metternich regime.

The *Burschenschaften* were German student organisations formed during the liberation struggle against Napoleon. They advocated the unification of Germany and combined progressive ideas with extreme nationalism.   p. 458

319 The *Hambach festival* was a political demonstration held by members of South German liberal and radical bourgeoisie at the Hambach Castle (in the Rhineland Palatinate) on May 27, 1832 to urge the unification of Germany,

constitutional reforms and the transformation of Germany into a federal republic.   p. 458

[320] Under the Hohenstaufen dynasty (1138-1254), the Holy Roman Empire (founded in 962) was an unstable union of feudal principalities and free cities, it incorporated Germany and several other Central European states, part of Italy and East European regions captured by German feudal lords from the Slavs.

p. 458

[321] Engels ironically paraphrases the refrain of Ernst Moritz Arndt's well-known poem "Des Teutschen Vaterland" written in 1813. Arndt's refrain is "Sein Vaterland muß größer sehn" (His fatherland must be greater).   p. 459

[322] See Note 220.   p. 459

[323] On the *Peace of Westphalia*, see Note 220.

The *Peace of Teschen* (Silesia) between Austria, on one side, and Prussia and Saxony, on the other, was signed on May 13, 1779 and concluded the War of the Bavarian Succession (1778-79). Prussia and Austria received parts of Bavarian territory, and Saxony was granted financial compensation. Russia acted as mediator in the conclusion of the treaty, and together with France, as its guarantor.   p. 459

[324] Silesia, part of the Austrian Empire since 1526, was seized by Prussia during the War of the Austrian Succession (1740-48) caused by the claims of several European rulers, above all, King Frederick II of Prussia, to the Habsburg domains, which, in default of a male heir on the death of Emperor Charles VI, went to his daughter, Marie Theresa.

Initially adopting a stance of benevolent neutrality towards Prussia, France openly sided with the anti-Austrian coalition after Prussia's first victories over Austria. In that war, Frederick II twice betrayed his allies by concluding separate peace treaties with Austria in 1742 and 1745; in 1742, Prussia received the major part and, after the war, the whole of Silesia.   p. 459

[325] See Note 177.   p. 459

[326] The reference is to the debate on and approval by the *Regensburg Imperial Diet* of the decision proposed by France and Russia to settle territorial issues in Rhenish Germany (see Note 177). The Diet was the supreme body of the Holy Roman Empire and consisted of representatives of the German states. It was in session almost uninterruptedly between 1663 and 1806.   p. 459

[327] See Note 171.   p. 460

[328] Here Engels uses the expression "*Mehrer des Reiches*" which was part of the official title of the Holy Roman Emperors.   p. 461

[329] The reference is to the secret Paris treaty of February 19 (March 3), 1859 concluded by France and Russia. Russia undertook to adopt a "political and military stand which most easily proves its benevolent neutrality towards France", and not to object to the enlargement of the Kingdom of Sardinia in the event of a war between France and Sardinia, on the one hand, and Austria, on the other. France pledged to encourage a revision of the articles of the Paris peace treaty of 1856 which ended the Crimean War, since they restricted Russian sovereignty on the Black Sea.   p. 461

[330] On December 2, 1851, Louis Bonaparte carried out a coup d'état by dissolving the Legislative Assembly and declared himself President of France in violation of the 1848 constitution.   p. 461

331 The *Carbonari* were members of secret political societies in Italy and France in the first half of the 19th century. In Italy, they fought for national independence, unification of the country and liberal constitutional reforms. Louis Napoleon was a member of the Carbonari organisation in 1831.

As special constable, Louis Napoleon approved the preventive measures taken against the Chartist demonstration on April 10, 1848.   p. 462

332 The so-called "nationalities principle" was advanced by the ruling circles of the Second Empire and extensively used by them as an ideological screen for their aggressive plans and adventurist foreign policy. Posing as a "defender of nations", Napoleon III exploited the national interests of the oppressed peoples to strengthen France's hegemony and extend its frontiers. The "nationalities principle" was designed to stir up national hatred and to turn the national movements, especially those of small nations, into a tool for the counter-revolutionary policy of the rival powers.   p. 462

333 The reference is to the French frontiers established by the Luneville peace treaty concluded by France and Austria on February 9, 1801 after the defeat of the second anti-French coalition. The treaty extended France's frontiers by annexing the left bank of the Rhine, Belgium and Luxemburg, and sanctioned its actual rule over the republics created in 1795-98: Batavia (Holland), Helvetia (Switzerland), Liguria (Genoa) and Cisalpine (Lombardy).   p. 462

334 Engels is referring to an attempt on the life of Napoleon III by the Italian revolutionary Felice Orsini on January 14, 1858. In this way Orsini hoped to encourage revolutionary action in Europe and advance the campaign for Italy's unification. The attempt failed, and Orsini was executed on March 13 of that year.   p. 462

335 The two monarchs, the Austrian Emperor and the Russian Tsar, took joint action against revolutionary Hungary. In mid-June 1849, the Tsarist army entered Hungary to assist the Austrian counter-revolutionary forces. The intervention was tacitly endorsed by the ruling quarters of France and England. The combined forces of the Habsburgs and the Tsar suppressed the Hungarian revolution.   p. 462

336 The war of the Kingdom of Sardinia (Piedmont) and France against Austria, which lasted from April 29 to July 8, 1859, was launched by Napoleon III, who, under the banner of "liberating Italy" (in his manifesto on the war, he promised to make it "free up to the Adriatic"), sought territorial gains and needed a successful military campaign to shore up his regime in France. Piedmont's ruling circles were hoping that French support would enable them to unite Italy under the aegis of the Savoy dynasty. The war caused an upsurge of the national liberation movement in Italy. The Austrian army suffered a series of defeats. However, Napoleon III, frightened by the scale of the liberation movement in Italy, abruptly ceased hostilities. On July 11, the French and Austrian emperors concluded a separate preliminary peace treaty in Villafranca. France received Savoy and Nice. Lombardy was annexed to Sardinia; Venetia remained under Austria.   p. 463

337 The *Basle Peace* was concluded on April 5, 1795 separately between France and Prussia, the latter being a member of the first anti-French coalition. Prussia's refusal to unconditionally assist Austria against France in 1859 generally made a bad impression in Germany.   p. 463

[338] The *free-hand policy* (die Politik der freien Hand)—a phrase coined by the Prussian Foreign Minister Alexander von Schleinitz during the Austro-Franco-Italian War of 1859, which defined Prussian policy at that time, neither to align with any of the warring powers nor to declare neutrality.   p. 463

[339] The *Crédit Mobilier,* short for the *Société générale du Crédit Mobilier*—a French joint-stock bank founded in 1852 by the Péreire brothers. The bank was closely connected with the Government of Napoleon III and, protected by it, engaged in speculation. It went bankrupt in 1867 and was wound up in 1871.

The bank's activities were described in a number of Marx's articles published in the *New-York Daily Tribune* (see present edition, Vol. 15, pp. 8-24, 270-77 and 357-60).   p. 464

[340] The *Confederation of the Rhine* (Rheinbund)—an association of sixteen states in Southern and Western Germany established in July 1806 under the protectorate of Napoleon I, after the latter had defeated Austria in 1805. Later, twenty other states in Western, Central and Northern Germany joined the Confederation. It fell apart in 1813 after the defeat of Napoleon's army in Germany.
    p. 464

[341] After the defeat of Austria by Napoleonic France in July 1805 and the formation of the Confederation of the Rhine (see Note 340), which announced its separation from the German Empire, Francis II, Emperor of the Holy Roman Empire of the German Nation, who had earlier accepted the title of Emperor of Austria under the name of Francis I, on August 6, 1806 rejected the German imperial crown. The German Empire ceased to exist.   p. 465

[342] The reference is to the fortresses of the German Confederation located mostly along the French border. Their garrisons were formed from armed units of major member-states, mostly Austria and Prussia.   p. 466

[343] The reference is to the reactionary government of Prince Schwarzenberg formed in November 1848 after the defeat of the bourgeois-democratic revolution, which had been launched by the popular insurrection of March 13, 1848 in Vienna.   p. 466

[344] In August 1863, a conference of German princes was convened in Frankfurt-am-Main on the initiative of Emperor Francis Joseph of Austria to discuss a plan for the reform of the German Confederation providing for Austrian supremacy. King William I of Prussia refused to attend; several minor states also failed to extend full support to Austria, and the conference proved fruitless.   p. 466

[345] The term *Realpolitik* was used to describe Bismarck's policy, which, his contemporaries believed, was based entirely on cool calculation.   p. 466

[346] The reference is to Frederick II's conversation with Beauvau, the French envoy to Berlin, not long before the War of the Austrian Succession (see Note 324).
    p. 469

[347] When territorial issues were settled by the so-called Imperial Deputation in 1803 (see Note 177), Prussia received as compensation the secularised Münster bishopric and some other possessions in Western Germany.   p. 469

[348] The reference is to the events of the wars waged by the third and the fourth coalitions of European powers against Napoleonic France. The third coalition was formed in 1805 and embraced Britain, Austria, Russia, Sweden and the Kingdom of Naples. Prussia refused to join it, declaring its neutrality, and in

November 1805 concluded a treaty with Russia pledging to act as a mediator between the coalition and France, and, should its efforts fail, to join the campaign against Napoleon. However, after Austria's defeat at Austerlitz on December 12, 1805, Prussia signed a treaty with France, under which it received the Electorate of Hanover, for certain territorial concessions on the Rhine. The establishment of Napoleon's rule in Western and Southern Germany and his action to the detriment of Prussia again prompted the latter to side with Russia and Britain, who were still in a state of war with France. The fourth coalition was formed and encompassed Britain, Russia, Prussia and Sweden. In October 1806, in the battles of Jena (see Note 220) and Auerstedt, the Prussian army was routed by French troops which then occupied Prussia.

p. 469

349 The *Customs Union* (Zollverein) of German states (initially embracing 18 states), which established a common customs frontier, was founded in 1834 and headed by Prussia. By the 1840s, the Union embraced all German states with the exception of Austria, the Hanseatic towns (Bremen, Lübeck, Hamburg) and some of the smaller states. Formed due to the need for a single German market, the Customs Union subsequently promoted Germany's political unification. It ceased to exist in 1871. p. 470

350 *Landwehr*—the army reserve formed in Prussia in 1813 during the struggle against Napoleon. In the 1840s, it consisted of men under forty who had done three years of active service and not less than two years in the reserve. In contrast to the regular army, the Landwehr was called up only in case of extreme emergency (war, or threat of war). p. 471

351 *Kulturkampf*—the term used to designate the campaign of the Bismarck government in 1871-75 against the Catholic Church and the Party of the Centre closely associated with it, which expressed separatist and anti-Prussian tendencies widespread in Western and South-Western Germany. A number of laws were passed for the purpose of weakening the influence of the Centre and the Catholic clergy which supported it. However, the Church refused to comply. In the second half of the 1870s and early 1880s, against the background of the growing workers' movement, Bismarck, seeking to unite all reactionary forces, effected a reconciliation with the Catholic Church; the majority of the laws were repealed. p. 471

352 Here Engels has in mind the liberals who advocated the transformation of Germany into a federative state after the model of Switzerland, which was divided into self-governing cantons. p. 471

353 The song about Burgomaster Tschech (*Tschech's Attentat*)—a folk satire mocking Frederick William IV of Prussia in the context of the abortive attempt on his life staged on July 26, 1844 by Heinrich Tschech, former burgomaster of Storkow (Prussia).
The song about the Baroness von Droste-Fischering—a folk satire of the Catholic clergy mocking the tricks played by the so-called "healers" who operated in Trier in the 1840s. p. 471

354 The reference is to the coup d'état in Prussia in November-December 1848. On November 2 of that year, the counter-revolutionary Brandenburg-Manteuffel government came to office; on November 8, by a royal edict, sessions of the Prussian National Assembly were transferred from Berlin to Brandenburg; the majority of the Assembly, which continued meeting in Berlin, were dispersed on November 15 by General Wrangel's troops; the coup d'état ended

when on December 5, the Assembly was disbanded and a Constitution granted. It introduced a two-chamber system and empowered the King not only to revoke the chambers' decisions but also to revise some of the articles of the Constitution itself. In April 1849, Frederick William disbanded the chamber elected on the basis of the imposed Constitution, and on May 30 passed new electoral legislation which introduced a three-class voting system based on high property qualifications and unequal representation of the various groups of the population. The King managed to get the new Constitution adopted with the support of the majority in the new chamber of representatives, and it came into force on January 31, 1850. Prussia retained the upper chamber, which consisted mostly of representatives of the feudal nobility (chamber of the gentry). The Constitution gave the government the right to set up special courts to deal with cases of high treason. In December 1850, the Brandenburg-Manteuffel ministry was replaced by the Manteuffel ministry, which remained in office until November 1858.

p. 472

[355] Since Frederick William IV of Prussia suffered from a mental illness, his brother, Prince William, was appointed his deputy in 1857, and regent in October 1858. In January 1861, following the death of the former, the Prince was proclaimed king under the name of William I. In November 1858, the Prince Regent dismissed the Manteuffel ministry and brought to power moderate liberals headed by Karl August Hohenzollern-Sigmaringen. The term of this ministry's office (up to March 1862) came to be known as "the New Era". However, the liberal ministry did not introduce any radical reforms and was replaced by a conservative cabinet headed by Prince Adolf von Hohenloe. In September 1862, Otto von Bismarck became Prussian Prime Minister.

p. 472

[356] In February 1860, the lower chamber (chamber of representatives) of the Prussian Provincial Diet refused to approve the plan for the army's reorganisation proposed by the War Minister von Roon. The government however managed to secure from the chamber of representatives the means to maintain the army already in existence, and this allowed it to begin the reorganisation. When in March 1862 the liberal majority in the chamber refused to approve the military budget and demanded the establishment of a ministry accountable to the Provincial Diet, the government disbanded the latter and announced new elections. In late September 1862, Bismarck's ministry was formed, which in October of that year dissolved the Diet and launched the military reform without waiting for it to approve the expenditure. This constitutional conflict, as it was called, between the Prussian government and the bourgeois-liberal majority of the Diet was settled only in 1866, when, after Prussia's victory over Austria, the Prussian bourgeoisie capitulated before Bismarck.

p. 473

[357] On Prussia's war against Denmark in 1848-50 and the mobilisation of 1850, see Note 309.

p. 473

[358] Under the London Protocol on the integrity of the Danish monarchy, signed on May 8, 1852 by Russia, Austria, Britain, France, Prussia, Sweden and representatives of Denmark, Schleswig-Holstein and Denmark could be bound only by personal union. Holstein remained a member of the German Confederation. In 1855, a constitution was published which was valid for all parts of the Danish Kingdom and covered both these duchies; only in 1858, under pressure from the German Federal Diet, did the Danish government

agree to exclude Holstein from the provisions of the Constitution, but on condition that it make a contribution to national expenditure. On November 13, 1863, the Danish parliament approved a new constitution which declared the annexation of Schleswig to Denmark.   p. 474

359 The *National Association* (Deutscher National-Verein) was a party of the German liberal bourgeoisie which advocated the unification of Germany (without Austria) in a strong centralised state under the aegis of the Prussian monarchy. Its inaugural congress was held in Frankfurt in September 1859.

After the Austro-Prussian War of 1866 and the formation of the North German Confederation, the National Association announced its dissolution in November 1867.   p. 474

360 The reference is to the Russo-Prussian convention initiated by Bismarck and signed on February 8 (January 27), 1863 by Russian Foreign Minister Alexander Gorchakov and the Prussian representative Gustav von Alvensleben. Under the convention, Prussia undertook to render Tsarist Russia comprehensive assistance in suppressing the Polish uprising of 1863.   p. 477

361 See Note 332.   p. 477

362 The reference is to Austria's role in the Danish-Prussian War of 1848-50 (see Note 309), especially in its final stage, when Prussia sided with the duchies of Schleswig and Holstein, which were waging an armed liberation struggle against Danish rule. Together with Tsarist Russia and other European states, Austria supported Denmark and brought pressure to bear on Prussia to make peace. On July 2, 1850 a treaty was signed which preserved Danish supremacy over the duchies. Advocates of their secession continued hostilities, but Prussia did not support them, and the Schleswig-Holstein army was routed. In the winter of 1850-51, on Austria's initiative, a commission of the German Confederation (see Note 171) escorted by Austrian and Prussian troops was sent to the duchies. The Schleswig-Holstein army was disbanded, and Danish rule over the duchies restored.   p. 477

363 The war of Austria and Prussia against Denmark, caused by the latter's refusal to give up its plans to annex Schleswig, began in February 1864 and ended in July with a total defeat of the Danish army. Under the peace treaty signed in Vienna on October 30, 1864, Denmark lost its rights to the duchies of Schleswig and Holstein, as well as to the small principality of Lauenburg, which were declared the joint possession (condominium) of Austria and Prussia.
                                                                      p. 477

364 In the original, Engels used the term *Haupt- und Staatsaktion* ("principal and spectacular action", "main and state action"), which has a double meaning. First, in the 17th and the first half of the 18th century, it denoted plays performed by German touring companies. But this term can also denote major political events.   p. 479

365 The Warsaw Protocol of June 5 (May 24), 1851, signed by Russia and Denmark, as well as the London Protocol of May 8, 1852 (see Note 358), established the principle of the integrity of the Danish Crown's territorial possessions, including the duchies of Schleswig and Holstein.   p. 479

366 The reference is to the armed intervention in Mexico by Britain, France and Spain in late 1861-early 1862. Its aim was to suppress the Mexican revolution and turn the country into a colony of the European powers. Hostilities were

conducted by the French troops, as Britain and Spain soon recalled theirs. By mid-1863, the capital, Mexico City, and a number of other major centres were captured. Mexico was proclaimed an empire with the Austrian Archduke Maximilian at its head. However, the insurgents managed to win several important victories. The French troops sustained heavy losses and were forced to leave the country in early 1867. p. 479

367 See Note 171. p. 480

368 The phrase "a refreshing jolly war" ("ein frischer fröhlicher Krieg") was coined by the historian and writer Heinrich Leo in June 1853 in the *Volksblatt für Stadt und Land*, No. 61 and used later also in a militarist and chauvinist context.
p. 480

369 The *North German Confederation* (Norddeutscher Bund)—a federative state formed in 1867 after Prussia's victory in the Austro-Prussian war to replace the disintegrated German Confederation (see Note 171). The North German Confederation included nineteen states and three free cities, which were formally recognised as autonomous. The Confederation ceased to exist in January 1871, when the German Empire was formed. p. 480

370 The reference is to Bismarck's diplomatic preparations for the Austro-Prussian War of 1866 (see Note 172). In early March 1866, Robert Goltz, the Prussian Ambassador in Paris, obtained Napoleon III's consent to observe benevolent neutrality towards Prussia in the event of it becoming involved in a war with Austria. Simultaneously, Bismarck conducted negotiations in Berlin to explore the possibility of forming a Prusso-Italian coalition spearheaded against Austria. The other party in the negotiations was the Italian general Giuseppe Govone, who was given to understand that, France being agreeable, Bismarck would not oppose Italy annexing the German territories lying between the Rhine and the Mosel. The treaty on a defensive and offensive alliance between Prussia and Italy signed on April 8, 1866 provided for Italy to receive Venetia in the event of victory over Austria. p. 480

371 Fighting in the Austro-Prussian War of 1866 on the side of Austria were Saxony, Hanover, Bavaria, Baden, Württemberg, the Electorate of Hesse, Hesse-Darmstadt, Nassau and other member-states of the German Confederation; on the side of Prussia—Mecklenburg, Oldenburg and other North German states, as well as the three free cities.
In early June 1866, Austria lodged a complaint with the Federal Diet against Prussia's violation of the treaty on the joint administration of the duchies of Schleswig and Holstein. Bismarck refused to comply with the decision of the Diet which, on Austria's proposal, declared war on Prussia. During the war, the headway made by the Prussian troops forced the Diet to move from Frankfurt to Augsburg, where on August 24, 1866, it announced its dissolution. p. 481

372 The Austro-Prussian war ended in the signing of the peace treaty in Prague on August 23, 1866.
On Prussia's annexation of three member-states of the German Confederation and one free city, see Note 172. p. 481

373 Louis Bonaparte was nicknamed "the Little" by Victor Hugo in a speech in the Legislative Assembly in November 1851; the nickname became popular after the publication of Hugo's pamphlet *Napoléon le Petit* (1852). p. 481

[374] In September 1866, the Prussian Chamber of Deputies voted 230 against 75 for the so-called indemnity bill proposed by Bismarck on exempting the government from responsibility for the expenditure that had not been legally approved at the time of the constitutional conflict (see Note 356).   p. 483

[375] The Prussians defeated the Austrians on July 3, 1866 neaɪ the village of Sadowa, in the vicinity of the town of Königgrätz in Bohemia.   p. 483

[376] The *Customs Parliament* (Zollparlament) was formed following the signing of a treaty between Prussia and the South German states on July 8, 1867. It consisted of members of the North German Confederation's Reichstag and specially elected deputies from South German states: Bavaria, Baden, Württemberg and Hesse. It was to deal exclusively with trade issues and the customs policy. Bismarck's wish to gradually broaden its prerogatives extending them to political questions, met with stubborn resistance from the South German representatives.   p. 484

[377] The river Main formed the boundary between the North German Confederation and the South German states.   p. 484

[378] Under the peace treaty with Austria concluded in Vienna on October 3, 1866 Italy, which fought on the side of Prussia in the Austro-Prussian War, annexed Venetia. However, as a result of Prussia's opposition, its claims to the South Tyrol and Trieste, the property of Austria, were not satisfied.   p. 486

[379] In his despatch of August 6, 1847 to Count Apponyi in Paris, the Austrian Chancellor Metternich wrote "L'Italie est une expression géographique". Later he applied the expression to Germany as well.   p. 486

[380] The London Conference of diplomatic representatives of Austria, Russia, Prussia, France, Italy, the Netherlands, Belgium, Great Britain and Luxemburg on the issue of Luxemburg was held between May 7 and 11, 1867. Under the treaty signed on May 11, the Duchy of Luxemburg was declared neutral. Prussia undertook to promptly withdraw its troops from the Luxemburg Fortress, and Napoleon III was to renounce his claims for annexing Luxemburg.   p. 486

[381] See Note 308.   p. 487

[382] See Note 350.   p. 488

[383] On August 6, 1870, in the battles of Spicheren (Lorraine) and Wörth (Alsace), Prussian troops defeated several French corps. These victories, won at the initial stage of the Franco-Prussian War of 1870-71, allowed the Prussian command to launch an offensive, in the course of which the French army was broken up into two groups and then surrounded and smashed to pieces.
On the *Battle of Sedan*, see Note 224.   p. 488

[384] The news of the defeat of the French army at Sedan gave rise to mass revolutionary action in Paris, on September 4, 1870 which led to the fall of the Second Empire and the proclamation of a republic. Power, however, was captured by bourgeois republicans. The provisional government headed by General Louis Trochu declared itself "the Government of National Defence" but, scared by the revolutionary outburst, in fact chose a policy of national betrayal and collusion with the enemy.   p. 489

[385] The reference is probably to the proclamation addressed to the French nation on August 11, 1870 and signed by King William I of Prussia.   p. 489

[386] The *Landsturm Statute*, passed in Prussia on April 21, 1813, provided for the organisation of volunteer units ("francs-tireurs"), without a uniform, who were to carry on guerrilla warfare in the rear and on the flanks of Napoleon's army. All able-bodied men not in active service were urged to join the *Landsturm*.

The brutalities perpetrated against the French francs-tireurs by the Prussian army that occupied France at the time of the Franco-Prussian War of 1870-71 are described by Engels in a series of articles "Notes on the War" (see present edition, Vol. 22, pp. 163, 167 and 198-202).   p. 489

[387] Engels is referring to the Battle of Héricourt (near Belfort) on January 15-17, 1871 between German troops and the French Eastern Army under Charles Bourbaki, which advanced to the southern Vosges planning to deal a flank strike at the main communication line of the German army besieging Paris. The attacks of the Eastern Army were rebuffed by the Germans, it was forced to retreat to the Swiss border and was interned on that country's territory. In the meantime, on January 28, 1871, Bismarck and Jules Favre, a representative of the National Defence Government, signed a convention on the armistice and the capitulation of Paris.   p. 490

[388] Several hundred civilians were killed and many wounded in street fighting on March 18, 1848 in Berlin. The insurgents took over the guarding of the Palace, and on the morning of March 19 forced the King to go out onto the balcony and bare his head before the corpses of the fallen fighters.   p. 491

[389] After the signing of a convention on the armistice and the capitulation of Paris on January 28, 1871, the hostilities between France and Prussia were not resumed. On February 26, 1871, the French government headed by Thiers concluded a preliminary peace on the terms dictated by Bismarck. The final peace treaty was signed on May 10, 1871 in Frankfurt-am-Main. It confirmed Germany's annexation of Alsace and eastern Lorraine. Under the Frankfurt Treaty, the terms on which France was to pay the 5-milliard francs contribution were made harsher, and the German occupation of the French territory was prolonged. That was the cost of Bismarck's assistance to the Versailles government in the suppression of the Commune.   p. 491

[390] See Note 220.   p. 491

[391] Under the Peace of Westphalia, which concluded the European Thirty Years' War (1618-48), Strassburg remained incorporated in the German Empire, although Alsace became part of France. By order of Louis XIV issued on September 30, 1681, French troops occupied the city as belonging to Alsace. The Catholic Party of Strassburg headed by Bishop Fürstenberg hailed the annexation and did its best to prevent resistance to the French troops.

p. 491

[392] *Reunion chambers* (Chambres de réunion) set up by Louis XIV in 1679-80 were to give juridical and historical grounds for France's claims to territories of neighbouring states, which were then occupied by French troops.   p. 492

[393] See Note 337.   p. 492

[394] The reference is to the preliminary peace treaty signed on October 5, 1735 in Vienna by Austria and France. It ended the War of the Polish Succession (1733-35) between Russia, Austria and Saxony, on the one hand, and France, on the other. Russia and Austria supported the claims to the Polish throne of

Elector Friedrich August of Saxony (the future King August III of Poland), while France promoted Stanislaus Leszczynski, Louis XV's father-in-law. Under the treaty, Louis XV recognised August III as King of Poland provided the Duchy of Lorraine was given over to Stanislaus Leszczynski. On his death, it was to pass over to the French crown. The terms of the preliminary treaty were confirmed by the Vienna Treaty of 1738. On Stanislaus Leszczynski's demise in 1766, Lorraine was incorporated into France.   p. 492

395 The reference is to the strong fortified position formed by North Italian fortresses of Verona, Legnago, Mantua and Peschiera. Engels wrote about the role of these fortresses as a stronghold of Austrian rule in Northern Italy in his works "The Austrian Hold on Italy" and "Po and Rhine" (see present edition, Vol. 16, pp. 183-89 and 227-29).   p. 494

396 In his speech in the Reichstag on February 6, 1888 during the discussion of the bill on the reorganisation of Germany's armed forces, Bismarck, who insisted on the need to boost the country's military might and who actually recognised the possibility of an anti-German coalition between France and Tsarist Russia, extolled Alexander III's policies towards Germany, counterposing them to the anti-German campaign launched by the Russian press.   p. 495

397 In the winter of 1886-87, Bismarck capitalised on a slight deterioration in relations with France and demanded that the Reichstag pass a law providing for a substantial increase of the army and approve a military budget for the next seven years. The majority of the deputies refused to approve the budget proposed by Bismarck and suggested a three-year budget, after which the Reichstag was dissolved. At the elections of February 21, 1887, a majority vote was received by the pro-Bismarck parties—conservatives, "free conservatives" (see Note 403) and National Liberals (see Note 170), who formed a so-called cartel. The new Reichstag approved the budget proposed by Bismarck.
                                                                        p. 497

398 Engels is referring to the conferral of the title German Emperor on King William I of Prussia in Versailles on January 18, 1871.   p. 497

399 See Note 252.   p. 499

400 The reference is to the economic crisis which struck Germany in May 1873. It was preceded by rapid economic advance accompanied by the feverish establishment of new enterprises and extensive speculations.   p. 499

401 The reference is to the bourgeois-liberal Party of Progress (Fortschrittpartei), formed in 1861 in Prussia. It voiced the interests of petty bourgeoisie and the sections of middle bourgeoisie engaged in foreign trade. The party supported the idea of the country's unification under the aegis of Prussia, but demanded that a parliamentary system be established. In 1866, its Right wing split off and formed the National Liberal Party (see Note 170). In 1884, the men of Progress entered into a union with the Left wing of the National Liberal Party and formed the German Party of Free Thinkers (Deutsche Freisinnige Partei).
                                                                        p. 500

402 The reference is to the General Association of German Workers (Lassalleans) set up by Ferdinand Lassalle in 1863, and the German Social-Democratic Workers' Party (the Eisenachers), whose inaugural congress took place in Eisenach in 1869. The former was a nationwide political organisation of the working class which employed mostly legal forms of class struggle. The latter

was set up with Marx's and Engels' assistance and was headed by Bebel and
Liebknecht; it was affiliated to the First International. Despite a number of
erroneous propositions in its programme, it pursued a revolutionary and
proletarian line on the issue of Germany's unification and on other questions.
At the Gotha Congress in 1875, the two trends merged into a single party,
which up to 1890 was called the Socialist Workers' Party of Germany.

p. 500

[403] The *Conservative Party* (the so-called *Kreuz-Zeitung's* Party, see Note 168) was set
up in 1848 and promoted the interests of the Junkers, the aristocracy, the
generals, the Lutheran clergy and top officials. In the first years after the
unification of Germany, it was in opposition to Bismarck's government,
believing that Prussian supremacy in Germany was not secure enough. In 1866,
a Free Conservative Party split off from it which expressed the interests of big
landowners and a section of industrial tycoons, and unconditionally supported
Bismarck. In 1876, the Party was reorganised into an all-German Conservative
Party.

p. 501

[404] See Note 170.

p. 501

[405] The treaties with the South German states (Baden, Hesse, Bavaria and
Württemberg) on their joining the North German Confederation were signed
in November 1870. They accorded a greater measure of independence to the
Confederation's member-states, the relevant provisions being incorporated into
the Constitution of the German Empire of April 16, 1871. Bavaria and
Württemberg retained the special tax on beer and spirits and special rights in
the management of the postal and telegraphic service; Bavaria, moreover,
retained a degree of independence in administering its army and railways.

p. 503

[406] Under the Constitution of the North German Confederation, which came into
force on July 1, 1867, the Reichstag, which had a right to approve the budget,
was elected by universal suffrage. The Federal Council, whose functions were
confined to approval of laws, consisted of representatives nominated by
governments of all member-states of the Confederation.

p. 503

[407] On the revisions of the Constitution of 1849-50, see Note 354.

Engels uses the term *Manteuffelism* alluding to the constant violations of the
Prussian Constitution that occurred under the Ministry of Otto von Manteuffel
(1850-58).

On the *constitutional conflict,* see Note 356.
On the *Battle of Sadowa,* see Note 375.

p. 504

[408] Under the *Law on Imperial Treasury Notes* of April 30, 1874, banknotes to the
total sum of 120 million marks were issued. All member-states of the German
Empire were obliged to exchange and withdraw their paper money from
circulation.

The *Law on the Imperial Bank* passed on March 14, 1875 regulated the
emission operations of all banks on the territory of the German Empire.

p. 506

[409] The reference is to courts (Schöffengerichte) that sprang up in the Middle Ages
in the part of Germany where Frankish law was in force (Westphalia, Saxony,
cities on the Lower Rhine and Mosel). They disappeared by the 18th century
but were resurrected after Germany's unification in 1871 as "an innately
German institution". They consisted of a judge and two Schöffen (assessors)

who, unlike juries, took full part in passing sentences, in other words, defined the extent of the punishment together with the judge as their chairman. To fulfil a Schöffen's functions, a person had to meet certain age, property and residential qualifications. p. 507

410 See Note 69. p. 507

411 The reference is to the Imperial Press Law of May 7, 1874. p. 507

412 The reference is to the administrative reform of 1872 in Prussia which abolished landowners' hereditary rule in rural districts and introduced elements of local self-government: elective elders in the communities, district councils under the Landrats, elected in conformity with the estates system, etc. The purpose of the reform was to strengthen the state apparatus and to promote centralisation in the interests of the class of Junkers as a whole. p. 507

413 The reference is to the local government reform in England. The Local Government Bill was introduced by the Salisbury government (1886-92) in March 1888 and approved by Parliament that August. Under the reform, the sheriff's functions were given over to the elective county councils in charge of taxation, local budgets, etc. All persons who enjoyed the right to take part in parliamentary elections, among them women over 30, could take part in council elections. p. 508

414 See Note 351. p. 509

415 *Ultramontanism,* an extremely reactionary religious and political trend in Catholicism, which emerged in the 15th century. Its adherents opposed the independence of the national churches and advocated the idea of the Pope's supremacy and his right to interfere in the affairs of any state. Its mounting influence in the second half of the 19th century led to the formation of Catholic parties in some of the European states and the declaration of Papal infallibility at the first Council of the Vatican in 1870. p. 509

416 On September 20, 1870, troops of the Italian Kingdom entered Rome, which until then had been under the Pope's rule. On the basis of the plebiscite held on October 2 in the Papal States in which the majority voted for annexation to Italy, the government announced that it was henceforth incorporated into the Italian Kingdom. This completed the country's political unification. The Pope's secular rule was abolished. The Guarantee Law passed in 1871 secured the Pope's state sovereignty only within the boundaries of the Vatican and Lateran palaces and his country residence. The Pope reciprocated by excommunicating the instigators of the occupation of Rome, refused to recognise the Guarantee Law and declared himself "the Vatican prisoner". p. 509

417 The reference is to the small groups of deputies representing the Poles and Alsatians in the Reichstag, as well as the so-called German-Hanover separatist party formed after 1866 and embracing champions of the independent Hanover monarchy headed by the Guelph dynasty, which had ruled there prior to Hanover's annexation to Prussia in 1866. p. 510

418 See Note 312. p. 511

419 See present edition, Vol. 25, pp. 146-71. p. 511

420 *Woodhull & Claflin's Weekly* published the *Manifesto of the Communist Party* on December 30, 1871 in an abridged form.

Le Socialiste also printed an abridged version of the *Manifesto* in January-February 1872.

p. 516

421 The first Russian translation of the *Manifesto of the Communist Party* appeared in 1869 in Geneva in the Volnaya Russkaya Tipographia (the Free Russian Press) publishing house, the ownership of which Herzen handed over to Chernetsky, a staff member, in 1867.

p. 516

422 The 1882 Russian edition of the *Manifesto of the Communist Party* appeared as a third instalment of the Social-Revolutionary Library published by Pyotr Lavrov. Engels made a mistake, naming Vera Zasulich as the author of the translation: it was the work of Georgy Plekhanov. In 1894, in an afterword to the article "On Social Relations in Russia" (see present edition, Vol. 27), Engels himself wrote that the translation was that of Plekhanov.

Marx and Engels wrote a special preface to the 1882 edition (see present edition, Vol. 24).

p. 516

423 The Danish translation in question (K. Marx og. F. Engels, *Det Kommunistiske Manifest,* København, 1885) had some omissions and inaccuracies, which was noted by Engels in the preface to the fourth German edition of the *Manifesto* (see present edition, Vol. 27). The French translation appeared in *Le Socialiste* between August 29 and November 7, 1885, and was reprinted as an appendix in the book: Mermeix, *La France socialiste,* Paris, 1886. The Spanish translation was published in the *Socialista* in July-August 1886, and also as a separate edition: *Manifesto de Partido Communista* par Carlos Marx y F. Engels, Madrid, 1886.

p. 516

424 *Owenites*—followers of Robert Owen, the English utopian socialist whose ideas gained particularly wide currency in the 1820s-30s. According to his system for transforming the life of all mankind, "the communities" established on voluntary principles were to become a model for the development of the new productive forces (including the science of chemistry), the education of a new harmoniously developed man, and the establishment of new social relations. His most prominent followers were John Grey, Thomas Hodgskin, William Thompson and John Bray. Engels wrote in *The Condition of the Working-Class in England*: "English socialism arose with Owen" (see present edition, Vol. 4, p. 525).

Fourierists—followers of Charles Fourier, the French utopian socialist whose doctrine became especially widespread in the 1830s-40s. Advocating the establishment of a harmonious social system on the basis of the 18th-century materialists' ideas, Fourier admitted the presence in it of private property, classes and unearned incomes. He believed that the principal condition for the success of the new society was the growth of labour productivity that would secure universal wealth.

Fourier's doctrine made a major impact on the social and philosophical thought in a number of countries in Europe and North America.   p. 516

425 *Sturm und Drang*—a literary movement which evolved in Germany in the early 1770s and got its name from Friedrich Klinger's play of the same title. It conveyed the mounting general discontent with the feudal practices.

p. 520

426 This article was written by Engels in English as a preface to the American

edition of Marx's speech on the question of free trade delivered in Brussels on January 9, 1848 (see present edition, Vol. 6, pp. 450-65). Engels also looked through the translation of the speech made by Florence Kelly-Wischnewetzky and translated his preface into German. It was first published in that language in *Die Neue Zeit*, No. 7, July 1888. In the second half of August, it was published in the English original in *The Labor Standard* in New York. The publication of Marx's speech in pamphlet form was delayed, as many publishers refused to accept it, and it was not printed until September 1888 by Lee and Shephard Publishers, Boston. The concluding part of the article was also published in German in *Der Sozialist* (New York) on October 27, 1888.

p. 521

427 On the Brussels Congress on free trade, see Engels' essays "The Economic Congress" and "The Free Trade Congress at Brussels", present edition, Vol. 6, pp. 274-78 and 282-90.

p. 521

428 See Note 154.

p. 521

429 See Note 193.

p. 521

430 *The physiocratic school, Physiocrats*—a trend in bourgeois classical political economy that emerged in France in the 1750s. The Physiocrats held Nature to be the only source of wealth, and agriculture the only sphere of the economy where value was created. Although they underestimated the role of industry and commerce, the Physiocrats rendered an important service by shifting the search for the origins of surplus value from the sphere of circulation to that of production, thereby laying the basis for the analysis of capitalist production. Advocates of large-scale capitalist farming, they showed the moribund nature of the feudal economy and thus contributed to the ideological preparation of the bourgeois revolution in France.

p. 522

431 See Note 252.

p. 524

432 The reference is to the *American Civil War of 1861-65*. The Southern slave-holders rose against the Union and formed a Confederacy of the Southern states. The war was caused mainly by the conflict between the two social systems: the capitalist system of wage labour established in the North and the slave system dominant in the South. The Civil War, which had the nature of a bourgeois-democratic revolution, passed two stages in its development: the period of a constitutional war for maintaining the Union and the period of a revolutionary war for the abolition of slavery. The decisive role in the defeat of the Southerners was played by workers and farmers.

p. 525

433 "*Manifest destiny*", an expression widely used in the 19th century by the ideologists of the expansionist policy pursued by the US ruling quarters to vindicate this policy. It was first used by John O'Sullivan, editor of the *U.S. Magazine and Democratic Review*, in the July-August issue of 1845, Vol. XVII, p. 5.

p. 525

434 *Parliamentary train*—a name for third-class trains in England which, under the law of 1844, each railway company was obliged to run once a day at a speed of 12 miles per hour, fares not exceeding one penny per mile.

p. 526

435 In 1823, William Huskisson became President of the Board of Trade. On his initiative, a series of measures were introduced in the 1820s to reorganise the obsolete customs system. The prohibitive duties on corn were replaced by a

sliding tariff scale, under which import duties rose or fell depending on the fall or rise in grain prices inside the country.

The tariff reform of 1842 lowered customs duties on corn and other imported goods, but introduced income tax as a compensation for the treasury.

p. 528

[436] The reference is to the Ten Hours' Bill of 1847, which came into force on May 1, 1848. In August 1850, Parliament introduced an additional factory act which prolonged the working day for women and adolescents to ten-and-a-half hours on the first five days of the week and reduced it to seven-and-a-half hours on Saturday. See also Note 161.

p. 528

[437] See Note 349.

p. 529

[438] The need for a reform of the customs tariff so as to raise the duties on imported industrial and agricultural goods was stated by a group of Reichstag deputies in October 1878. In December, Bismarck submitted his initial rough draft of a reform to a specially established commission. The final version was debated in the Reichstag beginning in May 1879 and was approved on July 12 of that year. The new customs tariff provided for a substantial increase of import duties on iron, machinery, textile, grain, cattle, fats, flax, timber, etc.

p. 531

[439] The reference is to the trade agreement between Britain and France signed on January 23, 1860. The principal figure on the British side was free trader Richard Cobden. Under the agreement, France renounced its prohibitive customs policy and introduced duties that could not exceed 30, and later 25 per cent of the cost of the goods. The agreement granted France the right to export the bulk of its goods to England tax-free. One consequence of the agreement was mounting competition on the home market caused by the influx of English goods, which provoked displeasure among the French manufacturers and industrialists.

p. 533

[440] The *Standard Oil Company* was founded by John D. Rockefeller in the state of Ohio in 1870 with an initial capital of $1 million. In the 1870s, the company dominated the refining and transportation of oil and came to control almost the entire US oil industry. In 1882, the company was transformed into a trust of the same name, operating on a capital of $75 million. Later, the Standard Oil grew into one of the world's largest corporations.

p. 533

[441] The *American Sugar Company* (trust) was set up in 1887 and became the *American Sugar Refining Company* in 1891. In the first years of its existence, the trust came to dominate nearly all of the US sugar industry. Later, despite the formation of major competing companies, the trust managed to retain its position as the largest corporation in the branch by establishing control over some of its competitors and cooperating with others on a profit-sharing basis.

p. 534

[442] The *Manchester School*—a trend in economic thinking which reflected the interests of industrial bourgeoisie. Its adherents, known as Free Traders, advocated freedom of trade and non-interference by the government in economic life. The centre of the Free Traders' activities was Manchester, where the movement was headed by two textile manufacturers, Richard Cobden and John Bright, who founded the Anti-Corn Law League in 1838. In the 1840s and 1850s, the Free Traders formed a separate political group which later constituted the Left wing of the Liberal Party.

p. 534

443 This letter written by Engels (see Engels to Laura Lafargue, May 7, 1889, present edition, Vol. 48) in connection with the preparations for the international socialist congress was published in *The Labour Elector* on behalf of the French socialist Charles Bonnier, who was actively involved in the work. The decisive role in the convocation of the congress belonged to Marxist organisations, the German Social-Democratic and French Workers' parties, which acted under Engels' guidance. Opportunists, mostly French Possibilists (see Note 444) supported by the British Social-Democratic Federation, sought to prevent the consolidation of revolutionary Marxist forces and tried to take the organisation of the congress into their hands, but in vain. The International Socialist Workers' Congress, which took place in Paris in July 1889, highlighted the Marxists' victory. It paved the way for a new international proletarian association, the Second International. The alternative congress convened by the Possibilists and their allies failed to win the support of the majority of socialist organisations and proved a flop. p. 537

444 *Possibilism*—an opportunist trend in the French socialist movement that existed from the 1880s to the early 20th century. It was headed by Paul Brousse and Benoît Malon, who in 1882 effected a split in the French Workers' Party. The dissenters adopted the name of the Workers' Social-Revolutionary Party. Its ideological foundation was the reformist theory of municipal socialism. The Possibilists declared the "policy of possibilities" ("la politique des possibilitées") their principle. In the early 20th century, they joined the French Socialist Party.
On the *opportunists*, see Note 208. p. 537

445 The *Parliamentary Committee*—the executive of the British Trade Union Congress (up to 1921). p. 538

446 The International Workers' Congress was convened in London in November 1888 by the British trade union leadership. Represented at it were trade unions from several European countries. p. 538

447 This is Engels' letter to James Keir Hardie, editor of the *Labour Leader* magazine, where it was published without a heading in the "Mining Notes" section and supplied with the following introductory note: "The great miners' strike in Germany is over, and the men have succeeded in establishing their demand for an 8-hour day from bank to bank. Mr. Frederick Engels, the eminent historian of the labour movement, and the life-long friend of the great Karl Marx, sends me the following interesting note on the strike."
The Ruhr miners' strike was one of the major events in the German working-class movement in late 19th century. It began on May 4, 1889 in the Gelsenkirchen mining district and spread to the entire Dortmund area. Up to 90,000 people were taking part at its peak. Some of the strikers were under the influence of Social-Democrats. The main demands of the strikers were: higher wages, reduction of the working day to 8 hours, and recognition of workers' committees. The industrialists promised to meet some of the workers' demands, as a result of which work was partially resumed in mid-May. However, as the employers went back on their word, a miners' delegates' meeting held on May 24 passed a decision to continue the strike. Repressive measures, on the one hand, and fresh promises by mine-owners, on the other, prompted the workers to call off the strike in early June. p. 539

448 See Note 253. p. 539

[449] A three-man delegation of the striking miners was formed through the effort of some of the Reichstag liberal deputies who sought to curtail the influence of Social-Democratic ideas on the miners and used their relatively low level of political awareness. The delegation was received by William II on May 14.

p. 540

[450] In mid-May 1889, the strike movement launched by the Ruhr miners spread to Upper and Lower Silesia, where it involved a large part of the mines (20,000 people) and lasted from May 14 to 24, and to Saxony, where 10,000 people took part in it. In the Saar area, workers at some of the mines went on strike on May 14-16, and by May 23, the number of strikers reached 12,000. Somewhat earlier, strikes began in the Wurm mining district, involving about 8,000 men. Work was not resumed until May 31. A major miners' strike also took place in Bohemia, in the district of Kladno, on May 24.

At the end of May, strikes for higher wages and, in some cases, shorter working hours, were held in various towns and districts of Germany. On May 25, about 20,000 masons went on strike in Berlin; in Freienwalde, a strike was launched by railway workers, and in Stettin and Königsberg, by house painters and carpenters.

p. 540

[451] This article was occasioned by the campaign launched by the Possibilists (see Note 444) in France and their adherents in the Social-Democratic Federation in Britain in order to discredit the International Socialist Workers' Congress held in Paris between July 14 and 21, 1889, at which the Marxist parties of European countries clearly dominated. Initially, the Possibilists tried to take preparations for the congress into their hands and thus secure themselves a leading role but, having failed to do so, they convened an alternative congress in Paris, attended by only a few foreign delegates, their representation in most cases being purely fictitious. The attempt to unite the two congresses failed, since the Possibilist Congress made unification conditional on reverification of the credentials of the delegates to the Marxist congress.

p. 542

[452] *Three tailors of Tooley Street,* a well-known phrase originating from John Canning, a British statesman, who said that three tailors of Tooley Street had addressed the House of Commons in a petition opened with the words: "We, the people of England".

p. 543

[453] The *Carlists*—a reactionary clerical absolutist group in Spain uniting adherents of the pretender to the Spanish throne Don Carlos, the brother of Ferdinand VII. They relied on the army and the Catholic clergy, as well as on the more backward peasants in some regions of Spain.

p. 544

[454] This is an excerpt from Engels' letter apparently addressed to Eleanor Marx. The excerpt was printed by *The Labour Elector* and published in German translation in the *New Yorker Volkszeitung* on September 25, 1889 and the *Berliner Volks-Tribüne* on October 26, 1889.

The London dockers' strike from August 12 to September 14, 1889 was a major event in the British working-class movement of the late 19th century. Taking part in it were 30,000 dockers and over 30,000 workers of other trades; the majority were unskilled labourers who did not belong to any trade union. The strikers obtained higher wages and better working conditions. The dockers' strike introduced more organisation into the movement: a, dockers' and some other unions were set up which embraced a large number of unskilled workers and came to be known as the New Trade Unions.

p. 545

455 This article carried by the *Sozialdemokrat* aroused profound interest in the socialist quarters in many countries: on October 11, 1889, it was reprinted by the Vienna *Arbeiter-Zeitung*; on October 12, in a slightly abridged English translation, by *The Labour Elector*; on October 26 (with insignificant editorial changes and under the heading, "Was die Bourgeoisie nicht kann und was die Arbeiter können"), by the *Berliner Volks-Tribüne*, as well as by other newspapers in Germany and the USA. In 1890, the article was translated into Russian and published in the *Социаль-демократъ*, No. 1, 1890.

This article was published in English in full for the first time in: Marx and Engels, *Articles on Britain*, Progress Publishers, Moscow, 1971.   p. 546

456 The reference is to the first ballot to the French Chamber of Deputies on September 22, 1889, when the republicans received only 215, and the various monarchist groups (Legitimists, Bonapartists and Boulangists), 140 seats.

p. 547

457 See Note 454.   p. 548

458 Engels probably wrote this passage when working on *The Origin of the Family, Private Property and the State*. In content, it relates to the passage in Chapter IX of the book which deals with the survival of the gentile system in medieval aristocratic, patrician and peasant associations (see this volume, pp. 268-69). However, due to the absence of any other information, the dating of this fragment, written in longhand on a separate sheet, is only provisional. The title has been supplied by the editors.   p. 553

459 *Polis* (a city state)—a typical socio-economic and political organisation in Ancient Greece and Ancient Italy. The Greek polis emerged in the 8th-6th cent. B.C. It included the city proper and the adjacent agricultural settlements. Only its indigenous inhabitants who owned land and slaves possessed full civic rights. There were also free citizens who did not enjoy full rights, such as metoikos (see Note 108), they engaged in trades and commerce.

p. 553

460 Engels wrote these notes when preparing the new edition of his book *The Peasant War in Germany*. As is clear from his letters, specifically, to Friedrich Adolph Sorge of December 31, 1884, he intended to revise it completely presenting the peasant war of 1525 as "the pivot for the whole history of Germany" (see present edition, Vol. 47). This demanded that substantial historical data be added. The notes written on a separate sheet are probably a fragment and a draft plan for the introduction to the book. Engels' intention to publish a revised edition of *The Peasant War in Germany* was not realised.

p. 554

461 *Interregnum*—the period between 1254 and 1273 in Germany after the Hohenstaufen dynasty had ceased to exist. It witnessed the struggle between various pretenders to the Imperial crown, incessant strife between princes, knights and cities, and the mounting arbitrary rule of the princes in their estates. In 1273, Rudolf Habsburg was elected Emperor of the Holy Roman Empire.   p. 555

462 The *Hundred Years' War*—a series of wars between England and France lasting from 1337 to 1453. It was caused by the dispute between the two countries over the possession of the commercial and industrial towns of Flanders, the main consumer of English wool, and the English kings' claims to the French throne. During the war, the English managed to seize a considerable part of

France. However, as a result of a popular war against the foreign invaders, the English were driven out of French territory with the exception of Calais.

The reference is to the so-called *reconquista,* in the course of which the peoples inhabiting the Peninsula recaptured the territories conquered in the 8th-15th centuries by the Arabs and the Berbers collectively known as the Moors. By the mid-13th century, the Moors retained only the Emirate of Granada, which fell in 1492.

The reference is to the final period of Tartar-Mongol rule in Russia, which lasted throughout the 13th and 15th centuries. The popular struggle against the invaders resulted in the formation of the Russian centralised state. This enabled Prince Ivan III of Muscovy to refuse to pay tribute to the Golden Horde in 1476. After the unsuccessful campaign against Russia undertaken by Khan Ahmed in 1480, the country set itself completely free from the Tartar-Mongol yoke.

The *Wars of the Roses* (1455-85)—wars between the feudal houses of York and Lancaster competing for the throne, the white rose being the badge of the House of York, and the red one of the House of Lancaster. The wars almost completely wiped out the ancient feudal nobility and brought Henry VII to power to form a new dynasty, that of the Tudors, who set up an absolute monarchy in England.

                                                                                                    p. 555

[463] Engels may have written this unfinished work when he was preparing the new edition of *The Peasant War in Germany* (see Note 460). Its content shows that it was to serve as part of the introduction to the new edition. Engels also used his earlier notes on the history of Germany, namely the manuscript *Varia on Germany* (present edition, Vol. 23, pp. 599-610). The title has been supplied by the editors.

                                                                                                    p. 556

[464] *Municipium*—at the time of the Roman Republic, a city tied to Rome by a treaty. Municipia were of two categories, depending on the nature of the treaty with Rome, equal or unequal. The former usually enjoyed self-government and their citizens enjoyed full civil and political rights in Rome. The citizens of the latter did not have political rights in Rome but performed the duties of Roman citizens. A municipium had no permanent status.

                                                                                                    p. 556

[465] *The Lay of Ludwig* (*Das Ludwigslied*) was written in the Franconian dialect by an anonymous poet in the late 9th century. It is a panegyric of the West Frankish King Ludwig III celebrating his victory over the Normans at Sancourt in 881 (*Hausschatz der Volkspoesie,* Leipzig, 1846).

                                                                                                    p. 560

[466] The reference is to the extant texts in the Old High German and the Romance (Old French) languages—oaths of allegiance exchanged by the East Frankish King Louis the German and the West Frankish King Charles the Bald, as well as by their vassals in Strassburg in 842.

                                                                                                    p. 560

[467] The *Slavs of the Elbe (Laba)*—a large group of West Slavic peoples which at the end of the first and beginning of the second millennium A.D. inhabited the territory between the Laba and its tributary, the Sala (Saale), in the West, and the Odra (Oder) in the East. Beginning in the 10th century, German feudal lords launched a systematic campaign to capture the Slavic lands and set up military districts, the marks, on conquered territories. Despite the resistance of the indigenous population, in the second half of the 12th century the Germans managed to capture the last free territories of the Slavs of the Elbe. Some of the Slavs were annihilated, some were forcibly Germanised, and others managed to retain their ethnic and cultural features.

                                                                                                    p. 560

468 *Lotharingia* (Lorraine)—a state on the left bank of the Rhine established in 855 during the division of Emperor Lothair I's possessions and named after his son Lothair II, to whom it was handed over as an independent kingdom. Its position between the West and the East Frankish kingdom made it unstable and was one of the causes of the struggle for its territory. After the death of Lothair II in 870, Lotharingia was divided (roughly along the language frontier) between his brothers, the East Frankish King Louis the German and the West Frankish King Charles the Bald.   p. 560

469 The reference is to the English victories over the French in the Hundred Years' War (1337-1453) (see Note 462).   p. 563

470 The reference is to Wellington's campaign against France in the Peninsular War of 1808-13 and his victory at Waterloo (Belgium) on June 18, 1815. The best-known victories won by Wellington in Spain in the way described by Engels were the battles of Talavere in 1809 and of Salamanca in 1812.
                                                                            p. 563

471 Engels is referring to the refusal of the German Emperor Albrecht I of the Austrian Habsburgs to recognise the freedoms of the Swiss cantons confirmed by his predecessor, Adolf of Hassau. In the 14th-15th centuries, in their continued struggle for independence, the cantons managed to defeat the troops of the Austrian feudal lords and to secure for Switzerland the position of a state free from Austrian rule and subordinate only formally to the German Empire.   p. 563

472 At the *battle of Crécy* on August 26, 1346, the English, using a combination of knights and archers, defeated the French army, whose main force was cavalry. This battle was fought during the Hundred Years' War between England and France (see Note 462).
On the *Battle of Waterloo*, see Note 226.   p. 564

473 The reference is to the printing with movable type invented by Johann Gutenberg in the mid-15th century. This invention was one of the main factors which promoted science and literature in the 15th and 16th centuries, and eventually led to the growth of the productive forces throughout the world.
                                                                            p. 564

474 The Duchy of Burgundy, which was formed in the 9th century in the basins of the Saône, Seine and Loire and later annexed considerable territories (Franche-Comté, part of Northern France, the Netherlands), became an independent feudal state in the 14th-15th centuries. It reached the peak of its might in the second half of the 15th century under Duke Charles the Bold (1467-77). He sought to expand his possessions and this hindered the formation of a centralised French monarchy. King Louis XI of France managed to form a coalition of the Swiss and the Lotharingians against Burgundy. As a result of the Burgundian wars of 1474-77, the troops of Charles the Bold were defeated, and he himself was killed in the Battle of Nancy (1477). His lands were divided between Louis XI and Maximilian of Habsburg, the son of the German Emperor.   p. 564

475 Capitalising on Italy's political fragmentation and the discord between the Italian states, King Charles VIII of France invaded Italy in 1494 and occupied the Kingdom of Naples. Charles VIII's campaign was the start of the Italian Wars (1494-1559) during which Italy was repeatedly invaded by French,

Spanish and German troops and became the scene of a prolonged struggle for supremacy in the middle Mediterranean peninsula. p. 564

476 Here Engels has in mind the Huguenots' movement which unfolded in the 16th century under the religious banner of Calvinism and led to the Huguenot, or religious wars between the Catholics and the Protestants (Huguenots), which continued, with interruptions, throughout the second half of the 16th century. They produced economic dislocation and political anarchy, which worsened the conditions of the masses and provoked peasant revolts. Frightened by them, the feudal lords and the bourgeoisie rallied round Henry of Navarre, a former Huguenot leader, representative of the new Bourbon dynasty, who adopted Catholicism and became king under the name of Henry IV. p. 564

477 See Note 462. p. 565

478 The first attempt at unification of Poland and Lithuania was made in 1385, when the two states concluded a dynastic Krewo Union (after Krewo Castle, where it was signed), which was aimed mainly at joint defence against the mounting aggression on the part of the Teutonic Order (see Note 218). At the same time, it promoted the interests of both states, which sought to expand their territories at the expence of Ukrainian and Byelorussian lands. In 1569, the Lublin Union was concluded, under which Poland and Lithuania formed a single state under the name of Rzecz Pospolita. Lithuania retained its autonomy. The Union existed up to 1795. p. 565

479 This original research is based on materials carried by Chartist papers, Engels' own notes and personal reminiscences. In fact, it is a detailed synopsis of a work on the history of Chartism. It highlights the role of its Left wing, the influence on each other of Chartist agitation in England and the Irish people's liberation movement. Engels compiled the table at the request of the German socialist Hermann Schlüter to help him write a history of the Chartist movement. The chronology drawn up by Engels by late August 1886 probably provided the basis for Schlüter's book *Die Chartistenbewegung in England* which appeared in Zurich a year later. p. 566

480 "*A sacred month*"—the slogan advanced by Chartists in 1839, a call for a general strike. p. 567

481 The *Union* with England was imposed on Ireland by the English government after the suppression of the Irish rebellion in 1798. The Union, which came into force on January 1, 1801, abolished the autonomous Irish Parliament and made Ireland still more dependent on England. The demand for the repeal of the Union became widespread in Ireland from the 1820s. p. 572

482 The reference is to the Bill moved by James Graham for discussion in the House of Commons on March 8, 1843. It provided for the regulation of child and adolescent employment in factories, specifically, reduction of children's working day to six and a half hours. The Bill met with strong opposition on the part of MPs and the various public groups, e.g., the Dissenters (see Note 486). Graham withdrew his motion. On the factory legislation, see also Note 161. p. 573

483 *An Act to amend and continue for Two Years, and to the End of the next Session of Parliament, the Laws in Ireland relative to the registering of Arms, and the Importation, Manufacture, and Sale of Arms, Gunpowder, and Ammunition* was passed by the House of Commons in August 1843 following an upsurge

in Ireland in the movement for the repeal of the Union (see Note 481).

p. 573

484 *Rebecca Riots*—popular unrest in 1839 and 1842-43 in South Wales. They were triggered off by the imposition of charges at the toll-gates on the public roads. The name was borrowed from the Bible: "And they blessed Rebekah, and said unto her, Thou *art* our sister, be thou *the mother* of thousands of millions, and let thy seed possess the gate of those which hate them" (Genesis 24: 60). Many participants in the movement were associated with Chartism.   p. 573

485 *Educational Clauses*—a component part of the Factory Bill proposed by James Graham (see Note 482). Under these clauses, the children living in the industrial regions of Great Britain were to attend school not more than three times a week. However, this was opposed by the Dissenters (see Note 486), who constituted a significant part of the population there and were against the teaching at schools of the Scriptures based on the dogmas of the Anglican Church.

p. 573

486 *Dissenters* were members of Protestant religious sects and trends in England who rejected the dogmas and the rites of the official Anglican Church.

p. 573

487 The *Court of Queen's Bench* is one of the high courts in England; in the 19th century (up to 1873), it was an independent supreme court for criminal and civil cases, competent to reconsider the decisions of lower judicial bodies.

p. 574

488 The *Young Ireland* group was formed in 1842 by the Irish bourgeois and petty-bourgeois intellectuals.   p. 575

489 The reference is to *An Act for the Better Security of the Crown and Government of the United Kingdom* introduced in the House of Commons by the Home Secretary George Grey and passed on April 19, 1848.   p. 575

490 *Repealers*—supporters of the repeal of the Anglo-Irish Union of 1801, which had abrogated the autonomy of the Irish Parliament. In January 1847, the radical elements of this movement formed an Irish Confederation. Representatives of its revolutionary Left wing, who stood at the head of the national liberation movement, were subjected to severe repression in 1848. See also Note 481.   p. 576

491 The reference is to the *Habeas Corpus Act of 1679*. It introduced a writ of Habeas Corpus, the name given in the English judicial procedure to a document enjoining the pertinent authorities to present an arrested person before a court on the demand of the persons desiring to check the legitimacy of the arrest. The procedure does not apply to persons accused of high treason and can be suspended by decision of Parliament. The British authorities frequently made use of this exception in Ireland.   p. 576

492 See Note 351.   p. 578

493 The reference is to court proceedings instituted by Bismarck in 1876-77 against a number of conservative journalists and politicians, who exposed his involvement in the stock-exchange machinations, on the charge of insulting him in the press. The incident revealed the mounting tension between Bismarck's government and the conservatives, who criticised his policies from a Right-wing standpoint.

On the *Anti-Socialist Law*, see Note 174.   p. 578

494 The expression "to go to Canossa" dates back to the humiliating pilgrimage to the Canossa Castle in Northern Italy undertaken by the German Emperor Henry IV in 1077 for the purpose of persuading Pope Gregory VII to revoke his excommunication. It became a current phrase after Bismarck said in the Reichstag in May 1872: "We shall not go to Canossa."

In the late 1870s, needing the support of the Catholic Party of the Centre, because his old stronghold, the National Liberal Party (see Note 170) was losing its influence, Bismarck repealed nearly all anti-Catholic laws passed during the *Kulturkampf* (see Note 351) and forced the principal adherents of the anti-Catholic policy to retire. By using the expression "going to Canossa", Engels ironically alludes to Bismarck's concessions to the clerical circles in 1878-87, which in fact amounted to giving up the *Kulturkampf*.   p. 579

495 *Septennate* (a seven-year period)—the German law on army credits, fixed for seven years ahead. It also approved an increase in the numerical strength of the standing army in peacetime (401,000) for the same term.   p. 580

496 Engels may have written these notes in the second half of September 1888, when sailing on the *City of New York* from America, where he had spent over a month (August 17 to September 19, 1888) together with Eleanor Marx-Aveling, Edward Aveling and his friend Carl Schorlemmer. They travelled from New York to Boston, nearby towns, and the Niagara Falls, and took a voyage across Lake Ontario stopping over in Canada. Judging by the concise form of the notes, Engels probably intended to write an article about the trip. However, this plan was never carried out. The fragment "Impressions of a Journey Round America" (see this volume, pp. 584-86) is only the beginning of this work.   p. 581

497 The reference is to the establishment of a National Park near the Niagara Falls recounted by Engels in his letter to Laura Lafargue of September 5, 1888: "The State of New York bought up all the grounds (on the American side) about the falls, turned out all the touts, hucksters and exhortionists, and transformed the whole into a public park. ...And the simple fact of the Americans having done this compelled the Canadian government to do the same on their side..." (present edition, Vol. 48).   p. 581

498 The reference is to the American Civil War of 1861-65. See also Note 432.
                                                                   p. 583

499 The fragment is probably the beginning of Engels' proposed article on his trip to the United States (see Note 496).   p. 584

500 See Note 220.   p. 586

501 This is a draft reply, written by Engels on behalf of Eleanor Marx-Aveling to the *To-Day* editors over the publication (No. 1, April 14, 1883) of an English translation from the French of Chapter XXIII of *Capital* (corresponds to Chapter XXI of the German original). Its heading, "I.—The Serfdom of Work" was the editor's invention. In the letter, permission to publish the translation of one more chapter was made conditional on certain terms. They were fulfilled, as may be seen from the editorial note to the publication of Chapter "II.—The Lordship of Wealth" in the *To-Day*, No. 2, June 1883. "This chapter is translated from the second and third sections of Chapter X of the original. The selection published in our last issue was translated from

Chapter XXIII of the original. The translations are, of course, our own, and not those of the late Karl Marx." The sub-heading noted that the translation was from the French edition of 1872.   p. 589

502 The reference is to the first authorised French edition of Volume One of *Capital*. Under the agreement between Marx and publisher M. Lachâtre in February 1872, the work was to be published in instalments. It appeared between September 1872 and November 1875. When preparing this edition, Marx made changes and additions to nearly all parts of his work.   p. 589

503 This excerpt from the letter by Hermann Lopatin, a Russian revolutionary, to Maria Oshanina, a member of the Narodnaya Volya (People's Will) Executive, recounts his talk with Engels, naturally in his own interpretation, which bears the stamp of his Narodnik views based on utopian peasant socialism and revolutionary democratism directed against autocracy. However, writing under a fresh impression from the talk, Lopatin obviously gives an accurate account of some of Engels' ideas. Lopatin and Engels met on September 19, 1883, several months after the former had escaped abroad from exile in Vologda. The excerpt was first published on Pyotr Lavrov's initiative and with Engels' permission in the book: *The Foundations of Theoretical Socialism as Applied to Russia* (in Russian), Geneva, 1893.   p. 591

504 *Zemsky Sobor*—a central representative institution of social estates in Russia in the mid-16th-late 17th centuries. Its composition, convocation and sessions were not strictly fixed and changed in the course of time.

The interest in the convocation of the Zemsky Sobor at the end of the 19th century was evoked by hopes of limiting autocratic power and of changing the political system with the help of such representative institutions.   p. 591

505 The reference is to the letter addressed by the People's Will Executive to Tsar Alexander III on March 10, 1881 (after the events of March 1 of that year, when Tsar Alexander II had been assassinated by members of the organisation). The Executive agreed to renounce violence as a means of struggle on two conditions: 1) a general political amnesty, and 2) convocation of representatives of all the Russian people "to reconsider the existing forms of state and public life". The elections to the proposed Constituent Assembly were to be held on the basis of universal suffrage and guaranteed freedom of the press, speech, assembly and election manifestoes. The Executive further stated that it would comply with the decision of the future People's Assembly.   p. 593

506 The reference is to the Marx's ironic comment in the early 1880s on some sectarian and dogmatic mistakes made by the French Marxists in the struggle against the opportunist trend—Possibilism. Recollecting it, Engels wrote to Paul Lafargue on August 27, 1890 (present edition, Vol. 49) that Marx had said about these mistakes: "All I know is that I'm not a Marxist."   p. 593

507 This article was based on Engels' letter to Paul Lafargue of November 14, 1885 (see present edition, Vol. 47). On November 13 Engels was requested to write it by Lafargue, who was preparing Engels' biography for a series on outstanding international socialists carried by *Le Socialiste*. The article was anonymously printed by the newspaper on November 21, 1885 as the second part of Engels' biography. The paper also carried Engels' portrait by Clarus sent to Engels by Lafargue together with the letter of November 13.

Part of this article was published in English for the first time in Marx K., Engels F., *Writings on the Paris Commune*, New York-London, 1971, p. 234.

p. 594

[508] See Note 350.   p. 594

[509] See Note 432.   p. 596

[510] Engels thought of writing this article in October 1886, when the book by the Austrian bourgeois sociologist and lawyer Anton Menger, *Das Recht auf den vollen Arbeitsertrag in geschichtlicher Darstellung,* was issued. Menger attempted to prove that Marx's economic theory was not original and that he had allegedly borrowed his conclusions from English utopian socialists of the Ricardian school (Thompson et al.). Unable to ignore Menger's allegations and his falsification of the very essence of Marx's doctrine, Engels decided to reply in the press. However, fearing that a personal rebuttal may serve to give this third-rate scholar undeserved publicity, Engels considered it expedient to rebuke Menger through a *Neue Zeit* editorial or through a book review signed by the magazine's editor Karl Kautsky, and enlisted Kautsky's help in writing a piece against Menger. At first he intended to write the main part of the text himself, but fell ill and had to interrupt his work, so the piece was completed by Kautsky under Engels' instructions. It appeared anonymously in the *Neue Zeit*, No. 2, 1887; later, in the index to the magazine published in 1905, Engels and Kautsky were named as its authors. In 1904, the work was translated into French and printed by the *Mouvement socialiste*, No. 132, with Engels named as the author. The manuscript is not extant. Since it is impossible to ascertain which part of the work was written by Engels, and which by Kautsky, in the present edition it is published in full in the Appendices.   p. 597

[511] See K. Marx, *The Poverty of Philosophy. Answer to "The Philosophy of Poverty" by M. Proudhon* (present edition, Vol. 6, pp. 105-212).

In January 1849, Proudhon made an attempt to establish a "People's Bank" founded on the utopian principles of "free" credit that he was expounding. The bank, through which Proudhon intended to effect peaceful social reform by abolishing loan interest and introducing money-free exchange based on the producer's receiving a full equivalent of his earned income, collapsed two months after its establishment.   p. 606

[512] The reference is to the hostile campaign against Marx conducted in the 1870s by the German bourgeois economist Lujo Brentano, a leading representative of armchair socialism (see Note 289). He accused Marx of deliberately falsifying the phrase from Gladstone's speech delivered on April 16, 1863, which appeared on April 17 in almost all London newspaper reports of this parliamentary session (*The Times, The Morning Star, The Daily Telegraph*), but was omitted in Hansard's semi-official publication of parliamentary debates, in which the text was corrected by the speakers themselves. This gave Brentano a pretext for accusing Marx of unscrupulous misquotation. Marx retaliated in his letters to the *Volksstaat* editors on May 23 and July 28, 1872 (see present edition, Vol. 23, pp. 164-67 and 190-97). After Marx's death, the same accusation was made in November 1883 by the English bourgeois economist Taylor. It was disproved by Eleanor Marx in February and March 1884 in two letters to the *To-Day* magazine, and by Engels in June 1890 in his preface to the fourth German edition of *Capital* (see present edition, Vol. 35) and in 1891 in the pamphlet *Brentano Contra Marx* (present edition, Vol. 27).   p. 613

513 This inaccuracy in Marx's book was set right by Engels in the second German edition of *The Poverty of Philosophy* published in 1892. It also gave a more precise wording of the quotation used by Engels in the preface to the first German edition (see this volume, p. 280), and the correct date of the publication of Thompson's book. p. 613

514 The letter to the *New Yorker Volkszeitung* printed on March 30, 1887 and signed by Edward Aveling was written by Engels, as is seen from the rough copy. It was prompted by the conflict between Aveling and the Executive of the Socialist Labor Party of North America (see Note 295). p. 617

515 The reference is to Aveling's letter of February 26, 1887 printed at the press and sent out to the sections of the Socialist Labor Party of North America and other socialist organisations. It was a detailed reply to the charges advanced against Aveling. p. 618

516 Engels made the amendments to the programme of the North of England Socialist Federation at the request of John Lincoln Mahon, an English worker and socialist. In a letter to him of June 22, 1887, Engels voiced his appreciation of the programme, saying: "I consider it very good as a spontaneous working-class declaration of principles" (present edition, Vol. 48). Engels' amendments relate mainly to the introductory part of the programme; he made them on the leaflet containing the text of the programme.

The *North of England Socialist Federation*—a workers' organisation set up in Northumberland (Northern England) on April 30, 1887 during a major miners' strike that lasted from late February to June 24, 1887. The organisation was sponsored by John Mahon, Thomas Binning, Alexander Donald, et al. Throughout 1887, the Federation conducted active work among the workers but failed to consolidate its initial success and soon ceased to exist. p. 619

517 This letter, the original of which has recently been discovered by GDR researchers in the archive of the International Institute of Social History (Amsterdam), was written by Engels on the occasion of the expulsion from Switzerland, under pressure of the German authorities, of four leading editors and publishers of *Der Sozialdemokrat,* newspaper of the Social-Democratic Workers' Party of Germany, which was published in Zurich after the promulgation of the Anti-Socialist Law (see Note 174). The letter was to be sent out to the editorial boards of various newspapers for the purpose of informing English readers about the real causes and circumstances of this action by the Swiss Federal Council. When writing the letter, Engels most probably had the full text of the resolution on the expulsion, which he repeatedly quotes and which did not appear in *Der Sozialdemokrat* until April 28.

Engels apparently believed that the letter should originate with German Social-Democrats, and so it was despatched bearing Kautsky's signature. Apart from *Justice,* on April 28, 1888 *The Commonweal,* press organ of the Socialist League, featured a note about "an interesting letter from a comrade on this subject" and gave a summary of it. Publications in other English papers have not been found. p. 623

518 Engels gave this interview to a representative of the *New Yorker Volkszeitung* on September 19, 1888 at the end of his tour of the USA. Unwilling to meet certain members of German socialist organisations in America, towards which he had a negative attitude, Engels travelled incognito and did his best to avoid any kind of contacts with the press. However, Jonas, editor of the *New Yorker*

Volkszeitung, who had learned about Engels' stay in New York, arranged an appointment for him with Theodor Cuno, former activist of the First International, as his representative. The interview was published by the newspaper without obtaining Engels' approval of the text. It was reprinted by the *Chicagoer Arbeiter-Zeitung* on September 25 and *Wochenblatt der New Yorker Volkszeitung* on September 29. Later, on October 13, it was also reprinted by the *Sozialdemokrat.*

p. 626

[519] The *Landsturm*—an armed force, a second-rate militia, organised in Tyrol in 1809. In the 19th and the beginning of the 20th century, the Landsturm existed in Germany, Austria-Hungary, Holland, Switzerland and Sweden. It was called up in the event of national emergency (see also Note 386). p. 626

699

NAME INDEX

A

Adler, Victor (1852-1918) — a founder and leader of the Austrian Social-Democrats.— 542-43

Aeschylus (525-456 B.C.) — Greek dramatist and tragic poet.— 171, 210

Agassiz, Louis Jean Rodolphe (1807-1873) — Swiss naturalist, lived in the USA from 1846, opponent of Darwinism.— 160

Agrippa, Marcus Vipsanius (c. 63-12 B.C.) — Roman general and statesman.— 19-20, 22

Albedyll, Emil (1824-1897) — Prussian general, commander of the 7th Corps in Münster (Westphalia) in 1888-93.— 540

Albrecht I (c. 1255-1308) — Austrian duke; German Emperor from 1298.— 563

Albrecht, Karl (1788-1844) — German merchant; convicted for his involvement in the oppositional movement of "demagogues"; in 1841 he settled in Switzerland, where he propagated in a religious mystical form ideas close to Weitling's utopian communism.— 320

Alexander I (1777-1825) — Russian Emperor (1801-25).— 455, 490

Alexander II (1818-1881) — Russian Emperor (1855-81).— 414, 477, 480

Alexander III (1845-1894) — Russian Emperor (1881-94).— 406, 411-16, 593

Alexander of Macedon (*Alexander the Great*) (356-323 B.C.) — general and statesman of antiquity.— 168

Alexeyev, Nikolai Alexandrovich (1852-1893) — Mayor of Moscow (1886-93).— 413

Ammianus Marcellinus (c. 330-c. 400) — Roman historian, author of *Rerum Gestarum* covering the history of the Roman Empire from 96 to 378.— 59, 177, 199

Anacreon — Greek lyric poet (second half of the 6th century B.C.).— 184

Anastasius I (c. 430-518) — Byzantine Emperor (491-518).— 39

Anaxandridas (6th cent. B.C.) — King of Sparta from 560 B.C., shared the throne with Aristones.— 171

Anaximander of Miletus (c. 610-546 B.C.) — Greek philosopher.— 612

Appian (end of the 1st cent.—c. 170) — Roman historian.— 393

Appius Claudius Caecus (died c. 448 B.C.) — Roman consul.— 224

Ariovistus (1st half of the 1st cent.

B.C.)—chief of the Germanic tribe of Suebi, fought against Caesar.—11, 12

Aristides (c. 540-467 B.C.)—Athenian statesman and general during the Greco-Persian wars.—219

Aristones (6th cent. B.C.)—King of Sparta (574-520 B.C.), shared the throne with Anaxandridas.—171

Aristophanes (c. 446-c. 385 B.C.)—Greek comic dramatist and poet.—172

Aristotle (384-322 B.C.)—Greek philosopher.—212

Arkwright, Sir Richard (1732-1792)—English industrialist, invented the cotton spinning machine named after him.—573

Arminius (*Hermann*, or *Armin*), *the Cheruscan* (18 or 16 B.C.-A.D. 19 or 21)—leader of the resistance of Germanic tribes against Roman rule, annihilated a Roman army in the Teutoburg Forest in A.D. 9.—25-29, 31

Arndt, Ernst Moritz (1769-1860)—German writer, historian and philologist; took part in the national struggle against Napoleonic rule; deputy to the Frankfurt National Assembly (Right Centre) in 1848-49.—459

Arnold, Wilhelm Christoph Friedrich (1826-1883)—German lawyer and historian.—82, 95-97, 100-02

Artaxerxes—name of the three Persian kings from the Achaemenian dynasty: Artaxerxes I (reigned c. 465-c. 425 B.C.), Artaxerxes II (reigned c. 405-c. 359 B.C.) and Artaxerxes III (reigned c. 359-338 B.C.).—229

Ashley (*Cooper, Anthony Ashley*) (1801-1885)—English politician, Tory philanthropist.—569, 571

Asprenas (*Lucius Nonius Asprenas*) (c. 28 B.C.-A.D. c. 30)—Roman statesman and general, fought in the wars against the Germans.—25, 28

Attwood, Thomas (1783-1856)—English banker, economist and radical politician, adhered to the Right wing of the Chartist movement until 1839—566, 567

Auerswald, Hans Adolf Erdman von (1792-1848)—Prussian general, Right-wing deputy to the Frankfurt National Assembly; killed during Frankfurt uprising in September 1848.—109

Augustenburg, Friedrich (*Frederick*) (1829-1880)—Prince of Schleswig-Holstein-Sonderburg-Augustenburg, pretender to the throne of Schleswig-Holstein from 1852; Duke of Schleswig-Holstein under the name of Friedrich VIII from 1863.—478

Augustus, Gaius Julius Caesar Octavianus (63 B.C.-A.D. 14)—Roman Emperor (27 B.C.-A.D. 14).—11, 12, 18, 21, 22, 28-31, 35, 36, 38, 116, 223, 225, 246

Aveling, Edward (1851-1898)—English socialist, writer and journalist; one of the translators into English of Marx's *Capital,* Volume One; member of the Social-Democratic Federation from 1884; subsequently one of the founders of the Socialist League; an organiser of a mass movement of unskilled workers and unemployed in the late 1880s and early 1890s; husband of Marx's daughter Eleanor.—434, 617, 618

B

Babeuf, François Noël (*Gracchus*) (1760-1797)—French revolutionary, advocate of utopian egalitarian communism, organiser of the "Conspiracy of Equals", executed.—604

Bachofen, Johann Jakob (1815-1887)—Swiss historian and lawyer.—142, 150, 151, 158-61, 165, 188

Bailly, Jean Sylvain (1736-1793)—French astronomer, prominent in the French Revolution, a leader of the liberal constitutional bourgeoisie; as

Mayor of Paris (1789-91) ordered troops to open fire on a republican demonstration on the Field of Mars (1791), for which he was executed by sentence of the revolutionary tribunal in 1793.—126

Bakunin, Mikhail Alexandrovich (1814-1876)—Russian revolutionary and journalist, participant in the 1848-49 revolution in Germany; later an ideologist of Narodism and anarchism; opposed Marxism in the First International.—382, 422, 426, 449, 516

Bancroft, Hubert Howe (1832-1918)—American historian, author of several works on the history and ethnography of North and Central America.—146, 159, 161, 259

Bang, Anton Christian (1840-1913)—Norwegian theologian, author of works on Scandinavian mythology and history of Christianity in Norway.—238

Barbès, Armand (1809-1870)—French revolutionary, a leader of secret societies during the July monarchy; played a prominent part in the 1848 revolution.—313

Baring, Thomas (1799-1873)—head of the bankers' house in London, Conservative M.P.—574

Battenberg, Alexander, Prince of (1857-1893)—son of the Prince of Hesse, in 1879-86 sat on the Bulgarian throne as Prince Alexander I, pursued a pro-Austrian policy.—411, 412, 414

Bauer, Andreas Heinrich—German shoemaker, a leader of the League of the Just, member of the Central Authority of the Communist League; emigrated to Australia in 1851.—313, 314, 323, 327, 328

Bauer, Bruno (1809-1882)—German philosopher and journalist, Young Hegelian.—363, 365, 381

Baur, Ferdinand Christian (1792-1860)—German theologian and historian of Christianity, professor in Tübingen, leader of the Tübingen School.—112

Bayle, Pierre (1647-1706)—French sceptic philosopher, critic of religious dogmatism.—396

Beauvau, Louis Charles Antoine (1710-1744)—French marshal, sent on a diplomatic mission to the court of Frederick II of Prussia in 1740.—469

Beck, Alexander—German tailor, member of the League of the Just, at the end of 1846 was arrested for involvement in the League's case; a witness at the Cologne Communist trial (1852).—315

Becker, August (1814-1871)—German journalist, member of the League of the Just in Switzerland, adherent of Weitling; participant in the 1848-49 revolution in Germany; in 1853 emigrated to the USA where he contributed to democratic papers.—315

Becker, Hermann Heinrich ("Red Becker") (1820-1885)—German lawyer and journalist, member of the Communist League from 1850; sentenced to five years' imprisonment at the Cologne Communist trial (1852); in his later years a National Liberal.—329

Becker, Johann Philipp (1809-1886)—German revolutionary, participant in the democratic movement of the 1830s-50s and the international working-class movement; fought as an officer of the Swiss army in the war against the Sonderbund; prominent figure in the 1848-49 revolution; commanded the Baden people's militia during the Baden-Palatinate uprising of 1849; active member of the First International; friend and associate of Marx and Engels.—418-23, 446, 447

Becker, Wilhelm Adolf (1796-1846)—German historian, professor at Leipzig University, author of works on ancient history.—206

adherent of Christian socialism towards the end of his life.—106

Bornstedt, Adalbert von (1808-1851)—German journalist, supported the adventurist plan for the invasion of Germany by a revolutionary legion; member of the Communist League until his expulsion in March 1848; a secret agent of the Prussian police in the 1840s.—324

Börnstein, Arnold Bernhard Karl (1808-1849)—German democrat, a leader of the volunteer legion of German refugees in Paris (1848).—324

Bougeart, Alfred (1815-1882)—French journalist of the Left, author of works on the history of the French Revolution of the late 18th century.—126

Boulanger, Georges Ernest Jean Marie (1837-1891)—French general, War Minister (1886-87); strove to establish his military dictatorship in France.—416

Bourbaki, Charles Denis Sauter (1816-1897)—French general, commanded the Guard and later the 18th Corps and the Army of the East during the Franco-Prussian war of 1870-71.—490

Bourbons—royal dynasty in France (1589-1792, 1814-15 and 1815-30).—389

Bracke, Wilhelm (1842-1880)—German Social-Democrat, one of the founders (1869) and leaders of Social-Democratic Workers' Party (Eisenachers), associate of Marx and Engels.—309

Brandenburg, Friedrich Wilhelm, Count von (1792-1850)—Prussian general and statesman, head of the counter-revolutionary ministry (November 1848-November 1850).—304, 349

Bray, John Francis (1809-1895)—English economist, utopian socialist, follower of Robert Owen.—280, 285

Brentano, Lorenz Peter (1813-1891)—Baden democrat, lawyer; deputy to the Frankfurt National Assembly (Left wing) in 1848; headed the Baden Provisional Government in 1849; following the defeat of the Baden-Palatinate uprising emigrated to Switzerland, and then to the USA.—419, 447

Brentano, Lujo (1844-1931)—German economist, a leading representative of armchair socialism.—613

Bréquigny, Louis Georges Oudard Feudrix de (1714-1794)—French historian.—63

Bright, John (1811-1889)—English manufacturer and politician, a leader of the Free Traders and one of the founders of the Anti-Corn Law League, M.P. from 1843.—295, 571, 573

Broadhouse, John—see Hyndman, Henry Mayers

Brousse, Paul Louis Marie (1844-1912)—French socialist, physician; participant in the Paris Commune, lived in emigration after its suppression; close to the anarchists; joined the French Workers' Party in 1879, a leader and ideologist of possibilism, an opportunist trend in the French socialist movement.—593

Büchner, Georg (1813-1837)—German dramatist and writer, revolutionary democrat, an organiser of a secret revolutionary Society of the Rights of Man in Giessen.—313

Büchner, Ludwig (1824-1899)—German physiologist and philosopher, a vulgar materialist.—369

Bückler, Johann (c. 1780-1803)—German robber nicknamed Hans the Flayer (Schinderhannes); in a number of literary works depicted as a "noble robber" and defender of the poor.—294

Bugge, Elseus Sophus (1833-1907)—Norwegian philologist, professor in Christiania (now Oslo), researched into ancient Scandinavian literature and mythology.—238

Bürgers, Heinrich (1820-1878)—
German journalist, contributor to the
Rheinische Zeitung (1842-43); member
of the Cologne community of the
Communist League, an editor of the
Neue Rheinische Zeitung in 1848;
member of the Central Authority of
the Communist League from 1850;
one of the accused at the Cologne
Communist trial (1852).—123, 328

Burrows, Herbert (1845-1922)—English
official, radical, a founder of the
Social-Democratic Federation.—542,
543

C

Cabet, Étienne (1788-1856)—French
lawyer and writer, utopian communist, author of *Voyage en Icarie.*—516,
604

Caesar (Gaius Julius Caesar) (c. 100-44
B. C.)—Roman general, statesman
and writer.—6, 10-17, 18, 29-30, 35,
44, 53-55, 138, 139, 151, 196, 234,
236, 241-44, 246

Caligula (A. D. 12-41)—Roman Emperor (A. D. 37-41).—116

Calvin, John (real name *Jean Chauvin*)
(1509-1564)—prominent figure of
the Reformation, founder of Calvinism, a trend in Protestantism, characterised by particular intolerance towards Catholicism as well as other
trends in Protestantism.—395

Camphausen, Ludolf (1803-1890)—
German banker, a leader of the
Rhenish liberal bourgeoisie; Prussian
Prime Minister (March-June 1848).—
471

Carloman (715-754)—elder son of the
Frankish major-domo Charles Martel; ruler of Austrasia, Alamannia
and Thuringia (741-47).—86

Carolingians—Frankish royal dynasty
which ruled in France (751-987),
Germany (till 911) and Italy (till
887).—48, 58, 62, 67, 72, 73, 74, 82

Cavour, Camillo Benso, conte di (1810-

1861)—Italian statesman, head of
the Sardinian government (1852-59
and 1860-61); relying on the support
of Napoleon III pursued a policy of
Italian unification under the supremacy of the Savoy dynasty; headed
the first government of the newly
united Italy in 1861.—464

Charlemagne (Charles the Great) (c. 742-
814)—Frankish King (768-800) and
Roman Emperor (800-814).—59, 63,
65-67, 72, 74, 76-81, 252, 254, 346,
554

Charles VIII (1470-1498)—King of
France (1483-98).—564

Charles, Archduke—see *Charles Louis
Johann*

Charles Louis Johann (1771-1847)—
Archduke of Austria, field marshal,
commander-in-chief in the wars with
France (1796, 1799, 1805 and 1809),
War Minister (1805-09).—492

Charles Martel (c. 688-741)—Frankish
major-domo, became actual ruler of
the Frankish state in 715.—61, 65,
67, 72

Charles the Bald (823-877)—King of
West Frankish Kingdom (840-77),
Emperor of the Franks and King of
Italy (875-77).—68

Charles ("the Bold") (1433-1477)—
Duke of Burgundy (1467-77).—560

*Chernyavskaya-Bokhanovskaya, Galina Fyo-
dorovna* (1854-d. after 1926)—Russian revolutionary, member of the
Narodnaya Volya (People's Will) organisation.—592

Chilperic I (539-584)—King of the
Franks (561-84).—62

Christian, Prince of Glücksburg (1818-
1906)—heir to the Danish throne
from 1852, King of Denmark as
Christian IX in 1863-1906.—456

Civilis, Julius (A. D. 1st cent.)—chief
of the Germanic tribe of Batavi;
headed the uprising of Germanic and

Gaulish tribes against Rome (69-70 or 71).—240

Claudia—Roman patrician family.— 223

Claudius (10 B. C.-A. D. 54)—Roman Emperor (41-54).—31, 116

Clausewitz, Karl von (1780-1831)— Prussian general and military theoretician.—450

Cleisthenes—Athenian politician, in 510-507 B. C. carried out reforms aimed at abolishing the remnants of the gentile system and establishing a democracy based on slaveownership.—220

Clemenceau, Georges (Eugène Benjamin) (1841-1929)—French politician and journalist, leader of the Radicals from the 1880s; Prime Minister (1906-09 and 1917-20).—331-33

Clovis I (465 or 466-511)—King of the Salian Franks from the Merovingian dynasty (481-511).—95

Cobden, Richard (1804-1865)—English manufacturer and politician, a leader of the Free Traders and founder of the Anti-Corn Law League, M.P.— 533, 572, 573

Constantine I, the Great (c. 285-337)— Roman Emperor (306-37).—39

Copernicus, Nicolaus (1473-1543)— Polish astronomer, originator of the heliocentric theory of the universe.— 368

Cosijn, Pieter Jakob (1840-1899)—Dutch philologist, expert on the Germanic languages.—84

Cotton, Sir Robert Bruce, Bart (1571-1631)—English collector of ancient manuscripts, books, coins, etc., founder of the Cottonian library transferred to the British Museum on its foundation (1753).—82-83

Coulanges, de—see *Fustel de Coulanges*

Crassus (Marcus Licinius Crassus) (c. 115-53 B. C.)—Roman politician and general, crushed the revolt of

slaves under Spartacus in 71 B.C.; twice consul.—11, 15

Crawford, Emily (1831-1915)—Irish journalist, Paris correspondent of several English papers.—484

Cuno, Friedrich Theodor (1846-1934)— socialist, active member of the German and international working-class movement and of the First International; after the Hague Congress (1872) emigrated to the USA, contributed to the *New Yorker Volkszeitung.*—626

Cunow, Heinrich Wilhelm Karl (1862-1936)—German Social-Democrat, historian, sociologist and ethnographer.—168

Cuvier, Georges Léopold Chrétien Frédéric Dagobert, baron de (1769-1832)— French naturalist, author of works on comparative anatomy, palaeontology and the classification of animals.— 141

D

Dahlmann, Friedrich Christoph (1785-1860)—German historian and liberal politician; deputy to the Frankfurt National Assembly (Right Centre) in 1848-49; author of works on the history of Denmark and Germany.— 49

Daniels, Roland (1819-1855)—German physician, member of the Communist League, defendant at the Cologne Communist trial (1852); acquitted by the jury; friend of Marx and Engels.—329

Dante Alighieri (1265-1321)—Italian poet.—545

Darwin, Charles Robert (1809-1882)— English naturalist, founder of the theory of evolution by natural selection.—118, 372, 385, 517, 612

Dawkins, Sir William Boyd (1837-1929)—English geologist, anthropologist, palaeontologist and archaeologist; researched into the lives of the cave dwellers of Europe.—6, 33

Demosthenes (384-322 B. C.)—Athenian orator and statesman.—205

Descartes, René (1596-1650)—French philosopher, mathematician and naturalist.—368

Dicaearchus (4th cent. B.C.)—Greek scholar, disciple of Aristotle, author of historical, political, philosophical, geographical and other works.—206

Diderot, Denis (1713-1784)—French philosopher of the Enlightenment, atheist, leader of the Encyclopaedists.—373

Dietzgen, Joseph (1828-1888)—German Social-Democrat; philosopher who arrived at main premisses of dialectical materialism independently; leathermaker.—384

Dio Cassius Cocceianus (c. 155-c. 235)—Roman historian and statesman, representative of the Senate aristocracy, wrote *Historia Romana* running to 80 books in Greek.—11, 20-22, 24, 27, 29, 47

Diodorus Siculus (c. 80-29 B. C.)—Greek historian, author of *Bibliothecae historicae.*—238, 246

Dionysius of Halicarnassus (1st cent. B. C.-A. D. 1st cent.)—Greek historian and rhetorician, author of *Roman Antiquities.*—209

Disraeli, Benjamin, Earl of Beaconsfield (1804-1881)—British statesman and author, a Tory leader; Prime Minister (1868, 1874-80).—410

Domitian (*Titus Flavius Domitianus*) (A.D. 51-96)—Roman Emperor (81-96).—32

Domitius Ahenobarbus, Lucius (d. A.D. 25)—Roman general and statesman; in the early 1st century undertook expeditions to Germany.—11, 22, 23

Drusus, Nero Claudius (38-9 B. C.)—Roman general; headed expeditions against the Germans in 12-9 B. C.—19-21, 23, 31

Dühring, Eugen Karl (1833-1921)—German eclectic philosopher and vulgar economist, his philosophical views were a mixture of idealism, vulgar materialism, positivism and metaphysics; a lecturer at Berlin University from 1863 to 1877.—511

Duncombe, Thomas Slingsby (1796-1861)—British radical politician; participated in the Chartist movement in the 1840s; M. P. (1826-61).—569, 570

Dureau de la Malle, Adolph Jules Cesar Auguste (1777-1857)—French poet and historian.—230

E

Eccarius, Johann Georg (1818-1889)—German tailor, prominent figure in the German and international working-class movement, journalist; member of the League of the Just and later of the Communist League; a leader of the German Workers' Educational Society in London, member of the General Council of the First International; subsequently took part in the British trade union movement.—320

Edmonds, Thomas Rowe (1803-1889)—English economist, utopian socialist, drew socialist conclusions from Ricardo's theory.—280

Einhard (c. 770-840)—historian of the Franks, biographer of Charlemagne.—61

Eisenbart, Johann Andreas (1661-1727)—German physician, served as the prototype of Doctor Eisenbart in German folklore.—288

Elliott, Ebenezer (1781-1849)—English poet, supporter of the Anti-Corn Law League; in his works described the hard life of the English workers.—568

Elsner, Karl Friedrich Moritz (1809-1894)—Silesian journalist and radical politician, deputy to the Prussian

Frederick William (1620-1688)—Elector of Brandenburg (1640-88).—309, 475

Frederick William III (1770-1840)—King of Prussia (1797-1840).—346, 347, 358, 361, 469, 473

Frederick William IV (1795-1861)—King of Prussia (1840-61).—363, 491

Freeman, Edward Augustus (1823-1892)—English historian, liberal, professor at Oxford University.—133

Freiligrath, Ferdinand (1810-1876)—German revolutionary poet, member of the Communist League; an editor of the Neue Rheinische Zeitung (1848-49).—110, 111, 329

Frost, John (1784-1877)—English radical, joined the Chartist movement in 1838; deported for life to Australia for organising a miners' uprising in Wales in 1839, pardoned in 1856 and returned to England.—567-69, 575

Fustel de Coulanges (Numa Denis) (1830-1889)—French historian, author of works on the history of antiquity and medieval France.—208

G

Gaius (Caius) (2nd cent.)—Roman lawyer, systematised Roman law.—166

Galba, Servius Sulpicius (5 B.C.-A.D. 69)—Roman statesman, proclaimed Emperor in June 68, slain by the Praetorian conspirators, led by Othon in January 69 during the rebellion of troops and people against his rule.—116

Galle, Johann Gottfried (1812-1910)—German astronomer, discovered the planet Neptune in 1846, drawing on Leverrier's calculations.—368

Garibaldi, Giuseppe (1807-1882)—Italian revolutionary democrat; led the struggle of the Italian people for

national liberation and the unification of the country in the 1850s and 1860s; headed the revolutionary march to Southern Italy; participated in wars against Austria (1848-49, 1859, 1866).—307, 421, 463

George, Henry (1839-1897)—American journalist, economist and politician.—437-39

Germanicus (Julius Caesar Germanicus) (15 B.C.-A.D. 19)—Roman general, made several campaigns against the Germans, suppressed an uprising of Rhenish legions in 14 B.C.—15, 28, 31

Gervinus, Georg Gottfried (1805-1871)—German historian and politician, liberal; professor in Heidelberg.—470

Gfrörer, August Friedrich (1803-1861)—German theologian and historian, author of works on the history of Christianity and the Church, for some time a follower of the Tübingen School; professor at Freiburg University from 1846.—112

Giers, Nikolai Karlovich de (1820-1895)—Russian diplomat, Minister for Foreign Affairs (1882-95).—414

Giffen, Robert (1837-1910)—English economist and statistician, head of the statistical department at the Board of Trade (1876-97).—299

Giraud-Teulon, Alexis (b. 1839)—professor of history in Geneva.—143, 144, 170

Gladstone, William Ewart (1809-1898)—British statesman, Tory and later Peelite, a leader of the Liberal Party in the latter half of the 19th century; Prime Minister (1868-74, 1880-85, 1886, 1892-94).—210, 292, 411, 626

Godwin, William (1756-1836)—English writer and journalist, rationalist, one of the fathers of anarchism.—607, 614

Goegg, Amand (1820-1897)—German democratic journalist, member of the Baden Provisional Government

(1849); emigrated after the revolution; later member of the First International.—328

Goethe, Johann Wolfgang von (1749-1832)—German poet, dramatist and philosopher.—111, 148, 359, 361, 371, 496

Gould, Jay (1836-1892)—American millionaire, financier who gained control of several large railway systems.—475

Govone, Giuseppe (1825-1872)—Italian general and statesman, participated in the wars against Austria (1848-49, 1859 and 1866), negotiated with Bismarck in April 1866, War Minister (1869-70).—480, 482

Gray, John (1798-1850)—English economist, utopian socialist, follower of Robert Owen; an author of the "labour money" theory.—283-85, 289, 291

Gregory I (the Great) (c. 540-604)—Pope (590-604); canonised after his death.—63

Gregory of Tours (Georgius Florentius) (c. 540-594)—Christian priest, theologian and historian; Bishop of Tours (from 573), canonised after his death.—62, 240

Grey, Sir George (1799-1882)—British statesman, Whig; Home Secretary (1846-52, 1855-58, 1861-66) and Colonial Secretary (1854-55).—575

Grey, Sir Henry George, Viscount Howick, Earl of (1802-1894)—British statesman, Whig, Secretary of War (1835-39), Colonial Secretary (1846-52).—573

Grimm, Jacob Ludwig Carl (1785-1863)—German philologist, author of a historical grammar of the German language and of folklore adaptations; professor in Göttingen and then in Berlin.—18, 46-55, 80, 85, 87, 99, 237

Gröben, Karl Joseph, Count (1788-1876)—Prussian general, commanded a corps which took part in the suppression of the Baden-Palatinate uprising of 1849; member of the Prussian Upper Chamber from 1854.—420

Grosvenor, Richard, Marquis of Westminster (1795-1869)—English aristocrat, Whig.—574

Grote, George (1794-1871)—English historian, M.P. (1832-40), championed electoral reform.—205-08, 567

Grün, Karl Theodor Ferdinand (pen name Ernst von der Haide) (1817-1887)—German journalist, "true socialist" in the mid-1840s, petty-bourgeois democrat during the revolution of 1848-49, deputy to the Prussian National Assembly (Left wing).—365

Guérard, Benjamin Edme Charles (1797-1854)—French historian.—64, 80

Guizot, François Pierre Guillaume (1787-1874)—French historian and statesman.—389

Guntram, or Gontran (c. 525-592)—King of Burgundy (561-92).—62, 67

Gustav I (Vasa) (c. 1496-1560)—King of Sweden (1523-60).—554

H

Habsburgs (or Hapsburgs)—dynasty of the Holy Roman emperors from 1273 to 1806 (with interruptions), Austrian (1804-67) and Austro-Hungarian emperors (1867-1918).—127

Hadrian (Publius Aelius Hadrianus) (76-138)—Roman Emperor (117-138).—32

Hall, Charles (c. 1745-c. 1825)—English economist, utopian socialist.—607, 613

Hansemann, David Justus (1790-1864)—German capitalist, a leader of the Rhenish liberal bourgeoisie; Finance Minister of Prussia (from March to September 1848).—471

Harney, George Julian (1817-1897)—a leader of the Left-wing Chartists, editor of *The Northern Star, Red Republican* and other Chartist periodicals; was on friendly terms with Marx and Engels.—319, 512, 566

Harring, Harro Paul (1798-1870)—German writer, radical, emigrated in 1828.—319

Hartmann, Lev Nikolayevich (1850-1913)—Russian revolutionary, Narodnik, in 1879 participated in one of the terrorist acts of the People's Will against Alexander II, after that he emigrated to France, then to Britain, and in 1881 to the USA.—292

Haupt, Hermann Wilhelm (born c. 1831)—German business clerk, member of the Communist League; was arrested with other Cologne communists, gave evidence against them and was released before the trial; fled to Brazil.—328

Häusser, Ludwig (1818-1867)—German historian and politician, liberal, professor in Heidelberg.—470

Hecker, Friedrich Karl Franz (1811-1881)—German democrat, a leader of the Baden republican uprising in April 1848; after its suppression emigrated to Switzerland and later to the USA where he fought in the Civil War on the side of the Union.—418

Hegel, Georg Wilhelm Friedrich (1770-1831)—German philosopher.—269, 357-69, 371, 373, 377-78, 382-84, 386, 388, 391, 519-20

Heine, Heinrich (1797-1856)—German revolutionary poet.—109, 110, 357, 493

Henry IV (1553-1610)—King of France (1589-1610).—491

Herod (73-4 B.C.)—King of Judaea (40-4 B.C.).—229

Herodotus (c. 484-c. 424 B.C.)—Greek historian.—9, 151, 172

Herrfurth, Ernst Ludwig (1830-1900)—Prussian statesman, Minister of the Interior (1888-92).—540

Herwegh, Georg Friedrich (1817-1875)—German democratic poet, an organiser of the German legion in Paris in 1848.—324

Herzen, Alexander Ivanovich (1812-1870)—Russian revolutionary democrat, materialist philosopher and writer; emigrated in 1847.—449, 516

Hetherington, Henry (1792-1849)—English printer and publisher of workers' papers; took part in the organisation of trade unions, and later in the Chartist movement; was fined for his publishing activities and imprisoned on a charge of blasphemy.—569, 570

Heusler, Andreas (1834-1921)—Swiss lawyer, professor in Basle, author of works on Swiss and German law.—167

Heyne, Moritz (1837-1906)—German philologist, author of several works on the history of the German language; published items belonging to the Old German and Gothic literary heritage.—81-82, 89

Hildebrand, Hans Olof (1842-1913)—Swedish archaeologist, historian and numismatist.—38

Hildebrannus (8th cent.)—Charles Martel's beneficiary.—67

Hincmar (c. 806-882)—archbishop of Reims (France) from 845; author of the third part of *Annales Bertiniani* (861-82).—64, 78

Hincmar (830-882)—archbishop of Lyons (France) (858-79).—68

Hinkel, Karl (1794-1817)—German student, participant in the opposition student movement for the unification of Germany.—458

Hirschfeld, Karl Ulrich Friedrich Wilhelm Moritz von (1791-1859)—Prussian general, commanded a corps which took part in the suppression of the Baden-Palatinate uprising (1849).—420

K

Kalnoky, Gustav Sigismund, Count (1832-1898)—Austro-Hungarian statesman, ambassador to St. Petersburg (1880-81), Chairman of the Imperial Council of Ministers and Minister of Foreign Affairs (1881-95).—414

Kamensky, Gavriil Pavlovich (1824-1898)—Russian economist, agent of the Tsarist government abroad, sentenced in his absence to imprisonment by a Swiss court for counterfeiting (1872).—293

Kant, Immanuel (1724-1804)—German philosopher.—359, 367, 368, 370, 373, 381

Kaulbars, Nikolai Vasilyevich (1842-1905)—Russian general, military commissioner of the Tsarist government in Bulgaria in 1886.—414

Kautsky, Karl Johann (1854-1938)—German Social-Democrat; journalist, economist and historian, editor of Die Neue Zeit (1883-1917), author of several Marxist theoretical works; ideologist of Centrism among the German Social-Democrats and in the Second International.—521

Kaye, Sir John William (1814-1876)—British military historian and colonial official.—151

Kelley-Wischnewetzky, Florence (1859-1932)—American socialist, translated Engels' book The Condition of the Working Class in England into English; wife of the Russian émigré and socialist Lazar Wischnewetzky.—434, 517

Kern, Jan Hendrik (1833-1917)—Dutch philologist, Orientalist and Sanskritist.—83, 86, 89

Kinkel, Gottfried (1815-1882)—German poet and democratic journalist; took part in the 1849 Baden-Palatinate uprising; sentenced to life imprisonment by Prussian court; in 1850 escaped and emigrated to London, a leader of the petty-bourgeois re-

fugees; opposed Marx and Engels.—328

Klapka, György (Georg) (1820-1892)—general of the Hungarian revolutionary army (1848-49), emigrated in 1849; during the Austro-Prussian War of 1866 commanded a Hungarian legion organised by the Prussian Government in Silesia and intended for participation in the war; after the amnesty returned to Hungary in 1867.—307, 481

Klein, Johann Jacob (born c. 1818-died between 1895 and 1897)—Cologne physician, member of the Communist League, a defendant at the Cologne Communist trial (1852), acquitted.—329

Kolb, Georg Friedrich (1808-1884)—German politician, journalist and statistician.—530

Kopp, Hermann (1817-1892)—German chemist and historian of chemistry.—376

Korff, Hermann—former Prussian army officer, democrat; manager of the Neue Rheinische Zeitung (1848-49); later emigrated to the USA.—306

Kossuth, Lajos (1802-1894)—leader of the Hungarian national liberation movement, headed the bourgeois-democratic elements in the 1848-49 revolution and later the Hungarian revolutionary government; after the defeat of the revolution emigrated first to Turkey and then to Britain and the USA.—328

Kotzebue, August Friedrich Ferdinand von (1761-1819)—German writer and journalist, extreme monarchist.—422

Kovalevsky, Maxim Maximovich (1851-1916)—Russian sociologist, historian, ethnographer and lawyer; politician, liberal; author of a number of works on the history of primitive communal system.—165, 167, 168, 232, 236, 241

M

Macaulay, Thomas Babington, Baron (1800-1859)—English historian and politician, Whig, M.P.—308

Macfarlane, Helen (pseudonym Howard Morten)—contributor to Chartist newspapers Democratic Review (1849-50) and Red Republican (1850), translator of the Manifesto of the Communist Party into English.—512

M(a)cLennan, John Ferguson (1827-1881)—Scottish lawyer and historian.—140, 157, 169, 192, 232

Maine, Sir Henry James Sumner (1822-1888)—English jurist and historian of law.—186

Malon, Benoît (1841-1893)—French socialist, member of the First International, member of the Central Committee of the National Guard and of the Paris Commune; after the Commune was defeated emigrated to Italy and later to Switzerland where he adhered to the anarchists; a leader and ideologist of Possibilism, an opportunist trend in the French socialist movement.—593

Manteuffel, Otto Theodor, Baron von (1805-1882)—Prussian statesman; Minister of the Interior (1848-50), Prime Minister and Minister of Foreign Affairs (1850-58).—304, 349, 472, 504

Marat, Jean Paul (1743-1793)—a Jacobin leader during the French Revolution.—126

Marcianus (c. 5th cent.)—Greek geographer.—35

Marcus Aurelius Antoninus (121-180)—Roman Emperor (161-180), Stoic philosopher.—35, 38

Marius, Gaius (c. 156-86 B.C.)—Roman general and statesman, consul (107, 104-100, 86 B.C.)—11, 30

Maroboduus (second half of the 1st cent. B.C.-A.D. 37 (41))—leader of the Germanic tribe of Marcomanni

(8 B.C.-A.D. 19), brought together the Germanic tribes of the Rhine area; fought against Rome, from A.D. 6 maintained neutrality towards Rome.—12, 22, 23, 28, 34

Marx, Jenny (née von Westphalen) (1814-1881)—Karl Marx's wife.—320

Marx, Karl (1818-1883)—109-10, 118-20, 123-28, 131, 141, 147, 150, 165, 166, 170, 173, 176, 204-07, 211, 256, 264, 277-83, 291, 297, 302-06, 311, 312, 315, 317-23, 326, 328, 330, 335-40, 364, 381-82, 403, 422, 426-27, 433, 438, 442, 448, 464, 495, 512-13, 515-24, 535, 545, 591, 593, 595, 599, 601, 604, 606-14, 626-27

Marx-Aveling, Eleanor (1855-1898)—took part in English and international working-class movement in the 1880s-90s; journalist; Marx's daughter, Edward Aveling's wife from 1884; member of the Social-Democratic Federation and later of the Socialist League; active in organising the mass movement of unskilled workers; an organiser of the dockers' strike in London in 1889.—434, 589

Maurer, Georg Ludwig (1790-1872)—German historian, studied the social system of ancient and medieval Germany.—78, 201, 239, 241

Mazzini, Giuseppe (1805-1872)—leader of the national liberation movement in Italy; an organiser of the Central Committee of European Democracy in London (1850).—313, 316, 328

Meitzen, August (1822-1910)—German statistician, historian and economist; worked in statistical departments in Prussia and in Germany (1867-82).—348, 350-51

Melbourne, William Lamb, Viscount (1779-1848)—English statesman, Whig, Home Secretary (1830-34), Prime Minister (1834 and 1835-41).—566, 570

Menger, Anton (1841-1906)—Austrian lawyer, professor at Vienna University.—600-09, 610-16

Menke, Heinrich Theodor von (1819-1892)—German geographer, revised Spruner's *Hand-Atlas für die Geschichte des Mittelalters und der neueren Zeit.*—96, 559

Mentel, Christian Friedrich (b. 1812)— German tailor, member of the League of the Just; in 1846-47 was imprisoned in Prussia for his involvement in the League's case.—315

Merovingians—the first royal dynasty in the Frankish state, (mid-5th cent.-751).—58, 61, 63, 65, 71, 73, 76

Mestorf, Johanna (1829-1909)—German historian and archaeologist.—34, 37

Metternich-Winneburg, Clemens Wenzel Lothar, Prince von (1733-1859)— Austrian statesman and diplomat, Minister of Foreign Affairs (1809-21) and Chancellor (1821-48), an organiser of the Holy Alliance.—465, 486

Mierosławski, Ludwik (1814-1878)— prominent figure in the Polish national liberation movement, took part in the Polish uprising of 1830-31 and in the 1848-49 revolution; commander of the revolutionary army during the Baden-Palatinate uprising of 1849.—420

Mignet, François Auguste Marie (1796-1884)—French historian.—389

Mikhailovsky, Nikolai Konstantinovich (1842-1904)—Russian sociologist, journalist and literary critic, ideologist of the liberal Narodniks; an editor of the magazines *Otechestvennye Zapiski* and *Russkoye Bogatstvo.*—311

Milde, Karl August (1805-1861)— Silesian manufacturer, moderate liberal; Minister of Trade in the Auerswald-Hansemann Ministry (from June to September 1848), President of the Prussian National Assembly (Right wing).—471

Mirbach, Otto von (born c. 1800)— retired Prussian artillery officer, democrat; commandant of Elberfeld during the May 1849 uprising; emigrated from Germany.—595

Mitchel, John (1815-1875)—Irish journalist and historian, prominent figure in the Irish national liberation movement, leader of the revolutionary-democratic wing in the Young Ireland group; favoured union with the Chartists; for preparing a revolt in Ireland was deported to colonies in 1848; escaped in 1853 and emigrated to the USA.—575

Moleschott, Jakob (1822-1893)—Dutch physiologist and philosopher; lectured in Germany, Switzerland and Italy.—369

Molière (real name *Jean Baptist Poquelin*) (1622-1673)—French playwright.—266

Moll, Joseph (1813-1849)—German watch-maker, a leader of the League of the Just, member of the Central Authority of the Communist League; President of the Cologne Workers' Association (from July to September 1848), member of the Rhenish District Committee of Democrats; killed in battle during the Baden-Palatinate uprising of 1849.—314, 321, 323, 326

Mommsen, Theodor (1817-1903)— German historian of Ancient Rome.—206, 225-29

Mone, Franz Joseph (1796-1871)— German historian and philologist.—99

Moore, Samuel (1838-1911)—English lawyer, member of the First International; translated into English Volume I of Marx's *Capital* (together with Edward Aveling) and the *Manifesto of the Communist Party;* associate of Marx and Engels.—518

Morgan, Lewis Henry (1818-1881)— American ethnographer, archaeologist and historian of primitive society.—131-35, 139-43, 147, 152, 156, 189-92, 194, 206, 207, 210, 211, 213

Morny, Charles August Louis Joseph, duc de (1811-1865)—French politician,

Bonapartist; an organiser of the coup d'état of December 2, 1851; Minister of the Interior (December 1851-January 1852).—476

Moschus (mid-2nd cent. B.C.)—Greek poet.—184

Motteler, Julius (1838-1907)—German Social-Democrat; deputy to the Reichstag in 1874-79; an émigré in Zurich and later in London at the time of the Anti-Socialist Law; was responsible for transportation of the *Sozialdemokrat* and illegal Social-Democratic literature to Germany.—623

Moxon, Edward (1801-1858)—English publisher; for publishing Shelley's poems, was brought to trial in 1840 on a charge of blasphemy levelled by Hetherington; found guilty in June 1841 but was not punished.—570

Mülberger, Arthur (1847-1907)—German journalist, physician.—425

Müllenhoff, Karl Victor (1818-1884)—German philologist and historian, expert in Germanic antiquities, mythology and medieval literature.—10

N

Nadler, Karl Christian Gottfried (1809-1849)—German poet, wrote in the Palatinate dialect.—105

Napoleon I Bonaparte (1769-1821)—Emperor of the French (1804-14 and 1815).—123, 175, 192, 309, 347, 375, 415, 455, 459, 463, 465, 469, 495, 506

Napoleon III (*Charles Louis Napoleon Bonaparte*) (1808-1873)—Napoleon I's nephew; President of the Second Republic (1848-51), Emperor of the French (1852-70).—29, 109, 297, 302, 411, 412, 421, 460, 461, 463, 464, 475-77, 479-82, 484-89, 494, 498, 578, 580

Napoleon the Little—see *Napoleon III*

Nearchus (c. 360-c. 312 B. C.)—Macedonian navigator, a fellow campaigner of Alexander the Great, described an expedition of the Macedonian fleet from India to Mesopotamia (326-324 B.C.).—168

Nero (*Nero Claudius Caesar Augustus Germanicus*) (37-68)—Roman Emperor (54-68).— 35, 40, 116-17

Nicholas I (1796-1855)—Russian Emperor (1825-55).—456, 460, 461, 477

Niebuhr, Barthold Georg (1776-1831)—German historian.—206, 208, 228, 269

Nothjung, Peter (1821-1866)—German tailor; member of the Cologne Workers' Association and of the Communist League; one of the accused at the Cologne Communist trial (1852).—328-29

Novikova, Olga Alexeyevna (1840-1925)—Russian journalist, lived in Britain for a long time; was in fact a diplomatic agent of the Russian government under Gladstone's administration in the 1870s.—292

Numonius Vala (died A. D. 9)—legate; commander of Quintilius Varus' cavalry; killed when fleeing after the Roman defeat in the Teutoburg Forest.—28

O

Oastler, Richard (1789-1861)—English clergyman and politician; sided with the Tories in opposing the Free Traders; favoured a reduction of the working day by law.—574

O'Brien, James (pseudonym *Bronterre*) (1805-1864)—Irish journalist, ideologist and prominent figure in the Chartist movement, an editor of *The Poor Man's Guardian* in the 1830s, an organiser of the National Reform League (1849).—569, 575, 576

O'Brien, William Smith (1803-1864)—Right-wing leader of the Young Ireland group; sentenced to death in

1848 after an unsuccessful attempt to organise an uprising, commuted to life deportation; amnestied in 1856.—573, 576

O'Connell, Daniel (1775-1847)—Irish lawyer and politician, leader of the liberal wing of the national liberation movement.—572, 574-76

O'Connor, Feargus Edward (1794-1855)—a Left-wing Chartist leader, editor-in-chief of *The Northern Star*; reformist after 1848.—566-70, 572-75

Odoacer (c. 434-493)—German military leader in the service of West Roman emperors; dethroned Emperor Romulus Augustulus in 476 and became king of the first "barbarian" kingdom in Italy.—245

Olga (d. 969)—Grand Princess of Kiev, Regent of the Russian state from 945, after the death of her husband Igor, her son Svyatoslav being still a minor.—235

Orleans—branch in the royal house of Bourbons (1830-48).—416

Orosius, Paulus (c. 380-c. 420)—Roman historian, Spaniard by birth; author of *Historiarum adversum paganos.*—20

Orsini, Felice (1819-1858)—Italian democrat, republican; prominent figure in the struggle for Italy's national liberation and unification; executed for his attempt on the life of Napoleon III.—462

Oshanina, Maria Nikolayevna (née *Olovenikova*) (1853-1898)—Russian revolutionary, member of the Executive of the Narodnaya Volya (People's Will) organisation; emigrated to Paris in 1882; representative of the Narodnaya Volya's Executive abroad.—591-93

Otfri(e)d (9th cent.)—monk from Wissembourg in Alsace; wrote a poem entitled *Liber Evangeliorum domini gratia theotisce conscriptus* (c. 868), which included all four Gospels.—86, 105

Otho, Marcus Salvius (32-69)—Roman statesman, legate in the province Lusitania; in January 69 organised praetorians' plot against Emperor Galba, had him murdered and proclaimed himself emperor; took his own life in April 69.—116

Otto, Karl Wunibald (born c. 1810)—German chemist; member of the Cologne Workers' Association and of the Communist League (1848-49); one of the accused at the Cologne Communist trial (1852).—329

Ovid (Publius Ovidius Naso) (43 B.C.-A.D. 18)—Roman poet.—29

Owen, Robert (1771-1858)—British utopian socialist.—599

P

Palgrave, Sir Robert Harry Inglis (1827-1919)—English banker and economist, editor of *The Economist* (1877-83).—300

Palmerston, Henry John Temple, Viscount (1784-1865)—British statesman, Foreign Secretary (1830-34, 1835-41, 1846-51), Home Secretary (1852-55) and Prime Minister (1855-58 and 1859-65).—461, 477

Pare, William (1805-1873)—British economist, active in the co-operative movement, follower of Owen.—609

Pattison, James (1786-1849)—English politician, liberal M.P. (1835-41 and 1843-47).—574

Peel, Sir Robert (1788-1850)—British statesman, moderate Tory; Home Secretary (1822-27, 1828-30), Prime Minister (1834-35, 1841-46); repealed the Corn Laws in 1846.—528, 570-73

Pepin (or *Pippin*) *III* (*the Short*) (714-768)—Frankish mayor of the palace (741-751), first king of the Carolingian dynasty (751-768); son of Charles Martel.—64, 65-67

INDEX OF LITERARY AND MYTHOLOGICAL NAMES

INDEX OF QUOTED
AND MENTIONED LITERATURE

WORKS BY KARL MARX AND FREDERICK ENGELS

Marx, Karl

Конспект книги Льюиса Т. Моргана "Древнее общество". In: *Архив Маркса и Энгельса*, т. IX, М., 1941.
— *Marx's Excerpts from Lewis Henry Morgan, "Ancient Society"*. In: *The Ethnological Notebooks of Karl Marx*. Assen, 1972, pp. 95-241.— 131, 134, 141, 150, 156, 158, 165, 166, 170, 190, 194, 197, 205-08, 210-11, 225, 264, 276

Capital. A Critique of Political Economy. Volume I. Book One. The Process of Production of Capital (present edition, Vol. 35)
— *Das Kapital. Kritik der politischen Oekonomie.* Erster Band. Hamburg, 1867.— 131, 279, 335, 340
— *Le Capital.* Traduction de M. J. Roy, entièrement revisée par l'auteur. [Vol. 1] Paris, s.a. [1872-1875].— 589
— *Das Kapital. Kritik der politischen Oekonomie.* Bd. 1. 3. vermehrte Aufl. Hamburg, 1883.— 336-40, 433, 438
— *Capital: A Critical Analysis of Capitalist Production.* Translated from the third German edition, by Samuel Moore and Edward Aveling and edited by Frederick Engels. Vol. I. London, 1887.— 340, 522

Capital. A Critique of Political Economy. Volume II. Book Two. The Process of Circulation of Capital (present edition, Vol. 36)
— *Das Kapital. Kritik der politischen Oekonomie.* Von Karl Marx. Zweiter Band. Buch II: Der Cirkulationsprocess des Kapitals. Herausgegeben von Friedrich Engels. Hamburg, 1885.— 336

The Civil War in France. Address of the General Council of the International Working-men's Association (present edition, Vol. 22)
— *The Civil War in France.* Address of the General Council of the International Working-men's Association. London, 1871.— 518

The Class Struggles in France, 1848 to 1850 (present edition, Vol. 10)
— *Die Klassenkämpfe in Frankreich 1848 bis 1850.* In: *Neue Rheinische Zeitung. Politisch-ökonomische Revue.* Nr. 1, 2, 3, 5-6, 1850.— 604

A Contribution to the Critique of Political Economy. Part One (present edition, Vol. 29)
— *Zur Kritik der politischen Oekonomie.* Erstes Heft. Berlin, 1859.— 280-81, 283, 291

Critical Marginal Notes on the Article "The King of Prussia and Social Reform. By a Prussian" (present edition, Vol. 3)
—Kritische Randglossen zu dem Artikel "Der König von Preussen und die Sozialreform. Von einem Preussen". In: *Vorwärts!* Nr. 63, 64; 7., 10. August. Paris, 1844.—315

The Eighteenth Brumaire of Louis Bonaparte (present edition, Vol. 11)
—Der achtzehnte Brumaire des Louis Napoleon. In: *Die Revolution.* Erstes Heft. New York, 1852.—302
—Der achtzehnte Brumaire des Louis Bonaparte. 3. Aufl. Hamburg, 1885.—302

General Rules and Administrative Regulations of the International Working Men's Association (present edition, Vol. 23)
—Published as pamphlets in English and French in November and December 1871 and in German in February 1872.—517

The June Revolution (present edition, Vol. 7)
—Die Junirevolution. In: *Neue Rheinische Zeitung,* Nr. 29, 29. Juni 1848.—126

On Proudhon [*Letter to J. B. Schweitzer*] (present edition, Vol. 20)
—Über P.-J. Proudhon. In: *Der Social-Demokrat,* Nr. 16-18, 1., 3. und 5. Februar 1865.—278

The Poverty of Philosophy. Answer to the "Philosophy of Poverty" by M. Proudhon (present edition, Vol. 6)
—Misère de la philosophie. Réponse à La philosophie de la misère de M. Proudhon. Paris-Bruxelles, 1847.—427, 613
—Das Elend der Philosophie. Antwort auf Proudhons "Philosophie des Elends". Deutsch von E. Bernstein und K. Kautsky. Mit Vorwort und Noten von Friedrich Engels. Stuttgart, 1885.—278, 281, 427, 521, 613

Preface [to *A Contribution to the Critique of Political Economy*] (present edition, Vol. 29)
—Karl Marx. [Preface] In: *Das Volk,* Nr. 5, 14. Juni 1859.—519

Provisional Rules of the Association (present edition, Vol. 20). In: *Address and Provisional Rules of the Working Men's International Association, Established September 28, 1864, at a Public Meeting Held at St. Martin's Hall, Long Acre, London.* [London,] 1864.—517

Revelations Concerning the Communist Trial in Cologne (present edition, Vol. 11)
—Enthüllungen über den Kommunisten-Prozess zu Köln. Basel, 1853.—312-13
—Enthüllungen über den Kommunisten Prozess zu Köln. Neuer Abdruck mit Einleitung von Friedrich Engels und Dokumenten. Hottingen-Zürich, 1885.—312-13, 328-29

Second Address of the General Council of the International Working Men's Association on the Franco-Prussian War. To the Members of the International Working Men's Association in Europe and the United States (present edition, Vol. 22). Published as a leaflet in English and in German in September-December 1870.—495

Speech on the Question of Free Trade. Delivered to the Democratic Association of Brussels at Its Public Meeting of January 9, 1848 (present edition, Vol. 6)
—Discours sur la question du libre échange, prononcé à l'association démocratique de Bruxelles. Dans la Séance Publique du 9 Janvier 1848. Bruxelles, 1848.—291

—Rede über die Frage des Freihandels, gehalten am 9. Januar 1849 [1848] in der demokratischen Gesellschaft zu Brüssel von Karl Marx. In: Marx, K. *Das Elend der Philosophie.* Stuttgart, 1885, S. 188-209. Anhang 2.—521
—Free Trade. A speech delivered before the Democratic Club, Brussels, Belgium, Jan. 9, 1848. Boston-New York, 1888.—521

Theses on Feuerbach (present edition, Vol. 5)
—First published in the Appendix to the separate edition of *Ludwig Feuerbach und der Ausgang der klassischen deutschen Philosophie.* Stuttgart, 1888.—520

Wage Labour and Capital (present edition, Vol. 9)
—Lohnarbeit und Kapital. In: *Neue Rheinische Zeitung,* Nr. 264-267, 269; 5.-8., 11. April, 1849.—127
—Lohnarbeit und Kapital. Separat-Abdruck aus der *Neuen Rheinischen Zeitung* vom Jahre 1849. Nottingen-Zürich, 1884.—277

Engels, Frederick

The Assembly at Frankfurt (present edition, Vol. 7)
—Die Frankfurter Versammlung. In: *Neue Rheinische Zeitung,* Nr. 1, 1. Juni 1848.—124

The Condition of the Working-Class in England. From Personal Observation and Authentic Sources (present edition, Vol. 4)
—Die Lage der arbeitenden Klasse in England. Nach eigner Anschauung und authentischen Quellen. Leipzig, 1845.—119
—The Condition of the Working Class in England in 1844. With Appendix written 1886, and Preface 1887. New York [1887].—399, 402, 434
—The Condition of the Working Class in England in 1844. With appendix written 1886, and preface 1887. New York-London, 1888.—517

The Housing Question (present edition, Vol. 23)
—Zur Wohnungsfrage. In: *Der Volksstaat,* Nr. 51, 52, 53, 103, 104; 26., 29. Juni, 25., 28. December 1872; Nr. 2, 3, 12, 13, 15, 16; 4., 8. Januar, 8., 12., 19., 22. Februar 1873.—424-25
—Zur Wohnungsfrage. Zweite, durchgesehene Auflage. Hottingen-Zürich, 1887.—424-26, 433

Ludwig Feuerbach and the End of Classical German Philosophy (this volume)
—Ludwig Feuerbach und der Ausgang der klassischen deutschen Philosophie. In: *Die Neue Zeit,* Nr. 4, 5, 1886 and as a pamphlet, Stuttgart, 1888.—519, 600

Preface [to the first German edition of *Capital,* Volume II] (present edition, Vol. 36)
—Vorrede. In: K. Marx. *Das Kapital. Kritik der politischen Oekonomie.* Zweiter Band. Buch II: Der Cirkulationsprocess des Kapitals. Erste Auflage. Herausgegeben von Friedrich Engels. Hamburg, 1885.—278

The Role of Force in History (this volume)
—Die Rolle der Gewalt in der Geschichte. In: *Die Neue Zeit,* Bd. 1, Nr. 22-26, 1895-1896.—578-79

Marx, Karl and Engels, Frederick

Address of the Central Authority to the League. March 1850 (present edition, Vol. 10)
— Ansprache der Zentralbehörde an den Bund vom März 1850. In: *Enthüllungen über den Kommunisten-Prozess zu Köln* von Karl Marx. Neuer Abdr. mit Einl. von Friedrich Engels, und Dokumenten. Hottingen-Zürich [1885].— 326

Address of the Central Authority to the League. June 1850 (present edition, Vol. 10)
— Ansprache der Zentralbehörde an den Bund vom Juni 1850. In: *Enthüllungen über den Kommunisten-Prozess zu Köln* von Karl Marx. Neuer Abdr. mit Einl. von Friedrich Engels, und Dokumenten. Hottingen-Zürich [1885].— 326

[Circular Against Kriege] (present edition, Vol. 6). Published as a lithographic circular in 1846.— 319

Demands of the Communist Party in Germany (present edition, Vol. 7)
— Forderungen der Kommunistischen Partei in Deutschland. Köln, 1848 (a leaflet).— 323

The German Ideology (present edition, Vol. 5)
— Die deutsche Ideologie. In: Marx/Engels, *Gesamtausgabe.* Erste Abteilung, 5. Band, M. 1932.— 173, 519

The Holy Family, or Critique of Critical Criticism. Against Bruno Bauer and Company (present edition, Vol. 4)
— Die heilige Familie, oder Kritik der kritischen Kritik. Gegen Bruno Bauer und Consorten. Frankfurt a. M., 1845.— 364

Manifesto of the Communist Party (present edition, Vol. 6)
— (anon.) Manifest der Kommunistischen Partei. Veröffentlicht im Februar 1848. London.— 120-21, 186, 312, 320, 441, 512-18
— Manifesto of the German Communist Party (published in February 1848). In: *The Red Republican,* Nos. 21-24, November 9, 16, 23, 30, 1850.— 512
— (anon.) Манифестъ Коммунистической партіи. Б. м. и г. [Женева, 1869].— 516
— Manifesto of the German Communist Party (first published in February 1848). In: *Woodhull & Claflin's Weekly,* New York, No. 7, December 30, 1871.— 516
— Manifeste de Karl Marx. In: *Le Socialiste,* New York, Nos 16, 17, 19-24, 26; 20, 27 janvier, 10, 17, 24 février, 2, 9, 16, 30 mars 1872.— 516
— Das Kommunistische Manifest. Neue Ausgabe mit einem Vorwort der Verfasser. Leipzig, 1872.— 518
— Манифестъ Коммунистической партіи Карла Маркса и Фр. Энгельса. Переводъ с нѣм. изданія 1872 г. Съ предисловіемъ авторовъ. Женева, 1882.— 516
— Das Kommunistische Manifest. Dritte autorisirte deutsche Ausgabe. Mit Vorworten der Verfasser. Hottingen-Zürich, 1883.— 118, 119
— Manifesto of the Communists. Published by the International Working-men's Association. New York, 1883.— 516
— Det Kommunistiske Manifest. Med Forfatternes Forord. (Efter den tredje avtoriserede tyske Udgave.) In: *Socialistisk Bibliotek.* Udgivet af Det socialdemokratiske Arbejderparti i Danmark. Bd. 1. Socialistiske Pjecer, København, 1885.— 516
— Manifeste du parti communiste. In: *Le Socialiste,* Nos 1-11; 29 août, 5, 12, 19, 26 septembre, 3, 10, 17, 24, 31 octobre, 7 novembre 1885.— 516

—Manifesto del Partido Comunista. In: *El Socialista*, Nos 14-17, 19-22; 11, 18, 25 Junio, 2, 16, 23, 30 Julio, 6 Agosto 1886.—516
—The Manifesto of the Communists. By Karl Marx. Assisted by Frederick Engels. London, International Publishing Company, 1886.—516
—Manifesto of the Communist Party. Edited and annotated by Frederick Engels. Third Edition, London, 1888.—119, 512

Preface to the 1872 German edition of the "Manifesto of the Communist Party" (present edition, Vol. 23)
—Vorwort. In: *Das Kommunistische Manifest*. Neue Ausgabe mit einem Vorwort der Verfasser. Leipzig, 1872.—518

Preface to the Second Russian Edition of the "Manifesto of the Communist Party" (present edition, Vol. 24)
—Предисловіе. In: К. Маркс и Ф. Энгельсъ. *Манифестъ Коммунистической партіи*, Женева, 1882.—627

Review. May to October [1850] (present edition, Vol. 10)
—Revue. Mai bis Oktober [1850]. In: *Neue Rheinische Zeitung. Politisch-ökonomische Revue*, Nr. 5-6, Mai bis Oktober 1850.—328

[Marx, K., Engels, F.] *To the Workers of Cologne* (present edition, Vol. 9)
—An die Arbeiter Kölns. In: *Neue Rheinische Zeitung*, Nr. 301, 19. Mai 1849.—128

Marx, K., Schapper, K., Schneider II. *Appeal* (present edition, Vol. 8)
—Aufruf. In: *Neue Rheinische Zeitung*, Nr. 147 (2. Aufl.) November 19, 1848.—305

WORKS BY DIFFERENT AUTHORS

Abendroth, H. von. *Terrainstudien zu dem Rückzuge des Varus und den Feldzügen des Germanicus*. Leipzig, 1862.—20, 28

Aeschylus. *Oresteia: Agamemnon.*—171
— *The Seven Against Thebes.*—209
— *The Suppliants.*—210

Agassiz, L. and Agassiz, E. *A Journey in Brazil*. Boston, 1868.—160

Altniederdeutsche Interlinearversion der Psalmen. In: *Kleinere altniederdeutsche Denkmäler*. Mit ausführlichem Glossar herausgegeben von Moritz Heyne. Paderborn, 1867.—83-84

Ammianus Marcellinus. *Rerum gestarum libri qui supersunt.*—59, 177

Annales Bertiniani. In: Roth, P. *Geschichte des Beneficialwesens von der ältesten Zeiten bis ins zehnte Jahrhundert*. Erlangen, 1850.—77

Appian of Alexandria. *The Roman History* (in 24 books).—393

Aristophanes. *Thesmophoriazusae.*—172

Aristoteles. *Politica.*—212

Arndt, E. M. *Des Teutschen Vaterland*. In: Arndt, E. M. *Lieder für Teutsche im Jahr der Freiheit 1813*. Leipzig, 1813, S. 99-101.—459

Arnold, W. *Deutsche Urzeit.* Gotha, 1879.—82, 90, 95-97, 100-02

Aveling, E. and Marx-Aveling, E. *The Labour-movement in America.* In: *The Time,* Nos 3-6, 1887.—434

Bachofen, J. J. *Das Mutterrecht. Eine Untersuchung über die Gynaikokratie der alten Welt nach ihrer religiösen und rechtlichen Natur.* Stuttgart, 1861.—142, 150-51, 158-61, 165, 188

Bancroft, H. H. *The Native Races of the Pacific States of North America,,* Vols I-V. New York, 1875.—146, 159, 161, 259

Bang, A. Ch. *Vøluspá og de sibyllinske orakler.*—238

Bauer, B. *Christus und die Caesaren. Der Ursprung des Christenthums aus dem römischen Griechenthum.* Berlin, 1877.—113

Becker, W. A. *Charikles, Bilder altgriechischer Sitte. Zur genaueren Kenntniss des griechischen Privatlebens.* Zweiter Theil. Leipzig, 1840.—206

[Beda Venerabilis.] *De Venerabilis Baedae Historia ecclesiastica gentis Anglorum.*—235

Berthelot, M. *Les origines de l'alchimie.* Paris, 1885.—376

Beust, F. *Kleiner historischer Atlas des Kantons Zürich.* Zürich, 1873.—99

Bevan, W. [Speech at the Twentieth Annual Trades' Union Congress at Swansea on September 6, 1887.] In: W. Binning, "The Trades' Union Congress", *The Commonweal,* No. 88, September 17, 1887.—515

Bible—112
   The Old Testament—111, 112, 163
      Genesis—162-64
      2 Samuel—325
   The New Testament
      The Acts—338
      Revelation—112-15, 117

Bonaparte, N.-L. *Des idées napoléoniennes.* Paris, 1839.—475

Borkheim, S. *Zur Erinnerung für die deutschen Mordspatrioten. 1806-1807.* Mit einer Einleitung von Fr. Engels. Hottingen-Zürich, 1888.—446, 449-50

Börne, L. *Schilderungen aus Paris (1822 und 1823).* In: Börne, Ludwig. *Gesammelte Schriften.* Neue vollständige Ausgabe. Bd. 3. Hamburg. Frankfurt a. M., 1862.—106

Bougeart, A. *Marat, L'ami du peuple.* T. I-II. Paris, 1865.—126

Braune, W. *Zur Kenntnis des Fränkischen und zur hochdeutschen Lautverschiebung.* In: *Beiträge zur Geschichte der deutschen Sprache und Literatur.* Bd. 1. Halle, 1874.—81, 84, 94, 105

Bray, J. Fr. *Labour's Wrongs and Labour's Remedy; or, the Age of Might and the Age of Right.* Leeds, 1839.—280

Bréquigny, L. G. O. F. de, La Porte du Theil, F. J. G. *Diplomata, chartae, epistolae, et alia documenta, ad res Francicas spectantia, ex diversis regni, exterarumque regionum archivis ac bibliothecis, jussu regis christianissimi, multorum eruditorum curis, plurimum ad id conference Congregatione S. Mauri, eruta.* In: Roth, P., *Geschichte des Beneficialwesens von der ältesten Zeiten bis ins zehnte Jahrhundert.* Erlangen, 1850.—64

Bugge, S. *Studier over de nordiske Gude- og Heltesagns Oprindelse.* Kristiania, 1881-1889.—238

Caesar, Gaius Julius. *Commentarii de bello Gallico.* In: *Die Geschichtschreiber der deutschen Vorzeit in deutscher Bearbeitung.* Bd. 1: *Die Urzeit.* Berlin, 1847-1849.— 12-14, 53-55, 139, 151, 236, 241, 246

Cosijn, P. J. *Kurzgefaßte altwestsächsische Grammatik.* Th. 1: *Die Vocale der Stammsilben.* Leiden, 1881.—84

Coulanges, Fustel de. *La cité antique.* Étude sur le culte, le droit, les institutions de la Grèce et de Rome. Paris-Strasbourg, 1864.—208

[*The Counterfeiters or the Agents of the Russian Government*] Фальшивые монетчики или Агенты русскаго правительства. Genève-Bâle-Lyon, 1875.—293

Cunow, H. *Die altperuanischen Dorf- und Markgenossenschaften.* In: *Das Ausland,* Nr. 42-44, 20. und 27. Oktober, 3. November 1890.—168

Dahlmann, F. C. *Geschichte von Dännemark.* Bd. 1-3. Hamburg, 1840-1843.—49

Dante. *Divine Comedy. Inferno.*—545

Dawkins, W. Boyd. *Early Man in Britain and His Place in the Tertiary Period.* London, 1880.—6, 8, 33

Demosthenes. *Against Eubulides.*—205

[Dietzgen, J.] *Das Wesen der menschlichen Kopfarbeit. Dargestellt von einem Handarbeiter. Eine abermalige Kritik der reinen und praktischen Vernunft.* Hamburg, 1869.—384

Dio Cassius. *Historia Romana.* In: *Die Geschichtschreiber der deutschen Vorzeit in deutscher Bearbeitung.* Bd. 1: *Die Urzeit.* Berlin, 1847-1849.—11, 20-24, 27, 29, 47

Diodorus Siculus. *Bibliothecae historicae quae supersunt.*—238, 246

Dionysius of Halicarnassus. *Roman Antiquities.*—209

Dureau de la Malle, A. *Économie politique des Romains.* T. 1, Paris, 1840.—230

Die Edda die ältere und jüngere nebst den mythischen Erzählungen der Skalda. Stuttgart und Augsburg, 1855.—147

Edmonds, T. R. *Practical Moral and Political Economy; or, the Government, Religion, and Institutions, most Conducive to Individual Happiness and to National Power.* London, 1828.—280

Einhardus. *Vita Caroli Magni.* In: Roth, P. *Geschichte des Beneficialwesens von der ältesten Zeiten bis ins zehnte Jahrhundert.* Erlangen, 1850.—61

[Enfantin, B. P.] *Les oisifs et les travailleurs. Fermages, loyers, intérèts, salaires.* In: *Le Globe,* No. 66, 7 mars 1831.—606

Engelhardt, C. *Thorsbjerg Mosefund.* København, 1863.—40

Espinas, A. *Des sociétés animales.* Paris, 1877.—144

Euripides. *Orestes.*—172

Ferguson, A. *An Essay on the History of Civil Society.* Edinburgh, 1767.—339-40

Feuerbach, L. *Fragmente zur Charakteristik maines philosophischen Curriculum vitae.* In: *Ludwig Feuerbach's sämmtliche Werke.* Bd. II, Leipzig, 1846, S. 381-414.—378

— *Grundsätze der Philosophie. Notwendigkeit einer Veränderung.* In: *Ludwig Feuerbach in seinem Briefwechsel und Nachlass sowie in seiner Philosophischen Charakterentwicklung.* Bd. I. Leipzig und Heidelberg, 1874, S. 406-412.—374, 378-79

— *Noth meistert alle Gesetze und hebt sie auf.* In: *Ludwig Feuerbach in seinem Briefwechsel und Nachlass sowie in seiner Philosophischen Charakterentwicklung.* Bd. II. Leipzig und Heidelberg, 1874, S. 285-294.—378

— *Das Wesen des Christenthums.* Leipzig, 1841.—364

— *Wider den Dualismus von Leib und Seele, Fleisch und Geist.* In: *Ludwig Feuerbach's sämmtliche Werke.* Bd. II, Leipzig, 1846, S. 347-379.—378

Fison, L. and Howitt, A. W. *Kamilaroi and Kurnai.* Melbourne, Sydney, Adelaide, and Brisbane, 1880.—153, 155

Florus, Publius Annius. *Epitomae de Tito Livio.* In: *Die Geschichtschreiber der deutschen Vorzeit in deutscher Bearbeitung.* Bd. 1: *Die Urzeit.* Berlin, 1847-1849.—20-21

Formulae Turonenses vulgo Sirmondicae dictae. In: Roth, P. *Geschichte des Beneficialwesens von der ältesten Zeiten bis ins zehnte Jahrhundert.* Erlangen, 1850.—73

Fourier, Ch. *Théorie de l'unité universelle.* T. 3. In: *Oeuvres complètes,* T. 4. Paris, 1841.—179

— *Théorie des quatre mouvements et des destinées générales.* In: *Oeuvres complètes.* T. 1. Paris, 1841.—255

Freckenhorster Heberolle. In: *Kleinere altniederdeutsche Denkmäler.* Paderborn, 1867.—84-85

Freeman, E. A. *Comparative Politics.* Six Lectures read before the Royal Institution in January and February, 1873. With *The Unity of History.* The Rede Lecture read before the University of Cambridge, May 29, 1872. London, 1873.—133

Freifrau von Droste-Fischering. In: *Historische Volkslieder der Zeit von 1756 bis 1871.* Bd. 2. Berlin, 1871-1872, S. 82.—471

Die Geschichtschreiber der deutschen Vorzeit in deutscher Bearbeitung. Bd. 1: *Die Urzeit.* Hrsg. v. G. H. Pertz, J. Grimm u.a. Berlin, 1847-1849.—11-16, 18, 20

Giraud-Teulon, A. *Les origines du mariage et de la famille.* Genève et Paris, 1884.—143-44

Gladstone, W. E. *Juventus Mundi. The Gods and Men of the Heroic Age.* London, 1869.—210

Glossae Lipsianae. In: *Kleinere altniederdeutsche Denkmäler.* Mit ausführlichem Glossar herausgegeben von Moritz Heyne. Paderborn, 1867.—84

Goethe, J. W. *Faust.* I. Teil.—359

— *Der Gott und die Bajadere. Indische Legende.*—148

Gray, J. *The Social System: A Treatise on the Principle of Exchange.* Edinburgh, 1831.—283, 291

Gregorius Turonensis. *Historia Francorum.* In: Roth, P. *Geschichte des Beneficialwesens von der ältesten Zeiten bis ins zehnte Jahrhundert.* Erlangen, 1850.—62, 240

Grimm, J. *Deutsche Grammatik.* Th. 1-4, 2. Ausg., Th. 1. Göttingen, 1822.—85

— *Geschichte der deutschen Sprache.* Bd. 1-2. Leipzig, 1848.—17-18, 46-55, 80-81, 85, 87, 98-99

Grote, G. *A History of Greece; from the Earliest Period to the Close of the Generation*

Contemporary with Alexander the Great. A new edition. In twelve volumes. Vol. III. London, 1869.—205-08

Guérard, B.-E.-C. *Polyptyque de l'abbé Irminon.* In: Roth, P. *Geschichte des Beneficialwesens von der ältesten Zeiten bis ins zehnte Jahrhundert.* Erlangen, 1850.—64, 80

Gutrun (Kudrun).—185

Hegel, G. W. H. *Encyclopädie der philosophischen Wissenschaften im Grundrisse.* The first edition was published in Heidelberg in 1817.—358
— *Grundlinien der Philosophie des Rechts,* Berlin, 1821.—269, 358, 361, 378
— *Phänomenologie des Geistes.* The first edition was published in Bamberg and Würzburg, 1807.—373
— *Vorlesungen über die Philosophie der Geschichte,* Leipzig [s. an.]. The first edition was published in Berlin in 1837.—388
— *Vorlesungen über die Philosophie der Religion,* Berlin, 1832.—378
— *Wissenschaft der Logik.* Bd. 1 (2 books), 2. Nürnberg, 1812-1816.—360

Heine, H. *Atta Troll.*—109

Herodotus Halicarnassensis. *Historiae.*—9, 151, 172

Heusler, A. *Institutionen des Deutschen Privatrechts.* Zweiter Band, Leipzig, 1886.—167

Heyne, M. *Kleine altsächsische und altniederfränkische Grammatik.* Paderborn, 1873.—81-84, 86, 89

Hildebrand, H. *Das heidnische Zeitalter in Schweden. Eine archaeologisch-historische Studie.* Hamburg, 1873.—38

Hildebrandslied.—237

Hincmar Remensis. *Annales Remenses: Annales ad annum 869.* In: Maurer, G. L. *Einleitung zur Geschichte der Mark-, Nof-, Dorf- und Stadt-Verfassung und der öffentlichen Gewalt.* München, 1854.—77-78
— *Vita Remigii.* In: Roth, P. *Geschichte des Beneficialwesens von der ältesten Zeiten bis ins zehnte Jahrhundert.* Erlangen, 1850.—64

Hinkel, K. *Jugend-Muth und -Kraft.* In: *Deutsche Volkslieder.* Mainz, 1849, S. 39-40.—458

Hodgskin, Th. *Popular Political Economy.* Four Lectures Delivered at the London Mechanics' Institution. London, 1827.—280

[Hoffmann von Fallersleben, A. H.] *Das Lied der Deutschen.* In: [Hoffmann von Fallersleben, A. H.] *Deutsche Lieder aus der Schweiz.* Zürich und Winterthur, 1842, S. 16-17.—459

Homer. *Iliad.*—170, 208, 211
— *Odyssey.*—170, 211

Höpfner, E. *Der Krieg von 1806 und 1807. Ein Beitrag zur Geschichte der Preußischen Armee nach den Quellen des Kriegs-Archivs bearbeitet.* Bd. I-IV. Berlin, 1855.—449

Horace (Quintus Horatius Flaccus). *Carminum.* III.—536

Huschke, Ph. *De Privilegiis Feceniae Hispalae senatusconsulto concessis.* Gottingae, 1822.—227

Im Thurn, E. F. *Among the Indians of Guiana.* London, 1883.—365

Irenaeus. *Refutation and Overthrow of Gnosis falsely so called. (Against the Heresies.)*— 116

Jordanes. *De origine actibusque Getarum.*—36

Karl Marx vor den Kölner Geschwornen. Prozeß gegen den Ausschuß der rheinischen Demokraten wegen Aufrufs zum bewaffneten Widerstand. (9. Februar, 1849). Aus der *Neuen Rheinischen Zeitung.* Mit einem Vorwort von Fr. Engels. Hottingen-Zürich, 1885 (*Sozialdemokratische Bibliothek.* II.)—304

Kern, H. *Die Glossen in der Lex Salica und die Sprache der salischen Franken. Beitrag zur Geschichte der deutschen Sprachen.* Haag, 1869.—83, 86, 89

Kleinere altniederdeutsche Denkmäler. Mit ausführlichem Glossar herausgegeben von Moritz Heyne. Paderborn, 1867. (*Bibliothek der ältesten deutschen Litteratur-Denkmäler.* IV. Band. *Altniederdeutsche Denkmäler.* II. Teil. Paderborn, 1867.)— 83-86

Kopp, H. *Die Alchemie in älterer und neuerer Zeit. Ein Beitrag zur Culturgeschichte.* Erster Theil: *Die Alchemie bis zum letzten Viertel des 18. Jahrhunderts.* Zweiter Theil: *Die Alchemie von letzten Viertel des 18. Jahrhunderts an.* Heidelberg, 1886.—376

Ковалевскій, М. *Первобытное право.* Вып. I, Родъ. Москва, 1886 г.—167-69

Kovalevsky, M. *Tableau des origines et de l'évolution de la famille et de la propriété.* Stockholm, 1890.—165-67, 232, 236-37, 241

Lange, L. *Römische Alterthümer.* Erster Band, Berlin, 1856.—227

Lassalle, F. *Das System der erworbenen Rechte. Eine Versöhnung des positiven Rechts und der Rechtsphilosophie.* In zwei Theilen. Th. II: *Das Wesen des Römischen und Germanischen Erbrechts in historisch-philosophischer Entwickelung.* Leipzig, 1861.— 275

Lelewel, J. *Pythéas de Marseille et la géographie de son temps.* Bruxelles, 1836.—10

Letourneau, Ch. *L'évolution du mariage et de la famille.* Paris, 1888.—143-44

Liutprand, *Antapodosis, seu rerum per Europam gestarum, libri VI.*—249

[Livius, Titus.] *Titi Livi ab urbe condita libri.* Neunter Band: Buch XXXIX-XXXXII. Berlin, 1864.—225

[Longus.] *Daphnis and Chloe.*—184

McLennan, J. F. *Primitive Marriage. An Inquiry into the Origin of the Form of Capture in Marriage Ceremonies.* Edinburgh, 1865.— 140, 157, 169, 192, 232
— *Studies in Ancient History comprising a Reprint of Primitive Marriage. An Inquiry into the Origin of the Form of Capture in Marriage Ceremonies.* London, 1876.—140

Maine, H. S. *Ancient Law: its connection with the early history of society, and its relation to modern ideas.* 3rd ed. London, 1866. The first edition appeared in London in 1861.—186

Manlius, J. *Loci communes.*—601

Marcianus. *Periplus maris exteri.*—35

Maurer, G. L. *Einleitung zur Geschichte der Mark-, Hof-, Dorf- und Stadt-Verfassung und der öffentlichen Gewalt.* München, 1854.—53, 78

— *Geschichte der Städteverfassung in Deutschland.* Erster Band. Erlangen, 1869.—239

Meitzen, A. *Der Boden und die landwirthschaftlichen Verhältnisse des Preussischen Staates nach dem Gebietsumfange vor 1866.* Erster Band. Berlin, 1868.—348, 350

Menger, A. *Das Recht auf den vollen Arbeitsertrag in geschichtlicher Darstellung.* Stuttgart, 1886.—600, 602-08, 610-12, 614-15

Molière, J. B. *George Dandin, ou le mari confondu.*—266

Mommsen, Th. *Römische Forschungen.* Erster Band. Berlin, 1864.—225-27
— *Römische Geschichte.* Erster Band. Leipzig, 1854.—229

Mone, F. J. *Urgeschichte des badischen Landes bis zu Ende des siebenten Jahrhunderts.* Bd. 1: *Die Römer im oberrheinischen Gränzland.* Karlsruhe, 1845.—99

Morgan, L. H. *Ancient Society or Researches in the Lines of Human Progress from Savagery, through Barbarism to Civilization.* London, 1877.—131, 141, 149, 156, 158, 166, 174, 190, 194, 197, 210-12, 220, 235
— *Systems of Consanguinity and Affinity of the Human Family.* Washington, 1871.—152, 190

[Mülberger, A.] *Die Wohnungsfrage.* In: *Der Volksstaat,* Nr. 10, 11, 12, 13, 15, 19; 3., 7., 10., 14., 21. Februar und 6. März 1872.—425

Mülberger, A. *Zur Wohnungsfrage (Antwort an Friedrich Engels von A. Mülberger).* In: *Der Volksstaat,* Nr. 86, 26. Oktober 1872.—425

Müllenhoff, K. *Deutsche Altertumskunde.* Bd. 1. Berlin, 1870.—10

Nadler, K. G. *Fröhlich Palz, Gott erhalts! Gedichte in Pfälzer Mundart.* Frankfurt a. M., 1851.—105

Nibelungenlied.—185, 423

Niebuhr, B. G. *Römische Geschichte.* Erster Theil, Berlin, 1827. The first edition appeared in 1811.—228.

Novikoff, Olga de. *The Russianization of England.* In: *Pall Mall Gazette,* No. 6192, January 15, 1885.—292

Orosius, Paulus. *Historiae adversus paganos.* In: *Die Geschichtschreiber der deutschen Vorzeit in deutscher Bearbeitung.* Bd. 1: *Die Urzeit.* Berlin, 1847-1849.—21

Otfrid. *Liber Evangeliorum domini gratia theotisce conscriptus.* In: *Beiträge zur Geschichte der deutschen Sprache und Literatur.* Bd. 1. Halle, 1874. In: Braune, W. *Zur Kenntnis des Fränkischen und zur hochdeutschen Lautverschiebung.*—86, 105

Ovidius Naso, Publius. *Ex Ponto.* In: *Die Geschichtschreiber der deutschen Vorzeit in deutscher Bearbeitung.* Bd. 1: *Die Urzeit.* Berlin, 1847-1849.—29
— *Tristia.* In: *Die Geschichtschreiber der deutschen Vorzeit in deutscher Bearbeitung.* Bd. 1: *Die Urzeit.* Berlin, 1847-1849.—29

The People of India. Ed. by J. F. Watson and J. W. Kaye, vols I-VI. London, 1868-1872.—151

[Persius Flaccus, A.] *A. Persii Flacci satirarum liber.* Lipsiae, 1881.—114

[Plinius Secundus, C.] *Plini Secundi Naturalis historiae libri 37,* vols I-IV. Hamburgi et Gothae, 1851-1853.—243, 246
— *Bellorum Germaniae libri XX.*—46

— *Naturalis historia.* In: *Die Geschichtschreiber der deutschen Vorzeit in deutscher Bearbeitung.* Bd. 1: *Die Urzeit.* Berlin, 1847-1849.—16-17, 33, 36, 47-49, 54, 56

Plutarch. *Short Sayings of Spartan Women.*—171

Plutarchus, Chaeronensis. *Vitae parallelae: Aemilius Paullus.*—10

Procopius, Caesariensis. *De bello Vandalico.* In: Grimm, J. *Geschichte der deutschen Sprache.* Bd. 1. Leipzig, 1848.—48, 177

Proudhon, P. J. *Système des contradictions économiques, ou Philosophie de la misère.* T. I-II. 2-me éd. Paris, 1850. The first edition appeared in 1846.—278, 606

Ptolemaeus, Claudius. *Geographia.*—33-35, 38, 41, 45-47, 49, 54-56

Pytheas von Massilia. *Periodos oder Über den Ozean.*—10

Regnault, E. G. *Histoire politique et sociale des principautés danubiennes.* Paris, 1855.—293

Ricardo, D. *On the Principles of Political Economy, and Taxation.* First edition. London, 1817.—279, 281-83, 612

Rodbertus [J. K.] *Sociale Briefe an von Kirchmann.* [Drei Briefe.] Berlin, 1850-1851.—279
— Zweiter Brief: *Kirchmann's sociale Theorie und die meinige.* Berlin, 1850.—279

Rodbertus-Jagetzow [J. K.] [Letter to R. Meyer of November 29, 1871.] In: Rodbertus-Jagetzow. *Briefe und Socialpolitische Aufsätze.* Bd. 1. Berlin [s.a.], S. 134.—279

— [Letter to J. Zeller of March 14, 1875.] In: *Zeitschrift für die gesammte Staatswissenschaft.* Bd. 35. Tübingen, 1879. S. 219.—283
— *Der Normal-Arbeitstag.* Berlin, 1871; and in: *Berliner Revue,* 16., 23., 30. September 1871.—283
— *Zur Erkenntniß unsrer staatswirthschaftlichen Zustände.* Erstes Heft: *Fünf Theoreme.* Neubrandenburg und Friedland, 1842.—279, 283-86, 290

Roth, P. *Geschichte des Beneficialwesens von den ältesten Zeiten bis ins zehnte Jahrhundert.* Erlangen, 1850.—61-63, 68, 71-75, 77-81, 253

Salvianus. *De Gubernatione Dei.* In: *S. Salviani Opera Omnia,* Tyrnaviae, 1752.—250

Sax, E. *Die Wohnungszustände der arbeitenden Classen und ihre Reform.* Wien, 1869.—425

Schaaffhausen, H. [Paper presented to the Sixth General Congress of the German Society of Anthropology, Ethnology and Early History on August 11, 1875.] In: *Correspondenz-Blatt der deutschen Gesellschaft für Anthropologie, Ethnologie und Urgeschichte.* Braunschweig, München, 1875. In the report, *Die sechste Allgemeine Versammlung der deutschen Gesellschaft für Anthropologie, Ethnologie und Urgeschichte zu München am 9. bis 11. August 1875.*—8

Schiller, F. *Die Worte des Glaubens.*—606

Schneider, J. *Die römischen Militärstraßen an der Lippe und das Castell Aliso. Nach eigenen Lokalforschungen dargestellt.* Düsseldorf, 1878.—23, 32

Schoemann, G. F. *Griechische Alterthümer.* Erster Band: *Das Staatswesen.* Berlin, 1855.—171, 210

Serno-Solowiewitsch, A. *Unsere russischen Angelegenheiten.* Antwort auf den Artikel des Herrn Herzen: "Die Ordnung herrscht!" (*Kolokol*, No. 233). Aus dem Russischen übersetzt von S. L. Borkheim. Leipzig, 1871.—449

Серно-Соловьевичъ, А. *Наши домашнія дѣла.* Отвѣтъ г. Герцену на статью «Порядокъ торжествуетъ» (III. *Колоколъ*, № 233). Vevey, 1867.—449

Spruner, K., Menke, Th. *Hand-Atlas für die Geschichte des Mittelalters und der neueren Zeit.* 3. Auf. von. K. v. Spruner's Hand-Atlas, neu bearb. von Th. Menke. Gotha, 1880.—96, 99, 102, 559

Starcke, C. N. *Ludwig Feuerbach.* Stuttgart, 1885.—357, 372-74, 378, 520

Stirner, M. *Der Einzige und sein Eigenthum.* Leipzig, 1845.—364

Strabo. *Strabonis rerum geographicarum libri XVII.* T. 6, Lipsiae, 1811.—168
— *Geographica.* In: *Die Geschichtschreiber der deutschen Vorzeit in deutscher Bearbeitung.* Bd. 1: *Die Urzeit.* Berlin, 1847-1849.—14, 16, 29, 45

Strauss, D. F. *Die christliche Glaubenslehre in ihrer geschichtlichen Entwicklung und im Kampfe mit der modernen Wissenschaft.* Bd. 1-2. Tübingen-Stuttgart, 1840-1841.—382
— *Das Leben Jesu.* Bd. 1-2. Tübingen, 1835-1836.—363, 382

Sturluson Snorri. *Ynglinga Saga.* In: Sturluson, S. *Heimskringla.*—148

Suetonius Tranquillus, Gaius. *De vita Caesarum: Claudius.* In: *Die Geschichtschreiber der deutschen Vorzeit in deutscher Bearbeitung.* Bd. 1: *Die Urzeit.* Berlin, 1847-1849.—21

Sugenheim, S. *Geschichte der Aufhebung der Leibeigenschaft und Hörigkeit in Europa bis um die Mitte des Neunzehnten Jahrhunderts.* St. Petersburg, 1861.—161

Tacitus (Publius Cornelius Tacitus). *Annales.* In: *Die Geschichtschreiber der deutschen Vorzeit in deutscher Bearbeitung.* Bd. 1: *Die Urzeit.* Berlin, 1847-1849.—15, 27, 30-31, 34, 45, 99
— *Germania.* In: *Die Geschichtschreiber der deutschen Vorzeit in deutscher Bearbeitung.* Bd. 1: *Die Urzeit.* Berlin, 1847-1849.—12, 15, 18, 25, 32-33, 36-37, 39-41, 45-49, 54
— *Germania.* In: *Operum quae supersunt.* Vol. II. Lipsiae, 1835.—139, 176, 199, 238, 240-45
— *Historiarum.* In: *Operum quae supersunt.* Vol. II. Lipsiae, 1835.—116

Taufgelöbnis. In: *Kleinere altniederdeutsche Denkmäler.* Mit ausführlichem Glossar herausgegeben von Moritz Heyne. Paderborn, 1867.—86

Thompson, W. *An Inquiry into the Principles of the Distribution of Wealth Most Conducive to Human Happiness; Applied to the Newly Proposed System of Voluntary Equality of Wealth.* London, 1824.—614
— *An Inquiry into the Principles of the Distribution of Wealth Most Conducive to Human Happiness.* A new edition by W. Pare. London, 1850.—609-11

Thucydides. *The History of the Peloponnesian War.*—212

Tschech's Attentat. In: *Historische Volkslieder der Zeit von 1756 bis 1871.* Bd. 2. Berlin, 1871-1872, S. 79-80.—471

Topographische Special-Karte von Deutschland. Hrsg. von Gottlob Daniel Reymann, fortges. von C. W. von Oesfeld und F. Handtke. Glogau, o. J.—96-98, 100, 105

Velleius Paterculus, Gaius. *Historia Romana.* In: *Die Geschichtschreiber der deutschen Vorzeit in deutscher Bearbeitung.* Bd. 1: *Die Urzeit.* Berlin, 1847-1849.—21-22, 24-26, 29, 46

Virchow, R. [Report at the session of the Berlin Society of Anthropology, Ethnology and Early History on December 21, 1878.] In the article: *Verhandlungen der Berliner Gesellschaft für Anthropologie, Ethnologie und Urgeschichte.* Jahrgang 1878. In: *Zeitschrift für Ethnologie,* Bd. X. Berlin, 1878.—8

Wachsmuth, W. *Hellenische Alterthumskunde aus dem Gesichtspunkte des Staates.* 1.-2. Theil. 1.-2. Abtheilungen, Halle, 1826, 1830.—172, 206

Wagner, A. *Vorwort.* In: Rodbertus-Jagetzow, C. *Das Kapital. Vierter socialer Brief an von Kirchmann.* Berlin, 1884.—284

Wagner, R. *Die Walküre. Erster Tag aus der Trilogie: der Ring des Nibelungen.* Mainz, s.a.—147

Waitz, G. *Deutsche Verfassungsgeschichte.* Bd. 1. Kiel, 1844.—50

Waldersee, F. G. *Die Methode zur kriegsgemäßen Ausbildung der Infanterie für das zerstreute Gefecht; mit besonderer Berücksichtigung der Verhältnisse des Preußischen Heeres.* Berlin, 1848.—473

Weerth, G. *Leben und Thaten des berühmten Ritters Schnapphahnski.* In: *Neue Rheinische Zeitung,* Nr. 69-72, 74, 92, 95, 103-107, 167, 171, 172, 176, 178; 8.-11., 13. August; 2., 6., 15.-17., 19., 20. September; 13., 15., 17., 19., 23., 25. Dezember 1848 und Nr. 185, 188, 201; 3., 6., 21. Januar 1849.—109

Weitling, W. *Das Evangelium eines armen Sünders.* Bern, 1845.—319
— *Garantieen der Harmonie und Freiheit.* Vivis, verl. des Verfassers, 1842.—315

Wermuth, Stieber. *Die Communisten-Verschwörungen des 19. Jahrhunderts.* Im amtlichen Auftrage zur Benutzung der Polizei-Behörden der sämmtlichen deutschen Bundesstaaten auf Grund der betreffenden gerichtlichen und polizeilichen Acten. Erster Theil: Die historische Darstellung der betreffenden Untersuchungen. Zweiter Theil: Die Personalien der in den Communisten-Untersuchungen vorkommenden Personen. Berlin, 1853-1854.—312, 322

Westermarck, E. *The History of Human Marriage.* London and New York, 1891.—144, 147

Wiberg, C. F. *Bidrag till kännedomen om Grekers och Romares förbindelse med Norden och am de nordiska handelsvögarne.* Gefle, 1861.—34
— *Der Einfluß der klassischen Völker auf den Norden durch den Handelsverkehr.* Aus dem Schwedischen von Mestorf. Hamburg, 1867.—34, 36-40

Wolff, W. *Die schlesische Milliarde.* Abdruck aus der *Neuen Rheinischen Zeitung.* März-April 1849. Mit Einleitung von Friedrich Engels. Hottingen-Zürich, 1886. (*Sozialdemokratische Bibliothek.* VI).—341
— *Neue Rheinische Zeitung,* Nr. 252, 255, 256, 258, 264, 270-272, 281; 22., 25., 27., 29. März; 5., 12.-14., 25. April 1849.—127

Worsaae, J. J. A. *Die Vorgeschichte des Nordens nach gleichzeitigen Denkmälern.* Ins Deutsche Übertragen von J. Mestorf. Hamburg, 1878.—35

Zeuß, K. *Die Deutschen und die Nachbarstämme.* München, 1837.—46, 48, 54

Zurita, A. de. *Rapport sur les différentes classes de chefs de la Nouvelle-Espagne, sur les lois, les murs des habitants, sur les impôts établis avant et depuis la conquète, etc., etc.* In: *Voyages, relations et mémoires, originaux pour servir à l'histoire de la découverte de l'Amérique,* publiés pour la première fois en français, par H. Ternaux-Compans. Vol. 11, Paris, 1840.—168

DOCUMENTS

Ancient Laws and Institutes of Wales; Volume the First. London, 1841.—233

Annual Report of the Secretary of the Treasury on the State of the Finances for the Year 1887. Washington, 1887.—527

Archiv für die Geschichte des Niederrheins. Hrsg. v. Theod. Jos. Lacomblet. Abth. 1. Bd. 1. H. 1. Düsseldorf, 1831.—75

Bismarck, O. *Ansprache an die Einwohner des glorreichen Königreichs Böhmen.* In: *Königlich Preußischen Staats-Anzeiger,* Nr. 164, 11. Juli, 1866.—481

— *Rede bei der zweiten Berathung des Gesetzentwurfs, betr. Aenderungen der Wehrpflicht* [6. Februar 1888].—495

Capitularia maiorum domus.—62, 74, 78-81

Code Napoléon.—170, 392

Friedrich Wilhelm III. *Edikt den erleichterten Besitz und den freien Gebrauch des Grund-Eigenthums, so wie die persönlichen Verhältnisse der Land-Bewohner betreffend. Vom 9ten Oktober 1807; Verordnung wegen Zusammenziehung bäuerlicher Grundstücke oder Verwandlung derselben in Vorwerksland, mit Bezug auf die §§ 6. und 7. des Edikts vom 9ten Oktober 1807., den erleichterten Besitz und den freien Gebrauch des Grund-Eigenthums betreffend. Für die Provinzen Ostpreußen, Litthauen und Westpreußen. Vom 14ten Februar 1808; Verordnung wegen Zusammenziehung bäuerlicher Grundstücke oder Verwandlung derselben in Vorwerksland, mit Bezug auf die §§ 6. und 7. des Edikts vom 9ten Oktober 1807., den erleichterten Besitz und den freien Gebrauch des Grundeigenthums betreffend. Für das Herzogthum Schlesien und die Grafschaft Glatz. Vom 27sten März 1809; Publikandum, betreffend die, durch das sub dato Memel den 9ten Oktober 1807., ergangene Edikt, erfolgte Auflösung der persönlichen Erbunterthänigkeit in der Provinz Schlesien und in der Grafschaft Glatz. Vom 8ten April 1809; Verordnung wegen Zusammenziehung bäuerlicher Grundstücke oder Verwandlung derselben in Vorwerksland, mit Bezug auf die §§ 6. und 7. des Edikts vom 9ten Oktober 1807., den erleichterten Besitz und den freien Gebrauch des Grundeigenthums betreffend. Für die Provinzen Kur- und Neumark und Pommern. Vom 9ten Januar 1810.* In: *Sammlung der für die Königlichen Preußischen Staaten erschienenen Gesetze und Verordnungen von 1806. bis zum 27sten Oktober 1810.* Berlin, 1822.—347

— *Edikt die Regulierung der gutsherrlichen und bäuerlichen Verhältnisse betreffend. Vom 14ten September 1811.* In: *Gesetz-Sammlung für die Königlich-Preußische Staaten.* Berlin, 1811.—347

— *Deklaration des Edikts vom 14ten September 1811, wegen Regulirung der gutsherrlichen und bäuerlichen Verhältnisse. Vom 29sten Mai 1816.* In: *Gesetz-Sammlung für die Königlichen Preußischen Staaten.* Berlin, 1816,—346

— *Ordnung wegen Ablösung der Dienste, Natural- und Selbstleistungen von Grundstücken, welche eigenthümlich, zu Erbzins- oder Erbpachtsrecht, besessen werden. Vom 7ten*

Juni, 1821. In: *Gesetz-Sammlung für die Königlichen Preußischen Staaten.* Berlin, 1821.—347

Friedrich Wilhelm IV. *Gesetz, betreffend die Ablösung der Dienste in denjenigen Theilen der Provinz Sachsen, in welchen die Ablösungsordnung vom 7. Juni 1821 gilt. Vom 18. Juli 1845; Gesetz, betreffend die Ablösung der Dienste in der Provinz Schlesien. Vom 31. Oktober 1845.* In: *Gesetz-Sammlung für die Königlichen Preußischen Staaten.* Berlin, 1845.—348
— *Gesetz, betreffend die Sistirung der Verhandlungen über die Regulirung der gutsherrlichen und bäuerlichen Verhältnisse und über die Ablösung der Dienste, Natural- und Geldabgaben, sowie der über diese Gegenstände anhängigen Prozesse. Vom 9. Oktober 1848; Verordnung, betreffend die interimistische Regulirung der gutsherrlich-bäuerlichen Verhältnisse in der Provinz Schlesien. Vom 20. Dezember 1848.* In: *Gesetz-Sammlung für die Königlichen Preußischen Staaten.* Berlin, 1848.—346
— *Gesetz, betreffend die Ablösung der Reallasten und die Regulirung der gutsherrlichen und bäuerlichen Verhältnisse. Vom 2. März 1850.* In: *Gesetz-Sammlung für die Königlichen Preußischen Staaten.* Berlin, 1850.—349

Hêliand. Mit ausführlichem Glossar herausgegeben von Moritz Heyne. Paderborn, 1866. In: *Bibliothek der ältesten deutschen Litteratur-Denkmäler. II. Band. Altniederdeutsche Denkmäler. I. Teil.*—89

Kolb, G. Fr. *Handbuch der vergleichenden Statistik der Völkerzustands- und Staatenkunde.* Für den allgemeinen praktischen Gebrauch. Siebente, auf Grundlage der neuesten staatlichen Gestaltungen bearbeitete Auflage. Leipzig, 1875.—530

Leges nationum Germanicarum or Leges barbarorum.—42, 47, 59, 73, 82, 86

Notes, échangées avec le plenipotentiaire de la Prusse, concernant l'extradition des criminels. 1885, le 1 (13) janvier.—292

[Palgrave, I] *Address by R. H. Inglis Palgrave, F.R.S., F.S.S., President of the Section.* In: *Report of the Fifty-Third Meeting of the British Association for the Advancement of Science; held at Southport in September 1883.* London, 1884.—300

Protocole de Varsovie, signé le 5 juin 1851, entre la Russie et le Danemark, relatif à la succession danoise.—479

[*Report of the Agrarian Commission of the Prussian Second Chamber on the Draft Redemption Law of March 2, 1850.*] In: *Stenographische Berichte über die Verhandlungen der durch die Allerhöchste Verordnung vom 30. Mai 1849 einberufenen Zweiten Kammer.*—350

Report of the Royal Commission on the Housing of the Working Classes. England and Wales. 1885.—401

Rules of the Communist League (present edition, Vol. 6). In: Wermuth und Stieber, *Die Communisten-Verschwörungen des 19. Jahrhunderts.* Erster Theil, Berlin, 1853, S. 239-243.—321

Strafgesetzbuch für das Deutsch Reich. Mit Erläuterungen aus den Motiven und der Rechtsprechung königl. preuß. Ober-Tribunals. Zweite Auflage. Breslau, 1872.—290

Traité conclu à Berlin, le 5 août 1796 entre la République Française et la Prusse, pour l'établissement de la ligne de démarcation destinée à assurer la neutralité du nord de l'Allemagne.—469

Traité de paix conclu à Bâle le 16 Germinal an III (5 avril 1795) entre la République Française et le Roi de Prusse.—463-66, 469

Traité signé à Londres, le 8 mai 1852, entre le Danemark d'une part, et l'Autriche, la France, la Grande-Bretagne, la Russie et la Suède de l'autre part relatif à l'ordre de succession dans la monarchie danoise.—490

Verfassung des Deutschen Reichs. In: *Reichs-Gesetzblatt.* 1871. Berlin, [s.a.], Nr. 16.—504

Wilhelm I. [Die Proclamation an das französische Volk 11. August 1870].—489

ANONYMOUS ARTICLES
AND REPORTS PUBLISHED IN PERIODIC EDITIONS

New Yorker Volkszeitung, Nr. 10, 12. Januar, 1887: *Aveling und die Sozialisten.*—618
—Nr. 52, 2. März, 1887: *Affaire Aveling noch einmal.*—617

[*Novoye Vremya*] *Новое время,* № 3666, 15 (27) мая 1886 г.: *Утренняя почта. Среда, 14-го мая, Москва, 13-го мая* (Телеграфная корреспонденция Правител. Вестника).—413

The Times, No. 31352, January 24, 1885: *Extradition by Russia and Prussia.*—292

INDEX OF PERIODICALS

L'Ami du Peuple. Journal politique et impartial—a newspaper published by a Jacobin leader Jean Paul Marat from September 12, 1789 to July 14, 1793; appeared under this title from September 16, 1789 to September 21, 1792, and then as *Publiciste de la République française.*—126

Das Ausland—a magazine on geography, ethnography and natural science published from 1828 to 1893, first daily and from 1853 on weekly (initially in Munich and from 1873 in Stuttgart).—168

Deutsche-Brüsseler-Zeitung—a newspaper founded by the German political refugees in Brussels and published from January 1847 to February 1848. From September 1847 Marx and Engels regularly contributed to it and under their influence it became an organ of revolutionary communist propaganda.—319

Deutsche-Jahrbücher—a Young Hegelian literary and philosophical journal *Deutsche Jahrbücher für Wissenschaft und Kunst* published in Leipzig from July 1841 under the editorship of Arnold Ruge. In January 1843 it was closed down and prohibited throughout Germany.—363

Deutsch-Französische Jahrbücher—a German-language yearly published in Paris under the editorship of Karl Marx and Arnold Ruge; only the first issue, a double one, appeared in February 1844. It carried a number of works by Marx and Engels.—318

Frankfurter Zeitung und Handelsblatt—a daily published in Frankfurt am Main from 1856 (under this title from 1866) to 1943; newspaper of the petty-bourgeois democratic party of Southwestern Germany—the German People's Party—in the 1880s.—307

Le Globe, Journal Politique, Philosophique et Littéraire—a daily published in Paris from 1824 to 1832; organ of the Saint-Simon school from January 18, 1831.—606

Justice—a weekly of the Social-Democratic Federation published in London from January 1884 to December 1933; appeared under this title in 1884-1925 and then as *Social-Democrat Incorporating Justice.*—537

Kölnische Zeitung—a German daily published in Cologne from 1802 to 1945; it took an anti-revolutionary stand and attacked the *Neue Rheinische Zeitung* in 1848-49; it expressed the interests of the Prussian liberal bourgeoisie in the 1850s.—128, 335, 489

Колоколъ (*The Bell*)—a revolutionary-democratic newspaper; it was published by Alexander Herzen and Nikolai Ogaryev from 1857 to 1867 in Russian and in 1868-69 in French (*La Cloche*) with Russian supplements; it was published in London until 1865, then in Geneva.—516

Kreuz-Zeitung—see *Neue Preußische Zeitung*

The Labour Elector—a weekly of the socialist trend published in London from June 1888 to July 1894.—537

The Leeds Mercury—an English weekly (until 1861) founded in Leeds in 1717; in the 1840s became the organ of the Radicals.—571

The Manchester Guardian—a daily founded in 1821; a newspaper of the Free Traders and, from the mid-19th century, of the Liberal Party.—484

Missouri Republican—a daily of the US Democratic Party; published in St. Louis under this title from 1822 to 1888, and as *St. Louis Republic* until 1919.—408

Neue Preußische Zeitung—a conservative daily published from June 1848 to 1939; newspaper of the Prussian Junkers and Court circles, also known as the *Kreuz-Zeitung* because the heading contained a cross bearing the device: "Forward with God for King and Fatherland!"—124, 307

Neue Rheinische Zeitung. Organ der Demokratie—a daily newspaper of the revolutionary proletarian wing of the democrats during the 1848-49 revolution in Germany; it was published in Cologne under Marx's editorship from June 1, 1848 to May 19, 1849, with an interval between September 27 and October 12, 1848. Engels was among its editors.—109-11, 120, 123, 128, 277, 306, 325, 349, 595

Neue Rheinische Zeitung. Politisch-ökonomische Revue—a theoretical journal of the Communist League published by Marx and Engels from December 1849 to November 1850.—328

Die Neue Zeit—a theoretical journal of the German Social-Democrats; published monthly in Stuttgart from 1883 to October 1890, and then weekly till the autumn of 1923. Engels contributed to it from 1885 to 1895.—520

New Yorker Volkszeitung—a German-language socialist newspaper, published from 1878 to 1932.—408, 617, 626

The Northern Star—a weekly, central organ of the Chartists; published from 1837 to 1852; first in Leeds, then in London. Its founder and editor was Feargus O'Connor, George Harney being one of its co-editors. Engels contributed to the paper from 1843 to 1850.—319

The Pall Mall Gazette—a conservative daily which appeared in London from 1865 to 1921.—292

The Red Republican—a Chartist weekly published by George Julian Harney in London from June to November 1850; it carried the first English translation of the *Manifesto of the Communist Party* by Marx and Engels.—512

La Réforme—a daily newspaper of democratic republicans and petty-bourgeois socialists published in Paris from 1843 to 1850.—319

Rheinische Zeitung für Politik, Handel und Gewerbe—a daily newspaper founded on January 1, 1842, as the organ of the Rhenish bourgeois opposition. It was published in Cologne till March 31, 1843. From October 15, 1842 to March 17, 1843, it was edited by Marx and assumed a strongly pronounced revolutionary-democratic complexion, which led to its suppression. Engels was one of its contributors.—363

Science—an official press organ of the American Association for Advancement of Science published in New York from 1883.—397

Severny Vestnik (Northern Herald)—a literary, scientific and political monthly of a liberal Narodnik trend published in St. Petersburg from 1885 to 1898.—311

Der Social-Demokrat—an organ of the Lassallean General Association of German Workers. It was published under this title in Berlin from December 15, 1864 to 1871; in 1864-65 it was edited by Johann Baptist von Schweitzer.—278

El Socialista—a weekly, central organ of the Socialist Workers' Party of Spain published in Madrid from 1885.—543

Le Socialiste—a French-language weekly published in New York from October 1871 to May 1873; a newspaper of the French sections of the First International in the USA from December 1871 to October 1872.
The *Manifesto of the Communist Party* was published abridged in it in January-February 1872.—516

Le Socialiste—a French weekly founded by Jules Guesde in Paris in 1885; up to 1902—press organ of the Workers' Party; from 1902 to 1905—of the Socialist Party of France; from 1905 to 1915—of the French Socialist Party, Engels contributed to it in the 1880s-90s.—333

Der Sozialdemokrat—a weekly central organ of the Social-Democratic Party of Germany published during the Anti-Socialist Law in Zurich from September 1879 to September 1888 and in London from October 1888 to September 27, 1890.—111, 449, 472, 623-24

The Star—a daily of the Liberal Party published in London between 1888 and 1909.—542

Time—a socialist monthly published in London from 1879 to 1891.—434

To-day—a socialist monthly published in London from April 1883 to June 1889; was edited by Henry Mayers Hyndman from July 1884 to 1886.—335, 589

Der Volksstaat—central organ of the German Social-Democratic Workers' Party published in Leipzig from October 2, 1869 to September 29, 1876, first twice and from 1873, three times a week.—424-25, 449

Der Volks-Tribun. Organ des Jungen Amerika—a weekly founded by German "true socialists" in New York; published from January 5 to December 31, 1846.—319

Der Vorbote—a monthly of the German sections of the International in Switzerland, published in Geneva from 1866 to 1871 under the editorship of Johann Philipp Becker; on the whole, upheld the line pursued by Marx and the General Council, regularly published documents of the International and information about its activity in various countries.—422

SUBJECT INDEX

Usury, usurers—215, 219, 248, 266, 274, 432, 558

V

Value—279-84, 286, 288, 429-30, 605, 609-10
Vienna Congress of 1814-15—410, 455, 459
Vindili—17, 47

W

Wage labour—183, 271, 274, 289, 536, 600, 603
Wales—232-33, 235
War of Austrian Succession, 1740-48—459-60, 469
War of Bavarian Succession, 1778-79—458
War(s)—496
—between tribes—198, 203, 212, 256
—in slave-holding society—30, 37, 261, 264
—in feudal society—67, 555, 556, 569-62, 565
—in capitalist society—307, 443-44, 450-51, 580
—and revolution—415-17, 456, 592
See also *Austro-Italo-French war, 1859; Austro-Prussian war, 1866; Crimean war, 1853-56; Danish-Prussian war, 1848-50; Danish war, 1864; Franco-Prussian war, 1870-71; Hundred Years' War, 1337-1453; Italian wars, 1494-1559; Military art; Napoleonic wars; Peasant war in Germany, 1524-25; Seven Years' War, 1756-63; Thirty Years' War, 1618-48; War of Austrian Succession, 1740-48; War of Bavarian Succession, 1778-79; Wars of the First French Republic (late 18th-early 19th cent.)*
Wars of the First French Republic (late 18th-early 19th cent.)—462, 492, 493
Wealth—132, 139, 262-63, 267-68, 275, 337, 536
Weitlingianism, Weitlingians—279, 315, 316, 317, 319-20, 326, 517

Westphalia—32, 97, 428, 469
Will—187, 264, 275, 333-34, 373, 387, 391, 476, 478, 480
Workers' aristocracy—299-301, 403, 626
Workers' Party of France—333-34, 407, 415-17
Working class—118, 121, 272, 317, 319, 322, 329, 330, 365, 390, 401, 404, 424-25, 432-33, 435, 438, 440, 456, 500, 515-18, 535, 536, 550, 599-600, 602
—in Britain—296-301, 389, 400, 626
—in France—122, 125, 271, 303, 389, 456, 472, 512
—in Germany—121-22, 305-06, 317-18, 329-30, 407, 428, 431-32, 472, 476, 500, 502, 539, 541
—in Italy—463
—in Prussia—305
—in the USA—402-03, 434-37, 439-40
Working-class and socialist movement—120, 128, 313, 316, 318, 321-22, 391, 404, 406, 425, 435-37, 439-41, 455-56, 512, 515, 517, 599-600
—in Austria—543
—in Belgium—426, 442
—in Britain—299, 432, 545, 626
—in Denmark—442
—in France—303, 313, 316, 409, 442, 546
—in Germany—122, 305-06, 312, 314, 315, 317, 319, 325, 328-30, 397-98, 407, 418, 428, 432, 472, 476, 499, 502, 539-41, 546, 580
—in Holland—442
—in Hungary—543
—in Ireland—626
—in Italy—426
—in Portugal—442
—in Spain—442, 544
—in Sweden—442
—in Switzerland—314, 320, 442
—in the USA—402-03, 434-41
See also *Chartism, Chartist movement; Communist League; German Social-Democracy; German Workers' Society in Brussels (from 1847); Ideological struggle in the working-class movement; International Working Men's Association (First International); Knights of Labor (USA); League of the Just; Paris Com-*

GLOSSARY OF GEOGRAPHICAL NAMES[a]

Abyssinia	Ethiopia	Etsch	Adige
Adrianople	Edirne	Fiume	Rijeka (Rieka)
Aix	Aix-en-Provence	Frisches Haft	Zalew Wiślany
Aliso	Alise-Sainte-Reine	Glogau	Głogów (Głogów)
Bardengau	Lüneburger Heide	Gravelingen	Gravelines
Bardenwik	Bardowick	Greifswalde	Greifswald
Barmen	Wuppertal	Guyana	Guiana
Bečva	Bečzwa	Havana	Habana
Bohemian Forest	Šumava, Český Les	Hal	Halle
		Haspelscheid	Haspelscheidt
Branibor	Brandenburg	Homburg	Bad Homburg vor der Höhe
Breslau	Wrocław		
Britlinga	Brietlingen		
Bromberg	Bydgoszcz	Horsadal	Roßtal
Castrop	Castrop-Rauxel	Jaxartes	Syr Darya
		Karninschesberg	Kaninchenberg
Constantinople	Istanbul	Kerprich	Kerprich-Hemmersdorf
Crastlingi	Krassum		
Crettenach	Crettnach		
Cyrene	Cyrenaica	Königgrätz	Hradec Králové
Danzig	Gdańsk		
Drontheim	Trondheim	Lestines	Estinnes du Mont
Edingahûsun	Edemissen		
Ems	Bad Ems		

---

[a] This glossary includes geographical names occurring in Engels' articles in the form customary in the press of the time but differing from the national names or from those given in modern maps. The left column gives geographical names as used in the original; the right column gives corresponding names as used on modern maps and in modern literature.—Ed.

Lower Silesia	Dolny Śląsk
Lützelstein	La Petite-Pierre
March	Morava
Massel	Masłow
Mederiacum	Brück
Memel	Neman
Merzig	Messancy
Montabaurer Höhe	Montabaurer Wald
Mülhausen	Mulhouse
Neufahrwasser	Nowy Port
Nimwegen	Nijmegen
Oberbarmen	Wuppertal
Oesel	Saaremaa
Ölandsund	Kalmar Sound (Kalmarsund)
Olmütz	Olomouc
Otlinga	Ötlingen
Oxus	Amu Darya
Pillau	Baltiisk
Pomerania	Pomorze
Reekheim	Reckheim
Riesengebirge	Karkonosze
Saarburg	Sarrebourg
St. Petersburg	Leningrad
Silesia	Śląsk, Slezsko
Sinkfal	De Honte or Westerschelde
Soonwald	Soon Wald
Stedieraburg	Steterburg
Taschberg Moor	Thorsbjerger Moor
Tilsit	Sovetsk
Thebes	Thivai (Thevai)
Trebnitz	Trzebnica
Troy	Ilium
Upper Silesia	Górny Śląsk
Widau	Wied Au